BOOKNOTES

ON AMERICAN CHARACTER

Brian Lamb is also the author of:

Booknotes: America's Finest Authors on Reading,
Writing, and the Power of Ideas

Booknotes: Life Stories
Notable Biographers on the People Who Shaped America

Booknotes: Stories from American History

Also by C-SPAN:
Traveling Tocqueville's America

Who's Buried in Grant's Tomb?
A Tour of Presidential Gravesites

Booknotes
ON AMERICAN CHARACTER

Brian Lamb

PUBLICAFFAIRS

NEW YORK

Published in the United States by PublicAffairs™, a member of the Perseus Books Group.
All rights reserved.
Printed in the United States of America.

No part of this book may be reproduced in any manner whatsoever without written permission except in the case of brief quotations embodied in critical articles and reviews. For information, address PublicAffairs, 250 West 57th Street, Suite 1321, New York, NY 10107. PublicAffairs books are available at special discounts for bulk purchases in the U.S. by corporations, institutions, and other organizations. For more information, please contact the Special Markets Department at the Perseus Books Group, 11 Cambridge Center, Cambridge, MA 02142, call (617) 252–5298, or email specialmarkets@perseusbooks.com.

Book Design by Robert C. Olsson
Set in 11-point Adobe Garamond

Cataloging-in-Publication Data
    Booknotes : on American character / [compiled by] Brian Lamb.—1st ed.
        p.   cm.
Collection of essays by various authors based on interviews originally held on the television program Booknotes.
    Includes index.
    ISBN 1–58648–232–7
    1. National characteristics, American—Anecdotes.   2. United States—Civilization—Anecdotes.   3. United States—History—Anecdotes.   4. United States—Politics and government—Anecdotes.   5. United States—Biography—Anecdotes.   6. Authors, American—20th century—Interviews.   I. Title: Book notes   II. Lamb, Brian, 1941-   III. Booknotes (Television program)
E169.1B74   2004
973—dc22

                                                                    2004040033

First Edition
10 9 8 7 6 5 4 3 2 1

Contents

America at War

A Nation of Law & Order

American Inventors and Businessmen

Our Cultural Heritage

Introduction

A book on "American character" that begins with chapters from Ann Coulter and Michael Moore? Absolutely!

Ann Coulter and Michael Moore, commentators whose worldviews could not be more different, both wrote books that landed them on *Booknotes*. More importantly, both authors also landed on *New York Times'* non-fiction bestseller lists. Their simultaneous popularity demonstrates the great divide in American politics today. America in 2004 is a 50–50 nation. We see evidence of this in many places: the election of 2000 had to be settled in the Supreme Court; the United States Senate is split 51–49; the U.S. House has a Republican majority of only two dozen seats; and the Supreme Court remains consistently divided at 5–4.

The great divide is also reflected in my *Booknotes* mailbag:

"It's a pity that Mr. Lamb's style . . . is so ill-suited to a propagandist, liar, and fascist like Ann-thrax Coulter."

RAYMOND DUSAY

"Last Sunday [with Ann Coulter] must have been one of the few times in C-SPAN history when a viewer (in this case, myself) stood for 60 minutes and cheered at the TV. The neighbors must have thought I was watching pro wrestling. Thank you."

SHAGGY DOG

"I just finished watching your interview with Michael Moore. I found him, as always, fascinating, entertaining, and one hundred percent right on all the issues."

RACHEL R. PIERRE

"I can't believe you had that fat, atheist, America-hating bastard, Michael Moore, on your show. It wasn't bad enough that you had him on, but that he was not questioned on his ridiculous views. If you had to survive in the fair market, you would all be homeless."

DUKE LOGAN

E-mails like these are making it an adventure to log onto my computer these days. Callers to C-SPAN's talk programs frequently decry the heated political climate, saying "We've never been more divided." Yet as this book shows, America has a long history of highly partisan politics, often bitter, sometimes even violent. Here are some of the stories you'll read:

• **Roy Morris** recounts the Hayes–Tilden election of 1876, a contest which dragged on for four months of political infighting and maneuvering. Hayes took the oath in the middle of the night to avoid violence in the streets. Morris says, "He entered the presidency under a real cloud—he was called 'His Fraudulency' or 'Ruther-fraud B. Hayes'. . . . the *New York Sun,* which was a Democratic newspaper, habitually when they ran his photograph after he was president, would print the word 'fraud' across his forehead."

• Discussing the rise of American Imperialism in the early 1900s, writer **Warren Zimmermann** describes Theodore Roosevelt's controversial policies towards the Philippines, saying: "There was a huge opposition in the United States to what we were doing in the Philippines. It was led by people as famous as Mark Twain and included Andrew Carnegie. . . . Theodore Roosevelt had a lot of impatience with liberals who wanted good government and tended to be pacifistic or to shrink from the manlier virtues and he and called these people 'goo-goos' (good government) . . . to their faces and in public."

• Fast forward to the mid-twentieth century and the rise of modern conservatism. Of Barry Goldwater, author **Rick Perlstein** says, "What most people remember about the Barry Goldwater campaign, [was] how hated he was. He was seen as a fascist, an American Hitler." By contrast, "Lyndon Johnson might have had a mile wide of popularity, but it really was ultimately an inch deep, whereas people would send Goldwater telegrams as he was preparing for the convention: 'I'd give my marrow, my bones for you. I'll stand by you like a soldier in combat.' These were people who believed that liberalism had to be stopped. . . . Literally, a matter of the survival of Western civilization."

And of course, many of us experienced firsthand the turbulent 1960s with its political assassinations and protests over civil rights and the Vietnam War. Several chapters in this book recount authors' personal involvement in these and related events. Yet, *Booknotes: On American Character* isn't just about our periods of national divisiveness. It offers seventy-eight contemporary nonfiction writers whose topics span 225 years of the American experience. You'll read essays on American exceptionalism and of the leaders who promoted it; there are stories of Americans' penchant for ingenuity and technological prowess. Some authors demonstrate the benefits of American capitalism while others chronicle its downsides. Several chapters remind us of America's willingness to take up arms to promote democracy, while other writers capture our domestic struggles with violence and racial prejudice. And a few stories, such as Michael Paterniti's travels with Einstein's brain, are included because they are fantastic, only-in-America, kinds of tales.

Booknotes: On American Character was published on a special day for C-SPAN—March 19, 2004, our network's twenty-fifth anniversary.

A quarter-century ago, it would have been hard to imagine a day when we would be publishing books. Our concerns were much more immediate: would our just-barely-installed satellite dish, the first privately owned uplink in Washington, D.C., function properly? Could our staff of four successfully pull off the first nationally televised debate from the floor of the U.S. House of Representatives? March 19, 1979, you see, was the first day the U.S. House permitted television cameras to cover its debates. The cable industry had committed to carrying those sessions via a new not-for-profit channel it was funding, called C-SPAN. That morning when the gavel came down on the first televised Congress, the stakes were awfully high for C-SPAN and the cable television industry, both anxious to demonstrate our technological prowess to national representatives in the capital city and to citizens across the U.S.

Happily, our technology worked and history was made. Instantly, 3.5 million homes as far from Washington, D.C. as Yankton, South Dakota or Lafayette, Indiana could watch Congress in their living rooms. And, once it was successfully launched, C-SPAN began to grow. By 1982, this part-time service that only transmitted House debates became an around-the-clock channel, with a full schedule of other public affairs programming. The network that linked three and a half million homes in March 1979 today connects 88 million households. And, C-SPAN, which had only those four employees on its first day, now employs 280 people. Our single channel of programming has become a family of information services with three TV networks—C-SPAN, C-SPAN2 and C-SPAN3; a Washington, DC FM radio station that is carried nationally by two satellite radio services; and ten different web sites. We even have two 45-foot buses, fully equipped with television technology, which travel the country to teach young people about C-SPAN and Washington. In ten years, the buses have visited over 2,000 high schools.

In 1989, with a decade of political television under its belt, C-SPAN ventured into a new programming arena with regular coverage of non-fiction books. *Booknotes* arrived on TV screens in April of that year, promising viewers an uninterrupted hour with nonfiction authors each week. By 1998, we introduced *BookTV*, which offers forty-eight hours of nonfiction book programming every weekend on C-SPAN2. *Booknotes* marks its fifteenth anniversary this April having presented nearly 800 authors such as British Prime Minister Margaret Thatcher, China expert Bette Bao Lord, theologian Michael Novak and Eleanor Roosevelt biographer Blanche Weisen Cook. If you're interested in seeing who has been on the program, the appendix of this book lists every author interviewed since 1989 and the series' website (www. booknotes.org) has the transcript of every *Booknotes* interview stored in a fully searchable archive.

In 1997, publisher Peter Osnos took *Booknotes* from the television screen to the bookstore, publishing *Booknotes: America's Finest Authors on Reading, Writing, and the Power of Ideas* (Times Books). Two additional books followed, *Booknotes: Life Stories* (Times Books, 1999), a collection of American biographies and *Booknotes: Stories from American History* (PublicAffairs, 2001), an anthology of American historical events. Peter, who published three of the four *Booknotes* books, suggested "American character" as this book's theme. Recognizing the debate about American values raised by the September 11th terror attacks, Peter argued that this new collection of *Booknotes* interviews, spanning two centuries of American history, would offer an interesting window on our national psyche.

All of the material in *Booknotes: On American Character* is presented in traditional C-SPAN style—without commentary, allowing readers to form their own judgments. This book follows the formats of its three predecessors in which transcripts of our hour-long *Booknotes* interviews have been edited into essays. My questions are omitted in the editing process but we take care to retain the author's original intent and the uniqueness of his or her own voice. Our goal with all four *Booknotes* volumes is the same—to introduce you to new authors and encourage you to find their books and read more of what they have to say.

What is particularly enjoyable about all of our *Booknotes* projects is their collaborative nature. As the series' interviewer, I'm responsible for the final selections of the featured books and I read every one of them, a fact attested to by the annotated copies lining the shelves in my office near Capitol Hill. I also have a great deal of help: On the television side, producer Andrew Murray scouts for books and schedules the authors. Hope Landy has served for many years as the series' editorial assistant. Connie Doebele, a longtime C-SPAN colleague and our Executive Producer for books, oversees the series with the guidance of our Vice President of Programming, Terence Murphy. Brett Betsill has directed several hundred of the interviews, joined in recent years by Maurice Haynes.

Assembling this book from those hour-long interviews involved a different team of people. Executive Assistant Carol Touhey and Vanessa Melius, a community relations representative, both worked on prior *Booknotes* books and were C-SPAN's editorial leads for this project, skillfully aided by Kate Darnton, Lindsay Jones, and David Patterson at PublicAffairs. C-SPAN's Molly Woods, Clare Levy, Maura Pierce, Andrew Nason, and Peggy Keegan assisted in editing and fact-checking chapters. Susan Swain, our network's co-chief operating officer, has been the guiding hand behind all four of the *Booknotes* books. Susan's sharp eye for important content and her unusually good edit pencil have kept this fourth *Booknotes* book on mission. Our other co-COO, Rob Kennedy, always makes sure we meet our contractual obligations.

These are just a few of the 280 people who work at C-SPAN. During the past twenty-five years, 1141 people have come to work with us and each played a part in helping C-SPAN grow. Sixty of those here today have spent more than ten years at C-SPAN, none longer than Jana Fay, who was with me on that first day in 1979 and now serves as our Vice President of Finance.

Other people who played a critical role in the development of C-SPAN are those in the cable industry who make the C-SPAN networks available to their customers and pay the affiliate fees which fund our operations. Their twenty-five-year commitment to C-SPAN is an important public service by private industry. Representing them are the 125 men and women, top executives in the cable industry, who have served on C-SPAN's board since 1979. I especially want to thank the thirteen chairmen who committed a great deal of their scarce personal time to our network—from our founding chairman, Bob Rosencrans to our current Executive Committee chairman, Steve Burke, CEO of Comcast Cable Communications.

Putting today's world in some perspective has been the greatest benefit of my fifteen years of *Booknotes* interviews. I started out in journalism knowing far too little about American history; these years full of reading have helped me improve upon that knowledge and enriched my life. Speaking on behalf of my C-SPAN colleagues and our cable system affiliates, in this season of C-SPAN anniversaries, I'd like to express our hope that C-SPAN—in particular the *Booknotes* television series and the books associated with it—has given viewers and readers some valuable learning experiences of their own.

Brian Lamb
Washington, DC
March 19, 2004

On American Character

Views from the Right

by

ANN COULTER

Political analyst, lawyer, and columnist Ann Coulter is currently one of the most vocal figures of the American right. Coulter has worked for the Senate Judiciary Committee and the Center for Individual Rights, a Washington-based public-interest law firm. In her book Slander: Liberal Lies About the American Right, *published by Crown in 2002, Coulter argues that the left, aided by the media, unfairly maligns conservatives and distorts the national debate. Ms. Coulter appeared on* Booknotes *on August 11, 2002.*

[I DECIDED TO write this book] after the Clinton trial, after the impeachment and the acquittal in the Senate, technically. . . . I sat back and literally was shocked that Clinton had gotten basically the entire Democratic Party and liberals to line up behind him on the basis of his argument, "My opponents are right-wing Republicans." That argument worked [for him]. That was a good argument.

Neither I nor anyone I know would have defended a Republican under similar circumstances, and that was when I first started thinking, "They really hate us. What is this about? Is it just abortion? Is it socialism they want?" I started asking my liberal friends, "What are you afraid of? If [House Republican leader] Tom DeLay were czar of the universe, what are you afraid he'd do?" . . . It was just craziness. "Republican Party—racist, sexist, anti-Semitic, homophobic."

I realized there is no serious dialogue or engagement of ideas between the left and the right in this country. There's a lot of fertile debate going on the right. We argue with one another all the time and come up with lots of great new interesting ideas that people are talking about, like school choice, flat tax, welfare reform, quality-of-life crimes. It's amazing how productive debate can be when one isn't constantly being called a racist.

THE RELIGIOUS right chapter—that was an example of how it actually paid to be in Aspen over New Year's. I was talking to one of my really smart financial friends, a banker in Atlanta, basically a Republican. Many of my friends see me as the representative of the Republican Party, and they're always telling me what the Republican Party should be doing. He said, "You know, the problem with the Republican Party is the religious right. They've got to get rid of the religious right."

I was so struck by this. I said, "You sound like a crazy person. Why not 'They have to get rid of the green people?' What is the 'religious right'?" So I thought I'd write five or ten pages on the religious right and how it's just this vague, totemic symbol. The more I started researching it and reading every mention of the "religious right," the more fascinating a subject it became. I mean fascinating in the clinical sense. I ended up with an entire chapter on it.

It really is like trying to nail Jell-O to a wall to figure out what the left even means by "religious right." It's this apocryphal enemy, and half of America not only believes it exists but actually is afraid of it!

You never hear about the "atheist left." It's just this crazy totemic symbol that the masses are trained to laugh at and sneer at. People are constantly denouncing this apocryphal religious right and are always hailed for their courage.

[Former Minnesota governor] Jesse Ventura, when he gave an interview to *Playboy* magazine, said something to the effect that "People who go to church are weak-minded." He then quickly had to explain [that] he was just talking about the religious right.

It was stunning how the entire media erupted in praise for his courage, his genius, in standing up to the religious right. It's bad enough that liberals have to be bullies to people who happen to believe in God. To be hailing people for courage and for standing up against the powerless on behalf of the powerful is really more than people should have to bear.

I WAS CONFIDENT [this book] was going to sell well. I seem to have a fan base. You can sort of sense these things. Fortunately with the Internet—various Web sites carry my column—they can tell how many unique users have clicked on to read a column. I know I have a very popular column, and I get a lot of fan mail, especially since 9/11. I think I may be the only controversialist whose standing has gone up after 9/11.

But I was completely delighted [that my book went straight to the number one spot on the *New York Times* best-seller list]. I think it was more of a surprise to the New York publishing industry, none of whom would publish my book for two months. . . .

As I describe in my book, the New York publishing industry—except, thank God, for Crown Books and my wonderful publisher and editor—reacts to books by conservatives as, "Well, this won't sell," even though they've been best-sellers for fifty years now, and especially now with the Internet. But for two months, my agent shopped [this book] around and no one would buy it. I've kept some of the snooty rejections, my favorite being that "This book does not move the national dialogue forward." That was from Doubleday. . . .

I e-mailed my agent, Joni Evans, back and said, "You know, that's funny because I thought book publishers made money on the basis of how many books they sold. I didn't realize it was how many yards they moved the national dialogue forward."

I think it's an important book, and I want people to read it. If I can't get liberals to read it—though I think by attacking so many of them, I may have enticed some of them into flipping through a few pages—I would at least like Americans to read through it so that they will hoot with laughter the next time, for example, they hear a Republican presidential candidate called "stupid."

Every Republican presidential candidate since Calvin Coolidge [has been called "stupid"]. If you are not stupid, the less popular way of dismissing a substantial conservative is to portray him as scarily weird. Nixon was scarily weird rather than stupid. George Bush, senior, was saved only by his lightning-rod vice president, Dan Quayle. They couldn't simultaneously say that Dan Quayle was the stupidest man ever born of woman and so was George Bush, his boss. So he took most of the heat off the former President Bush, though even President Bush was ridiculed as a simpleton who was constantly stumbling over his words.

I think, most stunningly, the "stupid" argument was used against Eisenhower, the bumbling old guy who won the Cold War. I cover that quite a bit because Americans remember him, and they remember that he wasn't stupid. And now, most recently, the comparison between Bush and Gore—it's just always the same thing.

The Republican is always an idiot, an idiot, an idiot. Any small mistake he makes will be reported and then justified on the grounds that it reinforces impressions. Well, where did those impressions come from? Because you always call every Republican stupid and the Democrat is always such a genius, so intelligent that when he then goes on to lose, that is always explained as "He just couldn't connect to the common voter, couldn't connect to the common man," like Adlai Stevenson.

I THINK [the mainstream media] are less likely to write about [my book if I criticize them]. I've never been able to game things. It's hard enough to figure out what you think and then write about them in a way that you think is persuasive. I write what I think is true. It did cross my mind now and then, "I attack a lot of people in the major media. I wonder if they'll refuse to have me on now?" But what am I going to do, not write it? I mean, it's not like they're doing me any favors now anyway.

I can assure you, if what I wanted was network attention, was fawning write-ups in *Vanity Fair* or reviews in the *New York Times*, I wouldn't say the things I do. I wouldn't write the things I do. It's very easy, as every "moderate Republican" knows, how to be billed as a genius in the *New York Times,* or how to be billed as the "new intellectual leader on the Supreme Court" in a cover story on the *New York Times Magazine.* [After he voted to uphold *Roe v. Wade,*] David Souter knows. Sandra Day O'Connor knows. Everyone senses how you get called an "intellectual titan" by the mainstream media: support abortion; be a liberal.

AFTER PRESIDENT Clinton blamed Oklahoma City on Rush Limbaugh and other talk radio hosts . . . that got repeated and ricocheted through the media sound chamber. And when talk radio hosts did not instantly admit complicity in the bombing but instead objected to this preposterous, vicious attack on talk radio hosts, [*Washington Post* media critic] Howard Kurtz started referring to this as "the blame game" on both sides.

That really is one of the biggest pieces of propaganda, one of the biggest lies, always made. Liberals viciously attack conservatives, compare them to Down syndrome, wish them dead of cholesterol-induced heart attacks, accuse them of trying to bring back slavery, and then they say, "Oh well, both sides do it."

The point of my book is that both sides do not do it. This [is an] easy equation of just backing off and saying, "Oh well, you guys do it, too." I've just written my book showing that they do it. I'd like to see a carefully documented thirty-five pages of footnotes of them showing how we do it, because we don't. We couldn't get away with it.

THE EVIDENCE is so overwhelming that the Democratic Party represents these Malibu Marie Antoinettes and Park Avenue matrons, and the Republican Party represents the middle class, the working class, the average American who wants his taxes cut and believes in God. But for years, just through power of repetition, somehow Democrats have been able to portray Republicans—or liberals have been able to portray conservatives—[as] the party of the powerful, the party of the rich; whereas, Barbra Streisand and Martha Stewart, that's the party of the people.

I think the paradigm is out there in front of people, but because of repetition they can't see something going on right in front of them. . . . It's really amazing how Democrats just try to associate the Republican Party with corporations. It's a springboard from the idea that Republicans represent the rich. The rich? *Au contraire!* We represent the middle class. You guys are representing the soccer moms on Park Avenue.

THE REASON conservatives still have the White House, and my book is doing well, and we still have the House . . . is because of the great common sense of the American people.

But think how great our country would be if they weren't being propagandized to on a daily basis, day in and day out, from ABC, NBC, CBS, *Washington Post, New York Times, Time, Newsweek,* and *U.S. News and World Report.* It really is amazing that the conservatives ever win any victories at all with this propaganda machine and the colleges and the public schools.

The left really does control these three incredibly crucial nerve centers, and I just say, "Off with them. You've nearly wrecked the country. Be gone."

As I described in my book, in all of the media where there's competition—books, talk radio, and the Internet—yes! Americans are actually very clever people, and they keep choosing conservatives. So it's interesting that instead we get a whole series of Democratic hacks delivering the news to us on ABC, NBC, and CBS.

MY HOBBY [politics] has become my life. I have the greatest life imaginable. I think I have a greater life than anyone in the universe, in fact. I sleep until noon. I work in my underwear. I'm my own boss. No one can fire me. The only people who could ever fire me are the American people—if they don't want to hear me anymore, if they don't buy my books, if they don't read my columns. But other than that, I don't have a boss. I'm happy all the time. I have a wonderful life. I love to have people come up to me and praise me and tell me I say the things that they can't say. And it does, in fact, happen in places like L.A. and Manhattan, not just [out in the rest of] America.

Views from the Left

MICHAEL MOORE

Flint, Michigan, native Michael Moore first gained attention by attacking his hometown's biggest employer, General Motors, in the 1989 film Roger and Me. *Today, he is one of the most outspoken voices of liberalism in the United States. In* Dude Where's My Country?, *published by Warner Books in 2003, Moore attacked both Republicans and centrist Democrats for allowing conservative forces to dominate the nation. Mr. Moore joined us on* Booknotes *on November 16, 2003.*

[My BOOK] IS part humor, part serious, a bit of satire, a bit of a rant. It comes from a person who seriously loves his country and is wondering what has happened to it.

Some of the things I'm saying in this book, even I have a hard time believing. When I was writing it, I just thought, "People are not going to believe this. People are not going to believe that there may have been a business relationship between the bin Laden family and the Bush family that dates back to the 1970s." You have to go, "Wait a minute. What are you doing—spending too much time on the conspiracy-theory Web sites?" No, actually, this is all well documented.

I.F. Stone, investigative journalist from the 1950s, 1960s, 1970s, had this belief: He said that the stuff that you need to dig up is already there. It doesn't really require that much work. Some of the best stuff is in those little two- and three-paragraph stories, the filler stories, or maybe it's a paragraph or two that's buried someplace.

I was reading the *New Yorker* magazine two months after September 11, in an article by Jane Mayer, and she just nonchalantly, in the middle of this article, says that in the days after September 11th, twenty-four members of the bin Laden family and their associates were allowed to be picked up by a private jet that flew around the country to pick them up and take them to Boston, and eventually to Paris.

I was stuck in Los Angeles on 9/11, and we were going to fly that day back to New York, and instead we had to drive 3,000 miles. And I'm just thinking, I had to drive 3,000 miles, and you're telling me that the only way you could fly on September 12 or 13, 2001, was if your name was bin Laden or if you were a member of the Saudi family? What is that all about?

I'm not drawing actual conclusions. I'm not saying, "Well, it's definitely this or that." I don't really know. It's kind of a not-so-silent plea from an average citizen who's saying, "There's smoke here. Where's the fire?" Is there a fire? I'd like to know. I'd like to know what the relationship is between the Bushes and the Saudi royal family. How does that affect our foreign policy? And how does it affect things that have happened to us here, such as 9/11?

I'd like to know why the Taliban were coming to Houston in the late 1990s, while George W. Bush was governor, to meet with Bush's friends in the oil and natural gas business, having a number of negotiations in Houston—these are Taliban leaders in Houston—to discuss building a pipeline across Afghanistan.

It's not to say just because your name is bin Laden that you're guilty of anything. I'm not saying that. I'm just saying in a normal police investigation, if your brother committed mass murder, chances are that the police are going to pay you a visit and ask you a few questions: "What do you know? Who do you know? Can you help us? What do you think? Where do you think he is? When you go back there, will you stay in touch?" Normal police work.

It wasn't done in this case and this came right from the White House, the approval to allow this private Saudi jet to fly around and pick up these people and then scoot them out of the country without hardly a question being asked.

Let's give them the benefit of the doubt. It could just be basic human nature. If the son of a good friend of mine was just involved in something really bad, I might be worried for the family. It could just have been a natural thing. Maybe George Senior—who's involved in the Carlyle Group, which is funded in part by the bin Ladens—just said, "We should do something nice here. There's no reason these other bin Ladens have to suffer." It could just be something as simple as that.

It also could be that this pipeline deal went sour. Part of what's connected to this is that the Cheney energy meetings that took place in 2001—we still to this day don't know who was at these meetings, what was being discussed—but it has been reported in a number of papers that part of the discussion involved this Taliban pipeline. In fact, they had reopened negotiations with the Taliban to again consider building this pipeline to bring natural gas from the Caspian Sea region through Afghanistan and into Pakistan.

Did that have something to do with this? Was this all about a bad pipeline deal? Then I start to think other things. I know a little bit about airplanes. . . . The Pentagon is a five-story building. The World Trade Center, though it's tall, is only a block wide. If you're off by this much at 500 miles an hour, you're in the river. You're not hitting the building.

To be so exact and so precision-like in their ability on that day to hit those buildings . . . , maybe we framed it wrong here. Why did we just jump to the immediate conclusion that this is what we call a terrorist attack? Why don't we ever consider the possibility that it was a military attack?

These pilots were well-trained. These people knew what they were doing. My own common sense will never accept that they learned how to do this at some rinky-dink flight training school in Florida, on a little video game playing their little Pac-Man buttons. And if it was a "military" attack, whose military was it, or whose part of which military? Was this a rogue element within a certain regime? And why can't we read the twenty-eight pages? Why can't we read these pages that are in the congressional 9/11 report that have been blacked out, that apparently are about Saudi Arabia?

What's great about this, we live in a free country and it's an open society. That means we have to have a free flow of information. The citizens can't make the best decisions unless they have this information. So to withhold information like this, it just smacks of "What going on here?"

These are the questions I'm raising. I'm hoping to give a bit of a jolt, whether it's to the media or whether it's to the Democrats in Congress. [I want them] to do their jobs, and ask these questions, and don't accept either being ignored or being given some answer like, "Well, we were worried about the bin Ladens, and so we wanted to help them, because we were afraid something would happen to them on that day."

Imagine if after Oklahoma City, Bill Clinton had said, "You know, we're really worried about the McVeigh family. Why don't we go up there, fly up to Buffalo and send a private plane, pick them all up and send them to Paris for a while until things calm down here?" Can you imagine what the press and the Republicans would have done with that? [What if] then it was revealed that there was a financial connection between the Clinton and McVeighs that dated back many years?

I'm sure that President Bush was as affected by [September 11th] and those who died that day as all of us were. But I think that after the sorrow of the tragedy started to wear off, he, and especially his advisers, realized this bonanza that essentially had been handed to them in the form of this tragedy, which is that, "We can now use this. We can use this for anything. All we have to do is say, because of 9/11, because of terrorism, we have to do this. We have to drill for oil in Alaska because of 9/11. And people will go for it. They'll listen to us. If we tell them that Saddam Hussein was connected to

9/11, they'll actually believe it." And they did. The majority of Americans actually believed this complete, complete fallacy. And it worked.

I, personally, am offended to use the dead of that day of September 11 for an excuse to pass the Patriot Act, to take away people's civil liberties, to lock people up without even charges being brought against them, to drill for oil in Alaska, to do all these other things that they want to do. I always say it's because of that. If I had a relative who died that day, I would be personally offended. I would not want their death to be used by politicians who are trying to push this right-wing agenda.

I READ IN *National Geographic* last year this survey that they did of young adult Americans, eighteen to twenty-five-year-olds, asking them geography questions. Something like 85 percent didn't know where either Iraq or Israel was on the map. Nearly 60 percent didn't know where Great Britain was. And 11 percent of these young adult Americans could not find the United States on the globe.

Now, that's scary. . . . You have a citizenry who are charged with and given the vote to make decisions, and they don't even know where they are in the world and they don't know where the rest of the world is. First of all, if you're going to bomb another country, the majority of its people should know where that country is. In fact, maybe that should be a new rule. There has to be a test handed out. If you can't find Iraq on the map, you are not allowed to let your air force bomb that country.

[Invoking "God bless America"] is unique to us and it's an arrogant statement. It's not, "May God," or "Please, God," bless America. It's "God bless America." God bless America! When people around the world hear that, they're just going, "Who the hell do you think you are? Eight-five percent of your people can't find Iraq on the map. Get real here. God isn't playing favorites." God created all of us equally. He loves everyone equally. We don't have the express lane to him, like he's going to listen to our prayers as we bomb Iraq. I don't think that's what God is up to.

THE MAIL I started to get [after my previous book, *Stupid White Men*, was not from] readers that were from the church of the left. These were not people who are hard-core liberals or progressives or lefties, or whatever. The people who read this book were people who lived in middle America and who have very middle-American values.

The response to it was overwhelming and it was very profound. So when I started to write this book, I thought, "I need to speak to this new audience, this very wide audience that I now have . . . , as just a middle-American person, as someone who's from the Midwest." I don't come from a left community. My whole thing isn't based in Berkeley. I come from Flint, Michigan. I have a high school education and so I'm a lot like the people that are now reading my books.

What I feel is an enormous responsibility that I have to . . . encourage the people who come [to hear me speak] to not look to Michael Moore as the leader who is going to lead us somewhere. I am really just another Joe, and what I want to say to them is, "We all have to do this together. Don't leave here tonight [unwilling] to do your part as a citizen, to be an active citizen—democracy is not a spectator sport. It is a participatory event, and if the people fail to participate, it ceases to be a democracy." We live in a country, as we know, where half the people don't vote. Forget about getting involved in other ways in the democracy.

I've been trying to figure out, why it is that the American public hates that word [liberal] and they don't like liberal leaders? They don't like to vote for them, because it seems like an oxymoron, "liberal leader." Liberal leaders usually don't lead. They're very wishy-washy. They're wimpy. . . . Our side, we don't have fighters. . . . They've got Trent Lott, Newt Gingrich, Tom DeLay, people that believe in something.

So what I'm saying to liberals in the book is, "Let's get the courage of our convictions here. Let's stand up for something." [The editorial page of the] *New York Times*, before the war, said, "I think the war is not a good idea. We shouldn't go to war." And then as soon as we've gone to war, [it said,] "OK, we're at war. I guess we better support the war."

No wonder they're so attractive to so many people, the conservatives and the right-wingers, because at least they stand for something. They've got conviction and I think the American people would rather have that. They'll vote for a conservative, even though they don't agree with the conservative, even though, as I point out in my book, on all the issues, the American public is very liberal. The majority of Americans now are pro-choice. They're pro-labor. They're pro-environment. They want a higher minimum wage. You go down the whole list of things, they're liberal on the issues. And yet they'll vote for Republicans and conservatives because when it comes to leadership, they're voting for a leader, someone who will lead. They'd rather have that and . . . if they don't like some of the things they stand for, that's OK. They just want to know whoever's in charge is going to be in charge.

I never have [met Ann Coulter]. . . . I'd love to meet her. I think she's got a great act. I think she knows that I believe in what I believe in. She can't believe in half that stuff she says. She's very smart, and she knows how to work it. . . . When I say Ann Coulter doesn't believe in those things, I'm not disparaging the fact that she is a conservative. I respect her for believing those things, but the way she takes it is kind of extreme ends. I got to believe that she knows it's good camera time for her, for herself—and those legs.

The Nation's Leaders

Benjamin Franklin:
Printer, Scientist, Founding Father

by

JAMES SRODES

Benjamin Franklin is remembered as something of a Renaissance man: pamphleteer, inventor, and diplomat. Journalist James Srodes goes further, describing Franklin as one of the most pivotal players in the fight for American independence. In May 2002, Mr. Srodes appeared on Booknotes *to discuss his book* Franklin: The Essential Founding Father, *published by Regnery in 2002.*

WITHOUT FRANKLIN, we would not have had the American Revolution we did.

He was the catalyst. He was that one ingredient that took all the other contributions of all the other founding fathers and mothers and really created something that was going to succeed. Without Franklin, I don't know that we would be a sovereign nation. And I can argue that we probably would still be a very small country clinging to the Atlantic coast.

Franklin lived a long time, which is part of the reason he played such a big role. He lived from 1706 to 1790. He was eighty-four when he died, which was a ripe old age. [Franklin was the only person] to sign the Constitution, the Declaration of Independence, and the Treaty of Paris.

He was the leading American representative in London for nearly twenty years before that, fighting, in essence, to stop the revolution, to get the British government to roll back much of its punitive taxation and impositions. When he arrived home in defeat in 1775, he became the focal point of people who were coalescing around this very frightening idea of breaking with England. England, after all, was how they identified themselves.

He took a role in the Declaration. He helped Jefferson write it, and Jefferson freely acknowledged that help. And then because of his international prominence as a scientist and as a politician, he was sent back to France to try to win French support for what was going to be a very long and bloody war. And he did that.

It was that support—the guns, the tents, the clothing, the gunpowder, which we could not make, and the money—that won the war. I say Washington won the battles, Franklin won the war.

FRANKLIN WAS A very utilitarian man. His interests were all over the map. In fact, some Harvard medical people have suggested he may have had attention deficit disorder. But he was basically a utilitarian. He invented bifocals because he got tired of taking one set of glasses off and putting another set of glasses on. He invented a fireplace because he got tired of having cold rooms that were full of smoke. He got into electricity because lightning burned down a lot of houses and killed a lot of people. So he was a very utilitarian person, and that affected his politics.

He made the connection between lightning and static electricity, the kind you get when you shuffle your foot on the rug and then touch a doorknob and get that jolt. He discovered and proved to others—that's the important point—that they were both the same thing, that the cause was an imbalance in charges. And he showed other people all around the world how to prove that to themselves. So even before he flew his kite, the Franklin experiments were being tried successfully in France and England and even Russia. And that's where his fame came from, not just the discovery but because he shared it and shared it with a very clear writing style that was accessible to everybody.

FRANKLIN SOLD his prosperous printing business, sold his newspaper, and "retired" in his mid-forties because, he said, "I don't have an awful lot of time left." Men really didn't live past fifty. So it was this period between 1747 and 1754, when he really got into a frenzy of invention—rocking chairs, stepladders for libraries. He experimented with ants and how ants communicate. His interests were extraordinary, and his experiments with electricity, which first began to be publicly known in 1751, just rolled on through the 1750s.

[FRANKLIN WAS] born in 1706 to a Boston candle and soap maker named Josiah Franklin and his second wife, Abiah. Josiah Franklin had seventeen children by his two wives. It was an extraordinary, crowded family. Thirteen of them were around at any one time, by Franklin's reminiscence. They weren't poor, but they were scrapping.

Josiah was a Congregationalist, which meant that he was constantly reexamining his conscience, trying to perfect himself. And while Benjamin left that church almost as soon as he could, that stuck with him, that constant perfection, inward-looking effort to improve oneself, to find virtue, which wasn't a single quality but a multiple of qualities that you sought. It stuck with him all of his life.

He was apprenticed to a half-brother as a printer apprentice. He didn't have much formal schooling, only had three years in a school, but became an omnivorous reader and turned to writing very skillful parodies, which he had published anonymously, without his brother's knowing, in his brother's newspaper. He ran away when he was seventeen, got to Philadelphia, and then managed to get to London, which was the center of printing skills, where he perfected his techniques. By this time, he was a really strong guy. People think of Franklin as being fat and sedentary; this was a real horse of a guy.

To be a printer in those days, you had to be extraordinarily robust and have great upper-body strength. He was also a quite well-known swimmer and at one point considered taking up the trade of professional swimming instructor and aquatic star. But he stayed with printing, came back to Philadelphia, bought a newspaper. By the time he was twenty-seven, he was running the most popular, widely read newspaper in the colonies.

He was an exhausting pamphleteer. Pamphlets were an extraordinary political device. He wrote his first one while he was still a printer in London, a dissertation on morals, which was terribly embarrassing because he was very superficial and young. But he became probably the best pamphleteer of the age. He published the pamphlets anonymously, he published them under other people's names, and he published them under his own name, and kept up a drumfire of agitation for American rights that drove the British government mad.

Almanacs were a profitable line that most printers produced, and they were ostensibly to tell the farmer when to plant and when the moon would be full and other useful items. Franklin took the basic almanac format and added humor and satire and a little political insight, a little political editorialization . . . He created this fictional character, Poor Richard Saunders, who was an astrologer and was down at the heels, and Saunders's wife was always nagging at him. He created really the first great literary character in America. Everybody had a wife or knew somebody whose wife was as naggy as Richard Saunders's wife. And there were pranks that he played. And basically, the crop information and the phases of the moon were accurate enough.

Because Franklin was also the postmaster general and because so many of his relatives had printing shops and were postmasters under his patronage, *Poor Richard's Almanac* became the most popular almanac in America. It sold 10,000 copies a year, which would be 2 million copies today, at 10 pence, which would be $40 or $50 today. It was an enormous source of profit, but it was also an enormous source of influence.

YOUNG BEN FRANKLIN saw slaves being auctioned under his father's shop sign. By the time he hit his forties, he began to make and write an economic criticism of slavery, that slavery didn't really pay the owner, that it was a poor way to use manpower. By the time he got to England, there was already the beginning of an anti-slavery groundswell of opinion. He met many of the leading abolitionists and became the president of an effort to build schools in America for young blacks.

HIS SON WAS illegitimate. It was known instantly and it was publicly known. His enemies used it as a stick to beat him. The woman is not known, although [two books were written about it,] each nominating a different character. It is probably true that she was a prostitute, or at least someone that he had no intention of marrying. The woman he did marry, Deborah Read, took William in as an infant and raised him as what he was, Franklin's first son. They had two more children of their own.

Their marriage, by the way, was a common-law marriage because she'd married before and that husband had run away and she couldn't prove that he was dead.

They were married for forty-four years . . . and twenty-six of those years he was gone. Even during the years he was in America he was gone.

HE CROSSED THE Atlantic eight times and spent twenty-six years of his life outside the United States in France and in England. This was a man for whom travel was like vitamins. He said often, "If I don't travel, I don't feel well."

He first went to London as a very young man, to work for close to two years as a young printer. Then he came home. So that's one round trip. Then he went back in 1757, and he was there till 1762, as the colonial agent, the lobbyist, if you will, for Pennsylvania, Georgia, New Jersey, and, lastly, Massachusetts.

He visited France during his second tour in London, where he was celebrated and honored as the electrician and the new Newton. He met Louis XV and was celebrated and honored and made a fellow of royal academies in Germany and Brussels and in Russia, and so on. And so he traveled widely in Europe.

That was his first contact with the French intelligentsia. And it was where I was able to find and demonstrate that he made the first contacts with the French merchants who were rounding up supplies and shipping things in speculation that we were going to go to war with Britain.

[The relationship between France and Britain in those years was] an antipathy that transcended anything we've ever known. The Cold War was like a minuet compared to how the French and English hated each other. There had been nearly 150 unbroken years of warfare between them. They had nearly destroyed each other, and they were in intense competition for these world-wide colonies, which were subsidizing the life of the nations at home. You couldn't have these kings and these courts if you didn't have people laboring in the rice paddies and the cane fields of places millions of miles away.

Franklin came home in 1762 in kind of disgrace because he'd tried to get the king to take the royal charter for Pennsylvania away from the Penns, and it was a no-hoper. (A), the king didn't have the money, and (B), he didn't have any more desire to run Pennsylvania than the Penns did. There was a huge political upheaval. All during this time, Franklin had been a member of the Pennsylvania General Assembly. He found himself voted out of office one month, and then a couple of months later, he found himself being unanimously chosen to go back to London. So he went [to London] in 1764, and he was there till he sailed back in 1775.

While he was there, he was again trying to get some sort of reform because the whole nature of the American colonies was changing. The Americans knew it, and the British refused to acknowledge it. Colonies were supposed to feed the mother country. No decent Englishman went out to a colony and planned to stay. The only people who planned to stay in colonies were people who were on the run, religious dissenters and people of the second class.

[KING GEORGE III took over] in 1760. He was a very young man. He succeeded his grandfather, George II, and was very popular at the beginning because he was supposed to have been raised in a reformist household. And so Franklin thought, "Well, now, here's our chance to get a benevolent king who'll take over and save the colonies." It turned out that George III wanted none of it, no reform, no innovations, nothing.

While Franklin was coming back on this third trip, Lexington and Concord occurred. The war was on. So the question was, do we go ahead with the war? Do we declare independence? This debate lasted all the way through 1775 and 1776 and was really an open question until that convention in the summer of 1776. There were numbers of people—George Washington, Thomas Jefferson, Samuel Adams—who said, "Oh, no. We've got to get some last-minute deal." There was a petition in the summer of 1775, which Franklin drafted, a last petition to the king, saying, "Look, you've got to stop this." George III refused to even look at it, and indeed, turned the screws, sent more troops. Franklin [then] undertook this extraordinary journey.

He went all the way to Canada [at close to seventy years of age] to try to talk the Canadians into joining [the fight], and they wouldn't have any of it.

So he had to come all the way back, nearly died, got back on his feet, and was there for the Declaration of Independence.

Right after the Declaration of Independence, just as the British troops were coming in earnest to land on Long Island . . . the French sent secret emissaries to say, "Look, if you're really serious about this war, we'll help you. We don't want to get into war with the British, but there are these islands down in the Caribbean where we'll ship stuff under our own flag, and then if your people can get them into these hundreds of little waterways that dot your Atlantic coast, we'll sell you stuff. We'll lend you stuff. We'll take tobacco and jute and things in trade. What do you say?"

So the Continental Congress sent a number of people to France, but most importantly, they sent Franklin as the person to get a formal declaration of recognition of the United States and a trade treaty. That was really important. They empowered two other people, who turned out to be just awful and enemies of Franklin, to help him and to seek similar treaties from Spain and Holland and the other courts of Europe. Franklin disapproved of this. He said, "Come on. These monarchies aren't going to help us. The only reason the French king is interested in helping us is not out of any love of liberty. It's to get back at Britain."

FRANKLIN WAS far more radical and suspicious of power than [philosopher David] Hume. Hume believed you could set up checks and balances. Franklin believed that the only way you could check unlicensed power was to limit it. He believed in one-year terms in office. He believed in a plural executive. In other words, when he was governor of Pennsylvania during the time between his return at the end of the war and the Constitution, he shared that office with two other men. He believed that the presidency should be a three-man job. [For the legislature, he argued for] one house, popularly elected. But then when that stalled, when that became impossible, he came up with the Senate compromise.

FRANKLIN INVENTED his own form of deism. Thomas Jefferson was a deist, although I think Jefferson put Jesus a little higher in the category of ancillary divine beings. Jefferson, of course, as you know, cut up a Bible, took the four Gospels of Matthew, Mark, Luke, and John and cut out all the extraneous matter and left only Jesus' statements. That book is still available. It's called the Jefferson Bible.

There were a lot of deists. This is part of the Enlightenment. As I said in the book, once you cut off a king's head, once you've cut off God's anointed monarch, then you can ask any question you want. You can talk to God, directly. And if you don't get the answers you want from God, you can invent your own answers.

Franklin got tired of churchmen. For the same reason he didn't like lawyers, he didn't like ecclesiasticals. He felt that too many of the clergy's interests were in making docile parishes and not enough in really working toward virtue and getting to God. So his God, whom he called God, but most of the time called Providence, was way out there. He was beyond our mortal reach. But you could reach God through Buddha, through Allah, through Moses, or any of the Talmudic intercessors. But the best thing you could do to reach God and to please God and to ensure your own salvation was to help other men. And he believed that with great sincerity.

FRANKLIN WROTE [his autobiography] in two installments. He wrote one installment, which was really in the form of a letter to his son, William, who by that point was about to be named a royal governor of New Jersey. It was more of a letter like Lord Chesterfield's to his son, pointing out how you overcome personal vice and how you become more virtuous. Then he wrote a second installment many years later. He never wrote a complete autobiography, but he wrote about the most interesting and least public of his years, his growing up, his family background, and his own struggles with immorality and licentiousness.

It confirmed in my mind that you ought to read people's autobiographies, but you ought to read them with a very large spoonful of salt. The first part was a letter to his son, saying, "Look at the mistakes I've made. Here's how you ought to improve yourself. You're a lot like me. You tend to be a bit of a jerk about women. You tend to spend too much money. You like the easy life. Now, take it from me. Try to be a better guy."

And then the second part, which he wrote at a friend's home in France, was really more of a justification of his political career up to the revolution.

I'VE ALWAYS been interested in Franklin because I'm from Pennsylvania and he was part of my childhood history. I was scouting around for another book idea . . . and I started reading more about Franklin, and most of the previous historians of Franklin's life confess a frustration in coming to grips with who Benjamin Franklin was. The more I read, the more . . . I began to say to myself, "I think I know this guy. This is a guy who's really hypercharged and hyperenergetic, and very cold-minded, very tough, and not the fat, jolly fellow that we think of. This is a tough customer." And I said, "I think I can get this guy."

The Louisiana Purchase

by

JON KUKLA

When Thomas Jefferson made the Louisiana Purchase in 1803, he doubled the size of the nation and laid the foundations for expansion across the continent. Jon Kukla examined the complex origins of this famous deal and the diplomacy that made it possible in his book A Wilderness So Immense: The Louisiana Purchase and the Destiny of America, *published by Knopf in 2003. Dr. Kukla, chief executive officer of the Patrick Henry Memorial Foundation, appeared on* Booknotes *on July 6, 2003.*

[THE UNITED STATES] bought the land by treaty in April of 1803.

It was the western watershed of the Mississippi River and what they called then the Isle of Orleans, which was the city of New Orleans or now Orleans Parish. Depending on how you count them up, it [would equal] thirteen states and little parts of a couple of others.

We bought it because it was offered to us. That vast territory was incidental to what the United States really wanted, which was simply the city of New Orleans, the port of New Orleans. The port of New Orleans controls the navigation of not only the Mississippi River but also the Ohio River, at that point, of course, the United States was all east of the Mississippi River and the farmers and merchants in Kentucky and Tennessee were desperate to have the use of the Ohio River to export their crops.

We paid $15 million. [The purchase was financed] for twenty years at 6 percent, so by the time all the notes were paid off in 1823, the price was about $23 million. When you hear that it was 4 cents an acre, that's the figure for that computation.

It was an enormous deal. Jefferson was just flabbergasted when the word came back, at the extent of the piece of property that had been purchased. He got word, roughly, around the 3rd of July, 1803, and wrote a number of letters. The responses from people that he wrote to are interesting because half a dozen of those folks said that the Louisiana Purchase was equal in importance to the Declaration of Independence and to the writing of the Constitution.

What it did was to secure the western watershed of the Mississippi River and the use of the Mississippi River. In that way, it put an end to the regional tensions that could have split the country at the peak of the Appalachian Mountains because the Westerners desperately needed to use the river. There had been some separatist movements in the 1780s in Kentucky and Tennessee. And then, of course, it meant that the nation was going to be able to expand considerably across the continent to the Rockies without having a neighbor on the west.

At the time, there were about 50,000 people [living west of the Mississippi], a relatively small population. That would be 50,000 Europeans. In fact, part of the pressure that the Spanish had exerted . . . in the decade before the Louisiana Purchase was one of population—there was a significant movement of people over the mountains into Kentucky and Tennessee. If you start immediately after the American Revolution—let's say 1785—there were roughly 30,000 Americans who had gone over the mountains into Kentucky and Tennessee, and there were roughly 30,000 French and Spanish inhabitants of Louisiana. By 1800, Louisiana had about 50,000 inhabitants, but the numbers in Kentucky and Tennessee were roughly 326,000. So the increase in population was sevenfold, at least.

THIS DIPLOMATIC story [of the Louisiana Purchase] is the story of elite, white leaders making decisions based on information that they had to glean from all kinds of sources. But they had never themselves set foot in the territories that were being affected by their decisionmaking.

LOUISIANA WAS founded about 1682 by the French, and it was named for King Louis XIV. Then at the end of the Seven Years' War, or in American history, the French and Indian War, the French gave it to the Spanish in order to keep from having to surrender it to Britain. They'd essentially lost in North America to Great Britain—they lost Canada, for example. So the Spanish took possession and administered Louisiana from the 1760s up until just weeks before the Americans took possession of it in 1803. That Spanish domination of Louisiana is often missed. You go visit Louisiana and you ride the streetcars down Saint Charles Avenue. For the longest time, when I first got to Louisiana, I figured that Saint Charles Avenue, that was probably named for Charlemagne. Well, in fact, it's named for Carlos III, who was the king of Spain right on the eve of the Louisiana Purchase.

Carlos III, the father, was probably one of the most able monarchs in all of Spanish history, and his son has an equally strong claim to be one of the most inept. It made a big difference that you had a less able man facing the challenges of the French Revolution and ultimately of Napoleon.

ONE OF NAPOLEON'S goals was to try to reestablish the French domination of Haiti, which was then Santo Domingo. [He wanted] the sugar colony there, which had had such an enormous role in the French economy. What Napoleon wanted to do was send an expedition to conquer Santo Domingo, put down the revolt of the slaves there, reinstitute slavery, and get that sugar economy working again.

And in fact, this was what caused Napoleon to be interested in Louisiana. He wanted to use Louisiana as a place to supply food and firewood and all kinds of mundane commodities that weren't very profitable. The idea was that you didn't want to waste slave labor and expensive land in this tropical plantation economy of Haiti, which could be put to use making sugar, particularly, but also coffee, indigo, and chocolate. That stuff's profitable. So the idea was that you brought in these other mundane supplies from Louisiana. So that was Napoleon's imperial vision, and that was why he pressed the Spanish to cede Louisiana back to him in 1800.

[Sugar was] something like [20 percent of the gross national product of France,] and it had a phenomenal role in French overseas trade. What happened was that the French would bring the sugar in from Santo Domingo, particularly, but Martinique also. And the British were, frankly, doing the same thing in Barbados and Jamaica. But the French would bring it in and then process it and market it throughout Europe. So it represented something like 60 percent of the foreign shipping of the French shipping trade. It was a phenomenally important part of the French economy.

This was 1800. Jefferson was elected in 1800, took office in 1801. . . . When the Americans learned that the Spanish were ceding Louisiana back to the French, it was at that point that Robert Livingston and the Americans started working on the idea of, "We can't let this happen."

In 1801, France was being run by Napoleon. It had gone from Louis XVI, who was beheaded at the beginning of the revolution. It had gone through a whole bunch of turmoil and different forms of government. Napoleon was first consul [for life] in 1802, and then, later on, early in 1804, he crowned himself emperor.

ROBERT LIVINGSTON was a New York statesman, and he was Jefferson's minister to France. . . . He had been foreign minister for the Continental Congress in the American Revolution, was experienced in diplomacy, [and therefore] was Jefferson's choice to go represent the United States to France when Jefferson came to the presidency.

Livingston had worked on the idea of trying to get hold of New Orleans. He'd been working on that for months, then late in the game, James Monroe arrived with special authority to negotiate for those purposes. Monroe, I don't think, ever realized how much work Livingston had done before his arrival, so he had an inflated notion of what he had done. As far as what Monroe saw: he arrived, they went through three weeks of negotiation, they ended up with a treaty. It looked like that's when it all happened, but as I pretty well document in the book, Livingston had worked long and hard in order to create the situation in which the treaty came about.

After the treaty had been signed and sent back to the United States for rat-ification that summer, Napoleon began to have second thoughts. It was at that point that Monroe, who was even closer to Jefferson than Livingston and had been with him more recently, and so on, had the self-confidence to say, "We've been authorized to spend $2 million. Let's give it to him." Liv-ingston was not sure that that was a good idea. Turn over $2 million to some-body who's about to back out of a deal? What happens?

Monroe insisted that this was the right thing to do. Only Monroe could have done that. You could argue about whether Monroe or Madison was closer to Jefferson, but Monroe was very, very close personally and politi-cally to Jefferson, and so he had the wherewithal to say, "Let's do it." And that did, in fact, quell those fears that Napoleon would try to back out of the treaty.

JEFFERSON HAD scruples about the constitutionality of the Louisiana Pur-chase. The thing that most people jump to, of course, was that there wasn't the authority to buy this big piece of land. Jefferson wasn't terribly troubled about the land deal, and the language that he used to describe the situation is that this was "beyond the Constitution." His basic feeling was that had the guys at Philadelphia thought that anything like this could have happened, they would have, of course, written it [into the Constitution] and so on.

He contemplated writing an amendment to the Constitution to sanction what had been done. The trouble that he and others had was in bringing into the Union all of these people who were not accustomed to the democratic ways of American society, who didn't speak English, who were Catholics and so on. Bringing [the inhabitants of Louisiana] into the Union was what trou-bled Jefferson and the others.

The reality [was they were adding] people in large numbers in one big event—people who were very different from what most Americans thought of as living there. [The inhabitants of Louisiana] were certainly not Boston's former Puritans and they were not Jefferson's yeoman farmers. These were different folks. In fact, they had a substantial proportion of the population of

New Orleans that was free people of color and who were recognized as having a role in society.

WHATEVER YOU want to say about any other parts of Jefferson's career—and there are other brilliant parts and parts that people argue about—his handling of the diplomacy of the Louisiana Purchase was absolutely brilliant. He decided that he wanted to bring about a peaceful resolution of it. He used his representatives, both Livingston and Monroe, beautifully. He also used Pierre DuPont as a kind of back-channel messenger to the people around Napoleon. He just played this beautifully.

[In 1801], you can pretty much count on a message getting across the Atlantic in four weeks, sometimes longer. It took three or four weeks for a message to get from New Orleans to Washington. There were no railroads, there were no cell phones. Part of the key here was that Jefferson had been an ambassador, and he had been in France trying to represent his nation for five years with the same limitations on communications. So what he did when he appointed Livingston was that he took Livingston into his office. They spent several days together going over alternate scenarios, so that by the time Livingston went to France, he knew Jefferson's mind, he knew how he would react to this, that, or the other thing.

When he got a chance to send Monroe, Jefferson did the same thing. He brought Monroe to his office and they spent a week. By the time Livingston and Monroe got over there, they knew Jefferson's mind, they knew what he wanted, they knew how he'd react, because they had played all of these things out in speculation. They had had his full confidence and they did a magnificent job.

THE TREATY WAS negotiated in April, and it was dated April 30, 1803. The Senate passed it in three readings. Because Napoleon was said to be having second thoughts, Jefferson wanted it to push through.

THERE ARE TWO reasons [anyone should care about this purchase, 200 years later]. The one that jumps to people's mind is the land transaction—the size—and clearly, that's phenomenally important in American history because it reshaped the continent of North America.

Speculate on what North America would look like if there hadn't been a Louisiana Purchase:

Canada's boundaries would probably have extended down from Lake Erie to St. Louis. There'd be a Spanish or a French regime in charge of New Orleans and what's now the state of Louisiana, the state of Arkansas, and so on. It's likely that if the government under the Constitution of the thirteen original states had not been able to secure the navigation of the Mississippi and the Ohio Rivers for the Kentuckians and the Tennesseans, those states would have split off. There was a secessionist movement in New England that probably would have pulled it apart, too. And so we would have had a Balkanized map of North America, with all of the attendant irritants and abrasion that go with that. So there's that geographic response to the purchase's significance.

The other significance is one that we can now understand, 200 years after the event. . . . To engage in a broad caricature, the first 200 years of American history, from Jamestown in 1607 to the Louisiana Purchase in 1803, had created a white male agrarian Protestant civic world on the East Coast. At New Orleans in 1803, that world confronted French, Spanish, and free people of color, which was an extraordinary shock to the American understanding of race relations in an urban setting. I see that as the beginning of an encounter with diversity, and that encounter with diversity—both through immigration and through expansion—has characterized the second 200 years of American history.

So for those geographical and the human dimensions—those are the two ways in which I think it's worth pausing to contemplate the significance of this event.

Character and
Characters in the U.S. Senate

by

JOSEPH MARTIN HERNON

In 1956, Senator John F. Kennedy won the Pulitzer Prize for his book, Profiles in Courage, *an admiring portrayal of eight of his senatorial colleagues. Forty years later, Joseph Martin Hernon provided his own study of
the most influential U.S. senators in his book* Profiles in Character:
Hubris and Heroism in the U.S. Senate, 1789–1990, *published by M.
E. Sharpe. Hernon argued that the most influential American senators are
not necessarily the most celebrated. Each chapter of his book pairs a famous
senator with his lesser-known counterpart, producing a history of the Senate through sixteen men. Mr. Hernon, University of Massachusetts Professor of History Emeritus, joined us on February 15, 1998, to discuss several
of these senators and their impact on American politics.*

PRESIDENTS HAVE their presidential libraries, which are all very fine, with
big staffs and court historians, and we have many, many biographies—more
than we need of some—of the presidents. Yet a lot of the senators are ignored
and were extremely significant politically.

I CONSIDER Thomas Hart Benton more significant than Daniel Webster,
Henry Clay, and John C. Calhoun put together in his thirty years in the Senate. [Benton was] one of the first two senators from Missouri, the man who
inched his way toward opposition to slavery, the man whose son-in-law was
the first civil governor of California, John Charles Fremont. Benton was
involved in almost everything over that thirty-year period, and he finally

came to oppose slavery. This was the principal issue between him and Calhoun from the annexation of Texas in 1845 to 1850. [Benton and Calhoun] became the principal focal points between 1845 and 1850 for the struggle of the soul of the Democratic Party over the slavery question.

The whole question of a Civil War would have come up earlier if [the Democratic Party had] accepted Benton's position of opposition to the extension of slavery into the West. They selected John C. Calhoun's position and nominated Northern Democrats like Franklin Pierce and James Buchanan to appease the South and postpone the Civil War for another ten years. I might just [point out] that in studying these senators, one can see clearly the role of race in shaping our politics over the last 200 years.

Thomas Hart Benton perhaps profited from an early sin, or mistake, when he was expelled from Chapel Hill, the University of North Carolina, at the age of sixteen for petty thievery. That haunted him for the rest of his career and perhaps prevented him from ever running for president. Martin Van Buren wanted him as his vice president, but he turned it down and it made him stronger in the Senate. That's another theme of this book, that many of these people who were in the Senate for thirty years or so are more significant than most of our presidents.

[Benton was] kind of a frontiersman. He killed one man in a duel. He wounded Andrew Jackson, almost killed him, and then they become close friends after they got into the Senate. He was this incredible character. He had his body scrubbed down with a horsehair brush by his servant every day. He would say, "Why do you do this?" "The Roman gladiators did it, sir." Benton had this huge ego, yet he had a great sense of history and what history was all about.

THE CIVIL WAR and Reconstruction are incredibly important, the watershed in American history. And as much as I admire all of the studies on the Civil War, including the wonderful documentary by Ken Burns, you notice that it ends conveniently with the assassination of Abraham Lincoln. The next twelve years, the Reconstruction, help to explain why the civil rights movement was postponed for another century as blacks were abandoned. Historians have been very reluctant to get involved in the quagmire of the Reconstruction because it's so complicated. I think I've made a little more sense of the Reconstruction in focusing on Fessenden and Sumner from 1865 to 1868, but I leave it up to historians to decide for themselves.

I wanted to zero in on someone like William Pitt Fessenden, who's almost completely unknown and whom I raise almost to the level of Lincoln. I call him the "Down East Lincoln".... Lincoln was a folksy Midwesterner. Fessenden was a laconic Down East Maine senator, who's buried in an unmarked grave in

Portland, amazingly. I've been up there. It's the family plot, and Fessenden was illegitimate. Daniel Webster was his godfather. That's the reason why Fessenden did not run—I speculate anyway—for the presidency in 1858 when he was told that all of New England and Pennsylvania were ready to support him for the Republican Party nomination in Chicago in 1860. Fessenden said, "I'm going fishing." He didn't want to get involved. He was happy being in the Senate.

Charles Sumner was the great hero of the anti-slavery movement who was brutally caned by [South Carolina Senator] Preston Brooks in 1856 on the Senate floor. Massachusetts kept open his Senate seat for four years until he returned to the Senate in 1860. [He was hurt] very badly. According to a couple of historians, he suffered from psychogenic neurosis. Fessenden said—they had been good friends in 1856—that he found him a changed person. Their differences from 1864 on, in the Republican Party, shaped so much of the Reconstruction, [issues] like the wording of the Fourteenth Amendment and the impeachment of Andrew Johnson. After the death of Lincoln, Fessenden and Sumner were the two that are crucial for understanding that period from 1865 to 1868.

I would really like to get to know Fessenden, who was so mysterious and had a very acerbic tongue. Stephen Douglas called him "the greatest debater in the Senate," and Lincoln's friend, Benjamin Brown French, called him "the greatest man in the country." When Lincoln was desperate for reelection, he plucked Fessenden out of the Senate and made him secretary of the treasury, a kind of prime minister, for eight months in 1864.

Fessenden was born illegitimate. He had an incredible life. He was engaged to Longfellow's sister, Elizabeth, for six months and then she died. He had three sons, unlike most politicians, who fought in the Civil War. His youngest son, Sam, was killed in the second battle of Manassas. Two other sons were wounded. One of them, Captain James Fessenden, trained the first black soldiers, but [his unit] was disbanded by Lincoln as too controversial. This was down in South Carolina and some of these volunteers joined the famous unit on which the movie *Glory* is based.

The record of the Joint Committee of Fifteen on Reconstruction, the most important congressional committee in history, was published in 1914. In that, you see Fessenden's draft of the Fourteenth Amendment. His draft is so broad that it would have made the Fifteenth Amendment, granting the right to vote to black males, unnecessary. Thaddeus Stevens called it too radical, and yet Fessenden has been labeled a conservative because he opposed the impeachment of Andrew Johnson.

GEORGE FRISBIE HOAR was a Mr. Pickwick-like character and a man who should be truly honored. He was the first person to call for the vote for women, and the only one in the Congress to oppose the exclusion of the Chinese in 1882 and 1902. He stood up for the rights of Irish Catholics and opposed the annexation of the Philippines. Albert Beveridge, another senator from Indiana, said in a famous speech that it was our destiny to civilize the Philippines. And, of course, Teddy Roosevelt and William McKinley were fathers of twentieth-century imperialism. Hoar got up and said, "What about the Declaration of Independence and the Constitution?" Hoar was the grandson of Roger Sherman of the Connecticut Compromise that brought the Senate into being.

Hoar [was] very humane in the sense of applying the principles of the Declaration of Independence and the Constitution. . . . He said, "There is no Chinese question, the problem is with Congress bringing it into politics." And he said, "The ultimate liberation of the Negro will come with the liberation of the white, of the Saxon." In other words, he was an amazing person in his views of not only domestic issues but foreign policy.

WILLIAM BORAH was one of the great orators of the Senate, senator from Idaho from 1907 to 1940, a great character. In the 1920s, President Calvin Coolidge joked that "Congress was occasionally out of session, but Borah was always in session." In 1924, so the story goes, Coolidge decided on Borah as his running mate and Borah was out horseback riding in Rock Creek Park. The Secret Service found him; he came riding into the White House and he walked into the president's office. Calvin Coolidge said to him, "Senator Borah, we want you on the ticket." And Borah replied, "Which place, Mr. President?" Borah was quite content being chair of the Foreign Relations Committee. He was also known at the end, unfortunately, as a kind of champion of appeasement against Hitler.

Borah had affairs with two of Washington's most prominent women who were rivals for his affection—Alice Roosevelt Longworth and Eleanor "Cissy" Patterson. Though married to the speaker of the House, Nicholas Longworth, "Princess Alice," daughter of Teddy Roosevelt, soon became known as "Aurora Borah Alice," especially after Senator Borah reportedly fathered her only child, Paulina. At the time it was known only in scuttlebutt, but in a 1988 biography, it all came out. Princess Alice died in 1980 and Mary Borah, who was known as "Little Borah," lived to be 106—she died in 1976. It wasn't until after their deaths that they could publish these stories. "The stallion of Idaho," was his nickname in Boise.

William Borah was born in downstate Illinois. He ran off to become a Shakespearean actor in a traveling troupe. At the age of sixteen, he played the role of Mark Antony. Then he went off to the University of Kansas for a year, then took a train west. He was going out to Washington state. I guess he was gambling on the train and lost some money and a gambler said, "Well, why don't you get off here?" That was Idaho. He ended up in Idaho and became a famous lawyer there and then was elected to the Senate in 1906.

FRANKLIN ROOSEVELT called George William Norris of Nebraska the "perfect, gentle knight of American conservatism." . . . I deal with him over a thirty-year period, including the last time, when he was defeated in 1942. What he's most famous for would be relevant today. He left the Senate in 1943 and refused to take a penny in pension. [He had been] in Congress for forty years. Thirty years in the [Senate.] He said that it would be immoral because he had voted on all of those pension bills.

I LIKED JOHN Kennedy very much. I was an early volunteer, one of the earliest for him. But I felt that I had to be fair, and I think all the evidence indicates that there was some kind of manipulation in his winning the Pulitzer Prize, with this provision: There's manipulation all the time in these prizes behind the scenes. And so, was it wrong for Joe Kennedy to make every effort to use his influence to win the Pulitzer Prize for his son to help in the presidential campaign? I'm just pointing out that this was a kind of hubris.

In the same way, [I can] put in a positive note about one of the Kennedys, Bobby Kennedy. Some people would say that when he entered the presidential race in 1968, this act, as a senator from New York itself was one of hubris, [he was] seizing the limelight from Eugene McCarthy. But on the other hand, those last two months Bobby Kennedy demonstrated a kind of heroism—from the assassination of Martin Luther King until his own assassination. He was freed up with this realization that he may not win the presidency, and he was addressing issues that were really important in the country.

ARTHUR VANDENBERG of Michigan from 1945 to 1951, is perhaps one of the unsung senators. Many people have read David McCullough's wonderful biography of Harry Truman, but there's no available biography of Vandenberg. Vandenberg from 1945 to 1947 was chairing the Senate Foreign Relations Committee, was president pro tempore of the Senate, led Truman, especially in foreign policy. Vandenberg and George Marshall, the new secretary of state in 1947, worked very closely together. The Vandenberg Resolution was the basis of NATO and our mutual assistance pacts around the world. He is a major figure who's been largely ignored because he's not a president.

THE MOST disagreeable [senator I profiled] would be Henry Cabot Lodge. Lodge was brilliant, but he was incredibly cynical. The death of his son, Bay Lodge, who died of food poisoning in 1909, and then his wife's death shortly afterward, really made him very cynical. He was largely responsible for getting Warren Harding the nomination, but he just laughed at him, at Harding's bloviations. He sneered from his balcony, looking down on the American populace. He became very bitter. . . .

Cabot Lodge had a very superior attitude. He came from the Boston Brahmin elite, a Ph.D., and he was an accomplished historian himself. . . . He opposed Woodrow Wilson, to some degree, because of his ego.

HUBERT HUMPHREY and Strom Thurmond . . . both played roles in the Democratic Convention in 1948 when Humphrey gave his famous speech supporting civil rights. Thurmond became the States Rights candidate, opposing the civil rights plank, and broke with the party, running as a Dixiecrat in 1948. Thurmond's significance is in understanding the role of the Southern strategy. Thurmond was very important in electing Nixon in 1968 and Ronald Reagan in 1980. Lee Atwater, his assistant, became George H. W. Bush's campaign manager. Future historians will look upon Thurmond as a kind of modern-day John C. Calhoun, the way he elevated South Carolina to a very important place in the Electoral College, in electoral history.

Thurmond was prune juice, teetotalism. There's a fundamentalist element. He felt that he was God's muscle man in the Senate. Amazing [was] his adaptability to change—a man who said the *Dred Scott* decision was right in 1964, then hired the first black on his staff in 1971, and got about a third of the black vote in South Carolina.

HUBERT HUMPHREY was the victim of Vietnam. He was one of the most wonderful, warm human beings you could meet. But Lyndon Johnson took advantage of his good nature, and as Humphrey reminded people in 1970, he made a mistake in letting Lyndon Johnson push him around in 1968 when he was a candidate for president and barely lost to Richard Nixon. So Humphrey was really a victim of Vietnam as, indeed, the Democratic Party was a victim of Vietnam, from the 1960s up until the election of Bill Clinton.

THE INSCRIPTION on Taft's statue [on the Capitol grounds] . . . says that the state should be its people's servants. It's essential that that happen. It's dangerous if the people become the servants of the state. It reflects a quote from Alexis de Tocqueville that it's a great danger to democracy, that democracy could turn to despotism, when the people of a state begin to look upon themselves as servants. Many of these politicians would talk about the character of the senators being based on the character of the people themselves. So basically, people get what they deserve, what they vote for.

Leadership in Wartime

by

ELIOT A. COHEN

In his book Supreme Command: Soldiers, Statesmen, and Leadership in Wartime, *Eliot A. Cohen examines four civilian wartime leaders—Abraham Lincoln, Georges Clemenceau, Winston Churchill, and David Ben-Gurion—who succeeded through their intimate involvement in the details of their respective wars. Mr. Cohen, director of strategic studies at the Paul H. Nitze School of Advanced International Studies of Johns Hopkins University, joined us on September 22, 2002, to talk about his book, published by The Free Press that same year. He discussed what a modern president might learn from these leaders' stories; in fact, President George W. Bush read the book prior to the war in Iraq.*

THESE WERE FOUR statesmen [Abraham Lincoln, Georges Clemenceau, David Ben-Gurion and Winston Churchill] that I'd always admired enormously. The more structured reason [I chose them], I suppose, is this: that I wanted a certain kind of historical continuity, starting with the middle of the nineteenth century and going up to the middle of the twentieth century. I wanted to look at four democracies . . . I wanted just one American, one Frenchman, one Brit, one Israeli.

I thought each of the four was so different from one another, and yet they had so much in common that the tension worked quite well.

OF COURSE, Abraham Lincoln was probably our greatest war president, I would say even greater than Roosevelt. The thing that entranced me about Lincoln—and still entrances me—is the way in which he was "deceptive." That is probably a harsh word, but this is a man who worked extraordinarily subtly and indirectly. My favorite quotation, which I put in the book, is from

Willie Herndon, his law partner, who said, "Any man who ever took Lincoln for a simple man usually found himself lying flat on his back in a ditch." And so a lot of that chapter is about Lincoln's cunning, if you will.

GEORGES CLEMENCEAU was the prime minister of France in the very last year of the First World War. He is, in some ways, the most interesting character, the one about whom I think I knew least before I began work on the book. The thing that is amazing to me is that he became premier at age seventy-six, and he took charge when France was really in terrible shape. It's not at all clear that France was going to win the war. In fact, he was thinking about the possibility that they may have to withdraw, even lose Paris. And he was determined to fight to the end.

His interesting challenge was he had to weigh the advice of two very different military professionals, Ferdinand Foch and Philippe Pétain, who had very different attitudes to how the war ought to be fought. And there was this seventy-six-year-old doctor sorting it out.

WINSTON CHURCHILL is my hero. Winston Churchill I find utterly fascinating. It'd be very hard to write a book about civilian wartime leadership without talking about Winston Churchill. There is the standard narrative that this is the man who gives the lion's roar, who's tremendously inspiring, who has, of course, this magnificent command of the English language but has terrible judgment. That's really been the standard account. The more I dug into Churchill, the thing I found most interesting is the way in which he was actually a man of system. He was a man who was much more thorough and deliberate than he's been portrayed. Teasing that out was really quite interesting. Also, Churchill is the one who knew how to ask questions, and his questioning I just found marvelous.

BEN-GURION IS probably the one least known to an English-language audience. He's the founding father of the state of Israel. A lot of the material for him is really still available only in Hebrew. There's some of it that's been translated. . . . I was able to look at his wonderful wartime diaries that he kept. He was a tremendously compulsive diarist, just writing nonstop.

The thing that I liked about Ben-Gurion was the way in which he had this ability to apply an enormous amount of common sense to a problem and say, "You're thinking about it all wrong." There's a kind of a brutal honesty about it. The other thing is that for a man who was, in many ways, personally quite unpleasant and a man of terrific temper, and so on, he had a quality of moderation about him which is actually shared by these three other statesmen, which I found fascinating.

But what happened was, after he retired from politics the first time, in 1953, he decided to move to this little kibbutz in the southern part of Israel, and he decided that he wanted to take part in the reconstruction of the land, or "pioneering," as he talked about it. And so he was in this poor, impoverished little kibbutz, and he was living in this house, which wasn't that much bigger than a trailer, honestly.

When I visited it, because it's now located next to the main research site where they have his archives, the thing that struck me was the images that he had. There are four different images which really say everything there is to say about his life.

There's a picture on his desk of one of his old comrades from the Socialist movement, a fellow named Berl Katznelson, and that really gets to his roots in the Socialist movement in what was then Palestine. There's a replica of Michelangelo's *Moses,* so there's his connection to the history of the Jewish people. And in this little sitting room that he had, there is a micrograph of Abraham Lincoln that's been made out of the words of the Emancipation Proclamation. That's the more general humanist side of him.

Then in his little tiny bedroom, there is the most surprising thing of all. I've always asked people who are curious about this, "Well, OK, what picture do you think he would have hanging in his bedroom?" It's a picture of a contemporary. The answer is Mahatma Gandhi, which nobody would ever guess—Gandhi, the pacifist. Ben-Gurion was a man of war. But it says something about what a tremendous range there was in him and what an understanding of the importance of a spiritual power. It's fascinating.

ONE OF THE things that attracted me to these four is that there were these threads between them, these connections between them. Clemenceau had actually visited the United States just at the end of the Civil War. I think he'd like to say that he got to Richmond before Lincoln did. He was a great admirer of Lincoln. Churchill was a tremendous admirer of Clemenceau. And in fact, if you look at some of Churchill's speeches, some of his best lines, including the motto of his Second World War memoirs, are, you have to say, lifted from Clemenceau. Ben-Gurion was a tremendous admirer of Churchill, but also of Lincoln. So there are connections there, as well.

IF YOU WERE one of their military subordinates, you probably felt that all four of them were meddling in different ways—if you mean by "meddling" asking lots of questions, even making suggestions about things like particular troop movements, and so on. You'd have to say that all four of them were playing quite an important role [in the tactics of war].

This is not a book which is a mandate to politicians to begin barking orders to their generals and say, "Do this" and "Do that." It's really a book about the nature of the dialogue that goes on and that should go on between political leaders and their military subordinates. That's really the heart of it. It's what I call the unequal dialogue, because the politicians ultimately have to be in charge. My central argument is that, really, there's nothing that in principle [political leaders] can't get into because there can be larger ramifications from even very technical things.

[An example of this is] in the spring or early summer of 1943, when Churchill ended up making this decision about whether or not the Royal Air Force in its bombing raids over Germany is going to be using chaff, strips of aluminum foil, to jam German radars. Well, why on earth should a prime minister who's also minister of defense end up having to make that decision? Isn't that an example of micromanagement and meddling?

If you unpack it, actually, it's revealing. First, the military doesn't agree with itself. You have the Royal Air Force's Bomber Command, which wants to use this stuff, obviously, to save bomber crews and be able to deliver the bombs more effectively. On the other hand, you have the Air Defense Great Britain, which is the successor to Fighter Command, knowing that they have no counter to this, being very much afraid that they were going to have more German air raids, being deathly afraid that if the Germans see how well this works, they'll do exactly the same thing back to the British.

So you have a deadlock. There is no expert military opinion on whether or not you should use chaff, code named WINDOW. And it ended up getting bucked up to a political leader to make. Now, that's a particular kind of case, but I think it illustrates the way in which sometimes even seemingly quite small decisions can actually have much larger implications having to do with risk or political objectives, where the politicians have to be involved.

LET'S JUST TAKE Lincoln, who was in many ways the most interesting of the group because he was, in many ways, a very gentle man. He stayed up late at night trying to figure ways to commute sentences of sentries who had fallen asleep on guard duty and were being sentenced to be shot. He wrote these extraordinary letters of condolence—one to the daughter of a friend of his who fell in battle—to women who were paying a price.

[During] the Battle of Fredericksburg, in which Ambrose Burnside—one of his less able generals—had hurled . . . numerous armies at a completely open slope, Marye's Heights, he suffered ten, twelve thousand casualties. What Lincoln said to somebody in his office is, "If we just had a general who was willing to do this every day for week of days, at the end of this, the Army of the Potomac would still be a mighty host, the rebel army would be shattered, the insurrection would be over, and [the Union] restored. The war won't be over until we find a general who understands that arithmetic."

Now that, to me, is a pretty cold-blooded statement. This tremendously humane man was willing to support Ulysses S. Grant when they're taking these awful casualties in 1864, 1865; he's willing to do it.

TAKE A DIFFERENT example of ruthlessness and doing terrible things, Winston Churchill, who, again, had a very tender streak in him. But one of the most brutal decisions that he made, and certainly one of the most brutal decisions that he felt he made, was in June of 1940. After the French had been practically knocked out of the war by the Germans, in order to prevent the French fleet from falling into German hands, he ordered the Royal Navy to attack it and its harbors in Algeria. They killed something like 1,300 French sailors. Now these were people that had been fighting side by side with them a few weeks earlier. Churchill's description of that is extremely eloquent. He said, yes, this was the hardest decision he ever made. He said there was great tragedy, but it was absolutely necessary. Then he laid out why he thinks that was the case.

THERE WAS A dark side to Clemenceau. He was actually much more up front about it. He once said something like this, "I had children, they turned against me. I had a wife, she left me. I had friends, they betrayed me. I have only my claws and I will use them." So he was a guy who was not terribly bashful without saying what a tough fellow he was.

During the war, [he was premier of France] only for a year, and then his [term ended], in 1920. . . . But [he] was pretty willing to have people arrested. He was willing to have people shot. He was ruthless in terms of foreign generals, which doesn't sound very hard. But one of the arguments I make is that people always very substantially underestimate how difficult it is to fire a general in wartime. There's so much pressure, so much uncertainty, so many potential political repercussions. And all four of these people were completely willing to cashier general officers. As I said, it sounds easy, but in truth, it's an extraordinarily difficult thing to do.

BEN-GURION REALLY cleaned out the complete high command of the Haganah.

The Haganah was the underground Jewish army before the creation of the Israeli state. But it was really quite elaborate and it had a regular general staff. He was moving people around. He also got rid of the guy who effectively had been the civilian head of the Haganah. First, he marginalized him, and then he eventually simply pushed him aside.

[The vote in the U.N. to make Israel a country] was a very close vote. There was tremendous uncertainty in the Jewish community in Palestine whether this was even going to be a good idea. The odds against them seemed so terrible. [They felt] that the Third World was mobilizing against them. But the decision was made, and they went through with it. For me, the poignant thing about that is that after the vote, there was this eruption of celebration in Tel Aviv, and in Jewish communities in places like New York. There's a beautiful phrase in Hebrew, which I can't really translate, but Ben-Gurion says that he looked at the dancing crowds and he said, "I felt like a mourner amongst those who rejoice." It's because he knew what this was going to lead to.

ONE OF THE things that all four of these leaders had, which seemed to be a tremendous requirement of good political leadership, is [what Lincoln's assistant secretary of war] Charles Dana says about Abraham Lincoln: He had no illusions. That's one of the reasons why I think all four of these people were also melancholy: They were men without illusions.

The question with Lincoln is, "Who didn't he fire?" He went through a long series of generals. He began with Irwin McDowell; he fired him. George McClellan, he kept him a little bit longer; McClellan was in for a year, fired, brought back and fired again after a month. George Meade was . . . in reality there for about nine months.

There's a poignant part which brings out Lincoln's ruthlessness. McDowell later appealed, and he's got these generals making the case for him. This came to Lincoln just after this poor major—who was desperate to get back into war, because he was basically a patriotic man—had just made the ultimate sacrifice. His son, who was the captain of the Ohio infantry, had just been killed. What further patriotic testimony can you ask for? And Lincoln said, "I'm terribly sorry. I've got to make an example of you."

The first thing I think of with Lincoln would be the importance of correctly judging the character of your subordinates, particularly your military subordinates. And Lincoln was ultimately quite a good judge of character. [Lincoln kept saying, "Stop worrying about the capital in Richmond and worry about the generals and troops in the middle."] That means that you don't just accept what the military seniority and promotion system coughs up, that you may have to reach down and find some rather unprepossessing soul who looks like Ulysses S. Grant. Very early on in the war, Lincoln kept an eye on Grant, about whom he had heard both good things and bad things, and he tried to figure out, is this the kind of person who's right for the job? So in this sense, Lincoln . . . devoted an enormous amount of effort to try to figure out what somebody's character was and how far he could push them.

With Clemenceau, [I think of] firsthand knowledge. Clemenceau was out there one day a week on the front lines. I think it's tremendously important to get out there and get a feel for the troops, get a feel for the leaders.

With Churchill, it's questioning, the importance of asking lots and lots of questions and not being cowed by anybody saying, "Do you really want to get into that level of detail?" And with Ben-Gurion, it's really making sure you've got the first order of questions right: What is this all about? What are we trying to achieve? Who is our enemy?

WHAT . . . a president [would] take away from a book like this, would be, first, the importance of asking lots of hard questions and not simply accepting a plan that's presented to you, and being quite insistent on options.

The other thing I would say for presidents to take away from the book is the importance of remaining on top of the process all the way through. One of the chapters talks about the United States, from Vietnam through the Gulf War and a bit beyond. It seems to me pretty clear that the civilians were in control all the way through at one level, but at another level, they didn't really think hard through the conclusion of that war. . . . It's quite clear that General Norman Schwarzkopf, the theater commander in Iraq in the first war, went into armistice negotiations with his own terms of reference that he drafted. All that happened was the State Department changed the word "negotiate" to "discuss," because only the State Department can negotiate. Hopefully, somebody read that and took it seriously, wouldn't allow that to happen again.

Abraham Lincoln

by

FRANK J. WILLIAMS AND

EDWARD STEERS JR.

Abraham Lincoln is usually ranked as one of the greatest leaders in U.S. and world history. Over the years, numerous authors have appeared on Booknotes *to offer their insights into the sixteenth American president. In* Blood on the Moon: The Assassination of Abraham Lincoln, *published by the University Press of Kentucky in 2001, Edward Steers Jr. examined the collaboration behind Lincoln's assassination. Mr. Steers, a writer in West Virginia, joined us on* Booknotes *on February 17, 2002. Frank J. Williams, author and chief justice of the Rhode Island Supreme Court, analyzed Lincoln's political career and his character in* Judging Lincoln, *a collection of nine essays, published by Southern Illinois University Press in 2002. Mr. Williams appeared on* Booknotes *on November 10, 2002.*

FRANK J. WILLIAMS

THE FASCINATING part about Lincoln is that he was an enigma. As much as we know about him in the historical record in his utterances, in the collected works of his writings and speeches—almost a million words—he still kept many things very close to his chest. He was a very private person. So the challenge is to try to detect what was really going on his mind and what his motivations were and the Machiavellian nature of his personality.

Each of us has a dark side and a light side, and Lincoln had a dark side, too. He had a temper. Most people don't know that. Fortunately for us, and himself, he was able to keep it in check most of the time. I think his views on race are ambivalent, at best, and racist at worst. Of course, this was the culture in which he lived. We see that in comments he made at the Lincoln–Douglas debates. But as other scholars have said, he probably would not have won the race for president if he had taken a position more closely aligned to the abolitionists.

In our current generation, there's more a sense of reality, that Lincoln really was not a godlike figure, that he was a human being. [Some generations believed] he was raised to the heavens after his death, which is unfortunate. He shouldn't be treated as some kind of votive candle on the shelf somewhere. He did have human foibles. He was a hypochondriac. He was suspicious. He misjudged his generals during the war until he himself developed the necessary judgment to retain generals that could win battles. But this is all part of the growth of a human being in the first instance, and a leader in the second.

The president is commander in chief, as well as chief magistrate of America. His role in both capacities was important for me to study. I'm pleased with the way he managed, on the whole, with these dual roles. He struggled mightily, as every president does. . . . Many of the issues that Lincoln had we now have, now that we are at war with terrorism—the security of our country versus civil liberties. . . . That's why Lincoln remains such a relevant person in our current life.

GENERAL GEORGE McClellan . . . was Lincoln's troublesome general. He had been commander in chief initially. He had "a case of the slows," to quote Lincoln. Lincoln reinstated him as general after the second battle of Bull Run. After Antietam, when McClellan refused to follow up the so-called victory, Lincoln finally had the courage to fire him. Remember, McClellan was very popular with his troops.

Lincoln sent a messenger with an order relieving McClellan from command and appointing Ambrose Burnside, a Rhode Islander, to take his place as commanding general of the Army of the Potomac. Burnside did not want the command. He knew he didn't have the competence for it, and we saw that at the Battle of Fredericksburg in December 1862.

Since McClellan was so popular with the troops and America . . . the Democrats, the loyal opposition, chose him as the Democratic candidate for president in 1864. But there was a conflict from the beginning. Here they're making this former commanding general of the Army of the Potomac the Democratic candidate, but then the peace lovers acquired a peace platform, in which there would be an effort at peace without the end of slavery, without necessarily reunion. This doomed the Democrats in the 1864 election.

LINCOLN IS sometimes criticized for curtailing civil liberties, like suspending the writ of habeas corpus. We could talk about that forever. But here's a president and a commander in chief who allowed the elections to go forward in wartime. And initially in 1864, he thought he was going to lose. That's why he wrote the "blind memorandum" in August and had all of the Cabinet members initial the back of it. He expected to lose, and if he did, he would work with the incoming president to terminate the war or prevail in the war.

This election was the first time in American history that soldiers in the field were allowed to cast ballots. So Lincoln took a big gamble, and yet he believed in the basic tenets of the democracy: that you should not curtail this necessity of having elections every two years.

[Lincoln was able to win the soldiers' votes because of his] ability to transcend politics and strike a responsive chord in many Americans, including the soldiers in the field. These were the people who were being sent into battle, receiving the casualties and the deaths that followed. Yet they believed in this person they came to call "Father Abraham." And they were able to differentiate between him and McClellan, who, under the peace platform, would end a war in which they fought so hard to prevail.

THE THIRTEENTH Amendment outlawed "involuntary servitude," to use the exact language, slavery, forever. It was added to the Constitution in 1865. But Lincoln campaigned for this amendment long before the reelection in 1864, which took a lot of guts and courage. He didn't have to say anything, but he did campaign for it. It was so important to him that he logrolled, used patronage. We never found any illegal acts that he may have committed to get votes, but the important thing is he wanted the old Congress, that is, the Congress that would go out of existence after his inauguration in 1865, to be the one to pass the resolution that would go to the states for ratification. He succeeded in February 1865.

It's a close call on whether his offer of patronage to congressmen to get their vote ran afoul of an antibribery statute that was already part of the United States code. He came very close, we think. No money [changed hands], but clearly there was the implication that if you were to vote for this resolution, you might be taken care of, with one of your constituents or relatives being given a job in the government.

[The Thirteenth Amendment was ratified in] December of 1865 by enough states to make it part of the Constitution but, in February of 1865 it had been passed by the House and Senate to send to the states for ratification. And Lincoln was reelected in November.

EDWARD STEERS JR.

I PLACE [the Lincoln shooting at] approximately 10:20 P.M. in the presidential box at Ford's Theater.

The theater is on 10th Street in Washington, D.C., not far from the White House, which is at 16th, of course, and in the center of Mr. Lincoln's neighborhood.

John Wilkes Booth was, at the time, one of America's greatest tragedians, of the famous Booth family, a Maryland family, from Bel Air, Maryland. John Wilkes Booth by 1864 had become certainly one of America's greatest actors and a matinee idol—extremely handsome, personable, well liked, generous, outgoing. Seems he had everything going for him, and everybody liked him. He basically had no enemies at all.

He was in his twenty-seventh year. At the time of the assassination, he was one month short of his twenty-seventh birthday.

Booth shot Lincoln point-blank with a .41-caliber derringer, a single-shot pistol, probably within two feet of the back of his head.

Booth entered the theater, which was crowded, by the way, virtually standing room. He had easy, full run of the theater, being a famous actor, a very close friend of the Ford family, of John Ford and his brother, Harry Clay Ford. So Booth could come and go in the theater at will. He had reconnoitered the theater earlier in the day, made all of the arrangements, knew what he was going to do and knew when he was going to do it. So he simply entered the theater, made his way up the staircase to the dress circle or balcony, and then slowly made his way across the back of the theater to the box.

Abraham Lincoln and his wife, Mary, were sitting on one side, and on the other were Major Henry Rathbone and his fiancée and stepsister, Clara Harris. It was just the four of them.

[The bullet] entered the lower left base of Lincoln's skull, and while there's some controversy as to the path of the bullet, most people agree that it traversed diagonally across the brain, lodging behind the right eye.

Lincoln just went comatose. He slumped in his chair. It wasn't a violent reaction on his part; his head just fell forward. Mary Lincoln, of course, who was sitting right next to him, holding his hand, screamed and pandemonium broke out. Major Rathbone realized what had happened, jumped up, and began to grapple with Booth.

Booth had a large bowie knife. He stabbed Rathbone in the arm and then vaulted over the balustrade onto the floor of the theater stage. He turned toward the audience, by most accounts, and yelled "Sic semper tyrannis"—"Thus always to tyrants"—which was Virginia's state motto at the time, and is now. He then exited stage right, went out the rear door into the alley behind the theater, known as "Baptist Alley"—Ford's Theater had originally been the 10th Street Baptist Church—where his horse was being held by a young boy who worked for the Fords.

He struck the boy, mounted the horse, wheeled around and galloped down the alley, turned left, went up onto F Street, turned right, and headed for the Capitol grounds.

Laura Keene was starring in the play and it was a benefit performance for her that evening. That is, all of the proceeds from that evening would go to Laura Keene as a reward and appreciation for her role as the star. She was starring in the play *Our American Cousin*, which is a British spoof on American bumpkins, a play that Lincoln would really enjoy very much.

She made her way to the box. That's interesting, how she was able to make her way to the box—but she did. She asked Dr. Leale if she could rest Lincoln's head in her lap and he said yes, and so she did.

They tried to administer to Lincoln in the box. There were several doctors in the theater. The first doctor to get to the box was Charles Leale, who was an army sergeant. And at first, he didn't know how the president was injured or to what extent, but he began to examine him, thinking that perhaps he had a chest wound, had been stabbed. At one point, he ran his fingers through Lincoln's hair and noticed blood on his hand. And then, of course, he found the entry wound. A blood clot had already formed, which essentially suppressed Lincoln's breathing. Leale removed the blood clot, and Lincoln began to breathe quite normally and his pulse restored.

At that point, several other doctors came into the box. They consulted and pretty much agreed that they had to move Lincoln.

They probably moved him over to the Petersen house directly across the street between 10:45 and 10:50.

[AFTER THE assassination, Booth] headed over the Navy Yard Bridge, over the Anacostia or eastern branch of the Potomac, directly into southern Maryland. He went straight to the Surratt Tavern, which was approximately thirteen miles southeast of Washington, where he picked up a carbine and a pair of binoculars and some whiskey, and then headed on directly to Dr. Mudd's house, where he arrived at 4:00 A.M.

The [myth surrounding the Lincoln assassination] that I like the best, of course, is that Mary Surratt and Samuel Mudd were innocent victims.

Mary Surratt was the woman who owned the tavern, Surratt Tavern in Surrattsville, and the boarding house in Washington not many blocks from Ford's Theater, which became a center for the conspirators to meet, including John Wilkes Booth. Several of the conspirators actually boarded for a brief period at Mary Surratt's boarding house.

Mary Surratt was one of the four that were condemned to death by hanging and became in some ways a cause célèbre.

[She was the first woman to ever be hanged in America] by the federal government. Of course, there were many women that had been hanged, but she was the first by the federal government.

[The myth about] Dr. Samuel Mudd was [that he was] nothing more than a simple country doctor who was persecuted for nothing more than administering the Hippocratic oath to an injured man who was seeking medical attention. [The injured man was] John Wilkes Booth. Booth and [co-conspirator David] Herold arrived at Dr. Mudd's house four and a half hours after the assassination.

[THIS HAPPENED] on April 9th. So this was five days [after Lee met Grant at Appomattox]. Lee had surrendered the Army of Northern Virginia. Washington was celebrating wildly every day. There were illuminations throughout the city, which [are] hard for us to understand today, but they are rather spectacular, where everything is illuminated with all forms of light. And so, Lincoln and Mary Lincoln were having a night out of relaxation, enjoyment, and celebrating what would effectively be viewed as the end of the war.

But this is an important point, particularly from Booth's perspective. Of course, it wasn't the end of the war. There were still 175,000 Confederate troops in the field—about 85,000 in North Carolina under Joe Johnston, about 55,000 in the trans-Mississippi area under Confederate General Kirby Smith, and then about 35,000 scattered in various places throughout the South. That's a substantial number of Confederate troops. Now, while it was impractical, the idea was if there was some way to join up those troops, you would have a formidable force that could face Sherman and Grant and perhaps continue the hopes of the Confederacy.

ONE OF THE most prominent [myths surrounding the assassination] is that Edwin Stanton, Lincoln's secretary of war, was somehow behind Lincoln's assassination, that he engineered it together with radical Republicans to eliminate Lincoln now that the war was over, and won, so that the radical Republicans could have their way with the South.

Stanton was secretary of war and, of course, a very powerful man. [He and Lincoln were] very close. Again, it's another one of the myths that have come out of the Civil War and this episode that Stanton and Lincoln were somehow estranged.

[That night, Stanton] was home. He was preparing to go to bed when word came by a pound on the door. A messenger that said that Secretary of State William Seward had been killed at his home and the president had been shot. There was little bit of confusion because Stanton thought that Seward and Lincoln had been attacked together. Of course, Seward was bedridden.

He was recuperating from a very serious carriage accident. But Stanton soon realized that they were two separate incidents. He went downstairs, got a carriage, and went to Seward's house, where he met Gideon Welles, the secretary of the navy, arriving at the same instant. They went upstairs and checked on Seward. It was a horrific sight. There was blood everywhere. Seward was all right. His wounds were superficial. He had been attacked by one of the conspirators, Lewis Powell . . . a key figure, and one of the four to be hanged.

This was going on at the same time, approximately, that Booth was shooting Lincoln, approximately at 10:30. So it was coordinated, and that's an important [point].

Seward's wounds were disfiguring. He was stabbed in the face, and it was a very serious cut that ran from ear to jaw, which disfigured him for life. But it wasn't in any way life-threatening to him. He actually fought back, even though he had a broken jaw—that's what he was recuperating from in bed. He struggled with Powell until help came in the way of [a male nurse named] George Robinson. Powell then fled. He turned, ran out of the room, down the stairs, out the front door, presumably screaming, "I'm mad. I'm mad." David Herold was supposed to be tending his horse outside. Herold, who was one of the conspirators in the plot and one of the four to be hanged, had accompanied Powell to Seward's house. But when Herold heard the sounds coming out of the Seward house and the screaming, he apparently panicked. We don't know that for sure, but that's the suspicion. He turned and rode away, leaving Powell's horse there but abandoning Powell.

THAT NIGHT, four [conspirators] participated—Booth, George Atzerodt, Herold, and Powell. Now, we haven't talked about Atzerodt, but he was the man who was assigned to assassinate Andrew Johnson, the vice president. Andrew Johnson was currently living at the Kirkwood Hotel, which is at 12th and Pennsylvania, a short distance away from Ford's Theater. Atzerodt had taken a room early that morning in the Kirkwood Hotel and at approximately 10:30 was to go to the hotel, knock on the door, and assassinate Andrew Johnson.

He did go to the Kirkwood House and ordered a drink at the bar. He was within feet of Johnson's room, but apparently his courage evaporated and he turned and fled. He mounted his horse, rode about the city, saw and heard the commotion on 10th Street, and realized that Booth had carried out the assassination of Lincoln. Atzerodt returned his horse to a stable and boarded a trolley and went down to the Navy Yard and tried to stay there with a friend, but the friend refused to have him. So he came back into the city on the trolley and checked into the Pennsylvania House and spent the night there.

THERE IS NO direct evidence or even smoking gun that can place this [plot] on the desk of Jefferson Davis. But certainly, the Confederate secret service knew about it and was involved in helping Booth assemble his conspiracy and in helping him afterward to escape. There are those who say—and I happen to believe this myself—that those agents would have never acted on their own and involved themselves with John Wilkes Booth. They weren't rogue agents. This information they would have reported up to their superiors, and their superiors clearly would have reported this up to Richmond.

THERE WERE TEN conspirators that were eventually charged with Lincoln's murder, but there were certainly many more people that had knowledge of the conspiracy and participated in the conspiracy, mostly after the fact. There were a few, Thomas Harbin being one, who were brought into the conspiracy beforehand by Dr. Mudd. There were, by my count, probably twenty-six people who could have been charged under Stanton's edict of aiding and abetting Booth both before and after the assassination.

The Disputed Election of 1876

by

ROY MORRIS JR.

In 1876, New York Democrat Samuel Tilden lost the presidential election by one electoral vote, the narrowest margin in U.S. history. Although Tilden almost certainly won the popular vote, a series of manipulations by Republicans in Southern states tipped the balance in favor of Ohio Republican Rutherford B. Hayes. Roy Morris Jr. recounted this sensational and corrupt election in Fraud of the Century: Rutherford B. Hayes, Samuel Tilden, and the Stolen Election of 1876, *published by Simon & Schuster in 2003. Mr. Morris, Tennessee historian and biographer, appeared on* Booknotes *on April 6, 2003.*

W E ALL REMEMBER the 2000 election—the butterfly ballots and the hanging chads and the election officials looking through microscopes at ballots. The whole media buildup was very much farcical, not in the outcome but in the transpiring. [The year] 1876 was more of a tragedy, particularly for the 4 million-plus black citizens of the South who, at least as an indirect result of this election, were put back into a condition of involuntary segregation for the next ninety-plus years.

[THE YEAR] 1876 was the last year of Ulysses S. Grant's second term. It was also the centennial year in American history, and there were celebrations going on throughout the year, particularly in Philadelphia, where the centennial exhibition was based.

The country was not in very good shape. There had been a succession of scandals, especially in Grant's second term. In fact, Grant himself wanted to run for a third term, but the scandals and the depression which set in in

1873, the worst depression in American history to that point, had precluded him from being able to get a nomination. So there was a great deal of unrest and uncertainty, coupled with the fact that in the South, redeemer governments had taken control of seven of the ten former Confederate states by then. Three states were still under Reconstruction governments. They happened to be South Carolina, Florida, and Louisiana and they all three figured very prominently in the 1876 election and its aftermath.

RECONSTRUCTION WAS a process that had been underway since the end of the Civil War, in fact a little bit before the end of the Civil War. The former Confederate states, in order to get admitted into the Union again, had to revise their state governments, approve the Thirteenth, Fourteenth, and later Fifteenth Amendments, giving equal citizenship and voting rights to black citizens. The former Confederates, many of whom were disenfranchised and lost the right to vote for a while, had to petition to get the right to vote again. Essentially, there were a number of steps set out by Congress for these states in the South to meet these guidelines before they could be fully represented again in Congress.

There were thirty-eight states then, Colorado being the thirty-eighth admitted. And in fact, it admitted just prior to the election. Colorado had three electoral votes at the time. No one thought that it would be an important state one way or the other. In fact, Colorado's territorial representative had been a Democrat, and he guaranteed that the state would go Democratic in the election, so the Democrats, who controlled the House of Representatives in 1876, agreed to let Colorado enter the Union. Of course, they were badly surprised because on election day, Colorado went Republican.

The Republicans still controlled the Senate. The Democrats had gained control of the House in 1874 primarily because of the panic and depression of 1873, which put something like 3 million Americans out of work.

THE REPUBLICAN and Democratic conventions were in June, so [the presidential campaign] lasted for three or four months, going into November.

RUTHERFORD B. HAYES was very much a dark-horse candidate when the Republican convention was held. Maine congressman James G. Blaine was the front-runner for the Republican nomination. But Blaine ran into a scandal of his own right before the convention, in which he was accused of having traded on his influence as a congressman and Speaker of the House to help some railroad interests in Little Rock, of all places. He was badly wounded politically by this scandal, [but] he still went into the convention as the front-runner.

Robert Ingersoll, who was the noted orator of the time, gave a nominating speech for Blaine in which he called him "the plumed knight," which is something that stuck with him throughout his career. There was a big rush after Ingersoll's speech to nominate Blaine but the lights in the convention hall somehow malfunctioned, and it was later alleged that Blaine's opponents had done something to sabotage the lighting. So they postponed for the night the nominating vote.

During the night, the other candidates got together and decided that if no one could show sufficient strength to stop Blaine on the first ballot or two, that the support would go to Rutherford Hayes, who was the favorite-son candidate from Ohio at the time.

The Republican convention was held in Cincinnati. That was very much to Hayes's favor because Cincinnati was pretty much his adopted hometown from the time he was grown. He started a law practice there and was city attorney in Cincinnati before the Civil War. He also met his future wife, Lucy, who was attending college in Cincinnati. She later became the first First Lady to be a college graduate. So Cincinnati was very much his hometown, and he [had] a hometown backing that the other candidates did not count on.

Hayes was . . . in his third term as governor of Ohio. He had also been a two-term congressman from Ohio, [and a] Union colonel during the Civil War, in which he was wounded four times. He became the most wounded president in American history.

He was most seriously wounded at the Battle of South Mountain, before Antietam, when he was shot in the left arm above the elbow. It might very well have been a fatal wound, or he might at least have lost his arm, except for the fact that his brother-in-law was his regimental surgeon and was able to rush him to a nearby house and give him hands-on attention. So he survived that wound and went back and served, and by the end of the Civil War, had become a brevet brigadier general.

His horse was shot out from under him four or five times, as well; twice, I believe, in the same battle, at Cedar Creek.

The main impact of the Civil War for Hayes was that he entered the war as an untried soldier. He never had any military training. It was a rite of passage, as it was for millions of Americans, which taught him that he had strengths that he didn't know about. He was elected to Congress the first time while he was still serving in the army. He said then that he would not campaign and he would not leave the army, if elected, until the war was over because that was the place for him. It turned out to be a very effective campaign slogan.

SAMUEL TILDEN [the Democratic candidate] was a very cerebral politician. He was very reserved, quiet, a lifelong bachelor. He was very wealthy. He had made millions of dollars as a corporate attorney before entering politics. In 1876, he had been governor of New York for two years. He was elected primarily as a reform candidate because of his role in overthrowing Boss Tweed and the Tammany Hall ring, which was the political patronage machine in New York.

Before he became governor, he was chairman of the Democratic Party in New York State and had also served in the New York Assembly. Boss Tweed, through Tammany Hall, controlled for some years the entire political machine in New York, so there's some controversy as to Tilden's credentials as a reformer. Some people said he waited a long time to try to reform Boss Tweed because he worked with him for several years before he started leading the reform efforts to oust Tweed from power.

There were some innuendoes that Tilden may very well have been a homosexual. As far as I could tell, I don't think that's the case, but his campaign managers were worried enough about it to pass along rumors of their own that after the election, Tilden planned to get married. In fact, so many different women were suggested as his possible mate that one Republican newspaper editor said Tilden must be planning to become a Mormon after the election, as well.

As governor of New York State, which was the biggest state in terms of electoral votes—they had thirty-five electoral votes—he was in a very strong position politically. In fact, he didn't have a lot of opposition at the Democratic nominating convention in St. Louis. He was pretty much the front-runner from the start.

[THE REPUBLICAN vice presidential candidate William] Wheeler was a congressman from New York State. He was primarily picked because he had taken an active role in working out a compromise to solve the Louisiana mess from 1874, 1875. The Democrats in Louisiana agreed to give up their claims on the governorship in return for being allowed to take their disputed seats in the Louisiana legislature.

[THE DEMOCRATIC vice presidential candidate Thomas] Hendricks was governor of Indiana, which was a very important swing state. Also, secondarily, Hendricks was a leading proponent of what was known as soft money. He was contrasting, adding that element to the ticket because Tilden was what was known as a hard-money Democrat—a whole complicated issue about gold reserves and specie payments, greenbacks. Essentially, Hendricks and the Western Democrats wanted more greenbacks printed, whereas Tilden and also Hayes and the Republican Party supported returning to the gold standard.

[WHEN IT CAME to campaign issues involving the South,] Hayes and Tilden both personally tried to stay above the fray. Hayes's people in Washington had a series of meetings with Southern Democrats. [They offered a deal:] In return for the Southern Democrats not going along with the other members of the House of Representatives in trying to block Hayes's inauguration, Hayes, once he became president, would remove the last federal troops which were propping up the Republican governors in Louisiana and South Carolina. In effect, [this would] end Reconstruction symbolically as well as literally.

MOST PEOPLE thought that it would be a close election but that Tilden would win. Certainly, going into the final days of the election, Hayes thought so, as well. In his diary he mentions several times the fact that he was pretty convinced he was going to lose.

[On election day] about 8.5 million people voted.

HAYES AND TILDEN both went to bed believing Tilden had won. Tilden was 250,000 votes ahead in the popular vote. But late on election night, the Democrats seemed to be wavering in their confidence. They sent some telegrams to the *New York Times* saying, "Can you give us the estimates of Tilden's electoral vote count, particularly in South Carolina, Florida, and Louisiana?" These were the last three Southern states still under Reconstruction control.

THE LEAD character in the whole election-night drama was "Devil Dan" Sickles, who was a former Union general, a former congressman, and a notorious figure in American history. He had actually shot and killed the son of Francis Scott Key, the composer of the "Star-Spangled Banner." Key's son Phillip was having an affair with Sickles's wife. Sickles beat the rap by pleading temporary insanity, which was the first time that that had been used successfully as a legal defense. After the Civil War, Sickles had been minister to Spain and had rushed back to America to help the Republican Party campaign for Hayes in 1876.

Sickles also believed that Hayes had lost the election. In fact, on election night, he went to a Broadway play and a late dinner. He lived on Fifth Avenue, right down the street from the Fifth Avenue Hotel in New York City, which was Republican National Headquarters. Sickles popped in to see how the election was going, and the place was empty except for one clerk who was packing up the records. He said, "Tilden's won the election and we're all going home."

The clerk even told Sickles that Zachariah Chandler [the Republican National Committee chairman] had already gone to bed with a bottle of whiskey.

SICKLES LOOKED over the figures and had something of a brainstorm. . . . He added up the totals, and if you took the electoral votes from Florida, Louisiana, and South Carolina, which were nineteen electoral votes, and put them with Hayes's 166 electoral votes, then Hayes would have the bare minimum of electoral votes needed to be elected.

Sickles sent telegrams to the Republican governors in those three Southern states saying, "Hold on to your states." And he added, "Troops and money will be furnished."

So on the day after the election, Tilden woke up to find out that he was not necessarily president-elect anymore. [He had spent the night] in his home in Gramercy Park, about four blocks away from the Fifth Avenue Hotel. He had gone to bed around midnight, people said. He had no idea that when he woke up the whole election would be up in the air again.

[HAYES WAS IN Columbus, Ohio,] at home. He had a group of family and friends over to listen [through the telegraph] to the election returns. His wife, Lucy, who was ordinarily a very vivacious hostess, went up to bed sick with a headache. Hayes went to bed a few minutes later, and they both consoled themselves with the notion that now at least they wouldn't have to uproot the kids and move to Washington.

THE DAY AFTER the elections . . . almost all the national newspapers . . . said that Tilden had won. He had maybe 203 or 207 electoral votes by those accounts. The only two major newspapers that didn't concede the election to Tilden were the *New York Times* and the *New York Herald,* who both said it was too close to call.

AFTER SICKLES sent his telegrams and follow-up telegrams to the Republican governors, visiting statesmen from both parties rushed down to these states. In fact, William Chandler, a member of the Republican National Committee—no relation to Zachariah—literally took a carpetbag filled with $10,000 to Florida to disperse among members of the Florida Election Commission and other influential people.

With the three states contesting their electoral votes, it fell to the Election Commissions in those three Southern states to decide who would get the certification which was sent to Washington for the Electoral College. December 6th would be the final day for the pro forma reading of the returns.

The Republicans sent one slate of electoral votes saying that Hayes had won the election. The Democrats, who had [newly] elected governors in those three states who hadn't taken office yet, sent opposing slates saying Tilden was entitled to the electoral votes. Neither the Senate nor the House could agree which of these different electoral votes to accept. There was a big debate over whether the president pro tempore of the Senate, who is empowered under the Constitution to open the votes, whether it was his decision which of the two competing slates of electorate votes could be opened.

The House of Representatives was controlled by the Democrats. They said he could only open the votes when the electoral college met on December 6th, and that he would have to set aside any challenged votes. This meant the election would have been thrown into the House of Representatives as it had been in 1824, and back before that in 1800. Tilden would have been elected by a huge majority in the House of Representatives.

Because they couldn't agree on who had the power to determine the Electoral College results, for the only time in American history, they came up with what was known as the Electoral Commission, composed of fifteen members. It was supposed to be seven Democrats, seven Republicans, and one Independent, taken from five members of the House, five members of the Senate, and five Supreme Court justices.

THE ONE Independent who would be the swing vote was Supreme Court justice David Davis of Illinois. But before the Electoral Commission could meet and start hearing evidence into who deserved the electoral votes, Davis was elected to the U.S. Senate from Illinois [as a Democrat.] It was a total disaster for the Democratic Party, the Democrats in Illinois thinking that they would influence Davis's vote on the Electoral Commission.

Davis was supposed to be an Independent, and he immediately resigned from the Electoral Commission, partly, it's been alleged, so that he didn't have to have the responsibility of deciding who had won the election.

There were no more Independents on the Supreme Court. So they picked who they thought was the most likely to be independent in his thought among the Republican Supreme Court justices and that was Joseph Bradley of New Jersey. That left eight Republicans and seven Democrats on the Electoral Commission. After weeks of hearings and testimony and test votes and back-and-forth, the Electoral Commission voted eight to seven in each case to give the electoral votes to Rutherford Hayes and the Republicans.

[IN THE CONTESTED states] Louisiana, Florida, and South Carolina, it was very close, only a few hundred votes either way.

But the Election Commissions in those three states were all controlled by Republicans. They all threw out enough Democratic votes, which were challenged on the basis that black voters had been intimidated and kept from the polls in these states. Districts which had gone to Tilden were thrown out and his votes were given to Hayes instead. That was the crux of the whole issue—who actually had control of these votes, whether it was Hayes and the Republicans or Tilden and the Democrats.

THE LAST DAY of debate [in Congress] after the Electoral Commission had decided and after the electoral votes were all in was an intense . . . eighteen-hour day. Tempers were very high. Some members were pulling guns on other members. . . . Nobody was shot, but there were a lot of hot tempers that day.

AT THE VERY end, Rutherford B. Hayes had 185 electoral votes and Samuel Tilden had 184. It's the only time in American history that an election has been decided by one electoral vote.

HAYES PROMISED in his acceptance letter that he would only serve one term, primarily because there was so much controversy over the use of federal employees being used to run or support presidential campaigns. So Hayes, to blunt the issue of reform, promised ahead of time that he would only serve one term so that there would be no question of his being reelected by federal employees.

[THE WHOLE post-election process] had been going on for four months. People were somewhat exhausted by then. Before then, though, there was a lot of talk and a lot of rumbling about possible violence. There were rumors that the Democratic Party was forming a secret army known as the Sons of Liberty or the Tilden Minutemen that would march on Washington and set Tilden in the White House by force.

President Grant took the rumors seriously enough that he brought additional troops into Washington to guard the bridges and the old Civil War forts. He had warships sailing up and down the Potomac, in case this phantom Democratic army suddenly appeared and tried to descend on Washington.

GRANT WAS supposed to leave office on March 4th, but it fell on a Sunday, so Hayes could not be inaugurated president until March 5th, which was Monday. The Republicans were still so worried that the Democrats might try something at the last minute that Hayes was secretly sworn in as president at the White House two days ahead of time. [Later] he was sworn in in public, but he was already president, so this was just a bogus exercise.

He entered the presidency under a real cloud—he was called "His Fraudulency" or "Ruther-fraud B. Hayes" or "Old Eight to Seven" or the "Great

Usurper." The *New York Sun,* which was a Democratic newspaper, habitually when they ran his photograph after he was president, would print the word "fraud" across his forehead.

So he came in with a very, very slight mandate. By removing the final troops from the South, he's been historically criticized as the president who ended Reconstruction. However, I think Reconstruction, by that point, would have ended no matter who was president. Certainly Tilden would have removed the troops, too.

In fact, a year before the election, Grant had already signaled that he was unwilling to send troops back into the Southern states to try to yet again keep Southern Democrats from taking over or retaking power in their individual states.

[THE OUTCOME of the election] certainly didn't surprise Tilden, who pretty much from the day after the election seemed to act like he didn't feel like he was going to ever be inaugurated president anyway.

It was very frustrating to his supporters that he didn't take a stronger stand on his right to be inaugurated. . . . Immediately after he lost, he took a long trip to Europe. He was not in the best of health. In fact, he had always been fairly frail. He had had a slight stroke a couple of years before the 1876 election.

There was a lot of talk about Tilden running for president in 1880, but he said that he wasn't physically up to the task. As it transpired, James Garfield won the presidency in 1880 over Winfield Scott Hancock by the smallest margin in history in popular votes; he was 10,000 votes ahead.

EVERYONE IN both parties said that had Tilden run in 1880, he probably would have been elected in a landslide, so in a sense Tilden lost out twice for the presidency, once in 1876 and once by declining to run in 1880.

James A. Garfield

by

KENNETH D. ACKERMAN

Rutherford B. Hayes decided not to run for reelection in 1880, leaving the Republican Party split between the Stalwarts, who favored Ulysses S. Grant, and the Half-Breeds, who favored James A. Garfield. Thirty-six ballots later, Garfield, the Half-Breeds' candidate, was president with a Stalwart as vice president, Chester Alan Arthur. Kenneth Acker-man, a Washington, D.C., lawyer who appeared on Booknotes *on July 27, 2003, argued that Stalwart supporter Charles Guiteau took it upon himself to promote Arthur by assassinating President Garfield. The story is outlined in his book* Dark Horse: The Surprise Election and Political Murder of President James A. Garfield, *published by Carroll & Graf.*

THE IDEA FOR this book flashed in my mind while watching the presidential campaign of 1996 and watching the conventions that year. That was the year of Dole versus Clinton. The conventions that year were totally staged: They were scripted, nothing interesting happened. The networks that year talked about not covering them at all but for the final speeches.

I thought at the time: Wouldn't it be good to write a book about a political convention when they really mattered, when they were passionate, exciting, bare-knuckled contests, unpredictable fights? I started looking for a good one to write about and I came up with 1880, which was Garfield. You put that together with the Garfield assassination—one of the more misunderstood events in American history—and the fact that there was a line of causation between the convention and the shooting of the president made a compelling story for a book.

THE POLITICS AT that time, the Gilded Age after the Civil War, were very much dominated by factional contests, raw power struggles—very similar to what was going on in the business world, very similar to what was going on in the Western frontier. At that time, the big fight was between two groups in the Republican Party called the Stalwarts and the Half-Breeds. Garfield got stuck . . . between the two sides. His nomination came after a thirty-six-ballot deadlock because the two sides were having a very strenuous tug-of-war that year and he got caught in the middle. That's what eventually got him killed.

[IN 1880,] James A. Garfield was forty-eight years old. He was a career congressman. He had been in Washington for sixteen years, serving in the House of Representatives. He had been the Republican leader. He had been chairman of several committees. He was one of the up-and-coming members of the Republican Party. He was also a Civil War veteran, and that made him a very popular figure. He had a house on I Street in Washington, D.C. He was from Ohio. He had a farm that he had bought a few years earlier in Mentor, Ohio, just outside of Cleveland. He was the last man to go from the United States House of Representatives to the presidency, [which he won in 1880].

CHARLES GUITEAU was the man who pulled the trigger of the gun that killed Garfield. He was the assassin. He at the time, in 1880, was thirty-nine years old. He was living in Boston, Massachusetts, selling insurance.

Guiteau was from Freeport, Illinois. He was a shiftless character. He never held any job very long. He was brought up by a very strict father, Luther Guiteau, who had very strong religious beliefs. He was sent to the Oneida community in upstate New York, which was one of the utopian communities at the time. They believed in free love and shared labor. They had a socialist ethic. He didn't fit in very well there; he didn't get along with the other people. When he left, he sued them, at one point, for wages.

He wrote some religious tracts and tried to sell them, but never very successfully. He worked as a lawyer. He worked as a bill collector. He tried to start a newspaper at one point but couldn't get funding for it. He was married for a few years, but his marriage ended up in divorce because he beat his wife. He never had much money. He was always a step or two ahead of the bill collectors.

He came to New York City in 1880, at the time of the convention, and he was at loose ends in his life. Nothing he'd ever done had really amounted to much. He'd tried to do a lot of things, but nothing had really clicked for him. His marriage had fallen apart. None of his jobs had really worked. He decided at that point that he'd really like to get involved in politics. So he went to New York City, which at the time was where the national political parties had their national offices. He went to the New York State Republican

Committee—which was the largest, most important one—and volunteered for the campaign.

WHAT I TRIED to do that was a little different than other Garfield books was to show that the assassination of the president was not simply the result of a disappointed office seeker who took out his anger on the president. Charles Guiteau, while he may, in fact, have been insane, was someone who was very caught up in the political process. He was identified with one of the major factions; he worked with the Stalwarts. He considered himself a Stalwart. He went to New York at the beginning of the campaign and became chummy with the people. He hung out at the headquarters. He gave a couple of speeches. Even though the leaders of the Stalwart branch, people like General Grant and Roscoe Conkling considered him very minor, he considered himself very major. What happened to him was very much wrapped up with the larger politics of the era.

Geographically, the Stalwarts were all over the country. Within the Republican Party, there were two factions, and they went back to the time when General Grant was the president. The Stalwarts were the Republicans who were the most loyal to Grant and that's how they defined themselves. They were the hard-line true believers in General Grant. In a way, the radical Republicans of the Reconstruction era evolved into the Stalwarts of the post-Reconstruction era.

Half-Breed—that word came from the same era. It started out as an insult. The people who weren't very strong toward Grant were considered Half-Breeds. It was the way you would refer to someone almost as a traitor—that they weren't strong enough in their support of the team.

They were all Republicans. This is all within the Republican Party. After a while though, when the Grant administration became tarnished with scandal and Grant's reputation fell, the Half-Breeds—they started to view that name as a compliment. They included a number of reformers at first, but over time, they simply became the opposite side of the Stalwarts. They were led by two very strong personalities: the Stalwarts by General Grant and increasingly by a group of Senate bosses, primarily Roscoe Conkling. The Half-Breed side was taken over by James G. Blaine, who was their leader in 1880.

Blaine was an interesting character. He's probably the most like a modern politician, a very smart man, a very charming man. He was the speaker of the House of Representatives for about a dozen years and that was where he made his national reputation. He was a newspaper writer in Maine, one of a number of newspapermen at the time who went into politics and made that their base.

WHAT GUITEAU tried to do was different than what any other presidential assassin had tried to do. What he tried to perform was a regime change. It wasn't simply to kill a person. It wasn't simply to destroy the president. He wanted to replace one ruling group, the Republican Half-Breeds led by Garfield and Blaine, with a different ruling group, the Republican Stalwarts, led by Chester Alan Arthur and Conkling and Grant. That's what he was trying to do.

He was able to do it because at the convention, a compromise had been reached. Garfield won the presidential nomination, but as a payback to the Stalwarts—to give them something because they lost—they made Chester Alan Arthur, the Stalwart vice president. So what Guiteau was trying to do was to put Arthur, who had befriended him personally during the campaign, in the White House. That's very different from any other presidential assassination.

When Guiteau pulled the trigger, he said, "I am a Stalwart and Arthur will be president." For some time, Arthur had to live with that onus because people suspected that he may have had something to do with it, even though there's no evidence that he did.

GENERAL GRANT was not on good terms with Garfield. He very much wanted to win a third term in 1880, more than he let on. Grant was very known for not sharing his feelings, for having immovable features. Those words are used about him a lot, his not being very expressive. But in 1880, he wanted to be president. People close to him noticed how anxious he got around the time of the convention, how he was counting the delegates, how he was following the telegraph, the news coming in on the telegraph.

After the convention was over and his backers failed to win it for him, after this thirty-sixth-ballot tug-of-war, he was very bitter. He let some friends know it.

He was disappointed in Garfield, because Garfield didn't pay attention to him when he went to see him, asked for patronage for friends of his, made recommendations, or said, "You should support this person over that person." Grant was very close to Roscoe Conkling. Conkling had been very loyal to Grant over the years and so when Garfield and Conkling had their falling out, Grant took Conkling's side. After that, the feelings between the two of them were very tense.

Roscoe Conkling was one of the real personalities of the era, in a way. Someone asked me when they read this book, "Is there not a Roscoe Conkling cult in the country?" And my response was, "There really ought to be." Roscoe Conkling was the senator from New York State. He was the leader of the Stalwart wing. He was the leading senator, in the sense that they didn't have a majority leader of the Senate, as a formal position, at that point, but he really filled it. He was the most talkative person on the Senate floor. He was a very vain, arrogant, strong-willed, opinionated person. He was a brilliant orator. He was a credible candidate for president in 1876. He was very close personally with Grant. And after a while, he devoted his strength of personality to building up the machine in New York State.

WHEN ARTHUR was getting ready to become vice president, the way he prepared himself was he went on a shopping binge. The bill is sitting in his papers at the Library of Congress. He bought six suits, a new coat, several pairs of trousers, several shirts, got several old suits pressed for a total of not quite $800, which in modern dollars would be almost $20,000. And he paid in cash.

[BEFORE CHESTER Arthur became vice president of the United States, he had a job in New York, appointed by] Grant. [He held the job for] six years [and was fired by Rutherford B. Hayes] for tolerating corruption, even though no corruption on him was ever shown. He was collector of the Port of New York.

His fixed salary was about $12,000, which was more than the fixed salary of the vice president of the United States, the Cabinet, the members of the Senate—everyone but the president. Then in addition to that, as the head of the office, he was allowed to collect certain commissions or bounties. The reason this was such a powerful job was that three-quarters of all imports into the United States came through New York City.

The customs house was where the tariffs were collected and those tariffs made up the bulk of the United States Treasury. Over $100 million a year came in just through the New York custom house. Arthur, as the collector, was able to keep a certain percentage of uncollectables that took extra work to nail down. If there were disputed bills, for instance, he was able to keep a portion of that as his commission. It was something called "moieties," and it was later repealed by Congress. But if you add that to his salary, in most years, he was making more than the president.

The collector of the Port of New York was not only the most important financial operation outside of Washington, D.C., it was the most important political appointive post in the country—and clearly in New York State. The reason was because it controlled the patronage. It controlled about 2,000 jobs, plus a payroll of $2 million at a time when parties collected money by making federal employees pay a part of their salary to the party. So the collector of the Port of New York was an extremely powerful political position and it was very heavily fought over.

Roscoe Conkling, as the New York State senator representing the Stalwart wing of the party, insisted that he have control of that position. Garfield, when he became president, after some hesitation, after being pulled back and forth on this, ultimately decided that he, as the president, needed to control the position. He appointed to it a man who was a political enemy of Conkling, whom Conkling felt he had to defeat.

Guiteau made the decision he wanted to kill James Garfield in mid-May. It was two days after Roscoe Conkling resigned from the United States Senate because of the outcome of his battle with Garfield over the control of the New York Customs House. Guiteau very much recognized his fate as being tied up in the fate of these larger political players.

Guiteau, at the time, was lobbying very hard to become the consul to Paris for the United States government. He came to Washington after the election and decided he wanted a job in government. He wanted a political appointment. He felt he had worked in the campaign. He gave a couple of speeches. He was close to the Stalwart leaders. He had met Chester Alan Arthur several times during the campaign. He got a few recommendations. He decided he wanted a job.

He actually got as far as meeting with Garfield. They had a face-to-face job interview. It was a very strange one. Guiteau had written a speech for the campaign. He got in to see the president. He gave the president a copy of his speech to look at. Garfield started reading it and as he was reading it, Guiteau stood up and walked out of the room.

He felt it was enough that Garfield was reading his speech and he didn't want to press the point. It was three pages long. It was not especially striking, in the sense of being terribly good or terribly bad. It was a typical speech of the time, someone repeating the campaign slogans of the Republicans. It just wasn't a striking speech one way or the other.

HE GOT TO see the president just once. Then he walked over to the State Department and he got in to see Blaine. He got in to see Blaine repeatedly. In fact, Blaine would hold an open meeting several days a week so that people could come in and see him. You didn't need an appointment, you could simply walk in and see the secretary of state. Guiteau went repeatedly to those meetings. When he would see Blaine, most of the time Blaine would put him off. He would keep saying, "Well, we're not going to make a decision about Paris, France, until the deadlock in the Senate is cleared up." And once that did clear up, once there was an outcome, Guiteau went back to Blaine, and Blaine snapped at him. He raised it at a meeting one day and Blaine said, "Never talk to me about the Paris consulship again."

AT THIS POINT, Guiteau had decided he wanted to remove the president. He was a very methodical person. He would sit in Lafayette Park, and he would track the president's comings and goings. There was no Secret Service protection at the time—that would not start until about fourteen years later.

The president felt no compunctions at all about walking the streets of Washington himself alone at night.

Guiteau lived in a series of rooming houses around Washington, mostly in the neighborhood of what we would today call Metro Center, around 13th and 14th Streets downtown. It's about four or five blocks, easy walking distance from the White House.

He dressed shabbily in the sense that he couldn't afford new clothes. He didn't have a job in Washington. He didn't have a bankroll. So after a while, his clothes had rips that were never fixed. Several people pointed out that he wore rubbers instead of shoes, like the kind you wear in the rainstorm to keep your feet dry, but very thin. He came to Washington, and many of these meetings were in March in a year when there was snow on the ground. So he wore very thin clothes. He didn't keep up his wardrobe very well and that was very much noticed.

GUITEAU HAD delusions of grandeur about himself and in a way, they weren't unrealistic. He decided he was going to shoot the president. He recognized his gun would probably end up in a museum, so when he went to buy a gun—he didn't own one at that time—there were two that he saw on the shelf. One had an ivory handle and the other had a wooden handle. The calculation in his mind was this, "The one with the ivory handle would look better in a museum if I use that one to shoot the president." It cost an extra buck, but that's what he bought.

Guiteau had never owned a gun before and did not quite know what to do with it. So he would walk down 17th Street to the river—at the time there was nothing at the river, it was just a deserted stretch of waterfront—he would take out his gun and practice shooting. He would literally take out this English Bulldog gun and put the bullets in and practice shooting, either at a twig or at a bird or at just the water, just to see what it felt like to have a gun in his hand. He wanted to get used to the feeling of the discharge, the smell of the gunpowder, the way the gun would jolt back at him. He wanted to get used to having it, . . . be comfortable with it.

For the two or three weeks that he was actually stalking the president, which is a frightening thing to think about in itself, he was walking around with a gun in his pocket most of the time.

[THE MORNING of the assassination,] he went to the train station a couple of times. When Garfield came back from the Jersey shore, [Guiteau] met him at the train—he was there at the train station with his gun.

[CHARLES GUITEAU shot Garfield on] July 2 of the first year, [1881, of his presidency]. Garfield had been president for just about four months when he was shot. Guiteau shot him in the train station in Washington, D.C. It was the Baltimore and Potomac train station, which is on the site where the National Gallery of Art is today. It was about 9:30 in the morning.

IT WAS A revolver called an English Bulldog . . . a five-shot revolver. Garfield was shot twice. One bullet hit him in the arm and grazed him. The other one hit him flat in the back. One of [the bullets] was never found, the one that grazed him in the arm. The one that hit him in the back—this was a question of some debate. They did ultimately find the bullet. The body had formed a cyst around the bullet, which ultimately formed an aneurysm later on. During the time when Garfield was being treated by the doctors, they had no idea where the bullet was. They kept trying to figure it out. At one point, they even brought in Alexander Graham Bell, the man who invented the telephone. He had invented a very crude form of metal detector, and they tried to use it to find the bullet. But it turned out the doctors were so far off in where they thought the bullet was, that the machine never worked.

[ONCE SHOT,] Garfield lived seventy-nine days. For most of [that] time, he was in the White House. They turned an upstairs room in the White House into a sickroom for him, where the doctors took care of him—arguably where the doctors killed him—but where they treated him. Then for the last few days, he was in Elberon, New Jersey, at the ocean.

In fact, [what killed President Garfield] was part of Guiteau's defense. Guiteau claimed—and he had very good evidence behind him—that it was really the doctors who killed him. Guiteau shot him, but then the doctors examined him without washing their hands. In the end, Garfield directly died from infections, a combination of infections and blood poisoning.

ONCE GUITEAU was arrested, he felt no embarrassment, no shame at any of it. He felt that he would be a hero. He talked very outwardly about everything he did. He dictated a long autobiography of himself to the *New York Herald* that was published. He wrote several long letters and then he testified for several days. That was where the most valuable information on him came from. What I tried to do with Guiteau, which is a little bit different than what other historians have done, is to take him at his word. I did not start with the assumption that he was insane but just took him at his word to see how he fit into context.

It struck me that when you take him and put him into context, he oddly makes sense. I say oddly, because where his logic led him is a very scary place. He decided in the end that he had to remove the president of the United States. He decided in the end that God was telling him to remove the president of the United States.

However, even given his personal insanity, whether it's medical or not, it very much fit in the context of the largest public debate going on in the country at the time. It was a time when the level of partisanship, of bad feelings, of personal attacks had reached such a level that he simply took it one step further.

THEY WAITED until Garfield had died [before they held a trial,] because for one thing, they needed to know whether it would be a murder charge or an attempted murder charge. The trial started about a month after he died.

[Before he shot Garfield], Guiteau wanted to see what the jail was like. He wanted to see where he'd be serving time. The jail at the time was on the site where Robert F. Kennedy Stadium is today, near the Anacostia River. He walked all the way out there. He knocked on the front door and said, "I'd like to come in and look around." The jailer thought he was a kook, thought that he was a crank, and told him to get lost. And he walked away.

He ended up in that jail. He stayed there until he was hanged, early the next year.

HE'S ACTUALLY not buried. After he was hanged, they did an autopsy on him, partly because there had been such a huge debate over whether he was insane or not. They didn't really find anything very interesting and his skeleton, his brain, and, I believe, his spleen were kept in a medical museum in the Washington area. They didn't bury the rest of the body.

The McKinley Assassination

by

ERIC RAUCHWAY

When President William McKinley was murdered at the 1901 Pan-American Exposition in Buffalo, New York, Theodore Roosevelt became the nation's twenty-sixth president. Roosevelt used the assassination by alleged anarchist Leon Czolgosz to urge reforms that his predecessor had resisted and to bring the United States into the Progressive Era. On September 21, 2003, Eric Rauchway appeared on Booknotes *to discuss his book* Murdering McKinley: The Making of Theodore Roosevelt's America, *published in 2003 by Hill & Wang, in which he examined the causes and repercussions of McKinley's assassination. Professor Rauchway teaches history at the University of California, Davis.*

It's IMPORTANT TO the McKinley assassination to put it in a slightly more international context. In 1881, the Russian czar, Alexander II, was killed by a bomb exploding under his carriage. In that year, there were meetings of hundreds of anarchists in Paris and London who adopted the propaganda of the deed—which is essentially a euphemism for terrorism—as their model for attacking industrial civilization.

Over the next couple of decades, there were many bombings, many assassination attempts, and many assassinations. McKinley's fits into that context. There were bombs exploding in Paris and London streets. The French president, the Spanish prime minister, the Italian king, and one of the Hapsburg heirs were all murdered in the decade preceding McKinley's death. And that was the context in which people saw it at the time.

THE ASSASSINATION of William McKinley, is, in my opinion, one of the most important political events of the twentieth century, for obvious reasons and for less obvious reasons. The obvious reasons are that without the assassination, in all likelihood, there would have been no Theodore Roosevelt as president and no Franklin Roosevelt as president. You can see where this goes with American politics. Roosevelt was far too eccentric, far too independent-minded, possibly far too entertaining a person ever to be nominated as a presidential candidate for the Republican Party in the normal way of things. So it took some kind of extraordinary event to put him in the White House. That being said, you didn't need an assassination. It could be a streetcar that hit William McKinley, or he ate a bad clam, or something like that. But the fact that it was a political assassination is really the more important thing. It was this particular kind of assassination—an anarchist assassination, a radical political assassination—that gave Roosevelt an opportunity that he wasted no time in seizing.

Coming to the presidency, Roosevelt said, "We must, on the one hand, condemn anarchists and radicals as evil. They are criminals. They don't understand our American way of life. On the other hand," Roosevelt said, "there's something to these complaints that the radicals have about American society, and we really ought to regulate corporations, look a little bit more favorably on labor unions, address the circumstances of workers in factories, regulate the railroads," that sort of thing. And it was this "on the one hand, on the other hand" way of speaking and of doing things that made him such an effective president. It was the assassination that gave him the avenue into that strategy.

THE CENTRAL question of my book [is,] who was Leon Czolgosz? When they saw this young man—he was about twenty-eight; some accounts say twenty-five—with this very-difficult-to-pronounce name people thought . . . that he was an example of the new immigrant coming to our shores who posed a threat to American society. [There were] millions of young men who were coming to America for strictly economic reasons. A lot of Americans thought these people were taking American jobs and lowering American wages and that they didn't want to Americanize; they just wanted to take our money and go home. That's what people thought they were looking at when they saw Leon Czolgosz.

That was one of the things that gave a boost to Roosevelt's style of politics—dealing with the immigrant threat. . . . [However, Czolgosz] was not that kind of person at all. In fact, he was American-born. He was born in Detroit in 1873 to parents who had not come to this country for those chiefly economic reasons. They had come fleeing the specter of oppression in

Europe. They followed a much older pattern of migration, where the whole family would come over with a very specific intent of becoming Americans. It was not so much that Czolgosz was a foreigner, ultimately, that led him to an alienation from William McKinley's administration. [It was] the fact that he had hoped to find a certain kind of America and hadn't found it.

[McKINLEY WAS shot on September 6, 1901, at] a little bit after 4:00 in the afternoon in Buffalo, New York, where there was a Pan-American Exposition—a kind of World's Fair—going on to celebrate America's connections to the rest of the world. Like many world's fairs, it had marvels of new technology, wonders of other lands, this sort of thing. This is right on the morrow of America's acquisition of colonial colonies in the Philippines and in Puerto Rico, so America had become an imperial power. They were planning on building a canal through Central America to connect the United States to its new acquisitions. All of this celebration of American extension of power was going on in Buffalo.

This was an electrified exposition. The Edison Company had contributed to the Tower of Light at the exposition and there were lots of new uses of electricity on display, including the X-ray machine. The Temple of Music was the largest enclosed space at the Exposition and it was there that McKinley was simply doing what we now call a meet-and-greet with the people. There was a long line of people waiting to see the president; McKinley went to the head of the line and started shaking hands.

He was just starting his second term. He had been elected president in 1896 and had taken office in March of 1897, then was reelected in 1900 and had been inaugurated for the second time in 1901. So he was just a little ways into his second term. McKinley was tremendously popular, judging by the vote anyway. He was reelected by a comfortable majority. In 1896, it had been a bit closer . . . thing between him and William Jennings Bryan. The country appeared to be very strongly divided between this swath of Bryanites in the mountain states and in the South and then the outposts of McKinleyites in the Northeast and on the Pacific Coast. By 1900, it was a much more McKinley-supportive affair and he won by a much greater margin, again over William Jennings Bryan.

Leon Czolgosz had a revolver in his hand, an Iver-Johnson .32, and he had a white handkerchief wrapped around it. He simply stood in line until he got to the president, upon which he raised his hand and shot the president twice at close range in the abdomen.

There were Secret Service [agents there when the shooting occurred]. There were a variety of New York detectives and military men who had been detailed to the fair and they somehow failed to prevent the assassination.

Immediately afterward, pretty much every cop in the country began saying, "Well, had I been there, I would have done this and that, and they should have done the other thing." But at the time, they appeared to be doing more or less what they . . . should be doing.

Lots of people had thought there was a strong chance that this was a dangerous appearance for the president to be making. George Cortalyou, who was his personal aide, had a premonition that the president shouldn't do this particular meet-and-greet. The people who had planned the exposition were having a beer on the afternoon just before this appearance and said, "Wouldn't it just be Roosevelt's luck if the president were to be shot?" There was a general idea that there were radicals out there—anarchists—and they might take a shot at the president at any time.

Afterward, one of the Secret Service agents gave testimony that he had seen a swarthy man with a mustache in the line and that he thought that this was a suspicious person. So he was looking at this suspicious person instead of at Czolgosz, and that's why he let Czolgosz slip by. He had looked at Czolgosz and said, "Well, he looks like an ordinary young mechanic out for the day to meet the president. This swarthy guy is somebody I should be keeping an eye on." There was a strong chance that the swarthy guy with the mustache could have been James Parker, somebody the Secret Service man later [claimed] wasn't in the line. James Parker was a black man who was in line behind Czolgosz and who, according to newspaper accounts immediately after the shooting and up until about the time the president died about a week later, tackled Czolgosz first. The presence of Parker was something that was widely accepted in popular culture, even though it never went into the official record. It was widely reported in newspapers and Parker was interviewed.

At the time, it was well known that this was "the Negro who saved McKinley," as one newspaper said, because he had put his arm around Czolgosz's neck and given him a bit of a beating and borne him to the ground, preventing Czolgosz from shooting McKinley for a third time. If you take into account [that] the president survived for about a week after being shot, there were several news cycles in there, during which people said, "Ah, this African American hero is the man who saved McKinley." The Secret Service later wrote him out of the story because it made it look like they weren't doing their job. At least, that's what it appears.

McKinley was shot twice. The bullets went into his abdomen. One of them was deflected by the president's sternum and so didn't actually penetrate his belly. The other one went deep into the president's belly, and they never found it. They tried to get it while the president was still alive. They tried to get it after he died. And eventually, they were prevailed upon to stop looking for it. Apparently it did a great deal of damage to the president's pancreas and various other internal organs, which caused his body to poison itself, effectively going septic. I talked to a Buffalo doctor, a pathologist, who said, "When I was doing my residency here, there was a story going around that his stomach was on display and that you could see the bullet hole in the back of the stomach, but I never saw it." And apparently, nobody has. But it's part of Buffalo lore.

McKinley was first worked on, at or near the exposition, by some doctors who were present, who got the one bullet and set it aside and then tried to find the other bullet. Then he was put up in Buffalo at one of the exposition managers' houses—a man called John Milburn. He was recuperating there, under the attention of several physicians, for a week. Within the community of medicine, there's a sort of controversy as to whether all had been done that could have been done to save McKinley. I think it's basically resolved that, given the state of the medicine at the time, they had done about what they could do. Ultimately, he died because he had this sepsis in the abdomen, but the proximate cause was the gunshot. He wouldn't have died otherwise. He was fifty-eight years old. [His wife, Ida,] was by his side.

THEODORE ROOSEVELT was in Vermont, at the Vermont Fish and Game Club, doing what vice presidents tended to do in those days—which was not very much that was satisfying to somebody as energetic as Theodore Roosevelt. He received the message that the president had been shot and he made his way very quickly to Buffalo. Then, when it appeared the president was recovering, he left again. He was on his way up Mount Tahawus or Mount Marcy in upstate New York when he got a message from a park ranger that the president was, in fact, dying. He was about to be president and should come back to Buffalo.

THEY FIRST TOOK Czolgosz away to the Buffalo police headquarters for interrogation. . . . They had him in custody for a while and then he was taken to trial in the New York courts. He was tried in a very brisk trial over a couple of days and then was sentenced to electrocution where he was, in Auburn State Prison. He was electrocuted a little over a month after that.

[At the trial, Czolgosz] tried to plead guilty and the judge wouldn't admit the plea, apparently because he couldn't have a guilty plea in what was potentially a capital case. That was all Czolgosz ever said at the trial. He said a few other things at the sentencing, where he said he wanted to make sure that they knew he had acted alone and that there was nobody else in it with him.

[Buffalo district attorney] Thomas Penney . . . impaneled three doctors to determine Czolgosz's sanity for the prosecution and then, in a very shrewd move, also got a couple of other doctors to act on behalf of Czolgosz to determine whether or not he was sane. Both sets of doctors concluded that Czolgosz was sane and therefore responsible for what he had done, so Penney apparently decided at that point not to bring it up at all at the trial.

When Czolgosz's attorneys . . . were appointed to take his case, Czolgosz didn't want them because anarchists don't believe in the law. When [his attorneys], particularly Loran Lewis, got up to speak on his behalf, they introduced the concept of insanity as the only way the jury could find that Czolgosz should not be found guilty and put to death. They made a purely rhetorical plea for Czolgosz's insanity, without really presenting any evidence at all. In fact, it was a very shrewd tactic of courtroom rhetoric. Lewis was essentially pleading for the jury to do what the law wouldn't have allowed them to do, which was find Czolgosz insane without much of a case there.

Lewis [essentially said], "Wouldn't it be much nicer if we would find this man was insane? It would have been as if the president had been killed in a railway accident. We should regret it very much, but it would lift a great cloud off the hearts of the world . . . if it were that kind of accident rather than if it turned out to be the product of an anarchist plot."

Once Czolgosz had been sentenced to death and was simply awaiting death, there was a lull in the coverage of the case. Then it came out again when he was electrocuted, partly because the prison warden made an extraordinary decision [about] how to dispose of the body. They designed a special coffin and a special grave into which they were going to put sulfuric acid to dissolve the body more quickly, rather than the usual quicklime. The prison warden was trying to keep anyone from taking bits of the body away for medical analysis. Again, it's likely he'd wanted to make sure that there wasn't extended discussion of the case, that it was going to be open-and-shut. So they were effectively destroying whatever remains there were.

WILLIAM MCKINLEY had an elaborate state funeral. He was taken to lie in state in Washington and then to his hometown of Canton, Ohio. It provided, as these kinds of elaborate ceremonies can, a sense of the orderly transition of power in that they were grieving for this man who was tremendously popular in 1901. He was laid away in Canton, where he is still regarded as a local hero.

McKinley's friends were—many of them—very nervous [about Theodore Roosevelt becoming president]. Roosevelt was a very independent-minded man. Some people thought of him as being eccentric. He was somebody who took radicalism much more seriously than other Republicans tended to do. One of McKinley's friends and colleagues was the industrialist and campaign manager and later senator Mark Hanna. He is responsible for the well-known, possibly apocryphal quotation, "Now look at that damned cowboy as president of the United States," referring to Theodore Roosevelt, whom Hanna regarded as a loose cannon. When Roosevelt came to the presidency, his willingness to adopt this "on the one hand, on the other hand" rhetoric— "On the one hand, we must criminalize anarchism and wage war on it as if it were international piracy; on the other hand, we must do some things to eliminate the causes of radicalism"—was an attempt to navigate this distrust of him among Republican leaders.

THERE'S A SMALL amount of literature on presidential assassinations. Most of that literature centers on whether or not the assassin was sane, and there-fore, [on] why people would want to shoot the president. It obviously was the central question following the McKinley assassination. Even following Czol-gosz's execution, there was a little bit of a hue and cry within the psychologi-cal community as to whether they might have done a little bit more to determine his state of mental health. It was that investigation, that post-mortem investigation into Czolgosz's insanity that provided the bulk of the primary source material for my book—the notes that the psychologists took when they were interviewing his family and his friends. That hadn't been looked at in any great detail before.

In November 1901, not too long after the assassination, a Boston doctor named Walter Channing, who had in his employ another doctor named Lloyd Vernon Briggs, decided to undertake a private investigation of Czol-gosz's family history, with an eye onto determining whether or not he had been mad. [The question was] therefore, whether justice had been served in executing him rather than committing him. Channing had followed these kinds of crimes over the decades and had weighed in on the Guiteau case [President James Garfield's assassin] on the side of the assassin being insane. He took an interest in this particular problem of criminal versus insane assas-sins. Briggs was a younger man whom Channing employed simply to do the footwork for the investigation. Briggs therefore went to Auburn, went to Buffalo, went to Detroit, went to Cleveland where Czolgosz's family lived and interviewed dozens of people to find out what kind of man Czolgosz had been. That's how I know that Czolgosz was not what he appeared to be, because Briggs got the straight story.

[Czolgosz's interest in politics] came on the wake of the 1893 panic and depression, which was a really epochal event in American history. This panic came on the heels of a big boom, which was driven in turn by the desire to annex and consolidate our hold on the Western states. There was an enor-mous amount of railway construction, telegraph wire laid and barbed wire strung—all of which drove the steel industry into a big boom. The boom went bust beginning in the early 1890s and in 1893, there was this terrible panic. It was exacerbated by some not very wisely conceived laws that the federal government had adopted in the early 1890s. All of the gold went leaching out of the United States treasury and people began withdrawing their deposits from American banks. In response to this, credit obviously became very hard to get—as it does in recessions—and people who employ other people began laying them off, which is what happened to Leon Czolgosz and millions of other Americans at that time.

He was put out of work and it was then that he and his brother, Waldeck, began looking into why America wasn't doing for them what they believed it was supposed to do. They read around a lot. First they began to question Catholicism and then later on they began to question capitalism, but only in a very mild sort of way. Leon's favorite book was a very well-known, very well-selling novel by Edward Bellamy called *Looking Backward*, which was the most tepid form of socialism you could possibly imagine. It hypothesized that although . . . [Americans in the late 1880s] lived in this grim industrial world where people couldn't find well-paying, constant work, sometime in the future—Bellamy put that date as the year 2000—we would live in a society that had peacefully evolved into one that was much better managed. [Bellamy envisioned that] machines did most of the dirty work and people were free to enjoy their leisure. This was a tremendously popular book. It drove a political movement of its own. There were Bellamy clubs. Leon was a devotee of that political philosophy for most of the 1890s, as far as we can tell.

Anarchists at that time would not have agreed what an anarchist was. There is a kind of irony involving the notion of anarchist societies at all, but an anarchist in the 1890s was somebody who believed that there should be no government. [They believed] that any considerable accumulation of property was a form of theft, that laws existed therefore to reinforce theft. Government was therefore complicit in this form of oppression, and they looked forward to, as communists would have said, the withering away of the state and the coming of a socialist utopia. They disagreed over how that was going to happen and whether it was going to happen violently. If it were going to happen violently, should they try to precipitate the violence? Or should they simply arm themselves in anticipation of the state trying to stamp them out? Or should they just wait and hope? There were all stripes of anarchists in America at that time.

I don't think there is any evidence that Czolgosz was insane in the sense that he should have been committed rather than executed. But that's a very narrow legal sense. In my mind, anyone who shoots anybody in cold blood is, to some degree, mad. Obviously, that doesn't let them off the hook, but between that narrow legal sense of being responsible for your actions and the much larger sense of having an off-kilter view of society, there are a lot of shades of gray. I try to paint a picture of that world as Czolgosz lived in it and to give a sense of how he could have come to this pass, pointing out that these were not uncommon experiences. But alone among these many millions of Americans who had these experiences, he's the one who decided to shoot the president on account of them.

[THEODORE ROOSEVELT ran for president in 1912 on the Bull Moose ticket.] It wasn't technically going to be a third term, but it would have appeared to be a third term because he had served almost all of McKinley's second term. Roosevelt had only been elected once, in 1904, in his own right. He had decided in 1908 not to run again, partly amid press accusations that this would be third-termism—and that was unbecoming ambition.

[During the 1912 campaign, John Schrank shot] Theodore Roosevelt in Milwaukee, Wisconsin. . . . Schrank would say afterward that he didn't think anyone should have a third term and that was why he shot Roosevelt. . . . Roosevelt was getting into a car at his hotel on his way to an auditorium where he was going to give a speech. Then in a characteristic Roosevelt gesture, he decided to bounce up again and wave to the crowd and he was shot while he was waving. Roosevelt later made a joke about [Schrank's weapon,] saying, "It was not a large enough caliber to kill a Bull Moose."

The bullet went through Roosevelt's speech—which was in his breast pocket—and hit him in the fleshy part of the chest. He looked down at himself and didn't think that there was any arterial blood coming out. He coughed, which he said he remembered from being a soldier as one way to tell if there was internal bleeding. He didn't cough up any blood, so he said to himself, "I can go on and do this." This was a considerable risk. Whatever precautions he took, to go walking around with a bullet in your chest is never a good idea. But he thought it was worth the risk to achieve this political end of giving this important speech.

He stood before the audience and he pulled out the text of the speech, so that people could see that the bullet had passed through the speech. Then when he opened his jacket, you could see that there was blood on his shirt. It appears that it was somewhat surprising to Roosevelt, that he did not know how much blood there was or that the speech had been perforated at that point. In any case, it was a very dramatic gesture—and it gave Roosevelt this spur to deliver this fairly long, almost an hour, speech. He explained why he was running as a Progressive, why he was repudiating the Republican Party, why he was challenging Eugene V. Debs and Woodrow Wilson as demagogues of the left, why he was the sensible, centrist candidate, and why he was having such a good time doing it.

After the speech he went to the hospital and then he was given some medical attention and it turned out it hadn't been quite so bad. He was laid up—

he wasn't able to campaign much . . . and it was fairly close to the election. He was fairly discouraged, ultimately, after losing the election [to Woodrow Wilson], even though he knew he was probably going to do that. But that was just about the end of his political career, really, that election.

Schrank was committed because, they said, he was insane. He said a vision of William McKinley had come to him and told him that Roosevelt was his true murderer and that he should be avenged. Schrank had committed the crime in a state that didn't have capital punishment, which Roosevelt thought was a sign of his sanity. He had tracked Roosevelt through several other states. Roosevelt said, "He surely would have been lynched had he tried to shoot me in Tennessee."

[There] is in my mind a critical difference between the two assassination attempts. . . . The assassination of McKinley was politically very useful to Roosevelt, letting him say, "These people who would shoot our leaders are criminals, we must fight a war against them. Oh, and by the way, that includes anyone who'd give them aid and comfort, which means basically the entire Democratic Party and William Randolph Hearst and his newspaper chain." This gave Roosevelt a nice stick with which to beat his political opponents. On the other hand, he wanted to address what he believed were the causes of the misery in which Czolgosz had come up and had become alienated from society. So it was an extremely useful political tool for someone who was a genius at creating useful political tools—Theodore Roosevelt.

The assassination attempt on him in 1912 was not nearly so useful. This man, first of all, said he wanted to prevent Roosevelt from having a third term. This painted Roosevelt in a rather unflattering light as an excessively ambitious man, which was one of his vulnerabilities in the public mind anyway. Second of all, he was probably somewhat mad. . . . Roosevelt's appearing at that speech with a bullet in his chest was a tremendous gesture of political ambition . . . saying, "Here I have been shot and I appear before you with this bullet in my chest. I am doing this because I truly believe in the Progressive cause, and if I were to die, it would be worth dying. I have had an A-1 time in life and I am having one now." Even this to him was an opportunity to be seized.

THERE HAVE been attempts to connect [the four presidential assassinations in American history]. I don't know that I find any of them persuasive. The high-water mark of attempts to categorize presidential assassins was in the 1950s, which was also the high-water mark of social science and of psychology, generally. Saying that these were loners, that these were men who were alienated from their families, doesn't say a whole lot. There are an awful lot of people like that who never take a shot at the president.

Edith and Woodrow Wilson

by

PHYLLIS LEE LEVIN

After World War I, Woodrow Wilson, America's twenty-eighth president, began his campaign to establish the League of Nations. In the face of considerable American opposition, Wilson traveled around the country to gain support for his vision of international cooperation. During this tour, he suffered the first in a series of strokes, which were downplayed by both the administration and the press. Phyllis Lee Levin argued that Wilson was severely debilitated after his first stroke and that his second wife, Edith Wilson, played a key role in keeping him in office during the remainder of his second term. On December 9, 2001, Ms. Levin appeared on Booknotes *to discuss her book* Edith and Woodrow: The Wilson White House, *published by Scribner that same year. Ms. Levin, author and former* New York Times *reporter, lives in New York City.*

[WOODROW WILSON had a stroke] in his bedroom [in the White House]. He must have fallen on the floor of the bathroom and cut his head, according to Ike Hoover [the chief usher at the White House], but Edith Wilson said she never saw blood. But what Edith Wilson did do was call Hoover to call Dr. Cary Grayson to come immediately. Hoover and Grayson came immediately [and examined the president. Then they] opened the door, came out, made some motion as if to say, "Something's happened," and that was it. Then no one was able to see Wilson—Joseph Tumulty, his secretary, for three weeks; a stenographer, for four months. But what Grayson did do was call a conference, and a very respectable group of physicians came to analyze what was wrong with Wilson.

The major stroke was October 2, 1919. That was when he was found on the bed and that was really such a radical stroke that there were many consultants, maybe four or five were brought in. Dr. Grayson was quite a good doctor. At first, I was suspicious of him. He was very well trained and I thought maybe he didn't diagnose things well because he didn't have the background. But he did. He had good schooling and he was very, very bright. He and a Dr. Dercum, who was also an outstanding doctor, wrote these analyses, and Dr. Grayson read them to Edith Wilson and she said that was not the way it was to be. So from then on, if you look at the *New York Times*, which I did, . . . the diagnosis was always a nervous breakdown. He would get better.

We have Mr. Hoover's account of the night that Wilson fell ill—quite different than Edith Wilson's. I read her memoir and it was quite different, enough so that I went and got out Mr. Hoover's original papers. . . . As I read on, she made a lot of other differences. She made up a lot of stories along the way, and her versions varied considerably from what I found to be the truth of the versions when I went to the original papers.

She claimed that her husband was alive and alert after this attack and that it wasn't serious at all. Of course, the doctors say that he had a stroke that made him unable to govern properly. Then . . . it was very sad to find out that about ten years ago, the original diagnoses were handed in to Professor Arthur Link, who had been the editor of the sixty-nine volumes of Wilson's papers. The original diagnoses were that Wilson was unalterably wounded by his stroke and unable to govern. But Mrs. Wilson prevented these diagnoses from being made public. So Dr. Grayson was co-opted into [reporting] what Edith Wilson perceived as a nervous breakdown. That was thought to be more respectable than a stroke.

Every time that Dr. Grayson would issue a press release saying Wilson was getting better, [the press would] just take it like it was. There were [people who questioned it], but very few. It seemed to be a gentlemen's agreement that you didn't question things. There were a couple of newspapers, something called the *War Weekly*, that wondered after a time, after several months, where Wilson was, because he wasn't seen until March. [His seclusion lasted from] October 1919 to March 1920.

[DURING THIS TIME,] votes were being taken in the Senate [on the League of Nations]. Senator Henry Cabot Lodge, who at some point was dismissed and so tarred and feathered as evil—it was a "but for him we would have joined the League of Nations," and that really isn't true. He was a very, very bright, intelligent man. I read all of his correspondence at the Massachusetts Historical Society, and he was in favor of a League at one point; he was in favor of some compromise. There's evidence of that.

Wilson didn't know how unlucky he would be with this thing. He could not get anyone to see that he [could not] compromise. Edith made one stab, and then according to her, he said, "Little girl, you, too?" as if she was betraying him. That was the end of it. Had he been married to [his first wife] Ellen Wilson, I don't think she would have allowed him to stay in office, being so ill. I don't think she could have been party to such a vast pantomime.

He wanted [the Versailles Treaty with the League of Nations] attached. That was a great, aggravating point. The whole idea was held up because he insisted that the Fourteen Points be part of everything, and he would not give an inch on it. They had signed the Versailles Treaty, but when it came to the League, he just couldn't let go. The crucial point was when the Democrats asked him how to vote: Would he allow them to vote for a compromise? And he said no. That was after several attempts, so that was the end of the League.

AND THEN HE thought he had to run for a third term; he would have to run for president again to champion his League, as sick as he was.

He had the stroke in October; all the voting took place in the following months. He was not out front [lobbying for his position, and lost the vote 53–38.] There was Senator Gilbert Hitchcock, who was a Democrat, who seemed to be his representative, and there were all sorts of maneuvering and private meetings. Then poor Colonel Edward House, [the president's adviser,] . . . Bernard Baruch, and different people came by, or wrote to ask him to please make the compromise with Lodge because it wouldn't matter—the small points could be ironed out. The big point was for us to have a League, that Wilson so wanted. I don't think he was well enough to understand, although a corner of me feels that he had been so stubborn [at other times] . . . that he might have stuck to his guns on this point as well.

SENATOR HITCHCOCK and Senator Albert Fall were the first people to see him from the outside. [They came in December, two months after the stroke.] It was just brilliantly laid. They covered his arm—it was his left arm that was paralyzed. . . . The lights were lowered. Dr. Grayson and Mrs. Wilson were in the room and everybody stood at attention. Mrs. Wilson took notes there in the bedroom because she didn't trust Fall to be honest. She was worried about what they would report. They apparently pulled it off, and the press gave Wilson high marks for it.

[WILSON'S FIRST wife was] Ellen Axson Wilson. That was a true love affair of a very young man and a very young woman and she was very intelligent. She was very educated for her time and she was an artist, and some of her paintings have been on exhibit at the Wilson House on S Street in Washington. She translated German for him. She was helpful, a wonderful helpmate all the way, and quite a wise woman and very eager. She was quite taunted because she was very interested in helping the poor and righting the slums and so on.

Ellen [died of] Bright's disease, a kidney ailment. She died August 6, 1914, just two days after the Germans invaded Belgium. . . . By March 1915, he had met his second wife.

There was an interim correspondence that Wilson had with a woman named Mary Peck, and how much of an influence it was on his marriage, I don't know. But I think she had somewhat of a nervous breakdown herself. Her family was very frail. I think that Wilson, in his great need to pour out his heart to someone, wrote these extensive letters to this Mary Peck, and during both [presidential] campaigns, it was a problem for him.

Wilson met Peck in 1907, and then the correspondence came. It dwindled radically when he met and married Edith Wilson. When he made a tour of the country on behalf of the League of Nations, trying to sell his Fourteen Points, he did stop in Los Angeles. He asked Mary Peck to come to lunch and introduced her to Edith Wilson. So there was some sentimental connection for all his life. Whatever the depths of it was, I don't know. But he had great need of her.

Dr. Grayson, [Wilson's] physician, [introduced Wilson to Edith]. . . . He knew Edith when he was an intern, and it may be that he had known her when she gave birth to her child. She had a son by her first marriage, who didn't live. Grayson had his eyes on Edith, thinking she might cheer the president up. [Wilson] was really in the depths of despair and the White House was just the most gloomy place in the world, and as described by his brother-in-law, they just sort of sat around and reminisced about what old times had been.

At any rate, Dr. Grayson then persuaded Edith Galt, as she was known, to come and meet this cousin of Wilson's. Her name was Helen Bones. There is this picture of two ladies having tea. In came Wilson and Grayson from a ride on the golf course, and Wilson was immediately taken with Edith, who in her memoir says she was glad she was wearing a marvelous French outfit. He invited her immediately to come back for dinner, and it was a done deal.

Edith Wilson was one of the first women to own an automobile. She was somewhat of a Henry James character in that she traveled abroad quite a lot as a widow, bought her dresses where Edith Wharton bought hers, and so on. And she ran a business. She claimed she had little to do with her husband's business, but she kept a fine eye on Galt Jewelers, and that's where her money came from. That's what supported her whole family. But she loathed the suffragettes and said so in her own handwriting. That's in her diary. She brought the issue up several times. She really couldn't stand them.

[WILSON WAS popular because] he kept the flame alive, the flame of a united world. Mrs. Wilson and President Wilson chose his biographer, Ray Stannard Baker, brilliantly. That perpetuated his reputation, embellished it, and then [a film] was made, word for word from her memoir. Mrs. Wilson had total control over it—if you read the papers of the correspondence between the producer, director, and herself. Geraldine Fitzgerald played her, and Alexander Knox was Mr. Wilson, and it was all just a beautiful story. The only thing that was wrong was Henry Cabot Lodge.

I believe Mrs. Edith Wilson started [her memoir] because Mary Peck had published her own memoir as a magazine serial. It was suggested that Mrs. Wilson was so angry that she wrote her memoir on the train and everywhere, and did scraps and scraps of it. She got very, very angry, and used very bad language in her diary. Then Bernard Baruch had a very renowned journalist named Marquis James come and look at [the memoir], and James said, "This is yours and you must keep your spirit in it." That's what was published.

I GIVE WILSON credit for caring and for being brave enough to go over [to Versailles] and think that he could do something. But the fact that he had no way to get along with these people and no background in understanding them was too bad. If you realize he didn't consult with his secretary of state, he didn't consult with anyone when he was over there, anyone to speak of— how could he know what's going on? He sat home in the evenings with Mrs. Wilson and Ray Stannard Baker and Miss Benham, [secretary to Edith Wilson] who became Admiral Helms's wife, which was a rather narrow circumstance to represent the world and take care of the world.

WOODROW WILSON was president from 1912 to 1921. I thought he was looked on as quite a hero until it came to his illness and entering in World War I and the peace conference. He wasn't well, even in Paris, and he also was almost a naive American in Paris as [Georges] Clemenceau and David Lloyd George perceived him. He didn't understand the complications and the history of war. He was so idealistic, he thought everything could be overcome, and it couldn't. Then, of course, he was ill. He listened to no one.

He didn't want to go into World War I, but . . . the Brits needed help, the French needed help, and the French had helped us in the Revolutionary War. There were people who were very anti-German in this country and there were people who were very pro-German. For example, Teddy Roosevelt was very angry with him. Wilson was elected partially because he would maintain peace, but he didn't maintain peace, and he finally declared war when there was enough pressure on him to do so.

MY CONCLUSIONS are how little we know about what really happens at the seat of power; how little we are privy to, how vulnerable leaders are. I used to, when I was very small—and not so small—think that they had maybe some charisma, some knowledge, some intellect that was so profound that they would lead us through anything. Now I know they're just regular folk who happen to have more ambition or energy and they land in the seat of enormous power. One hopes they have enough humility and enough intelligence to seek lots of opinions, because [as a nation] we keep repeating ourselves. I was astonished to find a setup: To prove that Wilson was able to run again for the third term, a *New York Times* photographer and a *Times* reporter would write [a puff piece about Wilson and] won a Pulitzer Prize. So you have to examine everything. They won the prize for the story of how strong Wilson was and how well he was. And it was all a setup.

Walter Judd:
Doctor, Missionary, Congressman

by

LEE EDWARDS

Walter Judd, politician and physician, was born in Nebraska in 1898. Working as a missionary in China, he was held captive for five months in 1938 when the Japanese invaded the northern city of Fenchow. Judd began his political career late in life; he was elected to Congress in 1942. During two decades as a Republican congressman, Judd played a crucial role in bringing the United States out of its isolationist stance. Lee Edwards joined us on September 2, 1990, to discuss Judd's career. His book, Missionary for Freedom: The Life and Times of Walter Judd, *was published by Paragon House in 1990. Dr. Edwards is a senior editor at* The World & I *magazine and a senior fellow at The Heritage Foundation.*

WALTER JUDD WAS an extraordinary man, someone whose career extended some sixty-six years, from 1923 to 1989. I really believe there isn't any other American who talked to as many people, was heard by as many people during those more than six decades than Walter Judd.

It was important to tell this man's story as a politician—that it was possible for a politician to be honest and principled and to get reelected. It's an incredible fact, but it still is a fact, that he never raised one dollar for himself during all of his campaigns. He was in Congress for some twenty years. And he never asked anyone to vote for him. All he said was, "If you agree with what I say and my positions and what I believe in, then vote for me. But don't vote just for Walter Judd. Vote for what I stand for."

Walter Judd was a liberal on domestic issues and was for the GI Bill and was for increases in Social Security and increases in the minimum wage. But at the same time, in the foreign policy field, he was a very strong anti-Communist. Regarding him as an anti-Communist makes him a conservative in the minds of many, many Americans. But he was both a liberal and a conservative. Actually, if you want to know what Walter Judd was, he was a Jeffersonian Democrat, that is to say, he was for individual freedom, limited government, and a strong defense.

I FIRST SAW him in 1960 . . . with his very famous keynote address in Chicago at the Republican Convention. That was pivotal—it was a classic bit of political oratory. It was very important for his career, and it could have been very important for American history because the keynote address really stampeded the convention in 1960. There were people who were saying, "Judd for vice president. Judd for vice president."

Richard Nixon, who had already gotten the nomination, had already picked his man, Henry Cabot Lodge. Well, the voice of the people was so loud that Mr. Nixon said, "Well, maybe I've got to think about someone else." He called Walter Judd in and he said, "Look, Walter, it's down to two people: Cabot or yourself. Do you think that you can be a better candidate than Cabot Lodge?" Dr. Judd, being the physician that he was, trying to be as objective and scientific about himself as he was trained to be, at the same time being trained not to talk about himself or to promote himself, said, "Well, I think that Cabot can be good in the Northeast. I think he can be good because he's an attractive figure. He's been working against the Soviets in the United Nations. Myself, I think I can be strong in the Midwest and the South. But really, you have to make the judgment, Dick."

He has said since that if he had pushed himself a little bit harder and sold himself a little bit more that Richard Nixon might very well have picked him. What would that have done? Would that have made any difference in American history? As a matter of fact, Richard Nixon sent a telegram to Walter Judd several years later, when neither of them was in office anymore, and said, "Walter, if I had picked you instead of Cabot, we'd both still be in Washington, D.C."

Judd was a doer. He felt that he ought to be about the business of what he called "serving the cause." The cause to him was freedom—not so much that he was an anti-Communist, but that he was pro-freedom. He felt that communism during his decades—when he was in public service and even since then—was the greatest enemy of freedom around the world and particularly for the Chinese people.

HE WAS BORN in Rising City, Nebraska—a small town of about 500 [people], a little farming town in the middle of the prairies. His father owned a lumber yard in Rising City. This was 1898. He grew up, went to school there in a little one-room schoolhouse with his brothers and sisters. Then he decided that he wanted to go off to college and become a missionary. . . . There were so few medical missionaries, so few medical doctors in China in the 1920s, so that's where he wanted to go. He was very much inspired by David Livingstone, the famous explorer and missionary, and what he had done in Africa. He hoped to emulate him in some small fashion in China.

He first lived [in China] from 1925 to 1931 as a medical missionary in the south, up in the hills in a little town named Shaowu. . . . He would have stayed for the rest of his life perhaps, but he had to leave because he had so many attacks of malaria that, finally, he almost died. He had forty-four different attacks of malaria. He left in 1931, came back to the States, and then decided he needed a little bit more to do in terms of learning how to be a surgeon. He had performed so many operations when he'd had to, he really wanted to know more about the art of surgery. So he picked the Mayo Clinic. The Mayo Clinic didn't want him. The Mayo Clinic said, "You're awfully old, Dr. Judd. Usually we take students right out of medical school." He said, "I think I know what your problem is." He was talking to the Admissions Office there. "You think that I won't perhaps be willing to get down and take the urine samples," he said, "I'll do anything if you'll just let me in here to the Mayo Clinic."

He was there for a couple of years in residency, got a scholarship, had among the highest grades of [those] trying to get into the Mayo Clinic. Then the call came from his church, the Congregationalist Church [asking if he would] like to be a medical missionary again, but in the north of China, not in the south, where he would have been much too prone to get malaria. He said yes. He dropped what would have been, I'm sure, a very successful career because he always felt himself to be a missionary.

In 1937 the Japanese invaded China and he had a choice to make: Should he stay or should he go back with his family? He was married to Miriam by this time. In 1937, he had two children—two girls, aged two and four. Miriam was pregnant with their third daughter.

When the Japanese invaded and began moving west toward Fenchow from Beijing, he said, "I'm going to get the family out," and they went all the way down by train to Hankow trying to get out. This is in August of 1937. But the streets [were] like a scene out of *Casablanca*. The foreigners were there trying to get out of Hankow. The city was being bombed by the Japanese—biplanes coming in and bombing it. . . . There were only two or three planes leaving every week. The Judds were there for several weeks trying to get tickets for one of the last planes to leave Hankow.

Finally, Judd was able to put his pregnant wife, Miriam, and the two children on the plane, and waved good-bye. He was never sure that he would see them again. He went back up north to Fenchow, feeling that as a missionary, as much as he loved his wife and his children and his family, that his obligation was to the mission and to those some 1,000 Christians who were still there in Fenchow.

That was in the fall of 1937. The Japanese kept coming west, and they took the city in February of 1938. So from February until July of 1938 he was a prisoner, in effect, of the Japanese, who had taken this old city of Fenchow in north China.

He felt that the Japanese had to be understood. He felt, as he got to know them more and to talk with them, that it was important to show strength against the Japanese; that if you gave in to them that they would take advantage of that. He became determined and began praying and desperately seeking ways to get out of Fenchow, to get back to this country and warn the American people about what the Japanese might very well do to us. He had seen that they were able to take over this large country, China—400 million people at the time. He was fearful that Americans would not understand that Japan could be a very formidable adversary for us as well. But yet he stayed there month after month after month. There was no rescue in sight, no way of leaving. How was he going to get out of Fenchow?

Finally, one day . . . a Korean interpreter came to him and said, "The Japanese commanding general wants to see you, but he wants to see you at night and privately." Judd said, "Well, of course. I'll be happy to." He came the next night, and this very proud Japanese general said to Dr. Judd, this foreigner, this barbarian, if you will, "I have a venereal disease. I don't dare go to my own doctors, because if I do, they will have to report it. That will be a disgrace to me and to my family. Will you cure me? Will you treat me?"

Dr. Judd, feeling that although this man was Japanese, although he had done these terrible things to the Chinese people in the course of the war, raping and pillaging, he was a man who needed his help as a doctor. He had taken the Hippocratic oath. So he treated him over the next several weeks for this venereal disease and was able to cure him, and nothing more was said at that time. Several days passed, the Korean came back and said, "Is there something that the general can do for you? Would you like to see your family?" Dr. Judd said, "Of course. Yes, I would like to very, very much." The Japanese general gave him a pass out of Fenchow, back to Beijing and back home.

He had a choice. What should he do? He was forty years old. He had a family to take care of, as he found out, including a third young daughter. "What should I do? Should I try to go back to my medical practice and to my medical career or should I try to warn the American people about what might very well be coming?" He determined—again, as a missionary in this sense of mission, this sense of a cause that he had to follow—that the important thing for him to do was put aside the medical career, and to go out and carry the message of what Japan might very well do to America, to the American people.

For the next two years, he made 1,400 speeches. I don't think anybody, even Gary Hart or Jimmy Carter or Ronald Reagan, ever made as many speeches over such a short period of time. He had a very simple message: "I'm not saying that we have to have a military invasion or military incursion of Japan. All I'm saying is, 'Let's stop giving them the means to build up; let's stop trading with them; stop giving Japan the wherewithal, the sinews of war, if you will, to fight us.' That's all." As he said over and over again, "Give up silk stockings now or your sons later."

Unfortunately, as we know, his warnings were not heeded—although there was something of an embargo, which finally, in 1941, under President Roosevelt, did come up. By this time, Judd felt that he had done the best that he could. He took up his medical practice in Minneapolis, and it was there on December 7th of 1941 that he learned about the war being started at Pearl Harbor. People came to him and said, "You were right about the possibility of our going to war with Japan. We didn't think that those people sitting on those volcanic islands would attack us. But they have. Well, we'd like you to run for Congress." Judd said, "That's crazy. I never thought about being a congressman. I'm a doctor. I may be a missionary, but I'm not someone who should go to Congress."

But they kept pressing him. Finally, they said, "Look, you keep telling us about what our mission is and what we should be doing, what our public duty is, and yet you won't follow your own public duty, which we say is for you to run for Congress." So he did.

He ran against a Republican in the Republican primary, a very famous name in Minnesota politics, Oscar Youngdahl, and beat him, to everybody's surprise. But [he won because of] that wonderful conviction of his, that passion, that certainty which he had and this ability he had to talk about what was going on over there in Asia—because there were very few people this time who knew much about Asia, who knew much about Japan or China or the Far East. He truly was an expert at a time when there were very few.

JUDD WAS A wonderful orator because he marshaled his facts. He spoke with this utter certainty that what he was saying was the truth and ought to be heard. He also had a facility for using phrases which would impact on the people. For example, in testimony before the House and the Senate in April 1939—they heard about his speechmaking and they brought him down there to testify—he called the war between China and Japan a "totalitarian war," a total war, which was probably one of the first times that phrase was ever used.

Later on, when he was talking about communism, he was the first public official to refer to communism as a "cancer"—these very vivid phrases. Or he would say that during the Cold War, in our protracted conflict with the Communists, that they wanted us to play on our side of the fifty-yard line; never wanted us to advance. He also said, for example, that the Communists were like any quarterback; they were always practicing deception. So he was able to use these very homely similes and metaphors to get people's attention, and these vivid images would stay in people's minds for decades.

WHEN HE WAS nineteen years old and an undergraduate student at the University of Nebraska, he had a very bad case of acne and he went to a doctor and said, "Look, can you clear up this acne?" He was very self-conscious about it and he wanted to date and go out with the girls. This doctor said, "Well, there's a new cure that we've just run across." This would have been about 1917. "It's called X-rays." And he exposed Dr. Judd's face without any protection to X-rays. Well, as a result of that, for several weeks of treatment, his face swelled up, became red. When it dried, his face was just ravaged, like a prune.

It had killed, in the process, not only the acne, but many cells throughout the entire skin so that, twenty-one years later, when he was in China, a cancer appeared [on his lip] and then they had to take it out by surgery. So for the rest of his life . . . he had twice-a-year operations, either with lasers or with surgery, to take away this skin cancer. He just accepted it. He said, "Well, you know, that's just the way things are," and just went on about his business.

He felt self-conscious, as you might suspect, with this rather unattractive face. Yet he determined that he was either going to be someone who would sit back and hide in a room or else he was going to overcome that through this force of personality, this conviction, this passion, this mission which he felt that he must carry out.

The Committee of One Million was extraordinary, maybe the first special-interest group in American politics, founded in 1953 by Walter Judd with the help of a man named George Meany, who was head of the AFL at that time—later on, the AFL-CIO—and also with the help of the American Legion. These organizations and such people as George Marshall, former secretary of state, some very prominent bankers and lawyers, and Arthur Schlesinger Sr. founded the Committee of One Million against the admission of Communist China to the United Nations. The idea was that we should not reward Communist China for its aggression in the Korean War by bringing it into the United Nations.

The committee was successful for eighteen years, from 1953 to 1971. Then, finally, in 1971, Richard Nixon sent a mixed signal. On the one hand, he told our ambassador at the United Nations to maintain the membership of the Republic of China—Taiwan, as it's more commonly known—in the United Nations. By the way, our U.N. ambassador was a man named George Bush, [who went on to become the forty-first president].

So while Ambassador Bush was fighting for the Republic of China over here, Mr. Nixon sent Henry Kissinger to China to arrange for Nixon's historic visit to China the following year. These mixed signals were read by the members of the United Nations as an indication that the United States cared more about the People's Republic of China than the Republic of China. So they voted for the expulsion, in effect, of the Republic of China from the United Nations, where it had been an original member since 1945.

China became Communist [in 1949] because Mao Tse-tung beat Chiang Kai-shek and the Nationalist Chinese at the end of a civil war which was fought from 1945 to 1949. There is a great debate: Who lost China? It's a good question, and it's an important question. . . . A major factor in the defeat of Chiang Kai-shek was not only his own conduct, his own inability or unwillingness to handle a certain amount of corruption around him. He himself was very straightforward, a man of rectitude, a man of civility, someone who did not personally engage in corruption, but there was some around him.

What happened was the Chinese people were worn out after four years of a civil war, which had followed eight years of war between China and Japan from 1937 to 1945. Finally the Chinese Communists, when they promised peace to the Chinese people, the people said, "OK, we'll go that route." But certainly a factor in it was a determination by the U.S. government to side with the Chinese Communists rather than with the nationalist Chinese. Walter Judd fought against that.

Why did he fight against it? . . . Dr. Judd always used to like to say that if you look at Asia, that China is the pond, the Middle Kingdom, the center of Asia. All the other countries are fingers that come off it—Korea or Japan or Vietnam or Thailand or the Philippines. He said [that] as long as China is under a nonbelligerent government, one which is friendly to the West and to the cause of freedom, we don't have to worry about Asia. We don't have to worry about these fingers.

Of course, he realized that with China going Communist in 1949, it was quite possible that some terrible things could happen in the peninsula of Korea. As a matter of fact, in January of 1950, Walter Judd predicted that South Korea would be overrun. It would not have been overrun, there is good reason to believe, if China had not been Communist, had been in the hands of a non-Communist government.

[AFTER TWENTY years in Congress, Judd] tried to quit, wanted to quit, said he was going to quit. Then this extraordinary outpouring of telegrams and letters from Republicans and Democrats and people in high places and not-so-high places came in, saying, "You've got to reconsider. We need you." This was 1962. . . . As a matter of fact, he got two telegrams from a man named Dwight David Eisenhower who really wanted him to run again. As a little parenthetical thought, it just shows the extent to which Eisenhower was a man very much involved in the fortunes of the Republican Party. Two years after he was out of office as president, he was still concerned about who was going to run for Congress from Minneapolis.

As a result of that, Walter Judd decided to run again, knowing, in all likelihood, that he would be defeated because the district had been gerrymandered by the Minnesota legislature. Many of the Democratic-Farmer-Labor Party people, the DFL, were now in his district, whereas they had not been there before. He knew it would be a very, very tough race for him to win. He gave it his best. It was a very close race; he lost 52 to 48 percent, which is not bad.

WALTER JUDD played [an important role] in bringing this country out of its isolationist mode and the Republican Party out of its isolationist stance. He was one of those rare people, like Arthur Vandenberg in the Senate . . . who saw that we were now in an interdependent world and isolationism was no longer possible. Through his good offices and through his arguments and through his rhetoric and through his marshaling of facts, he was able to get, for example, the Republican Party to support things like the Truman Doctrine, the Marshall Plan, NATO, the World Health Organization, the Voice of America, a great variety of initiatives.

In 1961, he was voted by his Republican colleagues as the man they most admired in the House of Representatives. When both sides asked who were the most influential members of the House and of the Senate, leaving aside the Senate majority leader and the Speaker of the House, there were ten men named. He was the only Republican who was named as being among the most influential.

JUDD WAS sixty-four when he actually retired. He decided that he had been a medical missionary in China, he had been a political missionary in the Congress, and now he was going to be a missionary at large to the nation and, particularly, to young people. So he began speaking on campuses about freedom—what it requires and what it demands from young people and from all people if it's going to be maintained. In 1964, [he began] a whole new career. He became a radio commentator. . . . From 1964 to 1970, he had a daily radio commentary, five minutes, which eventually was carried on 1,000 radio stations. It was the largest public affairs commentary program of its time.

He kept speaking to campuses. He kept going with, first, the Committee of One Million, then the Committee for a Free China, because he felt that there should be maintained the right kind of political, as well as economic and social relations, between the U.S. and the Republic of China. He kept writing for the *Reader's Digest*; he was a contributing editor for the *Digest* throughout most of the 1970s.

One of his last articles is one of my favorites. It's called "Everyone Wants Economy—Without the *Me*." His point was that we're all for doing away with government programs or government spending as long as it doesn't affect *me*. He was reaching out to young people, saying that, "Look, you have one life to lead. What kind of life are you going to lead? Are you just going to settle back and be concerned only about yourself? Or are you going to use your talents to help this country and to preserve the freedom which this country has had for this generation, for generations to come?"

Harry Truman
and Dwight Eisenhower:
A Presidential Partnership

by

STEVE NEAL

General Dwight D. Eisenhower first met President Truman during World War II when he was chief of staff of the U.S. Army. The two men worked closely between 1945 and 1952, reconstructing the army after the war and launching NATO. However, Eisenhower ran as a Republican in the 1952 presidential campaign, and their partnership soured when Truman supported Governor Adlai Stevenson for the Democratic nomination. Chicago Sun-Times *correspondent Steve Neal appeared on* Booknotes *on February 10, 2002, to discuss the presidents' complex relationship, their decade-long dispute, and their eventual reconciliation. Mr. Neal's book,* Harry and Ike: The Partnership That Remade the Postwar World, *was published by Scribner in 2001.*

OVER THE LAST twenty years I have done several surveys of leading historians that rank the presidents. In each of these surveys, Truman and Eisenhower ranked [among] the best presidents of the last half century. When I was getting rid of some of my books, I noticed that the Hopkins edition of Dwight D. Eisenhower's papers had a lot of letters to and from Harry Truman. They probably worked together, I found from reading their letters, more closely than any two presidents of the twentieth century. . . . There were all these wonderful letters, and I thought that there was a book there.

TRUMAN AND Eisenhower first met in Washington, D.C., in June 1945, just after the Allied victory in Europe. Ike spoke before a joint session of Congress

[and] paid tribute to President Truman. Truman decorated him on the lawn of the White House. He whispered to Eisenhower that he, Truman, would rather have the medal than the presidency. Then he had a dinner for him that night at the White House.

President Truman wrote his wife, Bess, that night that "Ike seems like a heck of a fellow. They're talking about him for president. I'd give him the job now, if I could." Truman was just getting into the job. This was new for Ike, too, because he had been so close to Franklin D. Roosevelt, and he hadn't quite known what to expect of this new president that he hadn't known much about.

IKE WAS BORN in 1890, and President Truman was born in 1884. . . . They really come from the same generation. What I found fascinating was that for fifteen years—from 1945 until January of 1961—our country was run by [these] people who grew up in small towns 150 miles apart from each other in the heart of America.

Ike was born in Texas but grew up in Abilene, Kansas, an old cattle town. . . . Even though Missouri and Kansas are both thought of as Midwestern . . . when you're in Abilene, you really feel like you're in the West. It is not that much of a drive to Colorado. You see all the Western historic sites. . . . So though geographically they're only 150 miles apart, Ike, in some ways, is as much a Westerner as Midwesterner.

The Eisenhowers really were from the poor side of the tracks. . . . The Trumans also came from a very modest background. Both Harry and Ike grew up on the edge of poverty. Truman's father went broke at one time. So did Eisenhower's. At the same time, they both had self-confidence and did not feel insecure about where they came from, [like] Richard Nixon or even Lyndon Johnson. Ike, in the famous speech after World War II, in London, [said] "I come from the very heart of America."

Ike's parents were hardworking people. His father was the foreman in the local creamery. His mother, Ida, was very well read [and] disciplined, and it was partly from her that he got his drive and ambition. . . . His father was a very humane, decent guy, but the mother had more of the drive. That was also the case on President Truman's side. His mother had more spark, and his father, like Ike's, sort of struggled.

Ike had been a terrific athlete in high school. . . . One of his close friends was going to the Naval Academy, [and he] applied to go to Annapolis, but the opening was for West Point, and so he wound up going there. Oddly enough, it was President Truman's ambition . . . to go to West Point, but because of his poor eyesight, he was ineligible. Truman served in the reserves and National Guard, and the military played a very important part in shaping President Truman.

Ike was not an academic star at West Point, unlike General Douglas MacArthur, for example, who graduated [first in the class of 1903]. Ike was a so-so student, but he was very well liked. He got a lot of demerits. He once said later in life he thought anyone who didn't go through West Point with a number of demerits wasn't worth their salt. He was a tough guy, a very strong person, which I think the public doesn't understand about him.

After getting out of West Point, he went, among other places, to Fort Sam Houston, where he met and married Mamie Doud, who was from a wealthy family from Denver. When the U.S. entered World War I, Ike was anxious to serve overseas, and he was frustrated because he was given a job training soldiers here, including running a camp in tank warfare, which was a relatively new technology. Among the challenges he had was they didn't even have tanks for him to teach with. But he was very good, very efficient. He had orders at one time to go over, but he was asked to stay in the States, which was a very bitter pill for him. Finally, when it looked like he was going overseas, the Armistice was signed. And so he felt that the world had passed him by.

TRUMAN WAS born in Lamar, Missouri. . . . While still in grammar school, he moved into the town of Independence. He was very rooted on the farm because he had grandparents who had a farm which stayed in the Truman family for many years.

Truman was a little guy. He was not athletic. He loved to read. He later said that he read every book in the local library in Independence. . . . One thing I found is that Truman and Ike read a number of the same things. They both liked military histories. They both admired . . . some biographies of Hannibal that came out around that time. They both were interested in the Civil War. I think the chance to go into Independence and to go to a larger school really opened up horizons for Truman.

Harry Truman was the last president of the United States who did not have a college education. There is no doubt that Truman . . . would have been a very good student. . . . But his family had financial setbacks, and his father expected him to work and help support his family, and Truman did that. . . . There was one point that I found very moving: He was in Kansas City, not long out of high school, [and he] had a job in a bank in Kansas City. He was doing pretty well, but the father asked him to come back and work on the family farm. Truman did this in a minute, never questioned it. He thought he was going to be stuck on the farm for a long time, [but] he also really cared for his mother and father, honored his family. At the same time, he was interested in courting Bess Wallace. It was a long courtship, and they didn't get married until after he returned from World War I.

THE U.S. INTERVENED in World War I in 1917. . . . Harry Truman was in the Missouri National Guard, [promoted to] captain of his battery and served in Europe. [He] saw combat, and emerged really as a leader.

One famous incident: There was a confrontation with a superior officer when a member of Truman's battery was wounded. Truman [put] the soldier on a horse, and Truman was told, "Get him off. He can't do that. Only officers ride horses." But Truman stood his ground. He felt this bond with his men for the rest of his life. In the Truman Library, you see this wonderful correspondence between him and the people he served with. . . . I think that one of the reasons he was effective as president was that he had this experience of serving in war.

Truman married Bess on his return, and he opened the haberdashery with his friend Eddie Jacobson. For a brief time, they were successful. But then when the economic downturn hit, there was a recession, and he went broke. He was determined to pay off his creditors, and he did. It took him a long time. It was not [paid off] until he was a number of years into the Senate.

When his business failed, Truman had a network of friends from his World War I service. He got to know in the service, a member of the Pendergast family who . . . ran the Kansas City Democratic machine. Truman got slated for the job called judge of Jackson County. It actually was more like a county commissioner. He got elected and was a very productive member of the Jackson County court . . . but in one of the Republican landslides in the 1920s, he got defeated. Some people would have dropped out of politics; Truman sort of enjoyed it. He came back and was elected chief judge of Jackson County, which was like being the head of county government in one of the great metropolitan areas in this country. He made a terrific record, built a number of roads, and built new courthouses. He was admired for his honesty. Though he was among our more partisan presidents, Truman worked well with Republican people across the aisle, with the business establishment, and [with] organized labor.

IKE GOT HIS first star right before the U.S. went into World War II. Ike was so frustrated during the 1920s and 1930s because there were so few promotions. The army was really downsized after World War I so that he almost became the military correspondent for a national newspaper chain. He was frustrated working under General Douglas MacArthur, [when MacArthur served] as army chief of staff, and later in the Philippines.

So when it became apparent that the U.S. was going to enter World War II, he was very anxious to serve because he'd missed out in World War I. He returned home and became a star in what was known as the Louisiana maneuvers, the largest peacetime maneuvers in history. Ike was a terrific strategist and tactician. His star really rose. It was General George Marshall and President Franklin Roosevelt who promoted Ike and recognized his potential.

TRUMAN HAD great admiration for Eisenhower as a soldier. In Truman's diary, he put Ike on this pedestal with General Marshall and Robert E. Lee and he disdained the brass-hat type, the MacArthurs, Pattons, and George Armstrong Custers.

[There was a photograph taken in occupied Berlin] . . . and the flag was flying over the U.S.-occupied zone. It was on that day that President Truman stunned General Eisenhower . . . when he looked at him, he said, "General, there's nothing that I wouldn't do for you, and that specifically includes the presidency in 1948." Well, Ike was stunned. You had the president of the United States, in effect, offering to support him for the presidency.

Ike laughed and said, "Mr. President, I don't know who your opponent will be in 1948, but it will not be I. . . ." But Ike returned late that year and was named by President Truman as General Marshall's successor as army chief of staff and he served Truman. This was a job that Ike found distasteful, because after leading history's greatest invasion, he presided over the dismantling of the army. It was very frustrating. . . . Ike didn't want to leave the nation vulnerable because there was a question of Soviet expansionism at that time.

Truman persisted with his idea of approaching Eisenhower about running as the Democratic nominee for president in 1948. Truman . . . was a very modest man, in many ways. He also knew that the Democrats, particularly after the 1946 election [in which they lost both houses of Congress], could have a hard time in 1948. He saw Eisenhower as one person who could preserve the New Deal coalition. . . . Ike was consistent, though. . . . He stepped down as chief of staff in 1948 and wrote a letter to a New Hampshire publisher saying he didn't believe that people in the military should go into politics.

President Truman was so grateful that he gave Ike a tax break on his book *Crusade in Europe*. . . . It ranks with General Grant's memoirs as one of the great books written by an American soldier. This made Ike a wealthy man. . . . President Truman called the IRS commissioner and talked to the secretary of the treasury and said, "I want you to do this for Ike." I found a document confirming that in the Truman Library. Ike got this huge advance, which would be comparable to up in the millions now.

Now, Truman sort of resented that years later, when . . . he had to sell off part of the family farm to make ends meet. There was no presidential pension at the time when he left office. He almost lost money on his memoirs, although he was paid a six-figure advance, serialized in *Life* magazine. He did not make money on it because he didn't get the special break that Ike did. . . .

Truman thought Ike earned it for his service to the country, and so he never flinched at doing that for Eisenhower.

THEY WERE STILL close when Ike went to Europe as supreme Allied commander of NATO. Truman was pretty sure he didn't want to run for reelection in 1952 ... and offered to back Ike again as a Democrat. Ike, in November of 1951, told him that if he ran, it would be as a Republican. Truman could accept this [since] he has great respect for Eisenhower.

When Ike came home from NATO in June of 1952, [Truman] decorated Ike, had him upstairs, and they had a drink in the White House study. Ike was complaining about being attacked [in a] whispering campaign by the right wing. Truman said, "If that's all there is, it's nothing to worry about." Ike was nominated in 1952 at the Republican Convention. Truman thought he would lose to Bob Taft for the nomination, [but] Ike just barely won the nomination.

[Today], General Eisenhower would be a moderate Republican; he certainly was an internationalist. But in domestic affairs, in some ways, he was to Bob Taft's right. Eisenhower would not have run for president in 1952 if Senator Taft, leader of the Senate Republicans, had endorsed the Truman foreign policy in Europe, the right of the U.S. to participate in NATO. Taft declined to do that, and so that was a factor in Ike's decision to run.

Ike also supported Truman in his decision to fire General Douglas MacArthur for his very public insubordination. Truman fired MacArthur for publicly defying administration policy in Korea and for writing a letter to the House Republican leader, Joe Martin, disagreeing with administration policy that, as supreme Allied commander, MacArthur was supposed to be carrying out.

The U.S. intervention in Korea was right after the North Korean invasion of June of 1950. Ike was in New York when he got the news. ... He was president of Columbia University from 1948 until his resignation in 1953 on being elected president of the United States. He was on leave for much of that time because half that time he was working for President Truman as his chief military adviser after the 1948 election. ... Then in June 1952, he was made supreme Allied commander of NATO, so he really believed strongly in the Truman foreign policy.

[IKE'S SON,] John Eisenhower, is an old friend [of mine]. ... He was concerned that this book would make the conflict [between Eisenhower and Truman make both] look bad. In fact, their collaboration is a story that [makes them] both look pretty good. The conflict was unfortunate. John's take on what happened was that his father should probably have been more attentive to Truman's ego at times and that Truman should have been less personal in some of his attacks on his father during the 1952 campaign.

The break started in August of 1952. Ike was staying at the Brown Palace Hotel in Denver, his [campaign] headquarters. Truman had a briefing at the White House with Governor Adlai Stevenson of Illinois.

President Truman invited Eisenhower to this same briefing with the CIA director, Walter Bedell Smith, Ike's World War II chief of staff, and with Secretary of State Dean Acheson and the Cabinet, Ike respectfully declined and put out a telegram saying that in his new role, he did not feel it was appropriate for him to do so. Truman wrote him a letter [and] said that . . . he thought that Ike had allowed some crackpots to come between them because he had threatened the bipartisan foreign policy of which Eisenhower had been a big part. Truman said finally that he was sorry if he caused him any embarrassment, "from one who always meant to be your friend and always tried to be."

Ike wrote back a handwritten note, very respectful, saying, "Mr. President, you've caused me no embarrassment, but I feel that since there was no emergency, it was not urgent for me to be there." It might be misunderstood if he went and attended this briefing. But, Eisenhower was, in fact, insulted. . . . Now, President Truman felt that Ike had shown disrespect not just for Harry Truman but for the office of the presidency of the United States. Truman always differentiated those. Ike had always come [to Washington] before when Truman had called, but Eisenhower had always been his subordinate in the past.

Ike was running [for president against] some people that he didn't really care to be in the same room with, such as . . . Senator Joseph R. McCarthy of Wisconsin. . . . Ike was advised not to go to Wisconsin, because he would be on the same stage as McCarthy. There was sharp dissension in the campaign. Eisenhower ultimately decided to go to Wisconsin because Truman had carried Wisconsin and there was some question that this would be a close election. Eisenhower was booked to be on the same stage and ride the train with Joe McCarthy.

Then it was published in the *New York Times* that Eisenhower had, in effect, surrendered to McCarthy and shared the same stage with him. Truman now had an issue to go after and ripped into Eisenhower. Truman went all across the country saying that this showed moral cowardice, that you can't trust someone who doesn't stand by their friends. He said, "I have great respect for General Eisenhower, but he's bowed to expediency." Truman became increasingly vitriolic in his attacks.

IKE, RIGHT BEFORE the election, pledged that if elected, he would go to Korea. This turned a close election into a rout because there was no American soldier with more prestige than Dwight Eisenhower. He pledged to end the war in Korea. Truman attacked this as campaign demagoguery at its worst and noted that Ike, as chief of staff, had been part of the decision to withdraw Korea from the U.S. defense perimeter. But Ike was genuine in his commitment to go there and try and do something to end the war. . . . Ike was again incensed and didn't know if he could even ride down Pennsylvania Avenue with Truman, he was so angry.

Truman, once the election was over, thought that bygones could be bygones. . . . He put together the first formal transition office and worked very hard to have a smooth transition. That was the only meeting Truman and Eisenhower had between June of 1952 and that famous ride in January of 1953, when they rode to the Capitol together.

President Truman was offended when he and Mrs. Truman invited General and Mrs. Eisenhower to the White House for coffee and sandwiches before going up for the inaugural ceremonies. They declined. President Truman thought that this was an insult to Mrs. Truman. Ike, having been in the military all those years, did not really understand partisanship. Truman had been friends with many people who had savaged him far worse than he'd gone after Eisenhower. But this was a real rift. . . . It would be a number of years before there was a warm conversation between Truman and Ike.

They didn't actually have a conversation until General Eisenhower broke the ice late in 1961, when he called on President Truman at the Truman Library. They had a friendly conversation. Truman gave him a personal tour of the library. Then a week later, they went to the funeral of their friend, Sam Rayburn, the great House Speaker, in Texas.

What really brought them back together was that terrible weekend in 1963, when John F. Kennedy had been shot. Truman and his daughter, Margaret, were staying at Blair House. Former president Eisenhower and Mrs. Eisenhower drove down from Gettysburg. They went to JFK's service with the Trumans, and they went to the grave site with the Trumans. There have been so few people who have been president of the United States that I really do think they felt something of a bond and remembered some of the great things that they had done together. That weekend, the reconciliation between these two great figures, was a very bright thing, a good thing for the country at this sad time.

They had a warmer relationship, but it was still formal. It was never as it was during the great years between 1945 and 1952.

THEIR LAST meeting was in 1966 in Kansas City, and it fittingly was at a luncheon for the United Nations, which they both believed in very strongly . . . .

[The real problem between the two of them] was a difference in backgrounds. Ike, as a five-star general, had not been used to the criticism that came in politics. He did not understand that when Truman went after him with these vitriolic attacks, that this happens in politics. In the case of President Truman, I think he probably did go too far in some of those. At the same time, I think Truman was very hurt.

President Eisenhower would die in 1969. President Truman lived until late 1972 and died just a few weeks before Lyndon Johnson. . . . Harry Truman did not go to Dwight Eisenhower's funeral. He was in frail health himself, but he issued a very gracious statement recalling their great service together.

Senator Richard Russell of Georgia

by

GILBERT C. FITE

Native Georgian Richard B. Russell began his long political career as a state representative, shortly thereafter becoming governor. In 1932, Russell was elected to the U.S. Senate, where he became one of its most respected and powerful members. Gilbert Fite, professor of history at the University of Georgia, appeared on Booknotes *on August 2, 1992, to discuss Russell's political career, his personal life, and in particular, his refusal to support civil rights legislation. Mr. Fite's book,* Richard B. Russell, Jr.: Senator from Georgia, *was published by University of North Carolina Press in 1991.*

RICHARD RUSSELL WAS a very distinguished politician for his day. Later, we may talk about some of his problems, but generally, he was in the mainstream of American history [during] the time he was in the Senate. He came to Washington in January of 1933, and stayed there until he died in 1971. He was in Washington for thirty-eight years in a very important period of American history, and he had much to do with many of the issues that the country was involved in during those years. . . . The United States Senate named one of its office buildings after him.

Russell was a senator when he died, and was president pro tempore of the Senate. . . . Senator Russell had as much or more respect by his colleagues than most any senator [in the period from 1933 to 1971], at least on the Democratic side. And he got along well with his colleagues on the Republican side as well. That was partly true because he was a master at doing favors for people in a behind-the-scenes way. His colleagues came to admire him for a variety of reasons. One was that they could absolutely depend upon his integrity. If Richard Russell gave you his word, you didn't have to worry about it; you didn't have to have it written down. Not only did he have great integrity, but he was fair, and people recognized that. So he built up a series of friendships and a high level of respect that very few senators had.

He was a humble individual, although he held high office and was chairman of the Appropriations Committee during his last years, and was on the Appropriations Committee all the thirty-eight years that he was in the Senate. He was the kind of person who would always be prepared on an issue; he worked hard to know more than other people on it.

OTHER THAN on the civil rights issue, Richard Russell was very much in the mainstream of Democratic politics, except, possibly, right at the end—he and Lyndon Johnson [disagreed] over a good bit of the Great Society program. But other than that, he was a New Dealer in the early years, supported Franklin Roosevelt all the way through, and supported such things in the early years as federal aid to education. He was not out of tune, except on this one issue, with the main thrust of the Democratic Party.

He changed views on many other issues—for instance, in his early years he was a strong isolationist. He got away from that in his later years. But on this issue of race, he lived in a time, was raised in a community that was strictly segregated, and just could not, for some reason or other, bring himself to see that this was wrong.

[He would have said blacks and whites should be] separate . . . but my view is that they can't be separate and equal. So Dick Russell would have argued with me on that point—or with anybody. And, he did. The *Congressional Record* is full of the arguments. [And unlike some of his Senate colleagues who gradually changed their views on race, Russell never did.] Part of this was due to his understanding of history. He was a great reader of history, particularly the Civil War and Reconstruction. And the history in that period tried to show that blacks were totally irresponsible when they got in positions of influence, as they did in some of the Southern states there during Reconstruction. With that understanding and with the stories that the older men in his community used to tell him about the Civil War and about Reconstruction, he believed that blacks could not handle the kinds of responsibility that he could. He was sort of bound by his understanding of history and how blacks had functioned in American society at a particular time. He never changed his mind, and there was no reasoning with him on that point, although he was a most reasonable man on almost every other issue. But not that one.

RICHARD RUSSELL came from a family of thirteen children. He was the first son and the fourth child of a family of thirteen. His father was a very ambitious man—a lawyer and a judge—and a man who pushed his son very hard.

Judge Richard Russell, his father, was very concerned about his sons succeeding. Richard Russell was born in Winder, Georgia, which is not far from Atlanta; a small town, probably had about 1,000 people at that time, and it was an area where they raised cotton—it was a rural town. He went to a private school, Gordon Military Institute, for his secondary education, and then he went to the University of Georgia for his law degree, which, at that time, was a two-year degree. So he was from a big family with an ambitious father who pushed him, and he lived in this rural community, although I should say that he did travel a good deal as a youth. He came to Washington. He was here, in fact, for Woodrow Wilson's inauguration with his father in 1913. But he was raised in a rural community and he never got over that feeling of agrarianism. He was a great agrarian.

He never married. As a young man, he did a lot of courting, as they called it in those days. When he was a teenager, he was literally pursued by young ladies. They thought that he was a catch, so to speak, if they could get a date with Richard Russell. I found in his files many of the letters that these girls wrote to him when he was sixteen, seventeen, and eighteen years old. Whenever any one of them would get serious, then he would drop them, but he almost got married in 1938.

He met a young lady here in Washington who was a professional person, and they came just within an ace of getting married, but they didn't get married because of religious differences. It seems not very important today, perhaps, but in the 1930s, a mixed marriage, which was, at that time a Protestant and a Catholic, didn't go over. The young lady was a Catholic and she wanted to have a Catholic wedding, with Catholic rites, and he didn't. He wanted his brother, who was a Presbyterian minister, to marry them.

When he came to Washington in 1933, he lived alone, either in a hotel room or in a small apartment. He also had a sister in Washington at that time and he visited her frequently. But generally, he lived alone; spent his evenings reading, getting ready for the Senate business the next day, or reading history. He had a great love of history and he probably knew more about the Civil War than most professional historians.

His pattern at the end of the day was [to] stay until about 7:00. Some of the staff used to say they wished he would get married so he'd have to go home for dinner. But he would stay until about 7:00, finish his correspondence, and in the early years before television, he'd listen to the news on the radio while he was having a couple of drinks of Jack Daniels, which he kept in his desk drawer—and then go out to a local restaurant to have dinner. He kept up that pattern during most of his years in Washington.

[He frequently saw his senior staff and the secretary who took his correspondence,] but the people who worked in the front offices, who took care of the daily routine, he didn't see them very often. He always went in his private door, or almost always. He was not hale and hearty and well met. He was a very reserved Southern gentleman. He called the ladies in his office "Miss So-and-So"—whatever their first name was.

He was a very intelligent person. He didn't show this in his early years in school because he liked to play rather than study. But once he got through law school—with a little better than average grades—and started practicing law, and went into politics in 1921 when he went to the Georgia legislature, from that time on, his intelligence showed in about everything that he was involved with.

He was never defeated in an election. When he was twenty-three years old, he ran for the state House of Representatives; he won that against an older man in the county who was well established—beat him better than two to one, as I remember it. Then when he ran for governor in 1930, a lot of people thought he was just testing the water, so to speak. That used to be characteristic in Georgia and probably other states—run and get known. He said, "No, I'm going to run to win" and he beat some of the best old-line politicians that the state had.

[One of them was] Eugene Talmadge, who had a lot of support from rural Georgia; that was his base. A lot of people thought that he would give Russell a real battle in 1936. [Russell was first elected to the Senate in 1933 to fill out the remaining term of a deceased senator,] so he came up for election in 1936. A lot of folks in Georgia thought that Talmadge could beat him because Georgia was predominantly rural at that time and he had a farm, and in his past political history, he had appealed to the rural element.

But the surprising thing for many people, including me when I began to study it, was how much support Russell had from farmers, yet he never acted like a farmer. He hardly ever campaigned without his shirt and tie in those rural areas, yet he got the farm vote because they felt, "He's giving it to us straight. We can depend on what he says." Russell didn't make many promises to farmers, but he still got their vote.

He was chairman of the Subcommittee on Agriculture Appropriations in the 1930s. The United States was very rural in the late 1930s, and he did a lot of favors for senators all over rural America, which was a good share of America at that time.

[I give him credit for establishing the school lunch program,] which first got its support from those who were trying to do something for farmers and get rid of the farm surpluses—"We are buying all these commodities, so why don't we distribute them to the schools?"—which they began to do in the late 1930s. And finally, in 1946, Russell was mainly responsible for getting a separate school lunch law passed in Congress. Originally, it had come out of the Department of Agriculture, mainly.

There was another thing about Richard Russell: If you told him something in confidence, you could be sure it was never going to be repeated. And so, over the years, his stature just increased, with more and more of his colleagues respecting him. Seniority played a big part because seniority was a lot more important in those days than it is now. When you got to be chairman of the Armed Services Committee, which he was for sixteen years, or chairman of the Appropriations Committee, which he was after 1969, you had a lot of power.

He could have been Senate minority leader in 1953 or majority leader in 1955. He did not want the majority leadership because by the time he could have had it, he and President Truman had a sharp difference over the civil rights question. Russell said, "I do not want the responsibility of handling the administration's program, as I would need to do if I were majority leader, with this civil rights issue in it as a main part of Truman's program."

RUSSELL'S SOUTHERN colleagues put a lot of pressure on him to run for president in 1952. He had been nominated in 1948, but he never joined the Dixiecrats; he went ahead and supported Truman, although he had been nominated [by fellow Southerners because of] the civil rights issue. So he said he wouldn't run anymore, but he had a lot of pressure from Southerners to run for president in 1952, and so he finally decided that he'd take a swing at it, and he did.

Russell had a lot to do with making Lyndon Johnson [Senate] minority leader and then majority leader. Russell liked Johnson from the beginning, and Johnson courted Russell as he did other people. When Johnson came to Washington, the Johnsons almost immediately began to entertain Russell—inviting him for dinner and that kind of thing, and courting him unmercifully, really. So Johnson and Russell [developed] a fairly close personal relationship early on. What Russell liked about Johnson was his ability to get things done and his ability to work with different elements in the Democratic Party. That is one of the main reasons that he supported Johnson for majority leader.

Russell could see the Democratic Party dividing over the question of civil rights by the late 1940s, and he felt Johnson would be the best person in the party, that he knew of anyway, to keep the two elements in the Democratic Party together. He worked hard toward that end. He admired Johnson. He liked Johnson; they were just the very opposite. If the old saw is right that opposites draw one another, here's a good example of it, because Russell was private, he was reserved, he was polite, while Johnson was often boisterous and demanding. But they got along very well together.

[Russell spent a lot of time in the White House with Johnson.] After Johnson became president, he spent more time with Johnson than any other senator.

HE GOT ALONG pretty well with Richard Nixon, and Nixon greatly admired Russell. That was a sort of a mutual admiration society. We have a taped interview with President Nixon in regard to Russell, and there's no question but he greatly admired him. In fact, he was the president who called Russell a "president's senator." So they had a good working relationship during that short time Russell was still in the Senate and Nixon was president. Nixon had one criticism of Russell, that he wasn't very effective in the electronic age. Nixon thought that public officials needed to do this, to communicate with the public in the electronic age, and Russell just shied away from that, and he did it on purpose.

Russell was very critical, in fact, of his colleagues, whom he said instead of tending to day-to-day business, were running to the television stations to get on TV so they could send their message home. He thought we'd have better government if everybody did their work and paid attention to the day-to-day operations more than trying to get publicity for themselves. The way we spend money nowadays on elections would have simply been abhorrent to Richard Russell. Now, of course, he did have the good luck of not having any opposition after 1936, so all he had to do was to raise enough money to file his candidacy. But he never spent much money, and the idea that members of Congress could keep a certain amount of campaign money—Richard Russell would have thought that was the worst thing in the world. If he had any extra money left over at the end of a campaign, he always sent it back, if he could find the people to send it to. When he couldn't find the people to send it to, he gave that money to the University of Georgia in his will.

SOME PEOPLE thought that Johnson and Russell really came to a parting of the ways over the Great Society program. It's true that Russell opposed most of that program, but they still had very close social relations all during the 1960s up to 1968. Russell nominated an old friend and political supporter, a rather distinguished lawyer, for a judgeship in south Georgia. The man had earlier made some anti–civil rights statements and took some anti–civil rights positions. This had been almost a decade before. Some of the civil rights people and the attorney general's office said, "We'd better look into this a lot more carefully."

Groups began to oppose the nominee. Russell thought that the president ought to put it right through. [Johnson] told Russell that "I'm finally going to appoint your nominee, but I've got to solve some political problems that I've got here with the appointment beforehand." Russell thought he was too slow and was embarrassing his nominee, so he wrote the president a red-hot letter. In fact, it was so hot that Johnson told one of his aides that he didn't want to keep it in the file, although he did.

The appointment was made, but Russell never forgave him. After Johnson decided he wasn't going to run for president and went back to Texas, he tried to mend the split, but he was never successful. In fact, when they were doing a book on Johnson and wanting some of his former colleagues to say some kind things about him, Russell didn't even answer the request until, finally, one of his assistants said, "We've got to write something," so they did. Russell was unforgiving in that situation.

He had no respect for some of his colleagues whom he thought really weren't prepared for the issues that they were dealing with in the United States Senate. He studied a great deal. The story is that when he first came to Washington he read the *Congressional Record* in its entirety every day. He wanted to be informed. He was a man who believed that knowledge was power and that if you knew more than the people you were arguing against or working against on a particular political issue, then you were more likely to win the battle.

He kept the filibuster rule in force, and even tightened it up in some cases, so that a minority had more power than it had had earlier. It wasn't until the Civil Rights Act of 1964 was passed that the rest of the Senate was strong enough to override that small minority. If Russell and the Southern caucus could have gotten the thing in committee—the Civil Rights Act—they might have blocked it even longer. In 1964, there were enough votes to put it directly on the calendar, and so there was no way for a committee to block it. Of course, that was done in a purposeful way by the people who wanted civil rights legislation passed.

[If Russell had had his way, the Civil Rights Act would not have been passed.] Now he knew the 1957 law was going to pass, but the most effective parts of that law, he and Lyndon Johnson arranged to cut out. Johnson became a strong supporter of civil rights because he wanted to become president. He saw that no person in American history, from this time onward, would probably be elected president without supporting civil rights. So he and Russell made a deal and they got the law passed, but it wasn't a very effective law. Neither was the 1960 law. It wasn't until 1964 that Johnson had built up enough support that they were able to put it past this minority that would have talked forever to keep it from passing if they'd had a chance.

[The idea of a relocation commission] had floated around. A number of people had that idea, of relocating blacks from the South to the North. Russell, on the racial issue, did not believe in integration in any form whatever. He believed that both races would be better off if they were separate—physically separated. So as the civil rights movement developed, Russell and people who held those views in Congress said, "Well, if we're going to have integration, why don't we have it in the North as well as in the South?" So he favored this relocation bill. If any black family wanted to move, at least one of the bills said that they'd be paid $1,500 to move to some other community. Of course, that got nowhere in Congress, any more than the idea that had been around during quite a little of the nineteenth century of moving blacks to Africa. These were mostly ideas to deter or to turn aside the main drive for civil rights. Russell and the Southern caucus started out with about twenty senators and finally declined until it only had about twelve or thirteen left that they could really depend on to oppose civil rights legislation. By that time they were just trying to slow the process up. As Russell said on many occasions, "If I could just stop this for twenty years," or something like this.

I have seen nothing in the record where his colleagues challenged [his views on race.] I believe it was Hubert Humphrey that once said that Richard Russell was in the mainstream of the Democratic Party, except on this issue of civil rights. I never saw any record of Senator Humphrey or any of the other strong pro–civil rights people criticizing Russell in the broad sense because of this one issue. I think that's just because they did have deep respect for him, but on this one issue [their feeling was] "Dick, you don't know what you're talking about, and we're going to change it." And they did.

Two Presidential Memoirs

by

MICHAEL KORDA

Michael Korda joined the book publishing industry in 1958 as an editor for Pocket Books, a division of Simon & Schuster. He eventually became editor in chief of Simon & Schuster, where he remained throughout many major shifts in the publishing industry. In his twelfth book Another Life: A Memoir of Other People, *published by Random House in 1999, Korda described his four decades of encounters with authors, editors, and publishers. On July 11, 1999, Mr. Korda appeared on* Booknotes *to discuss his book and, in particular, the experiences of editing the memoirs of two presidents—Ronald Reagan and Richard Nixon.*

First of all, my book is not called *A Memoir of Other People* for nothing. Anybody reading this book will get to know as much as they can possibly want to know about me, but I'm in the background, Zelig-like. The focus is on people like Ronald Reagan, Richard Nixon, Graham Greene, Larry McMurtry, Carlos Castaneda, Joan Crawford, Jackie Susann, Harold Robbins, Irving Wallace. The people that I published are what the book is really about.

[I've been with Simon & Schuster] forty-one years. I'm still editor in chief. I've been editor in chief for thirty-one years. I can't go any higher, and it would be embarrassing to everybody if I were demoted lower. So I think I'm stuck at this rank.

[I got to know Ronald Reagan] in what was then thought of as a terrific coup. Dick Snyder bought Ronald Reagan's presidential memoirs at the very height of the president's popularity, paying a fabulous amount of money for it, for the day—[roughly] $8 million—a lot of money. And since I'm the editor in chief of Simon & Schuster and also something of a historian, it was thought appropriate that I should be Ronald Reagan's editor. It was sort of fitting, because that's what they expected, anyway. They asked for me.

There was a minor glitch and problem, because I was also Kitty Kelley's editor. Kitty Kelley was then writing a biography of Nancy Reagan, which Nancy feared with considerable depth of fear. That proved to be an embarrassment for everybody, and I had to give up editing Kitty Kelley, which made me very sad because she's a friend and because she's a wonderful biographer. I then took on editing Ronald Reagan, which was sort of strange, because the president, of course, did not write his books. There was a ghostwriter, Bob Lindsey, whom we picked. Rather famously, at the end of the whole procedure, we had a press conference at which Ronald Reagan and I were photographed ostensibly editing his book. We sat in front of the television cameras and were given two sheaves of perfectly blank white paper, and a ballpoint pen. We sat there, the two of us together at this table, busily pretending to scribble editorial notes and things, and hand them back—on totally blank pieces of paper. Not for nothing did the president come from the movies. He was wonderful at it. Anybody watching this would [note] the concentration, the firmness of his handwriting, his total immersion in what he was doing. It was the movies.

After this had taken place and this scene had been recorded for all the television shows, the president stood up, and he walked to the door—the cameras were still on him, of course—and he turned around and waved, and he said, "I'm sure the book is great. I'm looking forward to reading it when I have the time." It's true, he had only the most tangential connection to this book.

I went out to see him in California. I liked him very much, politics apart. I thought he was a wonderful man. He used to phone constantly, and it was nice. Usually a telephone operator said, "The president will be on the line; please hold for the president." With Reagan, he's a great horseman, loves horses, and my wife, Margaret, is a very successful three-day eventer. Her whole life revolves around horses. So I would come home and hear Margaret on the phone. She'd be sitting there, talking about horses endlessly—this horse and that horse and what it did. After about twenty minutes, because I wanted to get a drink or something, I would say "Who is it?" And she would say, "It's President Reagan." He would place calls. He would pick up the phone, and he would say, "Hi. This is Ron Reagan. Is Michael Korda there?" And he would talk to whoever was on the line. He was the friendliest of men.

But I was actually sent out to him because he had neglected to mention, in taping the material that we were going to use for the book, his marriage to Jane Wyman. When I had pointed this out, I encountered this wall of resistance. For the first time, the president was actually rather stiff with me. No, he did not want to discuss Jane Wyman. Well, that's kind of a problem. As I pointed out to him, it isn't that anybody wanted him to say anything about Jane Wyman, but if reviewers find he hadn't even mentioned his first marriage, they might conclude that if he could leave that out, he'd leave other things out, and therefore, that the book couldn't be relied on.

So I was sent out to California to negotiate this point with a very reluctant president. I said, "You don't have to say anything about it. Just one sentence—on such-and-such a day, I was married to Jane Wyman, but the marriage, unfortunately, ended on such-and-such—that's it. That's all you need to do. Just so her name is in the index." No. Well, it did not take me very long to work out that the actual opponent to the mention of Jane Wyman was not, of course, the president, but Mrs. Reagan. I managed to negotiate that by saying, "It would make the president look foolish if he didn't at least mention [her]." Overnight, the president came back and said, "It's just fine." We wrote out by hand one sentence and put it in the book.

He was always, whenever I worked with him, the kindest and the nicest. . . . Of the three presidents I've worked with, I liked him by far and away the most, and I would have liked him even if he hadn't been president. He was just a very endearing and nice man.

[One day] the president came in with this brown paper bag. He said, "These are homemade chocolate chip cookies, made by our maid, and I brought them in for us to have with our coffee." And we put them on a [plate]. But these cookies looked weird. I think she was Latin American and they looked, in fact, like chocolate chip cookies that had been made by somebody who'd never seen a chocolate chip cookie. They were too thick and too burned at the edges. But he loved them, so we put them on the plate, and as we were having our coffee, we passed them around the table. There were about six or seven of us around the table, all of us working on these proofs except for Ronald Reagan, who was looking out the window and wishing he were doing something else. Everybody had one of these chocolate chip cookies, and when the plate got around to the end of the table, it's put back in front of the president, and there was one cookie left on the plate.

After about fifteen or twenty minutes, I realized that the president was paying no attention whatsoever to what we were saying, that his mind was fixed on something else. What it was fixed on was this one remaining chocolate chip cookie. It was perfectly clear to me that he wanted that second chocolate chip cookie with his coffee. But having been brought up properly in Dixon, Illinois, he had been taught as a maxim that cannot possibly be broken, that you do not take the last cookie on a plate, particularly when you're the host. So he couldn't take it. To break the spell, I said, "Mr. President, those chocolate chip cookies were delicious." And he held up the plate and he said, "Oh, yes. Yeah, they're good, weren't they? They're homemade," and he went through the whole thing. He said, "Would anybody like the cookie?" He passed the plate around the table, and it went around everybody, got to me, and I passed it on to Bob Lindsey, who's sitting between me and the president. You could see the relief on the president's face, and nobody had touched the cookie. And just as it reached Bob Lindsey, without even looking at it, Lindsey took the cookie and swallowed it. I looked, and Ronald Reagan's face was such a picture of sadness that my heart went out to him. Even though I don't agree with him politically, I just felt for him. He almost had it, he had that cookie in his hand. He was counting on it, and he didn't get it.

We probably printed about 300,000 or 400,000 [copies of the Reagan book], and I would be very surprised if we sold 15,000 or 20,000 in the end. It was total disaster, probably the largest disaster of modern publishing. The answer to that is that although people loved Ronald Reagan, they didn't necessarily want to buy his book, and I think that's often true of presidential memoirs. They didn't feel that they would really learn something new and different, as indeed they didn't, although it was quite a fine book in its own way. It's always struck me that presidential memoirs tend, by their very nature, to be non-books. The last readable one was written by Ulysses S. Grant, because he wrote it himself in longhand while he was dying of cancer. It's actually a very fine book. It was published by Mark Twain. But since then they've mostly been put together.

I PUBLISHED Richard Nixon for several years, many years, in fact. I was first introduced to him by his daughter Julie Nixon Eisenhower, a dear friend of mine—two of whose books I published—who took me to lunch at Nixon's house when he and Mrs. Nixon were living in New York City. We were upstairs in the dining room. Nixon was delayed by something downstairs and came up, and when he came in he was tremendously affable. He came across and shook my hand and said, "Very nice to see you; very, very nice." Then, without a change in tone or anything else, he went across and shook Mrs. Nixon's hand and said, "Very nice to see you," in exactly the same tone of voice, and sat down and started his soup. I thought, "This is really bizarre." But I came to recognize that he had this difficulty in communicating to people in some way.

When I went out to Saddle River, New Jersey, to dinner at Nixon's house there, he came down the stairs. We were gathered in the foyer, and he came down, and when he was two or three steps above us, he raised his arms—it was in a strange gesture—and said, "The good news is, the bar is open." Nixon found it very difficult to [communicate], he was shy. It was difficult for him to communicate with people, and he had this weird habit of referring to himself in the third person, which I mention in *Another Life*. He would say, "It's interesting you should say that. When Nixon was president, and leader of the free world," as if leader of the free world were a title, but always in the third person. But he would actually say to the butler, "Freshen Nixon's drink, would you?" Bizarre! I describe all of this. I describe [that] he was baffling; the fact that he couldn't find his way around his own house when he gave us a tour, myself, the Chinese ambassador, and the interpreter. He kept saying, "And this is Nixon's study," and he would open a closet door. "No, that's [not it] . . . " We had to go through three or four doors before he would finally open the door and say, "Well, that's it."

Then, when he wanted to give the Chinese presents, he opened this drawer of his desk, reached in, and said, "I'm going to give you one of the most important books of the twentieth century." They're standing there waiting, and he's got a desk drawer full of hard-cover copies of Whittaker Chambers's *Witness*. So he gives them each a copy. I thought, "What are they going to make of this when they get back to Peking and have it all translated?" The Pumpkin Papers, Alger Hiss—what [is the] possible significance? Twenty years from now, people are still going to be figuring out what message Nixon was trying to convey by giving them *Witness*. But there was an endearing quality—again, politics to one side—about the man, because he was so shy, so nervous about contact with people that you couldn't help liking him because he made such an effort.

He came to lunch at Simon & Schuster—I arranged a lunch for him to meet our senior executives. With considerable difficulty, it was set up and he came in. He was very gracious, very nice. And as he sat down to lunch, his assistant, a very, very nice young man, John Taylor, handed us each a three-by-five lined card on which there was a typed question. He explained, "When I give a signal to you, ask this question of President Nixon." And so we were sitting having our soup, and John Taylor snapped his fingers at me, and I picked up this card, and said, "Mr. President, given our present relationships with Europe, how would you compare them to what they were when you were president?" And Nixon said, "Ah, Michael, I'm glad you asked that question," and for ten minutes gave this very interesting, succinct lecture on American relationships with Europe. Then John Taylor signaled somebody else, who read their cue. So the entire lunch passed like that, and then Nixon shook hands and was gone. It was carefully staged so there could not be an unexpected question or a personal contact, even though he was, in fact, quite fond of me and I of him. There was this barrier of shyness that he could not break through.

A PUBLISHER HAS to [publish a wide variety of books]. I don't think publishing should be ideological. I think publishers should offer a broad range of books to people. It's in much the same spirit that I am happy to do first novels, and happy to publish and edit Graham Greene or Larry McMurtry, but I don't see why that should prevent me from publishing Jacqueline Susann or Harold Robbins. You should do the best and the most interesting of everything there is, and do it with conviction. To go down an ideological pathway for a publisher is to enter an ever-narrowing path, and you end up being unable to publish a broad range of books. I would never want to do that.

Social Movements

and Political Visions

Carry A. Nation, Prohibitionist

by

FRAN GRACE

*Fran Grace, an associate professor of religious studies at the University of Red-
lands, spent seven years researching the life of Carry A. Nation, whose strong
religious faith led her to a central role in the temperance movement. In 1900,
she used a hatchet to destroy a saloon in a small town in Kansas for its failure
to adhere to a prohibition amendment. She continued smashing saloons
across the country and was arrested more than thirty times before adopting a
less forceful approach. Grace shared Nation's story with* Booknotes *viewers
on August 16, 2001. Her book,* Carry A. Nation: Retelling the Life, *was
published by Indiana University Press in 2001.*

CARRY NATION IS not the woman that we normally think of. . . . She was
more than [what] she became after age fifty-four when she took her hatchets
and started smashing saloons.

She was a complex woman, not the flattened version that we often read
about in the three biographies that have been written about her so far. She
was a complex woman who was very expansive in terms of her personality, in
addition to the rigidity of her prohibitionism. She was a very religious
woman. . . . That is the reason we know about her, because she felt she was
called by God to go into saloons and address a concern that she had a lot of
passion for, but no avenue to express. As a woman, she couldn't vote. She
tried every other avenue to try to address the issue of prohibition, but they all
closed down. Finally, who else to turn to but God? God directed her toward
her smashing method, a method that she said had been used in the temple by
Jesus. So she was just carrying on a tradition that was well established.

CARRY NATION lived from 1846 until her death in 1911. One hundred years ago, everybody in the United States would have known her.

HER FIRST [SALOON] smashing was in a little dusty town in Kansas right near the Oklahoma border in June of 1900. She had been going through this dusty stopover town when she lived in Oklahoma in the 1890s, and she'd go back up to a place that she was very much identified with called Medicine Lodge, Kansas. Kiowa was a little town right in between, so she went here a lot. There were saloons in this town that she would try to instruct in terms of her prohibitionism and the saloon keepers just couldn't really give a rap about her messages. She would stop in there, and she felt like, "I've given those people fair warning. Things are really needing a lift here in terms of the prohibition movement, and so it's time for me to really make a statement." So she went down to Kiowa and smashed up several saloons. . . .

A few years earlier she went into a drugstore in Medicine Lodge, but a drugstore was a different thing from a saloon. She did it with a lot of other women and it was a group effort. It wasn't quite as radical to go into a drugstore as it was to be a woman walking into the male bastion of the saloon with your hatchet in hand and your rocks that you're going to throw to completely wreck it. It's a different thing to go into a drugstore and say, "Let me see that barrel underneath that counter," and then roll it out into the street and smash it there. The difference is that five years later, she actually took that step. She walked into a saloon, which women rarely did, except maybe to get bottles of milk. She called it a den of vice and called the saloon keepers "saturn-faced, beak-nosed donkey bedmates of Satan." That was what people thought about saloons, people like Carry Nation.

What was happening in Kansas was that there was a prohibition amendment, and so [the saloons] were illegal. But the saloon keepers wanted to keep selling liquor, and they would pay off public officials; they would pay them fees. In one case in 1900 in Arkansas City, Kansas, the whole town shut down. The fire department closed and the electric company closed because the temperance people had come in and gotten rid of the saloons momentarily, so the fees that were filling the coffers to run the city were gone.

So there was this connection between the revenue from illegal saloons going into the public coffers, and that was one thing that really angered a person like Carry Nation. In fact, that was why she ultimately picked up her hatchet. It wasn't that she was crazy or menopausal or sex-repressed. It's that she was angry that the people who were supposed to enforce the law were not doing it, and that's why she had so many followers, as people were fed up with this. They had voted for an amendment and they wanted to see it enforced.

BUT SHE DIDN'T always smash. See, this is what we don't understand. She was discriminating in her smashing. She focused her smashing attention on those saloons that were illegal. She did go in sometimes to saloons or to bars that were selling alcohol legally. For example, Union Station in Washington, D.C., in 1909, she busted up a saloon there, and who knows? I'm not sure why she did that.

When she first started out she didn't have much of a repertoire. She would go the night before and do some reconnoitering. . . . She would try to talk to the barkeeper: "You know, you shouldn't be doing this. This picture of Cleopatra at bath, this painting on your wall, is really an abomination. Please take it off. This statue, please cover it up." If she went back the next day and nothing had changed from when she'd gone in for her initial look at it, then she would go in the next day with her rocks, and she would start throwing them at the mirrors, at the paintings that she found so offensive. She would take the glasses and shove them off [the counter], and when she had her hatchet, she would look at crates and beer kegs and start smashing those.

A lot of people wanted to join in, mostly women, but also some men and sometimes some children. At one point in Topeka, she had probably several hundred, close to 1,500 people behind her, and that got out of hand. This became her problem, once she started her crusade, because it was out of her hands. . . . Sometimes people would, of course, call the police. Or, once she got started, the police knew and they caught her before she was going to start smashing and arrested her for causing a riot. As soon as she walked off a streetcar or into a street, people knew she was coming. There would be hundreds of people in these little town squares, and people were shoving and trying to see her and trampling over others. She was that kind of figure. The people who were in charge of public order hated it when she came.

SHE WENT TO jail at least thirty-one times. It could be more, including in Washington, D.C.

Praying . . . was her favorite pose for photographs that were taken of her in jail, and there were many of them. She wanted to be photographed in a petitionary position, a prayerful position with her Bible open, because—you have to understand—as a woman, to pick up a hatchet during those times and do anything out in public, speaking reform, she needed justification. She couldn't say, "I'm doing this because I want to."

IN SOME OF the photographs of her, she has, in addition to her hatchet and Bible in hand, a bag that she carried with her. In that bag, you would have found probably several hundred of those little hatchets. She would sell them to earn money to pay for her legal fines. She was very enterprising that way, and it was very interesting to read the diaries and the records of people from that time who would not have really paid any attention to her prohibitionism, but they wanted a hatchet. That's how popular she was. They wanted a hatchet. They were consumers of the performance and the excitement that she gave.

THE NEWSPAPERS all across the country gave reportage of her, and the newspaper reportage was different according to the regions. In the Midwest, sure, some people were appalled by her. Not everyone joined her smashing crusades on the streets of Midwestern towns, but they didn't comment on her ugliness, so to say. They didn't comment on what she wore. They didn't comment on her as a woman in the same condescending way. Then in the Northeastern press, which is really where we get our mythology about her in American history, they didn't like what she was doing as a woman. They didn't like prohibition, and they didn't like Kansas.

"HATCHETATION" WAS her word that she substituted for agitation. Extreme circumstances, she said, called for extreme agitation and activism. Once she started that, she got all these calls from Broadway, from vaudeville, from Chautauquas, from college universities—"Carry Nation, come tell us about your crusade"—because she was a very comedic, lively entertainer. This is something we don't know about her either. She wasn't just a kind of flattened-out, pinched-face, blue-nosed puritan. She had life to her. People liked to go to her performances. So the college campuses just loved it.

The folks at New Haven, the male students at Yale sent her a telegram: "Please, come save us. Please, come to New Haven. You wouldn't believe what we have to eat in the cafeterias. We have to eat meals that are soaked with brandy sauce and champagne sauce and all kinds of liquor-lubed meals." Of course, they were teasing her. They wanted a show. They wanted her to come and have a blast with her. I think part of her knew that, but she got on the train because she thought, "OK, I could do some good here. Get these boys at Yale straightened out." So she got off the train and people were there to greet her because they heard that she was coming.

She did her speeches here and there. Then she went to her hotel room, and she was sitting there quietly and she heard a knock at the door. These young men, these Yale students come, and they said, "Oh, Carry, please, can we ask a favor?" And she said, "Well, first, you have to sign an abstinence pledge." So they did that. They walked in and they said, "We would really like a photograph with you." Pleased, she sat on the bed and invited them to sit around her, and the lights go out so that the flash can occur. Unbeknownst to her, they brought out these gin glasses and beer steins and cigarettes. So there is this picture of Carry Nation and it's still in New Haven at Mory's Club.

SHE HELPED TO pass a prohibition [amendment] to the Constitution in Oklahoma in 1907, and then she decided, "OK, if I'm going to get that serpent of alcohol, I've got to get it at the head, so I'm going to Washington, D.C. . . . " She tried valiantly to get into the White House and was refused at the door. Her comment was that it was gender discrimination and that it was because she was a woman, a representative mother. "You can't, if you're a woman, get in to see the president, but if you're a brewer or if you're a tycoon, you can get in to see whomever you want."

She traveled a lot. She was born in Kentucky and moved several times, continuing to go north and to Missouri. Then, during the Civil War, she and her family went down to Texas. She was about sixteen or so, at that time. Then [just before] the war was over, they went back to Missouri. She married her first husband there, and he died [sixteen months later]. She married her second husband there, and he wanted to go down to Texas to try out farming, so they went down south again. She was a woman who moved a lot, and that's part of her story, which created a kind of fragmented history.

She did have a very complicated childhood. Her parents were not an ordinary pair. Her father, George Moore, was a farmer. He'd lost his first wife after having several children, and then married a woman named Mary Campbell. Mary was several years younger than he was, and she too had been married before and suffered the loss of a husband and two children. So both of them came to their marriage in grief.

There's this whole part of the mythology of Carry Nation that her mother was a lunatic, that her mother believed that she was Queen Victoria, that she hallucinated. [It's said] that this really is the genetic reason why Carry Nation started smashing, because her mother was a lunatic and so was Carry Nation. Well, there isn't a lot of evidence for that. There's evidence that Carry Nation had a difficult relationship with her mother, like a lot of children do; that she found her mother somewhat imperious, somewhat picky in terms of taste. She didn't, apparently, like to be around Carry, who was the eldest daughter [she had with George]. She had Carry sleep with the Africans whom the family enslaved, so Carry spent a lot of time with the family's slaves.

[Her time with the slaves] was really important in terms of her religious development. Here you have her father and mother, who were participating in a very rationally oriented, cognitive, withdrawing religion. Then she goes to the [slave] meetings. They would get together, often outside or in the cabins that they had, and there would be a lot of emotional expression and singing and what was termed shouting. Carry really resonated with the shouting. This was a very self-expressive and transcendent, ecstatic experience. So she had these two competing, opposing experiences of religion early on and both of them formed her. She kept them. Again, she's a complex person, not the flat

Carry Nation that we hear about. She's this complex person who both experiences religion in terms of pragmatics and the heart, and it's the heart that she got from the enslaved of the Moore family.

So here you have a passionate woman who is very lively and very religious and driven. So why alcohol? That is a crucial question. It's a complex question. She fell in love when she was in her early twenties, and she never really loved anyone with the same degree of idealism and romantic passion as she did this man, Charles Gloyd. He was an alcoholic. She didn't know it, and her parents tried to tell her. Soon after they were married, he would come home in a drunken state. She smelled it on his breath. He was withdrawn, and they were married a very short time, and then he died [just after the birth of their first child]. This was a very tragic story, and she wrote about in her diary for years afterward, when she was still going to his grave in sorrow.

He was an alcoholic, and he was a doctor and was trying to get established with a practice in a little town in Holden, Missouri. The pressure was on him to get this practice established because her parents didn't like him. They pressured her and said, "We're not going to let you marry him until we can see that he's really going to take care of you." So the pressure was on him. And he just got pretty sick and died.

She mourned for a series of years, really, four to five years. She was working. She had gone to Warrensburg, Missouri, for the Normal School, which was where she got a teaching certificate. Mostly, there were single women who were going to school there, and so already she stood out. She had to support herself, and here she was a single mother with no money. She had rejected her parents in marrying this man, and then he disappeared. So she was on her own, except for the mother-in-law, Mother Gloyd, whom she was with until Mother Gloyd died. So they were together as part of the same family unit for decades.

SHE HAD ONLY one child by birth. She ended up having several stepchildren. [A man named David Nation's] wife died, and he was left with several children still at home. He started a correspondence with a woman that he knew in town who had just been widowed, Carry Gloyd, who had one daughter. The tone of their correspondence was purely pragmatic, despite some rhetoric that's flowery and romantic. It's pretty much down to the brass tacks of "You know what?" as he says later, "I needed someone to run my house. I needed a woman in the house to keep house and to look after my kids." So she took on that role as stepmother.

DAVID NATION comes into the picture quite a lot earlier on than previous biographers have said. He and Carry knew each other when they were living in Missouri and she was married to Charlie. David and his wife came down from Indiana to take a ministry position. David became the minister of a Campbellite congregation in Holden. They would have gone to the same church, they were neighbors, according to the census records. So David's wife died, Carry's husband died, and then her teaching career didn't work out, so she needed money and he needed a mother in his home. They worked out this agreement to marry, join their lives together, and it was a great disappointment to her.

For her, it was a disappointment because she was a person who was passionate and who wanted that returned and he wasn't that kind of person. I think she had that expectation that they could build a life together that was mutually fulfilling and mutually religious, focused around ministry. Even though he was a minister, she didn't think he was a "real minister," a real Christian. For him, it was disappointing because what he wanted was a housekeeper. He wanted a mother for his children and she turned out to be a very assertive woman.

His claim for their divorce to be on the grounds of both desertion and cruelty did not happen; the court granted him the divorce on the grounds of desertion because Carry said, "I'm not coming back to David. I'm happy to have my own career, and I don't plan to come back." But his claim that she had been cruel to him throughout their life, that she'd been bossy and that she'd left him in his sickbed and she hadn't cooked meals and this and that, the court said, "No, we won't grant that." So they split up their possessions, and they went their separate ways. He died a couple of years later.

But it was the relationship with her daughter that really was the most tragic in her life. Again, this is something that other biographers haven't emphasized but is, of course, very important to a woman like Carry Nation, who presented herself, in her words, as the representative mother. This was the whole argument for why she would go into saloons. She called herself a home defender. If you call yourself a home defender and a representative mother and your own daughter's whole life is filled with sorrow and disappointment, what does that say about you? So she had this whole very complicated sense of her own motherhood.

She had a lot of jobs. First of all, I think one has to say that she didn't want to work. Any woman growing up in her time period expected to marry a man who was economically provident enough that she wouldn't have to work. So it was an extreme disappointment to her to have to work. She started out teaching. And then when [she and David] moved down to Texas because he wanted to farm, that didn't work. They were in constant fear of debt and not being able to pay their taxes. So she was forced to sell farm products—butter, eggs, and this and that.

When that didn't bring in enough income, she went to downtown East Columbia, Texas, and rented a hotel and started feeding people and having people stay there, travelers mostly. That's at the point in the divorce petition where David Nation says she became bossy, when she started to support the family. Then they moved back up to Kansas, because he got a ministry job, and that failed and they moved to Oklahoma on the Cherokee Strip there. Again, he had a ministry job, but it wasn't bringing in enough income. So she became an osteopath, one of the early osteopaths, which was a form of medicine and healing even though it had a strongly metaphysical content.

She did that probably till the end of her life, about ten years; the most concentrated years were before her smashing. Osteopaths are part of the American Medical Association, but back then, when it first started in the 1890s, they were considered quackery and not scientific at all.

She was trained. I still haven't been able to find out where. She was very familiar with the Kirksville, Missouri, American School of Osteopathy because she had planned to go there. But I can't find traces or records that she actually was a student there. There were other places, satellite places that she could have gone to.

SHE ALSO performed on Broadway. She performed in vaudeville. It was really interesting to read these accounts of her because you don't picture this woman with her nunlike attire and a Bible in her hand in vaudeville, but people really resonated with her. She would come onto the stage after you'd had the humorists and the women in their red taffeta, much abbreviated skirts, as the New York papers reported it, with her big black dress and her Bible, and she'd start preaching to these people. She'd say, "You are utter sots. You're ruining your lives," and they would cheer her.

EUREKA SPRINGS, Arkansas, for Carry Nation, was [the kind of] oasis that people who, at the end of their life, after they've worked really hard, it's what they longed for. It was a period that was not long enough for her. She only lived there two years or so. But she made a decision in 1909, after coming back from an extended tour in Britain, that it was time to rest. It was time to retreat from public life, not completely, but in the same way that she had been living it, smashing up saloons and lecturing everywhere, because she was in constant movement. She never really had a home. So she turned to Eureka Springs, where her husband had been healed of a certain rheumatism or some kind of arthritic [affliction].

She went to Eureka Springs, and she settled into a lovely little street area with a big house that she named Hatchet Hall. It's a place where she had women come who were fleeing from marriages to alcoholic husbands. She tried to extend a safe place to elderly women who had no one to care for them and had no money to support themselves. Then pre-college children came to learn from Carry Nation. So Hatchet Hall in Eureka Springs in 1909 and 1910 became a place where people could seek refuge if they needed it, where people could go and sing. Carry Nation was a singer and she had a parlor organ, and they could go for meals that were cheap. There were workers who would walk that street, miners or whatever, and they would stop in for cheap meals.

SHE DIDN'T LEAVE as much money after she died as you would think. She had given most of her speech performance proceedings away to the poor people who were living in the towns where she had her performances. So, for example, if she went to Atlantic City and she spoke and there were a lot of fees that came in from that, she gave it to the poor kids there. When she sold her hatchets, she made money, and when she bought her property, she made money. But she left the sum of approximately $7,000 that was to be split up, some going to the Free Methodist Church, which was very influential in her life, and then some to her grandchildren and a niece that she'd traveled to Great Britain with.

I THINK I would have found her a real turnoff, which I'm fairly blunt about. . . . I don't agree with her coerciveness on morality. I don't agree with that at all. But I loved her liveliness and her passion and her commitment to her cause. So [my views of Carry Nation] would have been some yes, some no.

The Triangle Fire

by

DAVID VON DREHLE

On November 24, 1909, thousands of New York City garment workers went on strike. Their demands for industry reform were not heeded until two years later, after one of the worst disasters in the city's history. On the afternoon of March 25, 1911, a fire broke out at the Triangle Waist Company in Greenwich Village. Most of the 146 workers who died were young female immigrants. In his book Triangle: The Fire That Changed America, *published by* The Atlantic Monthly Press *in 2003, David Von Drehle examined the tragic fire and its impact on the burgeoning New York labor movement. Mr. Von Drehle, a staff writer for the* Washington Post, *joined us on* Booknotes *on October 5, 2003.*

THE TRIANGLE FIRE actually started at about 4:40 P.M. [on March 25, 1911]. The Triangle Waist Company was the largest blouse-making factory in New York City at the time, making what were called shirtwaists, women's blouses, on the eighth, ninth, and tenth floors of what was then a high-rise building in New York. The eighth floor was where they cut the pattern pieces for the garments, and when they were done cutting them, they would sweep the remnants off the tables into big boxes under the tables. Somehow, a cigarette butt or something went into one of those boxes full of cotton scraps and tissue paper, and it went up like a bomb.

The fire unfortunately burned for about five minutes before an alarm was sounded. This is one of the great tragedies of the event, because it's possible that everyone could have been saved, if only the alarm had been put out immediately—not by the firemen so much as by evacuation. But the manager of the factory, a man named Samuel Bernstein, was on the eighth floor when the fire broke out. There had been previous fires in the Triangle factory, and they had always been extinguished by hand. Bernstein had put some out. Isaac Harris, the owner of the factory, had put some out. There were pails full of water around the factory, and they would grab a pail of water and dump it on the fire and everything would be fine.

That was Bernstein's impulse when he saw this fire on the eighth floor. He tried to put it out, first with fire pails, then by getting the fire hose from the stairwell. For some reason—not entirely clear why—the water wouldn't come on from the interior fire hose. He fought the fire for three or four, maybe five minutes before he gave up. And by then, the eighth floor was beyond hope and there was really nothing to be done. If, instead of trying to put out the fire, he had tried to alert the people on the ninth floor, I think people could have been saved. It's hard to second-guess him, because his personal courage in the fire was enormous. He saved many, many scores of people through his efforts, but he made a disastrously wrong judgment at the beginning.

The eighth floor, which had about 200 people on it, mostly young women, was safely evacuated, but just barely. The last people off the eighth floor were running through flames. The tenth floor was the executive suite, the offices for the owners and the salesmen, also the packing and shipping operation. They escaped up to the roof. It was the people on the ninth floor, which was the main sewing plant, that had difficulty getting out. They got the word very late that there was a fire in the building. It was 4:45, right at closing time, when they discovered there was a fire, basically by seeing the flames outside the windows coming up from the floor below. There were about 250 workers, mostly young immigrant women, mostly Italians and Eastern European Jews, and they didn't know what to do.

Some of them ran to the fire escape, a rickety fire escape in the rear air shaft behind the building. It quickly became overloaded and collapsed. Some of them went to the stairwell on the northeast corner of the factory and got down before the flames blocked that route. Some of them knew enough to go up to the roof and barely escaped before that route was sealed off by the flames in the air shaft. There was one other door at the southwest corner of the factory, clear across the room, two elevators, and a door to the stairwell. That door was kept locked at closing time because the factory owners didn't want the workers stealing garments, so they made all of them leave through one door, where they had a night watchman search their purses. They locked that other door.

The elevators on that corner kept running—amazing courage on the part of the elevator operators, going up again and again until, finally, they couldn't go anymore. They saved, I'm sure, over a hundred lives through their courage. But in the end, the elevators couldn't run any more. The exits were sealed off, either locked or in flames. And the last 146 people on the ninth floor either jumped from the windows to their deaths [as fifty-four of them did] or died in the flames.

The tallest ladder in New York went up to the top of the sixth floor. One of the heartbreaking scenes of this fire was the workers trapped in the ninth-floor windows of what was called the Asch Building, watching as they hand-cranked the ladder up, and it came up and up and up, closer and closer to them, but then stopped two floors below.

The building was right off Washington Square [in] New York City. It's still there—a fireproof building of concrete and steel. The contents, unfortunately, were flammable. . . . It was a beautiful early spring afternoon, Saturday afternoon, and so thousands of people were walking the streets, were out in Washington Square, which is the most useful, loveliest park area in that part of the city. And so all these people were able to run to the fire and stand there in horror as this unfolded before their eyes.

A SHIRTWAIST is a woman's blouse, basically. At that time, though, it was the fashion sensation of modern time. The nearest parallel I can draw to how important the shirtwaist and skirt set was for women around the turn of the century and the first decade of this century is what blue jeans have become. It's a fashion trend that just didn't go out of fashion from 1890 to World War I. It symbolized women's freedom, women's liberation.

This was the time of the suffrage movement. Women were going to work in record numbers. They were coming off the farms and going into the cities. You have to remember what women were wearing before this. They were wearing hoops and bustles and severe girdles, as if they were imprisoned in their clothes. All of a sudden, here was this fashion of loose, comfortable skirts, high enough off the ground to walk in comfortably, and these light cotton blouses called shirtwaists.

The most famous artist of the day was Charles Dana Gibson. He created the Gibson Girl. . . . He was hugely influential, and he loved the shirtwaist. He drew so many of his Gibson Girls in shirtwaists, and once he did that, everybody had to look like that.

[The average age of the Triangle Waist Company workers was] around nineteen or twenty. Some of the ages are not precisely known, so we're roughly calculating. Two fourteen-year-old girls died in the fire, Kate Leone and Sara Maltese. One of the things that makes this story so compelling, or did for me, was the chance to learn what the immigrant experience was like for these young women. There are stories of amazing courage, and the stories of the women who died in this fire were the piece of the tale that had been most completely lost.

The newspapers in those days were very competitive on the daily breaking news, but they didn't go very deeply into the lives of the people who died, and so virtually nothing has been known about them. I spent a lot of effort to try to bring at least a couple of them back to life and . . . get a complete list of everyone known to have died in the fire. What you find are young women, in many cases traveling to the United States by themselves to earn money to send back to their families in Russia and in Italy, alone in the city, working six days a week, back-breaking labor—keeping nothing for themselves, sending it all home.

I LIVED IN New York for a couple of years as a reporter. My apartment was a block from the building of the Triangle fire, and I used to walk by there and look up at the windows and wonder what went on in there, what exactly was that story. One of the first stories I covered in New York was a fire in the Bronx, an arson fire, in which eighty-seven people had died. By coincidence, it was on March 25, 1990, and that day, the old hands in New York said, "You know, this is the anniversary of the Triangle fire." I come from Denver, Colorado. Everyone who grows up in New York knows the name, at least, of the Triangle Shirtwaist fire. I'd never heard of it before. That planted it [with me]. Then I found myself walking down the street and saw a historical marker on the building, and that was the beginning of what turned into this book.

What surprised me was how little of the primary material about this fire had been preserved. You go back to the newspapers and the rhetoric of the day and you see people saying, "We will never forget this day"—it was a searing event for New York City and the consciousness of the city. But when I got to doing the research, I found that document after document—the coroner's investigation, the fire marshal's investigation—had been lost. To my amazement, even the transcript of the trial—there was a manslaughter trial of the two owners—had been lost for thirty-five years.

I looked and looked. I finally found, through a number of coincidences, that the defense attorney for the owners—who was in his day the most famous lawyer in New York, probably the most famous in America—had, when he died, left his own personal copies of his greatest cases to the New York County Lawyers Association, which was a small bar association in downtown New York. So I called them and asked them if they had this record, and their immediate answer was no. Thankfully, the librarian kept looking, and they found down in a corner of the basement, these old records of Max Stever, including two volumes of the three-volume transcript. That was the breakthrough. A number of nuances, particularly, about this story came through in that transcript, which hadn't been seen by anyone in forty years.

MAX BLANCK and Isaac Harris were the owners of the Triangle Waist Company—the Shirtwaist Kings, as they were known. They were not related themselves, but they were married to two cousins. And they, like many of the workers at the factory, were themselves Russian Jewish immigrants. They had come over in the early 1890s, ten or fifteen years before the people who died, and so they were that much farther up the road of advancement into American society. Very successful businessmen, but they started out with nothing and ultimately were ruined by the fire.

There's no evidence that the fire I write about was an arson fire. It happened when everybody was at work, including Blanck and Harris. They were there and had to escape to the roof. Two of Blanck's daughters were there. He was going to take them shopping. They were terrified and had to run past flames to get out. So it doesn't make any sense that this was deliberately set. But there had been three or four other fires at Triangle and at another shirtwaist factory that they owned, which looked extremely suspicious. They all happened in the very early morning hours when nobody was in the factory. They all destroyed the contents of the factory and were all reimbursed by insurance. Nobody was hurt. And they all came, interestingly, right at the end of the season. If you've made too many shirtwaists and you're not going to ship them, it would be real nice to get an insurance check for those, rather than having to simply write them off as unsold inventory.

I do believe that Harris and Blanck had torched their premises before. They might even have been planning to set a fire at the end of this season, because there was a tremendous amount of stock in the factory that day. That's part of the reason that it burned so quickly and disastrously. Unfortunately, in New York City at that time, the method of insuring companies was extremely corrupt; it was run by the insurance brokers. The more insurance the brokers could sell, the more commissions they got. So there was no incentive in New York City in that time to take any precautions to prevent fires, only to make sure that you had enough insurance. Blanck and Harris, who by any measure should not even have been able to buy insurance, because of all the previous fires, were not only insured, but overinsured. They made a profit on this fire.

Blanck and Harris were indicted on one count of manslaughter. The one count was because the penalty for one count of manslaughter and 146 counts of manslaughter at that time would have been the same. The prosecutor, a politically ambitious guy named Charles S. Whitman who later became governor of New York, decided to press the case that Blank and Harris knew that the door on the tenth floor was locked. It was illegal to have a locked door during working hours and [he hoped to prove] that locked door caused the death of one of the workers named Margaret Schwartz, who did die in the flames right next to that exit. If they, by knowingly breaking the misdemeanor of locking the door, had caused her death, they would have been guilty of manslaughter.

Blanck and Harris were acquitted after a three-week trial with 155 witnesses. The judge in the trial, a Tammany Hall operative named Thomas Crain, gave a very unexpected jury instruction: He told the jurors that it wasn't enough to find that that door was locked. They had to find that Blanck and Harris knew that it was locked at that particular moment when the fire broke out. These jurors didn't feel that they could crawl inside the heads of the two men to decide beyond a shadow of a doubt—or a reasonable doubt—that they knew, as a matter of fact, that that door was locked on that day at that time. The prosecution had simply shown that it was normally kept locked.

What I rediscovered—it wasn't even remembered at the time—was that six years before this fire, Thomas Crain had been the tenement house commissioner of New York City. A terrible tenement fire had happened on Allen Street. Twenty people were killed. Most of them died behind a locked skylight. The fire escapes failed. [The victims were] immigrants. People had jumped from windows. The parallels were amazing, and Crain was blamed for that fire. He was hounded out of office as tenement house commissioner. At the time, he thought his career was over. The editorials in the newspapers were mocking and scornful. So I find it hard to believe that in his heart of hearts, Crain didn't have some sympathy, some fellow feeling for Blanck and Harris. That might explain why he gave such a favorable jury instruction. But the jurors got back in the room and they couldn't reach the decision, and they acquitted Harris and Blanck. I think as many as five of the twelve initially supported a guilty verdict. But they argued and negotiated and took, ultimately, four votes, and the last one was for acquittal.

Blanck and Harris soldiered on in the shirtwaist business in New York City all through World War I. The blouse business got weaker. To my surprise, they tried to keep the Triangle name going for six years after this fire, even with all the infamy attached to it. Then Blanck organized a number of other shirtwaist companies—Normandy Waist Company, Trouville Waist Company—all these French-sounding companies. But ultimately they left New York City around 1920.

THERE ARE several prevailing myths [about the fire]: One is that the Triangle was a sweatshop. This is true in modern-day terminology. It's certainly what we now would think of as a sweatshop: It was a crowded factory full of long rows of sewing machines, with women and some men bent over their sewing machines, working long hours for low pay. But they would not have thought of the Triangle Waist Company as a sweatshop at all. To them, a sweatshop was a tiny, crowded tenement factory with a few people, usually working pedal-powered sewing machines, hunched over, pedaling all day to sew. The Triangle was the epitome of the modern, up-to-date factory, where all of the sewing machines were powered by electricity. There was light. There was air. So this idea that the Triangle was the most notorious sweatshop in New York at its time—that is not quite right.

CLARA LEMLICH was one of the great female labor organizers, labor agitators in American history. She was a young Russian immigrant shirtwaist worker at this time. She didn't work for the Triangle factory, she worked for a big factory owned by Louis Leiserson. But in 1909, it was a season of wildcat strikes in the garment district, and Clara Lemlich took her factory out on strike and then led the movement across New York to call a general strike in the shirtwaist industry.

You have to understand that even though there were 40,000 shirtwaist workers, roughly, in New York at this time, only about 100 of them belonged to the union when Clara Lemlich got the idea that she should call a general strike. It was an incredibly audacious, bold stroke. The men who ran the American labor movement didn't support the idea. They didn't want much to do with it. But she was supported by a group called the Women's Trade Union League, which was mostly wealthy, well-to-do progressive women who thought that women workers should be unionized.

Clara Lemlich, in late November 1909, stood up at a rally of shirtwaist workers and called for a general strike, and the movement was carried by acclamation. The next day, to the astonishment of New York, 15,000 or 20,000 shirtwaist workers went out on strike. By the end of the week, it was 35,000 or 40,000 workers. The shirtwaist industry was shut down. This strike was the first great galvanizing moment for urban labor, the garment industry, and for women workers in the garment industry. It was the making, in a sense, of the International Ladies' Garment Workers' Union. And it all started, really, in a way, with her.

Anne Morgan was the daughter of the richest man in America, J. P. Morgan. . . . When this general strike happened, she decided that she was on the side of the strikers. She began to raise money for them, to organize events for them, and to recruit rich, prominent women to go down and walk on the picket lines with them so that the police would be afraid to arrest strikers. They wouldn't know when they were going to get a rich one and wind up on the front page of the paper. Never in the history of New York—probably in the history of the United States—had wealthy people come in on the side of the strikers. And that made the shirtwaist uprising a historic event for feminism, as well as for labor, and for Progressive politics in the United States.

Alva Smith Vanderbilt Belmont came from a plantation in Georgia, moved to New York, married a Vanderbilt—William K. Vanderbilt—and instantly became one of the most prominent women in New York. She married her daughter off to the Duke of Marlborough, which set off a fashion craze among rich people in America to get royal titles for their families by marrying their eligible daughters off to British royalty in need of money. She then divorced Vanderbilt, which was scandalous at the time, and married a Belmont, which is another one of the most prominent names in New York. After her Belmont husband died, she became the driving force for women's suffrage in America. She, too, took on the strikers' cause and organized huge rallies for them at Carnegie Hall. She sat through night court one night so that she could bail out some arrested strikers by putting up the deed to her Madison Avenue mansion. She was a great character.

[The Triangle fire and the cloak makers' revolt of 1910] were the two biggest organizing events for the garment workers in America. It made their union, which even today—they've merged with the textile workers—remains one of the most important unions in America. This is where they come from, from that strike and then the fire. It changed the Democratic Party of New York, as well.

New York City was run at that time by Tammany Hall, the infamous, notorious Democratic Party machine, which was led by a fascinating character named Charles F. "Silent Charlie" Murphy. He never spoke but ran the city from a dining room at Delmonico's restaurant, with all his spies reporting in on what was going on, and his orders going back out about how they were to conduct the business of the city.

When Silent Charlie Murphy came into power at the turn of the century, Tammany Hall, the Democratic Party of New York, was essentially a conservative organization. They were conservatives. They were pro-business. Their function in New York City was to keep the immigrants just happy enough that they didn't cause any trouble, but then to allow business to do what it wanted. That way, Tammany could remain in power on the votes of the immigrants but collect the graft that was possible through all their rich friends. This was changing, [however,] because the nature of the immigrants in New York was changing. They were no longer compliant.

Particularly, the Eastern Europeans were coming over with great political ambitions. They had the experience of not just poverty, but political oppression in Russia and they wanted to make a better society for themselves. They organized politically. They were politically radical and they were fueling the rapid growth of the Socialist Party in New York. This was creating pressure on the political left for the first time in New York history. The pressure had always been from the Republicans, and now they had the pressure from the Socialists.

Each year, with each passing election, this became more and more obvious a problem for Tammany and for Charlie Murphy. This fire came along and Murphy saw the chance to get on the right side of those immigrant Jewish garment workers who were filling up the Lower East Side. He seized the opportunity to pursue reform for the first time in the history of the Democratic Party and he put the reform reins in the hands of two young men—one, Alfred E. Smith; the other, Robert F. Wagner.

Tammany had just taken control of the state legislature. The assumption was that since Tammany had the state legislature, Murphy would put a couple of old hacks in charge. But to everyone's surprise, he put in Robert Wagner, age thirty-three, and Al Smith, age thirty-eight—both extremely loyal Tammany men—what we would call today "machine hacks." He recognized promise in these young men. Everyone derided him. They said he'd put the "Tammany Twins" in charge. "The kindergarten class had been promoted," was what one of the newspapers said.

Wagner and Smith set up a thing called the Factory Investigating Commission, a commission of the legislature that they appointed and ran. It had powers unprecedented before and after in the history of New York. They passed the most progressive set of labor and workplace safety laws in American history up to that time. They did it very quickly, in three or four legislatures. It launched Al Smith's career. [He went on to become governor of New York and ran unsuccessfully for the presidency.] It launched Wagner into the United States Senate, and their program became the program that Franklin Roosevelt took nationwide, known as the New Deal.

In a way [the fire] was, for that generation of New York, something like the experience of September 11, 2001, was for our generation. Never before had there been so many people standing, watching helplessly as people died in a fire above the street. . . . While it was a tremendous tragedy, it is also a story about how politics can work if people organize and vote and keep at it. They can make political institutions change.

The Civil Rights Movement

by

DOROTHY HEIGHT

Dorothy Height was born in Richmond, Virginia, in 1912, a time when more than three-fourths of the black population in America was still providing cheap labor in the rural South. Throughout her life she has worked toward racial equality, marching at major civil rights rallies, advising U.S. presidents, and leading the National Council of Negro Women. On April 11, 2003, Congress voted to award a Congressional Gold Medal to Dr. Height in recognition of her many contributions to the nation. Dr. Height joined us on August 3, 2003, to discuss her seventy years of fighting racial and sexual discrimination, as told in her memoir Open Wide the Freedom Gates, *published by PublicAffairs that same year. Dr. Height lives in Washington, D.C.*

I WAS NINETY-ONE in March. I go to work every day. I am the chair and president emerita of the National Council of Negro Women. Two or three years ago, we initiated a process of transition activity, so I've been a part of it. But I'm pretty active not only in the National Council of Negro Women; I'm chair of the Leadership Conference on Civil Rights and had an active role in civil rights.

All in all, I worked for the YWCA some forty years, but I was thirty-three years on the national YWCA staff. I went in to work on interracial education. For eighteen years, I was the director of training, and then as the civil rights movement moved and a lot of YWCA moved to implement its interracial charter, I became the director and an organizer of its Office of Racial Justice. So, I entered . . . a major national organization whose membership is drawn largely from the majority population, but which was inclusive of the changes that were made. Today, the YWCA has something I had a major hand in working on, which was the creation of the "one imperative" in 1970, and that one imperative is to thrust our collective power toward the elimination of racism wherever it exists and by any means necessary.

[I GREW UP] in a little town called Rankin, Pennsylvania. It was a borough of Pittsburgh, a tiny little town, population of about 7,800 people. . . . It was an interesting little community. My father was a building contractor. And while I had been born in Richmond, he was among those who in 1916 felt that there were better opportunities in Northern communities, and so . . . the family moved to Rankin. My mother was a nurse, and in fact, she was the head of nurses at a hospital in Richmond, Virginia, a black hospital. My father was very fortunate because he could find work. In fact, he employed people. He was self-employed all his life. But my mother, being a nurse, was not able to work in any hospital, nor was there a nurses registry that would take a Negro at that time.

I'd had a little experience with prejudice in that one of my little neighbors, whom I loved very much, told me one day that she couldn't hold hands and go down the hill with me as we went to school, as we had always done, because she found out that I was a "nigger." So that was my first shock. But I lived also with the realization of my mother's feelings about not being able to get the kind of job that she wanted.

Rankin was kind of a mission center, and some women from the YWCA had come out there and organized, and I had joined. I was chosen, actually, as one of the three girls to be on a YWCA poster emphasizing "mind, body and spirit." We had our little white blouses, blue ties, and middies on. And so I eagerly gathered up some friends, and we went downtown, a forty-five-minute streetcar ride to downtown, to Chatham Street, to the YWCA, because we thought, "Well, since we're Girl Reserves—as they were called then—we just wanted to swim."

When we got there, the person at the desk said, "I'm sorry. You cannot swim." Well, I had not heard any such thing before, but I said to my little friends, "Well, let us ask for the executive." So we went in and she did see us. Then the executive said to us, "I realize that you are Girl Reserves and you'd like to swim, but I cannot break the rules of the YWCA and have you swim in this pool." That was my first experience of protesting against discrimination.

I don't know [how long it took before a black person could swim in a pool in Pittsburgh]. But one of the things that I feel was significant for me was that the YWCA later changed its policy. But I don't know how long that particular association took, but it later proved to be one of the most significant organizations in terms of the inclusion of women of all races.

THERE WERE very few black students in our high school. As a matter of fact, as I looked back later, I realized that it was a kind of survival of the fittest because while we were few, for three years the black students graduated first, second, and third in the classes. It's an interesting thing because we had such a good relationship among the students in the school. I was on almost every kind of activity—the debating society, the basketball team. The reality was that only the best students made it.

My English teacher encouraged me to enter the impromptu speech contest. That was a kind of activity in which you have to be prepared on a wide range of subjects, and then you draw your number and you make your speech. My principal and my Latin teacher, who was also my coach, drove me to Harrisburg because I had been the winner in our county and in our area. When we got there, we went to the hotel, and the principal went in first, and then he sent for the teacher, who had been sitting with me. [The hotel wouldn't let me in.] And my teacher came back and she said, "I just don't know what to say," she said, "because they didn't know you were a Negro."

As we were getting ready to go on this trip, and they were going to drive, my mother had said to me, "Dorothy, no matter what happens, keep yourself together. You just keep yourself together." It was as if I could hear those words as the teacher was talking to me. I said, "That's all right." [My teacher] said, "But you have to make your speech, and you have to have some dinner and you have to get dressed." I said, "If there's a delicatessen, I can get something and make a sandwich and get some milk and graham crackers. And I can take my dress to the place, and dress in the ladies room." So that's what we did.

I drew my number—I was Number 17, and there were seventeen contestants. It was in the Carnegie Hall of Harrisburg, the state capital. I drew the number, of course, with no advantage because you only know what you're going to speak [about] . . . ten minutes beforehand. I drew the Kellogg-Briand Peace Pact, and as I made my little speech, I pointed out that Aristide Briand said the League of Nations could not produce peace; the League of Nations was an instrument to be used by people. Peace would come to the hearts of men, when men really wanted peace. . . . I said that the message of peace had come some 2,000 years ago, but if you remember, the parents of this child were turned away at the inn, like my principal and my teacher and I had been turned away that very day. I won the first prize with the unanimous vote of the judges, and the only black person in the room besides me was the janitor who had helped me find the drinking water when I was getting dressed. I was fifteen.

I GRADUATED from Rankin High School in 1929. I loved the sciences, and I had a brother who recommended to me Barnard College and I applied. My principal, teachers all gave me good marks, good letters. Then I went and took the exams, and I was later informed that I had been accepted. But when I went to take the placement test, the dean was so reluctant to talk with me . . . . Finally, she said, "I haven't rushed to talk to you because I didn't realize you were a Negro." And she said, "You know, we have two colored students already." Belle Tobias and Vera Joseph were the two. And she said, "We cannot take another until the fall because Belle Tobias will be leaving."

Well, that was a very low moment for me. And today, as I hear people talk about quotas, I react. I know what a quota can do. After she said all this, I just was about to give up, but my sister, with whom I was living, after a few days followed my brother's second advice. He said, "Try NYU." I was talking to Dean Ruth Schaeffer a few minutes before the close of registration, and she asked me if I had a diploma. And I said no. She said, "Well, have you applied to NYU?" And I said no. . . . My sister whispered to me, "Dorothy, show her your letter from Barnard College accepting you." So I showed her the letter. I'll never forget that she took the letter, she looked at it, and she said, "A girl that makes these kind of grades doesn't need an application." And she accepted me.

Later on, both Barnard and NYU gave me their highest honors. That said to me was that there had been a change [in our society]. . . . That's one of the reasons I say to people you can't get bitter about what happens to you. You have to keep working.

MARY MCLEOD BETHUNE was a woman born of slave parents, and yet she became an adviser to presidents of the United States. She's the only African American woman to have founded a four-year accredited college, which is Bethune-Cookman College. For me in 1937 to come under her tutelage, to have the opportunity to see how she worked with both the powerful people and the powerless, was really a critical element to my whole growth and development.

President Roosevelt had brought Mrs. Bethune to Washington as his adviser on minority affairs for the National Youth Administration, and later she became a special adviser to the president, which was a unique role. Mrs. Bethune for me was a person who dealt with the simplest matters as well as the larger issues in a fashion that always was without personal feelings or getting herself in the way. She was always [motivated] to see how she could make things better or how she could bring people together. And she, in establishing the National Council of Negro Women and calling women to learn to work together, was teaching coalition building and collaboration and networking long before those words became popular.

I FIRST MET Eleanor Roosevelt when I was on the staff at the Harlem YWCA. I had been there about a month. I was the assistant executive, and I had the assignment to escort Mrs. Roosevelt into a meeting that Mary McLeod Bethune was holding at the YWCA building in Harlem.

In 1938, I was one of ten young people that Mrs. Roosevelt called to Hyde Park . . . We spent the weekend with her, planning for what was called the World Conference of Youth, to be held at Vassar College. I felt it was a very good experience because Mrs. Roosevelt really took seriously helping us as young people understand how to stand for what we were, but also how to respect other people, how to work together. She followed the conference all the way through, but before that, she had prepared us in a very real way. I don't think any of us ever will forget that weekend at Hyde Park.

[Later] I was a member of a group called the Committee of Correspondents who brought women from all over the world to meetings. . . . Mrs. Roosevelt was the closing speaker. I had led the discussion. When the group was closing and Mrs. Roosevelt was about to leave, one of them said, "Mrs. Roosevelt, how did you come to be such a great woman?"

And it was interesting. She sat down on the nearest desk to her and said, "Because I was married to a great man, and he taught me many things." She said, "He was the governor of the State of New York, and he could not travel, but he sent me." She said, "I came to see people, to understand people, and I would come back to him and report and say, 'Oh, yes, I went to that orphanage and they were beautiful, and they have good meals and all.'" And he would say, "Eleanor, don't you think that when the wife of the governor appears, the meals are going to be better than usual? The next time that you go, don't go to do just what they have planned for you. Beforehand, find out the poorest neighborhoods, and then ask to go to those neighborhoods. And when you do, look at the clothes hanging on the line and they will tell you something about the people. And look out to see how many people are just sitting around the streets." he said, "And what are the men doing? Are they all off at work or are they sitting around wishing for work?" She said, "That made a difference."

I was in Taiwan a few years ago. A woman came up to me and she said, "You may not remember but I was in the group. I asked the question of Mrs. Roosevelt." And she said, "Mrs. Roosevelt's answer changed my life. I am now the champion of the poor people here." She told me she had been elected to office and what she was doing.

I FIRST MET Martin Luther King [in 1945], when he was fifteen years old. He had come to Morehouse College at a time when [one could] become a student at Morehouse College without graduating from high school because it was part of the gifted program. I was in Atlanta for the YWCA of the United States; I was director of training. My white colleagues would stay in the hotel, but I couldn't. That gave me the opportunity to stay with Dr. and Mrs. Benjamin Mays; he was the president of Morehouse. His wife invited me to come home early one evening [and] she said, "I want you to meet Bennie's favorite student." It turned out to be Martin Luther King, Jr.

I remember what an experience it was to sit around at dinner and then after dinner to just hear him [talk], like any fifteen-year-old would do, about what he wanted to do and what he wanted to be, whether he wanted to go into ministry, or medicine, or law. One of the things that struck me so mightily was I knew that I was in the presence of an unusual person, not only because he was gifted but because of the nature of the conversation. And then ten years later, when Rosa Parks refused to give up her seat, he was my leader, in 1955. It was a tremendous experience.

[THE 1963 Civil Rights March] was really a march for jobs and freedom. A. Philip Randolph, who called the march, had called one during the Roosevelt administration, but President Roosevelt issued Executive Order 8802 and so that march never was realized.

But this time, A. Philip Randolph called for the march . . . and the first call really helped to get the principle of fair employment practices moving. But this time, it was an effort to really speak up for jobs and for equality of opportunity.

There was a spirit [at the 1963 march]. There was a sense of righteous indignation. There was a coming together, as I have never seen. I think that any young person at that time had to have a feeling that they were witnessing a moment in America that was America at its best. It was the kind of experience that brought together people of all races, all ages, male and female, all denominations.

There was a sense of unity. That was the heart of that day, and it was only as years have gone by that we see that we lost that drive. The climate has changed.

For a long time, we put a lot of attention on dealing with prejudice and bigotry and building race relations, interracial groups. But we came to the realization that we were not dealing so much with interpersonal relations. And this is where the civil rights movement moved us to the realization that we had to change a whole system that was based in segregation. It took giving evidence of the way in which segregation worked not only to the people who suffer but to the whole community; [it took] direct nonviolent action to highlight, to really focus attention on the reality of segregation and discrimination.

[Taking part in the 1963 march] was being a part of what I think was one of the greatest experiences in America—and not only for me, but for everyone. Martin Luther King, Jr. made a great speech, and that was an unusual occasion. But also, I was one of the women, along with Mrs. King and Mrs. [Ralph] Abernathy, who were seated on the platform, and we tried very hard to get the opportunity to have a woman speak. Bayard Rustin, who was the executive for the program, said, "There are women members of all of the organizations—the unions, the churches, all of the different organizations which are represented—and so women are represented." We didn't convince him that while we were pleased to hear their male heads, we wanted a woman. We had a whole long list of women who could speak. . . . One of the things I'll never forget is that the only voice we could hear of a woman that day was Mahalia Jackson singing the national anthem. But we women nevertheless, took our seats. I don't think that would ever happen again.

I WOULD HAVE to say the leadership of Dr. King [has been the most effective in civil rights] because of the quality of his leadership, the teachings that he gave, and the recognition that we had to have freedom everywhere—and we had to have justice everywhere or neither would exist anywhere. In the white community, I can think of so many leaders—of course, Mrs. Roosevelt and women like that [who advanced civil rights]. But I would have to say that in a surprising way, the leadership that Lyndon Johnson gave in helping the country get the Civil Rights Act was very critical.

I met with Lyndon Johnson to let him know more about us, but also to talk with him about some of our concerns about issues related to women. I think all the way through the civil rights effort, there's been a need to still keep alive the issues related to women. We who are women, who are also colored, have double factors to deal against, both racism and sexism.

What I remember about LBJ that had a great impact on me was when he was the vice president, he held a meeting of the Negro leadership. In that meeting, he had just come into office, and he said, "I know that you have been reluctant knowing my history." He said, "You wanted John F. Kennedy, so you took me." And then he added, "But what you don't know is that Mary McLeod Bethune put my integration diapers on me when I was in the NYA movement." She was the head and adviser to the National Youth Administration, and he said, "I called her and said, I got this message to go to Tallahassee," he said, "but that's a colored school." Mrs. Bethune said to him, "Lyndon Johnson, I didn't ask you what color the people are." She said to him, "You are a representative of the United States of America and you go wherever you are assigned." And he said, "Believe me, I went." I often think of that [story] because of his own recognition of his steps along the way.

I have been associated with the National Council of Negro Women since 1937. Mrs. Bethune had called together two years before women from organizations, and she said what we needed was not another organization but one that would bring people together. And she said, "because the Negro woman"—and these are her words—"stands outside of America's mainstream of opportunity, influence, and power, what we needed was to harness our will and power so that we could deal with the problems that affected us, to try to make life better."

Civil Rights Years

by

VERNON JORDAN

During the Clinton administration, Vernon Jordan—then a Washington, D.C., lawyer and lobbyist—was known as an "FOB," a friend of Bill's. His memoir Vernon Can Read!, *written with Annette Gordon-Reed recounts his earlier life as a leader in the civil rights movement, including ten years as head of the National Urban League. Mr. Jordan joined us on December 23, 2001, to discuss his book, published by PublicAffairs in 2001.*

[ON MAY 29, 1980,] I got shot in the back in Fort Wayne, Indiana, about 1:00 in the morning, after having addressed the Fort Wayne Urban League's Equal Opportunity Day dinner. I got out of a car with a member of the local Urban League board, and as I got out of the car, all of a sudden something hit me in my back and I was sort of sailing up in the air. The next thing I knew, I was on the ground. The next thing I knew, I was bleeding. And the next thing I knew, I was hearing a wonderful sound—it's called a siren.

Ninety-eight days [of my life were spent recovering in the hospital]. A man named Joseph Paul Franklin, by his own admission [shot me]. We never had a conversation [about why].

He was acquitted in my case. The case took place in a different venue from Fort Wayne, in South Bend, Indiana. In that case, tried under Section 245 of the Civil Rights Act, he was acquitted. Why he was acquitted, the process, I didn't pay much attention to that because I had only one concern. By the time that he was tried, I was actually out of the hospital. I went and testified in the trial. Not much I could say except that I got shot. The best part about going to the trial is that I had an opportunity to spend time with Dr. Jeffrey Towles, the black surgeon who actually saved my life.

There was this marvelous story about Jeffrey Towles, whose mother cleaned the doctors' offices in a small town in West Virginia, and she, being a single mother, took him with her. He, as she cleaned, thumbed through these medical books and got carried away with the diagrams and the pictures. He went to school at West Virginia State, went to medical school at the University of Louisville and did his residency in trauma surgery at Detroit General Hospital. We had dinner the night before I was to testify, and he said, "When I was at Detroit General and in Louisville, I saw all kinds of wounds. I've never seen a wound like yours. Based on what I saw, you were not supposed to make it." But because of his expertise, here we were having a conversation.

[The wound was] in the left side of my back. It missed my spine by about a fourth of an inch.

MY UNDERSTANDING is that Joseph Paul Franklin is doing two consecutive life terms in a federal penitentiary. He was stabbed in prison. The intention, as I understand it, was not to kill him but to hurt him. He was stabbed thirty-eight times by black prisoners.

He befriended—as I understand it from Bill Webster, who was then head of the FBI—a black prisoner, and the black prisoner befriended him. At some point, the black prisoner, after he got close to him, said, "Did you shoot Vernon Jordan?" Franklin, as I understand it, said, "Yes." A couple of nights later, Franklin was cornered in the prison by four or five black prisoners with prison-made knives from tin cans, and they stabbed him thirty-eight times. I didn't see it; it was reported to me.

He has given some press interviews, wherein he has admitted that he, in fact, shot me in Fort Wayne.

I WAS THE president and chief executive officer of the National Urban League, founded in 1910 in New York City with the express purpose of helping blacks who had migrated from the South to the northern cities find work and adjust to city life. I was the fifth executive of the Urban League; the first of that group to be a lawyer, not a social worker. My predecessors, Whitney Young, Lester Granger, Eugene Kinckle Jones, George Edmund Haynes, they were all social workers. I sort of broke the mold in that I was a lawyer. My successor, John Jacob, was, in fact, a social worker. So it was a social service agency, historically, providing social services to black people in employment, in training, and in education. [There is a] huge program in vocational training. At the time that I succeeded Whitney Young, I inherited a baton that Whitney had taken beyond social services into advocacy and made it a real civil rights organization. It's a great American institution, the Urban League, and I'm very grateful for my stewardship there.

Martha Coleman was an Urban League member, a white woman, divorced. [There was some controversy at the time because the night I was shot,] after the dinner, we went to her home. If you traveled as much as I did in those days—180 days a year after what is generally not the best dinner, and generally, you don't have time really to eat it, you're shaking hands and you're greeting and you're taking photographs and you're thinking about what you're going to say. [After dinner,] on any given night in any given town, I could be with ten people, twenty people, or as in this case, one person. I've never selected people based on race, one way or the other, and so there we were. The notion that I was a civil rights leader and was out late at night with a white woman, some people tried to read into that something that was not there, whatever that was. The fact is that it is my judgment that I was shot in my back by Joseph Paul Franklin with a .30-06 [hunting rifle] because I was black and because I was a civil rights leader.

It hurt. That's for sure. It hurt for a long time. I was moved from Fort Wayne after ten days. President Carter sent a plane for me that brought me to New York, and I was in New York Hospital for eighty-eight days. The first month, I was in trouble because I kept running a low-grade fever, and they could not figure out what that was until I went into the CAT scan for the second time. They brought me back upstairs and stuck something like a gun in my back and found about a pint of what looked like spoiled orange juice. That dissipated the low-grade fever, and I began to get better and better. In September, I was out. Late October, I was playing tennis.

IN 1966, JIMMY Carter lost [his first bid for] the governorship [of Georgia]. It was shortly after that that David Gambrell, who ultimately became a United States senator, taking Senator Russell's seat, appointed by Jimmy Carter, brought the then-defeated candidate for governor to my office. David Gambrell had a vision. He said, "You two should meet because both of you are going places in this country." How David Gambrell knew that, I don't know. His daddy I knew very well, E. Smythe Gambrell, former president of the American Bar Association. David left Jimmy Carter and me alone in my offices at the Voter Education Project, and we became friends. Then in 1969, Paul and Carol Muldawer in Atlanta, two very good friends, hosted a cocktail party at which Jimmy Carter announced [a second bid] for governor. I demanded equal time, and I announced that I was going to be a candidate for the Fifth Congressional District seat of Georgia that had been held by

Charles Longstreet Weltner. The present incumbent was a Republican, Fletcher Thompson.

I didn't run, because two weeks subsequent to my announcement, I was offered the job as executive director of the United Negro College Fund. It was my judgment that there were many, many black men and women who could be able candidates for Congress, but I was the only one being asked to run the College Fund. It was a unique opportunity, and I wouldn't have to run for reelection, I wouldn't have to campaign, the job was mine. So it was an easy choice.

In 1974, C. Peter McColough, who was the chairman and CEO of the Xerox Corporation, of which I was a director, was my corporate campaign chairman at the National Urban League, which meant that he and I traveled around the country to raise money for the Urban League. We were going to Atlanta, and I called my friend, then Governor Carter, and said that Peter McColough and I were coming to Atlanta. Peter, in addition to being chairman of Xerox, was also the treasurer of the Democratic Party, one of the few CEOs in the country who was an acknowledged active Democrat. Carter was at that time [campaign] chairman of the Democratic National Committee.

So I said, "Why don't I bring him by to say hello, a photo-op?" Carter said, "Great." He called back and suggested that Peter and I come the night before and spend the night at the governor's mansion. Well, if you grew up in Georgia, as I did, an opportunity to spend the night at the governor's mansion is quite a nice thing. So I called Peter McColough, I said, "You want to go the night before and spend the night with Governor Carter?" Peter agreed, and we went, had a wonderful dinner. After dinner, he spent a good part of the evening talking about his presidency to the point that Peter was exhausted, went to bed, and Carter kept talking to me, followed me into the bedroom. I finally said, "Listen, Governor, you're not going to be president for three reasons. Number one, you won't be in office. Number two, nobody knows who you are, really. And number three, you're from the South." He said to me, "Vernon, I'm going to be president of the United States." I was wrong, and President Carter was right.

[At] the June 1977 National Urban League Conference . . . my keynote address attacked President Carter's policies on race. It was a speech based on the disappointment of black people in América with the then-President Carter, given the fact that we'd made a huge difference, especially in the South, in his election. I was echoing the sentiment that, once inaugurated, he had, as my grandfather would say, "disremembered" the constituents that had meant so much to his election. So that's what that speech was about. It had nothing to do with my personal relationships with the president. It had everything to do with the fact that I was head of the Urban League, a constituent leader in the black community, and he was the president of the United States, whose election he owed partially to us. So this was pay-up time, and he had to be reminded. Obviously, he was not happy. I didn't look too happy myself.

The tension [between us] did [dissipate]. We're still friends. That happens in this town [Washington, D.C.,] and in this country, that from time to time, you do have a public dispute with your friend. It doesn't end the friendship. He had some not-so-good things to say, but he apologized, and we're still fellow Georgians and friends. We've known each other since 1966.

[COMPARING BILL Clinton with Jimmy Carter? I see in Clinton] youthfulness, drive, ambition, caring. It's not that I didn't see all of that in Jimmy Carter. I just thought at the time, 1969, that Jimmy Carter would not be president. I just didn't believe it, and I was very wrong. But I was very right about William Jefferson Clinton.

[I met Bill Clinton in 1973 at a] dinner, the Urban League in Little Rock, where I was a speaker and this young law professor shows up. I knew then, based on my own intuitive notions, that he not only wanted to be president, but would be.

[Following] the 1992 election, [I was] head of the transition. I wanted to continue my time in the private sector. I had done my pro bono time from the time I got out of law school through the Urban League, and I wanted to continue on that track. I was very content, very happy with the practice of the law, did not want to interrupt it. Secondly, I did not want during the time that I was chairman of the transition to be in play for a job, thinking that I could do a better job of the transition. I thought it very important to say to the president-elect early on what my decision was about service in the administration. I think I was right about that.

[Today, I see] Bill Clinton a good bit. We're either on the phone or we're having lunch at the Sugar Hill Restaurant or we're having supper or a drink at his house or mine, or we're on the golf course. We will always be friends.

To some extent, my life in the public view was defined by the Clinton presidency, and it was very important to me for people to understand that the most exciting time in my life was before Clinton was president. It was the civil rights movement. It was the Voter Education Project, the Urban League, the College Fund, working for Donald Hollowell, organizing for the NAACP. That's a part of my life and a part of my time that I have had time to reflect and think about, and so I wrote about it.

[I TOOK A different route for college, by selecting DePauw University in Indiana.] There was an organization in New York called the National Service and Scholarship Fund for Negro Students, and it had historically worked with Dunbar High School in Washington [to send] their best students—some needing help, some not needing help—to predominantly white, Ivy League schools. A wonderful man, Paul Lawrence, an educator from California, showed up for a meeting of the National Honor Society at David T. Howard High School my senior year, and he made this speech about going north to school. I was captivated by him and fascinated with the idea . . . and so I applied to DePauw, and was accepted. Once you're accepted at DePauw University, everybody writes to you and says, "You must come here."

This was 1953. It was very small. I was the only black in my class. In a student body of 2,000, there were four blacks. There were no black faculty, no blacks in the administration. It was an institution where Percy Julian, the famous chemist, had graduated and taught in the 1930s. It has a rather distinguished but small black alumni.

I was the headwaiter at Longden Hall. I convinced Mrs. Elsie DePonte that I could not just be a waiter, that I knew enough about serving and food service that I should be headwaiter, and she actually gave me the job. I was headwaiter for about two and a half years. The Roy O. West Library was being dedicated in 1956, and Mrs. DePonte wanted her two best headwaiters to serve the head table, and so she selected Pat Sharp and me. I [was photographed at the event] with the then-vice president of the United States, Richard Nixon and President Russell Humbert of the university. . . . I saved that picture and in 1971, when I was appointed head of the Urban League, President Nixon, who had given Whitney Young's eulogy in the cemetery in Kentucky where he was buried at that time, invited me to the White House. . . . When we sat down on either side of the fireplace, I said, "Mr. President, I brought something for you," and I showed him this photograph. He asked, "Where was this taken?" I explained to him DePauw University and that he had come out to dedicate the library. He loved it and he wrote his name on it. And then I said, "Mr. President, this picture was taken at a time when both of us were on our way up." We had a big chuckle.

I WAS WORKING for Donald Hollowell as his law clerk immediately after law school. He was the civil rights lawyer in Atlanta at that time and hired me right out of law school for $35 a week. . . . As Don Hollowell's law clerk, I escorted Charlayne Hunter [now Charlayne Hunter-Gault, CNN South Africa bureau chief], through the mobs at the University of Georgia in January of 1961. We had won a lawsuit in Judge William Bootle's court in Macon, Georgia, admitting Charlayne Hunter and Hamilton Holmes to the University of Georgia—the first time black students had been admitted to that segregated institution.

She was a student at Wayne State University. She was born [in South Carolina] and reared in Georgia and wanted to go to her state school, as did Hamilton Holmes, who was reared in Georgia. He was a student at Morehouse College. They were plaintiffs already by the time I got out of law school in June of 1960, and Hollowell was a lawyer, Constance Baker Motley and Thurgood Marshall from the NAACP Legal Defense Fund were their lawyers, and so I was just thrown into it.

Shortly after I was out of law school, there I was, new degree in one hand and a subpoena for the governor in another.

[IN 1973, THERE] was this conference on civil rights that Lyndon Johnson had at the Johnson Library in Austin. Johnson was out of office. We had this conference on civil rights, and he asked me, as the new head of the Urban League, to keynote it. There was former Chief Justice [Earl] Warren, Hubert Humphrey, former cabinet members in his administration, the entire civil rights leadership. It was a great honor. After the speech in the green room . . . he was saying to me, "You know, you and I have a lot in common." And I said, "What's that, Mr. President?" And he said, "We were both born poor in the South, you black and me white," and he said, "and we both succeeded great men under tragic circumstances. I succeeded John Kennedy after his assassination, and you succeeded Whitney Young after he was drowned." He said, "People didn't have that much confidence that we could do a good job." He said, "I was a good president with the possible exception of Vietnam. And I brought you here to make sure you're going to be a good president of the Urban League. That's why I wanted you to keynote this meeting."

And then he said, "I have some advice for you," and he said, "it's advice that I couldn't use." He said, "Get your own people. I couldn't get rid of Bobby Kennedy and I couldn't get rid of McNamara and I couldn't get rid of [MacGeorge] Bundy because the nation was in mourning and they were more in mourning for this young president than they were pleased about this old succeeding president. So I couldn't do that. But you can. Get your own people." Lyndon Johnson was right.

[I SERVE ON numerous] corporate boards. [I have] a law degree, a bachelor's degree, and about sixty honorary degrees. [Some of my major jobs have included:] NAACP; clerkship with Donald Hollowell; assistant to Leslie Dunbar at the Southern Regional Council; deputy to Wiley Branton at the Voter Education Project; director of the Voter Education Project; attorney consultant to the U.S. Office of Economic Opportunity; back to be the director of the Voter Education Project; then the executive directorship of the United Negro College Fund; and then the big job of my life was succeeding Whitney Young as head of the National Urban League.

I was at the Urban League for ten years. That was the end of my 501(c)(3) stewardship. After that, I left the nonprofit arena and became a lawyer at Akin Gump Strauss Hauer & Feld, where I'm still of counsel. But I've spent most of my time as a senior managing director at Lazard Frères in New York.

I'm the beneficiary of unique parents, the beneficiary of wonderful institutions—St. Paul AME Church, the Butler Street YMCA, the Gates City Day Nursery, the elementary schools, the David T. Howard High School, the counselors at the YMCA, and the teachers in those schools who cared about me and who taught me and who pushed me. I have also been very blessed with a line of mentors—Don Hollowell, Leslie Dunbar, Wiley Branton, Ruby Hurley, Gardner Taylor, Howard Thurman, and also friendships—Franklin Thomas, whom I talk about in the book, and Ron Brown, John Jacob.

Also I have been the beneficiary of having marvelous compatriots in every organization—the NAACP, the Urban League—people who work with me, who worked for me, we worked together. And so, what I know is that I did not get here by myself. I stand on many, many shoulders.

Friedrich Hayek,
Free Market Philosopher

by

ALAN EBENSTEIN

Friedrich Hayek's economic philosophies championed the free market at a time when a global debate was occurring over socialism. An Austrian-born economist, he is best known for his 1944 book The Road to Serfdom. *In 1974, Hayek was awarded the Nobel Prize in Economics, and his theories heavily influenced Ronald Reagan and Margaret Thatcher's governments. On July 8, 2001, economist and author Alan Ebenstein appeared on* Booknotes *to discuss* Friedrich Hayek: A Biography, *published by St. Martin's Press.*

FRIEDRICH HAYEK is possibly the most important political philosopher of the twentieth century. In the same way that Karl Marx, during the nineteenth century, put forward ideas that were implemented during the twentieth century, I think that Hayek's ideas in the twenty-first century may be of great importance.

Hayek was born in 1899, and he died in 1992. He was from Austria and grew up in pre–World War I Austria-Hungary, the Austro-Hungarian empire. He then moved to London during the 1930s and 1940s, and subsequently went to Chicago, and then back to Europe for his later decades. So he was a man whose life spanned almost the entire twentieth century and who lived throughout the European and American worlds.

Hayek actually was a student in America in 1923–1924, and that was vital to his intellectual development. So as a young student, he came to America and studied at New York University. He studied economics. After being in the United States for a year, he returned to Vienna. Subsequently he went to the London School of Economics. He was in America [again] from 1950 to 1962, at the University of Chicago. Milton Friedman was at the University of Chicago at that time, and others. Hayek's most well-known book, *The Road to Serfdom*, was published in 1944, so he really became known in the United States several years before he came here to teach.

When Hayek first attempted to publish *The Road to Serfdom*, it was taken to three different publishers, none of whom accepted it, and one of the reviewers wrote back that although the book might do well, it had an ideological viewpoint that wouldn't be appropriate to be published by a leading publishing house. So it was the case that at that point in time, the views that Hayek was putting forward were not popular views.

The crucial idea of *The Road to Serfdom* is that without economic freedom, there cannot be political freedom. Hayek tried to tie political freedom and economic freedom together, and this was a very different idea than existed during the 1930s and 1940s, when there was the idea of democratic socialism—that there could be socialism, government control of a nation's economy, and yet still have democracy. Hayek said that that would not be possible, that instead, without a free market system, there could be no democracy.

HAYEK WAS A formal man. He was not particularly outgoing or warm. He was more an aloof intellectual. . . . James Buchanan received the Nobel Prize in Economics . . . as Hayek did, and Hayek and Buchanan were close, through an organization called the Mont Pelerin Society, an international society of classical liberals and libertarian free market–oriented economists. Though Hayek was reserved, he was a man who was an excellent teacher. Many of his students speak to his knowledge and his great intellectual ability, and at the same time, they speak of him being a reserved man, not someone who would talk readily about his family life or his personal life but rather someone who was most interested in ideas and their consequences.

The Nobel Prize in Economic Sciences was first given in 1969. Hayek received the Nobel Prize in Economics in 1974, and he was the first free market economist to receive the prize. Prior to that time, it had primarily been Keynesians who had received the Nobel Prize, so when Hayek received the prize in 1974, it was a real event, because the free market view, a pro-capitalist view, was being acknowledged as a respectable way of looking at the world.

This is something that was very different from the way Hayek had been treated earlier in his career when he had written *The Road to Serfdom* and some of his other works. He had been considered virtually a reactionary crank for the views that he put forward. So it was something that the Nobel Prize had a great influence on Hayek in terms of bringing him to national and international attention again.

[WHEN *The Road to Serfdom*] was originally published in 1944, it was a best-seller. . . . Hayek came to the United States from England at that time, and participated in a whirlwind tour . . . of the United States, and it sold a lot. It's since sold hundreds of thousands of copies, so all told, there's probably 300,000 to 400,000 copies of *The Road to Serfdom* that have sold. It's been translated into over twenty languages, sometimes unauthorized foreign-language translations to countries in . . . Eastern Europe and the Soviet Union.

Before the Berlin Wall fell, Hayek's works would be circulated in typewritten, translated copies, so he's someone who has had a great influence not just in the Western world but in the formerly Communist world. He's considered to be one of the greatest intellectuals who put forward the idea that it's not possible to have an effective command economy. It's not that it would be ethically or morally undesirable to have a socialist system, where the government owns all the land, runs all the businesses. It's simply that a system like that doesn't work. When he put forward these ideas in the 1930s, this was not a position worth considering. However, it's since become the conventional wisdom, almost. Since we've seen the collapse of the Soviet Union and of the economies in Eastern Europe, Hayek's [predictions have] largely been vindicated by events. . . .

The Road to Serfdom was originally put into a digest form by the *Reader's Digest*; this was before the TV age. The *Reader's Digest* at that time had a circulation of something like 12 million people, so it was a much more significant part of the American intellectual scene than it has subsequently become. All of a sudden he was not just well known within academic and literary circles, but by the general public, and so his lecture tour in the United States changed from a rather scholarly, sedate tour to a more popular tour.

HAYEK IS A thinker who appeals to individuals of all political perspectives. When Marx wrote, during the nineteenth century, he was not well recognized during his time. In the reviews of Marx before the Russian Revolution in 1917, he's referred to as a socialistic commentator and agitator. That might be the view of Hayek today, in that he's known in a broader circle, but he's not famous in the sense that some others are famous. Keynes might be a better example of an economist, or Milton Friedman, who's the most well known today.

Hayek's renown is not as great as either Keynes or Friedman, but Hayek is someone who enunciated a vision, a way of looking at the world, a world that could be different than the way that it is. That's why some people refer to him as a liberal and some people refer to him as a conservative. Hayek would have referred to himself as a "nineteenth-century liberal." He didn't particularly like the word *libertarian,* but that was the view that was closest to his own. He did not like conservatism. His postscript to his 1960 work, *The*

Constitution of Liberty, is explicitly titled: "Why I Am Not a Conservative," and he criticizes conservatism for its power-adoring characteristics, for the idea of a very establishment social order, for the idea of power in society. He didn't like those ideas—nongovernmental sources of power in a society.

A reaction that many have when they first read Hayek's works [is] that it's a new way of looking at the world. There are many individuals who say that reading *The Road to Serfdom* or some of Hayek's other works have had a significant influence on them. What's so important about Hayek's work is that he's really challenging the way people look at the world. Particularly in regard to socialism, the argument wasn't that socialism would be undesirable or that people weren't altruistic enough to be social for socialism to work. Rather he argued that factually, socialism couldn't deliver the goods—in order to have an effective economy, you have to have prices, you have to have profits, you have to have the ability for people to exchange goods and services. This is a different idea than much of the [world's] mind-set and ideology, so it's something that when people read it, it often changes their way of looking at the world.

HAYEK AND KEYNES knew each other well. During the 1930s, as Hayek came to the London School of Economics, he immediately started out with a blistering confrontation with Keynes on some of the economic issues of the day. Hayek wrote a blistering review of one of Keynes's books, and then Keynes did a response to Hayek's review where he said that "Professor Hayek's review is an outstanding example of how a logician starting from a wrong premise can end up in Bedlam."

Notwithstanding that rather inauspicious start, they became good friends. During World War II, the London School of Economics was relocated to Cambridge, where Keynes was. Keynes and Hayek would take turns at night watching for fires, as Britain was being bombed, from the top of King's College in Cambridge. So they knew each other well.

The primary difference between Keynes and Hayek is that Keynes was a welfare state interventionist. He was not a socialist. He did not believe in government management and operation of a nation's economy. But he believed in a large role for government in a nation's economy though demand management, through active support for unions, for a strong welfare state, whereas Hayek is more a pure free market economist, more of a libertarian. Hayek's view is that the smaller the state, the less government, the better. So they differed in their views in that regard.

HAYEK WROTE over twenty books, and they range from technical economics to the history of ideas to psychology and then, later in his career, primarily in the area of political philosophy, political theory, and the history of ideas, all wonderful books. . . . *The Road to Serfdom* is probably the easiest book for a general reader to get into.

The Road to Serfdom remains a valuable book for understanding the essence of a free market economy—why it is that a free market economy is economically productive. But more than that, [he argues] why a free market economy is the only free society that's possible. If people don't have freedom in their economic lives to buy and sell as they wish, to exchange on the terms that they see fit, that really there's not much political freedom, either. So as an introduction to the idea of a tie between economic freedom and political freedom, I think it's an outstanding work for that.

Originally, the title of *The Road to Serfdom* was going to be *The Road to Servitude*, which is a line from Tocqueville. Hayek decided to change that to *The Road to Serfdom* because he thought that it sounded better. But Hayek was definitely in that school of nineteenth-century political writers who believed also, as Thoreau put it, "That government is best which governs least." So it is a different idea than government as it's emerged, and Hayek's analysis is a sophisticated analysis of how those ideas are applicable to the twenty-first century as well as the nineteenth.

In England, it also has had quite a bit of influence because they had many industries that were nationalized. The arguments against the welfare state are more difficult, and Hayek had difficulty with: "Where do you draw the line of government?"

Within the United States, there are aspects of Hayek's message that appeal both to Democrats and to Republicans. From an economic perspective, Republicans are probably closer to Hayek's message, but from a civil liberties perspective, Democrats are probably closer to Hayek's message. The idea of less government is an idea that, in different ways, appeals to both sides of the political spectrum.

RONALD REAGAN once met Hayek and mentioned to him that he'd read one of his books and learned a great deal from it. The same goes for Barry Goldwater, [who] was a great admirer of Hayek; Margaret Thatcher, and Winston Churchill, as well, read *The Road to Serfdom* in England. . . . Hayek is someone who's had great influence, particularly on the leading economic conservative, political leaders in the United States and England during the last half century.

Thatcher was very friendly toward Hayek and looked at him as her leading philosophical inspirer. At the same time, it shouldn't be thought . . . that they were on the phone constantly. She saw him perhaps only several times a year, often in a semisocial manner. He was more an inspirer of thought and someone who put forward philosophical ideas rather than someone who was an active government adviser on the issues of the day. Occasionally he'd get involved on an individual basis, but it wasn't from the perspective of his thought.

HAYEK WAS AN agnostic, so he did not have a religious view of the world or a supernal view of morality. His idea was that the justification for capitalism, for free market libertarianism, is that it creates more material goods, that people have a higher standard of living, that it leads life to be more flourishing, more abundant. It's the medical breakthroughs, the technology that allows us to have a higher standard of living and from his nonreligious perspective of the world, life has no purpose but itself. That was his message in *The Fatal Conceit*.

Hayek was someone who had a genuinely interdisciplinary approach. It's not something where he was just an economist or just a political philosopher or just a moralist. He's someone who really was trying to look at a wide variety of issues and discover their interconnections: How do the economic system and the political system and the moral system interact? How do all the aspects of a societal order function together? It's not something that can be looked at in isolation. It's something that has to be looked at in a more holistic manner. That's really Hayek's ultimate message; the moral aspect, in terms of the questions of politics and economics, are not just questions that are technical questions that have objectively right and wrong answers. They are questions about how people want to live; how are people organized; how can we create the best society?

Hayek's argument was that because there are so many people, knowledge is fragmented. Because knowledge is so fragmented among all the members of a society, you have to create a society in which fragmented knowledge can be most utilized. This is most likely to happen in a capitalist society; it's a society where, in particular, prices and profits play a crucial role. They are ways to communicate information, that that's how we should look at prices and profits, as way to communicate information on individuals who have divided knowledge.

THERE'S A FEELING that whatever exists now is the way things always are going to be, and the way they've always been. If there's one thing we learn from history, it's that the future will be completely unlike the present. We don't know how it's going to be, but we should know that it's going to be completely different. Hayek is someone who really had a completely different view of the world, and he tried to enunciate it, and, obviously, it's a view that has inspired many people.

Barry Goldwater and the Rise of Conservativism

by

RICK PERLSTEIN

Former Arizona senator Barry Goldwater lost the 1964 presidential election to Lyndon Johnson by a large margin. However, Rick Perlstein argues that Goldwater's unsuccessful campaign marked the beginning of the rise of modern conservatism. Mr. Perlstein, a Brooklyn-based writer, appeared on Booknotes *on June 3, 2001, to discuss Goldwater's political life and the movement to define and build American conservatism. His book* Before the Storm: Barry Goldwater and the Unmaking of the American Consensus, *was published by Hill & Wang in 2001.*

WHY BARRY GOLDWATER? I started reading books about conservatism. I didn't know conservatism even had a history. It seemed to me that there had always been these conservatives, and they'd always fought liberals. The liberals were the Democrats, and the conservatives were the Republicans. Immediately when I started reading a bit of history and seeing just how marginal this movement was in the 1950s, I just began pursuing the plot: How did conservatives become more powerful? Every road led to Barry Goldwater and this 1964 campaign. It was the glue that tied together hundreds of disparate elements.

[The year] 1964 was the Goldwater–Johnson election, Barry Goldwater against Lyndon Johnson. Goldwater lost in the biggest popular landslide up to that point, even worse than Alf Landon in 1936.

Barry Goldwater won six states. He won quite comfortably in five states in the Deep South. . . . He won Arizona, his home state, only by a whisker. Of course, the guy who beat him was Lyndon Johnson. The Wednesday after the election, people were saying conservatism was finished for good, that we now lived in a liberal republic, that if the Republican Party ever veered from the center and embraced conservatism as its organizing principle, there wouldn't be a Republican Party, and there might not even exist a two-party system. That's how discombobulating this whole thing was in American history.

[CLARENCE "PAT" MANION] was a figure that's been obscured by history. He was a law professor at Notre Dame, a former New Deal liberal who really made a quite dramatic conversion to conservatism in the 1940s. The bridge to conservatism, ironically enough, was that he was anti-interventionist. He didn't believe America should get involved in World War II. That was both a left-wing and a right-wing kind of movement.

[Manion] just became more and more convinced of this calling to spread the gospel, in the McCarthy mold, that the New Deal was this cancer on American society and that internal subversion from communism was rotting America from within, so that he became more and more activist. He retired as dean from the Notre Dame Law School. He started this radio program, . . . the *Manion Forum of Opinion*, and he preached the conservative true religion to whatever stations would take him. He would have guests like Barry Goldwater and segregationists from the South. He became more and more driven by the idea of winning conservative political power.

[Manion] set the bomb in that they were casting about for someone to run in 1960. He came to like Barry Goldwater, and he came up with this idea, "Why don't we ghostwrite a book for Barry Goldwater, put his name on the cover?" They talked to Goldwater; he said, "Well, whatever. Do it. If I like it, I'll sign off on it," and [he] didn't think much of it because people were always coming to him with these crackpot schemes. This was just one more crazy idea. They literally put this book together on a shoestring—guys who had never been involved in publishing; made all kinds of mistakes. There were comic mistakes; Keystone Kops mistakes. But the book came out—they actually called it a pamphlet—*Conscience of a Conservative*. Within a few years, it had sold 3.5 million books. Shepherdsville, Kentucky, where the printing plant happened to be, suddenly became the center of the publishing world.

I think that the hardcover sold for $3. A dollar went to the "Draft Goldwater for President" campaign in 1960; a dollar went to whatever guy happened to sell it, whether it was a bookseller or a conservative activist who might buy 10,000 copies and give them out to his friends and put the dollar in the kitty anyway; and a dollar went to this publishing company.

The guy who wrote *Conscience of a Conservative* was a *National Review* editor, Brent Bozell Jr., William F. Buckley's best friend. He married William F. Buckley's sister. For those who care to follow these matters, his ideology was a little different from that of the Manion conservatives. The Manion conservatives still had this one foot in isolationism, which was really being rolled over by the juggernaut of history.

Bill Buckley really counted himself as a political pragmatist, and his great goal in founding *National Review* was to create a conservative platform on which a presidential candidate could run. He just didn't think Barry Goldwater was the guy. He had distrust in Goldwater's abilities. In fact, he was button-holed by a *Time* magazine reporter at a party who said, "You don't really believe that Barry Goldwater could actually be a successful president?" Buckley said, "Well, of course not." He almost threw a little cold water on the whole Barry Goldwater campaign in 1964 as it was gearing up. He saw it as a lot of people involved did—as not an attempt to win the presidency so much as to build a movement that could lose, but go on to fight a hundred battles more.

[GOLDWATER] REALLY emerged as a national figure in 1957 and 1958. That came through a highly published and dramatic showdown with the union leader Walter Reuther, a self-professed Socialist or Social Democrat in the European mold. He really, more than any union leader before him, saw the goal of the union movement as sharing in state power and working tirelessly for the promotion of a left-wing social agenda. . . . Because of his politics and because of what seemed like the rising power of the union movement, Reuther was basically seen as a potential totalitarian dictator of the United States by the kind of people who listened to Clarence Manion.

Barry Goldwater was a member of the Air National Guard and he was a jet pilot, and he was damn proud to be a jet pilot. He loved to tool around in the latest planes that the defense contractors were building. That was part of this image that made him so attractive to the likes of Bill Buckley and especially Clarence Manion. Conservatives were seen as stodgy, old, fat, greedy. He was youthful, attractive, well spoken, adventurous. Another thing that made him attractive to Clarence Manion was [this]: on the one hand, you had Southern segregationists who weren't particularly economically conservative and you had Northern Republicans who might be conservative, but the Republican Party was just so hated in the South, so they couldn't decide whether their conservative candidate would be a Democrat or a Republican. But as Barry Goldwater won his reelection in 1958, in a year when most Republicans had lost resoundingly, he emerged as this Republican hero. One of the things he started doing was speaking down South at meetings of these nascent Republican Parties in Southern states like South Carolina, saying, "Well, I don't think *Brown v. Board of Education* was such a good idea. Maybe you guys in the South have it right. Maybe the federal government shouldn't be meddling in states' rights." That was new. That was a new concept, a Republican who appealed for popularity in the South.

[When] you see Barry Goldwater, you see his cowboy hat, you see his suede jacket, his blue jeans, the rifle on his knee, with Camelback Mountain, that great, beautiful element in the Phoenix landscape in the background. It looks like he's the Marlboro Man. . . . [However,] Barry Goldwater was a pretty self-dramatizing guy. He really bought into the mythos of the West and the individual conquering the frontier. But, of course, he hadn't done any conquering himself. By the time he came along, his father was a millionaire. He gamboled around Phoenix and didn't have to carry any money, because every store would just charge whatever he wanted to his father. He was a rich, comfortable man. And, in fact, the Goldwater fortune, as I go to great lengths to remind people, really wouldn't have existed if it weren't for strong federal intervention into the economy of Arizona. One of the goals of the New Deal was to economically develop the South and the Southwest. And one of the ways the party of Franklin Roosevelt was later rewarded was that the South and the West largely turned against the New Deal and the government programs that had been so instrumental in turning these areas from wastelands without electricity and water into worthy parts of American civilization.

[WILLIAM REHNQUIST], a segregationist, was great friends with Barry Goldwater. He was a leader in Phoenix Republican circles. . . . Barry Goldwater was not a segregationist. He was a man who really saw, "Everyone isn't equal," and was extremely honorable in his personal dealings on matters of race. In fact, one of the things he worked for was an open housing law in Phoenix; that same law, Rehnquist testified against as a local lawyer. He said, "Our aim should not be to have an integrated society or a segregated society, but a free society." He thought people should be able to rent to people for whatever reason they chose, including their race. Barry Goldwater thought that was abhorrent, but he also thought that the federal government shouldn't have any say in the matter.

One thing that happened during the campaign that was particularly historic was the debate over the 1964 landmark Civil Rights Act. It was voted on [by the Senate] June 19th, not long before the Republican Convention was set to go into session. Barry Goldwater was extremely torn. It was a time of enormous racial tension. The Southerners were filibustering the bill, and African Americans were outraged. It really looked like a Civil War situation. Goldwater had to decide whether to buck his constitutionalist principles and vote for a law that he really thought was unconstitutional because it dictated the behavior of private business. Under Title VII of the Civil Rights Law, employers are not allowed to discriminate on the basis of race, but Barry Goldwater, like a lot of conservative businessmen of the period, thought that people should be able to hire whomever they wanted. He thought that it would take a federal police force to enforce the law. He envisioned it as making America an ugly place, a distrustful place. He had to decide whether to vote for a bill that he probably knew would improve the conditions of blacks or uphold his abstract principles. He really did agonize over it. One of the things that helped tip the balance was a memo from his friend Bill Rehnquist, who said, "You should have no hesitation about voting against the Civil Rights Bill."

RONALD REAGAN's October 27, 1964, speech, nationally televised, on behalf of Barry Goldwater [was] a week before the election. There was all kinds of *Sturm und Drang* within the high circles of the Goldwater campaign, whether they should allow this crackpot actor to take their precious television time. All of Goldwater's biggest California funders threatened to withhold their money unless they put Reagan on the air. He was their hero. . . . Ronald Reagan went on the air, and he just [held the nation] spellbound. People would call their conservative friends the next day and say, "You've been talking all this crazy talk for the last months about Goldwater. I've seen this Reagan guy, and I finally understand what you're talking about." The Republican Party was really looking to end the campaign with a rather profound economic deficit, but so much money started pouring in after Ronald Reagan went on the air that they ended the campaign in surplus.

It made [Ronald Reagan] the man of the hour. He was able to inherit these armies that were built up in the process of trying to nominate and elect Barry Goldwater. Reagan won the governorship of California . . . in 1966. He said things that were similar to what Barry Goldwater was saying, but he had a sparkling [manner]—he was the "Great Communicator." He was able to use these metaphors that connected with people, whereas Barry Goldwater assumed that people already knew what he was talking about. Goldwater was used to talking to Republicans, used to talking to conservatives. He didn't really think he had to meet people halfway. He was a good speaker to conservatives; he was a poor speaker to a general audience. One of the things [Reagan's] speech said was that Social Security should be made voluntary. Goldwater had said that early on in the campaign, in the New Hampshire primary, and that had done so much political damage to him that he never mentioned it again. But Ronald Reagan was able to explain it in a way that it didn't sound crazy anymore.

But place yourself in Barry Goldwater's shoes, which is something I've been doing all this time. He had suffered the vilest possible abuse for months and months, totally unfair abuse about how he was going to blow up the world. That is what most people remember about the Barry Goldwater campaign, how hated he was. He was seen as a fascist, an American Hitler. He busted his hump for months and months to try and get his message across. Suddenly, in comes [Reagan] on a magic carpet who seemed to be scooping up all the hard-earned, organizational support that he had helped build with his hands.

CONSERVATISM WAS a crusade. It was a struggle for the soul of Western civilization. . . . Lyndon Johnson might have had a mile wide of popularity, but it really was ultimately an inch deep, whereas people would send Goldwater telegrams as he was preparing for the convention: "I'd give my marrow, my bones for you. I'll stand by you like a soldier in combat." These were people who believed that liberalism had to be stopped, that we needed to take a firm, belligerent stand against the Soviet Union. They didn't think it was just a matter of personal preference, but, literally, a matter of the survival of Western civilization. If you believe that, you have no problem licking a couple of envelopes to help the cause.

The Coors Family

by

DAN BAUM

Adolph Coors emigrated from Prussia to the United States in 1868, found-
ing the Coors Brewery in Golden, Colorado. A hundred years later, the
Coors family had made its mark not only in beer but in politics as major
funders of various conservative causes. Journalist Dan Baum discussed the
history of the Coors family and their influence on contemporary politics in
Citizen Coors: An American Dynasty, *published by William Morrow in*
2000. Mr. Baum appeared on Booknotes *on June 11, 2000.*

[IN THIS BOOK, READERS] not only get the story of this very odd
family—these people are very odd ducks indeed—they get kind of a history
of the twentieth century. The Coors family committed to the idea that the
twentieth century was basically a bad idea, and they were going to do everything they could politically, and in their business life, and in their personal
lives, to stop the twentieth century from happening, and they lose. At the
very end of the century, they are defeated by it, but they put up a very good
fight. So you get the rise of the right [because] these are the original financiers
of the new right; you get a thumbnail history of the labor movement in the
last thirty years; you get a great labor defeat and then a labor victory; and a
pretty cool business story.

THE ORIGINAL Adolph Coors? I'm as cynical a reporter as the next guy and I
start this book and I think, "Well, I'm gonna find the holes in this [story]
because they put forward this immigrant miracle story."... [In 1868,
Adolph Coors came from] Prussia, Dortmund, ... and God help me, it's
true. It's one of these classical bootstrap immigrant miracle stories.

Adolph stowed away on a ship because he didn't have the fare, landed in Baltimore, where he could have stayed. He didn't speak any English. There were a lot of Germans in Baltimore. It would have been a very comfortable thing to do. But he wanted a brewery. . . . He came out to Illinois and he worked in a brewery for a while, but he wanted his own. He got on a train and went to Denver four years before the Battle of Little Bighorn. This was the dawn of time; Denver was about 50,000 people. He finally founded his own brewery—he had a partner for a while—on the banks of Clear Creek, on the site where the brewery is now. They never moved. He brewed good beer is the only explanation for his success, because there were other breweries in Denver. Within a few years, he was winning prizes at Chicago exhibitions.

HE WAS AN amazing man, an unhappy man, a taciturn, brooding man. . . . Family meals were silent and there was this Prussian discipline in the household, and he had no interests whatsoever outside the brewery, outside of making beer. There was a flood and he almost lost the whole brewery in this flood, but he bent Clear Creek to save his brewery. I use that as a metaphor: He bent a river; not even nature is bigger than the will of Coors.

The nineteenth century was very good to this family and then at the beginning of the twentieth century, prohibition was imposed, in 1916 in Colorado. . . . Now they can't make beer anymore. They keep the business open by making malted milk, and the lesson that they take away is, "Government is the enemy. Government is the bad guy. With a wave of its imperious hand, government can take away the livelihood of an industrious, hardworking, ingenious entrepreneur." They never got over it. In 1929, Adolph threw himself out of a window and killed himself. . . . [He was] eighty-three years old.

[His son] Adolph Jr. [was] the old man in the black suit; he dressed like that every day until he died in 1970. He walked around looking like he was playing Martin Van Buren in a stage play—an alpaca three-piece suit with a high-button collar and a black bow tie and high-button shoes, a walking anachronism; emblematic of how the family thought of themselves.

[BILL COORS AND Joe Coors] are the two main characters of the book . . . because they're the ones who pretty much take over the brewery from their father in the 1950s—the father is there until the 1970s, but they're really running the place. And then the next generation is Peter Coors, who is the man we see in the commercials; he's Joe's son, Bill's nephew.

Adolph III, who is Adolph Jr.'s oldest son, [was murdered]. This is so important, because . . . the Coors way was to hand the brewery from Adolph to Adolph to Adolph, and from the day he was born, Adolph III was raised to run that brewery.

Now as it turns out, he really wasn't all that well-suited to run the brewery. He didn't like beer very much; he was allergic to it. And he had a terrible stutter, which made him ill-suited to be the front man for the company. But it didn't matter whether he was suited for it or not. He was Adolph III, and by God, he was going to run that brewery.

He was kidnapped in 1960, and it was a particularly painful kidnapping because . . . he disappeared one day, and the family got a note from the kidnapper demanding ransom and agreed to pay the ransom, and then nothing ever happened. The kidnapper disappeared, and Ad was just gone, for nine months. Then his body was found; he had been killed in the attempt to kidnap him, as it turned out, and the kidnapper made the ransom demand but then lost his nerve. He has since been caught, tried, served his whole sentence, and while I was doing the book, was paroled. I tried to get to him and couldn't.

The significance of the kidnapping and the murder is that Bill, the second son who was a very good engineer, a man who never wanted to work in the brewery, who wanted to be a surgeon or a concert pianist, comes back and serves the family. He is now going to be the oldest son, and this is a position for which he was never trained, never raised. He has the skills to do it. This is the irony: He is in many ways way more qualified than his older brother ever was to run that brewery, but he's not Adolph III. In fact, after Adolph III's death, Adolph Jr., the father, would read a little eulogy to his son before every board meeting started and would always end with, "This company will never be the same." That said, Bill was free to try his best. But Bill always understood that in a way, he was a usurper, he was an impostor.

THE COORSES, being ideologically conservative, were always offended by having a union in their brewery. The year 1977 was really the worst imaginable time for them because Miller Lite had appeared two years earlier and was eating up their market share, and they decided finally they were going to get rid of the union, once and for all. They did it with stunning speed. It was childishly simple for them to force the union into a strike. The union didn't have any kind of ideological underpinnings the way the Coorses did. The union immediately fell apart and they busted the union, hired strikebreakers. There was a vote to decertify and the union was out—the first American brewery, and still the only large American brewery, to be non-union.

No brewery in its right mind would want to be non-union. Beer is a working-man's beverage, and if you're a brewer interested in prospering, you don't go out and pick a fight with the unions. But the Coorses, always being more interested in making good beer and doing the right thing as they saw it politically, they didn't care about picking a fight with unions. They wanted to pick a fight with unions. And they did, unfortunately for them. After the strike collapsed, George Meany, the president of the AFL-CIO, handed over to a former brewery worker named David Sickler the responsibility for the boycott [of Coors beer]. In Sickler, for the first time, the Coorses had an ideological match. David Sickler was as committed to the cause of unionism and to the left as the Coorses were to the right. Sickler organized the most successful boycott against a single corporation in modern times; a boycott that, although it was officially called off ten years later, still continues; there are a lot of people who won't drink Coors.

THERE ARE TWO threads running in this book: There is the political story and the business story. The business story is one of a seventy-year battle or a one-hundred-year battle against the forces of marketing. These are people who just abhorred the idea that you should have to try to sell your product. They say you make a good product and if you price it fairly, people will buy it. And they make excellent beer, always have made excellent beer, and, for a long time, that worked.

But in the 1970s, the whole beer industry changed, certain dramatic things happened, and the need for marketers in that brewery became apparent. They fight it and fight it, and, finally, by the early 1990s, they can't fight it any longer and they end up giving absolute command of the brewery to a marketer from Frito-Lay, a man who has no history in the brewing business, no sense of the tradition of brewing—their worst nightmare, their worst enemy. It's like handing over the keys of the city to savages. They walk out of the brewery and never go back. Peter Coors is nominally chairman, but it doesn't matter what his title is, he has very little to do with the running of the brewery.

THE OTHER GREAT thread in this book is their political story. Joe Coors, in particular . . . was really the first big-time financier of the new right. In the 1950s, in the early 1960s, there really was no conservative movement as we now know it. Lionel Trilling, at the time, wrote that "liberalism is not only the dominant ideology, it's the only ideology in America." The *National Review* existed, but that was about all there was to bring together people of conservative politics, and so conservatives back then, each was on his own, thinking he was wandering in a liberal wilderness.

Joe is very conservative from the lessons that this family learned in the end of the nineteenth century and the beginning of the twentieth century. [The Coorses are] very conservative, very rich, and have no desire to spend any money on themselves. These are very simple-living people; they drive old cars, live in unassuming houses . . . , are personally modest people. [In 1973, Joe] looked around for something he could do to help turn the country to the right . . . and through a series of circumstances, founded the Heritage Foundation, which gave the conservative movement in the United States its first piece of real estate.

[He accomplished this through] money. He . . . wrote a letter to the Republican senator from Colorado, Gordon Allott. Allott was out of town, and so the letter landed on his press secretary's desk—this young guy from Wisconsin named Paul Weyrich, who now, of course, is one of the pillars of the new right. Coors said, "I want to spend money on the conservative movement; I want to do something." As Richard Viguerie explained it, Weyrich said, "What the movement needs is real estate." As he put it, "The Jews were the world's whipping boys until they had Israel; and the Mormons were wanderers in the desert until they had Utah. We need an address. We need a place, a place for reporters to call, a place to do research for Republican members of Congress, a place to give somebody to the conservative movement, a gathering place with prestige." And that's what Joe did. He also started a television network way before its time. What he did, he started a news operation to deliver to television stations film reels . . . of pre-made news stories to air all with a conservative bent. It failed. He spent a lot of money on it. It failed for a lot of reasons, but it was a visionary thing to do. [The man he hired to run his news operation was Roger Ailes.]

Among the people that we have the Coorses to thank for is for Roger Ailes, James Watt, and Ronald Reagan. Joe Coors noticed Ronald Reagan. Ronald Reagan in 1964 made a famous televised speech before the campaign, and it was more a speech about conservative principles. . . . I don't think he mentioned [Republican presidential candidate Barry] Goldwater's name at all in this speech. . . . This is where he says, "Are we going to condemn our children to 1,000 years of darkness, or is this going to be the last, best hope of mankind?" Joe Coors flew out and shook Ronald Reagan's hand, and he not only became a financial backer of Ronald Reagan, they became good friends.

One of the good interviews I did for this book was with Lynn Nofziger, who was Reagan's political director. Nofziger describes himself as an ideological kook. . . . Nofziger worked for Reagan in the governor's mansion, in California, as press secretary. . . . He always made sure that Reagan got time with Joe Coors because not only did Joe have deep pockets and was willing to write checks, but Joe Coors kept Reagan centered and focused on these conservative principles. Nofziger said, "I really didn't have to do much because they really became close friends." Reagan would fly out to Colorado and just hang out with Joe and Holly and have dinner with them and sit around the house and talk.

I don't know if you remember the radio addresses Ronald Reagan used to do. . . . These were well before he's president. . . . These are the shows on which he coined the term "welfare queen." These were very conservative, quite strident addresses he was giving on the radio. . . . Coors Brewery was the national sponsor. Even in places where Coors wasn't sold, Coors Brewery was the national sponsor.

[RUSSELL KIRK, Barry Goldwater, and Bill Buckley had a big impact on Joe Coors;] Russell Kirk, more than anybody. In fact, one of the questions I always ask people when I'm writing about somebody who—I can't talk to is, "What do they read?" The only book I ever heard anybody talk about the Coorses reading was Russell Kirk's *The Conservative Mind*, which came out in 1953, the first articulation of an American conservative ideology. It's a remarkable book, and it really foretells the Reagan revolution and the Gingrich revolution beautifully. . . .

JOE THOUGHT the Corporation for Public Broadcasting was the next thing to the propaganda arm of the Kremlin, and he wanted a seat on that board. The last day of Richard Nixon's presidency, Richard Nixon appointed him to a seat on the board of CPB. Joe already had started this right-wing network. It was an obvious conflict of interest, first of all, but then Joe wrote a letter to the president of CPB complaining about a show about the funeral industry based on Jessica Mitford's book and tried to strong-arm the president of Public Broadcasting, and Congress just ate him alive.

But they would have eaten him alive, anyway. These were folks who went out of their way to draw attention to themselves as strident conservatives. They wanted everybody to know it, and because of that, they got clobbered in the [beer] boycott, and they never understood. The boycott was launched in 1978, when the Carter presidency was in its last two years, and Reagan was ascending. . . . Then Reagan was elected, and for Reagan to be elected, for them it was like the second coming. It was the grand moment. It was everything they dreamed of. And it was the worst thing that could have happened to a brewery.

[IF YOU'RE Joe Coors you sit back and say, "I had an impact on this country and changed things, through the Heritage Foundation, through Ronald Reagan."] They're very proud of that. The ironic thing is, it worked—they turned the country rightward, but they had to change their practices within the walls of their beloved brewery because they were so beaten up by this boycott.

THE MORAL of the story is that everybody plays by the rules sooner or later. Nobody is bigger than the tide of history. The Coorses made the strongest effort anybody has ever made, probably, to turn back the hands of time, and they got beat, and they were defeated by it. Modern times caught up with them like they catch up with everybody else.

Libertarianism

---

by

DAVID BOAZ

Libertarianism, the political philosophy emphasizing individual rights and limited government, only entered American political terminology in the mid-twentieth century. The roots of this philosophy, however, reach back much further. In his book Libertarianism: A Primer, *published by The Free Press in 1997, David Boaz outlined the history and central principles of libertarianism. He argued that the influence of the socially liberal, economically conservative baby boomer generation points to a "coming libertarian age." Mr. Boaz, executive vice president of the Cato Institute, a libertarian think tank, appeared on* Booknotes *on January 26, 1997.*

W HAT I LIKE best about libertarianism is the fact that I can live here at the end of the twentieth century and have unprecedented access to ideas and music and goods and travel and all those things that make life really worth living. [This] wonderful, modern society we live in, it's not quite as libertarian as I would like, but the modern world—since the American Revolution and since Adam Smith sort of summed up the notion of spontaneous order in free markets—is built on the ideas of John Locke and Adam Smith. We do have a society in which people are largely free to make their own decisions, in which free markets have created tremendous prosperity.

I'M SURE YOU have people on your [C-SPAN] shows every day complaining that some people are poor, that we can't get certain things, that health care is not good enough—all kinds of problems with the economy. But if you look at it in historical perspective, for tens of thousands of years, people were desperately poor. They suffered backbreaking labor. And about 150 years ago, we had the Industrial Revolution. We started having free markets. Karl Marx called it capitalism because he thought capital was the point, but that's not the point. The point is people working freely, allowed to trade and exchange, and they created this tremendous wealth. We can sit here in this television studio, and you're going to film this and be able to broadcast it nationally, internationally. Millions of people are going to be able to watch this. You have put some of this information on an Internet site, and people can access it any time of the day—tremendous advances in society and the economy, and that's because we've had a relatively libertarian society.

This is a libertarian country. All the founders were basically libertarians, and in an earlier generation, we would have called them "liberals" or "classical liberals." They would have called themselves Whigs, perhaps. But we can look back at their ideas and say they were basically libertarians. They believed in individual rights. They believed in government only by consent. They believed in free markets.

[The Declaration of Independence is] one of the greatest pieces of libertarian writing ever. The second paragraph of the Declaration—"We hold these truths to be self-evident that all men are created equal, that they are endowed by their creator with certain unalienable rights, that among these are life, liberty, and the pursuit of happiness"—that is a beautiful, succinct, eloquent statement of what libertarianism is. It goes on to say that "[i]t is to secure these rights that governments are instituted among men." That's why we have government, not to give us midnight basketball, not to tuck us in at night. We have government to secure our rights. That paragraph goes on to say that when any government ceases to do that, it is the right of the people to alter or abolish it. That was where you got from the libertarian theory to the right to rebel against an oppressive government.

Thomas Paine was one of the great libertarians of all time. He was known as a rabble-rousing writer. Everyone reads *Common Sense* when they're in college. *Common Sense* is a great essay. One of the great things about Thomas Paine is that he put together two elements of libertarian theory: One is the theory of justice, of individual rights—that adult individuals have the right to live their life the way they want to. The other is a theory called spontaneous order, the theory of the self-regulating society. Academics would say it's not the normative theory, it's the positive theory. It observes the world and says, "If you leave people alone to trade and exchange and make their own decisions, a self-regulating order will emerge. You don't need the government to create order. Order emerges." Thomas Paine put those two ideas together, and so in that sense he's a really key libertarian thinker.

THE DIFFERENCE between the Federalists and Anti-Federalists was over issues of how much power you can give to the federal government. The Federalists wanted to give a tiny amount of power to the federal government, and the Anti-Federalists thought that even a tiny amount of power was too much. We're still judging that argument, because if you look at what the Federalists gave the government in the Constitution, it's a pretty libertarian grant of power. The government was not granted the power to go out and do everything from Social Security to midnight basketball; it was granted the power to regulate commerce between the states and to handle foreign affairs, and that was about it. The Anti-Federalists said, "You do that and it will get too powerful. It will exceed its bounds. You will not bind down the government by this Constitution." And clearly, on that score, you have to say the Anti-Federalists were right.

Whether that means we should have stuck with the Articles of Confederation and not tried the Constitution is a more difficult question. But if you look at George Mason and James Madison, you're talking about two Virginia libertarians who disagreed over whether the Constitution was too risky.

ALEXIS DE TOCQUEVILLE was a libertarian, one that you might call a conservative libertarian, very concerned about tradition and order in society, something of an aristocratic approach. I really don't know what [modern libertarians] think they see in Tocqueville. He was a brilliant critic of American democracy. He was a great admirer of it, but he pointed out the kinds of things that could happen, that could be foibles of a democratic society, which was a new experiment. People didn't know. He was really predicting. There's an essay of his, "What Sort of Despotism Democratic Nations Have to Fear." We know what sort of despotism nondemocratic nations had. Could there be despotism in a democratic nation? And he warned about a government that would beneficently cover the surface of society with minute and petty rules and regulations. I have to say that was pretty prescient. . . . Today we've got regulations on everything from how long you have to stay in the hospital after you have a baby to what drugs you can take if you're sick and your doctor recommends something the FDA doesn't, all for our own good. The government is always beneficent to us, and yet they're covering our society with this network of rules.

SLAVERY IS ABOUT the greatest violation of individual rights there can be, and so abolitionism was clearly the libertarian cause of its day. William Lloyd Garrison and Frederick Douglass were libertarians. If you read their writings, they talk about individual rights. They talk about how "no man is empowered to govern another," and they call slavery "man stealing." The reason they call it "man stealing" is that they are saying, "You are trying to steal the very essence of a man from himself." They rested their argument on self-ownership, which is an old libertarian theory. In my book, the first reading about slavery is from

Richard Overton, who was one of the Levellers in England. Self-ownership, the idea that I own myself, that is the base of my individual rights. Nobody owns me; I don't belong to the collective; I don't belong to other people. I own myself. And if I do, slavery is an attempt to steal me from myself.

Sarah Grimké and Angelina Grimké were sisters. They were abolitionists. In the struggle for abolitionism, they began thinking about their own rights as women and realized that they didn't have full equal rights, either. Women did not do a lot of public writing at that time. They did do public speaking. . . . One of the reasons they're in my book is partly because feminism and abolitionism were clearly libertarian causes, but another reason is that [their arguments] rest the case for abolitionism and women's rights squarely on the notion that each adult individual holds moral responsibility for his own actions. So to try to control his actions, either to make him a slave or to forbid him from entering into contracts, which was a way women were treated at the time, was to take away that moral responsibility. It tells him, "You can't be"— or to tell her, "You can't be a full and complete adult because you don't have the responsibility to enter into actions and be responsible for them."

THE *NATION* WAS a libertarian magazine in the first half of its life. I believe it was founded around the time of the Civil War, and, throughout the nineteenth century, it was a classical liberal magazine. It advocated free markets, the rule of law, decolonization, international peace, but very much free markets. An essay actually written in the *Nation* in 1900, looking back on the nineteenth century, says, "Look at the tremendous achievements that free people, freed from vexatious meddling of governments, have been able to produce." But alas, today it seems that people have forgotten the principles of the Declaration of Independence that brought us to this happy state. We are going to be doomed to a century of war and statism before we get back on the path. That was pretty prescient. We have been through a twentieth century with a lot of war and a lot of statism because we forgot the principles of the Declaration of Independence.

H. L. MENCKEN generally was [a libertarian]. He was probably the greatest journalist of the first half of this century. He was, interestingly enough, known as a liberal back during the era of Harding and Coolidge. He was this great liberal journalist who was always railing against the pomposity of the complacent bourgeoisie of the Republican administrations. Then, when Franklin Roosevelt came in, Mencken started to be considered a conservative, because he also railed against the excessive government and the pomposities of the New Deal. What he really was, was a libertarian all those times. He believed in the individual, and he didn't much believe in government.

FRIEDRICH HAYEK died in 1992. He was ninety-three. When I met him, he was a very old man, and so I remember a very old man of old-fashioned, European demeanor, a gracious gentleman, a scholar who was always so careful and precise to state his objections to other people's ideas without ever criticizing other people personally. He dedicated his book *The Road to Serfdom* to the socialists of all parties. I think he was very sincere in wanting to say, "I share your aspirations. I understand your dreams. But please read this warning of what will happen if you let government have too much power." And he kept that respect for all of his adversaries to the end of his life.

WE NEED A government to protect our rights. We need a government to protect us from people who might hurt us on our own streets. That's why we have police. We have courts to settle disputes. And we need a national defense to protect us from people who might hurt us overseas. But if you look at the history of the world, there have been so many instances of governments getting into wars to aggrandize themselves, to gain land, to gain power. It used to be that kings would say, "I did it to get better known." Fortunately, the liberal libertarian impulse in modern life has been so strong that a king can't say that anymore. But we still have too many countries getting into unnecessary wars, sending off kids to die, exploiting the society, seizing money to be spent on military expenditures. We need a strong national defense. We need to be secure from our enemies. But in the present context, I don't think that means that we need American boys in . . . all the places around the world that our government seems determined to meddle.

My father was very interested in politics. He was a judge in our local community, and he was very interested in political ideas and he talked about the role of the government. He felt the federal government was way too big, and I guess that got me thinking in that direction. Then, as I started reading, I found a lot of evidence that I felt that was true, and I now probably think it's a lot more "too big" than he would have thought.

For one thing, we can see more of the problems than, say, we would have when my father was my age. But for another reason, I just read different things, thought about things differently, and decided that there was a more fundamental indictment of the size of government, that there is something about human beings that means they ought to be free to live their lives the way they want to and that intrusion by government into that process is wrong. And that came to seem very consistent and very right to me.

Six Views of Race
in American Society

EUGENE ROBINSON

FRANK WU

THOMAS BYRNE EDSALL

RANDALL KENNEDY

DERRICK BELL

JOHN MCWHORTER

Fifty years after the Brown v. Board of Education *decision ruled segregated schools unconstitutional, racial issues continue to percolate in American society. Over its fifteen years, numerous authors have appeared on* Booknotes *to participate in the ongoing debate about racial identity, including the six featured here: Eugene Robinson, assistant managing editor of the Style section at the* Washington Post, *joined us on November 7, 1999, to discuss* Coal to Cream: A Black Man's Journey Beyond Color to an Affirmation of Race, *published by The Free Press that same year. Howard University law professor Frank Wu visited us on March 31, 2001, to talk about his book* Yellow: Race in America Beyond Black and White, *published by Basic Books in 2001. On December 15, 1991,* Washington Post *reporter Thomas Byrne Edsall discussed* Chain Reaction: The Impact of Race, Rights, and Taxes on American Politics, *coauthored by Mary Edsall and published by W. W. Norton & Company in 1991. Harvard Law School professor Randall Kennedy appeared on* Booknotes *on March 3, 2002, to talk about his book* Nigger: The

Strange Career of a Troublesome Word, *published by Pantheon Books that same year. On November 15, 1992, New York University Law School professor Derrick Bell discussed* Faces at the Bottom of the Well: The Permanence of Racism, *published by Basic Books in 1992. Finally, John McWhorter, associate professor of linguistics at the University of California–Berkeley, joined us on March 2, 2003, to discuss* Authentically Black: Essays for the Black Silent Majority, *published by Gotham Books in 2003.*

EUGENE ROBINSON

THE BOOK STARTED with this fascination with color and race and Brazil that all came together. I was correspondent down there for the *[Washington] Post* in South America. I was living in Buenos Aires, Argentina, but spent a lot of time in Brazil.

I thought it was really interesting because here was a country that was so like the United States in so many ways; [it had] a history that was parallel to ours in a lot of ways, yet an entirely different idea of race had evolved, one in which I sometimes felt very comfortable. But I had questions about it. So I was trying to understand that.

THEY DIDN'T outlaw slavery in Brazil until 1888. Slavery in Brazil was different in that it was, in some ways, more brutal. It was African slavery. For many years, for centuries really, during the whole Middle Passage importation of slaves, far more slaves were taken to Brazil than to the United States. The numbers dwarf the number brought to the United States. One difference is that in the United States, for whatever reason, slaves were considered valuable property and so were taken care of. Families were split up, but the population grew. In Brazil, slaves tended to be worked very hard, and when they died, more were brought over. So it was very rough.

In other ways, it was different. There were some slave revolts in Brazil in which slaves took chunks of territory and held them for long periods of time. Also, arguably, slaves' families were not separated in Brazil in the way they were separated here. I think that contributed, at least in the places where there was the heaviest concentration of slaves, in actually preserving a little bit more culture of West Africa, which was translated to parts of Brazil.

THERE'S A LOT more miscegenation in Brazil than there was in the United States, a lot more intermarriage, and over the whole society, it seems like a much more continuous color spectrum. When I looked at that society, when I looked at the people I saw around me, I saw a lot of people who, in the U.S.

context, would not have been thought of as white, although they often thought of themselves in the Brazilian context as white, and were.

In Brazil [looking] at the color of someone's skin, the literal color—the amount of melanin and the amount of pigmentation—is something that they do all the time. It's the way they think of themselves. Here we don't. We see white people and black people, but we don't really mean those colors. And in fact here, if we put an olive-skinned Greek person up next to an olive-skinned person from Ethiopia, we see two different races, even though they could be exactly the same hue.

When I came back [to the United States], I looked around in the way that I had learned to look in Brazil.

If you go to very low-income areas in our society, you tend to see a greater proportion of very dark-skinned people than you do see in the upper socioeconomic ranks of black America. In part, it grows out of what, in years past, in decades past, was a more overt color discrimination or color line, unspoken but there, in the black community. There's also this very substantial gap in wealth between even middle-class white Americans and middle-class black Americans with same levels of income, but their wealth is strikingly different.

[My friend, journalist Mac Margolis] had spent more time in Brazil than I had. . . . What he started teaching me or helping me see, was that the initial view I had of race in Brazil, which was that here was some sort of racial paradise . . . wasn't that simple; that there was a pattern that shaped the society in which whites really were at the top, but that some tended to be black in the rest of society. And these were things that you ought to take into account.

I did [change my mind about race in Brazil while I was living there]. I went thinking for a while, and feeling more important than thinking, that the Brazilian model was one that we might think about. It was very comfortable and wonderful in a lot of ways.

I eventually came to think that our way of struggling with race—friction, confrontation, all the problems we've had with it over the years, which stems from my sense of racial identity—has produced a lot more in terms of benefits and progress than the Brazilian system has.

Lord knows we've got a long way to go, but . . . I don't know of another society where a minority like black people in the United States have made as many strides, concrete strides, in terms of closing [the] income gap, closing employment gaps. We've come an enormous way. Got a lot more to do. There are still very important gaps, in addition to the percentage of black America that's mired in the direst of circumstances in the inner cities.

But I'm not aware of a place that's come as far as we have, and it's because we wrestle with it. We don't say everything is OK if it's not. It's uncomfortable at times, and it would be nice, just in terms of going about your daily life without tension, without racial friction. Brazil is a great place, but the society is more unequal than this one.

FRANK WU

SOMETIMES WE TALK about race as if everyone is either black or white, and that's it. When you talk about race that way, you leave out not just Asian Americans. You leave out Hispanics. You leave out thousands of people, millions of people of mixed-race background. It's as if they don't exist.

I'm suggesting it doesn't matter who you are, what your identity is, what your politics are, what sort of policies you think we should have—if you can't see yellow and brown and red and all the different shades, then you leave out a huge proportion of the population in California, on college campuses, and in the future of our nation because it's changing incredibly rapidly.

But I'm also trying to move us beyond black and white in a different sense, in a figurative sense. Sometimes we talk about race as if you've got villains on the one hand—hard-core bigots who are doing bad things—and then you've got victims on the other hand.

Now, we still do have villains. The KKK is out there. You see skinhead groups using Web sites to try to bring the young to their hateful cause. But sometimes it's not just villains and victims. Sometimes we all have a responsibility, even if my family wasn't here when there were slaves. My family wasn't even here when there was Jim Crow.

Sometimes none of us is to blame. You just have these situations where the people to be blamed—they're long dead and gone. Nonetheless, we still have this mess to muddle through.

Now, most biologists recognize race is sort of a fiction. It's the kind of thing we make up. There aren't clean, neat lines. A whole lot of people out there who are characterized as black, in fact, are more white than black. And there are a lot of people who are white, whom we treat as white, who, in fact, have some black ancestry.

Then these lines blur, and most of us share more genes than we know, and the differences are tiny. And the differences within racial groups are every bit as big as between racial groups.

I think it's important to recognize that we may be past these formal tables, but we still socially and culturally construct them. So that even if race is fictional, it has a social reality. It affects people's lives.

I wouldn't classify anyone [racially]. I would allow people to declare for themselves. An Asian American is—well, it's a strange concept. There aren't Asian Americans in Asia. For one thing, the people in Asia—well, they're there. They're not here. And for another thing, there isn't a pan-Asian identity, except for sort of a bad one, when one nation wants to conquer another nation.

So the people who are Asian Americans—well, they're people whose grandfathers or great-grandfathers would have hated one another, would have been at war with one another. But here, we recognize we have a common cause. Sometimes people say, "Well, why do you have to be Asian Americans? . . . Aren't you breaking up into little groups?"

Actually, Asian American [is] a coalition identity. It brings together people from about two dozen different national origins: You've got Pakistani, Indian, Hmong, Vietnamese, Cambodian, Thai, Korean, Japanese, Chinese, all sorts of different ethnicities, languages, walks of life, class backgrounds, different stories as to how they got to the United States. What they've recognized is that being Asian American can be empowering, that even though our forefathers may have hated one another, here we've got a common cause.

And even though, growing up, I didn't know very much about Koreans or Thais or Pakistanis, I realized, in the United States, we have this shared identity and a set of experiences, even though we're incredibly diverse—different politics and different cultures—there is a common thread. It's that "When are you going home, where are you really from" thread of being a perpetual foreigner. And we can turn that into something empowering and positive.

[TEACHING AT historically black Howard University,] I'm in an environment where not just my students but my peers, my boss, my boss's boss and my boss's boss's boss is African American. I've learned as much as I've taught. This has really changed my life. Although *Yellow* is a book by an Asian American . . . it's not just about Asian Americans and not just for Asian Americans.

It's meant to talk about race more generally. Many of the examples are about African Americans because I realized that I face prejudice; I face stereotypes. Sometimes that's not recognized. Sometimes I'm annoyed. And sometimes, in some instances, Asian Americans can face serious hate crimes and bias. But by and large, what I face doesn't compare with what African Americans face.

So I realized if I'm going to be serious about this work, civil rights work, I have to stand up and speak out not just when it's someone who happens to look like me but when it's others, when it's African Americans. Their cause is my cause.

I should make clear I think this is a great nation. It's different. This is a nation where we say we believe anyone can come here and become an equal and become a full participant in this great dialogue. And I want to be a participant in that dialogue. I want to make us live up to our ideals. It's because I'm proud to be here, proud to be an American, that I want to do this.

THOMAS BYRNE EDSALL

YOU CANNOT RUN a [political] campaign in America appealing to race. With the American people, there is a great sense of equity and fairness. There are, though, in racial issues questions that really go to the heart of what is America, what is fairness. Should policies try to make the field a level playing field with everyone at the beginning of the race starting equally, or should policies attempt to correct for past discrimination, the history of segregation and slavery? Racial issues have provoked fundamental conflicts over what is the meaning of equality, what is the meaning of fairness. These are unresolved conflicts.

Democrats care [about minorities] to the extent that they need the minority vote. It's essential. Republicans care in that they get a benefit by capitalizing in a negative way, many times, on the problems of the underclass, on welfare dependency, on the emergence of a Jesse Jackson who was himself a very divisive candidate. You'll see Republican literature or Republican campaigns now using images of Jesse Jackson as a way to attack. But I don't think this was a productive effort. What you have in America is a very interesting phenomenon where overall, if you look from the 1940s to the present, black America has made great strides. Overall, the integration of America has progressed, and it is a success story.

The size of the black middle class has grown by leaps and bounds, way faster than the size of the total black population. At the other end, though, you have an underclass that hasn't particularly grown, but their problems have worsened and they've become geographically concentrated and they are very threatening. The underclass problems sort of reinforce in the worst possible ways racial stereotypes—the illegitimacy, the crime, the unemployment, the nonwork. It is like the Bill Moyers TV show where he interviewed teenage boys who were fathers of one or more children, taking no responsibility. These are the worst stereotypes that people hold of black America, and they are being reinforced constantly by shows that show them as perpetrators of crimes.

So you have this minority segment of the black community driving the politics of race in many respects when, in fact, the majority has been quite successful. There has been considerable integration, workforces have changed. The *Washington Post* newsroom is a different place than it was twenty years

[ago], as is the floor of AT&T and GM. The workforce of corporate America has changed and become far more diverse. There is a great deal of success there, but at the bottom there are problems, and those problems tend to drive the whole political system.

RANDALL KENNEDY

NIGGER IS A very powerful, provocative word that provides a very interesting window on American culture.

It's a word that, first of all, has an interesting history. It's first and foremost a slur that provides a window on some of the ugliest aspects of American history. But it's not simply a slur. It is a word that means many things. It's been used in an ugly way, as a weapon, but it's also a word that has been used as a term of endearment. It is a word that has been used as an anti-racist weapon. So it's an interesting word, and that's why I found it worthwhile to spend my time and energy writing a book about it.

Nigger is a word that has a very violent history. There are many instances in the book where I talk about the violent episodes. It's a word that has violence. It has blood around it. It's a word that in many instances justly causes fear. It's a menacing word. And so it has connotations that are different than just your regular sort of curse words.

The word is derived from N-I-G-E-R, which was Latin for "black." How it actually became an insult is unclear. *The Random House Historical Dictionary of American Slang* has a very nice treatment of *nigger,* as does the *Oxford English Dictionary*. Both of those dictionaries take the word back to the seventeenth century. So it's got a long lineage.

One of the interesting things about the word is initially, it was not used, apparently, as a slur. We do know, though, that by the early nineteenth century, certainly by the 1830s, it was a very well-known slur. By the 1830s, the word *nigger,* first of all, was prevalent, and it was well known as a slur. How it actually got that way is not altogether clear.

The "N" word has been thoroughly stigmatized in American culture. No politician can be elected president of the United States if he is captured on tape using the word *nigger.* I would set that forth just as an ironclad proposition. And it's a good thing. Let me back up a moment. If he's using that term in a way that bespeaks either enmity or that bespeaks indifference or contempt, he cannot be elected president of the United States. And that's a good thing.

Do I ever use the "N" word? One of my favorite albums, comedy albums, is an album by Richard Pryor called *That Nigger's Crazy*. I talk about that album in my book. I have repeated on many occasions jokes from *That Nigger's Crazy*. I think that that album is a wonderful album that tells us a lot about black American culture, a lot about American race relations. As far as I'm concerned, one of the treasures of American culture. And it is part of our cultural inheritance.

Another instance would be Mark Twain's *Huckleberry Finn.* I've repeated what Mark Twain had to say in *Huckleberry Finn.* Mark Twain uses *nigger* on over 200 occasions in *Huckleberry Finn.*

So have I repeated the word? Have I used the word? Yes, I've used it. I don't use it as a word to wound people. I don't use it as a word of racial put-down. But do I think that the word *nigger* has a place in American culture? The answer would be yes.

My position with the word *nigger* is, "It all depends." It all depends on how somebody's using it because *nigger,* like every other word, takes its meaning from the circumstances. I can insult somebody calling them "sir." It all depends on how I use the word *sir.* It all depends on the inflection of my voice. It all depends on the other words that surround my use of the word *sir.*

So *nigger*—it all depends on how you use it. You can assault somebody with it, but you can also embrace somebody with it.

DERRICK BELL

BLACK PEOPLE ARE the faces at the bottom of the societal well—most of [the] whites in America who are only one level above, also denied opportunity, also oppressed in a certain way, are fascinated in looking down on us, rather than looking back at the top to see where the folk at the top are manipulating both groups.

Only if they, in effect, let down their ropes, join with us, can both groups ever climb up and challenge and confront those at the top who make all the money, who have all the opportunity. And some do, but most seem fascinated simply making sure that we stay below them. It's a kind of a metaphor that, it seems, reflects much of what has happened in the history of race in our society. And it's the challenge that faces our society and it is the reason—because thus far that challenge has never been effective—that I've concluded that racism is a permanent part of the American scene.

What my publisher said—Martin Kessler, who has really supported me with this book—"Derrick," he said, "your book is unremittingly despairing." [Is racism permanent?] Very few blacks would ask that, though some do, particularly professional civil rights people. They mean that, "Gee, racism is permanent? Where does that leave us?" But most blacks say, "Yes, it is, now let's deal with that. Thank you for saying it." You see?

Because if you really are a part of this thing, if you really sense where you are, regardless of how much money you may make and what have you—that you are part of a group that's at the bottom of the societal well—then any truth, any insight about your status is not despairing, because the truth is not despairing when you see it as the truth. In fact, it's almost enlightening, because you say, "Ah, that's what it is. It's not this thing over here. It's not this thing over here."

For blacks [this book] was to provide this enlightenment, to give a different sense of where they are, of what is the cause of the sense of subordination that they feel and they experience. It is also to say to whites that racism, in its permanence, is not a condemnation of you but rather a challenge to you to recognize that you, too, are victimized by this—unless you are at the very top of this system. Even then, the crime that afflicts our communities that is mostly black crime is not limited to black people, you see? And so, there is something there for all of us.

Brown v. Board of Education was decided two years before I graduated, and the world generally felt—knowledgeable people, experienced people—that, well, with *Brown* decided, a discrimination based in law being condemned by the Supreme Court, it was all over. All we needed was enforcement, sort of a rearguard action to take care of the folk who were persistent and hard-liners.

I was told that I was born fifteen years too late to be a civil rights lawyer, you see. And, well, now we see that that was wrong; that was far, far too optimistic. The question I've been asking—and I have the luxury as a law teacher that I didn't have as a litigator, that I didn't have as an administrator—to step back and ask, "Look, what keeps these patterns going again and again, in different forms, but continuing over 200 years?" It seemed to me that the conclusions that I found from that question led to the title of my book, that racism is a permanent part of the American scene.

JOHN MCWHORTER

I THINK NOWADAYS a great many black Americans are caught in a kind of a bind. There is a sense that to be authentically black, to have a kind of sophistication about your color, that your job is to emphasize black victimhood in public. Your job is—I hate to say it—to exaggerate the extent of your victimhood in public. And in general, when race issues come up when white people are around, you are supposed to cloak the race in tragedy and downplay the progress that has been made. The idea is that we're not all the way there, and that whites are on the hook, as it's often put. Don't let white people off of the hook.

And the reason for this is because it's often felt by many people, in a certain level of their consciousness, that if whites are let off the hook, if whites start getting too comfortable, then that will spell the death of the black community, or at least the part of the black community that's been left behind.

It's become especially clear in my mind over about the past two or three years. And that was just the first part. The second part is that this is not the way black people talk to each other. This is not what you hear at one of our Thanksgivings or at one of our Christmases. This victim routine is not something that the typical African American feels in their bones. It's not something that you pass on to your children.

Most black Americans, I would venture, in private, when we're just among ourselves, sound an awful lot like Shelby Steele, sound an awful lot like Clarence Thomas. None of that stuff is difficult. Most of it is quite logical. But there's a sense that you're supposed to have a different idea when you go out in public, and that informs what we see so much of, in terms of the black presentation of the black condition.

That's what I mean by "authentically black." There's a sense that you're not authentically black unless you are in touch with your victimhood. And while this is understandable, it creates a lot of cognitive dissonance. It distracts a lot of young people from educating themselves, both in a literal way, and in how to get along in a less-than-perfect but still very promising world for them. I think that we need to address that. It's the kind of thing that needs to be given a name. It's this new "black double-consciousness."

There are people who love that idea of the salad bowl, as opposed to the melting pot. But it's very simple. There's a very simple fact: to my knowledge [there's no society]—and I've asked a bunch of people about this who know better than me, and none of them has been able to come up with an example—where groups of people live largely separately, rarely marrying out, in perfect peace. In any situation where you've got partitions like that—i.e., this salad bowl—then the reason for it is because one group is oppressing another or [there are] caste boundaries of some kind in the culture. There's no such thing as the salad bowl except as a transition.

Getting past race doesn't mean whites will love us to death, and in the meantime, we will hunker down behind this barrier, kind of warily eyeing these people who hurt us in the past. That's not getting past race. Getting past race is, Lord forbid, all of us mixing together. Now, sometimes we don't like to talk about that because it sounds like the black person saying he doesn't like what color he is. And that's not true. We now are in our time, and I'm perfectly happy with it.

But the future . . . means letting go of the Africa routines because, like it or not, we're right here. I like Africa. I study Africa. I am not African. I am an African American, and I use that term because we're used to it. But I'm more of an American.

It's perfectly understandable why a lot of black people are uncomfortable with that characterization. Are you more American than you are black? Or are you more black than you are American? . . . We won't get past race until we get beyond that.

Now, getting white racism out of the way—that was very important. Getting white residual racism out of the way—that's something we can work on. Although I don't think that it's a necessary condition, as many people seem to think it is. But another thing we have to get by is that we have to allow ourselves to be open to getting past race.

American Multiculturalism

by

ARTHUR M. SCHLESINGER JR.

The controversial metaphor of America as a "melting pot" originated with Israel Zangwill's 1908 play of the same name. Although the play itself has largely been forgotten, its central theme—the idea that immigrants can be transformed into Americans, producing a new, hybrid culture—has not. In a revised edition of his 1991 book, The Disuniting of America, *reprinted by W. W. Norton & Company in 1998, Pulitzer Prize–winning author Arthur M. Schlesinger Jr. discussed the problems surrounding American multiculturalism. Mr. Schlesinger joined us on* Booknotes *on May 10, 1998.*

GUNNAR MYRDAL WAS a Swedish economist who was brought to the U.S. to study the race problem. . . . A foundation brought him; the idea was that he could bring a certain detachment and have a certain perspective which might be useful for Americans. [Gunnar Myrdal's book, *An American Dilemma,* is] an extraordinary book in the depiction of conditions half a century ago. If you read *An American Dilemma* . . . it's hard to deny that great changes, great improvements have taken place. We haven't gone far enough, but there have been extraordinary changes in American life.

Gunnar Myrdal also proposed an argument as to how these changes might come about. He identified what he called "the American Creed," and he felt that the American Creed put certain ideals in the minds of Americans; ideals which were imperfectly fulfilled, often betrayed, by white America, but that in the longer run, this struggle for America's soul would result in an increasing fulfillment of those ideals. . . . Also, the American Creed provided means by which those who were excluded from the full benefits of American citizenship could carry out a legal and constitutional fight for their rights. It's a remarkable book.

We have held together [as a nation], more or less, except, of course, for the Civil War. We are in a stage with the end of the Cold War where ancient tribal antagonisms, ethnic rivalries, . . . which had been repressed by the Cold War, are beginning to burst out. One nation after another is being torn apart by this: In the murderous form in Yugoslavia, where we have seen what horrors religious and national rivalries can generate. Even . . . a nation as tranquil and peaceful as Canada . . . is on the verge of bust-up because of different linguistic and ethnic traditions.

All this suggests that we ought to pay more attention to what holds the nation together. We're living in a time of the breaking of nations for ethnic, tribal, religious reasons. One reason why I wanted to revise the book, *The Disuniting of America*, was we're more sensitive now to the need to find things that hold us together than we were when the book first came out. The Yugoslav experience has reminded Americans that if you press ethnic rivalries too far, if you decide that people belong irrevocably to one or another ethnic community, that may be the road to trouble, and that there is some virtue in the older idea of assimilation and integration. That is, we are, after all, Americans. The melting pot has worked unevenly; it's worked imperfectly, but it has produced the ideal of one people.

[MOST HISTORIANS are liberal] because they see the necessity of change, that change is the essence of history and, therefore, are more sympathetic to change than conservatives. If change were not the essence of history, there'd be no point writing history—if everything stayed the same.

History is a weapon. History ideally strives for objectivity above the battle and so on. But historians, like everyone else, are prisoners of their own experience and their own times, and very active. The selection of facts from the past involves an interpretation, a sense of priorities, a sense of values as to what matters. History can be a very strong weapon for people who wish to construct a certain movement in a certain direction. History, for example, has been the victim of nationalism, often, [such as] what's happening in Yugoslavia, what's happening in Ireland.

George Mitchell, who did the superb job in bringing about the peace settlement in Ireland, once said to me, "You historians are worried about the fact that young Americans don't seem to know much of their history." And I said, "Yes, and we are baffled . . . people don't know when the Civil War took place and so on." He said, "The trouble with Ireland is that they know too much of their own history and they try to reenact it." And, of course, they're filled with resentments over grievances that took place half a century ago, a century ago, 300 years ago, back to Drogheda and Cromwell. History can be a weapon in the sense of vindication of people's desire to get back at somebody else or to move in one direction or another. One sees this in the construction these days of curricula, where the feeling is that people ought . . . to become proud of their ancestors. And so you get into a kind of ethnic cheerleading, which is at the expense of realistic history.

[THE AFRICAN-AMERICAN Baseline Essays are] a series of essays which were published some years ago as part of the Afrocentric movement. These essays attempt to show that most good things in the world originated in Africa. They talk about the glories of African kingdoms and so on. They're a gross form of ethnic cheerleading. They're rejected by most thoughtful black historians, but people felt . . . that if this made young black students study harder, if it made them feel better, why not use this as a basis for changes in the curriculum? A number of cities, for a while, played around with one version or another of the Afrocentric curriculum influenced by these standard treatises.

The vogue has passed partly because of the leadership of black intellectuals who feel that this is not the way to deal with the question, partly because there's no clear relationship between academic performance and the question of self-esteem. . . . Self-esteem really comes from achievement. It's not a cause of achievement, it's a consequence of achievement. And I've never noticed that telling Greek Americans about the glory that was Greece . . . or Italian American kids about the grandeur that was Rome [improved] their academic performance.

In 1900, America was the most literate country in the world and now we're forty-fifth]. . . . The decline of the public school system has been associated with the decline of the city and particularly the decline of the inner city, where public schools are valiantly carrying on. But so often they've been deformed by violence and by pressures to lower standards. We're more and more a society that depends on the filling out of forms, so illiteracy becomes a real problem. Other countries since 1900 have also become more literate, and that's another reason why we have declined in the standing.

HATE SPEECH IS SPEECH which incites racial, religious, or ethnic antagonisms of one sort or another. And the question is whether hate speech should be suppressed. And of course, the suppression of hate speech would require an abridgment of the First Amendment of the Constitution, as interpreted by the Supreme Court. Justice Holmes once said that the First Amendment is not just license for the speech with which we agree—obviously, there was no great virtue in that—but it's license for the speech that we hate. And to suppress [hate speech] raises the whole specter of censorship, and censorship of that kind would be hostile to the purposes of the First Amendment. Hate speech is hateful, but the way to deal with it, as Justice Brandeis said, is to have more speech, not less speech.

There [has] always been censorship with regard to pornography, the allegedly obscene materials and so on, and there is some point in that, particularly when children are involved. I doubt that when James Madison wrote the Bill of Rights that he had *Hustler* in mind or some of the pornographic magazines. But so far as speech having to do with public policy or artistic expression and so on, we have to fight for the full liberty of the First Amendment.

I can understand why college administrators would like to clamp down on abusive speech. They have [an] entirely understandable concern for kids who come from minority groups who are insecure and feel themselves intimidated by complacent white, bullying students. It's a very difficult situation for college administrators. Hence, the development of speech codes. Speech codes were means of prohibiting various forms of speech as a matter of administrative convenience, one can understand why administrators go to that. But they make a mistake. There are other forms of persuasion . . . The remedy, as Brandeis said, is more speech. . . . It's more of a challenge to college presidents, to college deans, to professors, faculty members to point out to the bullies and the racists among their students what the meaning of it is and what the implications of it are. That's [going to] do much more good in the long run than speech codes, which infringe on the First Amendment.

I'm of that generation which believes very strongly in integration and assimilation. . . .

MULTICULTURALISM is a fact of life. We've always been a multicultural country from the beginning. For a long time the minority cultures were diminished and excluded. But one of the great themes of American history has been the movement from exclusion to inclusion. It's been a faltering movement. It's still incomplete, but yet it's the kind of persevering direction in which we are going. And insofar as multiculturalism means recognition of the minority achievement, it's absolutely essential we should have much more of that insofar as it means looking at things with different perspectives—the arrival of Columbus, for example, from the viewpoint of those who met him, as well as from the viewpoint of those who sent him. That's very useful, too. The problem with multiculturalism is when it rejects assimilation and integration and when it tries to establish and perpetuate and celebrate separate ethnic and racial communities. Then you are moving in the direction of Yugoslavia, or at least of Canada.

It seems to me that the desire to protect people reaches kind of ridiculous proportions. Life consists of hard knocks and developing an ability to deal with them. The notion that anything that hurts or might be considered to hurt someone's feelings should not be said is a very dangerous standard. The insensitivity standard leads, in the end, to what happened to Salman Rushdie. Salman Rushdie wrote a book which the ayatollahs of Iran regarded as blasphemous, as offensive to true, believing Muslims. So they put a price on his head, the so-called *fatwa*. It's still operative; . . . poor old Rushdie can't move anywhere without bodyguards. . . . The hurt-feelings standard cannot survive in a free society. If we had the hurt-feelings standard throughout American history, that would've silenced Mark Twain, Ambrose Bierce, Mr. Dooley, H. L. Mencken, and so many other people who've enlivened and illuminated American life.

I don't think [this book is] conservative at all. It's a very liberal book. It's just defending the First Amendment. . . . There's a fallacy that militant multiculturalism is a liberal view. It's not a liberal view. It's really a view of the new left of the 1960s. And if you remember the 1960s, the new left regarded liberals as their main enemy. They weren't worried about conservatives, but the new left and the radicals of the 1960s were very much opposed to liberals. This is a book that most liberals wholly agree with. It's the aging radicals of the 1960s and their equivalents in the 1990s who feel that to talk about one people is injustice and who want to perpetuate ethnic and religious and racial differences.

[These people are] bound to lose. The most telling statistic is the rate of intermarriage, marriage across ethnic lines, marriage across religious lines, marriage across racial lines. More Japanese Americans marry Caucasians than marry other Japanese Americans. So many Jewish Americans marry non-Jews that people are worried about the future of a Jewish community, of a Jewish identity. The black–white marriages have quadrupled over the last generation. And the attitude toward what used to be called miscegenation has been absolutely transformed. I have confidence that love, or sex, will defeat those in the end who want to disunite America.

The Problem of Illegal Immigration

by

VICTOR DAVIS HANSON

Victor Davis Hanson is concerned about the large number of illegal aliens entering the United States and the trend toward multiculturalism, especially as they affect his native state of California. In his book Mexifornia: A State of Becoming, *published by* Encounter Books *in 2003, he argued that America's immigration policy is ineffective and must be addressed. Mr. Hanson, writer and professor of classics at California State University–Fresno, visited us on* Booknotes *on September 28, 2003.*

"MEXIFORNIA" IS A term that I discovered that was used by the La Raza left that was a connotation for a new hybrid-cultured California that would be not part of Mexico and not part of the United States, so the editors that I worked with embraced that as the title for my book. A lot of people think it came from the conservative right, but actually it didn't.

"La Raza" is a very funny word. It means "the race." There's a National Council of La Raza that's an advocacy group; people, they claim, of Mexican heritage. But I'm very worried about that nomenclature because it reminds me of the connotations of "Das Volk." Anytime you have a word for "the people," but it really means the race, I think it's outside the boundaries of the American assimilationist experience.

I LIVE ON a farm in central California, and I am a fifth generation [American]. I've lived with Mexican American people. My daughter's boyfriend is a Mexican American. I have a brother married to a Mexican American, and stepnephews and -nieces. So [my book] is a literary memoir of what I grew up with. It was prompted by the idea that I thought that the world that I used to know [was one] of assimilation. . . . Second- and third-generation Mexican Americans were such wonderful citizens, [and] this new generation was not getting the same opportunities. I was worried about some of the problems looming ahead for the future of California.

It's a very strange thing that's happening. We have the corporate conservative right who wants a perennial supply of cheap labor, who is in alliance with the therapeutic left that wants an unassimilated constituency. The language that we use—protectionist or racist—precludes discussion of this issue. . . . But we have this 800-pound gorilla of illegal immigration, and it doesn't have anything to do with Mexicans or Mexico or legal immigration. It's a particular illegal immigration from Mexico that's starting a whole series of inconsistencies and we're not discussing it.

We don't know [exactly how many illegal immigrants there are]. Nationwide, I think the U.S. census suggests there are 9 million illegal aliens. I've seen figures of 15, or 19, 20 [million] that advocates on both the left and right will use. In California, I've seen [estimates of] as many as 3 to 4 million. A term that's used now is "immigrants," meaning people who were born in Mexico, and that precludes the argument over whether they're here illegally or legally. But whatever the term we use, it's a radical shift since, say, 1970, where we had 400,000, not 4 million. Most of them were here legally and we had the assimilationist pattern, where we had no bilingual education, no Chicano studies. It was based on assimilation, intermarriage, and unity of the United States. I grew up in that generation, and the people that I knew—I was one of the few non–Mexican Americans in my school district—are all smashing successes now.

I'M A HOOVER fellow at Stanford University. I'm a professor at Cal State–Fresno. . . . I've had students that have come out of these therapeutic classes in Chicano studies that will be in my class, and they'll give prerequisites for their questions on Greek history or humanities or Western civilization. They'll say, "As a Chicana, I want to say . . . , " [using] this self-nomenclature. I've sometimes said, "Do you know where that [self-identification] leads? It leads to Rwanda. It leads to the Balkans. It leads to historically really disturbing things. How would you like it if I said, 'As a professor of classics, as a white person, as an Anglo, or as a Swede?'" So, we really want to get away from that. When you do that—you try to remind students that just because their professor has suggested that's a way of expressing ethnic pride, and that historically, it has a bad, bad, bad landscape around it—it works.

I am [annoyed by some academics.] If your real purpose is to have immigrants acquire the skills that we know from past immigrant experience would make them succeed, [then] that would be mastery of the oral and written

English language, a familiarization with the brutal laws of capitalism, and intermarriage. [These are] all of the things that allow people to succeed in America. People who are the ethnic shepherds in the universities, who advocate separatism at graduation, or revisionist history of the United States, or bilingual education are not giving [their students] the skills to compete.

It's very funny. People object to the term "separate," but what we have is separate [commencements]. On a typical Saturday, everybody graduates. But the real ceremony is on the day before, where people are given their diplomas. And at Cal State–Fresno, as at many California universities, we have a separate graduation ceremony for people of Chicano ancestry, where they'll wear the colors of the Mexican flag around their neck. They'll go to a special place. The prerequisites for participation in it are not academic achievement. They're none other than your racial identification.

In universities, the impetus comes from so-called Chicano studies departments who teach ethnic studies and they have for the last twenty years established this custom [of separate graduations]. The administrators, who are often transitory—provosts, presidents, deans—know that if you were to come to a California university, you're going to be judged basically on how you change the ethnic profile of the faculty or the students. You'll be rewarded if you increased it and punished if you got into any controversy. I can't think of anything more suicidal for an administrator to say than that he came to Cal State–Fresno and said, "I think it's unhealthy that we're participating in ceremonies based on race."

If you had a group called the National Council of Das Volk and you had a European American ceremony, it would be a catastrophe. Every once in a while, I have a naive student who will write me and say, "I want to start a European American ceremony" or "I want to have a European American group." And I say, "We know where that leads to, this ethnic separatism. We've seen that in the twentieth century, and don't do that."

[As] an example, my colleague at California State University–Fresno, Bruce Thornton, wrote a book about Joaquin Murieta, who's sort of this Robin Hood bandit of the nineteenth century. We have an actual ceremony in the Central Valley [of California] where we celebrate him. The myth that's taught [about him] in the universities was that a Mexican immigrant who was the subject of racism by white ranchers and white sheriffs had to steal from the rich to give to the poor. If you actually look at what we know of Joaquin Murieta, he probably could be classified as a mass murderer. He butchered people of all races, he was a thief, and he was hunted down and punished by the legal posse. So, [that is the difference] between the myth and the reality.

I find [ethnocentric teaching] very paternalistic because the students that I know [who] are Mexican American or immigrant Mexican, once they are educated and given the tools of inquiry and rationalism, are perfectly able to come up with their own analyses and conclusions about history.

I TALK TO young freshmen who come to California State University–Fresno. They know who Sojourner Truth is, but they have no idea who William Tecumseh Sherman or Ulysses S. Grant are. I try to tell them that whether you like Grant or whether you like Sherman, their contributions to the Civil War changed history in a way that Sojourner Truth did not. It's not a question of eliminating one particular aspect of history, but [concerns] giving proper weight to the sort of process that makes things happen.

We are creating a young generation that does not know traditional political and military facts, events, persons' names, and instead is interested in other [things], where the criteria is often race or neglect of the past. Sometimes it's valuable, as long as you realize what its simple core is.

This is my objection to this separatism between multiracialism and multiculturalism: Multiracialism is an American ideal that race is irrelevant because we all have this core adherence to democracy, capitalism, consensual government, and transparent society and we enrich it with food from the Philippines, music from Mexico, and fashion from Africa. But that's very different than multiculturalism, where groups come from different places, but then we in the elite say, "We are not going to privilege your culture versus your culture, versus your government, versus your judiciary, versus your attitude toward women." If we were to do that, there would be no reason that they came.

What I am saying, and why I am optimistic, is that race is just an abstract concept now in California. I have a neighbor whose daughter is half Japanese, half so-called white. She married a Mexican American fellow. I don't know what you'd call their grandchildren. You have a culture whose heroes are the Williams sisters, Tiger Woods, Penelope Cruz, Jennifer Lopez, and people are intermarrying, as I see at Cal State. The only problem is that one particular country [Mexico] is exporting human capital at the rate of hundreds of thousands a year, and it's taxing our ability to assimilate them. With the force-multiplying effect of multiculturalism, we've lost confidence in the powers of assimilation.

My point is to convey to the Mexican immigrant community that we ourselves are schizophrenic about [our attitudes]. For example, I talked to a farmer who employs illegal aliens and says, "Well, nobody will work, and these people are the hardest-working people in the world," which they are. Then he says, "But, I don't want to go to this restaurant in Salma with my family because everybody [who goes there] takes their clothes off. They stand out in their boxer shorts when they put their clothes in the washing machine. They sit there. And this is not civilized."

And I suggest to him, "Well, if you pay them cash and they're not legal citizens and they don't have the capital, then what do you expect them to do?" So we've also created in California this aristocratic lifestyle for upper-middle-class Californians that would be not possible elsewhere, where we have literally millions of Californians whose lawns are cut by people who are here illegally from Mexico, whose children are watched, whose houses are cleaned [by Mexican illegals].

But the problem is that these people don't just fly to Mars; . . . given the wages that they get . . . they can't participate in the civic life of California. Then we have to do something to give them the advantages that we do, and that means entitlements. We have a $38 billion deficit right now on an annual basis, and we're starting to see the wages of [our policies].

There's a cycle that's very disturbing that we don't want to talk about. Somebody comes at age eighteen from Mexico, say from Oaxaca, a very young, robust male, who's happy. We give him $10 an hour to pour concrete. He says, "This is ten times more than I make in Mexico." Everybody's happy. But then, suddenly, we're surprised when he would want to marry, have three children. He gets on his knees for ten years. A knee goes out. A back goes out. An elbow goes out, and then what happens? These are no longer rite-of-passage jobs. Our children don't do them anymore. They're not considered a stepping stone while you learn English and gain education, but they become a perpetual job.

When you're fifty and you're hurt and you have a family, then your children, who have never been to Mexico, don't feel that America was such a great deal. They have no method of comparison, but they do see that their parents work for somebody far more affluent, and [then] you get a range of bitterness. We have problems with graduation rates in high school. Four out of ten children of Mexican immigrants are not graduating.

The employer then looks at this phenomenon and says, "Well, don't bring somebody out who has a tattoo. Don't bring somebody out to the crew who speaks English. I want somebody from Oaxaca who's a hard worker. So we just cycle people as if they're commodities. It's really amoral, and we don't want to discuss it—left or right.

Even more disturbing is that 62 percent of the people in California who were born in Mexico are classified under the poverty level. And after twenty years, [there has not been] very much statistical difference. Twenty years of being here in America, doing unskilled labor, doesn't get you out of poverty. How could it, when it's unskilled labor and you don't have a redress of grievances? All the old mechanisms where we increase the power of the unskilled through unionization or legality are not there to help.

[TO GET TO the United States, an illegal Mexican immigrant] hires a "coyote" for $1,500 or $2,000. A coyote is a professional smuggler. Often it's quite dangerous, but he'll get across [the border]. He usually doesn't go live near the border, the jobs really aren't there. He'll go up to central California, find construction, which is booming, or agriculture, hotels, restaurants. He'll find other people in a similar circumstance. They'll rent an apartment, five or six together. They will pay cash for everything because they're often outside of the banking system. They don't have legal status, so they're often robbed. They're beaten up by people. They can't report these crimes because they're afraid of endangering their status.

But then, suddenly, after ten, fifteen years, they marry, they have children. They don't know about their legal status. They can't get a passport, can't get a driver's license. They don't make any more money than they did. Then we start to have the natural human reactions of bitterness, anger, and frustration. That lends them susceptible to an ethnic romance that says that racism caused all their problems and explains why Mexican immigrants from Mexico have not achieved the same level of parity as, say, Punjabis or Koreans or Chinese.

Most police departments—if they arrest somebody for speeding and he is an illegal alien, or if somebody goes into the hospital with a broken leg and she's an illegal alien—they will not call [the Immigration and Naturalization Service]. If they did call on INS, they probably wouldn't deport them. Because rather than confront the problem in the old American way of saying, "Look, this is a problem. We're going to have measured immigration. We're going to have it legal. We're going to have assimilation," we've just grown used to the advantages that accrue to everybody involved. The Mexican government gets $10 billion in remittances from its expatriate population. It loses hundreds of thousands of potential dissidents that might march on Mexico City for redress of grievances. It creates an expatriate community that romanticizes Mexico the longer and further it's away from it. The employer wants a perennial, perpetual supply of cheap labor that competes against poor, unskilled citizens and makes them not so competitive, and they can't unionize. The La Raza industry wants an unassimilated constituency.

And so we've sort of grown up with this. And the way we react to that is, "Well, we can't address the real problem because too many people benefit from it, so let's do something entirely new in American history. Let's give tuition discounts for somebody who's here illegally from Mexico, so that they will actually pay less tuition than a citizen from Nevada or Arizona in a California university. Or let's issue driver's licenses and not require them to have birth certificates, which we do of citizens." It's starting to be almost Orwellian in the society that's emerging.

WE SAY THAT legal immigration is always wonderful, but when you have illegal immigration and you have people here for years who don't know the English language, then how do you accommodate those residents within your system? It means you have to have bilingual translators. But we often forget in our emphasis on bilingual education, we assume that people who come from Mexico can read Spanish or even speak Spanish. In some cases, they don't speak Spanish well. They speak a native dialect that not a lot of people who are second-, third-generation Hispanics know.

When you have people come from Mexico and they are surrounded by people of all different races, in numbers that are greater, then you have the old process of osmosis. If you insist on English, then we have the paradigm that works so well. But when you have one person who is a native and four people who are here illegally, then you don't have the same cross-fertilization.

WE HAVE FAILED to inculcate [on] people who come from Mexico that the United States is unique, our Constitution is unique. It's part of a Western tradition of secularism, rationalism, consensual government, open markets, respect for the law, civic audit, and an independent judiciary. When you add all of those factors together, it explains why a wealthy country like the United States is prosperous and can attract people. Whereas in the case of Mexico, you go across the border to Mexico, and they have wonderful farmland, they have oil, they have natural gas, they have a good climate. But the paradigm is not similar, and therefore, Mexico cannot feed and clothe and house its 100 million people to the same degree that we can in the United States. People recognize that at a very gut level, and they vote with their feet to come north.

That being said, it seems to me that we who are an elite, who are educated and understand that process—not only in the concrete, but in the abstract—have a special duty to tell the immigrant, to articulate why they came across. "You came across, and this is why, and this is what we are going to do to make sure you are a success." Whereas if we do the opposite, if we say that "our culture is no different than yours," or "this was really your homeland," or "you really don't need legal status," or "English is no better, no worse than Spanish," or any of these issues that we often communicate, then we are failing our responsibility, and it's a moral responsibility. The result is we will create a Rwanda or a Balkan society, an apartheid community, which we have done in central California in some cases.

[REACTION TO the book has been] mixed. As I say to my wife, I don't want to get any more letters from what I call the far right, who attack the book because it argues for popular culture, intermarriage, assimilation and creating a multiracial society under one culture. They've been very critical. And then, I've also had the extreme left, in media, government, and especially academic life, where this is the third rail you don't talk about. But most people outside those extremes, 80 percent of the respondents, average people on talk shows or interviews, are very favorable and appreciate that somebody's talking about [immigration and race] in a way that doesn't just pander to a particular political point of view. We have an 800-pound gorilla in the living room that nobody wants to talk about, so I hope that the book will encourage discussion of this issue. . . . I was a little surprised at some of the invective, but that's part of the business of being an author. You have to get in the arena. You can't write a book without expecting criticism.

The Failure of the Welfare System

by

MARVIN OLASKY

Marvin Olasky's theories about welfare helped President George W. Bush develop his agenda of "compassionate conservatism." Dr. Olasky, a University of Texas journalism professor and columnist, argues that Americans were more successful at fighting poverty in the nineteenth century when the task was performed by community-based religious groups rather than the large government bureaucracies created by the Democrats' New Deal and Great Society programs. Dr. Olasky joined us on January 22, 1995, to discuss his book The Tragedy of American Compassion, *published by Regnery that same year.*

MY BOOK IS a history book. It's a book that describes how Americans successfully fought poverty before the government became involved big-time in poverty fighting during the 1930s and then further in the 1960s. It's pretty much an unknown history because the assumption of lots of historians has been that there really wasn't a whole lot in the way of poverty fighting until government did become involved. I spent a year . . . hanging in the Library of Congress, rummaging through the stacks, finding all these old reports and documents and memoirs and reporters' descriptions about these poverty programs in the nineteenth century that actually were a lot more effective than many of the programs we have today.

For homeless guys, they had lots of shelters [in the nineteenth century], but they were shelters that actually treated folks as human beings—not just as animals to whom you would throw a scrap of food. When a guy came to a homeless shelter, yes, they would give him lodging and food, but they would hand him an ax and say, "There's a woodpile next to our shelter. Why don't you chop some wood?" He could chop some wood for an hour, and in doing that, he would be providing for himself; he would also be providing for others who weren't able-bodied. The ax was given to people who were capable of doing it; there were other people who were physically incapable. What they were doing was telling the guy, "Hey, you are not just a taker. You also, despite what appears to be your lowly condition in life right now, can give. You can help someone else and the reason you can help someone else is because you're created in the image of God. You're not just an animal, you're not just someone to think of in material terms. You have a spiritual sense, and we're going to honor that and we're going to treat you as a human being, and that means helping others as well as being helped."

Today, this is done very rarely. At least from my brief experience at looking at homeless programs now, and from what I've heard from others, for the most part, homeless people are just there to take. I spent most of the year in Washington on leave for this book in the Library of Congress, but I did spend a couple of days on the streets dressed as a homeless person. I went around to about a dozen places during that time and was offered lots of things. There was food, there was shelter, there was medicine, clothing, but I was never actually asked to do anything. Even when eating a meal, if you go to McDonald's, you're supposed to—or at least this is the custom—to bus your own tray and take that away. Not there. There were nice young ladies bringing food to me and coming back and asking me if I wanted seconds, and then the custom was you just walk away, not asked to do anything at all.

I WENT [to live on the streets in March 1990] with a fellow who has been a professor at the Middle Tennessee State University named Dan McMurry. Dan actually has done this in a whole lot of cities. His particular specialty was urban sociology, and . . . he explained to me some of the tricks of the trade—things like putting some tape on my glasses and wearing a stocking cap, and he showed me the particular type of homeless shuffle to use and so forth.

I started out in Washington [at the] Center for Creative Non-Violence, which had the reputation as the largest homeless shelter in the world, 1,300 beds there, or so they claimed. Then I just went by word of mouth. Homeless people are not reading instructions for the most part—you ask a person, "Hey, where can I get lunch?" People would say, "Well, go up here." And I'd go over there and then go to other places, depending on whatever instructions I got. I found it interesting that they didn't ask any questions. I decided out of a certain sense of humor to identify myself as M, so if they have records there, they should have a record of Mr. M. You don't have to sign in. They just ask, "What's your name?" I said, "M," and they didn't ask about that. You see, back 100 years ago, they would immediately ask, "Where are you from?"—family, and work background, insurance, and stuff like that. They didn't ask about that. They just were quite ready to pass out medicine and so forth, whatever I needed.

I was curious. I went into their health clinic, because occasionally from spending too many hours at the computer I have some back problems. So I told them my back hurt, which indeed it did, and they immediately gave me some pills, which are actually fairly expensive pills which I've taken at other times for back pain. The doctor recommended that I do some swimming, and he said, "Here's where you can go swimming." I said, "Well, I don't have a bathing suit." And they said, "Oh, well, come at this time. We'll give you a bathing suit." A lot of stuff to give away right there.

I didn't spend the night there. I went on to other places . . . and just kept roaming around with Dan. There were lots of people who were just sitting around in the front [of the CCNV shelter]. One thing I found interesting is that all these guys, apparently able-bodied, were just sitting around, and there was a really trash-strewn lot right next door. It seemed to me simple enough to tell people just at the start, "Well, let's clean up this yard." But none of that was done.

At the Gospel Mission, if I'd gone over there, they had [Bibles], but no one directed me there. The places I was directed to, [there were] no Bibles. I spent one morning eating in the basement of a liberal church downtown and I figured, "They're going to have a Bible here to give me if I ask for it." There was a nice young lady who kept offering me food, pretty good food, for breakfast. It seemed to be a place that was a real neighborhood-friendly place where you can go all the time, although no one knows your name. There was a guy sitting across from me who had a beeper. He seemed to be a drug dealer, and it was a good place to go for a good free breakfast. After about the fourth time when she came back and asked if I wanted anything, I said in my homeless mumble, "Can I have a Bible?" She couldn't quite understand what I was saying, and so she asked, "Well, do you want a bag? Do you want a bagel?" She had both of those, but when I said, "No, I want a Bible," she said, "I'm sorry. We don't have any Bibles." That was an indication to me of what the priorities are at these places.

One hundred years ago, and still at some places like the Gospel Mission today, it was very different. They would treat people as human beings. They would say, "Here's a Bible, and we'd like to get you involved in Bible studies, and we'd like to provide some sort of work for you to see if you're able to do that and willing to do that. And, we have a whole bunch of anti-drug programs that are all based on this idea that you are more than just a material creature, to satisfy any immediate urges you have. You have a purpose in life because you're created by a holy and loving God."

YOU GET INTO questions [about effective programs for the homeless]: Is that really helping? These are the questions people asked a century ago. They're good questions to ask today: Am I helping? Am I helping a person to get out of the situation or am I just an enabler? Am I just working to sustain this person in the situation? . . . A lot of homeless guys are alcohol or drug addicts, and the thing about an addict is that any spare money you have, you're going to use to feed your addiction. So when you're providing free housing for folks, that's great. That's an advantage. You can just go and panhandle and feed your addiction or get money in whatever way you can, but you have the basic requisites of housing and food and so forth all provided for you. It's not a helpful situation.

In shelters I've met folks—one fellow used to work at the *Washington Post*. He showed me his clips and I checked into this, and he was a good writer when he was not doing crack. We often have the view that these guys are all stumblebums and pretty low on the bell curve and some are, but some aren't. There are a whole lot of personal reasons why people get into that situation, and as long as they are enabled to stay in it, some people will.

Today we have essentially a one-size-fits-all welfare system. If you're in a particular material situation, then you're entitled to get this benefit and that benefit. They didn't think in those terms [in the nineteenth century]. They thought in terms of values and individuals and different lifestyles the people had. They weren't afraid to categorize people: Here are people who will use resources well, here are people who won't; some people need a pat on the back, other people need a push.

Today we tend to think that the important thing is to give. It doesn't matter how you give, but giving is the important thing. It is, in a sense, a giver-centric view of the world, that whatever warm, fuzzy feeling you get from it, that's the central thing. [In the nineteenth century, they] didn't think in those terms. They wanted to be effective, so they emphasized discernment on the part of volunteers: Don't just give; give wisely, give in a way that will help and not hurt.

Work was real important. This started from the homeless shelters and the woodpiles next door. But other people came and they thought, "This is something that people are capable of doing." A lot of people may have gotten out of the habit of working. They may be drifting around, but it's real important to get people back into that habit as soon as possible.

Today we're often very worried about someone on the bottom rung of the ladder. How low is that rung? As a result, we tend to chop off those bottom rungs. Well, that sometimes leaves people without those entry-level jobs and without that opportunity to actually go and serve. My grandfather on my mother's side of the family . . . after he came to America, went around with a horse and wagon and picked up used mattresses and restuffed them. I don't think he'd be able to do that today. Today we have "Do not remove this tag under penalty of law." I don't know exactly how hygienic it all was, but it worked, and he got mattresses that people could afford, and he was able to work his way out of poverty.

[GOD] IS CRUCIAL and, from all I've seen now, the anti-poverty programs that work have a religious base. That's a grand generalization—certainly true historically—and my sense is that it's true now. Without it, people just don't change. Even today, the programs I've seen that are effective are ones that have this theocentrism and work on people's self-image—not by saying, "Hey, whatever you do, you're cool. We love you," but by saying, "You're pretty good because you are made in the image of a God who's wonderful, and therefore you have merit also." I've seen this all over the place.

In San Jose [there was a] group called CityTeam Ministries, which had a very effective anti-drug program. They had a success rate measured by whether a person stayed off drugs or alcohol a year after the program concluded. They had a success rate of about 75 percent, which is terrific, because most success rates for anti-drug, anti-alcohol programs are down in the single digits. The county people went to the people at CityTeam and said, "We can see that your program works, and we would like to give you a few barrels full of bucks in order to expand your program. Ours isn't working. Yours is working. Why don't you expand? We just want people off drugs and we'll be happy to do this. There's only one condition: You have to give up having worship services for these folks." The CityTeam people, to their credit, said, "Boy, we would love to expand. We just can't do it. This—our belief in God and sharing that belief with the people who come here—is the engine that drives our ship. You take away the engine, the ship won't go."

THERE WERE A lot of very well-intentioned people involved in [Lyndon Johnson's anti-welfare program, the] Great Society, but the whole process has been disastrous. I think there are three reasons why the war on poverty failed: It was a war on poverty, but it was also a war on shame. What really kept the welfare system, the star of the New Deal, from getting out of hand then was that there was a sense of shame involved in taking welfare unless you absolutely had to. People wanted to work, people wanted to be independent. . . . That was all lost in the 1960s. There was a sense of entitlement and that, in fact, if you could get welfare and if you didn't, that you were a chump.

That was a shame and really has hurt the whole process. There was a war on family because . . . prior to the 1960s, there was a sense that family was essential and that every child should grow up in a two-parent family. That all changed in the 1960s with the growth of feminism. . . . Since then, a lot of children [are] being born out of wedlock. Now we have about a third of children in the country being born to unmarried women. This is very tragic for those kids. The chief cause of poverty right now in the United States is not structural unemployment or anything like that. It's single-parent families with the moms in a very desperate situation of trying to both take care of kids and somehow make a living. That's very hard. But that's one of the results of the 1960s, the war on family.

The third thing that happened in the 1960s [was] a war on God. Up until then, even when you had governmental programs, starting in the 1930s, they tried to do things pretty much in the classic sense from the late nineteenth century. They tried to have those same emphases on work and family and God, even though it was a government program. In the 1960s, that all changed. By judicial fiat, essentially, God was excluded from governmental programs. As a result, if the only money you can pour into programs is money into programs where God is excluded, and if historically the programs that are the most successful are the ones in which God has a central place, then I think logically you are almost condemning yourself to failure. That's what's happened, and that's why the war on poverty hasn't worked.

The other side might argue that the reason the [Great Society] programs failed is that we didn't spend enough money, that they should have been even bigger. That would be one thing. Other people might say that they did not entirely fail, that a lot more people would be in poverty if it weren't for those programs. But I've walked around, for example, the Summerville area of Atlanta . . . with people in the community who point out to me various edifices of the Great Society, and they always refer to those edifices as the enemy. These were things designed to help people, but they were these big structures. They didn't do anything to actually help people in terms of their own families or fixing up their own homes and so forth. There were these big projects that could be labeled Great Society projects—"We're here to help you"—but it's been disastrous.

America at War

The American Revolution

by

GORDON S. WOOD

The first shots in the American Revolution were fired on the morning of April 19, 1775, in Lexington, Massachusetts. Fifteen months later, Congress issued the Declaration of Independence, but the war lasted until 1783, when Britain finally recognized its former colonies as an independent nation. Pulitzer Prize–winning author and Brown University history professor Gordon S. Wood examined the causes, character, and consequences of the War of Independence in his book The American Revolution: A History, *published by Modern Library in 2002. Professor Wood appeared on* Booknotes *on April 21, 2002.*

MOST HISTORIANS would say [the American Revolution started in] 1763, with the Peace of Paris, [which] created problems for the British empire that forced them to take steps to reform the empire. These efforts to reform became the trigger for the Revolution, which went beyond an imperial revolution to an imperial breakdown. Our revolution was not simply a colonial rebellion. It started that way, but by 1776, it had really become a world historical event, with larger implications.

In 1760, [the population of the colonies was] probably almost 2 million, 2 million by 1770. So it was still relatively small, compared to the 8 or 9 million of England. We were about a fifth of that, but we were growing much faster than Britain itself. So there was this prospect, as Benjamin Franklin saw it, that sooner or later, we were going to pass them. The demographic trajectory of the two parts of the imperial empire was that the Americans were going to outstrip the British. And sooner or later, he felt, the capital would have to be moved to America.

[KING GEORGE III became the monarch in Great Britain] in 1760. His father had died, so he inherited the throne from his grandfather, George II. He was a relatively young man, about twenty, and rather immature, but full of all kinds of visions of what the empire could be. He was naive, I guess we'd have to say, as a monarch. He wanted to rule in his own right. His grandfather and great-grandfather had been German-born and really didn't know England. He was the first Hanoverian coming from the House of Hanover, who was English-trained, English-born, and thoroughly Anglicized, with lots of ambition to be a real king.

Unfortunately, the modern British party government with the crown being a figurehead and really dictated to by a majority leader of the House of Commons hadn't yet evolved. That would take another half century. At the same time, George didn't quite understand the convention that his ministers really had to get the agreement of Parliament. So he appointed whomever he wanted as ministers. They were his ministers, after all, His Majesty's ministers. *minions*

He ran into a lot of trouble because these ministers didn't have the support—at least, at first—of the House of Commons. So one ministry after another would fall. He went through several ministries in the 1760s, until he got to Lord North, who did command a majority in the House of Commons.

It was one of these things where he simply couldn't grasp—who could blame him?—the future, that he had to somehow have the support of the House of Commons for his ministers. He simply hadn't fully understood the future. Historians who've criticized him for this, of course, have missed the point. He had every right to appoint whomever he wanted.

And of course, that's still true today. Technically speaking, Tony Blair is Her Majesty's minister. But she just appoints the person who has the majority support in the House of Commons. She doesn't have, presumably, any choice in the matter, at least politically. Constitutionally, she can appoint whomever she wanted, but it would be a constitutional crisis if she did so.

[THE BRITISH EMPIRE in 1760] was a huge empire, and the richest empire since the fall of Rome. It encompassed, in 1763, the Mississippi to India. It was an extraordinary phenomenon. It was the greatest phenomenon of the eighteenth century, the growth of this little island in the northwest of the European continent becoming a major world power. People were stunned and surprised by this. How could this little island do what it had done?

It was the empire that everyone attributed to Britain's success. So everyone thought the loss of the empire, or the North American part of it, at least, would diminish England. Of course, it didn't happen that way. Britain went on to have its greatest days in the nineteenth century, but everyone predicted that the loss of the North American colonies would be the end of Britain, which is why they stuck so long—eight years—in this long struggle to hold onto their American colonies.

SEVENTEEN-SEVENTY-FOUR was the first Continental Congress. [There was] a Stamp Act Congress earlier, in 1765, but the first Continental Congress met in 1774 in Philadelphia.

[We were] still colonies, and we were still under the king, and there was still a good deal of respect for the king, and there were still lots of people who were loyal.

Virginia was by far the biggest colony. We forget that now. We have to understand why four of the first five presidents were Virginians. It's because Virginia really was the United States. It made up a fifth of the population of the country and just took for granted that it was the leader. Although Massachusetts was certainly the leader in the radical movement, and that's where the Revolution really began. But without Virginia's support, the Revolution would never have been brought off because, as I say, a fifth of the population of the country was in the state of Virginia. And once the Virginians came on board—and they rivaled Massachusetts in their leadership—then the country was destined to break from Britain.

THERE WAS, [by the time of the Declaration of Independence], a good deal of resentment toward King George III. The reason they focused on the king was because that was the only tie left in their understanding of the empire. They had been forced to cut loose from Parliament earlier because the English said, "You're either under Parliament's authority or you're not under it." Given that choice, they said, "Well, we're not under it."

They had worked out by 1774 a notion that the empire was a kind of modern commonwealth. They were tied only to the king. So the king was the last tie, and that tie had to be broken. There was resentment of the king, at this point, because he had declared them outlaws. He or his ministers had made these Crown decisions to cut American trade, to regard the Americans as being beyond the pale of law. And so there was a certain amount of personal resentment.

THOMAS PAINE, writing in January of 1776, was the first major cry for independence. That focused people's attention because he referred to George III as "the royal brute" and wrote, "For God's sake, let's break from this royal brute." That was really seditious talk, and somehow it was left to him to make it, the first statement, even though he was a recent immigrant.

In the colonies, you had a good deal of what we might call, relatively speaking, for the eighteenth century, free press; and the press was very important during the Revolution. But a truly modern free press was a much later development. In some cases, not until the 1960s, with the *New York Times v. Sullivan* decision, did you get the kind of freedom that we now take for granted in the press.

GEORGE WASHINGTON was the crucial figure [of the Revolution]. People have called him the indispensable figure. I normally don't believe that any individual is indispensable, but in this case, Washington, as a leader, took seriously these responsibilities of virtue, of maintaining himself as disinterested, above interest. And he bought into the ideology of the Revolution and was sincere about it.

He could have become king, or he could have been a dictator. He refused all of these blandishments, all of these temptations. Every military leader we can think of, going back to Caesar through Cromwell, through Marlborough, through Napoleon, always expected political rewards commensurate with their military achievements. Not Washington. He had to be prodded into coming to the Constitutional Convention, and then to be president. He didn't want to be president.

He was reluctant, always reluctant, to assume civil power. That reluctance gave him his power. That reluctance to take power made him trusted. He's an extraordinary man, and we were just lucky.

I BECAME fascinated with James Madison because of his intellectual abilities. I've gotten less enthralled by him as time has gone on, but at the time, back in the early 1960s, I thought he was the most remarkable politician in American history because he was a thinker as well as a political figure.

He was actually much more ideological than I had thought and not quite as wide-ranging and as intellectually creative as I had originally thought. But he was still quite a remarkable man.

He was totally caught up in an ideology that you might call republican. His notion of an alternative to war, which is quite appropriate today, was commercial sanctions, and the embargo, which is usually identified with Jefferson, but it's really Madison's [idea]. He promoted using commercial retaliation as an alternative to using troops, which we would call economic sanctions. He was very much a proponent of that and very much caught up in it, which led to his peculiar behavior during the War of 1812 as president.

WE MAY HAVE had as many as 100,000 to 200,000 people [fighting against the British] at one time or another, which is a huge proportion of a population running 2 to 3 million people. The Revolution certainly had the largest death total. About 25,000 men were killed, which was the highest proportion of deaths of any war, except, of course, for the Civil War, in our history.

A lot of people were touched by the war. It was eight years long, the longest war in our history until Vietnam. Most families were touched in one way or another by the war, and it was the great cause that gave them a sense of unity, that helped to make the United States meaningful as a single nation for people, that eight years of experience.

THERE IS, of course, and has been over the last maybe thirty years, a good deal of criticism of [our past]. It's self-criticism. I don't think that's wrong. Any healthy democracy has to have a certain amount of self-criticism, and that often takes the form, for historians, of writing critically about the past. There can be excesses in that, and people who say that the American Revolution was a failure are making a mistake.

There are a lot of academics over the last thirty years who have emphasized that we didn't do enough [in the American Revolution]. We didn't, for example, free slaves. We didn't change the lot of women. Those are current issues. There is always a tendency in history to look at the past through the lenses of the present. We lament the fact that slavery was not abolished and that the lot of women did not change substantially and that the lot of Indians was worsened by the Revolution. Those facts are true, but it's anachronistic to apply twenty-first-century standards to an eighteenth-century world.

I don't think there's anybody writing today who thinks that [the American Revolution] was a terrible mistake. I do think that there are lots of historians who feel that we didn't do enough for these oppressed people, particularly black slaves and women. My answer to that is, of course, that the Revolution did really substantially change the climate in which slavery had existed.

For thousands of years, slavery had existed in the Western world without substantial criticism, and the Revolution marked a major turning point. It suddenly put slavery on the defensive. And that's the point that needs to be emphasized, not that Jefferson didn't free his slaves, but that as a man raised as a slaveholder, in a world that was dominated by slavery, he criticized it. That is what's new. That's the point that needs to be made. Where did that come from? Why did this generation suddenly become critics of slavery and put it on the defensive? That is an important point.

[During the period of 1760 through the Revolutionary War], most blacks were held as slaves—there were about a half a million. Most slaves were held by Southern planters, but every white colonist in one way, directly or indirectly, benefited from this institution of slavery.

There were probably less than 100,000 [black slaves in the north]. . . . In New York, about 14 percent of the population of New York was enslaved. Seven percent in my own state of Rhode Island. There were fewer slaves in the New England states and in the other Northern states, but slavery was still a national institution prior to the Revolution.

In the North, slavery succumbed to pressures—moral pressures that eliminated it everywhere in the North by 1804, at least on the record books. Now, slaves continued to exist in New York because they were grandfathered in, and so on.

None of the Revolutionary leaders ever condoned slavery, even though they were slaveholders, like Patrick Henry. He said, "I cannot justify the institution. I know it violates everything this Revolution is about. But I can't do without them." And Jefferson, too; he was a slaveholder through his whole life but never justified it. He always knew that there was something wrong with it.

There were many who did not have slaves who were critics, but there were also many critics among the slaveholders themselves. Actually, there were more anti-slave societies in the South, in the immediate aftermath of the Revolution, than in the North. So in the South, everyone thought the institution would die. It was an illusion, but they thought it would die. They thought that the ending of the slave trade, which was built into the Constitution, [meant that] Congress could act on the slave trade. Everyone assumed that once the slave trade was killed that the institution would die away. Well, they were wrong.

[Regarding women:] It was a patriarchal world. It always had been. What has to be said is that changes were afoot, in the air. Women didn't gain the right to vote until much later, but there is a direct line from the Revolution to Seneca Falls of 1848, the first women's convention. The first essays appearing in the newspapers claiming the equality of women came out of the Revolution. But women's lots, by today's standards, were just very dependent. They were considered to be like children in the household. Their husbands controlled their property, controlled their lives. They were regarded as little more than children legally. Now, of course, in actual fact, lots of women had lots of influence because of their personalities, and so on. But still, legally, they were like children when they married their husbands.

THE FOUNDING FATHERS wouldn't be that surprised [by the diversity in our government today]. Someone like Benjamin Rush, for example, really believed in the natural equality of people, that if you could educate people, there was no reason why anyone couldn't become a leader.

They couldn't have predicted everything, of course, but they would be really quite pleased to know that the United States had become a great nation. That was their dearest dream. They couldn't imagine the Civil War. They knew there was a possibility of a sectional problem over slavery.

But they wouldn't be totally surprised by what's happened. They would have said, "My God, this is a magnificent nation that's been created from these very tiny beginnings." I don't think that the fact that there are black representatives and women would have been beyond their imaginations. They actually did imagine a world where people could learn.

THE THING ABOUT the American Revolution is that it created the ideology that holds us together. Without that revolution, we would be like Argentina, a nation without any kind of adhesive. We have an intellectual, and ideological, adhesive that makes us one people, insofar as anything can, because we're so diverse.

We have this marvelous country which is held together by a set of beliefs that came out of the Revolution. It keeps us together. You don't have to be someone; you don't have to have a certain ancestor. You can learn to be an American by coming to believe in these things—liberty, equality, constitutionalism, and so on. You don't have to come from a certain race or ethnicity. That's not true of most of the world. . . . It's our history. Particularly the Revolution, but our whole history is what really holds us together. If people can come to believe in that history or in the ideals that come out of that history, then that's enough of an adhesive.

The End of the Civil War

by

JAY WINIK

In April 1865, the Civil War came to a dramatic close. These four weeks saw the fall of the Confederate capital at Richmond, General Robert E. Lee's surrender to General Ulysses S. Grant at Appomattox, the assassination of President Abraham Lincoln, and finally, the beginning of the country's reunification. In April 1865: The Month That Saved America, *published in 2001 by HarperCollins, Jay Winik reexamined the end of America's Civil War. Mr. Winik, a senior scholar at the University of Maryland's Center for International Security Studies, appeared on* Booknotes *on June 29, 2001.*

How wars end is every bit as important as why they start or how they're fought. Put differently, far too many civil wars throughout history end quite badly. Think of Northern Ireland. It's gone on for some 200 years. Think of Lebanon, Rwanda, Cambodia. Think of the horrors of the Middle East or the Balkans today. Our civil war could have ended just as badly, with the same terrible, tragic consequences, but didn't. Why? That's a question I wanted to answer and which I do answer in my book, *April 1865*.

In *April 1865* . . . I strip away the inevitability of events, so that rather than seeing the Civil War with the comfort of 136 years or 140 years of hindsight, you see the events as they take place; you see the decisions as they saw them; you see the turning points as they saw them; and you see how events could have just as easily gone one way or gone another way. It's that kind of richness of history that I wanted to bring alive.

ROBERT E. LEE was the moral conscience of the South, as General Wise, one of his top men, once said to him—and Wise was also a former governor of Virginia. Near the end of the war, they were talking about what would happen next. Wise had ridden through the lines. He dismounted his horse, and he had actually fallen in Virginia quicksand, and he was caked with red mud, and he looked ridiculous.

They joked a bit, but then they talked about the end of the war. Lee raised the dreaded concept of surrender, and he said, "What will the country think?" And Wise looked over at Lee, and he said, "Country? My God, man, you *are* the country to these men." So, in other words, Lee was the country to the Southerners. Whether or not he would decide to deal with the Northerners with honor and dignity and to become good citizens again, or with rage and continued civil war and civil violence, he would be the determinant of that.

CITY POINT IS in Virginia, and it's where Ulysses S. Grant, the commanding general of the Union armies, had his floating fortress. City Point was, in effect, an armed command post for the Northern Army as they were encircling Lee's army in Petersburg and in Richmond. They met on March 24th where Lincoln actually wanted to see the front lines and confer with his commanding generals.

It was from City Point that Lincoln, in that same meeting, spoke about his fears of guerrilla warfare and his fear that there would be a final bloody Armageddon; he did something quite unique. Abraham Lincoln said, "When this war is over, there must be no hangings, there must be no bloody work." What was looming large in his mind was the specter of the French Revolution, because it loomed large in the minds of all Americans. In the French Revolution, the revolutionaries started out with the best of intentions, and before everybody knew it, they were guillotining the opposition, and they were guillotining each other. Before everybody knew it, [violence] engulfed all of a continent.

In effect, what Lincoln said was, "There must be no French Revolution here." It was prescient, and it was visionary and it was one of Lincoln's finest acts and finest moments. And Grant would carry it out brilliantly at Appomattox during the surrender, where rather than treating Lee like a defeated, dishonored foe, he treated him with great dignity and grace. It was one of the most poignant scenes in our history. *remember the pageantry*

Just think about it, the morning that Lee had made this fateful decision that he's going to surrender. At that point, he straightened himself up, and he said, "Now I must go meet General Grant, and I would rather die a thousand deaths than do that." History has, more often than not, telescoped and simplified what happened. They have simplified it by describing it as Lee's vain, quixotic retreat. They've said then there's the dignity of Appomattox, end of war, end of story.

In truth, it's far richer. Let's ask the first question: How would Lee be treated when he went to meet U. S. Grant? He didn't know. What we do know is that Lee, that morning, was actually quite nervous, uncharacteristically so. He was speaking in mumbled half-sentences. And he should have been nervous because, throughout history, as he knew all too well, defeated generals and revolutionaries and traitors were typically beheaded, or they were hung, or they were imprisoned or, like General Napoleon, they were exiled.

In fact, that very morning, the *Chicago Tribune* editorialized: "Hang Lee." And just days earlier, in the Union capital of Washington, D.C., Andrew Johnson, the vice president of the Union, went out with several senators and before a thronging crowd of hundreds, maybe over 1,000, gave a rousing speech in which he said, "We must hang Davis, we must hang Lee. We must hang them twenty times." So, in fact, Lee didn't know what to expect. Grant would treat him with such tenderness and dignity, and it's such a rich scene. Grant was carrying out Lincoln's vision at City Point of no bloody work, no hangings. But it is really unique in the chain of history.

Interestingly enough, when they first walked into Appomattox Court House, Lee was wearing his finest uniform because, as he said, "Now I must become General Grant's prisoner," and Grant, who kept him waiting for thirty minutes, came in in a mud-spattered private's blouse. In fact, later on in history, he would apologize for how he was attired.

Picture this scene for a second: this small, little home, Wilmer McLean's house, in Appomattox Court House, this little village of about eight structures or so, and rolling hills. Outside in those rolling hills were thousands of men, who were standing at rapt attention to watch this amazing piece of historical theater take place. In fact, when the surrender was over—I'm going to digress for a second—everything would be ripped apart from the Wilmer McLean house: the desk, the pens, the floorboards, the wallpaper. Even a tree that Lee himself leaned against that morning would be ripped apart so there was nothing, except for a hole there, because everybody knew that day that history was taking place, and they wanted a piece of it.

But inside this small, little home, Grant came in and rather than talk about the surrender, they talked about the old days. . . . Grant said, "You know, I remember you from the Mexican War, and what was it we did?" Lee looked at him and he said, "All these times in this battle, I've tried to recall your face. I could never quite do it." They continued to chat happily. They continued on and on, and it was eventually Lee who said, "I suppose we must discuss the object at hand, the surrender."

So though they didn't know each other, the bonds that were forged and the closeness they had almost defied the fact that they were the greatest of nemeses one could imagine.

On April 9th, Robert E. Lee surrendered to U. S. Grant—that dignified, honorable surrender. Yet he only surrendered his army. There were still three Confederate armies in the field. There were over 175,000 men, their murderous gun barrels hot to the bitter end. There was Jefferson Davis, the Confederate president, calling for guerrilla warfare. Even Robert E. Lee's wife, Mary Lee—who was directly descended from Martha Washington, the great-granddaughter, and by marriage to George Washington—she said, "Robert E. Lee is not the Confederacy. Richmond is not the Confederacy." That's how volatile the situation still was.

How much longer would the war last? A week? Three weeks? Three months? Six months? As Lincoln knew and feared, throughout history such time spans had been enough to start, fight, and win wars, to unseat great dynasties or to complicate the reconciliation to come. And five days later, Lincoln was dead. He was killed on April 14th at 10:14 at night. And William Seward, the Union's secretary of state, was stabbed five times. His wife screamed, "They've murdered my son. They murdered my husband." Only Andrew Johnson escaped unscathed.

The irony of that night was [that] Andrew Johnson was invited to, of all places, Ford's Theater. He turned it down, saying, "I'm tired. I want to have a quiet, little supper and then turn in." He did this not realizing that on the very floor above him, in his hotel, was another deadly assassin who was going to plunge a knife into his heart. But at the last second, the assassin got cold feet, so Johnson escaped. But had Johnson been assassinated that night, there would have been a completed decapitation of the Union government.

[Seward's attempted assassin,] Lewis Powell, went by a number of aliases, from Lewis Paine to a number of other names. He was a big, hulking man who wore a broad hat. That night, Lewis Powell was dispatched by John Wilkes Booth, who was the murderer of Abraham Lincoln that same night. Powell arrived at the Union's secretary of state's house, knocked on the door, and pretended to be carrying medicine for Secretary of State Seward, because Seward had just been in a horse carriage accident. He had been knocked out, and he was in a neck brace lying down.

The irony is that when Powell went through the house and stabbed one person after another and finally found the ailing secretary of state, he stabbed him once, twice, and three, and then five times. What we know, or what is clear, was that he stabbed Seward a number of times in the neck brace, and that was the only reason why Seward wasn't killed.

I figured that the transition mechanism, vice president becomes president, was all very simple and laid out; end of story. In fact, the picture was far murkier and far more complex in April 1865. Because, as it turned out, when I went to check this question, the founders did not intend for the vice president to become president. They only intended for the vice president to temporarily act as president until there was an election. Then there would be a new president. So on that fateful evening, when Lincoln was shot, Seward was ailing with five wounds, and Johnson, who nobody ever expected to be president, had met with Abraham Lincoln only once by happenstance on the day of the assassination for thirty minutes. [He knew him before that] but not well. To this day, we still don't know what they talked about.

Johnson was widely written off as a buffoon in Washington circles. In fact, during the second inaugural, while Johnson was kind of rambling on and on because he was drunk that night, the attorney general said, "Take that deranged man out of there." That's how little regard they held Andrew Johnson in. In fact, Edwin Stanton was basically running things for the first day and a half. Temptations for a regency or Cabinet-style government were great, or for that matter, for a military-style intervention. After the assassination of Lincoln, there would be such turmoil, such chaos and anarchy gripping the Union capital.

In fact, the *New York Times* would editorialize: "If this were France, all the country would be in bloody revolution by twenty-four hours." They were in such turmoil that the Union Cabinet would soon be discussing whether or not, in effect, a Napoleonic coup was under way. Who did they think was behind it? None other than one of their greatest generals, Bill Sherman. That's why I think it's so important to go back and re-create the world, not as we see it with hindsight but as they saw it, so we can see the turning points that they confronted.

THE BENNETT HOUSE story is the story that we never hear about. Appomattox is usually viewed as the end of the war on April 9th. But, of course, there were still three Confederate armies in the field, 175,000 men, and Davis calling for guerrilla warfare. Five days later, there's a tripartite assassination attempt of Lincoln, Andrew Johnson, and Seward. The Union's in total chaos. What took place in the Bennett House in North Carolina was the final surrender of the other principal army of the Confederacy, which was commanded by Joe Johnston.

It was ten days' worth of negotiations where Sherman first sat down with Johnston and John Breckinridge, who was a former vice president, and Breckinridge rejoined them for the negotiations. At one point, the Confederates laid down such terms, and Sherman moved his chair back and said,

"Well, see here, who's surrendering to whom?" But in fact, Sherman gave very generous terms to the Confederates. In doing so, he thought he was carrying out Lincoln's vision. But he was sharply rebuked by the Union Cabinet, particularly after the death of Lincoln, the assassination. Grant was actually sent down to talk to Sherman. Now this was a fascinating scene, too, because in the Union capital when this happened, the attorney general, James Speed, said, "Well, what if Sherman decides to arrest Grant?" Speed and Stanton were convinced that Sherman was potentially thinking of some kind of a coup, and as they put it, he was getting ready to march northward with his legions to take over. That's the kind of chaos and anarchy that was gripping the North [in the] post-Lincoln assassination [period] while there were still Confederate armies in the field.

So if Johnston had decided to go to the hills and along with Lee start sanctioning some kind of guerrilla warfare, we would have been in a real mess. But Johnston instead followed Lee's example and he, too, surrendered, in this act of basic insubordination. In doing so, it really paved the way for this country to become not like the Balkans, not like the Middle East, not like Lebanon or Cambodia or these other civil war–torn countries, or Northern Ireland, but to become like America today.

American Imperialism

by

WARREN ZIMMERMANN

In the five years between 1898 and 1903, the United States gained increasing control over Cuba, the Philippines, Hawaii, Guam, Puerto Rico, Samoa, and Panama. Diplomat and writer Warren Zimmermann examined this significant period in the development of American foreign policy through the lens of five influential men: President Theodore Roosevelt, naval strategist Alfred Mahan, Senator Henry Cabot Lodge, Secretary of State John Hay, and colonial administrator Elihu Root. Mr. Zimmermann joined us on Booknotes *on January 19, 2003, to discuss his book* First Great Triumph: How Five Americans Made Their Country a World Power, *published by Farrar, Strauss, Giroux in 2002.*

I FOCUS ON 1898, the Spanish-American War, when the U.S. first became a colonial power. Theodore Roosevelt was a thirty-nine-year-old assistant secretary of the navy, and he considered that his major job was to get us into a war with Spain. He was the number one warmonger in the United States.

I came across a quote that Roosevelt made when he was a lieutenant colonel of volunteers on the troop ship going to Cuba in the Spanish-American War. He was going to fight the Spanish and he wrote his sister that, "If we are allowed to succeed in this, it will be the first great triumph in what will become a world movement." They did succeed, and it was.

What I wanted to do was make the contrast between the days when America was not a great power. . . . [Those days] ended in 1898. But we were quite a weak country as late as 1891.

William McKinley was a nice man. He was one of the nicest men that have ever held the presidency. He was limited a bit in his vision. He was the president of big business, but he was also a man with a real heart. He was a decorated hero in the Civil War, in fact, and he didn't like war. He once said, "I have seen war. I have seen the bodies pile up and I don't want to get us into a war." He said to Cleveland, who turned the presidency over to him in 1897, "I don't want to be a president that takes us into war with Spain." Yet he was.

THERE WERE two reasons why we went to war with Spain. The first was the more general human rights reasons. We went there because we believed we should defend the Cuban population against the abuses that the Spanish were perpetrating on them. But the second reason we went [was that] the strategists—naval captain Alfred Mahan foremost of them—believed that if we were going to be a great power we had to have a great navy. If we were going to have a great navy we had to control our borders and the seas around our borders. The most important of these was the Caribbean because there it was, right on our doorstep. And the most important piece of real estate in the Caribbean was Cuba.

THE DESTRUCTION of the *Maine* was enormously important. We were moving toward war with Cuba already for human rights reasons, because the American press and therefore the American people and Congress were exercised about the degree to which the Spanish were beating up on the Cuban population.

The strategists like Mahan and Roosevelt and Henry Cabot Lodge wanted to go to war with Cuba because they wanted to control the access to the Caribbean. They wanted to build a canal across Panama and they knew if we couldn't control Cuba we couldn't do that because there was Cuba, 600 miles long, controlling access to the Caribbean.

We were heading in the direction of war, but I don't think it was inevitable. The *Maine* was a battleship that was sent down at American initiative to protect the American population in Havana. [Americans were] coming under a lot of hostility and pressure from the Spanish population and from pro-Spanish elements in Havana because we had been very critical of what the Spanish were doing there.

The American consul in Havana said, "Send a battleship down as a show of strength to protect our population." So the *Maine* was sent down there on a courtesy visit, it was called, and the Cubans, because of naval protocol, couldn't exactly refuse it, so they covered up by sending a Cuban ship up to New York Harbor as a return courtesy visit.

The *Maine* sat in Havana Harbor in very shallow water and on February 15, 1898, it blew up in a huge explosion, about nine o'clock at night, and sank to the bottom. The bottom wasn't very far down because the superstructure of the ship was visible after the sinking of the *Maine*, but it did kill 268 American sailors. Of course, the Spanish were immediately blamed by war hawks like Roosevelt and William Randolph Hearst whose *New York Journal* flashed the headline saying, "The Spanish are responsible for this."

In fact, nobody today thinks the Spanish were responsible for sinking the *Maine*. Why would they have been so stupid to do that since it was almost certain to provoke a war with the United States which the Spanish were pretty clearly destined to lose? So there would have been no reason for them to do that. The general view now, and there have been investigations as late as the 1970s on this, is that the ship blew up because of spontaneous combustion in the soft coal in the bowels of the ship. This happened quite a lot in the U.S. Navy that there were small explosions.

This was a large explosion, so . . . it wasn't an act of hostility at all. It was an accident. Nevertheless, I think most people in the United States tended to blame the Spanish for it. This was all fanned in the press, so it made the road to war pretty inevitable.

One of the interesting questions is why didn't Cuba become a state? We turned Cuba back to independence after we were there for four years. We ran it as a military dictatorship for four years, from 1898 to 1902, then we gave it its independence. We had promised to do that, as a condition of our going into the war against the Spanish. I think there's a kind of revisionist feeling, which I share to a degree, that if we had held onto Cuba a little bit longer and prepared it either for independence or for statehood, we wouldn't be having the problems that we're having now with Castro and company.

THE PHILIPPINES is a fascinating case because when we went into the war with Spain in 1898, we were focusing entirely on Cuba. The Spanish were oppressing the Cubans. The Cubans were in a revolution against Spain. There was a lot of press interest in that, a lot of press interest in the human rights violations that the Spanish were perpetrating on the Cubans. It was not just the Hearst press—Hearst had two papers in New York and San Francisco—it was all of the American papers. All over the country, they were talking about how badly off the Cubans were and there was the view that the United States should go to help them.

Nobody paid any attention to the Philippines except a few naval strategists who decided that the Philippines would be a very useful piece of real estate for a Pacific strategy and for an Asian strategy. So when we declared war on Spain in April of 1898, Commodore G. W. Dewey, who was in Hong Kong, was ordered to take his small fleet to the Philippines and to defeat the Spanish navy there, which he did in about four hours. It was a very quick and massive victory for the United States.

Then we had the Philippines, and we had to decide what to do with it, whether to give it to the Philippine people, many of whom were also revolting against Spain and wanted to be independent, or whether to keep all or part of it ourselves. McKinley, whom I think had a real problem deciding on this, decided we ought to keep it. That's where the trouble started.

Arthur MacArthur was one of the military governors of the Philippines during that war, father of Douglas and very much like him—brilliant, imperious, opinionated, bigoted, arrogant. President McKinley did not like the idea of having MacArthur run the civil side of the Philippines, so he sent a brilliant lawyer and judge, William Howard Taft, out to the Philippines to take over from MacArthur, who had been the supreme ruler. Of course, MacArthur didn't like that at all. He left Taft cooling his heels for several hours before he would even receive him. But in this test of wills between MacArthur and Taft, Taft won because he had better lines back to Washington. He could go right to the president and to Elihu Root, who was the secretary of war and the head of the colonial administration. So Taft won. MacArthur was reassigned. And the Philippines came under civilian rule by the United States.

Taft [ultimately] did a brilliant job of helping to pacify a population which had been fighting us for a couple of years. He left with a lot of good will on the side of the Philippines. The Philippines remained a colony of the United States until 1946, but we've never had great hostility [between Filipinos and Americans] since that war between 1899 and 1902.

The Philippines is over 7,000 islands, so it was an enormously difficult country to pacify. Once we had gotten the Spanish out, we then had to deal with the Philippine revolutionaries, who had been revolting against Spain. They wanted to be independent, and they thought they had guarantees from the United States that they could be independent. They were probably wrong. I don't think they got any guarantees, but maybe some of the American military officers and diplomats around Asia were giving Emilio Aguinaldo, the Filipino leader, some intimations and some implications that, "If you help us, we'll help you get independence." There may have been some promises made.

In any case, he felt very disappointed when we cut him out of the surrender ceremony, when the Spanish surrendered to us. They didn't surrender to the Filipino revolutionaries. War broke out very soon after that, in February 1899, a war between Aguinaldo and his revolutionaries and the United States Army. The army had to be very quickly reinforced to deal with this war, which quickly devolved into a guerrilla war, with all the atrocities that go with guerrilla wars. We committed a lot, and the Filipinos committed a lot, as well. It was a very dirty war, and it lasted three years before we won it.

Nobody knows entirely [how many casualties the United States suffered]. It was a lot more than we lost in Cuba, which was a very short war. The Filipinos lost more. Probably most [of the] people who died in that war died of disease—the estimates for that go as high as 200,000 Filipinos dead of disease during the war.

Water was forced into the throats and stomachs [of the Filipino guerrillas]. The idea was to make them talk, of course. It was called the "water cure." It was a nefarious form of torture. Roosevelt, to his discredit—by then, he was president, when all of these atrocities were beginning to come out—tried to argue that it was a very humane way of dealing with prisoners. Of course, it wasn't. I don't think there have been any substantiated cases of people dying from the water cure, but it was certainly a very extreme form of torture, and we used it in a widespread way. It would certainly be against the Geneva protocol on torture [today].

There was a huge opposition in the United States to what we were doing in the Philippines. It was led by people as famous as Mark Twain and included Andrew Carnegie. It included Finley Peter Dunne—who wrote the "Mr. Dooley" essays, a famous journalist—and a number of people in the Congress, including the senior senator from Massachusetts, George Frisbie Hoar, who was a very strong opponent of what we were doing in the Philippines. So there was a debate, very much like the Vietnam debate that happened several decades later, over whether we should be there at all and over whether we should not be giving the Philippines independence instead of keeping them as a colony, as we did.

Theodore Roosevelt coined this phrase, "Goo-goo." He had a lot of impatience with liberals who wanted good government and tended to be pacifistic or to shrink from the manlier virtues, and he shortened the words "good government" . . . and called these people "goo-goos" . . . to their faces and in public as well. . . . For some of them, the reason they wanted the Philippines to be independent was they didn't want nonwhite peoples in the United States. There was a strong racist tinge to what a number of the "goo-goos" were saying. They thought that the quality of the political system in the United States would be debased by bringing in these millions of nonwhites, these Hispanics, the Polynesians, whatever, into the United States. So the "goo-goos," while they were liberal, were sometimes liberal for the wrong reasons.

HAWAII CAME effectively under the control of American sugar planters in the early 1890s, when the queen, Liliuokalani, was overthrown by them, with the assistance of the American consul, [by an] American naval ship that was in the harbor at the time. Ever since that time, this group, this junta, was lobbying for annexation by the United States; they wanted Hawaii to become an American colony. Grover Cleveland, who was not keen on imperialism, rejected this idea.

When McKinley came in, Hawaii came right back on the front burner. Roosevelt and Henry Cabot Lodge, the strong imperialists around McKinley, were arguing that Hawaii should be annexed. When we defeated the Spanish in the Philippines and Cuba, McKinley annexed Hawaii. He took advantage of the elation that came from these two major American victories in the Philippines and Cuba—they were both naval victories, by the way—in order to annex Hawaii. So Hawaii was annexed in the same summer that we defeated the Spanish in the Philippines and Cuba. It hadn't been a Spanish island, or set of islands, at all. But it was connected to the Spanish-American War because of the fact it was easy to annex once we had won these victories against Spain.

Alaska and Hawaii, when they were taken as colonies, they weren't intended to be states. They were to have a kind of a special status, but not to be states. It was really the effect of World War II and the contribution that Alaska and particularly Hawaii made in World War II that tipped the balance and got them to statehood.

Midway Island was taken at the same time, in the same summer as the Spanish were defeated, another flyspeck with a good naval-base possibility in the Pacific. So we ended up at the end of 1898 with a chain of islands, starting with Hawaii and going west, including Wake Island, Midway Island, and Guam, which we also took from Spain.

It was actually quite a comical Gilbert and Sullivan sort of thing when we took Guam. A naval vessel that was on its way to the Philippines to reinforce Dewey was told to stop off at Guam and seize it from the Spanish. So it sailed into the harbor and lobbed a few shells at the moldering fort there. The fort wasn't really defended by anybody; there were a few aging Spaniards there. They rowed out in a boat to tell the Americans that they were very sorry that they could not return the salute that we had just offered to Guam. And they were informed that that wasn't a salute, it was an attack, and that they were under arrest and Guam was American. Of course, we ran up the flag, and it stayed up.

Guam didn't become a state because it was too small. Hawaii and Alaska were large, of course. They were big geographically. They had significant populations. Guam really wasn't going to measure up by that criterion.

So from 1898, we became not only a Caribbean power—the Caribbean really had become an American lake—but we became a Pacific power with all of these islands in the Pacific. And the Philippines are only a few hundred miles from the Asian mainland.

Puerto Rico, like the Philippines, was a kind of afterthought. The whole thing was about Cuba. So we won a victory in Cuba. The Spanish surrendered. Then Mahan and the other naval strategists looked around and they said, "Hey, wait a minute. The Spanish fleet, what's left of it, can just go to Puerto Rico. We can't really control the Caribbean unless we control Puerto Rico, too."

Puerto Rico was the only other Spanish island in the Caribbean, so an expedition was fitted out to take Puerto Rico. The Puerto Ricans actually didn't have a grievance against Spain. The Cubans were revolting against Spain so there was a real reason there, but the Puerto Ricans weren't.

Puerto Rico had made a deal with Spain which was quite strongly in their interest, giving them a fairly independent political system, an elected parliament and so forth. That didn't mean anything to us. We crashed in for strategic reasons. We had to take Puerto Rico because we had to expel the Spanish [in 1898].

Puerto Rico was in a strange status. One Puerto Rican politician complained that we weren't paying any attention to it at all. He said, "We are Mr. Nobody from Nowhere," and that's probably a pretty fair description of how the United States dealt with Puerto Rico. We've had a very complex relationship with Puerto Rico. It's never fit into any of the categories that we had for other territories that we've controlled. We had territories in the American West, which were territories but which were going to become states. We had Alaska and Hawaii, which were territories which were not going to become states—at least that was the nineteenth-century idea. Then we had these new islands. We thought Cuba was going to be independent, the Philippines was going to be an American colony, and so was Guam.

Puerto Rico never became a state, and that is, to some extent, because the Puerto Ricans have chosen not to. They could become a state if they wanted to, but they would lose some tax benefits if they did that.

THEODORE ROOSEVELT was complicated. . . . If you went to university in the United States anytime between 1870 and 1900, . . . you would have been exposed at every great university in the United States, without any exception, to a theory that said that the Anglo-Saxon race is the superior race, superior to any other races, and has a God-given right to rule over other, lesser races. They got it from Charles Darwin, who would have been horrified to find that his Darwinism was applied in this way. They got it from proponents of eugenics who believed that there was an innate racial superiority that resided in certain races, particularly the Anglo-Saxon or the Teutonic race, and not in the others.

Roosevelt had a professor at Harvard, Francis Parkman, a famous historian, who wrote a book to say that the reason the British defeated the French in North America in the eighteenth century was because of their racial superiority. Then Roosevelt went to law school at Columbia and studied under a professor named John Burgess, who believed that we should stop immigration because we were bringing in too many people from Southern Europe who were debasing our culture. This was pretty crude stuff, so when you get to the people who were actually running our foreign policy, they all had been subjected to these really bizarre racist theories.

Henry Cabot Lodge bought these theories hook, line, and sinker. Roosevelt didn't quite. Roosevelt liked the idea of a melting pot, . . . the idea of bringing together people from different races. When he was police commissioner in New York, he loved the idea of mixing Anglo-Saxons with Jews and blacks and people from other ethnic groups. He enjoyed that.

Then, of course, Roosevelt helped to form the Rough Riders, the volunteer regiment that fought in Cuba of which he was the deputy commander and then commander. There was the captain of the Columbia crew. There was the Harvard quarterback. There were people who were in the Knickerbocker Club with Roosevelt. At the same time, there were cowboys. There were Indians. There were criminals. There were bartenders. It was a totally mixed group, people from the Southwest and people from New England, and Roosevelt loved that. He just thought that was terrific. [Roosevelt] certainly wasn't a racist by the standards of the nineteenth century, and I'm not sure he would be a racist even today. Now, he did write a four-volume history called *The Winning of the West,* which described the battles between the emerging American settlers and the American army and the Indians, in which he propounded the thesis that the Indians were an inferior race, were in the way of progress. They had to give way to civilization and they had to be eradicated or pushed away. It was a very ruthless theory.

At the heart of all of the imperial strategies by Roosevelt, Lodge, Mahan, and by the U.S. Navy, was the idea that we should build a canal across the narrow waist of Panama. This would let our ships through so we would have not only an Atlantic navy, we would have a Pacific navy. It was at the heart of the reasons we got into the Spanish-American War. Panama was part of Colombia, a rebellious province. . . . During the nineteenth century, American marines had landed . . . dozens of times to protect Colombia against Panamanian uprisings.

So we had essentially been the guarantors of Colombia's sovereignty over Panama, but things shifted very quickly after we became a Caribbean power in 1898. Theodore Roosevelt became president in 1901, and he immediately set out to do something about Panama. There was a revolutionary fervor in Panama against Colombia that had been building all during the last century and we had been putting it down.

We got in touch with these revolutionaries. We established contacts with some shady entrepreneurs, one a Frenchman, one an American lawyer, who had their own irons in the fire, all looking for the profit motive but who were in touch with what was going on in Colombia and in Panama.

To make a long story short, the Panamanians did revolt against Colombia. The American navy had ships down there because we had had early notice that this was going to happen, which helped to prevent the Colombians from putting down the revolution. So Panama became independent and asked the United States to recognize it. We did it instantly, within hours, and we signed a treaty with the Panamanians to build the canal across Panama.

We started [building the Panama Canal] in 1903 under Roosevelt. . . . The first visit by an American president abroad ever was Roosevelt going down to inspect the Panama Canal.

THERE ARE MANY definitions of imperialist. The one I like was actually Mahan's definition. He said that imperialism is national authority wielded over alien communities. So his definition didn't just mean that you control territory, it meant that you have influence.

Sinking the Lusitania

---

by

DIANA PRESTON

On May 7, 1915, a German U-boat fired a torpedo at the RMS Lusitania as it traveled from New York to Liverpool. The luxury liner sank in eighteen minutes, causing the deaths of roughly 1,200 civilians. Among the dead were 128 Americans, which in combination with Germany's 1917 announcement of unrestricted submarine warfare, influenced the U.S. decision to enter World War I. In her book Lusitania: An Epic Tragedy, published by Walker & Company in 2002, *Diana Preston examined the details of this event. Ms. Preston, a London-based author, joined us on* Booknotes *on June 23, 2002.*

M Y INTEREST [in the *Lusitania*] was really caught. I was researching something else in the docks at Liverpool, at the Merseyside Maritime Museum, and I saw this great bronze propeller sitting on the quayside, and I went to have a look at the little label underneath it, and it said this was the propeller of the ship *Lusitania*, sunk in 1915 by a German submarine. My interest really grew from there.

I'd always heard a little bit about the *Lusitania*, but I didn't really realize that there was a human drama at the core of that story as poignant, as moving as anything you'd find . . . with the *Titanic*, but also that it was a story which had deep political ramifications. It was a story of an event which really changed the nature of warfare.

LUSITANIA WAS OWNED by the Cunard Company. She'd been built up in Scotland, on the River Clyde, by the John Brown and Company, launched in 1906, made her maiden voyage in 1907, and really was the technological marvel of her age. It wasn't just that she was a uniquely beautiful, elegant ship, with suites and public rooms, modeled on the grand palaces of Europe, like Versailles and Fontainebleau. She was also very technologically advanced. She had revolutionary turbine engines. This was a ship that could cut through the Atlantic waters at a top speed of twenty-five knots. She was really the pride of Britain's merchant fleet.

The sinking was the 7th of May, 1915, just a few days after she'd sailed out of New York on May 1st, 1915. She was sunk about twelve to fifteen miles off the southern coast of Ireland. She was getting very close to the end of her voyage. At the time the attack happened, passengers were already starting to pack, ready for arrival in Liverpool the next day.

Roughly 2,000 people were on board. There were about 1,257 passengers. One of the great ironies was that this was her largest eastbound complement since the war in Europe had begun. And as well as those passengers, there were around 700 crew.

About two-thirds of the people who were on board were killed, around 1,200 people. One hundred and twenty-eight [Americans were killed].

THE *LUSITANIA* was sunk by the German U-boat, *U-20*, under the command of a thirty-year-old Berliner called Walther Schwieger. He had set out from his home port of Emden on the north German coast just the very day before the *Lusitania* had left Liverpool. It was just after lunch on the 7th of May that Schwieger was called to the periscope by one of his men, who had sighted the liner approaching over the horizon.

It was hit just after two o'clock. The torpedo slammed into the starboard side of the ship at ten minutes past 2:00 in the afternoon. And at 2:28 P.M., the ship, 30,000 tons of shipping, was gone. All you had was drifting debris on the water. Survivors, dead people in the water. Eighteen minutes.

It was an enormous shock to the world. If you look at the press reporting on both sides of the Atlantic, if you look at the American press, the British press—complete shock, complete outrage, a sense of a barbarous, unprecedented act. Here you had this ship with so many innocent men, women, and children on the transatlantic run. Of course, it was wartime. War had been going on in Europe since August 1914. But nobody genuinely believed, in the mind-set of the time, that an attack of that magnitude would actually be perpetrated.

A NOTICE WAS published in a number of United States newspapers, including the *New York Times*. It appeared the very morning that the *Lusitania* was due to sail out of New York, and it was warning people that a state of war existed between Britain and Germany, and it ended on a rather ominous note. It said, "Passengers intending to embark on a transatlantic voyage . . . are doing this at their own risk." So, of course, you can imagine the reaction on the docks that day. It was placed by the German ambassador, Count Johann von Bernstorff, of the German embassy in Washington, D.C.

IN 1915, the United States, under the administration of President Woodrow Wilson, was a neutral country. And Wilson [was] working hard to preserve the position of neutrality, if you like, having said in the early stages of the war to the American people, "We must be neutral in fact, as well as in theory."

But of course, does it actually work quite like that? There were certainly with President Wilson and other members of his administration cultural affinities with Britain; there were links there. Germany at this time, if you looked at her newspapers, you would have found virulent reporting of United States's pro-British stance.

[Germany] had a full diplomatic staff [in Washington], including two characters I found particularly interesting, the naval and the military attachés, about whom during the whole *Lusitania* saga, it became quite clear that they were associated with espionage and sabotage activities in New York and elsewhere.

WHAT HAD happened was she had twenty-five boilers, and on this last voyage, only nineteen of those were being used. Now, the reason for this was that the ships of that size were very heavy on coal consumption, so it was an economy measure for the war to shut down one of the full boiler rooms. That meant that her top speed on this last voyage was twenty-one knots, not the twenty-five knots that she'd been designed to achieve. She was going eighteen knots at the time the torpedo struck her.

It was . . . almost a Greek tragedy unfolding, this series of events impacting one another. There had been fog early that morning and Captain William Turner, a very precise, meticulous navigator, was not quite sure of his exact position off the Irish coast, so he had slowed his speed because of the fog. Secondly, keeping at a slow speed offered a straight line while his officers took a four-point bearing on the coastline to determine his exact position.

Passengers themselves were puzzled. They were disconcerted by the slow speed, and they thought it was asking for trouble in waters where everybody knew that U-boats were lurking. They were known to wait in the Irish Sea. Why were they going so slowly?

But it has to be said in Captain Turner's defense that at that stage in the war, no merchant ship that was capable of doing fourteen, fifteen knots plus had yet been successfully sunk by a U-boat, so at eighteen knots, he probably felt he was safe.

THE WATER temperature, according to the Irish Maritime Institute, whom I asked to look back over their records, was around about 51°, 52° [Fahrenheit]. That temperature doesn't sound cold, but imagine being in that for two to three hours. The survivors, already traumatized from the explosion, from having to get off the ship so fast, were having to last two or three hours in those conditions before the first ships got to them.

The great irony was that there were enough lifeboats. There were twenty-two wooden lifeboats, and there were also [twenty-six] collapsible lifeboats made of canvas, with sides that you could put up—plenty, plenty of space for 2,000 or so people on board, because the message of the *Titanic* had been taken very seriously.

Cunard had checked that there were enough. But what happened was that when the torpedo hit, it caused catastrophic damage. The ship began to list heavily to starboard. From the starboard side, you had the lifeboats . . . fall right out, so people had to jump six to eight feet to get in them. And it was very, very hard to lower them, they were tipping off, they were breaking off from their ropes and crushing down on the people already in the water.

On the port side, the lifeboats were swinging in over the deck. It took a mighty effort—they're really heavy—to push them out over the rail and lower them. And when they did manage to start lowering them, they were just ripped into matchsticks by the rivets protruding from the ship's side. So of all those lifeboats, only one got away safely.

WHAT HAD happened was that just a few weeks before the *Lusitania* disaster, Germany, which had been becoming concerned about the stalemate on the Western Front, had decided to unleash her U-boats and had declared what she called an "unrestricted submarine war." By that, Germany meant that her U-boats would attack any British or Allied vessel which they encountered in the war zone, which they had declared around the British isles. And as a result, since the middle of February, a certain number of merchant ships had been attacked, had been sunk.

But if you actually looked at the tonnage of shipping destroyed, it was not significant. At that stage of the war, something like over 95 percent of the merchant ships that were plying between the United States of America and Europe were getting through. So that was one of the reasons the British admiralty wasn't really taking the submarine threat seriously.

England and Germany had been at war since August 1914. Imagine the situation at this stage of the war in Europe. You have trenches which are stretching from Switzerland up to the North Sea. In terms of casualties, by this stage, Britain had already lost about a fifth of her regular army. Over on the eastern front, something like 3 million men were dead. Austro-Hungary had already lost [over 1.25 million] men.

So you have the Great War in Europe already in full flood and the *Lusitania* coming at a particularly critical point, when the war in the west seemed to have reached stalemate. Very little progress had been made. So you have Germany looking to her submarines, to her U-boats, as a mechanism for unblocking that, in the same way that Britain was looking to her campaign in the eastern Mediterranean, in the Dardanelles, to try and move things forward.

[AMERICA WENT to war] in April 1917, so you have a period between the sinking of the *Lusitania* in May 1915 and the spring of 1917. Many people are under perhaps a bit of a [misperception] that it was the sinking of the *Lusitania* that immediately precipitated the United States into war. It wasn't like that, but the event really soured relations between the United States and Germany.

In the aftermath, all this business of spying and sabotage was revealed. You had all kinds of acts of what we would now call terrorism, though that word wasn't used at the time. You had, in the aftermath, bombs exploding in the capital, assassination attempts on Jack Morgan of J. P. Morgan, who was involved in financing sales of American munitions to the Allies. You even had an assassination attempt on the British ambassador [Sir Cecil Spring-Rice] in Washington. All of these things in the background, souring the relationship between the United States and Germany. You had President Wilson saying to the German kaiser, "Look, this form of warfare, deploying submarines like that, attacking merchant ships without warning—that is against international law. This must stop."

You have the kaiser thinking about this for a while, eventually deciding to step back from that form of submarine warfare, but then bowing to the hawks in his own government, starting to resume it again in early 1917. You have more loss of American lives on the high seas. And it was that, coupled with evidence of Germany [seeking cooperation] with Mexico, as revealed in the Zimmermann telegram, that was really the last straw. So in April 1917, you have the United States going to war.

If you look at the headlines in the *New York Times*, you will find reports of soldiers advancing to the battle shouting, "Remember the *Lusitania*." And you'll find the comment which I think has great validity, saying, "In 1915, the *Lusitania* failed to deliver 200 American citizens to Britain, but in 1917, she delivered 2 million U.S. troops to the Western Front."

ONE OF THE fascinating things we researched in this book was how this new [submarine] technology had really come on the scene so fast. It's only around

1900 that you have the United States Navy ordering her first submarine, which was really the prototype for the submarines which Britain and Germany started to build. And yet by 1915, when the *Lusitania* was hit, this device had become a lethal weapon of war, and also something which was changing and challenging the very nature of the rules of war, which went back for centuries. People weren't prepared for the slim, 200 feet, "tin fish," as people called them, slinking under the water, attacking targets as large as the *Lusitania*.

I'M VERY CLEAR that Walther Schwieger only fired one torpedo that day, despite the way in which the British government sought to manipulate evidence, which was later given to the official inquiries in London into the sinking.

They were anxious because Germany was claiming that it was the munitions in the hull of the ship which had caused the *Lusitania* to sink so quickly. And they were saying, "Look, this is what happened and Britain—and by analogy her friends, the United States—is guilty of using passengers in a very hypocritical, self-serving way as mere human shields."

This accusation was starting to reverberate about exploding ammunitions hastening the ship's end. Britain was anxious that that might be the case; therefore, it was much better from Britain's point of view that it could be shown that there were at least two, possibly three torpedoes, and that those torpedoes alone caused the rapid sinking.

[I am] absolutely sure [there was only one torpedo] because one of the things I found at the British Public Record Office was an intercepted message. You have Walther Schwieger returning from his mission, back within radio contact of the German bases and radio stations, within 200 miles, he sent the telegram announcing, "I have sunk the *Lusitania* with one torpedo."

The British admiralty intercepted that message. They knew instantly the implications of it—what it meant—and it was that information they were so anxious to suppress. That's why witnesses, members of the crew, passengers who were determined to get evidence about what they'd really seen and heard that day, they were not allowed to do so. Even in the BBC archives, there is reference to the helmsman being taken aside before giving evidence to the official inquiry and being told that it would be very, in quotes, "helpful" if he would give evidence that there was only one torpedo. He said he wouldn't do that.

ONE OF THE things which intrigued me was there's often been this accusation about whether the British cynically put the *Lusitania* in harm's way as a mechanism to try and bring the United States of America into the war at that stage. And specifically, was Churchill, who was then the first lord of the admiralty—was he behind a plot like that? The conclusion I came to from research—letters, correspondence I looked at—was no, it wasn't like that. Churchill and the British admiralty were overly complacent about the *Lusitania* before the sinking, but there wasn't a plot deliberately to hazard her. They, on the other hand, were preoccupied with this campaign in the eastern Mediterranean. The idea was to try and knock Turkey out of things, to strike a blow at Germany that way. All the effort, all the thought, was going on big troop transports toward the Dardanelles in Turkey, to sending out misinformation to Germany about these troop movements. Everybody focused on that, nobody was giving a thought to this great ship setting sail 1st of May, 1915, to cross the Atlantic, setting sail on the very day Germany published a warning that it might attack.

[THERE ARE ALL kinds of controversies about Canadian military people being on this ship and having weapons, contraband, and all that and also about flying the American flag, versus the British flag.]

[These] points . . . all relate to accusations which Germany made against Britain, some of which were made with justice and some of which were spurious. If we take the one about flying other countries' flags to disguise the nationality of your shipping—yes, Britain did do that. It was a well-known *ruse de guerre* which they were quite enthusiastically following.

The Germans also alleged that there was contraband in the *Lusitania*, and more than that, that amongst that contraband there was war matériel being shipped from the United States. And again, this was quite true. If you look at the ship's manifest, which was published quite openly after the sinking, you will find 4 million live rounds of rifle ammunition. You will find shrapnel casings. You will find percussive fuses, as well as a whole lot of other matériel which could have been interpreted as contraband, down to leather to make belts and material to make uniforms. So that claim was legitimate.

But the Germans also claimed that the *Lusitania* was carrying guns on deck, that she was armed. Now, if that could have been proved to be true, it would have given legitimacy to Germany attacking without warning because it would have changed the nature of the *Lusitania*. She wouldn't have been just a merchant ship any longer. She would have been the equivalent of a naval ship. But there was never any evidence that there were guns on board. Passengers had heard these rumors. They looked. They could never find any.

And what else did the Germans allege that the *Lusitania* was carrying? Organized Canadian troops going off to the Western Front. And again, if that could have been proved, it would have justified the attack without warning.

[CAPTAIN WILLIAM Turner of the *Lusitania*] did survive. He was a remarkable survivor, really. He was washed off the bridge of his ship, and rescued eventually, after two or three fairly harrowing hours in the water. What happened was that one of his crewmen saw the sunlight glinting on the gold braid on the cuff of his jacket. He was rescued, picked up, put on board a fishing boat, brought into Queenstown, and within just hours of landing, this traumatized man was giving evidence to a local inquest in Ireland. And then, of course, he was asked to give evidence at the full official inquiry.

He found it all very traumatic. He resented the fact that his professionalism had been brought into question by the official inquiry. In his later life, he gave very few interviews. He would really only talk about what had happened to family and friends. And he clearly found it very stressful to give evidence at the inquiry. Even at the inquest in Ireland, we have him breaking down in tears.

The British admiralty [tried to blame Captain Turner for this]. It's very clear if you look in the files that the public record offers, you will see letters written by the first sea lord, a man called Admiral Jackie Fisher. He was the professional head of the navy. He reported to Churchill, who was the politician in charge of the navy.

If you look at the correspondence, you'll find memos written by Jackie Fisher saying, "I hope that Captain Turner is found guilty by the inquiry," and, "I believe he's guilty, and whatever the verdict, this man is a traitor."

They even had Captain Turner's background investigated to see if there was any potential for him perhaps having been a spy, having been in the pay of the Germans. But part of this "vilify Turner" campaign was a device to deflect any criticism away from the admiralty for having been negligent with the *Lusitania*.

THE *LUSITANIA* IS where she sunk, in about 200, 300 feet of water, about twelve miles off the coast. Her position is very well documented. Occasionally, there are dives on the wreck, but the Irish government are now very carefully controlling access to the wreck for a variety of reasons.

THE *LUSITANIA* WAS an image, a memory which had never gone away. That's why you find newspaper stories with soldiers advancing into battle shouting, "Remember the *Lusitania*." There are very powerful visual images on some of the recruitment posters. There is one of a woman in the water, a blue-green background, a woman in a white dress, her hair streaming like a mermaid behind her. Very poignantly, she's holding a baby in her arms and written in blood-red letters along the bottom is the word "enlist," and in the background of this drowning woman, is a sinking ship.

World War I in Flanders

by

WINSTON GROOM

Alabama author Winston Groom grew up learning only that "America won World War I for everybody." His grandfathers' guidebook encouraged him to learn more about Germany's invasion of France through Belgium, which launched a brutal four-year battle in the region known as the Ypres Salient. The German, English, and French armies fought in trenches for gains of several hundred yards. They witnessed some of the most poignant and most horrific episodes of World War I, including the Christmas truce of 1914 and the use of poison gas in the battlefield. Mr. Groom appeared on Booknotes *on September 1, 2002 to discuss this crucial battleground examined in* Storm in Flanders: The Ypres Salient, 1914–1918— Tragedy and Triumph on the Western Front, *published by the Atlantic Monthly Press in 2002.*

W AR HAS ALWAYS interested me for a lot of reasons. In this particular case, my grandfather was in World War I, went over, but did not fight in Flanders; he fought with the Americans, who mostly fought in France. When I was about fifteen or sixteen years old, I remember having a luncheon—Sunday dinner, they called it—at my grandparents' house. I was looking through the bookshelves and found this little, thin paperback book, which was the *Michelin Guide* to the battlefields of Ypres and Flanders.

My grandfather had gone over back in the 1920s just to revisit and had bought these little *Michelin Guides*. The Michelin people put out really stunning historical surveys of the war—I imagine to get people to burn up more tire rubber for the Michelin tire company. I began to look at this thing and thought, "What kind of destruction is this?" I was raised on World War II. My father was in World War II. But I looked at the pictures, both aerial photographs and ground photographs, and it looked like Hiroshima.

It occurred to me we never really were taught about World War I other than "America won World War I for everybody." So after that, I began just to read a little bit. And then I read more and more and more out of interest, not out of any desire at fifteen to sixteen years old to write a book about it, but there came a point a few years ago when I thought, "This story hasn't been told."

[WORLD WAR I took place] from 1914 to 1918. About 9 million [people died] . . . 9 to 10 million military people, which is an enormous number, and civilians were probably about that many. Far more civilians died in World War II because of the bombing on both sides. We blew up Hiroshima and Nagasaki, and so forth, and then the Germans murdered a great many people. But the number of military casualties—as a military war, World War I was extraordinary. I used to have the math, but if you [took] how many soldiers, sailors, marines, and so forth were killed, and divide it day by day into four years, it was a lot of people.

[THE FRENCH LOST] about 1.5 million. The British lost about 900,000. The French lost more, and a lot of them were lost in the first three weeks of the war, because they stopped the Germans; the Germans were right outside of Paris, looking at the Eiffel Tower.

The French stopped them at the Battle of the Marne. The British at that point were a relatively small army of about 80,000 to 100,000 men. They were sending more soldiers every week, so there is no way to just put a real number on it. But the French had millions and the Germans had millions.

[The Germans lost] about 2 million.

WORLD WAR I was fought all over the world, but primarily it was fought on the Western Front, which ran from the French border with Switzerland all the way 480 miles north to Ypres in the North Sea.

Then there was the Eastern Front with the Germans fighting the Russians, and that ran all the way almost along the entire Russian border. Then it was fought in North Africa, the same as it was fought in North Africa in World War II. It was fought in these strange little German colonies and French colonies and British colonies in darkest Africa, and the combatants would locate one tribe or another to fight with them. It was fought on the high seas everywhere.

WORLD WAR I was really about—and this is so controversial, we could be here for a week—but my short version is that Germany wished to expand. Germany, at this point, in the early part of the century, and especially 1912, 1913, and the beginning of 1914, had an enormously powerful army. And with her ally, Austria, Germany sought to expand herself. They wanted, based on what Hitler said, too, in World War II, *Lebensraum*. They wanted more land.

They didn't do it as overtly as Hitler did, who was quite an evil man. The kaiser of Germany at that point didn't wish war, but he was ready to fight it if it was coming. And of course, this tinderbox down in the Balkans and Sarajevo, where many bad things happened; a Serbian man assassinated the heir to the Austrian throne, and this set the whole thing in motion. The Russians felt that they had some sort of suzerainty in the Balkans because the Balkans were mostly Slavic people. The Austrians felt that they ought to have control of the Balkans. The whole thing was like a canoe that just rocked and rocked, and finally everybody fell out of it and then began fighting each other very viciously.

ON THE CENTRAL Powers side, which was the German side, you had, obviously, Germany and Austria-Hungary. Turkey got into it somewhat later. Those were the main powers. Then the Allies were France, which had a mutual defense treaty with Russia, so you had France and Russia.

Great Britain got into it because they had guaranteed the independence of Belgium, which was neutral. They did that because they knew that Belgium was sitting right on the English Channel and the North Sea. They didn't want anybody else coming in there. So Belgium had a treaty with England since 1839. . . . Then the British Empire, which was huge because it was India and all of the Caribbean nations that Britain controlled—they came in—Canada, Australia, New Zealand.

The Americans stayed out of it as long as they felt that they could. The Americans really did not take sides in this thing until after the Germans torpedoed the enormous passenger liner the *Lusitania* and 128 Americans were killed. But the Americans traditionally had a mistrust of England. We didn't get in it because of England.

We had problems with King George III in the American Revolution and in the War of 1812, the British came over and burned the Capitol and the White House. And in the Civil War, the British sided, at least tacitly, with the Confederacy, with the South, building them great blockade-running ships and selling them arms, and so on. Also, you had in America at that point, these enormous immigrations of Germans and the Irish, who despised England. So the Americans were not eager to get into this fight. They figured Europe's problems were Europe's problems.

BUT AFTER THE *Lusitania* and after the introduction by the Germans of gas warfare, there was a decided sway in public opinion and in the American press that Germans were not behaving properly here. It didn't take much. After the *Lusitania* incident . . . the kaiser realized he'd made a mistake and he called off unrestricted submarine warfare. Then, in 1917, he reinstated it and a number of American ships were sunk—nothing on the scale of the *Lusitania*; these were smaller boats. But Americans were killed. . . . If you were going to be what we call a civilized nation and go around just sinking indiscriminately any ship that comes within any distance of international waters, you were going to have to fight America. And that's what got us into it.

THE BATTLE [I wrote about takes place in an area] which was the key to the English Channel ports of Calais and Dunkirk and Boulogne. There's a question among historians—and of course, nobody ever knows all this "what if" stuff—but if the Germans had secured those ports and been able to not only deny them to the British, because that's obviously the supply route across the Channel, but to build submarine bases on those ports, conceivably they could have won the war. Also, then the Germans would have turned the flanks and been able to come down the English Channel and get behind the British and French armies who were fighting in France. So it was very crucial.

THE PROBLEM in Flanders—and it was not just limited to Flanders—but the fighting in that part of Belgium was basically fighting in mud. The subsoil in Belgian Flanders is a very thick blue clay, and it doesn't drain. And it's about two feet down. So when it rains, the water simply stays there. Well, these fellows had to dig trenches because of all this horrible artillery fire that's going back and forth, and the trenches simply didn't drain. They tried to pump them, but the pumping equipment was very primitive, as you can imagine, in 1914 to 1918.

And so most of the time, these guys simply waded around in water up to their knees, and all sorts of horrible repercussions came from that, such as "trench foot," which when I was in the U.S. Army, they called it "immersion foot," but it simply rots the feet. And then, of course, you've got all this water and you've got dead people, you've got dead animals. Very bad infections and diseases resulted from simply having to stand in water most of the time.

THERE WERE FOUR main battles [at Ypres], but the fighting there was really constant for four years.

What they called the "wastage"—that was the word that the British army used, meaning the casualties that occur every day without there being a major engagement going on—was anywhere from 1,000 to 2,000 men a day in Belgian Flanders. Every day, 365 days a year for four years. Just the wastage.

MAJOR JOHN MCCRAE was a physician with the Canadian army and he was in Flanders and one of his good friends who was a young lieutenant was blown to bits one day by an artillery shell. They had to sort of gather him up and put him in a bag or something in some way to resemble a human form.

McCrae conducted the burial services and afterward went and sat on the stoop of his ambulance, very depressed. . . . McCrae sat there and it was recorded that while artillery was reeling in the sky, the poppies were growing in Flanders field and he penned this poem [within twenty minutes]. [It was May 2nd, 1915.]

[He wrote it] right there very near the battlefield where the artillery was going off around him and didn't know what to do with it, showed it around a little bit, showed it to several British magazines, was turned down, and finally seven or eight months later, *Punch*, which is a British satirical humor magazine, published it, and it became emblematic, almost, of the war.

> *In Flanders Fields the poppies blow*
> *Between the crosses, row on row,*
> *That mark our place; and in the sky*
> *The larks, still bravely singing, fly*
> *Scarce heard amid the guns below.*

It was a great rallying cry to take up our quarrel with the foe. It's a remarkable piece of poetry. People wrote poetry in those days. Nobody much writes poetry anymore.

There are whole books just on the poem "In Flanders Fields."

SOME OF [the combat] was very much hand to hand in the beginning, especially because there were no trenches. There was no barbed wire, and these people were fighting over territory. They were fighting in the woods. They were fighting in the fields. They were fighting everywhere, and sometimes it was very much hand to hand.

Later, it became less of that. It became more of an artillery battle, meaning that the notion was simply to have the artillery, one would hope, erase all messages of living life and then the men would presumably go in and mop up. Well, that wasn't the way it was either, because as soon as the artillery stopped, the other side would come out of whatever hole they were living in and they would shoot you just like anything else.

IF THE BRITISH—and there were French involved as well at Ypres, but not to the extent that the British were—but if the Germans had driven the British out of the town of Ypres, out of Belgian Flanders, taken the English Channel ports, the entire war would have had a different complexion; meaning that depending on how the Germans used what they had taken, it could have resulted in a negotiated settlement earlier than the unconditional surrender, or it could have resulted in an immediate German victory and historians pretty much weigh with that.

FIRST, THE GERMANS used chlorine gas in 1915. The Germans were the manufacturer of [85 percent of the world's] chlorine. They had a huge industry, and people knew about poison gases. It wasn't like some strange secret weapon, but nobody thought of using them. It was inhumane, terribly inhumane.

People were getting shot out, and shelled out, and bombs were falling from the air, and suddenly to poison the very air that men breathe was considered barbaric, but the Germans thought it would give them the opportunity to break through up there at Ypres to get to those Channel ports. And so they released this horrible chlorine gas in 1915.

It was only the Canadians, who somehow managed by urinating in their underwear and putting it over their noses where the ammonia in the urine would counteract the effect of the chlorine gas who saved the day. The Germans could have just come pouring through and accomplished those things which I suggested, taking the Channel ports.

Then the Germans used another kind of gas, phosgene gas, which was, I read somewhere, . . . eight times as deadly as chlorine gas. My editor said, "How would they know it's eight times? What if it was ten times?" I said, "Okay, let's say ten times." But it was far more dangerous, because if it got in your lungs, it simply ate the lungs away.

And then mustard gas, which was the third gas the Germans introduced, in 1917, was probably the nastiest of all because it simply ate big holes in your skin as well as destroying your lungs and tissue. I've seen the most grotesque pictures and actually did not use one in this book because I just considered it too grotesque. It looked like leprosy or something. It just ate everything away.

And, of course, as soon as the Germans used it, the Allies began to use it. It never was a deciding factor in any battle, but it was just another horror—or frightfulness, is the way the British described it—of the war.

HITLER WAS actually an Austrian, but he joined the German army [as part of a Bavarian regiment] and was, by all accounts, was a fairly good soldier. He rose to the rank of corporal, never higher, and won the Iron Cross. He was at

Ypres for three of the four battles. He was gassed there in the end in 1917, and he was there for the great Christmas truce, which became a legendary element of World War I.

In 1914, in the beginning of the war, both the British and the Germans on Christmas Day simply quit fighting and went out and met in the middle of no man's land, played soccer, and exchanged gifts, and tobacco, and photographs, until the commanders found out about it and sent them back to shooting each other again.

Winston Churchill was there, [too]. Churchill had been the first lord of the admiralty, and he set in motion the fairly disastrous British adventure in Turkey at Gallipoli and afterward was drummed out because of that. He went to rejoin his old regiment at Ypres and by all accounts was a wonderful officer.

He was fairly old then for an officer. He was a major. I think later he became a colonel, but he was forty-two and had not fought a battle since the Boer War. He was a remarkable figure. His motto was, "War is a game to be played with a smiling face," and he would tell his officers, "If you can't smile, then you grin."

THE FINAL BATTLE of Ypres . . . came to be known as Passchendaele, one of those almost unpronounceable words, too many vowels in it. Passchendaele was a little village on a ridge; the ridge semicircled Ypres like an amphitheater, and the Germans were occupying the ridge and the British wanted it back because the British were being shelled by it.

The battles at Passchendaele, which lasted about four months, came to symbolize all of the horror and the suffering of the entire First World War. It was fought in mud, sometimes waist deep. It began to rain in the autumn of 1917 and it never stopped. It doesn't stop raining in that part of the world, Holland and that part of northern Belgium. It just rains all the time.

Sometimes it's a great big huge rain. Sometimes it's drizzle rain. They love the drizzle rain, but the ground, of course, fills up with water, and the men, the British who were attacking, had to cross this slop that had been torn up at this point, in that battle alone, by probably 4 to 5 million artillery shells. Each of those creates a crater, depending on the size of the shell, of some great dimensions. The craters fill up with water, and the craters were filled up with dead Germans, and the craters were filled up with blood.

And these fellows simply had to cross this ground maybe 200 yards at a time, maybe half a mile at a time, but they had to simply wade through this slop.

During that last fight in 1917 at Passchendaele, they sometimes had to have sixteen men carry one stretcher case out of the battle area, because of the struggling, and plus there was so much artillery, that inevitably many of the carrying parties would be killed or wounded.

THERE WERE SOME ideal trenches. The ideal trench would be about six by seven feet deep with what they call a "firing step" so that the men could move in the trench without having their heads blown off. But when they had to fight, they would step up on the step.

Ideally, the trench would have boards. There would be some sort of drains in the trench. Then there would be dugouts in the back side of the trench for the men to shelter themselves out of the weather and so on. That's the ideal trench, and it would be protected by barbed wire in front, sometimes more than 100 yards of it. One hundred yards out and strand after strand after strand.

There would be sandbags, parapets. . . . In Ypres, that really didn't work well because the water level was so high, two feet below ground, you would hit water. So the only way that they could really construct what we call a trench—what I call a fortification—was to build up. They'd get two or three feet and then they'd have to build up with sandbags. A bullet will go through a sandbag sometimes, so a man can be minding his business, standing there, smoking a cigarette; the next thing you know, his head is blown off. The trenches were very unsatisfactory in Ypres. They refined them more as the war went on. Concrete was used. Big timbers were used.

They had some metal corrugated things. Some men even wrote home for those little penny packets of flower seeds to plant flowers in their trenches— the British loved to plant flowers. The trenches became as homey as you could make them, but it was still a pretty rough business.

ABOUT 50,000 [Americans were killed in World War I], which is a lot of men, but compared to what the English and the French and the Germans and other powers lost, it is almost minuscule. It's horrible to say it, but we lost 58,000 or more in Vietnam, and we think of this as a huge figure. We have a big memorial right down the road here in Washington to those 58,000. I don't think there's a World War I memorial.

But just as an example, in this little corner of Belgian Flanders that I'm writing about, which is about the size of Manhattan Island, there are about 280,000 or 290,000 British alone buried there.

It's one of the biggest graveyards in the world. There are markers every-where. But 90,000 of the soldiers were never found; they were simply blown to bits. There is a wonderful memorial there at what's called the Menin Gate, which was the old medieval gate that the town of Ypres had to go [through] to [get] to the town of Menin, which was to the east. . . . In those days, dur-ing the war, it was simply blown apart. But that's where most of the British soldiers marched through to get to the battlefield, and after the war, they restored this gate in all of its splendor. There are 55,000 names of those British soldiers who were missing carved inside and burnished with gold.

The interesting [thing] was that they began to do this just after the war ended. A couple of years later, the British War Records Office determined that there were another 35,000 British soldiers missing. Because the memorial was already being built, there was nowhere to put their names, so they put them in Tyne-Cot cemetery, which is about four or five miles down the road.

You can imagine the horror of that conflict, where you had 90,000 men who were simply blown to bits. They couldn't find enough of them to put into a grave.

The Paris Peace Conference

by

MARGARET MACMILLAN

At the close of World War I, from January to July 1919, delegates from the Allied countries met in Paris to draft peace treaties. During these six months, the peacemakers, led by British prime minister Lloyd George, French premier Georges Clemenceau, and U.S. president Woodrow Wilson, divided up the defeated territories and shaped the future of Europe. The resulting Treaty of Versailles, which demanded reparations payments from Germany, was signed by the new German Republic on June 28, 1919. Margaret MacMillan appeared on Booknotes *on December 29, 2002, to discuss* Paris 1919: Six Months That Changed the World, *published by Random House in 2002, in which she contested the notion that the decisions made at the Paris Peace Conference paved the way to World War II. Professor MacMillan is provost of Trinity College in Toronto.*

[BEING THE great-granddaughter of David Lloyd George] has been nice in a way, I guess, to know that I have a famous ancestor. I never met him. On the other hand, it actually sort of inhibited me from doing this book because I thought, "I don't want to write a book that people will say, 'Oh, she's just doing it because of her great-grandfather.'" . . . So, I've had some mixed, ambivalent feelings about it, really.

THE BOOK COVERS six months in 1919. It has a bit of what happened before and it has a lot of what happened afterward, but what I really look at is the intense period of the Paris Peace Conference, which technically lasted for over a year. But the really intense period was when all the world leaders were there, and that was from January to June 1919.

Something like thirty-one countries were represented, and so you had a lot of people. They were there initially to settle the First World War, and that was a huge amount to settle because it covered not just Europe, but it affected Africa. It affected the Middle East. It affected the Far East.

The nations who didn't come—and this was later on to be an enormous point of controversy—were the ones who were defeated. The defeated nations expected that they would have the usual sort of peace conference that they had up to this point where they're defeated and the victor sat down and hammered something out, and this never happened.

The defeated were Germany, first of all—it had been the main linchpin in what were called the Central Powers—and then you had what had been Austria-Hungary, which by this point had broken up, and so you had a separate little Austria and a separate Hungary. They both were among the defeated; they were not invited.

What happened was—and this was really a mistake on the part of the Allies—that the Allies assumed that they would need a preliminary meeting to hammer out a common position. It took them so long to hammer out a common position that by the time they got it done—and it really wasn't done until the end of April 1919—that they really didn't dare sit down with the defeated nations. They thought, "If we try and open the whole thing again, we'll never get a peace."

The Germans were the first to be called to Paris, and basically the Allies said, "Here are your terms, take it or leave it. You have two weeks to send us in writing any comments you may have, but we may not pay any attention to them." The Germans, of course, resented that bitterly.

THE UNITED STATES came into the peace conference with no gains for itself in mind. None. At one point, they were asked and they considered taking over a mandate for Armenia. That was discussed. There was another discussion that perhaps they'd take over a mandate, an authority to run Armenia under the League of Nations for the area around Istanbul, the famous straits. There was no political support in the United States for that whatsoever, and so the United States really didn't have any territorial claims.

What it did have was, of course, a sense that America was now in a very strong position and perhaps it was a good time to get into markets and perhaps it was a good time to push American exports, but that was understandable because, in fact, it was.

GREAT BRITAIN came into the peace conference [with] two very clear goals. First, it wanted to destroy German naval power, because that's what had menaced Britain before the First World War. In fact, that's a very large part of what led to the First World War. And the British had a navy. They'd always wanted their navy to be the equivalent of any two other navies in the world, because for Britain the navy was its lifeline. It was its protection and its lifeline to all its vast empire and to protect its trade, and they wanted to destroy the German navy and they did.

Basically, that had been done by the time the peace conference opened. Germany had surrendered its submarines and its surface fleet to the British, and so the German submarine fleet went to the south of Britain and the German surface fleet went up to . . . Scotland. And so the British had done that.

The second thing the British wanted was more territory and that's where Lloyd George, the old liberal, suddenly becomes a real land grabber. What they grabbed were big bits of the Middle East. They also wanted to make sure that German colonies didn't go back to Germany. The British on the whole, with a few exceptions, didn't want the colonies themselves. You got some of the components of the British Empire now building their own little empires, and then there were some islands in the South Pacific which Australia and New Zealand took over.

FRANCE WAS interested in some of Germany's colonies and so they got bits of German colonies in Africa and, of course, they got bits of the Middle East. [Georges] Clemenceau's main interest was in protection against Germany. He was deeply apprehensive of Germany. He recognized it was stronger than France, and so what he wanted was some form of protection.

What some of his generals wanted and what some of the conservatives in his government wanted was actual territory. In fact, some of them even went so far as to talk about breaking Germany up into its component parts. Germany was a very new country. It had only really come into existence in 1871 and so some people in France said, "Well, why not have a Bavaria again? Why not have a Prussia again?" And, "Why not have some smaller states?" Woodrow Wilson and Lloyd George wouldn't have gone for it.

And there was some talk of taking the West Bank of the Rhine River, which was German territory. The Rhine makes a wonderful natural barrier and so some people in France said, "Why don't we take the West Bank of the Rhine, and make it part of France or perhaps make it into an independent state?"

Woodrow Wilson and Lloyd George wouldn't go for that. They said, "Look, the West Bank of the Rhine is German. If you take it away, you will create problems with German nationalism. It will just cause disruptions endlessly in Europe until Germany is reunited."

And so what Clemenceau settled for was control of German coal mines in an area for fifteen years, because France's coal mines had been destroyed by Germany, and a guarantee from the British and the French that if Germany attacked France, Britain and the United States would come to France's defense. This was known as the Anglo-American guarantee, and for Clemenceau, he felt that offered enough security.

It looks like what happened is that Lloyd George got what he wanted in the Middle East, and in return he promised the French that he would support their claims in Europe. Lloyd George later on denied this, but what that conversation was about was really dividing up the Arab territories of the old Ottoman Empire. The British and the French had already done a quiet deal during the First World War to do this. They certainly didn't want the Arabs getting independence.

The only [area] that they didn't bother to divide up between them was the Saudi Arabian Peninsula because they didn't think there was anything worth their worrying about.

But what they did is they divided the Middle East up so that the British were going to get what became Palestine, and France [would get] Jordan. The French were going to get Syria and Lebanon, and initially the French were going to have Mosul, which was in the north of what is today Iraq. The British wanted it because they suspected there was a great deal of oil there.

Clemenceau, much to the fury of his own people, including Pichon, his foreign minister, agreed, but we suspect that in return he got a promise from Lloyd George to get [the lost territories] back in Europe. But it was really old-fashioned imperialism. The British and the French didn't think the Arabs were ready for independence. They didn't think their wishes should be taken into consideration, and so they carved up the Arab Middle East really to suit themselves.

THE ITALIANS were not a major power. It was by courtesy they were considered one of the big four, but they were not as powerful as Britain, France, and the United States, and they tended only to talk when matters concerned them. And so they came with a very clear agenda, and they tended not to worry about much else.

Well, they got into a tremendous rout. They had claims. Italy had come into the war late, and it basically came in looking for the best deal for itself. It thought of joining either side. In the end, it joined the Allies because the Allies could promise it more.

What the Italians wanted was that great [area] of the east coast of the Adriatic, what is today Croatia, Slovenia, and Bosnia as you go from north to south. The Italians wanted to claim a lot of that on the grounds that it had once been Italian. There were still Italian communities living there.

Why they wanted it was because they didn't want any power across the Adriatic that could be a menace to them. The country that also wanted it was the new country of Yugoslavia that had just emerged. The Italians had been promised a certain amount of that territory during the war by the British and the French, but they wanted even more.

ONE OF THE real problems, and there were many problems at the peace conference, but one of the ones that really blew up was when the Italian claims were rejected by Woodrow Wilson, who said, "I'm not giving you territory which doesn't have Italians in it. I don't care what promises were made during the war by the British and the French. That is not what I stand for. I stand for a different sort of diplomacy where people aren't given away against their will to people to be ruled over by people of another ethnicity or nationality."

The Italians in a fury said, "All right, we're walking out," and it was a very crucial time of the peace conference. It was just around Easter 1919, as the German terms were being got ready.

So, the Italians walked out, which left a real problem—are there going to be enough nations there to enforce their will on Germany? And so there was huge rout. Woodrow Wilson was furious and decided to make an appeal directly to the Italian people. He believed that if he could speak directly to the Italian people, the Italians would see reason.

And so he issued an open letter, and unfortunately the Italian populace by that point was in no mood to see reason. There was a huge nationalist fervor in Italy.

At any rate, eventually what happened was the Allies made preparations for Britain, France, and the United States to simply go on and try and make the treaty with Germany anyway. The Italians came back rather reluctantly, but relations remained very, very bad.

LLOYD GEORGE was prime minister [of Britain] from the end of 1916 to 1922—six years—a very, very dominant figure. Eventually, he was head of a coalition government. He himself was a liberal, but during the war when things were going very badly, a section of the conservatives recognized that they needed a new prime minister and so did the liberals. He was put into office by a coalition, and in fact, most of his support came from the conservatives.

Lloyd George was a very controversial figure indeed. He was from a very nontraditional background in those days for British prime ministers. He wasn't an upper-class aristocrat. He came from fairly humble origins in Wales, and he really was a self-made man.

He was a great liberal and he'd never been much interested in foreign policy. That was one of the curious things, that he ended up having to do a lot of foreign policy. What he was interested in was domestic issues. He was interested in social welfare. He introduced the first old-age pension.

GEORGES CLEMENCEAU, the French prime minister at the time, was an old radical as well, rather like Lloyd George, although he came from a different background. He came from a more aristocratic background. He was someone who had seen France defeated, first by Prussia in 1870. He'd been in Paris when the Prussians had encircled Paris.

Clemenceau was in office from 1917 until the end of 1920. He'd been briefly prime minister before the war, and then he became prime minister again in the middle of the First World War.

It was said that when he died he wanted to be buried facing Germany, because Germany, which Prussia became the heart of, was a great enemy of the French. He is often portrayed as vindictive, but I don't think that's true. He recognized that France would have to deal with Germany if Europe were to be a safe and stable place, but he was worried about German power.

He was deeply cynical in some ways. He said about the League of Nations, which Woodrow Wilson was promoting, "I like it, but I don't believe in it."

WOODROW WILSON is the one I find the most puzzling. He was in many ways an extraordinary figure, a great idealist, a man of great vision. He was in some ways a great leader of the United States. He had a tremendous powerful oratory and he had an ability to inspire people, but he had these failings.

He failed to understand that people could oppose him and not be wicked. He tended to think if you disagreed with him, there was something wrong with you. It made him not very good at the usual cut and thrust and compromise of politics, and that in the end was part of his tragedy. He refused at the very end to compromise with the Republicans on his treaty, and it cost him very, very dearly.

[LLOYD GEORGE, Woodrow Wilson, and Georges Clemenceau] had a funny relationship, and yet they didn't like each other. Lloyd George got on with most people. He was one of these people who would have furious routs and then not bear a grudge. Wilson was much more prickly and tended once he conceived a dislike for someone never really to get over it.

Clemenceau didn't much like Lloyd George. He felt he was not a gentleman—for Clemenceau this was important—and felt he was not very well educated. Clemenceau didn't much like Woodrow Wilson either. . . . He said at one point in Paris, "I feel as if I'm sitting between Napoleon on the one side and Jesus Christ on the other," and he didn't mean either of those as a compliment.

WILSON WAS enormously popular, and he arrived in Europe in December 1918, and it was a Europe that was shattered by this war. In a funny way, the First World War affected the Europeans even more than the Second World

War. It was as if they had a <u>sense</u> that their civilization had inflicted irrepara-<u>ble damage on itself.</u> They'd lost these millions of young men and then, not just young men but men of military age. It's hard to imagine, but <u>the French lost, either killed or wounded, half their men of military age.</u>

People thought civilizations were collapsing. Austria-Hungary had gone. Germany had had a revolution. There had been a Russian revolution. Wilson came and people saw him as the hope. A lot of people in Europe really believed in his ideas. They thought the League of Nations was a very good idea.

Wilson was greeted as a savior, with huge crowds. His boat landed at Brest, the French port, and people who were there said that virtually every living being in Brest came out to welcome him. As his train went to Paris that night, his doctor woke up at about three in the morning, looked out, and there were French people standing along the railway tracks just watching the train go by.

THE FOURTEEN Points were among the various statements that Woodrow Wilson had made during the war, after the United States entered, about what the United States and its allies were fighting for.

He made them at different times. There were the Fourteen Points, which he made in January 1918, and then there were the <u>Four Principles,</u> which he made slightly later. There were a number of speeches, great speeches he made in the course of 1917 and 1918, but it's the Fourteen Points that really caught people's imagination the most.

<u>The Fourteen Points are about a new way of running the world,</u> about a new world order. That's what they're about—<u>about a peace without annexa-tions of territories, without retribution, about a just peace, about people's right to choose their own rulers.</u>

And that's often called "national self-determination," which gets us into a whole other difficult area, about a League of Nations. [That concept was] an association of nations which will <u>find ways of settling disputes other than going to war,</u> and about an <u>open diplomacy, about things being done more openly, no more secret deals,</u> no more secret promises. Woodrow Wilson and many people felt [this was what] had got Europe into this mess.

<u>The League of Nations was a noble idea.</u> A lot of people now look at it as a failure. I don't think we should, because it was the first time anything had been tried like this. The <u>League of Nations was set up.</u> What it was set up to do was <u>to provide collective security.</u> The idea was that it would be like join-ing a club. Everyone would join and then if anyone attacked a member of the club, everyone else in the club would come to that member's defense. The two mistakes it made, and it's easy to say this with hindsight of course, was that they didn't invite the defeated nations in immediately.

Germany, which had been told, "There's a new world order; things are going to be different," wasn't allowed to join the League of Nations, although it had to sign a treaty. The Treaty of Versailles, which Germany signed, incorporated the League of Nations. The very first part of the treaty was actually the covenant of the League of Nations, and that was one problem.

The defeated nations, although they eventually joined, never really trusted the League. They saw it as a league of victors. And the second problem was that the United States didn't join. That was a tragedy.

I DID [conclude that the Treaty of Versailles was not what caused World War II,] and I certainly didn't believe this when I started out. Like a lot of people, I thought it was a bad treaty, but I kept on thinking they did the best job they could have done. I kept on asking myself, if you're going to criticize them, what would you have done differently? Would you have driven Germany down into the ground and occupied Germany? There wasn't the will to do that in 1918. They'd already lost so many soldiers. The idea of going in and fighting door-to-door in Germany was not something that appealed. So, if you don't drive Germany down into the ground, you leave a very strong Germany at the heart of Europe. How do you deal with it? It was a problem, but I'm not sure that anyone knew how to deal with it, including the Germans themselves.

Like a lot of people, it also seemed [problematic] to me to say that something that happened in 1919 was responsible for something that happened twenty years later. Well, what about all the people in between and their decisions and their failures? You have to look at that as well.

Nazi Germany's Kulturbund

---

by

MARTIN GOLDSMITH

The Kulturbund, an organization composed exclusively of Jewish artists pre-senting concerts and plays for Jewish audiences, was supported by the Nazi Ministry of Public Enlightenment and Propaganda between 1933 and 1941 as a way to segregate Jews from German society. In The Inextinguish-able Symphony: A True Story of Music and Love in Nazi Germany, *Martin Goldsmith tells the story of the Kulturbund through the lens of his parents, who endured the Nazi regime until their escape to America in 1941. Mr. Goldsmith took the title of his book from the fourth symphony of Danish composer Carl Nielsen, who noted in the score, "Music is life and, like life, inextinguishable." Goldsmith appeared on* Booknotes *on January 7, 2001, to discuss his book, published by John Wiley & Sons in 2000.*

[IN THE YEAR] 1923, . . . Adolf Hitler staged his beer-hall putsch in Munich and the National Socialist Movement began. . . . [There were] 80 million people [living] in Germany back then. [Less than 5 percent were Jews.] It was a very, very small percentage, and yet the Nazis were able to convince the German citizens, apparently, that these small numbers of Jews presented a threat to them. My father does remember the April Boycott of 1933. He was going on twenty at the time. He remembers these storm troopers standing outside Jewish businesses with signs saying, "Germans defend yourselves. Don't purchase from Jews." My father remembers think-ing, "Defend yourselves? There's no threat." Joseph Goebbels was the inven-tor of the big lie, and if you repeat something over and over enough, you can convince a large group of people that a very small group of people somehow poses a threat.

THE YIDDISH or Kulturbund Jewish culture association came out of what the Nazis were doing the first few weeks and months after Adolf Hitler became chancellor of Germany on January 30th, 1933. The Nazis had many things on their plate, many things they hoped to accomplish. But one of the first things they did was to kick Jews out of German orchestras, German opera companies, and German theater companies to cleanse German art of the bad Jewish influence, they said.

And so by April of 1933, there were [thousands of] unemployed Jewish artists in Germany. Some of them decided to come together to form their own organization, Jews performing for other Jews. They quickly realized that it wouldn't get anywhere unless they had full Nazi backing. They nominated, as the artistic director of the organization, a remarkable man named Kurt Singer. He, in turn, found a fellow in the Nazi hierarchy named Hans Hinkel, who eventually rose to become the number two man behind Goebbels in the Ministry of Public Enlightenment and Propaganda, as it was called.

Hinkel and Singer worked out this plan for this organization. Only Jews could be a member of the Kulturbund; that meant whether you were a violinist or a flutist or an actor or you built sets or costumes or worked in the box office, you had to be Jewish. You could only attend performances of the Kulturbund if you were Jewish. The Kulturbund put on plays and operas and orchestra concerts, chamber concerts. They showed films, they sponsored lectures, all for the Jews of Germany. It became the only venue for Jews to attend cultural performances.

The Kulturbund raised its curtain for the first time on the 1st of October 1933, during the High Holidays that year, and was in business for eight years. It began in Berlin. By the end of 1933, there was already the first branch organization, which opened its doors in Cologne. By the high-water mark of the Kulturbund, in 1936, there were these organizations in forty-nine cities across Germany, and 70,000 people were members of the Kulturbund.

The Nazis not only allowed the Kulturbund to happen, but encouraged it for two important reasons: On the one hand, it was instrumental in the Nazis' desire to segregate Jews from mainstream German activities; and on the other, perhaps more important, hand, it aided in their propaganda efforts. They saw the Kulturbund as a wonderful propaganda tool. When there began to be complaints about reported German anti-Semitism, the Nazis could shrug their shoulders and say, "How bad can it be for the Jews? Look, they have their own orchestra, their own opera company. We're treating them just fine." So the Nazis were very encouraging of this organization, and they did subsidize it. The bulk of the funds for the Kulturbund came from subscriptions; people had to be monthly subscribers to the Kulturbund.

There were no walk-up sales allowed. But the Nazis also saw to it that certain monies from the Reich came to support their organization.

At the very beginning, the members of the Kulturbund were savvy enough to realize it probably was not a good idea to play music from Richard Wagner or Richard Strauss, German composers that the Nazis held in particular high regard. But at the outset, they could play other German composers: Beethoven, Brahms, Schumann. But eventually, again, the Nazis thought that for a Jew to perform German music or for a Jewish actor to speak the words of Goethe or Friedrich Schiller or other German playwrights, that was somehow to defile German music or German drama.

So the order came down that the Kulturbund was no longer permitted to play German composers, with one somewhat amusing exception. For a while, the Kulturbund was allowed to play music by George Frideric Handel, who was born Georg Friedrich Handel in Germany. But the Nazis apparently thought because Handel had composed such Old Testament oratorios as "Judas Maccabeus" and "Israel in Egypt," that he must be Jewish. So he was still allowed for the Kulturbund, until somebody pointed out to the Nazis that, well, yes, Handel is just as German as Brahms or Beethoven. So he was added to the verboten list.

And then in March 1938, when the Anschluss took place—the forcible takeover of Austria by the Germans—Austrian composers—Schubert, Haydn, Mozart—were added to the banned list.

MY MOTHER was the first to join . . . the Kulturbund Orchestra in Frankfurt when she was eighteen in the fall of 1935. A few weeks thereafter, after the passage of the Nuremberg Laws, which essentially stripped Jews of their citizenship, my father, who was studying the flute in the town of Karlsruhe, was kicked out of the music academy there. Like many a German Jew, he saw what was going on and decided he no longer wanted to live there. So for the next weeks and months, he made arrangements to move to Sweden. In fact, got himself an apartment over a milk bar in Stockholm. And he was all set to leave when, in March 1936, the phone rang, and somebody on the other end of the phone said, "There's this orchestra called the Kulturbund. Its principal flutist has a very bad cold. They need somebody to fill in. Can you play a couple of concerts?" My father at first said, "No, I really can't. I'm about to move. There are boxes all over the apartment," but the other fellow was persistent.

My father eventually agreed to play these two concerts with the Kulturbund Orchestra, one in Frankfurt and one in Hamburg. He played those concerts and then duly moved to Sweden, but he couldn't forget the lovely young violist he had met during those two concerts. A correspondence ensued between Frankfurt and Stockholm. When the same flutist, who had gotten sick in March, emigrated to Palestine in August, my father moved back to Nazi Germany to be with the woman who would become his wife and my mother. They played in the Kulturbund Orchestra of Frankfurt together for the next several years, until 1938, when they joined the orchestra in Berlin.

When they met, my mom was nineteen and my father was twenty-two. They got married in 1938; my mother was twenty-one, and my father was going on twenty-five. I, so many times, would say, "Dad, what was it like to be a Jew in Nazi Germany?" And he said, "Well, we were Jews in Nazi Germany. We were also young lovers in Nazi Germany." And they took time out, as often as they could, to go on the streetcar to the farthest reaches of Frankfurt and there to walk out into the hills, the Taunus Hills outside Frankfurt, where they would—like any twenty-five- or twenty-two-year-old people—pack a picnic lunch, go walking in the woods, and try to have as good a time as they could under the circumstances.

Not too long ago . . . a friend of mine said to my father, "Reading this book, do you feel more frightened in retrospect, looking back on what happened? Or were you more frightened when these things actually happened?" And he said, "Well, I'm more frightened now looking back and realizing the danger we were in. But at the time, certainly we knew there were things we couldn't do, things that were forbidden to us. We knew about dangers, but we were young. Perhaps we were foolish, but we had music and we had each other and we were happy, in some strange way."

My father's eighty-seven now, and he says if he lived to be 1,000, he will never forget that New Year's Eve, 1937–1938. He says he remembers so many details: how they took a streetcar and then they met a horse-drawn carriage, which took them up to this little inn up in the Taunus Mountains. He said it was snowing, and there was no electricity in the rooms, and everything was lit by candlelight. And there were big quilted feather comforters. And he says, "That was the first night that your mother and I made love." And after averting my eyes a little bit, I said, "That must have been wonderful." There are things that he does not remember whatsoever, but that New Year's Eve, that first night, he remembers quite well.

HENRY MEYER was one of the very youngest members of this organization, the Yiddish Kulturbund, the Jewish Culture Association. He joined the orchestra in Berlin when he was only seventeen years old and played with the orchestra, played chamber music with my parents in Berlin. In September of 1941, when the Kulturbund was shut down, he was still a member of the organization. . . . He and his brother were sent, first, to a munitions factory and eventually to Auschwitz. His brother perished within a few weeks of arriving in Auschwitz, but Henry Meyer managed to survive. He was incredibly fortunate. He was on the brink of death after being there for some time, and a Nazi doctor happened to be walking through the barracks. Henry Meyer said to him, "Look, I know what's happening tomorrow." He knew that there was going to be a selection the next day, and he assumed that he would not survive that process. And the doctor sat down and said, "What were you before you came here?" Henry Meyer said, "I was a musician. What were you?" The doctor said, "I was a doctor as well, practicing in Breslau." Henry Meyer said, "In Breslau, I played the Tartini Concerto there."

The doctor paused for a moment and said, "I was at that concert." And after a few more moments, the doctor got up, walked out of Henry Meyer's barracks, came back a few minutes later bearing a corpse over his shoulder. He plunked the corpse down on the cot next to Henry Meyer, picked Henry Meyer up, slung him over his shoulder, walked over to the next barracks, where he gave Henry Meyer a new name and a new identity.

Henry was able to survive long enough to be asked then to join the band in Birkenau that would play while prisoners were marched out in the morning and back into the barracks in the evening, before and after their work detail. He was told, "Well, since you're a musician, what instrument do you play?" Henry Meyer did not play a band instrument; he had played the violin, but, luckily, noticed a pair of cymbals leaning up against the wall and said, "Oh, I'm a real virtuoso on the cymbals." So he survived his last months in Birkenau playing the cymbals in that band. He said that he became a great favorite of the Nazi guards because they would often throw pebbles at him, and he would catch the pebbles with his cymbals. It made a loud noise, he said, which the Germans loved.

ALEX GOLDSCHMIDT was my father's father. He came to Oldenburg in 1906. He was the son of Moses Goldschmidt, who was a horse trader. Alex had four brothers, all of whom went into the horse trade, but he didn't. He decided to seek his fortune on his own. He entered into the woman's clothing game and came to Oldenburg in 1906, opened up a store in 1911.

In 1914, he marched off with his hometown regiment to fight in the First World War, and as a result, he didn't come home for any significant length of time, until after the Armistice. He came home in January in 1919, by which time my father was five years old. My father remembers this strange man coming up the stairs, and my father remembers turning to his mother and saying, "Who is that man?" and being told, "That's your father." Alex ran the store in Oldenburg from 1911 until the mid-1930s, when things began closing in on him.

He attempted to emigrate to the New World in 1939. He was born in 1879, so he was sixty years old.

THE LAW stipulated that as of January 1st, 1939, all Jews had to have these names affixed to their name. If you were a man, you became "Israel." So my father became Gunther Ludwig "Israel" Goldschmidt, and my mother was Rosemarie "Sara" Gumpert. To me, it was just one of all the horrible laws and strictures and edicts and curfews that were handed down; it was one of the most intrusive, certainly, before the advent of the final solution.

It was considered horrible that you might have a Jew in your background. Of course, there's the rumor that Adolf Hitler—whose name truly was Adolf Schickelgruber—may have been Jewish, and he did everything he could to stamp out that rumor. [Reinhard Heydrick, the head of the SS security service,] his grandmother's name was Sarah, S-A-R-A-H, which is not S-A-R-A, the way it was depicted on the passports after the 1939 law. And he had his grandmother's headstone blown up to erase any hints that that may have been the case.

HELMUT WAS my father's younger brother, Alex's younger son. Helmut hoped to emigrate to the New World in 1939. He was born in 1921, so at the time, he was eighteen years old. In 1938, right after the events of Kristallnacht, Jews were kicked out of German public schools. Helmut was one of the very last students to be asked to leave his public school in Oldenburg. I was gratified to learn when I made my last research trip to Germany a year ago, in November in 1999, that the students in his public school have adopted him as someone they want to memorialize. They're apparently finding money to put up a plaque in his honor as the last Jew to be kicked out of the school in 1938.

ADOLF HITLER was appointed chancellor of Germany. Anschluss was in March of 1938. That was when, under the threat of an invasion, the Germans simply marched into Austria, and there are stunning newsreels that one can see to this day how the city of Vienna just fell all over itself to welcome *der Führer*. He gave this triumphant speech overlooking the Heldenplatz, the Heroes' Square, in Vienna, and he proudly said, "I proclaim to the world that Austria has joined the German Reich."

November 9th, 1938, is remembered in some circles as Kristallnacht; in other circles, simply as the November Pogrom. It was the night that supposedly in retaliation for the assassination of a German official in Paris by a young Jew named Herschel Greenspan, Jewish businesses and Jewish synagogues and Jewish people were targeted for destruction. Synagogues were set on fire, businesses had their windows broken, many, many Jews were killed, many were arrested. Because of the broken glass that lay in heaps throughout Germany, the Nazis actually came up with the name Kristallnacht,

Night of Crystal, Night of Broken Glass, seeking to minimize the damage. For that reason, the Jews of Germany sometimes remember it simply as the November Pogrom, but I think the Nazis were a bit more poetic than they perhaps intended to be, and Kristallnacht does have a certain power, that name, that image.

On the night of November 9th, 1938, my father's father was arrested, and the following morning, he and forty-two other Jewish male citizens of Oldenburg were marched through the town, past the smoking remains of the synagogue. They wound through the streets of Oldenburg and eventually ended up at the Oldenburg prison, where they spent a night in jail and then were sent by train east to the concentration camp Sachsenhausen. Because of this march, about fifteen years ago or so the citizens of Oldenburg decided to do something extraordinary, which is on every 10th of November, to re-create that march, to follow the exact route that the marchers took at the point of Nazi guns.

At the time of the march, Helmut was still only seventeen years old, so he was arrested that night and brought to the Pferdmarkt, the horse market, in Oldenburg, where the march began. But at the beginning of the march, all women and children were dismissed, so Helmut didn't take part in the march and was not sent to prison that night and did not then spend the next three weeks in the concentration camp Sachsenhausen, where my grandfather did spend that time.

After being in Sachsenhausen for three weeks—this was a concentration camp just north of Berlin—my grandfather was released with the understanding that he had six months to leave the country or he would face rearrest. So after being released and recovering from the ordeal, he set about trying to book passage out of the country, and, in fact, booked passage on a ship leaving for Havana, Cuba. And he made arrangements for his younger son, Helmut, to accompany him. The idea was that they would move to Cuba, set up a household, and then send for the rest of the family.

Unfortunately, it was their ill luck to book passage on the ship *St. Louis*, which left Hamburg on May 13th, 1938, bound for Havana. In fact, it made it to Havana Harbor, where it dropped anchor. But because of power plays at the highest reaches of the Cuban government, they were not allowed to disembark. None of the passengers was allowed to disembark into Havana. The ship then sailed north to the coast of Florida and spent a couple of days treading water close enough so that the passengers could see the lights of Miami. They pleaded with the American government to be allowed to disembark in Miami, but for a number of reasons, President Roosevelt declined.

This was late June 1939 and President Roosevelt was beginning, I presume, to make plans for his unprecedented run at a third term as president of the United States. Immigration issues perhaps could have been touchy in the upcoming election. He wanted none of it.

Over 900 Jews were on that ship. At this time, 1939, the United States was still under the strictures of the 1924 immigration law, which said that a certain number of citizens from each country was allowed to come to America. Twenty-some thousand from Germany and from Austria. And so the argument went, "If we let in these nearly thousand Jews from Germany on this ship, that means that another thousand Jews who have been waiting patiently in line somewhere else will not be able to come in, so we have to adhere strictly to our immigration law." The ship was then turned away from Miami and sent back to Europe.

Certainly the events of Kristallnacht had been very, very well covered. There were headlines in major American newspapers across the country on page one in bold type about the horrors of Kristallnacht. It was well known what was going on. In fact, while the ship, the *St. Louis,* was treading water in the Western Hemisphere between Cuba and Miami, there were editorial cartoons in American newspapers. There were editorials about the *St. Louis.* There were demonstrations in various American cities. There was a telegram sent to President Roosevelt from such Hollywood luminaries as Edward G. Robinson, pleading with the president to allow the *St. Louis* to land. But all that was to no avail.

From a personal standpoint, [I feel] outraged, terribly unhappy. My grandfather and my uncle were within miles of freedom and safety, in Miami, had they been allowed to land. They were not.

The ship sailed back to Europe. A deal was brokered because everybody did not want the ship to sail back to Germany. Everyone thought, "Well, we can't have this happen." A deal was brokered whereby the over 900 Jewish refugees would be allowed to land in one of four countries: France, Belgium, Holland, or England. As it happens, the lucky ones disembarked in England. My grandfather and uncle disembarked in France. At the time, they must have thought, "Well, at least we're not in Germany." So there they were in late June 1939 as displaced persons in a camp near Le Mans. Within ten weeks, however, the Second World War broke out, September 1st, 1939. They metamorphosed overnight from displaced persons to enemy aliens. They were, after all, carrying German passports. Germany and France were now at war with each other. They were then sent to two camps in succession in the south of France, Rivesaltes and then Les Milles, camps that were not exactly concentration camps, but were very, very awful places to be interred. And they spent the better part of the next three years in those camps before, with the approval of the Vichy government, they were shipped from Les Milles via Drancy to Auschwitz.

My grandfather was at the time sixty-three years old, and he was part of a transport that left Drancy on August 14th, 1942. When they arrived in Auschwitz, he was one of the Jews immediately gassed. My uncle was only twenty-one years old, deemed fit to work. He was assigned his number and managed to survive another two months before dying officially of typhoid fever in October of 1942.

My two grandmothers, my grandfather, my uncle, and an aunt—so five in all [were] all killed by the Germans.

My grandfather and uncle ended up in Auschwitz. My mother's mother ended up in Trawniki in Poland, and my father's mother and my father's younger sister ended up in the ghetto in Riga.

Mr. Shapiro—my father only remembers him as Mr. Shapiro—was the man who in many respects saved my parents' lives. My mother's father ran this music conservatory in Düsseldorf, and one of his students had emigrated to America before Kristallnacht. On the occasion of Kristallnacht, the student, realizing all the terrible things that he saw in the newspaper, wrote to my grandfather Julian, saying, "Gosh, things look really awful there. Is there anything I can do?" My grandfather wrote back, saying, "Well, my daughter and her husband need to get out. Is there anything you can do?" And this fellow found this Mr. Shapiro, who was the man who agreed to sponsor my parents. At the time, if you wanted to emigrate to America, you had to find somebody who would stand up and say, in effect, "I will vouch for these people. They are fine, upstanding citizens. They will not end up on the public dole, and I will go on record as saying that." So it was Mr. Shapiro who was my parents' sponsor.

It was perhaps in late 1939 where they began filling out their official papers. They had begun playing not only in the Kulturbund Orchestra but also playing chamber music with friends, and they were invited by one of their friends to take part in a chamber music gathering that took place in, of all places, the American Embassy in Berlin. And there, they met a woman whom my father remembers only as Mrs. Schneider. And Mrs. Schneider took an interest in these two young people, and without being terribly overt about it, made it known to them that if they wanted to emigrate, she would help them fill out the necessary papers. She did. She also told them, "Look, you're probably going to have to wait a while." This was, again, 1940. President Roosevelt was beginning his run for a third term. And they waited for over a year, until late February 1941, before their visas arrived. Once they had their visas, they were able to get a passport and they then were able to book passage on what turned out to be the second to last boat to leave Lisbon carrying Jewish refugees. The boat left June 10th, 1941, and arrived at Ellis Island June 21st, 1941.

World War II Espionage

by

JOSEPH E. PERSICO

When Japan attacked the American naval base at Pearl Harbor on December 7, 1941, the United States suffered the greatest intelligence failure in its history. President Roosevelt responded to America's lack of preparation by focusing on the development of espionage. In his book Roosevelt's Secret War: FDR and World War II Espionage, *published by Random House in 2001, New York author Joseph E. Persico traced the expansion of U.S. intelligence, from FDR's private spy ring to the creation of the Office of Strategic Services and the construction of the atomic bomb. Mr. Persico joined us on* Booknotes *on November 11, 2001.*

THE UNITED STATES didn't go into the intelligence business in a serious way until 1941. We were probably the only world power that didn't have a professional intelligence service. Roosevelt relied very heavily prior to, let's say, 1940 on a circle of socialite friends as his sources. There was a group of them who styled themselves "The Club," and they had taken a shabby apartment on New York's Upper East Side. They had an unlisted phone number. They had a secret mail drop. It sounded like the spy games of boys being carried out by grown men. The chief figure in this outfit called The Club was Vincent Astor, one of the wealthiest men in the country.

Vincent Astor was the heir of a massive fortune in the United States. He was a socialite, but he was also a man interested in causes. He owned probably the biggest chunks of real estate in Manhattan. He and other members of The Club, while they seemed like dilettante amateurs, had this value for FDR: They were very highly placed. For example, Astor was a director of Western

Union, and consequently he was privy to the kinds of cables which were going from foreign embassies in the United States back to their homelands. Though it was illegal, he had these cables intercepted and he passed this intelligence along to FDR. Another member of The Club was Winthrop Aldrich, who, at the time, was head of the Chase National Bank. Aldrich knew about international financial dealings. He could report to FDR all the money that was going into and coming out of the Russian spy front in the United States, the Amtorg trading company. But this was a pretty unsophisticated level of intelligence for a country the size of the United States at that point.

Vincent Astor had a magnificent ocean-going yacht called the *Nourmahal*. It had a crew of over forty members. FDR asked Vincent Astor to cruise the Pacific, seemingly on a pleasure junket, and hit places in the Marshall Islands, which were then managed by Japan as a mandate, and to report on our preparations there. This was great fun for Vincent Astor and a great adventure. He subsequently thought this would lead to his becoming FDR's chief of intelligence, but he was up against tougher rivals in Bill Donovan and some others.

Bill Donovan was an authentic hero of World War I, a Congressional Medal of Honor winner, subsequently a vastly successful Wall Street lawyer. He became, in effect, the first head of a central intelligence agency in the United States. Franklin Roosevelt appointed him in the summer of 1941 to what eventually became the Office of Strategic Services (OSS). It was kind of a strange choice because Donovan was a staunch Republican, had run for governor of New York on an anti-Roosevelt, anti-New Deal platform. But he was also a man of irrepressible spirit, boundless optimism, full of ideas, and in a sense, he reflected the qualities of Franklin Roosevelt.

Donovan was a magnificent magnet for attracting talent. His OSS attracted college presidents, semanticists, philosophers, writers, journalists, photographers, actors, cameramen. Arthur Goldberg had been an OSS veteran, subsequently went on the Supreme Court. Historian Arthur Schlesinger Jr. was with the OSS. The French chef Julia Child was with the OSS. But what struck me about Donovan was the crack-brained ideas that he could advance, one of which was that his agents would somehow intrude into Hitler's diet substances that would cause the führer's breasts to swell, his voice to rise, and his mustache to fall out. Another idea that he came forward with was to drop leaflets over Japanese troops which show pictures of Japanese women involved in compromising positions with Caucasians, which presumably would demoralize them, seeing that their women were not being faithful. The thing that was surprising to me is that these crazy ideas did not turn FDR off at all. He didn't reject them out of hand because he loved the surreptitious, the furtive, the clandestine, and the covert.

JOHN FRANKLIN CARTER—interesting man—was a columnist in Washington. At one point, he wangled an appointment with the president in the Oval Office and he, in effect, said to FDR, "I have extraordinary contacts in journalism, among international government figures, among businessmen worldwide. I could easily set up for you a ring and I would report strictly to you." Roosevelt lapped that up. It was just the kind of thing that appealed to FDR—off the books, circumventing his own bureaucracy, something private, clandestine. A spy thriller kind of thing appealed to him. So he took money out of his own White House budget to set up the John Franklin Carter ring. He had this money transferred into the State Department, where presumably it was to buy reports about foreign governments. Carter operated throughout the war, directly reporting to FDR and the Oval Office.

The interesting thing was that we had an OSS that didn't necessarily know about the John Franklin Carter ring. We had John Franklin Carter who didn't necessarily know about the Astor ring.

[AT THE HEIGHT of the OSS, Donovan had 13,000 people working for him.] And that's starting from ground zero. We had no intelligence service to speak of, even the year before Pearl Harbor.

They did have intelligence. They had the information, but it came in a flood tide. Roosevelt didn't get intelligence decrypts that had been examined by analysts and placed together like pieces of a jigsaw puzzle. He got raw intelligence. It was very hard to sense, what's the direction of this? What's it warning us about? What is our antagonist likely to do next? Also we had nobody on the ground. We had no spies inside Japan, just as apparently we haven't done very much to penetrate the inner sanctum of our current adversaries.

The real parallel here is the shocking unexpectedness of Pearl Harbor and September 11th. How could this happen? After the fact, the strand of intelligence that leads from A to B to C to Pearl Harbor may stand out glaringly, and after the fact the strand of intelligence that runs from X to Y to Z to the World Trade Center and the Pentagon may seem to stand out glaringly. But before the fact, this intelligence didn't come in single strands, it came in great bundles. They were breaking the Japanese code, there were hundreds of messages available to the president. We now have the NSA [National Security Agency], which I understand does something like $3 billion of worldwide eavesdropping. What we had [during World War II] that was comparable was a flood tide of intelligence which seemed to overwhelm the circuitry. What we seem to be lacking then and now is careful analysis to say, "Well, we've got this tide of intelligence. What direction is it falling in? What do these jigsaw pieces tell us if we can put them together?" That was a failing prior to Pearl Harbor and is obviously a failing now.

THE U.S. CODE crackers were working very hard prior to 1940 in breaking the Japanese diplomatic code. They called it "Code Purple." They finally broke that code, it was broken by a team led by a man named Frank Rowlett. Rowlett and his people were then able, in effect, to place the president of the United States on the distribution list of the Tokyo Foreign Office because they were breaking these messages, and they were available in a very short time. There may have been a message from the foreign offices in Tokyo to the Japanese ambassadors in Washington. They were breaking that code and these messages got up to President Roosevelt very quickly. That's what the "Magic" operation was. It was very important because our breaking of the Japanese codes was responsible for our 1942 victory in the Pacific at Midway, which was a turning point of that war.

Frank Rowlett was operating out of a former girls' school in the northern Virginia suburbs of Washington called Arlington Hall. He operated with a very small group of people. I can't imagine they made a great deal of money. They worked for the army as cryptographers, but they were very dedicated. Their breakthrough was really a significant advance for us.

By breaking the Japanese codes, we also were able to find out German intent. How did that come about? Because the Japanese had an ambassador posted to Berlin. His name was Oshima. Oshima was a rabid pro-Nazi. Consequently, he won the confidence of Adolf Hitler. Hitler would bring in Oshima and say, "Mr. Ambassador, I'm going to send you to inspect the Atlantic Wall. I want you to see what I'm erecting to repel an Allied invasion of the continent," or he would say to Oshima, "I'm going to tell you how many divisions I have deployed in Norway, Denmark, in Belgium, and most importantly in France." Then he would say to Oshima, upon these rather critical revelations, "and I don't want you to breathe a word of this to anybody."

Well, Oshima did what a good diplomat does. He would report back to Tokyo, virtually verbatim, his conversations with Hitler through that diplomatic code that they were breaking, and these messages then were available to the president, to his secretary of war, to the military chiefs. One of the most significant revelations was when Hitler told Oshima, "I'll tell you where the Allies are going to strike. They're going to strike at the Pas-de-Calais," the narrowest part of the English Channel. He reported this back to Tokyo. They intercepted it. They now knew that Hitler expected the invasion there. Why was that significant? Because that was our deception plan. That's exactly what we wanted him to think, and we knew it was working.

There were something like 400 Oshima intercepts per year. General [George] Marshall said that he was our best source of information on German intentions. He was our best agent, an unwitting agent, albeit. For the president, it was not simply peeking at the other fella's hand; It was like holding the other fella's hand.

In 1942, after the Battle of Midway, the *Chicago Tribune* front-paged a story which practically blew the secret. The *Tribune* headline read, in effect, "Navy Knew Japanese War Plan." Well, how else would we have known it? The story was virtually saying they were breaking the Japanese code. Astonishingly, while any cabdriver in Chicago could have drawn that conclusion, the Japanese considered their code unbreakable. They used the same compromised code to the end of the war.

THE FBI HAD rounded up almost all agents operating with the United States. However, Hitler was very unhappy with the job being done by his intelligence service, the Abwehr, and pressured Admiral [Wilhelm] Kanaris, his intelligence chief, to do something more dramatic. The result was an operation called "Pastorius," in which eight Germans who had lived in the United States, two of whom had been U.S. citizens—men who had gone back to Germany—were recruited to form this team. They were put ashore in the United States via submarine in the summer of 1942 to carry out espionage. One of them decided to rat on his other comrades, thinking this would make him a hero. They were all quickly rounded up. This story is fairly well known.

What is far less known was Roosevelt's attitude toward these saboteurs. He immediately directed his attorney general, Francis Biddle, to organize the trial outside of the civilian courts through a military tribunal. He said to Biddle, in effect, "These are agents of the enemy. They've come ashore in wartime in civilian clothes. I don't think there can be any doubt as to what their fate must be." So he kept this case out of the civilian courts because the rules of evidence are strict, the opportunities for appeal seem to be endless. It was a military court, which he created and to which he named all the members, and then he directed his attorney general, Biddle, to prosecute the case, so that within eight weeks of these saboteurs setting foot in the United States, they were all condemned to death. Two of their sentences subsequently were commuted. What I found interesting was that this Hudson River patrician, this amiable, genial Franklin Roosevelt, was underneath as hard as nails. He expressed his only regret in this case that these men hadn't suffered the more ignominious fate of being hanged rather than being electrocuted.

IN THE BEGINNING, the United States and Britain were full partners in developing an atomic weapon. But as time went on and the United States launched the Manhattan Project and was putting millions of dollars into this, creating the facility at Los Alamos, we became the dominant partner and started cutting the British out of what was happening for security reasons. Churchill came to the United States at one point and saw Roosevelt at Hyde Park. He was furious. He accused Roosevelt of reneging. So a compromise was reached: The British would not get information on the A-bomb imported into Britain, but they would allow a small team of British physicists, mathematicians, and other scientists to work at Los Alamos. One of them turned out to be [Emil Julius] Klaus Fuchs. As we know, Klaus Fuchs stole major secrets of the bomb and gave this information to his Soviet controllers. He was at Los Alamos because of a deal cut between Franklin Roosevelt and Winston Churchill.

Klaus Fuchs had been a young, avid Communist in his native Germany. Things got very tough for Communists in Germany as the Nazis came to power, so he fled to Great Britain and eventually became a British citizen.

Klaus Fuchs was finally unmasked several years after the war in 1950. He was sentenced [to] a fourteen-year prison term. Eventually, upon his release, he continued his work in East Germany.

WINSTON CHURCHILL was very eager to have the United States join the war against Hitler, and consequently, British agents were to provide intelligence to help this happen. They told Roosevelt about the fact that the Germans had taken a map and cut Latin America into five future Nazi vassal states, that a Bolivian pro-U.S. government was going to be toppled by the Nazis, that we had 6,000 German troops in Brazil. Roosevelt used some of this information in his speeches and in his fireside chats. It was all fabricated by the British to help encourage the United States to enter the war.

[It] is frequently overlooked that the United States did not declare war on Germany; we declared war only on Japan on December 8, 1941. Why did Hitler do something seemingly so rash [as to declare war on the United States]? There was a leak of an important document called "Rainbow Five," a contingency plan that Roosevelt had called for: What would we need, should we go to war against Germany by 1943? How many divisions, how many ships, how many aircraft, how much fuel, etc.? The *Chicago Tribune* got hold of this secret plan and front-paged it, did not play it as a contingency plan. The *Tribune* played it as a war plan, and the headline said "FDR's War Plans: Goal Is 10 Million Armed Men, Proposed Land Drive by July 1943." When Hitler declared war on the United States four days after Pearl Harbor, he virtually quoted this. He said, "President Roosevelt intends to make war against us by 1943," so in declaring war against the United States, he didn't view it as being rash. He viewed it as anticipating the inevitable and getting the draw on the U.S.

FDR, BY HIS character and temperament, was ideally suited for secret warfare. He loved to trade in secrets. He was a master manipulator of people. He misled his own associates when it suited him. He seemed to enjoy subterfuge for its own sake. He said it best himself. He said, "I'm a juggler. I never let my left hand know what my right hand is doing." He left virtually no fingerprints. One of the most frustrating things that historians on the trail of Franklin Roosevelt complain about is the lack of written commitment to decisions that he made or explanations as to what he did.

World War II in North Africa

by

RICK ATKINSON

In November 1942, the United States launched its first military offensive against Germany when it invaded Northern Africa. Beginning with Operation TORCH, an amphibious invasion of Morocco and Algeria, American and British troops eventually forced a German surrender in Tunisia in May 1943. In his book An Army at Dawn: The War in North Africa, 1942–1943, *published by Henry Holt & Company in 2002, Rick Atkinson examined the importance of the North African campaign to the Allied victory in World War II. Atkinson, Pulitzer Prize winner and* Washington Post *staff writer, joined us on* Booknotes *on November 17, 2002.*

THE LIBERATION IN Europe is really a triptych—there are three panels that inform one another. The first one is North Africa; the second is Sicily and Italy; the third is Western Europe.

North Africa is really where we took the first blow against the German army, against the Wehrmacht. I started here because that's where the story begins; it's really where the great yarn starts. The circumstances of our going to North Africa are almost accidental, in some ways. After Pearl Harbor, there was a great hue and cry to retaliate against Japan, but there had been a decision between President Roosevelt [and] Prime Minister Churchill that Germany was the preeminent strategic impulse. The reason for that was a correct belief that if you could defeat Germany, then Japan would fall on its own.

So if you're going to fight Germany, where are you going to do it? The Americans wanted to cross the Channel in 1942 or 1943 and head straight for Berlin, drive right on Berlin. It's the American instinct for annihilating the enemy as quickly and as directly as you can. Churchill and the British, having been kicked out of Europe three times by that point, including at Dunkirk, recognized that, first of all, the Wehrmacht was a much more formidable foe than the Americans recognized; secondly, that it was important to blood the new allies, the Americans; and, thirdly, that there were benefits to be obtained by taking a Mediterranean approach. North Africa seemed like a good place to start. It was still controlled by Vichy France. If you could seize North Africa, wrest it away from Vichy France, you basically got control of the Mediterranean back again. That was very important because you would get control of Suez. You didn't have to send ships all the way around the Cape [of Good Hope] of Africa.

So, North Africa it was. And on the 8th of November 1942, there was a vast armada which had sailed from the eastern seaboard that landed in Morocco—[Major General] George Patton was the commander—and an equally sizable armada that had sailed from the west coast of Britain, through the Strait of Gibraltar, and landed in Algeria. The ambition, the game plan, was for those two armies to seize Morocco, to seize Algeria, and then swing into Tunisia, which would give all of North Africa to the Allied powers.

When Germany had rolled into France in the early summer of 1940, within weeks France was defeated. Hitler concocted a very clever armistice—he kept the northern two-thirds of France, including Paris, for himself, under German control. The bottom one-third of France, which would have its headquarters in Vichy, a small spa town, was left to the French to administer. Along with that portion of metropolitan France, the French colonies overseas were left to the French to administer. This way, Hitler didn't have to worry about Tunisia, Morocco, Algeria, and the other colonies that France controlled.

It was a deal with the devil. It is something that France wrestles with to this day. The leader of Vichy France was a World War I hero, Marshal Pétain, who was old and feeble. He was trying to do the best thing for France. Every Frenchman who had any sense of conscience wrestled with what was the proper course of action.

So North Africa was under the control of this rump state with its headquarters in Vichy.

THE BOOK STARTS on October 21, 1942. The admiral who was going to command the fleet that was leaving from Norfolk [Virginia] and other Eastern ports to go to Morocco, taking Patton and his soldiers there, was in Washington. He was flown up secretly from Norfolk for the day because he'd been summoned to meet the president.

His name was Henry Kent Hewitt. He was a wonderful character, a really interesting man. He's forgotten largely by most Americans. He ought not be forgotten. He was a genuine original [and] a very unformidable-looking man.

He wore a uniform, which looked like blue rummage on him. He was somewhat soft-spoken. When he was a midshipman at Annapolis, he was said to have been so terrified of heights in the sail loft that he squeezed the tar out of the rigging. But he was a pretty formidable sea dog. He'd won the Navy Cross in World War I. He had an amazing knack for navigation. The stars ate from his hand, he was so capable at figuring out where he was.

Hewitt had been given the task of taking this armada, more than 100 ships, across the Atlantic and depositing Patton and his men on three landing beaches in Morocco. He'd been summoned to the White House about a week before the fleet was to sail, for what was really a pep talk with the president. Patton was there, too. So the book opens with this scene of Hewitt landing at old Anacostia Field here in Washington, taking a staff car first to the Navy [Department] building and then to the White House, where Patton was waiting for him. They were escorted in a very circuitous manner around the White House, so no reporters would see them.

They spent about forty-five minutes with the president, who essentially wanted to wish them "Godspeed" and buck them up. Patton was ready to fight. Patton had qualms about the navy's tenacity. He was afraid that at the first sound of gunfire, the navy was going to turn around and come home. That wasn't the kind of man Kent Hewitt was, but Patton felt that by trying to buck him up with the president in the room that it would put some spine into Hewitt, where Patton suspected there was not enough spine.

[In October of 1942, there were] probably about 5 or 6 million Americans under arms. [The Battle of] Midway had occurred, that critical battle in the Central Pacific, which was really the beginning of the end for the Japanese ambitions of expanding into a greater East Asia co-prosperity sphere. We were fighting in Guadalcanal. The army and the marines had begun the island hopping that would last until the end of the war. We were not fighting anywhere in Europe, so this was the first opportunity to try to liberate the Continent. They started by trying to liberate the Continent just south of it, in Africa.

On the continent of Europe, the Germans had pretty well locked things down by November 1942. France was defeated. The Low Countries had been conquered. Spain was neutral. Switzerland was neutral. Italy, of course, was part of the Axis. The Axis was Germany, Italy, and Japan. They had a number of smaller fellow travelers, but that was the core of the Axis. The British were fighting a perimeter war, a war around the periphery. So there'd been fighting in Crete, brutal fighting in Greece. And in North Africa, of course, [Bernard] Montgomery, the British commander of the Eighth Army, was fighting the commander of the Axis forces there, Erwin Rommel. The great battle of El Alamein, which is in northern Egypt, began on October 23,

1942, almost within a few hours of the meeting between Hewitt, Patton, and President Roosevelt.

[In North Africa at this time,] there were probably about 200,000 British Commonwealth troops. It's important to remember that they weren't all British; they were Australians and New Zealanders, and—a very important part of the British war effort—South Africans.

Rommel had a very large force of Italians under him and a small force of Germans. His total force was probably in the same neighborhood, 200,000. The Italian army had been battered badly in North Africa, and Rommel had no fondness for them at all. He felt, in general, with a few exceptions that they were poor units that could not be relied on. This played out all the way across North Africa into Tunisia, and we see it again in Italy.

Rommel was a very interesting character. He was from southwest Germany. It's important to know that he's not Prussian. He didn't serve on the general staff. There's no "von" in front of his name. He was a very adroit military officer. We think of him as an armor commander, but he was an infantry officer in World War I. It's important to know that he was a very good German. He was a loyalist to Hitler almost to the end of his life. He had commanded Hitler's personal guard for a while at the beginning of World War II. He was sent to North Africa after the Italians had been routed badly in an effort to expand Mussolini's empire down there. Because Hitler could not afford to have the Italians overwhelmed in North Africa—there was the danger Mussolini would fall—he sent this young, very capable, very energetic, and very charismatic commander down there to try and stem the rout, which he did. For two years, the war between the British and Rommel swung back and forth across the northern littoral of Africa. It was a 2,000-mile-wide battlefield.

By the time he comes into our sights, and he arrived in Tunisia at the end of January 1943, Rommel was spent. He was worn out. He was physically ailing. He had blood pressure problems; he wasn't sleeping well. Two years of the stress of combat in North Africa on top of what he'd already experienced elsewhere, including as a commander in France, had really taken a toll on him. So when we see him, he's almost a shell of a man.

THEY BROKE the mold when they made George Patton. There's no doubt about that.

Patton was such a unique character, and [in this stage of the war] we see him really emerge. He began to ascend to the pantheon of the American military in Morocco because he was commanding the force that landed there. You see all of his great strengths as a commander and all of his great weaknesses as a commander right from the get-go in Morocco. [For one, he had a] terrible temper. When the landings were going badly, he was in the surf thrashing around, berating men, striking them, kicking them, screaming at them to get going, acting like a very immature lieutenant. He was actually a major general when the landings first occurred. Patton remained in Morocco as the drive toward Tunisia began.

[General Dwight] Eisenhower was his closest and oldest friend. They'd been friends twenty years at this point. Earlier in the year, Patton had written a letter to Eisenhower that said just that. So when Eisenhower got in trouble, when things went badly after Kasserine Pass, he called on his old good friend George Patton to go take command of the American forces there.

For about forty-three days, Patton was the commander of the II Corps, which was the overarching unit under which all American forces were fighting. He had a kind of checkered experience in those forty-three days. He won no great major battles other than the battle of El Guettar, where the Americans smartly repelled an attack by the Tenth Panzer Division, a very good German armored unit.

Other than that, Patton didn't do anything spectacular, and he left to go back to planning for the invasion of Sicily, which was to be his main job and turned the II Corps over to another up-and-comer, a classmate of Eisenhower's named Omar Bradley. Patton left feeling somewhat unfulfilled by this experience, knowing that he had not been great, that greatness still eluded him, and he was very driven to be great. You see this ambition in Patton from the beginning in North Africa and it carried on to Sicily, where he was the commander of American forces that went into Sicily, and then we saw him again, of course, in western France.

THERE WERE [over] 100,000 who landed initially [in North Africa], mostly Americans, some British in that first landing. By the end of the campaign, there were 460,000 there in May of 1943. The campaign lasted for seven months. There were 70,000 Allied casualties, 20,000 of those were American. About 7,000 of them were killed.

It took longer than anticipated. It was a harder fight. The Germans reacted with such alacrity and audacity really in getting to Tunisia that the fighting in Tunisia was much more protracted and much more brutal than Eisenhower or Roosevelt or anyone else had hoped. But, yes, we ended up defeating a very large German and Italian army, capturing 250,000 German and Italian prisoners, including a dozen generals, and clearing the shores of North Africa, winning back the Mediterranean. The first unimpeded convoy from Gibraltar sailed the Suez right after the campaign in Tunisia ended.

The Vichy French did fight. There had been diplomatic efforts, secret meetings, secret rendezvous, all kinds of efforts to try to get the Vichy French to throw in with us when we landed. All soldiers, including the Brits, wore American uniforms and American flags on their shoulders out of a belief that the spirit of Lafayette would obtain somehow and the Vichy French would not fire on Americans.

The Vichy army didn't fight very intensely. The French navy fought very intensely. There was a tremendous sea battle off the coast of Casablanca. They fought hard for three days. They, the French, suffered about 3,000 casualties and at the end of those three days they threw in the towel. After that, [the French] fought with us. They were not well equipped. They were not particularly well disciplined, but they did fight. They put together a division, and then more, and came into Tunisia with us.

FDR AND THE British prime minister, Winston Churchill, had met earlier at summit conferences, as we would call them today. They met in Washington in June of 1942, and a decision was made that they needed to have a face-to-face meeting with their respective military brain trust to decide where the war was to go from there.

Roosevelt wanted to meet in an exotic place. He wanted to meet in a warm place, and Casablanca sounded intriguing to him. Churchill had spent a lot of time in Morocco and persuaded him that it was a very exotic place to meet. It was done in great secrecy.

The president left Washington on the 9th of January, 1943, without telling anyone, really. He slipped out of town in the dead of night on the *Ferdinand Magellan*, his train. He was the first president ever to fly; he was the first president ever to leave the country during a war.

They spent about ten days in Casablanca deciding what to do next. The decisions made there were very important because for one thing, it affirmed this Mediterranean strategy. They decided that Sicily would be the next blow after the campaign in Tunisia was finished.

It was a wonderful place to meet. They took over a compound outside of Casablanca called Anfa, and along with all the serious business that was conducted, there were great hijinks. And, of course, since Churchill was there, there was great drinking and very little sleep and lots of exotic card games. You had field marshals building sand castles on the beach and so on. It's a wonderful story and it occurs right in the middle of this North African campaign.

THE IMPACT of the campaign in North Africa? I think it changed things in a fundamental way on several counts. First of all, it's where the United States first began to act like a great power, strategically, diplomatically, even tactically. It's where we muscled up for the first time. It's where the relationship between Great Britain and the United States changed. The British slipped into the role of junior partner because the preponderance of American power—including the preponderance of the American capacity to make hundreds of thousands of tanks and airplanes and so on—really became evident for the first time. It's really where the strategy for taking on Germany blossomed and the rest of the war in Europe followed from what happened in North Africa.

THE NORMANDY campaign lasted eleven months of the war [and] really is what most Americans think of as being our involvement in the war in Europe, in particular. I don't think you can understand what happened at Normandy and thereafter without understanding that there was a cumulative history to that army that went ashore in Normandy, and there was a cumulative history of the characters who commanded and peopled that army, and it started in North Africa.

The Bataan March

by

HAMPTON SIDES

Early in World War II, the U.S. Army found itself trapped on the penin-sula of Bataan, where it fought the Japanese for several months before sur-rendering on April 9, 1942. The Japanese led the American prisoners on the infamous Bataan Death March to a prison camp on Cabanatuan, where roughly 3,000 men died during three years of captivity. On January 28, 1945, the U.S. Army carried out a dangerous rescue mission to save the remaining 513 American and British prisoners of war. Hampton Sides appeared on Booknotes *on September 30, 2001, to discuss this rescue mis-sion as told in his book* Ghost Soldiers: The Forgotten Epic Story of World War II's Most Dramatic Mission, *published by Doubleday in 2001. Mr. Sides is a contributing editor for* Outside *magazine.*

THIS IS A STORY that is largely forgotten. It's a story that when you find out about it, you can't believe you weren't taught this in school—this res-cue that took place, one of the largest rescues in American history. When I first heard about it, I couldn't believe that this wasn't part of the shorthand of intrepid American acts like the Rough Riders at San Juan or the Alamo. This is one of those stories within the larger stories of the Pacific [in World War II].

This is the story of a gigantic group of people. Twenty thousand Ameri-cans between Bataan and Corregidor surrendered . . . but so many of these stories were never told because they returned to America after the war and didn't want to tell these dark stories, the dark chapter of an otherwise success-ful, or "good," war. It's only as they've come to the end of their lives that they have felt increasingly comfortable about telling these stories, and getting into it deeper.

BATAAN IS A peninsula that juts out into Manila Bay. It's full of volcanoes and jungles, and the American high command realized it was a perfect place to fight a protracted defensive war. When the Japanese invaded, very quickly General [Douglas] MacArthur realized that they were not going to be able to defend Manila, so they pulled back into this peninsula of land and held out as long as they could. The original war plan, which was known as "War Plan Orange," was to hold out just long enough for the resupply of ammunition, food, and medicines from the navy at Pearl Harbor. But there was no navy anymore because primarily, the navy was destroyed with the attack at Pearl Harbor.

Suddenly, these men on Bataan were caught without prospects for resupply on this peninsula. They held out as long as they could, three or four months, and then on April 9th, 1942, they finally pulled up the white flag and surrendered to the Japanese. The unthinkable thing had happened: The Americans had lost the battle. Of course, they'd never talked about a surrender. They didn't really have any plan or protocol for how you go about giving up your arms to the enemy. Thus began one of the darkest chapters of the war, what came to be known as the Bataan Death March.

The Bataan Death March started on April 9th of 1942 and lasted for [more than three weeks]. The Japanese led most of [the American POWs] from the tip of Bataan, a place called Mariveles, and went north, village by village, as fast as they could go. But, of course, that was the problem. By that point, the Americans were so sick and so depleted and so wracked with diseases that they couldn't move.

There were anywhere from 8,000 to 10,000 Americans who surrendered. It's hard to know the exact number because many of them swam across Manila Bay to Corregidor, the little island, and some just disappeared into the jungle, hoping to hook up with other Americans and develop a guerrilla force. Approximately 8,000 Americans went on this death march and approximately a thousand died en route.

CABANATUAN IS on the island of Luzon, about sixty miles north of Manila. It was the largest American prisoner of war camp ever established on foreign soil. It had as many as 9,000 people [8,000 Americans] there at one time, and it was a little tropical enclave of America. *Ghost Soldiers* really is the resonant phrase that refers to Cabanatuan. These guys referred to themselves as ghosts all the time, the ghosts of Bataan, because not only did they look like ghosts from having lived for three years in squalor and in starvation in these camps, but they felt like they had been forgotten by the land of the living and by their own country. They tried to establish some semblance of an American town. There was a Fifth Avenue, a Broadway, and a Main Street, as they called one of the thoroughfares. The place where they had the camp meetings was known as Times Square. They had a baseball diamond, a camp library, and a university. They called it a university, where the better-educated officers taught classes in astronomy and French to the enlisted men. They tried as best they could to carry on and have some semblance of American society there, to the extent that the Japanese would allow them.

The Japanese viewed prisoners of war very differently. They had ideas from their culture borrowed from the days of the Bushido code, of samurai days, that the ultimate shame was to fall prisoner. To surrender to the enemy was beneath contempt, and you were supposed to save the last round of ammunition for yourself. So this influenced the way they treated the American POWs. They didn't feel a necessity to treat the Americans with any delicacy, and they didn't.

Generally, with their treatment of the POWs, it wasn't like a Nazi policy of extermination or anything like that. Basically, [it was] letting them wither on the vine, not feeding them, not letting basic medicines come into the camp. By and large, these deaths of the American prisoners weren't the result of this sort of cruelty, but just basic diseases like dysentery and malaria that were flourishing in the camp because the Japanese command would not permit basic medicines like quinine to get into the camp. They just didn't feel it was necessary and didn't really understand why a prisoner of war should be treated with any delicacy. They didn't really get the whole Geneva Convention idea.

The prisoners died of dysentery, malaria, and beriberi and all sorts of insidious combinations of those three. Those were the big [causes of death]. They died of all kinds of nutritional deficiencies and a lot of esoteric ailments that cropped up when people were starved, not just for weeks or months, but years. They were primarily eating rice month after month after month, and they didn't have, for example, vitamin B and because they didn't have vitamin B, they were developing beriberi, which is a hideous disease. It causes the extremities to swell up, and eventually, you basically drown in your pus. It's a hideous way to go, and that's what happened to so many of these men.

Lots of other esoteric diseases cropped up. These guys became night blind or lost their vision altogether. Some of them lost their voices and some grew breasts. Their breasts swelled up and became tender. There was a strange disease called "limber neck" where they couldn't hold their heads up. Their necks became like rubber, and literally hundreds of men would walk around the camp holding their necks up with their hands. All these kinds of strange things were developing because they were getting a little bit to eat every day, but they weren't getting basic vitamins and minerals over a prolonged period of time and that wreaked havoc on their constitutions.

Captain Bert Bank, was from Tuscaloosa, Alabama. . . . His prison experience is that he went totally blind; this was probably from vitamin B or other vitamin deficiencies. One day, he was working out on the farm on this prison camp and he was supposed to be pulling weeds, but he was pulling up the actual tomato plants, and one of the guards came up and was going to give him a clubbing, and something happened. I guess the guard realized that the look on Bank's face was pretty vacant—it was clear that he couldn't see what he was doing. From that day on, his eyesight got progressively worse and he was moved inside to work on other details. He became totally blind.

After he got back, he underwent a vitamin regimen of some sort and was able to restore about 50 percent of his eyesight.

ONE OF THE main characters in the book is a guy named Dr. Ralph Hibbs, an army doctor. . . . I was interested in Dr. Hibbs because, to a large extent, this story is a medical story. Japanese cruelty certainly accounted for many deaths, but ultimately, this was a medical story—basic diseases, antique diseases; diseases that we had a handle on in civilized society were rearing their heads for an encore performance in this camp.

Without basic medicines, it was like going back to medieval times with doctors having to improvise, fake their way through operations without anesthesia. They used what they called "vocal anesthesia," which means the doctor just said, "This is not going to hurt much." They used folk remedies of various sorts, and the dentist would make artificial teeth from water buffalo teeth and improvise in all kinds of ways. The extreme measures they had to go to were heroic, and the improvising was just extraordinarily creative.

I MADE IT clear in the book that I was trying to understand the Japanese point of view, trying to understand the cultural factors that influenced the Bataan Death March and their views of the prisoner of war status. There were a lot of kind guards. There were a lot of instances of individual kindness that these prisoners I talked to remembered. Someone who is a Japan basher is not going to get much satisfaction from this book.

The Japanese were running the show from Manila. They wanted to use Manila Bay because it was one of the best harbors in Asia. They would come up from Manila and each commandant would have his own rules and regulations. They ruled with an iron fist. They went into this conflict thinking that the Filipinos would accept their rule because they were Asian and the Filipinos were Asian and the slogan was "Asia for the Asiatics." The Japanese felt that the Filipinos would forget American rule and turn their allegiance to a new power, but that didn't exactly happen. The Filipinos were still very loyal to the Americans, and although there were plenty of collaborators, by and large they didn't cooperate with the Japanese. There were underground and guerrilla organizations. They made life quite difficult for the Japanese occupation.

Usually around 100 Japanese guarded the prison, and it wasn't the cream of the Imperial Army. Most of these guys were either extremely young, green kids, fresh from Japan, or older folks out to pasture, people who were brought in after their military careers were really over. A lot of them were brought in from Korea and Taiwan, which were basically ruled by Japan, and they were stuck out there in the Philippines, a thankless post. So naturally, they were a little bitter and sulking and didn't want to be where they were, and I think this influenced the way they treated the American POWs.

The number of Americans inside the camp fluctuated wildly because the Japanese were continually moving them to one work detail after another. They worked on roads and bridges and shipyards. Through much of this period of 1942, 1943, and 1944, the number [of POWs in the camp] was somewhere around 5,000. Then as the Americans started winning the war and the tide was turning against the Japanese, they decided to start shipping the able-bodied American POWs north to Japan to work in the coal mines of Japan. So the numbers began to dwindle down, finally to 500 people, the last 500 who were left in the camp when the Americans returned.

About 3,000 people died in the camp and were buried in mass graves. All those people were disinterred at the end of the war and reburied in a military cemetery in Manila. More people died there than any other camp in American history, outside of the Civil War itself.

I OPENED THE book with an incident that happened at a different prison camp altogether called Puerto Princesa on the island of Palawan, also in the Philippines. . . . In this incident, the Japanese saw that the Americans were returning and decided to take their 150 POWs that were under their command and light them on fire. It was part of the Japanese policy to not let anyone be turned back over to the Americans for fear that maybe they'd become fighting soldiers again one day or live on to tell about the war crimes that they had witnessed.

One hundred and fifty Americans were involved in the incident [at Palawan], and 140 died. The rest survived, some for just a short while, and there were actually ten who survived, made it home, and told their story to the world. Yet it's an incident that is extremely obscure. The massacre at Palawan is not very well known today, even among the Bataan and Corregidor guys.

There are only two people still alive from the incident, and one is Eugene Nielsen, who's a Mormon gentleman and lives in the mountains in Utah. It's just an extraordinary tale of survival that he was able to escape this massacre. He basically jumped over a barbed-wire fence down onto a beach and hid in various cavelike folds in the coral reef. Eventually, he jumped into the bay and started swimming. He was shot three times, somehow swam for nine hours with bullet wounds, made it across the bay, dragged himself across a mangrove swamp, and eventually hooked up with Filipino guerrillas in order to tell his story to the army intelligence people. All of this figured in, ultimately, to the army intelligence, as they decided what to do with this other camp, Cabanatuan.

The massacre of Palawan happened in December of 1944. In January 1945, the American command returned to the Philippines. . . . They had found out about the existence of this other larger camp, Cabanatuan, and they were worried that a massacre much like Palawan was going to happen. They realized they had to do something, send some men back behind enemy lines and try to extricate these guys before another massacre like this would occur.

It took three days from when the Rangers [of the Sixth Ranger Battalion] got their mission to go in and liberate these men to the point where they got them safely back to American lines. The three days were January 28th, 29th, and 30th of 1945. . . . The Rangers were very helpful to me [in my research]. The Rangers were very modest. Their memories were not particularly complicated. They went in and did their jobs. They had an extraordinarily successful mission.

You had about 100 Japanese guards, and you had anywhere from 200 to 300 Japanese soldiers who were bivouacking in the rear of the camp, just using the place to sleep. Then there were another 1,000 Japanese soldiers one mile away and another 7,000 to 8,000 four miles away in the city of Cabanatuan. So the Japanese were everywhere.

[Colonel Henry Mucci] led the mission to Cabanatuan. . . . They called him "Little MacArthur" because he, like the supreme commander, had a high appreciation of the theatrics of warfare. He smoked a pipe, like MacArthur. He was a character; loud, very charismatic.

[Robert Prince] was the number two, the guy under Mucci who actually went into the camp and devised and planned and executed the assault on the camp.

One of the casualties was a doctor, which seems appropriate in some way to this story because doctors were so much a part of this story from the beginning—from the days of Bataan and now with the rescue, doctors figured into the story so intimately. This doctor, Jimmy Fisher, went along on the raid. He was the battalion surgeon of the Sixth Ranger Battalion, and he wasn't supposed to be at the raid itself. He was supposed to be in the nearby town getting the hospital ready for the casualties that they all expected were going to emerge from this operation. Dr. Fisher ended up being the main casualty of this raid. He was hit by mortar fire and didn't die immediately, but it took about twenty-four hours.

He was an amazing guy, a Harvard-educated guy who found it very important to be right there with his men. He didn't have to be there. He chose to be there at the point of greatest danger, and he paid the ultimate price.

A picture . . . was taken by a *Life* magazine correspondent named Carl Mydans, who did a great story just after the raid took place. The moment that he captured on film is the very moment that [the Rangers and former POWs] had crossed officially over into American lines. . . . The Rangers have big grins on their faces because they've just pulled off this spectacular raid. They'd been up for seventy-two hours, and they'd been popping Benzedrine. Basically, the U.S. Army was handing out speed to the Rangers so they could get through these long missions. The looks on their faces is one part that they are wired on amphetamines and one part elation from knowing that they pulled off this spectacular raid.

Whenever there's a mission like this, there's always somebody who gets left behind, somebody who just is clueless to the whole thing, and Edwin Rose was that man in this case. He was a stone-deaf British civilian, who somehow, through convoluted means, had ended up in this camp in the last few months of its existence. When the raid commenced and the gunfire started, Edwin Rose was sitting on the latrine. He had dysentery, and he was so deaf that he didn't hear the gunfire, and the raid began and ended. All the prisoners were removed and Edwin Rose missed it all.

He went back to his barrack, and went to sleep. He woke up in the middle of the night and realized something was wrong. He smelled smoke. He woke up right around dawn and realized there were Japanese corpses everywhere. Everything was different. He realized something big had happened, but he was still a little addled by the whole experience and his nutritional deficiencies.

It finally dawned on him that there has been a rescue and he'd been left behind. . . . He put on his best suit. . . . He shaved himself and tried to look sharp, went out with his bag to the front of the gate and just waited for something to happen. It could have been the Japanese that picked him up, but in this case, it was some Filipino guerrillas that intercepted him and brought him to safety. He said, "I knew someone would come." He was very optimistic that something good was going to happen, and it did. . . . He made it back to England.

The U-2 Spy Plane

by

PHILIP TAUBMAN

Philip Taubman, Washington bureau chief for the New York Times, *began covering intelligence issues for the paper twenty years ago. He used materials declassified by the federal government in the late 1990s to form the basis of his book* Secret Empire: Eisenhower, the CIA, and the Hidden Story of America's Space Espionage, *published by Simon & Schuster in 2003. He appeared on* Booknotes *on April 13 of that year to discuss intelligence gathering in the Eisenhower era, including the U-2 spy plane incident.*

[SECRET EMPIRE] IS about the creation of spy satellites in the 1950s, in the Eisenhower administration, and the whole vaulting of American spying from the conventional airplanes, up into the stratosphere with the U-2, and then on out into space. All this happened in a compressed period of about six years during the Eisenhower administration, and it essentially revolutionized the intelligence business and played a major role in stabilizing the Cold War and keeping it from turning hot.

[In U-2, the "U" stands for] utility. They couldn't figure out what to call the plane when they created it because they didn't want to identify it as an intelligence-gathering aircraft or reconnaissance aircraft. And they didn't want to identify it as a bomber or something that it wasn't. So they were trying to disguise the purpose of the plane. Somebody found in the air force manuals that there were so-called utility planes, and there was already a U-1 and a U-3, so they randomly called this the U-2.

The creation of the plane was a really amazing seat-of-the-pants operation that unfolded in 1953, 1954, and 1955, after a long process in which the air force had resisted the development of a specialized reconnaissance plane that would penetrate deep into Soviet airspace. It was only [advanced] because of science advisers that Eisenhower brought into play. He put a lot of faith in science.

He had a couple of people [advising him], particularly Jim Killian, who was the president of MIT, and Edwin Land, the man who created instant photography and the Polaroid Corporation. Those two men really were terrifically important in identifying the Lockheed plan for this exotic aircraft, which in its day was a revolutionary airplane.

The notion was that you would fly at 70,000 feet, which was way above any altitude where there'd been sustained manned flight until that point, and that you would cruise across the Soviet Union for thousands of kilometers, taking photographs that would reveal what kind of aircraft they had. The whole undertaking was basically improvised. The air force, in fact, had turned down the Lockheed plan that was the creation of this wonderful airplane designer named Kelly Johnson. Kelly's plan was discarded by the air force, and it was only through the intervention of Killian and Land and other scientists that Eisenhower reached in and said, "Let's build that plane."

And he did something equally revolutionary. Instead of giving it to the Pentagon to build, he put the whole project in the hands of the CIA.

THE U-2 IS basically a jet-powered glider, a rather ungainly looking plane. The wingspan was exceptionally long because under the laws of aerodynamics and of physics, in order to operate a plane at that altitude for that kind of sustained flight, you had to have tremendous lift from the wings.

It also made the plane very delicate. Under the Johnson plan—which is one of the reasons the air force didn't like it—it had no armaments. It had no military specifications of the kind that the air force would usually insist on. It was a very radical idea. The plane was so fragile that there was something that the pilots referred to as the "coffin corner." When you got up to your cruising altitude of about 65,000, 70,000 feet . . . you had to fly it between 388 knots and 394 knots—some very narrow window. If you went below that, the plane would stall, and because it was so delicately constructed, it would disintegrate. If you went above that speed, it would be too fast for the plane, and it would start being buffeted and it would disintegrate.

There's a great moment when one of the first pilots who used the plane took a look at it and tested the wings with his hands. They were so flimsy, he said, "This thing's made out of toilet paper." It was an amazing aircraft. It still is. We're still using it today. I think we have about forty that we use, and it's one of the few aircraft that have survived over the course of now a half a century.

The first test flight took place in mid-1955, and it went into service on July 4th, 1956—the first day that it was flown over the Soviet Union.

The goal was desperation: to find out what weapons the Russians had in those days. It's hard now, looking back, to imagine there was a time like this, although in some ways, it's not that dissimilar to what we face with groups like Al Qaeda, in the sense that there was a new threat emerging in the 1950s. It was the Soviet Union. Remember, they'd been our ally in World War II. Then quickly after the war, the relationship disintegrated, and we soon found ourselves in a Cold War, and we didn't know what kind of weapons the Russians had. We were desperately concerned that they were developing the means to deliver nuclear weapons to the United States in a surprise attack that would have been devastating. It would have made Pearl Harbor look like a pinprick.

Eisenhower became consumed with this. At one point early on in his presidency, he said the world was racing toward catastrophe, and he was right. He needed to have some kind of intelligence-gathering machinery that could look over the Iron Curtain, inside the Soviet Union, and see, at this point, what kind of bombers they had. Later, there was equal need to find out what kind of missiles they were developing.

FRANCIS GARY POWERS was trained by the CIA. Like the other U-2 pilots, he was plucked out of obscurity. Eisenhower did not want to have these planes manned by air force pilots. In fact, his original notion was to train foreign pilots. He didn't want air force insignia on the planes. This was one of the reasons he turned it over to the CIA. The theory being, quite correctly, that the penetration of Soviet air space was an act of war. He wanted to reduce the potential for these planes to set off some kind of confrontation with the Russians. So Powers, like other pilots drawn out of the air force, came from elite air force units. They went through something that was called "sheep-dipping," which was an idiomatic way of describing the process where you retired them, ostensibly, from the air force, they became civilians, and they went to work for the CIA. They went through a lot of training to learn how to fly this plane. They went through some crazy medical tests that were a preview of what later happened to the Mercury astronauts—at the same place, in fact, down in Albuquerque, at the Lovelace Clinic. Tom Wolfe made that famous in his book *The Right Stuff*.

A lot of them—I'm sure Powers among them—when they were plucked out of the air force and recruited to do these missions, assumed they were going to be flying an unbelievably futuristic aircraft. Some of them even thought they might be recruited to go into space. When they got out to this secret airfield in Nevada and they saw this really ungainly looking aircraft, they were stunned and disappointed.

[AS OF MAY 1, 1960,] we had probably no more than a dozen, maybe twenty U-2s. . . . The United States had flown, at that point, twenty-three missions over the heartland of the Soviet Union in the U-2. Along came Francis Gary Powers's flight on May Day. He was shot down over Sverdlovsk, and it created a huge international ruckus.

The Eisenhower administration had feared for some time that the plane might be vulnerable to attack. They put out the most reckless lies in the days immediately after the shootdown. At first, they didn't know that Powers had been caught alive. Khrushchev sprang a surprise on them. When one looks back at it, it was both a very volatile moment in the Cold War, and it was a moment that changed the perception of Americans about their government.

This was before Vietnam, before Watergate, but it was a moment in which the American government lied boldly to the American people. In the imme-diate days after the shootdown, first we said there was no spy plane going over the Soviet Union, it was simply on a weather reconnaissance mission. And then, when it became clear that it had strayed over the Soviet Union and might even have gone in deliberately, the most amazing story was put out by the White House: that the plane had gone up without the approval of any-body in Washington. This was ludicrous, of course. Within a day or two [on May 7, 1960], they had to retreat from that.

In going back and looking at this history, it became clear to me that this was, in a way, a preview of things to come: Americans [were] recognizing that their government was prepared to lie about activities in such a naked way that eroded confidence in the government.

In fact, this very mission that Powers flew started from Pakistan. We flew the plane out of various places over the years. They opened a secret base not far from Peshawar in Pakistan. The theory was that if you came in under the soft underbelly of the Soviet Union, over Afghanistan, and came in over those Asian republics of the Soviet Union, the radar coverage would be less intense than if you flew in from Western Europe. It turned out that was not really the case, and in fact, the second that Powers crossed into Soviet air-space, he was being tracked.

Unbeknownst to the CIA and the Eisenhower administration, the route that they had designed for this flight, unhappily and unluckily, took him right over a missile battery outside of Sverdlovsk, which is on the eastern flank of the Urals. In fact, it's the city that's probably better known as the place where Czar Nicholas II was assassinated by the Bolsheviks after the rev-olution. He and his family had been taken there and killed. [It's also] where Boris Yeltsin was born and grew up and where he made his career in the Communist Party before moving to Moscow. It's a gritty industrial city.

The route of flight for . . . the twenty-three previous missions had all been what they called "racetrack" missions, where they went in, did a big circle route, and came back out pretty much where they started. On this mission, it was the first one they were going to fly across the whole midsection of the Soviet Union, starting from the south and ending up in Norway. On the way, Powers was supposed to photograph some new missile test sites that we were concerned about and some aircraft factories.

They'd been tracking him from the moment he entered the Soviet Union because just a few weeks before, we'd flown another mission where they'd been ready to shoot down the plane, and because of bad communications and scrambling their aircraft belatedly, they couldn't catch up with it. Khrushchev was furious and said, "The next time they come, we're going to get them."

So Powers came in, and as he was flying over Sverdlovsk, they fired off three surface-to-air missiles. One of them hit a Soviet MiG fighter that was scrambled up to attack the plane, and the Russian pilot was killed. Another one went harmlessly by, and the third one blew up right behind the plane, knocking it out of commission. This plane, as I said, was so delicate, you could have hit it with a sledgehammer and it would have started to come apart.

The wings were seventy feet across, and the fuselage was about forty feet, so it's kind of like a gull. . . . We'll never know what piece came off. Powers realized instantly he was in big trouble, and it's a miracle that he survived because the plane went into a tailspin down to the ground. He managed to extricate himself from the cockpit. He was hanging on for dear life, connected by his oxygen hose, as the plane was coming down. He finally, just barely in time, managed to get the hose cut loose so that he could fall free of the plane and open his parachute.

The guy descended onto a collective farm outside of Sverdlovsk, where the farmers were looking up, thinking, "What the heck is going on?" They arrested him. And as I said earlier, Khrushchev did not say immediately that they had the pilot, so they kind of set a trap for the Eisenhower administration.

From 1956, when we started, to 1960, there were twenty-four flights—that's all, because Eisenhower was terrified of flying in because he feared exactly what happened with Powers.

THE SOVIETS knew [about the U-2] from day one. In fact, the first flight—we know it gave Khrushchev tremendous heartburn because it was July 4th, the American Independence Day. He was invited to the residence of the American ambassador, Charles Bohlen, in Moscow, Spaso House. And so there he was, receiving the hospitality of the United States, one of the few times that he was making a gesture to the Americans by going over there.

And that very day, we're making our first flight over the Soviet Union. He was burned up over it. In his memoir and his son's memoir, you can see how angry they were, and they were particularly humiliated because the plane, at that stage, was beyond their ability to shoot down.

POWERS, TRAGICALLY, was put on trial in Moscow. He was convicted of espionage, and then he was exchanged for a Soviet spy who was incarcerated in the United States. He came back, became a helicopter [pilot and] reporter in Los Angeles, and was killed when his helicopter crashed.

THERE ARE STILL a few [of the original U-2 pilots] around. I spoke to Martin [Knutson] and interviewed some others on the telephone. These men for years were not really able to talk about their careers, even after the Powers flight. When the existence of the plane became public, there was still a reticence on the part of the pilots to talk about their missions. And the truth is, as I said, the U-2's still in use today. So it was really only until recent years that the men who flew these original missions felt that the secrecy had finally ended.

In fact, it was only in 1998, not so long ago, that the CIA held a formal declassification conference on the U-2 and took a secret history that they had written internally and made it publicly available, which was invaluable to me in working on my book.

A GOOD DEAL of [this book is newly available information]. . . . One of the new things in the book is that just before the Powers flight, there was a lot of intelligence that should have told the Eisenhower administration that his plane was likely to be shot down. What I discovered in these declassified materials was that as of March 1960, the air force had concluded that the Russians had developed surface-to-air missiles that could reach the altitude and had the accuracy to knock the plane down.

From the day that that report landed, they should have ended the use of the U-2 over the Soviet Union, but they proceeded anyway. It's clear, in retrospect, as you look through these documents and you talk to people who worked with President Eisenhower, he was not adequately informed about the rising danger of a shootdown.

[U-2 FLIGHTS] made a huge difference. They basically stabilized the Cold War. The irony of the plane is that it delivered such invaluable service to the country . . . by allowing us to count the number of bombers that the Soviet Union had. These Bison intercontinental bombers that we feared so much— there were estimates that they were developing hundreds of them—and it turned out they had far fewer than we thought.

The fact that the plane was able to penetrate Soviet airspace was a very important factor in reducing tensions. It gave the United States the feeling that it was not as vulnerable to surprise attack, and yet, ironically, the missions ended with one of the most volatile moments of the Cold War when a plane was shot down.

It was frustrating to the builders of the plane that the flights ended in such a disaster that almost erased all the accomplishments that the plane had achieved up to that point.

TODAY, ANYWHERE there's trouble, we want to use [the U-2]. In fact, in Iraq, one of the issues that came up in terms of the weapons inspectors was whether the U.S. could fly the U-2 over Iraq. The Iraqis finally gave approval, at one point, and we started to use the plane.

WHAT HAPPENED in that era, which would be very hard to replicate today, was a confluence of factors. You had a president in Eisenhower who was committed to innovation and military technologies, who had the enlightened attitude of bringing top-flight scientists into a leading role in the White House. You had in the Oval Office a man who understood both the strengths and limitations of the Pentagon, as the man who had led Allied forces in World War II in Europe, a man who had been a five-star general. It took a lot of nerve. I'm not sure current presidents would have the nerve to say to the air force, "We're going to build an airplane, but the CIA is going to do it and the CIA is going to operate it." Then later he said to the Pentagon, "We're going to build spy satellites and the CIA is going to do it and you're not going to be the lead agency for that."

So you had a president who had this openness to innovation. You had an academic community and a scientific community which was reeling to some extent from the McCarthy witch hunts, particularly the banishment of Robert Oppenheimer—the head of the Manhattan Project that created the atomic bomb—who had lost his security clearance.

These were things that were very unpopular in the academic and scientific community, but people decided they would put their patriotism ahead of their concerns, and they would devote themselves to the national interest, in a way that ended with the Vietnam War. It has been very hard to rebuild since then.

This was, in some ways, the key to what happened with Eisenhower and these projects: He was not a captive of Washington. He brought in all these outside scientists to clear the air and tell him what the bureaucracies were [saying].

There are all kinds of things that we can do as a nation, in terms of technological innovation. Put your faith in science. This was Eisenhower's, in my view, greatest legacy to the nation as president, this abiding faith in science.

THE BIGGEST lesson I learned, which is applicable today, is that you have to have very special circumstances to create these breakthroughs in technology, and we need them again today to combat terrorism.

We need today to replicate what happened in the Eisenhower administration where we brought to bear the best minds in the country, and spared no resources, and had the patience to fail before we could perfect these systems.

In fact, not long after 9/11, the CIA brought back to Langley the very men who had created the systems I write about in my book . . . to talk to them for two days and ask them how can we replicate the environment that existed in the Eisenhower administration. It's something we must do.

The CIA's Covert Operatives

by

TED GUP

The 1949 Central Intelligence Agency Act exempted the CIA from disclosing information about its activities and its personnel. Therefore, the men and women who have died while serving the CIA are acknowledged with a star in the agency's Book of Honor, but many are not identified by name. Their contributions are not known. Ted Gup, professor of journalism at Case Western Reserve University and former investigative reporter at the Washington Post, *spent years unearthing the stories of these nameless officers. Mr. Gup joined us on August 27, 2000, to discuss* The Book of Honor: Covert Lives and Classified Deaths at the CIA, *which was published by Doubleday in 2000.*

THE BOOK OF HONOR is about the men and women who died in service to the CIA who were covert operatives overseas. In most of the cases, their identities were concealed, veiled in secrecy in some instances for ten, twenty, thirty, even fifty years. So the book reveals the identities of covert operatives killed in service to country and, also, the aftermath of those deaths, the burdens borne by the families and the secrecy they were forced to carry.

THE CIA STARTED in 1947. It was a recollection of the elements of the old Office of Strategic Services, the World War II entity. Following World War II, the OSS was quickly disbanded and the elements went to various places, the State Department, the Defense Department. There was quickly, with the rise of the Cold War, perceived to be a need for some centralized intelligence gatherer, hence the CIA. That was put together in 1947, largely bringing back together the disbanded elements of the OSS and modeled in no small part on that structure.

DURING THE [first] Gulf War, about ten years ago, I was at the agency doing a history of U.S.–Iraq relations for *Time* magazine, and I passed before what is called the "Wall of Honor," a marble wall with black lithichrome stars engraved, each one representing a fallen covert operative. In a bulletproof glass case is what is called the Book of Honor at the agency, listing the years each officer fell; and in more than half the cases, anonymous stars conceal their identity. That memorial touched me very deeply, and I decided then and there that I wanted to know the identities of those individuals.

Today, including those that have been added since my book was finished, there are seventy-seven fallen covert operatives. . . . [Only four are women, and that] reflects the history of the agency, in which there were not so many women on the front lines. In more recent times, there are a great number of women out there at risk.

WHY AM I interested in doing this? I'm haunted by the idea that we don't believe in the past, that it's not real for us, that it seems to be fiction. And I'm haunted by the oblivion to which people who gave their lives for country are subjected and by the fate of the families, the surviving family members who have been forced by the full weight of the U.S. government not to speak of their loved ones for many decades. Indeed, they are required to tell lies all those decades, to stick to the cover story at the time of their loved one's death. I found that haunting. Part of the reason I wrote this, in no small measure, was to try to lift some of that burden. It bothered me, and the more time I spent with the family members, the more it bothered me.

The first person that I interviewed was the chief of public affairs at the CIA. This was not done in any kind of sub-rosa fashion because I knew I'd be setting off trip wires and alarms left and right. I knew I was going to have to interview hundreds of covert officers and that probably the first time I made a call, it would get back to CIA headquarters. So I called their public affairs staff and said, "This is what I'm doing. I'm doing a project to try to unmask the identities of your fallen covert operatives. Can I get any help?" I don't want to sound as naive as I may sound in that. It was really a way of setting down a bookmark and saying, "This is what I'm doing. I'm not trying to end-run you. I want you to know this is what I'm up to." They had me over. We talked. They tried to dissuade me from doing it. And in the course of the total four years, they provided many courteous return phone calls and zero cooperation.

I interviewed more than 400 covert operatives, past and present, as well as several hundred family members. I would say it was 800 or 900 people all together over the course of four years.

I name about thirty-five who are nameless. Their names were not gathered under the Freedom of Information Act; that was of no help. This was all the old roll-up-your-sleeve, hard-core sleuthing. It was the only way.

It's a curious thing, but there's nothing off the record in this book. As sensitive and classified as it is, all but two families cooperated fully in writing this book. . . . I think that the reason that I got so much cooperation is that even those who have dedicated their lives to national security recognize that a lot of this is preposterous, that it still be veiled in secrecy.

DOUGLAS MACKIERNAN was a much-decorated World War II veteran who was at the very founding of the agency in 1947 and, about that same period, volunteered for one of the most remote assignments in the world in Urumchi in Xinjiang, China, far west China. His mission was, in large measure, to monitor the Communists as they surged to power and to do what he could to prevent them or at least harass them. The reason he's in the book—aside from the fact that he died in service—is that he underwent a 1,200-mile trek across desert and mountains, the Himalayas, trying to flee the Communists. He got within about fifty yards of safety, the Tibetan border, but a message from the U.S. government to the Dalai Lama granting Mackiernan safe passage was not delivered in time, and he was shot to death and beheaded within a few steps of safety.

[He left behind at his death a] widow, Pegge, and Mary and Mike, their one-year-old twins. The Chinese Communists accused him of being a spy, and indeed, the Chinese knew he was a spy. The only people who did not know he was a spy were the Americans. It played into the demonization of the Chinese and the Chinese government at the time.

The Americans know now with publication of this book that Mackiernan was a spy. But there was nothing before. A piece I wrote in the *Washington Post Magazine* in 1997 was the first confirmation that he was a spy.

I can't help but reflect on Douglas Mackiernan. When I called his widow, Pegge, I was the first one in forty-seven years to put together the fact that her late husband was the CIA. You can imagine the shock. To get a call out of the blue saying, "I'm putting together the pieces of a puzzle forty-seven years old," she was thunderstruck. Because for forty-seven years, the agency had told her, "You are not to talk about your late husband and if you do, you must say that he was an employee of the State Department, a vice consul." Again, the Chinese Communists knew Mackiernan was a spy and as evidence of that, they executed everyone that he had contact with within a year of his flight. It was no secret to the Chinese Communists. It was a secret to the U.S.

What happens is the U.S. paints itself in a corner. They say he was not a spy and then they lose credibility when they admit that he was. It also plays into the propaganda of the Cold War, that an innocent man was on the run and slain.

PERHAPS THE least glamorous of the people in the book, [is] Barbara Robbins, who was a twenty-one-year-old secretary in Saigon in 1965. She worked for the CIA. She was under State Department cover. One day she heard some noise in the street. She went to the window at the U.S. Embassy in Saigon to see what was happening. And at that very moment, a car bomb by a terrorist detonated and the grating around the window impaled her. She was killed instantly. I cite her because she came from a very patriotic family. Her father was a butcher outside of Denver, Colorado, and when I spoke to him, first in 1996 and 1997 and again in 1998, he told me that one of his final wishes in his life was to see his daughter's name inscribed in the Book of Honor, not just an anonymous star. He wanted her recognized. He died last year with that wish unfulfilled. His widow is still alive and shares that wish. I cite her because it's an egregious example of the CIA's obsession with secrecy. Why a twenty-one-year-old secretary who was killed thirty-five years ago cannot be identified after all this time is beyond my grasp.

Anyone is welcome to ask, but the CIA will neither confirm nor deny that Barbara Robbins was a part of the agency. It's the standard line that they've been issuing to these families decade after decade. They told me no more than they told anyone else in the public. There's a generic argument. A generic argument is that they need to protect sources and methods. "Sources" primarily means the individuals who've supplied them information. "Methods" are the ways in which they get that information, that intelligence. They're afraid, they say, that identifying these individuals will put foreign nationals and our own people at risk or will compromise the way that we gather intelligence.

I'm not someone that's made a living demonizing the agency, but the truth of the matter is that this is not an issue of national security. It's an issue of bureaucracy. There is simply no constituency pushing for the change, the lifting for the veil of secrecy. A butcher outside of Denver does not have enough power to lift the veil of secrecy, even on his own daughter's name. That's why it's remained this way year after year after year; it is the inertia of the bureaucracy. And unless and until someone plants a significant political powder keg under them, they're not going to change. This is the way it is. It's always easier to ignore than to change.

LARRY FREEDMAN was Jewish and very proud of the biblical tradition of Jewish warriors going back to the Maccabees. He was a Green Beret in Vietnam, he was in the elite Delta Force counterterrorist unit that made the aborted effort to rescue the hostages in Teheran. He was the first casualty in Somalia.

He was a hellion. He was a kid who, before he reached thirteen, held up a gas station with a bow and arrow, a real hunter's bow and arrow. He sawed off the top of a car to make it a convertible. He drove Harleys at high speeds. He got in more than a little trouble. Were it not for his finding the Green Berets and the military, I'm not sure exactly what would have become of him. But it was a perfect match, and it harnessed all of his excessive energy and his incredible courage and his patriotism. He became one of those who trained Delta Force at Fort Bragg, and was brought into the CIA upon retirement from Delta Force. He was renowned as a sniper. He could run five, six, seven miles with a full pack, set up his rifle and wait for two or three days for ten seconds of a window, when someone passed by, to do what he did as a sniper. He was deadly accurate, deadly patient, and a perfect physical specimen and very patriotic.

All of those resources and skills that he had were of no avail in Somalia. The vehicle he was in hit a land mine, a Russian land mine, and he was immediately killed. He was near Bardera, and he was there to ensure that airports were open so that food and relief supplies could reach the starving people of the country. He was not there in a capacity as a sniper. He was there as a kind of intelligence officer and liaison between the incoming U.S. military and the embassy and other elements of our U.S. government.

He was killed in December 1992. He's an anonymous star.

JOHN MERRIMAN'S story is particularly sad. He was killed in the Congo in 1964. His widow, Val, and son Jon are people that I've gotten to know quite well in the course of my reporting. They were at the director of central intelligence's office to receive a medal. Not long after they arrived, a call was placed from the White House inviting them to come over and meet the president [Johnson] and Lady Bird. They did go over there and there's no mention of it in the logs at the White House. I went through the Johnson Library. There's no reference. It was all hush-hush.

Merriman was flying a plane in the Congo, helping to suppress a Communist insurgency there, and he took ground fire and crashed. He was presumed dead, and the rest of the squadron returned to a remote base there. The next day, some indigenous people there drove up with a truck and a crumpled-up body in the back and it was the body of John Merriman, who was very much alive, although in agony. He was taken to the base hospital, which didn't even have aspirin, much less doctors or nurses. He had nothing to treat his pain. He had numerous broken bones, lacerations, internal bleeding. The straps from his seat belt had slashed into his skin. And he was allowed to stay there without medical attention for well over a week. He was in agony, passed in and out of consciousness. When he was conscious, all he said was, "Take me home. Take me home." He was allowed, essentially, to waste away in a Congolese hospital for another couple of weeks before any attempt was made to bring him home, and he died en route over the ocean.

The saddest part is that his widow was told that he died in a hospital in Puerto Rico, that he had asked for ice cream. They had brought him ice cream, and he died quietly in his sleep without pain. He was never in Puerto Rico. He never asked for ice cream. He died on a transport plane after great agony.

[handwritten margin note: embellished fiction) why?]

I'm not sure what part of the cover story they got, but the local newspaper in Tennessee, where his home was, reported as his death certificate did, that he was killed in a car crash in Puerto Rico, hitting an abutment.

I interviewed the Cuban pilots that Merriman trained and that flew with him. I interviewed the chief of station at the time at the agency. I interviewed probably forty or fifty people that were familiar with what he was doing in the Congo at the time.

The Cubans, after the Bay of Pigs, remained a resource for the CIA to conduct counterinsurgency activities. They hated Castro. There was nothing more the Cubans could do to dislodge Castro after the fiasco of Bay of Pigs. They had enough distance from the U.S. government, being Cuban, that they gave the U.S. government some deniability. Many of them were trained pilots from the Bay of Pigs, so they simply became a kind of surrogate air force for the CIA.

John Merriman was in the Congo to supervise the Cuban pilots. He was actually, technically, not supposed to fly, but he couldn't resist it. He was truly a flyboy. He loved to be in aircraft.

Merriman is named in the Book of Honor, but I asked probably fifty or sixty current covert operatives if they knew who John Merriman was. None of them knew who he was. None of them knew anything about him. They never heard of him.

HUGH REDMOND IS, unfortunately, in three different chapters because it reflects the sad attenuation of his life. He was supposed to be a businessman in Shanghai prior to the Communists' taking control of the government there. In fact, he was an NOC, under "nonofficial cover." He was a CIA person. Actually, he went over even before there was CIA and then became a part of the CIA when it came into being in 1947.

He was arrested trying to come home. He was helping nationalists within China conduct sabotage, supplying them with information and probably weapons as well. He was arrested, incarcerated for nineteen years, much of it held incommunicado. He was beaten. At points, he was starved. He suffered from malnutrition. He lost his teeth prematurely, just a terrible record of agony. He never admitted he was a spy. The U.S. government never admitted he was a spy; and if they had, he probably would have been released at that moment.

The Chinese government granted permission for the mothers of John Downey, Richard Fecteau, and Redmond, all three CIA spies held in Chinese prisons, to visit their sons who had been imprisoned for many years. And all the while, the U.S. government denied that they were CIA spies.

Redmond's star is nameless. It dates back to 1970, when it was said that he slashed his wrists with an American razor in the Chinese prison. We have no idea how he really died because the Chinese waited three months and then handed us an urn of ashes.

He was imprisoned in 1951, and he died in 1970. They cremated his body and turned the ashes over to the Red Cross, who carried it over the bridge, the Lowu Bridge, into Hong Kong and presented it to American Embassy officials there.

His mother pleaded with the government to do everything they could to get him out. She visited her son seven times. It was a horrible kind of strobo-scopic experience watching your son age prematurely. He developed all kinds of tics and ailments. He was never treated properly. He was very tough, but he was not immune to the kind of despair that one would encounter seeing your whole youth pass before your eyes. And his mother, it just disabled her with pain and regret to see this happen to her son.

It was very sad. The Yonkers, New York, community was completely behind Hugh Redmond's mother and every effort to free him. They had fund-raisers, they had all kinds of appeals to government. It was an incredibly cele-brated case, not only in Yonkers, but in the Northeast and, to some degree, around the country at the time. And the sad thing was that it was allowed to feed into the anti-Communist, anti-Chinese propaganda. The way the U.S. government allowed it to be played is that here was an innocent U.S. business-man held for nineteen years, when, in fact, he was a trained CIA operative probably engaged in direct sabotage or certainly assisting sabotage. I'm not sure what government wouldn't hold a saboteur in prison, but that conflicted with the Cold War objective, so they did not acknowledge that he was a spy.

RICHARD BISSELL WAS—I hate to use this word because it's so overused—but I think he was genuinely a genius. He was the father of the U-2 spy plane. He was really responsible, in no small measure, for the SR-71 Blackbird surveillance plane. He was instrumental in the first satellite imagery. . . . He was even prouder of his role in sponsoring covert activities overseas. He was a part of that era in the late 1950s when the agency had a carte blanche and were active all around the world. He was one of the architects of the disastrous Bay of Pigs, which is why he's in the book. Because despite all his triumphs, he'll forever be linked to and remembered, at least in part, for his role in that debacle.

There's a quote in there about Kennedy saying, "How could I have been so stupid?" But it really was an unmitigated disaster, and it was foreseen as such by many. That was the saddest part, is that they had a plan which may or may not have been workable, but at least it had the indicia of possible success. But it was continually cut back and curtailed to reserve presidential deniability and prevent the U.S. from being linked to it, which was absurd. Even as the operation was ongoing, the U.S. hand was all over it. So what we had done—the U.S., that is—is basically we had condemned ourselves to failure. Four American pilots died in the Bay of Pigs. Their identities were known within months, and their identities circulated in newspapers and books around the country for the ensuing three decades. But the agency refused to recognize their names, and they were nameless stars in the Book of Honor.

THE PRESS WAS always fed a lie. The press was always told that these were State Department employees or workers for AID, the Agency for International Development, or civilian employees of the Defense Department, or employees of foreign corporations. The press was never told who they really were, what they were really doing. The widows or widowers were informed of the loss.

There was a ritual in which the director of central intelligence would pen a letter to the widow or widower expressing his deep regret and sorrow, and that would be presented to the widow or widower along with a medal. And then both the medal and the letter would be promptly withdrawn within a matter of an hour or two. Usually immediately after the funeral, the agency would re-collect them and put them in a locked vault, so there was no evidence that they indeed worked for the agency.

ARTHUR MALONEY was a veteran of Normandy, a West Point grad, and a true combat officer. He was wounded after Normandy, and because of his wounds, he could not pursue his military career, and by default, he entered the CIA. He is in my book, both of his own right and also because his son became a CIA officer. His son was on a helicopter that crashed in Laos in 1965. His son's name was Mike Maloney. On the aircraft were two CIA case officers, Mike Maloney and Mike Deuel.

What the two Mikes on the helicopter had in common was that they were both the sons of senior CIA people. They'd both had very young brides. They were newly married. And both of their wives were pregnant at the time that they were killed. They were killed in 1965, and their identities hushed up.

The two Mikes were in Laos, part of what was then called "the secret war," which was increasingly becoming less than a secret. They were flying a helicopter, and they crashed near Pakse into a very dense jungle and were killed instantly. The U.S. press reported the death of two AID officers, and for thirty-five years, that stood. No one linked them to the CIA. In 1997 in a [*Washington*] *Post* article, I disclosed that Mike Maloney was CIA, not AID. What is sad about that story is that his widow, Adrienne, for years had asked the CIA to recognize her late husband by name, to put his name in the Book of Honor at agency headquarters for the benefit of her two sons.

She was told by then DCI, the director of central intelligence, John Deutch, "Write me a note. . . . We'll see what we can do about getting his name recognized in the Book of Honor." She wrote him a note, didn't hear anything. Sent a letter by registered mail, didn't hear anything; called, and was told her letters were lost. They basically ignored her and wanted her to go away. The day that my article came out, they called her and said they had changed their minds and they put his name in the Book of Honor.

SECRECY IS MORE of a threat to national security than lax secrecy, because when everything has been classified secret and top secret, people within the agency no longer take it seriously. Its credibility is eroded. What happens is that individual case officers make their own decisions. They say, "Well, it's classified, but it shouldn't be classified at this level." Or, "It's classified, but it won't hurt if I share this with someone." So what happens is someone like me comes along and I'm the beneficiary of that obsession with secrecy because many of those people who helped me should not have helped me under the rules of the CIA. But they took it upon themselves to make the judgment about what should and should not be classified. This is a direct result of the obsession with secrecy.

A Vietnam War Memoir

by

JOHN LAURENCE

During the Vietnam War, American television correspondents had relatively open access to fields of battle, providing dramatic footage of the conflict, though often at great personal risk. John Laurence was a CBS *News correspondent in Vietnam between 1965 and 1970. While he and his crew were embedded with a battalion of American soldiers, they produced the award-winning documentary* The World of Charlie Company. *Mr. Laurence appeared on* Booknotes *on January 20, 2002, to discuss his memoir* The Cat from Hué: A Vietnam War Story, *published by PublicAffairs that same year. Mr. Laurence lives in rural England.*

CBS SENT ME [to Vietnam in 1965 when I was twenty-five years old] as their radio correspondent. They had an extra camera crew. They'd sent the best combat crew they could find, Jim Wilson and Bob Funk, camera and sound, to Vietnam to work with Morley Safer, who had arrived a couple of months earlier. So they were going to have Morley and this great combat crew, and me as the radio reporter on his own, working separately. But Morley had discovered a marvelous Vietnamese cameraman that he enjoyed being with—they were well matched in many ways—named Ha Tu Kan. So when Wilson and Funk arrived, Morley was already happily partnered, and so Fred Friendly, who had hired me, decided that he would just try to see if I could do television.

I was convinced Vietnam was the right place to be. I was convinced it was a worthy cause. I believed in the military and the superiority of American fighting power, airpower, firepower. I believed that it was the right thing to do. I believed, probably, in the same way that young correspondents felt at the beginning of World War II when they went to Europe.

[MY FIRST STORY to air on *CBS News*] was a piece called "Dawn Attack: The 101st Airborne." One company of the 101st Airborne went into a village, a hamlet in the Van Thanh Valley—Happy Valley—just northeast of An Khe, and tore it up, just tore it to pieces looking for the Vietcong, some of whom they found and killed, but they burned the houses and threw a grenade in a bunker and killed a pregnant woman.

The area was what the American military and the South Vietnamese considered to be hostile territory. It had been controlled by the Vietminh and controlled later by the Vietcong. [The Vietminh] were the people of Vietnam who fought the French and drove them out, defeated them at Dien Bien Phu, led by Ho Chi Minh and his people. And the Vietcong were the indigenous South Vietnamese resistance, the National Liberation Front troops, the armed wing of the National Liberation Front.

A paratrooper was trying to clear some of the bunkers that were under each of the huts, or houses, in the hamlet, and just tossed a hand grenade. In fact, Wilson got a picture of it happening, and he, of course, would not have done that if he'd realized that there was a nineteen- or twenty-year-old girl in there. I'm just sure that the troops did not intend to kill innocent civilians. The company commander, as soon as he saw this, brought the body of the woman out and put her on the road, because they wanted every one of the soldiers, and us, to see what had happened. It was an accident. It was a mistake. It wasn't deliberate at all.

[The American troops] took a number of prisoners, some of whom were pretty assuredly VC, and tied them up and sat them in the sun. The company commander, right away, said, "No more hand grenades in the bunkers. Bunkers are like breezeways in America." He was a very, very bright, young West Point graduate—a young captain named Martin. So the troops stopped throwing hand grenades, but then they started throwing smoke grenades into the bunkers. They didn't want anybody in the ground whom they couldn't see. They were trying to flush out the VC. Wherever they found documents or a weapon or evidence of VC, they burned the houses down. First they blew them up, and then they burned them down.

I wrote a very sympathetic report about the soldiers. I didn't criticize them at all, and we didn't dwell on the fact that the woman had been killed. In fact, the shot lasted six seconds.

THERE'S A description [in my book] of Charlie Beckwith and his Special Forces Delta team. One of the first military operations that Delta ever did was to relieve the garrison at Plei Me Special Forces camp. This is in October of 1965 just before the . . . Ia Drang Valley battles. We were coming in—Wilson, Funk, and I, and an NBC cameraman named [Vo Huynh] and Charles

Mohr of the *New York Times*—with a South Vietnamese Ranger battalion, and it was ambushed. An armored convoy on its way to Plei Me, a South Vietnamese armored convoy, with lots of American advisers, was ambushed by a regiment of North Vietnamese. This was the first major contact between regular units of the North Vietnamese and American forces. The South Vietnamese held, with casualties; the North Vietnamese took a lot of casualties. The attack took place at twilight, and it was one of those beautiful, glowing, orange and blue sunsets behind us. American planes were sent; F-100s came in to bomb along the side where the attack was taking place. Both Charlie Mohr and I remarked, for years later, at how much a medieval duel it seemed like between the North Vietnamese anti-aircraft gunners and the American pilots. The tracers of the bullets shooting out of the airplane and the tracers coming up toward the airplanes were intersecting like crossed swords—very colorful, very bright, especially at that time of day.

The next morning, after the battle and after the North Vietnamese had retreated, our Ranger battalion walked down into the valley where the fighting had taken place. By chance, we came across that North Vietnamese anti-aircraft gun, and it was still pointed in the air and all the gunners were dead from the bombs the American pilots had dropped.

Wilson took a picture of a North Vietnamese soldier. He couldn't have been more than eighteen years old. Half of his head had been blown away, and it was exposed to the light, and it was an ugly thing to have to look at. [While writing this book,] I was sitting there at the computer, writing, trying to describe this young soldier's eyes looking at me and my reactions to it, and I remembered something that I hadn't taken a note about: Wilson got down on one knee with his big Oracon film camera and put the lens at the minimum distance he could to take a close-up—from the soldier's exposed head with the wound, and turned it on. He focused it and turned it on and rolled for about a minute, and he said, "They'll never use the shot," meaning they'll never use it in New York. That's where the film was processed and screened. He said, "But it'll sure 'F' up their lunch." He had a wicked sense of humor.

[By 1970,] TRYING to stop the war was a burning issue with me. Based on my experiences in Vietnam, I came to the conclusion that, first of all, the war could not be won; secondly, that what we were doing to the Vietnamese was wrong and cruel; third, that the Vietnamese would be better off under any kind of political system—democratic, Communist, didn't matter—that wasn't killing them. I felt a moral obligation, based on what I had learned, to do whatever I could to help to try to stop the war, and the only way that I could do that was as a correspondent for CBS. So we went back the third time in 1970 to make this documentary, to show people what it was costing us, as a nation, to keep our boys over there.

I went back with Keith Kay and Jim Clevinger as camera and sound, three guys commissioned by CBS to go and do a series of reports by living with American soldiers in the field. Before then, the best documentary I thought that had been made about the Vietnam War was . . . by Pierre Schoendoerffer, a fine, fine writer and fine documentary maker and filmmaker and a fine man. They'd called it *The Anderson Platoon*. They'd spent a few weeks living with a platoon from the First Cavalry in 1966 and made this marvelous documentary full of action and combat. It was very sensitively made and beautifully photographed.

We thought we might improve on that by doing an hour, doing it in color, and spending more time with a smaller unit, a squad, or even a fire team, twelve or four guys. We went to the First Cavalry division, and it turned out that the [senior public] information officer was an old friend of mine from the 1965–1966 days, J. D. Coleman, who was a major. J. D. knew my record and we told him what we wanted to do. He took us to the assistant division commander, [Brigadier] General Casey, who listened to what we had to say. He signed off on us going to live in the field without an officer in escort, or any escort—just simply living with the troops and trusting us to get it right.

We lived with a squad in Charlie Company, Second Battalion, Seventh Cavalry. We got to know them, they got to know us, and we trusted them as well. We were in an extremely hot area of War Zone C in the Dog's Head [forest] in the spring of 1970, just before the invasion of Cambodia. The North Vietnamese 95-C regiment was very, very active in that area and was just raising Cain with that brigade of the First Cavalry. Our battalion was very seriously attacked, and part of the artillery was overrun. They lost their commander as a result.

Charlie Company's sister companies were all hit—Alpha, Bravo, and Delta were all engaged in serious firefights, took serious casualties in the same period—and by some miracle, we weren't hit. Charlie Company was a very careful rifle company under a very careful and cautious commander, Captain Bob Jackson, who was on his second tour, had taught the troops, "Never walk down a trail." He had a heart attack in the field and was relieved by a younger captain, a very good man named Al Rice. Within the first week, Rice asked his troops to walk down a trail. They didn't want to do it; at least the lead platoon wasn't going to walk down the trail.

We photographed this, and recorded this, and reported this on "Cronkite." As a result, as much because of a *Newsweek* article that the troops got to read, there was dissension in the company; there was unpleasantness directed toward us, and we were expelled from Charlie Company for a time. About a month later, the Pentagon put enough pressure on the division commander to let us back in, to finish the documentary, and we did. They were gentlemanly enough to realize the project was unfinished. But they felt that we should not have shown that to the American public.

You see, the military likes to take care of its own house; this I've learned over the years. And they're very good at it. If you're an officer and you make a mistake, that's the end of your career, or it means you're unlikely to get a promotion. The more senior you get, the more difficult it becomes. They discipline their own very efficiently, but they don't like it to be seen in the outside world, and we had done that.

You might not get that kind of dissension today, because you've got an all-volunteer army. These soldiers, as good as they were—and they were excellent soldiers in Charlie Company—were mostly draftees.

Bill Ochs was the [First] Brigade commander, and it cost him his job, unfortunately. When you get up to general officer level in the army, the number of good people available for promotion every three years is greater than the number of slots available. So if you make a mistake or you don't know what's going on in your area of operation, if you slip up in any way—and I'm not suggesting that Bill Ochs did slip up—you're gone. It's just that as a result of the rebellion and the walking down the road, a B-52 strike was canceled, and the Pentagon doesn't like B-52 strikes being canceled. Bill Ochs was relieved of command sometime later, a month or so later, and that was the end of his career. He didn't make general as a result. But the army works that way. It will stop your career if you make a mistake.

The colonel and the information officer and some others came to meet us at Tan Son Nhut airport to ask us to change the wording of our script. We had prepared the film and were all ready to go with the rebellion story, to ship it to the States and have it edited. They wanted us to tone it down, to call it a "temporary refusal." I used the words "brief rebellion," and that was the best that I could do. I had to call it as we saw it and as it was captured on film. Looking back on it now, I probably would have changed it. If I knew then what I know today, if I was as experienced today, I might have changed the wording. It might have made it easier for us to finish the story, and that's one of the points in the book. If you can get along well enough with the military to be trusted and still trust your own conscience to report fairly and accurately and without personal bias, you can get along. . . . What I know is that if they don't know you and know that you're trustworthy, they're not going to let you get close to them.

JED DUVALL, who was a CBS correspondent about to go to Vietnam . . . argued that it was wrong to bring your personal attitudes, political attitudes, or humane attitudes—I think it was less political than it was our sense of humanity—to a story that we were going to cover. I argued with him that, in this case, it was an exception. I would agree with Jed that on 99.9 percent of all the stories that we American journalists cover, we should try to keep our personal biases out of it. But after five years of Vietnam and knowing the history and the little bit of the culture and what had happened and what we were doing, I felt that the more that I could do by reporting, [the better]. If you go back and look at those reports, you'll see that they're not biased. They're just showing a very detailed look of what the troops felt and less of what I felt.

I believe that a good journalist tries to help make a difference in the world. The very best journalists want to keep the American public as well informed as possible, even if it means risking their lives or losing their relationships or their sleep or their comfort or their health, which has happened in many cases. You go to Ethiopia, to the ends of the earth, to take pictures and do interviews and gather facts about people who are living through a famine and starving because you hope that people who see this back home will give twenty bucks to CARE or volunteer to join an organization that goes over there to help. What I've tried to do with this book is similar to that.

IF YOU READ this book all the way through, one chapter at a time, something happens. The people who have read the book, friends of mine, and some of my military friends, say that it is like a Greek tragedy. It is constructed as a tragedy, like a play, although it's not a play. It has all of the elements of an Aristotelian tragedy—ethos, and catharsis, and reversal, and there are a whole bunch of them: discovery, plot, magnitude, and, at the end, evaluation, what the Greeks called *dianoye*.

If you read the book through, you'll find yourself, like the narrator, going through all those steps, you go through a process of seeing that this was a vast landscape in Vietnam and that the stakes were so very, very great; that people were being killed. Greek tragedy always has suffering and death involved in it. There is a story which has a beginning, a middle, and an end—a plot, as there needed to be. And then the character changes; the reversal that's necessary happens, and out of that comes the discovery that something is wrong or something has caused this. There's causality, as in tragedy.

By the end of the book, it's my hope that, particularly, veterans of the war or people who lost friends in the war will see through what I write in Act 5— or Part 5—that all of this has a reason; that all of what happened in Vietnam has meaning for us today. That may not have been apparent before. I don't proclaim to have a cure for post-traumatic stress disorder, but I did have to resolve my own. It was difficult, but in the writing of the book, I think that has happened. It's my life's work, because I hope it may be helpful to others.

Vietnam POW Jim Thompson

by

TOM PHILPOTT

More than 800 American soldiers were seized by enemy forces during the Vietnam War. Among them was Special Forces Captain Jim Thompson, who was captured by the Vietcong during a reconnaissance mission in South Vietnam. Thompson endured nearly nine years of confinement and torture, more than any other known prisoner of war in U.S. history. Virginia author Tom Philpott revealed Thompson's experience as a prisoner and his difficult return to the United States in Glory Denied: The Saga of Jim Thompson, America's Longest-Held Prisoner of War, *which was published by W. W. Norton & Company in 2001. Mr. Philpott joined us on* Booknotes *on August 5, 2001.*

JIM THOMPSON IS the longest-held prisoner of war in American history. His story has been largely buried under an avalanche of tragedy for the last twenty-eight years. He's a stroke victim today. He couldn't tell his own story. I met him in 1984. I got his permission to tell his own story. And so my book *Glory Denied* is about what he went through in Vietnam. It's also about what his family went through in Vietnam and the family together went through after the war.

Alyce was Jim's wife. They had been married ten years at the time that Jim was lost in Vietnam and his captivity began. They met in New Jersey. Jim found in the army a place where he could realize his dreams and ambitions, but he was swept up in a war that he had no understanding of, that Alyce had no understanding of. She didn't know where Vietnam was, even at the time he was assigned there. It was very early in the war when he was lost and the war would affect all their lives profoundly.

He was an army captain in Special Forces. He was reluctantly in the Special Forces. Most Americans believe that the Special Forces are all volunteers. At the time John Kennedy said, "Let's build them up. We've got to fight communism around the world more aggressively." Jim Thompson was on recruiting duty, perfectly happy, a young army captain, and he was volunteered for Special Forces. He protested. That isn't what he wanted to be in. The protest went nowhere. He was assigned to it because that army needed officers for Special Forces. He was soon swept up in it. He was being trained at the time in 1962, to be assigned to the Congo. He was learning Lingala. Suddenly, Vietnam got hot and his team was told to train for Vietnam.

[HE WAS] shot down March 26th, 1964. He had been in Vietnam for three months. His assignment at that time was to be in charge of a Special Forces A-team. The A-teams were dispersed throughout Vietnam, and their mission was to win over the local populace, to train them to fight infiltration by the Vietcong. Khe Sanh . . . became much more famous in 1968 when there was a marine corps there. But in 1963, when Jim first arrived, it was a very remote outpost, quite a dangerous assignment, and his twelve-man team was there to work with the Nungs, who were sort of special forces from China, to work with the Montagnards, who were the native population there, and to work with South Vietnamese regular forces. None of them were as gung ho as the Americans.

[He was captured in 1964 and released] on March 16th, 1973, so ten days short of nine years.

PERHAPS I should tell you first how he was captured, which was with the A-team. They would be resupplied and receive their payroll from an air force plane that would fly in periodically. And if it had extra gas, one of the team members would hop aboard to see if they could see what Vietcong activity was like in the area. Jim Thompson didn't go on those flights. Usually it was his operations sergeant who did. But the sergeant was on R&R in Nha Trang on the coast.

So Jim hopped aboard. He thought he saw a bridge that had been newly built and he asked the pilot, an air force captain by the name of Richard Whitesides, to fly down below flight minimums, which was 1,000 feet, and they were shot out of the sky. Whitesides likely was killed from small-arms fire, but he was certainly lost in the crash. Jim was thrown from the crash. He had a broken back. He had a wound across his cheek. He had burns on his legs. He was in and out of consciousness when the Vietcong picked him up. He was kept for the next four years in jungle camps throughout South Vietnam. It was really quite a different existence than the pilots who eventually were shot down in the North and captured—all together they were a support group. But because Jim was isolated, he never had any of that kind of support structure. Additionally, he was exposed to so much more physically than they were up there just from trying to survive in a jungle environment.

IN THE FIRST couple of years [of his captivity], Jim went through some extreme torture. That was a typical kind of torture that the Vietcong and the North Vietnamese had done on prisoners of war. But Jim was suffering through it by himself.

Probably the worst time for him during his first four years of isolation in the jungles was when he didn't pay sufficient respect to the guards, so they threw him in a cage that he described as about two feet wide, two feet high, and five feet long, and he laid on his side for the next four months. They would bring him out of the cage every once in a while. . . . That's the typical kind of environment that he was kept in, just a bamboo cage under guard.

But this particular stint, a four-month stint, was unbelievably desolate and torturous, and . . . he survived. [When] they finally brought him out, [he went] from the cage, laying on his side for four months, to a room three feet wide by six feet long, and it felt like the Hilton to him.

He had . . . three relatively undramatic escape attempts . . . where he would walk away from his guards until other guards would find him and shoo him back to his camp. Within his first six months or so, though, he kept walking one day, and there was no guard to stop him, and he took off, and he ran all day as best he could. He was still injured from his crash in the aircraft, but he got to a riverbank that evening, and he hid in the brush until he thought it was dark enough to cross undetected.

The Vietcong had engaged the local Montagnards to look for him, and when Jim's feet went to cross the river, the bank on the other side exploded with Montagnards whooping and hollering and so forth, and soon Vietcong cadre were there and fired at his feet, and he was recaptured. The brutal treatment that he received really began in earnest after that. His head was slammed on the ground until he passed out numerous times. He was beaten with clubs and sticks, and it was quite grueling.

JIM WAS A very strong-willed individual. He spent five years in captivity by himself . . . so by the time he met up with others who had been captured six months, a year, he thought he should lead them. He was put into a situation where he wasn't with other military people. He was with civilians who were captured during the Tet offensive in 1968, and these civilians had been exposed already to the antiwar protests back home. They were in Vietnam to do civilian-type jobs. They weren't the gung ho militants that they saw Jim

Thompson to be. If they were employees of the Defense Department, he did command them—some of them realized that afterward—but many of them were contractors working for the Defense Department, and they didn't want to pay attention to Jim Thompson. They didn't want to be organized by Jim Thompson. They didn't want to escape with him.

Jim was blessed that one of his cell mates was Lew Meyer, who was this tough-as-nails navy fireman, a veteran himself, who believed Jim Thompson was in charge. Lew Meyer was an exercise fanatic. He wanted to stay in shape. He wanted to escape. When Jim Thompson and Lew were together for the first time, Jim saw Lew exercising. Jim jumped out of his bunk, tried to do a single push-up, and crashed on his face. He couldn't do it. He began to cry. Lew Meyer stopped his exercise program. He decided, "I'm going to build this guy back up. To keep myself in shape, I'll exercise while Jim is sleeping, but otherwise, I'll go along with his pace." So the two of them went through this extraordinary exercise regimen while he was captive.

Jim probably weighed—at his worst part—less than 100 pounds. He was a soldier, when captured, of about 180 pounds. He became a skeleton. . . . Mike O'Connor, who was . . . a warrant officer, an army pilot, who was shot down during the Tet offensive, looked through a crack in the door of his cell, and he saw this body up against the cell doors. He thought for sure the Vietcong were playing a joke on them, that that was a corpse, and then he saw the person wink and move, and he realized that it was a human being.

When other POWs saw him at that time—this is in 1968—some of them began to cry, because they said, "That's a look at Christmas future, that's what we will be." So . . . that was his nadir. When Lew Meyer met him, they were getting better food, they were able to live together, support each other, and then they began this regimen that would build them up so that they could [attempt] escape together in 1971.

JIM JR. WAS born the day after Jim was shot down. Alyce had made a decision about fifteen months later to move the family in with another man [named Harold] and to pose as the wife of this other man to put her life with Jim Thompson behind her. The reasons she did that were numerous, but her support system was breaking down. Alyce was the kind of woman who was very dependent upon her husband. There were some problems in the marriage, but nothing that Jim thought about much while he was in captivity because he idolized the marriage and the family. That was his dream, to get home.

Jim Thompson, soon after his capture, was tortured for a statement. He didn't write the statement; he signed the statement. He then read the statement. A lot of prisoners of war had been tortured and had to sign statements eventually. But unlike them, Jim Thompson didn't have somebody to rely on that he could bounce off what he had just been through. . . . But that statement that Jim had made was broadcast on Hanoi radio several months later. That was in November of 1964, so it was six months after Jim was lost. Alyce heard news reports of this, but she said that the army couldn't provide the tape for her. She could never verify whether it was actually her husband. The army had a problem finding the tape.

Several months later . . . she met an army sergeant at a bowling alley who had two children of his own that he wanted to raise. He asked Alyce if she'd like to move in with him, and they could be one family in Massachusetts. She made that decision. It would forever affect her life.

From Alyce's perspective . . . when her husband was lost, Jim was born, and she had three young daughters under the age of six. She found herself unable to cope. For a time, the commanding officer at the base at Fort Bragg, where Jim was assigned to Vietnam, was always there, a shoulder for Alyce to lean on, somebody providing the support that she'd need. "Alyce, if you want anything, if you want to go to any social events, just let me know." But if you're in the military, it's a transient life, and soon, after several months, the commanding officer was reassigned; a new commanding officer came in, didn't quite know her story. Neighbors would come home from work, have warm reunions, which Alyce could spy on from her close quarters; she lived on base. She found herself increasingly helpless to handle this situation. A woman who helped her out, Jean Ledbetter, lost her husband in Vietnam about six months later. The two of them met and were support for each other. But Jean soon learned that her husband had been lost and that she'd be moving off post. So another support for Alyce was gone.

[IN 1964, Jim was in the South being held by the VC, the Vietcong. Alyce was] living in Hudson, Massachusetts, with this Army sergeant. . . . For the next seven and a half years [Alyce and Harold] lived together . . . as husband and wife. Alyce wore a wedding ring, posed as his wife. If someone asked about her past, she would just say her husband was lost, and she'd try and avoid the conversation.

I THINK [the angriest character in the book] would have to be Jim Thompson. [When] Jim came back, three things, he said, had kept him alive in captivity: faith in God, faith in country, faith in the love of a good woman. When he got back, he found, eventually, none of that. The marriage was nothing as he had expected. He expected that while he was gone, they talked about him all the time, [that the children] knew their father, and they couldn't wait to see him; he wouldn't be unknown to his children. They would have shared stories over the years, pleasant things, their experiences at Christmas together. None of that was there.

Jim was released about a month after Everett Alvarez . . . in March 1973. When they arrived back in the Philippines, each of the POWs was given a file folder which contained love letters, report cards, drawings that the children had done. Jim Thompson's had only a pay stub. He called Alyce from the Philippines, and she said, "We need to talk when you get back." That's [the situation] he confronted when he got back, so he has to be the most angry in the story.

So he lost his faith in the love of a good woman. Also the country didn't embrace the warriors from Vietnam the way Jim had expected. He believed it was all propaganda while he was five years in isolation. What he was being fed by his captors was that your nation is divided over this war; there's great dissension; there are politicians who are saying, "Stop the war." Jim couldn't believe this until he met his first Americans and they said, in effect, "Yes, that's true."

JIM JR. WAS a playful youngster and when he came home from school, he would play outside. He barely checked in. This one particular afternoon, his mother called him in. The family was sitting around the table. She said to young Jim, "Harold is not your father. This man is your father." She pulled out a photograph and said, "And he's coming home." Jim Jr. was stunned. He didn't know what to say at that point. He went back outside to play. What affected Jim Jr.'s life so much was that the reunion of his parents was a very rocky affair for the next year and a half that they lived together. Incredibly, when Jim Thompson came back, Alyce was there waiting for him at Valley Forge. She told him how she had lived her life; invited him to divorce if he'd like, or they could try to make a family of it. Jim Thompson had dreamed of being reunited with his family, so he figured, "Let's give it a go." They went up to the house in Hudson, Massachusetts, took the furniture out, and moved on with their lives in the army. But for the next fifteen months, it was a terrible existence for the entire family.

[Harold was there in Massachusetts when they all got together.] One of the escort officers was also with him, and he said it was the most incredible tension-filled scene he'd ever been a part of. It was almost like Harold suddenly was this uncle who was just an observer as they went about picking up their possessions.

Jim Jr. was thrown into this family, and his father, this stranger in charge, was suffering not only from depression, he was trying to repair his family. He was the Rip Van Winkle of the army at that point. He was trying to repair his career and he was trying to reconcile how the country felt about the war. . . .

That was very tough. In that environment he became an alcoholic, or perhaps he always was one and the disease blossomed for him. He was suffering from severe depression. He was in need of some psychiatric counseling at that time and wasn't getting a significant amount. And in that environment, Jim Jr. was idolized by his father at first.

Among the four children, only the older daughter [Pam] had remembered her father, and she . . . kept a copy of his photograph hidden in her bureau drawer. The mother allowed her to keep it, but Jim Thompson's name was not to be mentioned in that household. The second daughter, Laura, had asked her mother at one point what happened to their father and Alyce said he died of a snake bite. The two younger children, Ruth and Jim Jr., didn't know they had another father. They believed Harold was their father. And so in this environment, when Jim returned, Pam, his princess, suddenly wasn't his princess any longer. She had changed. She had grown from a towhead youngster that he called Princess into this sort of gangly, studious teenager, bookish and not someone who found her father to be the Prince Charming that she expected [him] to be.

After fifteen months, the family fell apart. Jim Jr. went from being this coddled—spoiled, you might say—nine-year-old who was idolized by his father. Then one day his mother came up while he was visiting with relatives in Honesdale, Pennsylvania, and said, "Your father and I are getting a divorce. It's over." He wouldn't see his father again for years and years. At that point, his sisters said that he shut himself off. It was as if he closed down. This boy didn't want to be hurt anymore. Jim Jr. is a very good-natured, warm fellow, if you can draw him out. But he's a very quiet person.

He turned to alcohol himself in his early teen years. He dropped out of high school. He was a wayward son. Alyce didn't know quite what to do with him. And he became a truck driver and he had married . . . It was a tumultuous marriage. When he returned from the road, he found out that his wife had sold some $200 car that he treasured. He went to the Silver Dollar Saloon in Nashville looking for the person that she had sold it to. . . . Jim Jr. happened to be that night with a young lady who was a minor who had a handgun. When [the car purchaser] threatened him, according to the trial testimony, Jim shot him and was found guilty of second-degree murder.

The shooting occurred in 1990 and Jim Jr. . . . was convicted of second-degree murder [in 1991. He's now] been paroled and moved on promisingly with his life.

JIM THOMPSON SR., by that time, was a stroke victim living by himself down in Key West, Florida. He had retired on full disability from the army because of his stroke . . . in 1981.

I SPENT WEEKENDS and weeknights working on [this book] for approximately fifteen years.

At the time I was a writer for *Army Times*. . . . I was told that Jim Thompson was the longest-held prisoner of war in American history. That surprised me because I had always heard that Everett Alvarez was the longest-held POW. So I looked into the Thompson story and then went down to interview him. . . . He had lived for the past three years, at the time I met him, as a stroke victim. He was ambulatory. He could speak in broken phrases. He could understand everything that I said to him. But during our first interview together, Jim was very frustrated. I wanted him to tell his story and he could not. At some points, it looked like he was becoming tearful with his frustration. He got up, he went over to a small reel-to-reel tape recorder that he kept in his living room and he turned it on. I heard this vibrant, articulate, well-educated . . . person talking about his experience while held captive. He said, "Listen." And I listened. He provided me access to all his psychiatric records, health records, and his intelligence reports. Over the course of the next fifteen years, I interviewed 160 people who could tell a slice of Jim Thompson's story.

I THINK THIS story is unique in that it goes behind the scenes. It's almost like the underbelly of the James Stockdale story. There, you had a wife who built an organization while Stockdale was in captivity and kept the fires burning and they had a strong marriage which continues to this day. I think perhaps a more common story was a prisoner of war coming back, expecting things to be exactly the way he had left them, finding a woman who had learned to live on her own, to raise the family in a certain way, who wasn't ready to give up her independence. If she nevertheless had waited, they still had difficulty adjusting because they had gone on different paths during the captivity. An awful lot of the POWs' marriages ended a few years after they returned.

Creating the
Vietnam Veterans Memorial

by

MAYA LIN

As an undergraduate at Yale University in 1980, Maya Lin entered and won the national competition to design the Vietnam Veterans Memorial. The two years that it took to complete the memorial involved numerous political conflicts, as well as a struggle to maintain her design's artistic integrity. Lin, currently an architect in New York, discussed the creation of the Vietnam Veterans Memorial when she visited Booknotes *on November 19, 2000, to discuss her book* Boundaries, *which provides a look at her 1989–1999 work.* Boundaries *was published in 2000 by Simon & Schuster.*

[I DESIGNED THE Vietnam Veterans Memorial in] the fall of 1980. We were in class; we were studying funereal architecture. As a senior at Yale, you can choose your thesis. About six of us got together and decided we wanted to study architecture and how it relates to mortality—in other words, how man deals with his own mortality in the built form. We found an adviser, Professor Andy Burr, who agreed to be our professor, and we started designing projects. One was a memorial to World War II.

Someone saw a poster [about a] Vietnam Veterans Memorial competition, and we thought, what a great way to end the course; we'll have our own design [competition]. And so I designed it, but I had started researching it when I was researching the memorial to World War II. And so I had started working into an idea of, well, what is a war memorial? What has it been historically? What is it now?

Then I went to see the site. It was around Thanksgiving time. I had actually gone to see my parents, and then on my way back, I rendezvoused with a bunch of the students in the class and we went to see the site. It was a very cold day. I took one look at the site, and I thought it was a beautiful park, and again, I didn't want to make a piece that would overwhelm the site.

I saw this beautiful park, and I think in the essay, I said, "I still want the site to remain a park, a place where people could come." I still wanted you to be able to walk on to the site. And anything I've done has been a merger with the landscape. It's not been about creating some large, powerful form that in a way supplants the land; it's about working with [the land]. There's sort of a harmony going on.

And in a way, I had wonderful disagreements with the architects of record, Cooper-Lecky, because they could not understand why I [would] want to make such a thin, veneer surface. "This is a monument. Make those walls two to three feet thick." And I kept going, "No, no, no. I don't see it as a physical presence inserted into the land. I literally see it as a geode. I'm polishing the Earth and putting the names on that surface."

[WHEN I FIRST heard from the Vietnam Veterans Memorial Fund,] I was in class. I had entered the competition as an exercise. Students do it. It's good practice. I believed in it, but you don't enter something like this at the age of twenty, twenty-one [believing that you're going to win]. You forget about it.

I got a call from my roommate, and she called me out of class and said, "You just got a phone call from Washington. They're calling back in five minutes." You've never seen someone run faster out of a class. My professor was wondering, what's going on? And they called up, some people who said, "We're from the Vietnam Veterans Memorial Fund. Could we come ask you a few questions about your design?"

I was convinced I was number 100, not a big deal. They just were asking me a few questions, about drainage or something like that. And then, they all flew up. There were three of them, and they sat down in my dorm room. What they told me later is that they were freaking out because I wasn't just a student, I was an undergraduate. They were going to an undergraduate dorm in Saybrook College at Yale. They were all sort of hunched into the living room, and Colonel Schaet was talking in this very unemotional way about: "Well, this was the largest competition ever held, open to everyone, and you won."

And then he kept going. He didn't miss a beat. I was just listening, and my roommate caught it before I did. But I'm a funny person in that until it was built, I did not believe this would get built. I knew it was formalistically extremely different. I'm also someone who never counts on anything until it's real. And so, I basically braced myself, because having studied competition processes, as an architecture student will, [I learned that] it's very rare that something gets built the way it was conceived. It just doesn't happen that way.

THEY FLEW ME down to Washington to meet with the whole Vietnam Veterans Memorial Fund. I'm actually a very shy person, and I didn't know what to do. They wanted the thing kept very closed, so I called my parents, but they didn't want me talking to anyone, so I was fairly isolated.

[At] the very initial press conference, they made a model. They didn't talk to me, they just made the model and they had pushed the design way to the back. I said at one point, "You know, that model isn't accurate. . . ." "It's just a press conference model. Don't worry about it." And I'm going, "It is such a simple piece, everything matters." I instantly read that there were going to be interesting issues coming up as to how something like this was going to get realized.

I went through a very internal, very tough struggle as to who the architect of record would be, who would work with me to get the thing built. They took one look at me and to be fair to them, they thought, "She's a kid. . . ." I did a lot of publicity, because it was a direct fund–driven situation, and I was caught doing a lot of interviews. But basically, all I was concerned about was making sure that what I envisioned got built.

So I think from the start, we had cross-purposes. They assumed, "Oh, you wouldn't want to be interested, and you're just a kid. And it's [such a simple design]. It's so simple." Well, I'm [thinking], "I am obsessive about detailing, down to the whatever."

Anyway, the end result was that the architect of record selected, Cooper-Lecky, was [the firm that] Cesar Pelli, then dean of Yale's architecture school, had recommended. It was the absolute right choice. But there was a little bit of an internal power struggle that left grudges. And I think those grudges left a little bit of ill will, so that they didn't know where I was coming from and I didn't know where they were coming from. It all smoothed over in the end, but it made the entire process a little difficult going through.

THE CONTROVERSY was that people didn't like the design that was selected, after it was selected. I think people felt that for a lot of different reasons: It was not your traditional color; it was not your traditional shape; it was not at all vertical; it listed all the names; it did so chronologically; it was not usual. And it also was controversial partially because of who designed it. I was Asian, and I think that was misinterpreted.

And so, for a brief period of time—and I do want to say it was unusual how short a time it took to get this memorial built—it was very hotly debated. There were many criticisms that someone as young as I was, who could never have experienced or understood that war, how could she be the one left to design something?

I think, oddly enough, because I was too young to have been embroiled in the politics, I had made a choice. Unlike many of the designs that I've worked on since then, I consciously decided not to read anything about the politics surrounding that war. I made a call that the politics shouldn't get in the way of this work, that you were going to have people whose names are listed, [soldiers] who believed they should be there, and those who protested it, who went because they were drafted. I wanted both sides to be able to rest and not overtly get involved in forming an opinion.

I think this happens in many of my works. I think a lot of people say, "Well, you're a political artist," and I would [say], "No, not necessarily." I am drawn or have been drawn to work on issues: war, race, gender, but I don't have an overt political statement that I want to get across. If anything, my approach to the Vietnam Memorial was to make a piece that would be neutral and yet would ask us to face these individual lives lost on an individual basis. Now, that's new.

The veterans chose to have the names listed. Though I designed this for a class, I found out halfway through the design that they requested all the names to be listed. That inherently is a political statement, that we want to recognize these individual lives lost. A lot of artisan designers, when they saw that, almost looked at that requirement as a chore. So they'd find a form, and then they were trying to stuff the names on it. I allowed the names to be the memorial. That's it.

A lot of criticism was that the memorial was abstract: It's modernist, it's cold, it's inhuman. And I kept thinking, "Well, what's more realistic to bring back someone's memory than the person's name?" No one image, no one edifice is going to recollect and react to you the way a person's name will.

I had thought up what ideas I had about how I wanted to be honest about war, how I wanted to make it very honest about the names and about acknowledging loss. I thought about what a memorial to the Vietnam War should be. Then I put all that thinking aside and went to see the site. And it was on the site that I just decided I'd cut open the Earth.

ALL OF A SUDDEN, we were working with the veterans—and everything got politicized. We looked at Swedish black granite, we looked at Canadian black granite, and we looked at South African black granite. We settled on Indian black granite. I remember one of the comments from the veterans was it would be very hard to find a granite from Canada or Sweden because there were draft dodgers who went there, so they wanted a neutral territory.

By that point, it had become fairly highly political, and there were questions about one of the juror's being a member of the Communist Party, things like that. They wanted the thing to remain as neutral as possible because it had gone in under the Carter administration and it was being built under the Reagan administration. And at one point, a politician said, "Even though this is a neutral statement, we need to politicize the design."

And there was a real question as to the apex [of the design], because I had not put anything there. They came up with a paragraph that would have added sort of a political meaning. And I kept saying, ". . . just keep it very simple, keep it so that you don't add a political meaning. Let people come to this place and come away with their own thoughts."

The chronology [of war dead] begins and ends at the apex. It's like an open book: 1959, the beginning of the war, with the short prologue; 1975, at the bottom on the left. The beginning and the end of the war meet, the war comes full circle. It's a closed time line, but it's broken by the Earth. By having the names listed chronologically, any returning veteran can find his or her time on the memorial. In so doing, if you know one name, you'll find others in close proximity. I was trying to tap into a sense of bringing them back to that immediate memory. I talk about stopping time, where present, past, future all kind of comes to a point. By having to relive that past, it forces you to face it. And then you have to walk out into the present time.

[In designing the memorial,] I didn't think past one thought: I knew people would touch the names, and I actually knew people would cry. I don't know why I knew that. Other than that, I really didn't think of how it would be read as being such a popular piece. It's the only way I got through that time. I only could think of one person's reaction to it, always. That's the way I always am. It's a one-on-one experience, no matter how many people are there.

Fighter Pilot John Boyd

by

ROBERT CORAM

John Boyd produced a groundbreaking manual on jet aerial combat, contributed to the construction of the legendary F-15 and F-16 jet fighters, and devised military strategies that have been adopted around the world. Yet his contributions to military tactics have been largely overlooked. In his biography Boyd: The Fighter Pilot Who Changed the Art of War, *published by Little, Brown & Company in 2002, Atlanta writer Robert Coram tells the story of someone he says is of the greatest unknown heroes in American military history. Mr. Coram joined us on* Booknotes *on January 26, 2003.*

JOHN BOYD WAS one of the most important unknown men of our time. His ideas were responsible for our victory in the Gulf War. His ideas turned the U.S. Marine Corps around in the 1980s, changed the way they went into battle. His ideas are the basis for the time-based management theories that we have today. His ideas are gaining an ever-greater circle of respect around the world. He was a man who changed the world.

"Patterns of Conflict" was his great legacy to military theory. It made him the greatest military theoretician since Sun Tzu. It was a time-based theory of conflict that was responsible for our victory in the Gulf War.

[JOHN BOYD WAS in the air force] from 1951 until 1975. He started out as a fighter pilot, flew combat in Korea. Then he became an instructor at Nellis Air Force Base in Nevada, where he got a reputation as "Forty-Second Boyd," the man who defeated all comers in under forty seconds, or he paid them $40, and he never had to pay off. He was beginning to develop his theories of air combat at the time, but he knew he needed more. So he went from Nellis to Georgia Tech and got an engineering degree. Then he went to Eglin Air Force Base in Florida, where he developed the theory, and then came to the Pentagon, where he was responsible for the F-15 and the F-16 and the F-18.

He developed what was known as the Energy-Maneuverability Theory, or E-M Theory, and it's a clear line of demarcation between the old aviation and the new aviation. It gave a way to quantify the performance of an aircraft, to compare an aircraft performance with that of the adversary, and a way to design aircraft. When he was brought to the Pentagon to bail out what was then called the F-X, it was a plane that was about to go down in ignominy and have the navy force another salt-water airplane, as they're called, on the air force—another humiliation. Boyd salvaged the F-X, and that became the F-15.

I don't think [there are people out there who disagree with me]. There are some senior officers who were there when the aircraft went into production who would like to be known as the "father of the F-15." But by the time they came on board, the heavy lifting had been done. The people who were there and know what train delivered the goods to the station will tell you that John Boyd was the father of the F-15 and the F-16 and the F-18.

BOYD'S UNKNOWN because (a) he was in the military, and (b) he never wrote anything. Therefore academics have nothing to ponder over and explain what it means, and to perpetuate his legacy. Unfortunately, that's the way a lot of people are remembered, through their writings. He came from an oral culture. "Patterns of Conflict" is a briefing. Trying to read briefing slides is like reading a foreign language. It's impossible.

"Patterns of Conflict" was six hours long on some days. Some days it was longer. It depended on his mood. But his entire briefing, all of his works, [totaled] about fifteen, eighteen hours. He'd deliver them over two or three days.

[He would deliver this briefing] every time he got a chance. He would stop people in the halls of the Pentagon and say, "You got to hear my briefing." He delivered it hundreds of times. And as it became better known, he worked his way up the chain of command to ever more senior officers and eventually delivered it to a number of three- and four-star generals.

HE WAS ONE OF [the greatest fighter pilots in history]. Never defeated in air-to-air combat. He had [that] reputation as "Forty-Second Boyd." It's like a gunslinger. If you have a nickname and a reputation, you're always called out. He was called out by air force pilots, by marine corps pilots, navy pilots, and by exchange pilots from other countries. But he was never defeated in simulated air-to-air combat.

He was in World War II, briefly, as an enlisted man. He came out of a high school in Erie, Pennsylvania, and went in at the very end of World War II, but he was a swimming instructor. He flew combat in Korea, twenty-some missions, I believe.

He hit one [MiG]. He got a piece of one. But that's not really a good indication, because I know a man named Hank Buttleman, who was an ace, and he flew fifty missions without ever seeing a MiG. So it depends on being in the right place at the right time.

[Being an ace means] five airplanes shot down. A great cachet goes with being an ace, which is another reason a lot of Boyd's work is relatively unknown, because it's been overshadowed, if you will, by some of the writings of men who were aces.

In 1963, 1964, 1965, he used a computer to prove that the Soviet MiG was better than our F-111. He was a maintenance officer at Eglin Air Force Base. He came in asking for computer time, and the civilian threw him out of his office. He tried to do it the air force way, sent letter after letter saying, "What I'm working on will change aviation forever." He was dismissed [so] he stole a million dollars worth of computer time to develop his theory.

This was in the early days of computers. His theory was mathematically based and to run through all the variables would have taken him several lifetimes and then it might not have worked out. Computers short-circuited that process immensely.

He stole the time through the good offices of Tom Christie, who now works at the Pentagon. Christie was then in charge of an office at Eglin that did 60 or 70 percent of the computer work on the base, and he simply gave Boyd a project number that Boyd tied on to what he was doing and developed his theory.

Later on, the inspector general came down to investigate, wound up seeing what Boyd had done, the results of it, and exonerated Boyd completely. He turned his wrath on the civilian who refused him computer time.

No one believed [the Soviet MiG was better than the F-111]. Boyd briefed it to higher and higher levels, and finally he was briefing it to General Walter Campell Sweeney, then in charge of the Tactical Air Command. The briefing was to last for twenty minutes, but Sweeney heard enough then to know he wanted to hear more.

So the briefing lasted all that day and into part of the next day, at the end of which the general said, "I haven't seen the slides on the F-111," which was the pride of the air force. It was one of those do-anything planes. It could be a fighter plane. It could be a bomber. It could be a low level. It could do everything but dust crops, and it was the ultimate airplane.

BIGGER, HEAVIER, higher, faster, farther, that was the tradition of the air force. If you look at the long chain of fighter aircraft, each one was bigger, heavier, less maneuverable than its predecessor was, until Boyd came along.

He wanted about 30,000, 35,000 pounds, and a single engine. It became two engines, much heavier, and then it was "missionized," as the air force calls it, which means they kept adding equipment that degraded the performance even farther. So out of his disgust with what the air force had done to the F-15, he then went into the lightweight fighter project, and out of that came the F-16.

[Three men:] Pierre Sprey and Boyd and a fellow named Everest Riccioni forced the lightweight fighter, which became the F-16, onto the air force without the knowledge or consent of the air force. It was one of the most audacious projects ever hatched against the U.S. military.

Boyd would not think much of the F-15 and F-16 that the air force flies today, or the F-14 and the F-18 that the navy flies because of what they were in the beginning and what they could have been; what they were, and what the air force did to them after they were missionized.

[The F-16] was born as the most nimble, agile, fastest turning and burning aircraft ever made, the ultimate fighter airplane, famous for the buttonhook turn. Its performance has never been equaled before or since. It rivaled the performance, exceeded the performance of the F-15, then the darling of the air force.

The air force added a plug in the middle to make it longer. They added hard points for all the missions. They added more bombs and rockets. They added fuel tanks—everything to degrade the performance. They wouldn't make the wings significantly bigger, and they turned it from being a great fighter airplane into a little short-legged bomber.

[BOYD WENT TO Thailand for one year, to Nakhon Phanom, the secret air force base], toward the end of the Vietnam War in 1972. That part of the war was winding down when he was there. He shot down what was called the "McNamara line," the electronic sensors placed along the Ho Chi Minh Trail. He was vice commander of Task Force Alpha, and then he became the base commander [of the Fifty-sixth Combat Support Group] and turned around a base that had a severe morale problem, a lot of discipline problems. It was his only command, and he performed admirably.

He got out of the service in 1975. For the first year after he retired, he went into seclusion. He read the most daunting list of books imaginable. It was far beyond what most postgraduate degrees require. He came out of that with "Patterns of Conflict." That was what he had done during the year and a half he was away. And then another series of briefings and his work—he did a lot of work with the marine corps.

The air force takes great pride in the fact that John Boyd had no influence whatsoever on them. On the other hand, the marine corps, which had to make the biggest leap to embrace his ideas, did so.

One of the great untold stories of modern military history is how this retired air force colonel changed the way the U.S. Marine Corps does business. And if you know anything at all about military culture, that's extraordinary. He also turned the marine corps, unbeknownst to other branches of the service and to the public, into the most intellectual branch of the U.S. military. He did work with a fellow named Jim Burton, who was responsible for a lot of safety additions to the army's Bradley fighting vehicle. He was the heart of the military reform movement in the early 1980s.

The OODA Loop—the Observe, Orient, Decide, and Act cycle—that's his great contribution to thought today, both in business and in the military. If you go to the Internet and type in "OODA loop," you get about a thousand hits. Observe, orient, decide, and act. The military has tried to hardwire it to make it a linear high-speed cycle, and it's far, far more than that. Its impact is devastating if someone really understands its usage. It's devastating because if you can cycle through the loop quicker than the adversary, you cause ambiguity, uncertainty, confusion, mistrust in his mind, and time is stretched out for him, and at the same time, because you can cycle through it quicker, time is compressed for you. So you're getting ahead of his decision cycle, and he becomes confused. He turns inward instead of outward. He mentally collapses. It has happened in warfare and in business.

Observation—you see something. Then you become oriented to it, and the orientation phase is the most complex because into that comes the genetic heritage, your education, your background, so many intangibles, and they're different for all of us. So the orientation phase is different. Then you decide what you're going to do, and then you take an action. Once you become proficient at this and you have an intuitive understanding of how you relate to this evolving situation, you can go from the observation to the action phase, skipping, apparently, the orientation and decide, while the other person is still going through the full cycle.

[Boyd's voice was shrill.] He was loud. He was in your face. He smoked cigars. He even lit a couple of ties on fire. . . . He was a man with a mission and as long as you understood—or tried to understand—what he was about, he was accommodating and would help you along. But if you had what he called "an obstruction," that is, you disagreed with him or thought he was wrong, he had to bring you over to his side. And if he couldn't, he dismissed you forever. He had a knack for cutting people out of his life entirely.

[It's unclear what his politics were.] He came back from Vietnam surprised about the Nixon administration and stalked the halls of the Pentagon during the Watergate days. Keep in mind he's a colonel on active duty in the air force, accosting people in the halls of the Pentagon, saying, "Nixon is a crooked son of a bitch. We need to get rid of him." You don't hear many active-duty officers taking that position. I'm not sure that was politics as much as it was an issue of morality, because he always did the right thing, and he had no tolerance for those who did not.

Boyd had very little respect for rank. He thought most generals do nothing but get promoted, that they were careerists. Those generals are remembered for their contributions to their branch of the service, but Boyd is remembered for his contributions to his country.

He knew that what he was doing was right. His motives were the highest and the best. He was concerned not for his career, not for money, not for advancement, but for doing the right thing, for taking care of the men whom the military describes as being at the pointy end of the spear, the ones all of us should be concerned about. That was Boyd's life. And if someone thought more of their career or more of getting a job with a defense contractor after they retired, you bet he was on them in a minute. He had no patience with that sort of shortsighted careerism.

A lot of people were intimidated by Boyd. We're all intimidated by people who always do the right thing, who are models of probity and rectitude.

Boyd met [Dick Cheney] when he was the leader, the spiritual leader, if you will, of the reform movement. Dick Cheney, then a young congressman from Wyoming, heard his briefing, then had a number of one-on-one sessions with Boyd. When Cheney became secretary of defense, he was rare in that he knew more about strategy than most of his generals did. He called Boyd out of retirement in the early days of the Gulf War and got an updating, if you will. It was Boyd's strategy, not General Norman Schwarzkopf's, that led to our swift and decisive victory in the Gulf War.

He was responsible for all of the [first] Gulf War strategy. The multiple thrusts, the feints, the ambiguity, the marine feint. The early landing in Kuwait was his idea. He was behind every bit of it.

IT TOOK ME three years to write [this book.] This one took a lot out of me. There are still parts of it I can't read without getting emotional. Boyd was a man such as comes along very rarely. I was fortunate to be able to write this book. His life was sad. It was tragic. He was unknown and he did so much.

My father was a career army guy, thirty-one years in the army. I never had a childhood, I had a rather extended boot camp. So, for years, I was away from the military, I wanted no part of it. This book made me understand what my father was trying to teach me that I never got at the time. Boyd manifests the highest and best qualities we expect in all people in uniform, but not all of them have. Through Boyd, I learned what my dad was trying to teach me as a child.

I think he was the sort of man that all of us would like to be. He always did the right thing. He left his mark. He changed the world.

America's Modern-Day Military

by

DANA PRIEST

Since the Balkan conflict of the 1990s, the U.S. military has focused increasingly on peacekeeping as an essential part of its mission. Washington Post *reporter Dana Priest argues that the American military, traditionally reluctant to engage in non-wartime operations, is becoming an influential—yet largely unrecognized—force in foreign policy. Ms. Priest joined us on March 9, 2003, to discuss her book* The Mission: Waging War and Keeping Peace with America's Military, *published by W. W. Norton & Company in 2003.*

"THE MISSION" IS what the military is called upon to do today all around the world, which is a lot bigger than just fighting wars. They are asked to relieve humanitarian suffering. They are asked to rebuild nations. They are asked to train militaries who are unprofessional and often brutal, militaries that we normally would not have much contact with. But especially in the war against terrorism, the Special Forces, in particular, have been asked to go out and try to professionalize some of these militaries.

They actually do a whole other range of things, a lot of things that diplomats really should be doing, especially at the higher levels, at the four-star level. A lot of people in the military, when they saw that they were being asked to do a lot of these things in the last decade, they called it "mission creep." One could call it "mission leap," it is so big. And I just call it "the mission," because that has become what the military really does these days, a whole range of things.

I WAS A PENTAGON reporter for the *Washington Post* for eight years, and a couple years into the job, I one day happened to be in a military briefing for some army generals on an entirely different subject. I noticed the deployments around the world of army forces and the little deployments of Special Forces, things I'd never heard about before. So I started to inquire, "What are they doing?" After I peeled the onion back on that one, I found that the Special Forces at that time were in 125 countries, something we didn't know much about at all, including countries where the U.S. Congress had said we needed to cut off relations—Pakistan, Colombia, and Indonesia, in particular. The Special Forces had found their way around that in a sort of loophole of legislation that they and their bosses at the office of the secretary of defense had created. So they were out there in the world, doing all these things. I wrote a big story about that.

And then I just kept going. I kept saying, "Well, what else is the military doing out there?" In Europe, I found that they were sending hundreds of officers to help the former Soviet bloc states reform their militaries. Then I just kept going and going. And of course, we had peacekeeping and that sort of thing coming along, where I could go to Bosnia and look at what the troops were doing.

It really became a story that I thought was not in Washington. [Even though] a lot of us cover the Pentagon, you wouldn't be able to see it from Washington. But when you added the thousands of pieces of the puzzle together, you got actually a very big transformation of the U.S. military and what its role is. At the same time, you had the secretary of defense and the president, who had given the military an official new role, which was to shape—as they called it—the environment. Being good soldiers, that's what they did. The regional commanders in chiefs, called the CINCs, took that mission and said, "Let's take this seriously and find out in our region where we can engage people." They did that with hundreds of exercises, lots of humanitarian relief. They sent dozens and dozens of midlevel officers to do bilateral relations.

At the same time, you had our diplomatic corps, which was suffering quite a bit. Not only did it suffer budget cuts but terrible morale problems, a lot of accountability problems: Who are they? How good are they? You had a Congress that really wasn't interested in funding them. So you had this imbalance of resources that began to grow. The military took on many of the jobs that the State Department had, and they still have them today.

THE SPECIAL Operations Forces is an umbrella term that encompasses the navy SEALS. You also have the air force Special Operations units which are a whole variety of fixed wing, but also helicopters that are only flown under special circumstances. And then you have the army Special Forces, otherwise known as the Green Berets. You also have the Seventy-fifth Ranger regiment, which is really the larger combat force, and then you have the Civil Affairs and the Psychological Operations unit.

There is always this tension in the policy arena about where you send Special Forces. Do you send them into places where the human-rights record is not very good? After 9/11, a lot of that debate fell by the wayside, and we ended up sending troops to places like Uzbekistan where the military would go once in a while, but now they are going to be there in a much more routine way.

Part of what they do is training. That's a large part. They interact with the special forces of that country or, in the case of Nigeria where I went, they were actually training peacekeepers. However, as we know from Afghanistan, one of their main missions is to liaison with foreign rebel forces, so there are Special Forces . . . who meet up with the Northern Alliance warlords and troops to help call in air strikes against the Taliban. So they also have that combat role.

There are various degrees of secrecy. The A teams that I wrote about are the White Special Forces. They are not secret, although many of their missions are secret. The other group below them that we sometimes talk about is the Delta Force, and that is a clandestine unit. For all the time I covered it, the army never would admit that they even had a Delta Force.

Delta Force would do missions that are secret. They had the original counterterrorism mission, or either they would do hostage rescue under terrorist circumstances or they were supposed to also help the interruption or apprehension of weapons of mass destruction material and components.

THE U.N. ARE supposed to administer Kosovo. Kosovo doesn't have a political status that is defined yet. It is neither independent from Serbia nor really an integrated part. NATO pretty much punted on that question, it figured it would be so divisive. So what it did was put the U.N. in charge. The U.N. has their own administrators there, and many people think that the U.N. has a peacekeeping force. In fact, the U.N. is like pickup basketball; whenever there's a big crisis, the U.N. asks its countries to donate peacekeepers, and they cobble them together as a peacekeeping force. And then they have to try to work well together.

In this case, they have U.N. police [who] are often from countries where the police practices, I would say, are not so professional. Some of these people came because they were the brother of someone important and they knew they'd get a good-paying job if they became police officers in Kosovo. So they have no police training. They barely speak a common language, which is English, but many of them don't really speak English well. They don't want to get in trouble there. They don't want to put themselves at risk because it's Kosovo. It doesn't really mean much to them, other than a job. So you have the people who are supposed to be making sure that things are running right, who are supposed to be doing this detective work to find the bad guys, not wanting to do that at all. It's not safe, for one thing, and secondly, they're not organized in any way. They've never worked together. They speak five different languages. They can barely understand each other at some points.

MERITA WAS AN eleven-year-old Albanian girl in Kosovo. This is the story of what you get when you send infantry troops to a place to do nation building. Now, people in the administration don't like the words "nation building" because they say, "We don't send the military to do that. We send the military to create safe and secure environments." They make sure that people aren't shooting at each other anymore, cut down on crime, that sort of thing. So they had sent the Eighty-second Airborne to Kosovo right after the war in 1999, and they had been there for quite a while. I look at one particular town in Kosovo to really get to the bottom of what it is like: What do these troops do? What do they think about it? How do they perform? How do they figure out how to deal with a whole plethora of problems that they weren't expecting?

So in this case, this was one particular unit that had given its men a special task, to go and try to find the bad guys, in order to make this a safe and secure environment. They figured out that the bad guys were actually organized crime. They were Albanians who used to be in the KLA, the Kosovo Liberation Army, whom we were allied with during the Kosovo war. Those same people had become the underground political apparatus that really controlled Kosovo.

So these troops, they figured that out, and they said, "We got to go stop that." They tried to do that by becoming policemen, in a way. We see that in Kosovo, they're acting not as soldiers; they're acting as cops, gumshoes, detectives. And then we see that they abuse that power; they start pushing people around for no reason. These are very young nineteen-year-olds, in some cases. Lieutenants start interrogating people in very inappropriate ways because they're so frustrated. They see this violence all around them, and they see these people being killed. They want to stop it. They figured, "This is my mission, and I want to succeed."

What happened with Merita is that in this one company of the Eighty-second Airborne who were trying to do this detective work, you had a staff sergeant who was out of control. No one above him recognized it, as they should have. His name was Frank Ronghi. He had become the de facto leader of his platoon, mainly because the senior NCO in the platoon was not around, and he was replaced by a younger guy, and the lieutenant who was in charge was very new. He'd never commanded before—was straight out of West Point. So this guy—this big, burly weight lifter, charismatic, singer— was not only charming everyone in his platoon, but he was also intimidating them. And he became the de facto leader.

He went off on his own, it turned out, which was not allowed, and had relations with women, slipped away to drink, all sorts of things. He started to talk in very strange ways, calling himself "Nymphoman," saying that the girls of Kosovo were really getting to him. And then one day, when he went into these big yellow apartment buildings at the corner of Kosovo, which are an ethnic flash point because both Albanians and Serbs live there, he met Merita in the staircase as she was going up. He dragged her into the basement, and he raped her and killed her. Then he took her body and put it in some U.N. flour sacks, got a buddy, who wasn't sure what was going on, to drive him to a secluded location in the woods and buried her there.

That was such a tragedy in and of itself. People feel so guilty that it happened. They feel so remorseful. But it also became a part of the blackmail that the Albanian criminal network used against the U.S. peacekeepers, who are known as KFOR, Kosovo Force. The leaders of the Albanian community—thugs, really, most of them, hard-line political activists who want an independent Kosovo—used this to try to blackmail KFOR. They say, "We won't make a big deal about this if you release one of our leaders," whom they happened to have arrested the day before on a tip from an informant.

His name was Xhavit Hasani. And he turned out to be, actually, a very big deal. He was a Macedonian Albanian who funded a lot of the liberation movement in Macedonia and Kosovo. So he's probably the equivalent of a three-star general, but they don't know that. . . . But of course, they don't release him because they're not going to be blackmailed like that. So these troops have created an international incident by arresting him, first of all, then this terrible case of the murder creates another reason for these Albanians to go after KFOR. And it evolves into an international incident.

Merita was killed in the winter of 2000. It came out as a crime story—it is such an aberration to have a soldier kill someone like this, and people were wondering, would this spark some kind of big reaction or not? It did spark a localized reaction, but not a large one. So we all reported on it at the time. But we didn't actually do much in-depth look on this unit, which happened to be the one company that I had visited many months before, to do a story about peacekeeping, to see for myself what this was.

After the murder, the army leadership and the leadership of the Defense Department said, "How could this have happened?" So they asked the army to look into that, and they did their standard 15-6 criminal investigation. They had many people involved in it. They took dozens of statements from people who were there. They weren't at all looking at the murder. That was a criminal case. They were looking at the command climate, the unit climate, this sort of thing, to find out how could this have happened.

I went back a year later to see if anything had changed. The murder had happened. The army had responded. They had said they'd do peacekeeping differently, they'd train their troops differently. They do training now that they didn't do before. But the surprising thing to me when I came back was [that] none of the troops had known much about the murder. Most of them hadn't even heard about it.

[In Kosovo] 99.9 percent of the war was an American air war. [It was] done through NATO and there were some nations that participated in the air war, but the U.S. carried the vast majority of the burden.

The reason why they went to Kosovo was not only because of the humanitarian question but because it was on NATO's edge. They thought instability in the Balkans would bring instability throughout Europe, and so they had agreed that they needed to make this a stable place and they couldn't do it just with the status quo. So you have to make good on your promise. Now, if you've done the war, you've achieved that end. In order to achieve the lasting peace you have to do something, and the something that the U.S. government has is the military. . . . The alternatives that it has are very weak. That is the larger point in the book: Why should it be the military or nobody? And these many years after the Balkan peacekeeping first started, Bosnia was the first case where long-term nation building, peacekeeping, was going on since 1995. We still don't have an alternative.

We're still in the situation where people say this military shouldn't be doing this—they should be fighting wars. At the same time, there's no one else to send. The U.N. organization is not funded or organized properly, and the U.N. is a reflection of all of these countries. So there is a widespread frustration, not only in the U.S. government but in the world community, that militaries shouldn't do nation building, but there's no one else to do it. And, there has not been the political leadership to build another apparatus that could take that on—and that's the problem.

I had this fundamental belief that Americans don't know what their military does. I would test it with my friends and their friends and I would test it everywhere I went because like most book authors, I was obsessed with the book during the period of time I was writing it. A lot of people had the notion that our military—this is pre-9/11—wasn't doing much. Well, they were—to the contrary. The military is saying "We're overtaxed. We're in all these countries. We're doing all these things. We're out in the Middle East. We're in Central America in the drug war. They want us to help out with insurgents in Asia." So they were all over the place. I just wanted to give Americans who fund, who support, and whose history is here because of the American military, a better sense of what they actually do.

A Nation of Law and Order

John Marshall
and the Supreme Court

by

R. KENT NEWMYER

John Marshall, fourth chief justice of the United States, played a pivotal role in expanding the power of the U.S. Supreme Court. His most famous case, Marbury v. Madison *(1803), established the principle of judicial review, maintaining the Court's power to declare acts of Congress unconstitutional. R. Kent Newmyer appeared on* Booknotes *on February 24, 2002, to discuss Marshall's experience as a Federalist politician, his rivalry with Thomas Jefferson, and his role in shaping American constitutional law. His book,* John Marshall and the Heroic Age of the Supreme Court, *was published by Louisiana State University Press in 2002.*

THE SUPREME COURT in 2000 is a magnificent institution. It's ensconced in this beautiful marble palace. It has accumulated great authority, and—although it's always had its critics—great capital with the American people. . . . In the disputed election of 1800, it would have been an entirely different scene because the Court had no capital. It had no reputation. As a matter of fact, when John Marshall took over the Court in 1801 [as the fourth chief justice], the institution was pretty much on the ropes.

John Adams asked John Jay to return to the chief justiceship before he gave the job to Marshall. Jay turned him down for a number of reasons, but one of the reasons was Jay's conviction that the Court was destined to be the weakest of the branches of government and perhaps would even give way to the other political branches.

JOHN MARSHALL DIED at age seventy-nine, in 1835. He was born on the frontier of Virginia in Fauquier County. When the Marshall family moved there in the 1750s, there was really nothing there. It was really, truly frontier. They came from Westmoreland, and his father, in Marshall's words, was a planter of narrow means, which meant that he had a few slaves and a large ambition. He was obviously not born to the purple, although Marshall was descended on his mother's side from the Randolphs. It seems at times that almost everybody in Virginia was descended from the Randolphs; it was a mark of distinction.

Marshall served in the military for six years. He signed up in the summer of 1775 in the Culpeper militia, so he belonged to one of the numerous militia units that sprang up and was one of the first to sign up. His father organized a regiment, and in a sense, it was the father's influence that helped spur Marshall's patriotism, his early decision to join the military. He was nineteen when he signed up. He fought in a number of battles. The first battle he fought as a member of the Culpeper militia was what we call the Battle of Great Bridge, down around Norfolk. Then he fought at Germantown and Monmouth Courthouse.

MARSHALL'S FATHER, in 1772, was one of the first to subscribe to Blackstone's *Commentaries.* Sir William Blackstone was a Tory lawyer who gave a series of law lectures at Oxford. These were published in four thick volumes, *Commentaries on the Laws of England.* Marshall and every other lawyer in America, if there was one book they read—and many of them only read one book—it was Blackstone's *Commentaries.* Marshall's father put a copy of Blackstone's *Commentaries* in his son's hands in 1772, long before the Revolution. The great irony is that Marshall learned a lot of his law from a Tory lawyer.

John Marshall studied under George Wythe for two months in 1780. Marshall was technically still in the army, but was on leave. As a matter of fact, he didn't really see much action after 1780. His father was stationed at Yorktown, and Marshall came home to visit and decided to attend Wythe's lectures in the summer of 1780. Wythe had the first law lectureship in this country at William and Mary. Marshall was one of his very first students. We do have the account book, Marshall's notes, which he took when he was attending Wythe's lectures.

George Wythe was one of the great legal scholars of late eighteenth-century Virginia. He later became chancellor of the Virginia High Court of Chancery. He was one of these polymaths. He was a statesman, a lawyer, perhaps this kind of gentleman could only be produced in late eighteenth-century Virginia. But Wythe was a very learned man and dedicated to teaching, and the number of people that he influenced, including Marshall, Jefferson, and Madison was quite amazing.

THOMAS JEFFERSON was a second cousin [to John Marshall]. They were both descended from the Randolphs; that was the connection. Marshall never spoke of his family pedigree. He must have thought of it, but it was not something that was on his mind. He was forward-looking. He really didn't look back. I think it was that forward-looking quality, maybe nurtured on the frontier, which made him remarkably American, much more so than some of the other Founding Fathers.

He is a recognizable person to me. He's the kind of guy you could go out and feel comfortable having a beer with, or his favorite drink, a mint julep, and you could have had a good time. It wouldn't have been that easy with Washington, certainly not with Jefferson, maybe John Adams, but Marshall picked up some of the democracy from the frontier.

He ended up being a Federalist, a conservative, but personally he had all these remarkable democratic, egalitarian qualities. It was really that combination which was the key to his ability as chief justice. He was very egalitarian, very sensitive to other people, didn't stand on prerogatives, didn't stand on family.

Marshall was tall, sinewy, had a thick head of hair, was a socializer, nonjudgmental, devoid of malice, except maybe with Thomas Jefferson. I think he had a little tinge of malice that he reserved for Jefferson. He had an "easy conviviality, casual summer manner and frontier accent." The quote about the accent comes from John Randolph of Roanoke, who was another one of the Randolphs, who was very interested in family, very interested in Tidewater aristocracy, and very interested in Englishness. When he heard Marshall speak for the first time, there was a detectable "twang" was the word that Randolph used.

Randolph referred to Marshall's twang sort of lovingly, but it was evidence that Marshall wasn't quite of the real first-line families, was not quite the aristocrat that Randolph admired so much, although Randolph became a close friend of Marshall. Their friendship was remarkable because these guys were miles apart ideologically. Randolph was really one of the most romantic, states' rights, anti-national [Virginians]—and a very real critic of the Marshall Court. But he loved John Marshall.

THE IDEA OF being an American did not belong exclusively to any party. Both the Federalists, the party of John Marshall, and the Jeffersonian Republicans, the party which Jefferson founded, were patriotic. They both cherished the Revolution as the moment of conception for this great nation. What they disagreed on was what the nation was going to look like.

It was at this point that the terms "nationalism" and "states' rights" became, at least constitutionally speaking, much more meaningful because Jefferson, John Randolph, and John C. Calhoun were committed to a nation which was made up of states. One has to remember that at this time, state

state

government was the government that really touched people. State and local government was what counted. The reach of the national government was so flimsy at this time, it almost didn't exist.

People like Jefferson felt that the modicum of power which the national government had was too much. This was the basis of the personal and ideological antagonism [between Jefferson and John Marshall].

They knew each other from the 1780s and 1790s. I tried to figure out where the hatred started. I sometimes think it was a chemical disaffinity between these two guys. So where did these things actually begin to collide, these two different visions of America—the localist thing, as Jefferson saw it, the states' rights thing, and Marshall's vision of nationalism?

The national vision, of course, had an economic dimension to it. Marshall, in a sense, was a Hamiltonian to the extent that he not only saw the growth of an expanding market, but he saw the national economic unit as being the real foundation of American nationalism. If he could use the Court to enhance trade and commerce across state lines, he felt that maybe those economic sinews would bind the nation together, would overcome this localism which Jefferson saw. We're talking, really, about the roots of the Civil War.

THE JOHN ADAMS–John Marshall friendship is the key, ultimately, to Marshall's appointment as chief justice. Marshall was the chief defender of the Washington administration in Virginia. And of course, John Adams was vice president under Washington.

We're talking about the 1790s, and increasingly in Virginia, even a great man like George Washington [came] under attack by Jefferson and Madison. The Virginia Republicans came to look upon Washington, almost unbelievably, as a sort of traitor to the cause because he was talking too much nationalism. The Bank of the United States, a pro-English foreign policy, protective tariffs—all of these things begin to take shape in the 1790s, and the states'-rights nationalists felt they were anathema to their view of what the nation should look like.

It was Marshall who stepped forth to defend Washington's policies, especially his foreign policy and especially the Jay Treaty. This was a watershed moment in early American politics because Washington decided to settle outstanding problems with Great Britain in this treaty. The Jeffersonians in Virginia went nuts because they felt that this was a sellout to the former enemy at the expense of revolutionary France, which Jefferson particularly felt should be our friend.

Marshall emerged as a defender of federalism. When Adams became president, Marshall continued his affinity with the Federalist Party and his ability to defend Federalist principles. I don't have solid proof of this, but I'm sure Washington conveyed to John Adams his indebtedness to Marshall.

As a matter of fact, Washington became a kind of patron of Marshall, encouraged him to run for Congress, and so on. So Marshall emerged as the leading Federalist politician, even though he didn't like political parties. He was the most effective Federalist in Virginia. It was during this period, by the way, that he began to square off with Jefferson, who emerged in the 1790s as the leader of the Jeffersonian Republicans.

Adams was fighting on two fronts: One was the Jeffersonians, who held him in contempt; the other was the so-called high Federalists in his own party, led by Hamilton. Hamilton's cronies occupied key positions in Adams's cabinet, which was a holdover from the old Washington cabinet. It was a great mistake, Adams keeping these guys on—Secretary of State Timothy Pickering and Secretary of War James McHenry.

Hamilton, in the last two years of the 1790s, tried to subvert Adams's presidency, and Marshall was a constant support for Adams's moderate approach. The crucial issue was Adams's decision not to declare war on France. . . . There was a great rage in this country for a declaration of war. The Hamiltonians especially wanted war against France; this fit in their pro-English commercial thing. And Hamilton wanted to be the head of the army; he was an ambitious guy.

Adams put the kibosh on this and ended up firing these Hamilton spies in his cabinet. It was Marshall, really, who defended Adams all the way, both as congressman and as secretary of state. It was this, you might say, stalwart service in the cause of moderate federalism that convinced Adams finally that this guy had the qualities that would make a great chief justice.

[JOHN MARSHALL was nominated by President Adams, on January the 20th, 1801, and he was confirmed seven days later as the chief justice of the United States. That was also the time frame of the great case *Marbury v. Madison*].

Marbury v. Madison was a case that was not born great. If you look at the factual environment from which the case emerged, you would not have predicted that this would have been a great case. It originated in the Organic Act for the District of Columbia, passed in the last days of the John Adams administration. In the days before the Twelfth Amendment, the defeated Congress came back for a rump session in December. The Federalists were defeated at the polls. They came back for one more go-around, and they began to pass all these controversial acts. One of the acts was the Organic Act for the District of Columbia, one of the more innocuous of the Federalist acts, but it created forty-two justices of the peace for the District of Columbia.

It was a Jeffersonian sweep in the election of 1800, the Federalists had not only lost the presidency in the election, they lost both houses of Congress. John Marshall was nominated and confirmed by the Federalists, the old government. And he was chief justice for the next thirty-four years.

He was put there not just because of the services he had done Adams but because Adams felt that here was a guy who could turn the Court into a bastion of good sense against the radical persuasions of this new party, the Jeffersonian Republicans. So Marshall, in a sense, was put in this high office with a sort of mandate. Judicial review, which emerged from the case of *Marbury*, became the first instance where you might say he made good on the promise.

IN 1801, THERE were six [justices on the Court] counting the chief justice. Samuel Chase, William Paterson and Bushrod Washington were the key figures on the Court. They met in a basement room of the north wing of the Capitol. It was very modest chambers indeed, very cramped. As a matter of fact, the justices had to robe and disrobe in public; there was no conference room. I've often thought that Jefferson would have been pleased with the architectural arrangement because that's exactly where he wanted the Court—someplace in the basement of American government. And of course, it frightened Jefferson that his old enemy, Marshall—because they were ideological enemies by this time—[led the Court]. The stage was set for a showdown.

[The outgoing Adams government nominated the forty-two justices of the peace.] These folks, not surprisingly, were all Federalists. The commissions for the justices of the peace were, you might say, signed, sealed, but not delivered. The president had signed them. It was a completed deal except that they hadn't really been delivered. And so when James Madison, who was Jefferson's secretary of state, takes over March 5th, he finds on his desk forty-two justices of the peace commissions to be delivered, of course, all to Federalists. What Jefferson said is, "This is outrageous." By the way, this flagrant patronage move was one of the things which separated Jefferson and Adams. Jefferson felt that this was a real betrayal.

It was the refusal to deliver those commissions that was the factual background for *Marbury v. Madison*. William Marbury and four other guys brought a case. They took it under so-called original jurisdiction directly to the Supreme Court of the United States and asked Marshall and the Court to issue what we call a writ of mandamus to the secretary of state, showing cause why he shouldn't deliver these commissions.

ANOTHER ONE of the last-minute acts of the Adams administration was the Judiciary Act of 1801, which altered the whole structure of the federal courts. What it did was to relieve the Supreme Court of the United States of the obligation to ride circuit. The early justices were also trial judges. They were only in Washington, at the most, a month and a half during this period. The rest of the time, they rode circuit, where they sat with the federal district judges in the various states. It was a tremendous burden, and there was a lot of opposition among the justices to this onerous [requirement]. So the Judiciary Act of 1801 did away with circuit riding, created a whole bunch of new circuit courts, and sixteen new circuit judges. John Marshall's brother, James Markham Marshall, was one of these Federalist appointees. He was a circuit court justice.

One of the first things that the Jeffersonians did was to repeal the Judiciary Act of 1801, and so all of these new circuit judges were eliminated without really having taken office. That was part of the political environment.

James Markham Marshall figured in *Marbury* because he was called to sign an affidavit testifying to the existence of these mysterious commissions. When the case finally made its appearance in the Supreme Court—the preliminary arguments were made in 1801—Jefferson didn't allow any lawyers to appear. It was his way of repudiating, turning his back, stonewalling, if you will, the Marshall Court.

So the argument in the great case of *Marbury* was ex parte—it was from one side only. Only William Marbury, or Charles Lee, his lawyer, argued the case. All through this case, Jefferson refused to cooperate. Of course, Madison was the defendant in *Marbury v. Madison*, but Jefferson was clearly pulling the strings in the background. He would not allow people in the Department of State to testify to the existence of these disputed commissions.

Marshall [was faced with the question of] how do you get the existence of these commissions on the Court's records? So, he called on his brother, who testified to the fact that he showed up and actually saw those commissions. And, as a matter of fact, he took a couple of them because he wanted to deputize some marshals. And so you have this written affidavit from Marshall's brother in the case, testifying to the existence of these commissions. The purpose of all these shenanigans was to circumvent the stonewalling tactics of Thomas Jefferson and get the existence of the disputed commissions on the record so the Court could decide it.

This was all going on in 1801. The case would be decided in 1803. It was a unanimous decision. Six–zero. Something happened in that decision which is probably more important than the decision itself, in the great sweep of things. The Court abandoned what we call seriatim opinions. In the 1790s, the justices all wrote separate opinions. This was the English practice. This was the practice in the colonial and state courts. One of the first things Marshall introduced was the concept of a majority opinion, in other words, a single opinion speaking for the whole Court, written by one justice. That justice in the early period was usually Marshall, and that was the case in *Marbury v. Madison*.

So it's a significant case not only just because it declared an act of Congress unconstitutional but also because it was an opinion written by a single judge, Marshall, for the whole Court. It was that combination of a forceful majority opinion, and [an opinion] declaring judicial review.

[In his written opinion] Marshall gave this huge, long lecture. It looked like he was digging himself a huge hole, backing himself into the corner. But then, he finally says, "I'm sorry, but the Court can't help you." The Court can't issue a writ of mandamus ordering Madison to deliver these commissions because the authority for that rested on Section 13 of the Judiciary Act of 1789, which is a federal statute. That act, Marshall said, pretended to give original jurisdiction to the Supreme Court of the United States. When Congress attempted to bestow original jurisdiction to the Supreme Court, it violated Article 3 of the Constitution. Why? Because Article 3 of the Constitution talks about original jurisdiction—the notion being that original jurisdiction is not within the purview of Congress to change.

So Marshall declared Section 13 of the Judiciary Act unconstitutional. Marbury didn't get his commission, but the Court and Marshall got an occasion to explain why the Court had the power to declare Section 13 unconstitutional.

This is the great decision, maybe the most famous of all decisions, but there was not a great deal of hoopla about it in 1803. Perhaps Jefferson didn't realize that Marshall had stolen the family farm. It was a fairly narrow decision. Marshall justified judicial review, but he didn't say that Congress had to obey. He didn't say the Court had the final power to interpret the Constitution. What he did was lay out the theoretical foundations for the Court's power. Then, in subsequent decisions, Marshall put teeth in judicial review, where he really exercised power over acts of Congress. So it was a cumulative process building on *Marbury.*

[MARSHALL'S THIRTY-FOUR years as chief justice] is a huge, long period of time. Just think, he was chief justice while there were five different presidents. He belongs in the founding brothers, but he's always left out. That always strikes me as an anomaly. Here's the guy who put, as John Quincy Adams said, the Constitution on the sound foundation on which it rests.

John Knox and
the 1936 Supreme Court

by

DENNIS J. HUTCHINSON

John Knox was born in 1907 and served as law clerk to the famously dis-agreeable Supreme Court justice James C. McReynolds during the Court's 1936–1937 term. Knox's recently discovered memoir provides an insider's view of FDR's "court-packing" effort—an attempt to bolster his New Deal agenda. University of Chicago law professor Dennis Hutchinson appeared on Booknotes *on September 8, 2002, to discuss* The Forgotten Memoir of John Knox: A Year in the Life of a Supreme Court Clerk in FDR's Washington, *published in 2002 by University of Chicago Press.*

JOHN KNOX WAS a law clerk to Justice James McReynolds during the 1936–1937 term of the Supreme Court of the United States. Later in life, he decided to write a memoir of that term because, as it turned out, it was really the high point of his life. He spent eleven years writing up that one year, and when he was done, he had 978 manuscript pages. He tried for years and years to get it published, in whole or in part, and he failed. When he died in 1997, he left behind multiple copies of the manuscript. I came across several chapters of the manuscript in our law school library at the University of Chicago, where I work, and that made me curious as to where the rest of it was because this is a unique artifact. Law clerks don't write memoirs about working for the Supreme Court.

[The manuscript] gives an insight into how the Court operated between the wars. It gives an insight into what Washington society was like between the wars, which was very formal, very Southern. It humanizes an institution that we usually see only in sound bites or artists' sketches.

JAMES C. MCREYNOLDS, justice of the Supreme Court, had been the attorney general appointed by Woodrow Wilson. Wilson sent him to the Court, the rumor always was, [because] McReynolds was so difficult to deal with in cabinet meetings that once there was an opening on the Court, Wilson was glad to be rid of him. But Wilson admired his work as a trustbuster. McReynolds, indeed, had come to Washington as an assistant attorney general under the Theodore Roosevelt administration. That's how he came to Wilson's attention.

McReynolds served on the Supreme Court from 1914 to 1941. He was nasty, racist, anti-Semitic, gratuitously cruel, fixed in his ways, and lazy. He was a very severe man, and his anti-Semitism was notorious. For example, there's no photograph of the Court in 1924 because he would have to sit, as protocol required, next to Justice Louis Brandeis, who was a Jew, and he wouldn't do it.

He was from Elkton, Kentucky, border area Kentucky–Tennessee. He grew up in a very strict household, Disciples of Christ, the Campbellite wing. His father was known as "the pope," not for his Catholicism but for his infallibility, at least in the community.

JUSTICE JAMES MCREYNOLDS was a Democrat appointee from Woodrow Wilson, but he was very conservative. The so-called Four Horsemen, as they were epithetically called—Justice George Sutherland, Justice Willis Van Devanter, Justice Pierce Butler, and Justice McReynolds—were just rock-ribbed conservatives who thought that the New Deal was straight out of Hell, as well as being unconstitutional. [It] was a recipe for socialism, and they were going to stand in the way at every point along the way.

On the other side of the spectrum, you had Justice Benjamin Cardozo, Justice Harlan Stone, and Justice Brandeis, who were more liberal by common denomination and more willing to let the government try to deal with the horrors of the depression—massive unemployment, problems with wages, prices, and the like.

Then there were two figures in the middle, Chief Justice Charles Evans Hughes and Justice Owen Roberts. Depending on where those two justices went, Roberts was really the linchpin. He's the one who changed during this term. Either the New Deal was going to be constitutional and was going to run, or it was going to face one roadblock after another.

[In 1936,] Roosevelt had just finished his first term. As the first term wore on, the Supreme Court was striking down various aspects of the New Deal, such as the Agricultural Adjustment Act, the National Industrial Recovery Act, and the Bituminous Coal Conservation Act of 1935, on grounds that either Congress lacked the power because it wasn't interstate commerce or that the states had the power under the Tenth Amendment to regulate these affairs [more than] the federal government did. It was driving Roosevelt crazy. He thought that it was an affront to his political authority and it was a poor reading of the Constitution, but he couldn't do anything about it during his first term because there were no vacancies on the Court. Like Jimmy Carter, he went through a full term without being able to appoint anybody to the Court.

[FDR ANNOUNCED the court-packing bill on February 5, 1937. For] any justice seventy years of age or older who did not retire, a new seat would join him on the Court. Six were seventy years of age or older.

The Court reacted strangely to it. One of the actual historical facts that Knox's memoir contributes was the sense that several members of the court had a foreboding that the president was going to do something [like this] after the election.

Knox recounted in his memoir: "I've discovered carbon copies of letters Justice McReynolds wrote to the family, and this is before February 5th. The Justice is very nervous. He's afraid something is going to happen. He's been talking to a stock brokerage and talking to advisers in New York. He's afraid he's going to be forced off the Court."

And then the court-packing plan was announced on the 5th and the Court's response was twofold: The chief justice of the United States agreed to provide a letter to Senator Burton Wheeler on the Senate Judiciary Committee that essentially took the president head on in saying, "We're up to date in our business. We don't need more people."

The other thing the Court did was slow down, and Justice McReynolds inspired that. They just didn't issue any significant opinions for a period of about two and a half months because they have the power to issue the opinions whenever they want to.

Up until the spring of this [1936–1937] term, [Justice Owen] Roberts had stuck with the Four Horsemen, but he switched in the spring. That's the so-called "switch in time that saved nine," because . . . [his switch] kept the Court at nine.

JUSTICE MCREYNOLDS never talked about the court-packing bill [to John Knox], never talked about the most controversial New Deal cases. The constitutionality of the National Labor Relations Act was the huge case, a set of cases in fact, [and they] never discussed it. Knox was obviously hurt by that. That's one of the reasons he recounted it in the memoir. But for McReynolds, why should he talk to a staff member about that? He knew what he thought.

[JOHN KNOX NEVER, ever wrote an opinion on behalf of Justice McReynolds.] As far as I can tell, that's accurate and much different from today.

One of the things that's interesting as you compare the court's workload and output is they wrote a lot shorter opinions in those days. You'll notice Knox recounted from time to time, "The opinion took up five pages," he reported; "14 pages," he reported. Well, the school vouchers opinions [last] term are nearly 100 pages by the time you get everybody's opinion factored in.

JOHN KNOX GREW up in the near-western suburbs of Chicago. His father wrote and published how-to books for traveling salesmen. Knox went to the college of the University of Chicago. He went to the Northwestern University Law School in Chicago, where he took his initial law degree, and then he did two years of a graduate degree at Harvard Law School.

[In] the summer of 1930, even as a teenager, before [he] went to college, he'd write away to celebrities, particularly those who had served in the Civil War. He was fascinated by the romance and valor of fighting. Oliver Wendell Holmes was a Civil War veteran, had been wounded three times during the Civil War. Knox was thinking of going to law school, so Holmes was a two-fer. He wrote Justice Holmes and volunteered to drive to Beverly Farms, Massachusetts, from Chicago to visit him. Holmes apparently couldn't think of a good reason to say no, so he let him come and had lunch and talked about the Civil War, though not very extensively, to Knox's regret.

[In 1936,] Knox was twenty-nine, turned thirty just after the term ended. . . . Knox talked his way into [his job as the clerk or the secretary to Justice McReynolds]. He developed a pen pal relationship with Justice Willis Van Devanter. Van Devanter was someone who had tangential associations with the Civil War, a relative who'd fought in it. But Van Devanter's great attraction to Knox was that he responded extensively to letters that Knox wrote to him out of the blue.

I have no idea [why the justice corresponded with Knox]. At one point, I say in the introduction that the justice was either beguiled or bored by this sycophantish, constant letter writing—"Can you give me professional advice? Is it appropriate to refuse alcohol at professional parties? Should a young lawyer get married immediately upon beginning his career, or should he delay it?"—questions no one would ask today out of the blue, and certainly not to a Supreme Court justice.

Gradually, as the correspondence built up over a period of three or four years, he asked Justice Van Devanter if he would serve as a reference for him. Never met the man. After he had met him, he felt [even] more comfortable in asking for a reference, and finally Van Devanter said, "Oh, I really can't do that, but if you're interested in clerking at the Court, perhaps something could happen." And then nothing happened.

Then six months later, Van Devanter wrote him fairly formally—this was right near the end of Knox's second year at the Harvard Law School—saying, "There might be an opening. Would you be interested? Are you married? What are your formal credentials?" And on the day that Knox took his L.L.M. from the Harvard Law School, he got a letter from Justice McReynolds, not Van Devanter, saying, "I understand you're interested in a clerkship. I have some questions for you, and could you meet me in Washington on a certain date?" So he turned a pen pal relationship with Van Devanter into an interview with McReynolds. And McReynolds hired him.

THE FIRST MEETING [between John Knox and Justice McReynolds] was in June of 1936, and McReynolds interviewed him, decided that he was appropriate for the job. Knox was a graduate of Harvard. Van Devanter had said well of him. He was single, and he didn't smoke. Those were the critical criteria, as far as McReynolds was concerned. Knox was disappointed with the interview. He got none of the raconteurship that he enjoyed with Van Devanter, none of the warmth and outreach that he had seen from Justice Cardozo, whom he had also called on in the previous few years.

One of the interesting features to me of the memoir is Knox's frustration at not being able to get close to McReynolds. He wanted a mentoring relationship. He got a little bit of that when he called on Justice Cardozo. He didn't get it from Van Devanter, who as soon as Knox came to work for McReynolds, said, "I can't talk to you anymore because it would be inappropriate for me to give advice to someone who's working for another member of the Court."

[JOHN KNOX's responsibilities while he worked for the justice were to] "arrive by nine o'clock in the morning and no later; be there all day, so if I call and I need you, you can do whatever needs to be done; leave by six o'clock unless I let you go early or I need you later."

The first order of business was to pick up the mail from downstairs in the lobby of 2400 16th Street, N.W., to bring it to McReynolds, answer all social invitations immediately, according to the justice's direction, and then proceed to whatever court work was imperative.

Knox was paid $2,400 by McReynolds. Harry Parker, McReynolds's messenger, told Knox that he just wasn't going to be able to afford to live in Washington on $2,400.

JUSTICE MCREYNOLDS lived [at] 2400 16th Street, N.W. It's now called the Envoy, still standing, still an apartment house. At the time that McReynolds lived there, cabinet secretaries, members of Congress lived there. It's right across from Meridian Hill Park.

Justice McReynolds had thirteen [rooms]. It was a huge apartment. It's now been chopped up in the refurbishment into much smaller ones. But he had thirteen entire rooms.

John Knox worked in the justice's apartment at 2400 in a small cubicle. He lived downstairs at 2400 at least for the first several months, but it was extremely expensive. He felt totally isolated, and he was living in a pretty rare social atmosphere in the building, and he eventually moved out to a place at 2700 Connecticut Avenue, N.W.

[THE COURT] had just moved into the new building at 1 First Street, N.E. We think of it as being the Supreme Court and always being there, but it had only opened in 1935, after being on the drawing board for a long time. This was only the second year of the building's operation. The justices, though, were very set in their ways, on the whole and by and large, and they tended still to work out of their homes. Indeed, only two members of the Court [that term] actually used the new building. That was Chief Justice Hughes and Justice Roberts. The rest of them had law libraries in their homes. They had one staff member, usually. A couple of them had two. Knox served as effectively both a law clerk and as a social secretary.

THERE WERE LOTS of bright young folks who came to Washington during the New Deal, and [there was a] circle that Knox kind of stumbled into unwittingly, and then got very nervous about because they were all New Dealers. . . . Knox was working for the most arch-conservative on the Supreme Court, and at the Supreme Court—socially, you're out [if] you're not one of the boys. At the time that he's attending these so-called club meetings, as they called them, there were cases pending before the Supreme Court from the agencies that some of these young men were working for.

Even though he had had a fairly active social life, certainly, in Cambridge, when he came to Washington, he was immediately told by Justice McReynolds's messenger, Harry Parker, that he had to get calling cards—a professional card that identified him as law clerk to Justice McReynolds.

Knox discovered very quickly that one of his chief functions was dealing with social invitations that McReynolds received during the year. [That required] dealing with the calling cards because apparently during this period in Washington there was a very strict protocol about how you dealt with calling cards.

If you dropped off a personal calling card at someone's place and you were, say, Justice McReynolds, you turned up the right-hand corner to indicate that you had [personally delivered] it and not your chauffeur. If you just had your chauffeur or your law clerk or somebody drop it off, you just left the card flat. Correspondingly, when a card came into the McReynolds residence that had an upturned corner, it got high-priority attention because the protocol was that you had twenty-four hours after receiving a card to acknowledge it. If you acknowledged it, then you were in that social circle.

One can tell, particularly from the memoir, that Justice McReynolds viewed himself as quite a ladies' man and had a number of wealthy widows that he socialized with, played golf with at the Chevy Chase Club, and spent a fair amount of time with.

The problem that Knox had going from this busy social life that he had in Cambridge to Washington is that he felt isolated living in the building. He didn't know many people and those that he was most immediately exposed to were within McReynolds's circle, and he turned out to be fairly charming with these widows that McReynolds socialized with. Harry Parker warned him. He said: "If the Justice finds out about you socializing with his lady friends, he's going to fire you on the spot."

[Eventually,] the roof fell in. There's even one beautifully dramatic moment in which Knox was really tacking into the wind and was attending a tea. This happened to be a tea in Mrs. Savage's apartment, which was one floor above McReynolds's apartment, and the justice rolled up on a Sunday afternoon unannounced.

Fortunately, Mrs. Savage's maid saw him . . . and got Mrs. Savage to scoot Knox and his friend out of the apartment before the justice saw them.

I WAS FASCINATED to see how self-absorbed Knox was and how much he was leaning on any of the justices, but particularly his own justice, for a mentoring relationship. . . . Justice Butler and Justice Sutherland were the only justices that Knox didn't see during the year. And again, Harry Parker told him, "What are you doing going over to see Brandeis? What are you doing going over to see Cardozo? You shouldn't do that. They're both Jewish. McReynolds is going to find out about that. He will fire you on the spot." But this was how Knox got the job in the first place, and it's what he saw the payoff as being.

HARRY PARKER was technically the messenger to Justice McReynolds, paid by the Court. He also acted as chauffeur. He cooked the justice's lunch. He did all his [shopping]. He did a fair amount of the evening cooking. And as one of the justice's lady friends said, he did everything but breathe for the justice.

Harry was worried all year that Knox was going to get fired, either for socializing with the justice's lady friends or being absent from the apartment where he should be to answer the telephone if there was an official call or if the justice himself called.

And, as the year wore on, particularly as the bar examination got closer and closer, Knox was spending more time away from the apartment studying for the bar in the air-conditioned corridors of the new Supreme Court Building. Harry warned him again. He said, "You better be around here."

Mary Diggs . . . was maid and part-time cook. One of the many values of this memoir is it recaptures not only a social Washington in the 1930s but African American Washington. Harry Parker's mother served as a cook in the McKinley administration. He himself was a well-known caterer. There are families who worked in the African American community in Washington for years for the government, giving fabulous service, but who were all but invisible because of the staff positions they had.

"Pussywillow" was the name that Harry and Mary had for Justice McReynolds. They wanted to be able to talk about the justice and his lady friend and their social schedules and not have the justice suddenly overhear and be concerned about what was being said, so they had nicknames for the justice. "Madam Queen" was apparently the number one girlfriend at that point.

[The three—Harry, Mary, and John Knox—] obviously got along very well; again, this is Knox's account. It's a memoir. I can't verify every single word of it by any means, but it rings true. And, Harry and Mary said to him, "Why don't you join us for lunch?" Mary says, "I'll throw an extra pork chop on the fire." He says, "Oh, that would be wonderful." He was very hungry at this point, and so the meal was cooked. Two tables were set up in the kitchen: one for Harry and Mary and one for Knox. Knox sees the two tables and can't believe it. This is how far segregation operates in Washington and in this household. He says, "I'll sit with you," and Mary is kind of thrown by that.

During duck hunting by Justice McReynolds, Harry had to be the dog. Twice there's a reference, an account, of McReynolds going out to the Eastern Shore to hunt ducks in the fall and taking Harry with him, and Harry's job was to retrieve the kill, to wade through icy waters and bring back the ducks. There was a very poignant moment at which Harry says, "I'm getting too old to do this. I'm going to get pneumonia. I wish you wouldn't do that."

It's just the most demeaning image, and Knox is totally affected by it. He's really offended. It's one thing to talk about the bigotry and anti-Semitism in a public or direct sense, but doing this to a staff member, it obviously curdled Knox's stomach.

THERE ARE A couple of examples in the memoir of gratuitous cruelty. One is on a fairly low level where McReynolds assigned Knox an opinion to write and Knox wrote four drafts of it, spent the entire weekend doing it, took up a

Sunday doing it, and Harry told him, "You're wasting your time. The justice ain't going to use it. He's just trying to keep you busy." Knox was trying to prove himself or maybe to reassure the justice that he could do the job. And sure enough, when the justice got back, he took the opinion, and tossed it in the wastebasket.

Another time, . . . the justice went on and on working on an opinion, dictating, so that Knox would be hard pressed to attend a reception at the White House. That was the annual reception for the judiciary, and Knox had gone to lengths to get his tuxedo cleaned and pressed and was very eager to do it. But by the time McReynolds finished dictating the opinion, it was just too late, and Knox was sure that McReynolds staged it that way.

[Another example came when] King Edward was abdicating his throne "for the woman I love, Wallis Warfield Simpson." The abdication speech at the time was the most listened to radio address in history, and Knox was sure that the justice would allow Harry, Mary, and him to listen to it on the radio. They were all getting ready to do it, and when they finally asked permission, the justice said, "No, it won't be heard tonight. No."

JOHN KNOX . . . resumed his diary in the 1960s, and he wrote in 1962 that "I'm a pathetic failure at this point." He never married. He moved back to Chicago. He worked as a lawyer. He flunked the bar several times before he was admitted to practice. He worked in New York for a while during World War II. Then he moved back to Chicago, back to his family's residence in Oak Park after the war to take over his father's business, which was beginning to flounder. He ran that business as well as he could, even rewrote some of his father's little salesmen chat books for a while, but the business went belly up in the early 1970s. He became an insurance adjuster for Allstate.

Frank and Jesse James, Outlaw Brothers

by

TED P. YEATMAN

The legend of Frank and Jesse James began in 1869 when they were accused of robbing a bank in Gallatin, Missouri. Although this may not have been the James brothers' first bank heist, it earned them enormous media attention. Their spree came to an end in 1882 when Jesse was killed by a member of their own gang, Bob Ford, who'd been working with the government as an informant. Frank James surrendered and was tried for his crimes, but he was acquitted twice. On September 16, 2001, author Ted P. Yeatman appeared on Booknotes *to discuss* Frank and Jesse James: The Story Behind the Legend, *published the previous year by Cumberland House.* 〰2000〰

I was living in Nashville, Tennessee, back in the mid-1970s, and back about 1975, I decided for just the heck of it, I was going to, for a year, try to track down everything I could on the James brothers when they were living in Tennessee. They lived there for about four years from 1877 to 1881. I kept finding more and more new material, and I just couldn't quite put the subject down. And about twenty years later, I picked up and got a book contract and started work on the book.

THE JAMES brothers were born in the Kearney, Missouri, area. Frank was not born at the actual farm, but Jesse was born at what's now the James Farm, which is a historic site out at Kearney. It's owned by the county.

Frank and Jesse's father [Robert Sallee James] was a Baptist minister. As a matter of fact, he was one of the founders of William Jewell College in Liberty, Missouri. It's not the type of family background that you would normally figure for an outlaw. . . .

[Robert James] had quite a reputation as an evangelist in Missouri. He went out to California during the gold rush and was in one of the mining camps there just a few weeks and came down ill and died. And that was pretty much it. As a matter of fact, a number of people speculated what would have happened if he had possibly lived.

The widow James, Zerelda Cole James, remarried a fellow named Benjamin Simms. Simms and the boys apparently didn't get along too well. Zerelda James and Simms ended up [deciding to] divorce, which was something that was rather unusual for that day and age. [Simms died before the divorce was finalized, and] Zerelda later remarried Dr. Reuben Samuels. The relationship with Samuels continued on until his death. He died in 1908, and she died in 1911.

THE FIRST ACTUAL robbery that was pinned on the James brothers was the Gallatin, Missouri, robbery. They robbed a bank in December of 1869. This is the first one that [historians] actually have some reason to feel that they were in, although there is some evidence that Frank James may have been involved in another bank robbery in 1866 in Liberty, Missouri. As a matter of fact, they call [the bank in Liberty] the Jesse James Bank Museum. It's still there today and you could go in, see the bank vault and the counter and everything pretty much as it was back at the time of the robbery.

They just more or less came in, rode into town. There were about a dozen people. Some of them went into the bank; some of them more or less hung around out in the streets to keep an eye on things. The folks in the bank—one of them hopped over the counter, had a flour sack, and more or less said, "Fill 'er up." They took . . . about $60,000 worth of money and negotiable securities, and maybe even some non-negotiable securities in there, also. They were fencing these; they found some of the bonds as far away as Cincinnati.

[GADS HILL, January of 1874] was the first train robbery that Jesse pulled in Missouri. It is illustrative of the typical train robbery that they [pulled]. It was one that was rather colorful because Jesse, at the end of the robbery, left a press release to be telegraphed into the St. Louis newspapers.

JESSE MAY HAVE killed as many as six or eight [people], and that's just a guess. The bulk of the killing that was done was probably during the Civil War period, and we'll never know how many of those there were. . . . [During the Civil War], they were out in Missouri with the guerrilla groups that were under William Quantrill and Bloody Bill Anderson. Quantrill was a guerrilla leader out in the Kansas City–Independence area.

[FRANK JAMES was responsible for] a number of [killings]. As a matter of fact, he probably killed the bank teller at Northfield, [Minnesota,] although that was kind of hushed up for several decades, right up until after his death.

That [robbery] pretty much spelled the end of the James–Younger gang. The Youngers were captured right after the robbery at Northfield [in 1876]. It was a badly bungled robbery. They tried to get in the vault. The teller claimed that there was a time lock on the vault, and there's some question whether he was bluffing them there, but they didn't bother to check. They assumed, I guess, that it was locked. Then in the meantime, the townspeople heard that the bank was being robbed and were out in the streets with shotguns and old Civil War carbines and anything that would shoot, basically. [The robbers] just barely managed to get out of town alive, and right after that, they had several thousand folks after them combing the state in posses. It was one of the biggest manhunts Minnesota's ever had, before or since. The Youngers were captured, I guess it was about two or three weeks after the robbery, and the Jameses somehow managed to give the posses the slip, get on across to just about where the Dakota line is and then slip down into South Dakota and Iowa, and then somewhere down in that area they managed to get back to Missouri, apparently.

BOB FORD [killed Jesse James on April 3, 1882]. . . . Bob had ingratiated himself into the gang in the latter part of 1881, early 1882. But he was acting more or less for the law enforcement people in the Kansas City area and had met with Missouri governor Thomas Crittenden. He was providing information about Jesse's whereabouts, and they were possibly going to either bring him in somewhere or other. . . .

I'M NOT SURE that [the governor] was interested in killing Jesse. The reward actually was for bringing him in. But in this case, Bob just went ahead and pulled the trigger. I think he figured that "If I don't shoot him now, that's one opportunity blown, and we won't be able to get him in, and this fellow will probably come back and shoot me."

Why did Governor Crittenden want to get Jesse? Jesse had been on a train-robbing spree and Crittenden had campaigned for governor of Missouri on a campaign platform that included eliminating all of this outlawry that was going on in the state. It was getting big news headlines all across the country. You could see it in the *New York Times*, the Chicago papers. It had become a big political football in both Missouri and on a national level, and Crittenden was a Democratic governor and the Democratic Party was sometimes being accused of taking a lenient attitude toward this. One of his platforms was "We're going to eliminate the outlawry." He managed to get funding from some of the railroads to put up a huge reward. And this was the big factor. Whereas these folks might have figured, "Well, I'm not sure about doing it," when in point of fact, they could make, in one shot possibly, the amount of money that they would pull off of a major robbery. You have to figure that it was something like $5,000 or $10,000 they were offering for Jesse. You have to figure that that's several times that in current dollars.

They did a rather ineffective job of hunting the James brothers down for the first decade or so. It was only after Crittenden got in and posted the rewards [that they found them] . . . Jesse, at this point in time had made some very bad blunders. He had apparently killed one of the members of the gang, and this didn't go down too well with some of the other people, although he didn't come out and advertise this. As a matter of fact, that gang killing had something to do with Bob Ford plugging Jesse.

[BOB FORD] pulled a pistol on Jesse, who had laid his guns down on the bed, and Ford fired a shot and that was it. They put the body up for public viewing after they had taken it to the funeral home. They had a number of photographs that they took of the body. There was this constant thing that would happen every few years where somebody would come forward—say, after the turn of the century—and claim that he was the secretly surviving Jesse James and there would be some big furor in the press over this. Actually, there are people that are claiming now that their ancestor in Texas, who died sometime back in the 1940s, was Jesse. The last living claimant that actually claimed to be Jesse died in 1951.

Bob Ford actually, believe it or not, after he shot Jesse, [pled guilty to murder charges] and was convicted and sentenced to hang, and Governor Crittenden telegraphed a pardon. So this shows how things were going. Jesse had not actually been brought in formally and charged [with any crimes]. They'd never served the papers or anything on him. There was a large percentage of the population that thought maybe he was not guilty of any of this, that he was being persecuted by the Republicans, who were using this for political gain. This is what I mean by how this became politicized.

JOHN NEWMAN EDWARDS is the fellow who is often credited with being the creator of the James legend, and he was a newspaper editor. He was editor of the *St. Louis Dispatch* and several other newspapers. He is the one who issued a number of florid editorials defending Jesse James and saying that he was being persecuted and that all of these robberies . . . were being pulled by someone who was very clever and very theatrical and so forth. So he tended to blink at what was going on, and he later had a good bit to do with Frank James. When Frank came in and surrendered, he was brought in by Edwards, who had a lot to do with the negotiation between the Missouri authorities and Frank. He also apparently had a lot to do with some of the wire-pulling in the trials there.

[FRANK JAMES was tried for his crimes]. As a matter of fact, he went through several trials, at least two full trials that I know of. He was acquitted in both cases. One of them was for the Winston train robbery, which was one of the last things that the gang did. It was vague as to whether Frank had been there—at least they were able to prove that he might not have been. I think it was basically a matter of reasonable doubt. Whether he actually was or not, that may be another story, but he was able to beat the rap.

In the case of the Muscle Shoals, Alabama, payroll robbery, he was actually in Nashville at the time the robbery occurred, and there was some pretty good evidence to indicate that. I went over the depositions, and it looked like they had a rather weak case.

I'D GUESS THAT [my favorite character] would probably be Frank James. He was the most interesting one to do the research on because I never could figure what I was going to turn up next on him.

Frank's career in show business . . . started about 1901. Frank had tried running for the doorkeeper of the Missouri House of Representatives, and he had been thwarted in this. [Democrats were in control.] Frank wasn't a Republican at this point. He was a Democrat. As a matter of fact, that had something to do with why he switched parties [in 1904]. But he felt that he had lived an exemplary life after all of this [robbery] business and that he was entitled to be shown something for it. So when he was passed over for this position, he decided to go and join a traveling theatrical troupe and was in a number of melodramas that were put on in the Midwest, and at least as far east as Pennsylvania, as far as I know, and then as far west as [Texas].

[THE 1912 STORY of the shooting of Theodore Roosevelt in Milwaukee is in this book] because Frank offered to raise a bodyguard of 100 men to protect Roosevelt. He sent a telegram off to Roosevelt's aide offering this [after the shooting]. I think [the aide] was probably thinking, "Oh, my gosh, how are we going to deal with this?" because in one way, it was a possible plus, but at the same hand, it was also a possible minus that you've got this fellow that is noted as a bandit and an outlaw saying that he's going to raise a group of bodyguards. So he kind of sidestepped it and said, "Well, Mr. Roosevelt is not planning on doing any campaigning further here, but we want to thank you, and he wants to say that he's feeling as hearty as a Bull Moose." Frank was such a supporter of the Bull Moose Party, in fact, that he used to call the livestock in at his farm by yelling as loud as he could, "Bull Moose!"

[FRANK] DIED at the James farm [at age seventy-two], but he lived several other places. He lived in Nevada, Missouri, for about a year or two, I guess. Sold shoes over there. And then he went down to work as a salesman in a department store in Dallas, Texas.

[People knew who he was.] They were using him as a draw. This was one of the things, the fact that you had Frank James working in your store would bring in crowds of people. He ended up . . . working as a horse-race starter for a number of years. As a matter of fact, he did that right on up until close to the time of his death. . . .

JESSE IS BURIED up . . . in Mount Olivet Cemetery in Kearney, Missouri, which is about . . . twenty miles outside of Kansas City.

[Jesse James was exhumed in the summer of 1995 because] they wanted to do some forensic testing, DNA testing. Professor James Starrs and other forensic scientists got an exhumation order from the Clay County court because there was no record of an autopsy having been performed. And the only way they could do this was if there was no autopsy of record and the person had met their end through means that [were] somewhat violent, you might say. This was approached more or less as a regular forensic crime examination, just like you would have in a modern instance.

I wasn't able to make it over [to the cemetery when the exhumation was conducted], but I did a good bit of the historical research that they used for finding out certain things. In other words, they were trying to see if there were any wounds that Jesse had had earlier in his life that might be visible, say, on the bones or something like that.

[When they] dug him up, they weren't even sure that they were going to get him up. The remains had decomposed in certain areas. What they were looking for specifically was DNA evidence, but they were also trying to look for evidence of the bullet hole in the skull and things of that nature, so maybe they could tell something about the caliber of the weapon that was used to kill him. [The remains were confirmed to be those of Jesse James.]

THE [JAMES] legend came from the media. A lot of it comes from the early histories. There were histories of the gang that were being published even while they were robbing trains. There was an ad in one of the St. Louis newspapers for *The Border Outlaws* and *The Border Bandits*, [a two-volume book,] by James William Buel. One of the hooks for the sale of the book was this new train robbery that had occurred outside of Kansas City. . . . And as each new robbery occurred, they would publish an update to the book.

Afterward, you had a slew of dime novels that were these cheap pap. They were about the size of, say, *Time* or *Newsweek* magazine, but they would have content like a modern [paperback] Western, although they were even a little less than that. I'd say the ancestor of the dime novel would be some 1950s television series, as on the Old West, where they'd have one stock character in there that would go through a series of adventures—Buffalo Bill is one that pops to mind—. . . and he would be dealing with these other famous people in the Old West, maybe have a Wild Bill Hickock or Jesse James, or whatever. They'd go through however many adventures they could dream up, basically. [Jesse James's] name was alliterative, and the Robin Hood image was brought out very often, so you had this myth and this mystique that developed over the years.

[THE REASON the Jesse James legend is so well known] goes back to a lot of folklore motifs. . . . The other thing you'll notice with all legendary outlaws that achieve immortality—be it Robin Hood, Billy the Kid—all are killed by someone they trust. In the Robin Hood legend, it's the prioress that Robin Hood trusts. Billy the Kid, it's Pat Garrett, one of his former buddies. In this case, it's Bob Ford, one of the members of the gang. So it's all treachery.

A History of Violence in America

by

FOX BUTTERFIELD

1995

In his book, All God's Children: The Bosket Family and the American Tradition of Violence, *published by Alfred A. Knopf in 1995, Fox Butterfield examined the roots of violence in America. By tracing the family history of Willie Bosket, one of New York's most violent criminals, Mr. Butterfield argued that present-day black violence has its roots in a long tradition of white Southern violence. Mr. Butterfield, Boston bureau chief for the* New York Times, *joined us on* Booknotes *on March 31, 1996.*

THIS STARTED OUT as a story about a young man named Willie Bosket, who, as a boy [in 1978], murdered [two] people on the subway in New York. When I began to look into his record, I found that his father had also been convicted of murder. And then I found that his grandfather and great-grandfather had also been violent criminals. Eventually, I traced the family back to a county in South Carolina which has long been known to historians as being one of, or perhaps the most, violent county in the country. So where I started out looking at one young boy in Harlem, I ended up, really, in a way, with a history of violence in America.

It opened up a way to understand violence in a very different fashion than we normally do—that violence does not grow out of the causes that we usually associate it with. It turned out murder is not something new that grows out of our cities. It didn't have anything to do with race or with poverty or with the broken family or with television. In fact, it had a very different origin. The high homicide rates that characterize the United States really have a geographical origin in the white, rural pre–Civil War South.

I began looking into Willie's background, and then I learned about his father having also been convicted of murder and having been sent to the same reform school at the same age, and it seemed like a very powerful tale, which might help us understand why we're in this predicament today. You know, one of the surprising things is that when you look at crime rates now, most crimes rates in the United States are not all that different from those in Western Europe, the countries that we usually compare ourselves to. There's more burglary in London now than there is in New York. There are more car thefts in France per capita than there are in the United States. But in murder, we're off the charts.

IF YOU LOOK at young people in this country, young people commit homicide at a rate sixty times that of young people in England. There's something very wrong there. If other crime rates are that close, why do we commit so much violence? As I went back in this story, I found an explanation going way back into South Carolina, into the early history of the country. The explanation has a lot to do with what white Southerners in the nineteenth century called honor, or reputation. It was the notion that a person derives their worth from the opinion of others, so that if somebody insults you or your family, you have to take action. White Southerners in the antebellum South did not believe in going to court. Andrew Jackson's mother—and Andrew Jackson was born in the western part of South Carolina—once said to him when he was a boy, "A true gentleman does not go to court. If somebody insults you, you always settle them cases yourself."

In fact, we know that in the South, that among the upper classes, this notion of honor led to dueling. In South Carolina, dueling was outlawed in 1812, but it continued on. The code book for duelists in South Carolina was written by the governor of the state. In it, he said that he deplored the Christian doctrine of turning the other cheek. He said that because such forgiveness is utterly repugnant to human feelings; mere words can never be satisfaction for swords. Dueling stopped in the North, but it continued on in the South into and after the Civil War. Among the less affluent and less educated, honor led to a game that they called "rough and tumble" or a savage form of what was known then as "wrassling." The object of this was to chomp off your opponent's nose or ears or even chew off their fingers or gouge out their eyes. Again, this practice was outlawed in South Carolina back at the early part of the eighteenth century, but it continued. They made it a capital crime, but only if you gouged out the eyes or chewed off the fingers. The nose and the ears were OK.

WILLIE, AS A boy of fifteen, murdered [two] people on the subway in New York and before that he already had a kind of legendary criminal record. He had committed, by his own count, 2,000 crimes, including 200 armed robberies. Later, as an adult, when he was in prison, he continued to commit crimes in prison. He attacked his guards, he threw feces on them, bit their fingers, and, in one case, stabbed a guard in the chest with a homemade shank.

Today, he's in a cell in a prison in New York State. It's actually the most solitary confinement of any prisoner in the entire country. They have built a special cell just for Willie. The guards call him "Hannibal Lecter," like the character in the movie. When you go to the prison, you have to go through the regular prison and then you have to go through the normal solitary confinement block. Then you go through another set of doors and gates, and then you come to the area where they have Willie.

He's kept in a kind of Plexiglas cage. The iron bars are covered over with extra-heavy Plexiglas so he can't throw anything out or bite his guards. He's not allowed to have books, newspapers, magazines. He can't listen to the radio or watch TV. In fact, there are four TV cameras kept trained on him from outside his cage twenty-four hours a day, even if he wants to take a shower or go to the bathroom, to keep him under watch. The guards are not supposed to speak to him. It's really total solitary. They even removed the light fixtures from the ceiling of his cell because at one point, he took to eating the light bulbs to show how violent he really could be.

The prison is in the Catskills. It's in a place called Woodbourne. Oddly, it's not a maximum-security prison, but it's where they could build the most secure confinement area just for Willie. It wasn't just what he did on the outside, it's what he's done in prison. Every opportunity he got, he was waging what he called a "war on his guards." It was a war with the system. He thought that the criminal justice system was like a surrogate mother because he's been locked up since he was nine years old, either in a juvenile reformatory or an adult prison. He sees all the guards as his enemy and he wants to prove that he's the toughest, meanest guy there ever was. So when he had an opportunity, he would throw hot coffee on a guard or he would throw feces on them. Or if a nurse was giving him his medication, sometimes he would bite the nurse's finger.

WILLIE WAS BORN in Harlem. He had a normal delivery, and as a child, what was exceptional about him was that first, he was very bright; second, that he always seemed to be getting in trouble and his mother couldn't understand it. But she did frequently—when she looked at him—tell him he reminded her of Willie's father, of her husband.

She would say to him, "Willie, when you grow up, you're going to be bad. You're going to be real bad, just like your father." She didn't at first tell him what his father had done. She wanted to protect him from that terrible truth. So

Willie's imagination ran wild and he began to wonder what his father had done. When he was seven, he saw a picture on his grandmother's dresser of a man in fatigues and he asked who it was. And his grandmother said, "That's your father. He's in prison. He killed two men." Willie, in a rather perverse kind of way, thought this was great. His father was the baddest man you could be.

Willie and his father, Butch, never met. The first time they ever got in touch was when Willie had been arrested at the age of fifteen for murder and he was in a juvenile prison. The warden, in effect, arranged for Willie to get in touch with his father.

THERE'S A SIMILAR story about his father, Butch, who was in prison and wanted to escape. His father, after many years of being in prison, really tried to go straight. He worked very hard to get a college degree, to get an education, although he'd never been to school as a boy; he'd been locked up at the age of nine. In fact, both Willie and his father were sent to the same reform school at exactly the same age—nine. His father spent all those years locked up. But as an adult, he began to get an education and he found that he was very good at school.

Butch finally got out. He used his education as a way to get out. The prison system felt that he had been rehabilitated and he got two jobs, not just one. He got one job working in an aerospace company as a computer programmer. This was in Milwaukee. He also got a job teaching a course at the University of Wisconsin for computer science for undergraduates. He seemed to be doing well. And then, suddenly, he was rearrested. It was a charge of sexually assaulting a young girl. [He was convicted and imprisoned.] He said he was innocent, but he despaired and he plotted with the girl's mother, who claimed that Butch was innocent. He resorted to an old prison ruse, that if you swallow enough salt, it will cause a kind of ulcer in your stomach and make you cough up blood. He saved up enough salt from these little packets that the prison provided with his lunches and he swallowed them all at once and he did then cough up blood and the prison authorities didn't know what had happened, so they took him to a hospital. It happened to be kind of an unguarded hospital. And he then arranged for his girlfriend to come in disguised as a nurse.

She was a white woman who was a beautician and she came in, put on a nurse's uniform and brought in two guns. She managed to disarm the sheriff's deputy who was guarding Butch in the hospital room. They got the handcuffs off Butch, put them on the sheriff's deputy, chained the sheriff's deputy to the wall, and then they took off.

They would have made a clean break except for a small irony. When they turned out of the hospital room, they turned to the right instead of to the left. . . . The sheriff's deputies were alerted that he was on the loose, so the sheriff's deputies closed in and Butch used all the bullets that he had to shoot out with the sheriff's deputies except for the last two. When he realized he was down to his last two bullets, he took the gun and put it to the head of his girlfriend and killed her, and then he put it to his own head and shot himself. That was 1985.

BUTCH'S FATHER was named James. James had been born in South Carolina; was brought to Augusta, Georgia, as a young boy. He grew up very, very poor and turned to a life of crime as a young man when his marriage wasn't working out. James had married a woman and they'd had a child, Butch. James walked off and abandoned that child at the age of just a few months. He took a train north from Augusta to Washington and began robbing stores and was caught and put in prison a number of times for armed robbery. In a terrible turn of events, the mother also abandoned Butch when he was really still a baby. Butch was left to grow up on his own, largely on the streets of Augusta in a very poor section of town. He would go out and beg, and he soon joined a gang. He would rob stores. And we know from the records that are preserved that by the age of nine, he actually had a gunshot wound in one leg and he had a case of gonorrhea. This was diagnosed by a doctor.

James's father and Butch's grandfather was a man who was called Pud Bosket, who in some ways is the most interesting member of the family. Pud was born in 1889 outside a little town in South Carolina. His family were sharecroppers. His father had been a slave. Pud grew up in the 1890s, which, in many ways, was the worst decade for Afro-Americans in American history. It was a period which we remember now for the height of lynching. It was a period when the Jim Crow laws were imposed, segregation, when blacks lost the right to vote. One of his cousins was hung there, the first man to be hung in [Saluda] County, and Pud was at the hanging.

Pud, or Pudding, was a nickname that he was given from the time he was a boy. He never got any education. The family was really dirt poor, sharecroppers. He went to work farming a white man's land, and he became very resentful of the way his family and blacks were being treated. Where he worked, the white farmer would still whip his hands. This was still legal in South Carolina thirty, forty years after the end of the Civil War. It was a vestige of slavery. And one day, Pud got tired of that and he turned around as the white man was going to whip him and he grabbed the whip from the white man's hand and said, "This is the last nigger you're going to whip."

After that, he could never get another job because no white person wanted to employ him. So he began robbing stores and got put on the chain gang. But instead of becoming an outlaw, he became a kind of folk hero to other

African Americans in that community. It was a period that there were a number of black bad-men heroes that were springing up all over the South. These were the people who were celebrated in the early blues songs.

PUD'S FATHER was a man named Aaron, who was born a slave, whose family had been bought and sold a number of times, who himself, as a young slave boy, was bought and sold several times. I was very lucky to be able to trace the family back that far, back to Aaron's father, who had been probably born in Maryland. He was then sold off as a very young slave boy and put into what was called the long-distance slave trade; was sent in a coffle with other slaves, chained up, and ended up being sold in South Carolina. The family was bought and sold three or four times. At one point, one of their owners was a man named Bauskett, which is where they got their surname, from the white slave owner. Later, they were sold to a man named Francis Pickens, who actually became governor of South Carolina and, as governor, led South Carolina into secession. He was the governor who ordered the shots fired on Fort Sumter.

It's a very powerful story which gets at the roots of violence in America, that violence is not something that just started in our cities recently; these very high homicide rates which characterize American violence go back a long way, back into the nineteenth and even into the eighteenth century, perhaps. The county where Willie's family came from, Edgefield, was a small county. Its largest town was a village of 300 people. But in the nineteenth century, it had a homicide rate as high as New York City today, which is flabbergasting when you think about it.

PRESTON BROOKS was a congressman from South Carolina from this little county called Edgefield. In one of the most famous incidents in American history, in 1856, he was very upset when a famous senator from Massachusetts named Charles Sumner, who was the leading abolitionist, gave a speech in which Sumner excoriated South Carolina for upholding slavery and also attacked one of Brooks's relatives who was a senator from South Carolina named Butler. This was offense to the family's honor, and honor was incredibly important to Southerners in the nineteenth century.

Preston Brooks thought this over and he wanted to avenge his family and his state's honor, so he walked over . . . to the Senate. It was at noontime. Unfortunately, there were still some ladies in the visitors' gallery, and so as a matter of honor, he had to wait till the ladies left. Then he walked up to Senator Sumner's desk. Preston Brooks had a gold-headed cane, a walking stick he used because he'd been wounded in the knee in an earlier duel in South Carolina. He went up and began flogging Senator Sumner right on the floor of the Senate and flogged him so hard that he left the cane in shreds.

[Sumner never fully recovered from the beating.] Brooks resigned his seat, went back to South Carolina, but he was unanimously reelected. In fact, some local merchants bought him another cane and inscribed it, "Hit him again." For a lot of people in the North, this was regarded as the first act of the Civil War; the attack on Sumner was seen as a vicious criminal act.

STROM THURMOND'S father was a man named J. William Thurmond, who was the prosecutor or district attorney or, as they call them in South Carolina, the solicitor, for Edgefield County in 1896–1897. And one spring day in 1897, when J. William Thurmond was sitting in his office at the courthouse, a traveling salesman came by and began berating Thurmond. The traveling salesman was drunk and was insulting Thurmond about his politics and called him a liar and a scoundrel. This was an affront to honor, this old Southern notion of honor. And so Thurmond reached into his jacket pocket—and Southern gentlemen in those days always had their jackets tailored with a pistol pocket inside—pulled out his Colt revolver and shot the man dead on the spot.

He was put on trial for murder, but the jury acquitted him in thirty-five minutes because he pled self-defense; it had been an affront to his honor. It was a clear violation of that code. And at that time, the political boss of South Carolina, who was also from Edgefield, was a man named "Pitchfork" Ben Tillman, the first populist racist governor, an antecedent to George Wallace. . . . He went to the president of the United States and got the president to make J. William Thurmond the U.S. attorney for South Carolina as a kind of reward for having been charged with murder. Murder was no bar to high office in those days in Edgefield. If it was committed in the name of honor, it was acceptable.

I INTERVIEWED two hundred people [for this book]. Some of the most interesting ones were very elderly people in South Carolina who remembered back to the 1890s, what, for me, was the crucial decade in this whole process, where black Southerners began to adapt some of these notions from white Southerners.

Just in the same way that white Southerners talked about honor and reputation, African Americans picked that idea up in a way. The important point here is the attitude toward the law. White Southerners saw themselves above the law. Honor and slavery gave them that idea. But blacks in the nineteenth century found themselves outside the law. They couldn't go to court to seek redress because the sheriffs, the police, the judges, and the juries were all controlled by whites. So their only recourse, really, was to take things into their own hands.

Now this is one of these very surprising things which I came on in the research. Most of us know that if your father is a doctor, a lawyer, or a farmer, policeman, when you grow up, you're probably going to go into their line of work. What doesn't occur to us, because we don't have that experience, is that if your father is a violent criminal who's been in prison, that also is going to have a very powerful, if perverse, attraction for you. That's exactly what happened with Willie. When he found out his father was a violent criminal in prison for murder, Willie wanted to emulate him. In fact, he began telling his teachers and his schoolmates, "Don't mess with me. My father was a murderer. When I grow up, I'm going to be just like him."

In fact, there's some good news here, which we haven't talked about. Go back and look at violence in this country. We know now that we're not nearly as violent as our ancestors were. There are some very good recent historical studies in England and Holland and Germany and Italy which show that violence in the Middle Ages was ten times worse than it is now. The rate of homicide in London in Chaucer's time was ten times what it is in current London. From the sixteenth and seventeenth centuries onward, there was kind of a civilizing process. As the power of the state grew and courts spread, people didn't have to settle disputes out among themselves; they had another way of doing it.

In the nineteenth century, this process really sped up with the Industrial Revolution. As people went to work in factories, they had to be more disciplined to answer to the foreman, the bell, or the whistle. The spread of public schools in the nineteenth century, institutions like the YMCA, Sunday schools—all these made us a much more orderly people. So we now know, in fact, that in our big cities in this country—take New York or Philadelphia, Boston—the homicide rate in 1960 was only about half what it had been in 1850. So for a full century, our cities were getting safer.

The Child Molestation
Cases of the Early 1980s

by

DOROTHY RABINOWITZ

No Crueler Tyrannies: Accusation, False Witness, and Other Terrors of
Our Times *is a study of the American criminal justice system in the 1980s
and 1990s. Longtime* Wall Street Journal *writer Dorothy Rabinowitz
recounts a spate of cases that accused day-care providers of child abuse and
undermined the faith of a nation of working parents in their day-care
workers. It was a time when anonymous phone call tips sent often innocent
people into a legal system to defend themselves against recovered-memory
therapists and hungry prosecutors. Ms. Rabinowitz appeared on* Booknotes
on May 4, 2003, to discuss her book, which was published that year by
Wall Street Journal Books.

I CAME TO THE *Wall Street Journal* on the wings of one case like this. I had
an editor in chief at the *Journal,* Bob Bartley, who instantly recognized the
importance of this event that was taking place, this sweep of false accusations
of child sex abuse. He recognized that there was a larger issue here called
prosecutorial zealots—that is, runaway prosecutors who, quite simply, in
many cases don't care. They don't really care if you're guilty or you're not
guilty and who'll never give up the conviction. [So it's] all of that—runaway
prosecutorial zealots combined with the pathos of the cases of American citizens. Most of them—almost all of them—are lower-middle-class people who
got up and saluted the flag and were genuinely believers in our society. They
believed in law and believed that if you are falsely accused of something, our
system of justice is there for you and you will be rescued. Someone will come

forward. In every case I wrote about, these citizens said, "It's a mistake. Someone will come forward." And they believed it to the end.

THE AMIRAULTS were caught up at the height of 1984, which may seem like a long time ago to people, but it really wasn't. In 1984, 1983, 1982, there began a great sweep, a tidal wave of false mass abuse—that is, twenty school teachers accused [of child abuse]. There was the famous McMartin case in California. Prosecutors all over America picked up on nursery schools; that was where the great thrust of all of these cases were. Nursery school teachers, child-care workers, all of them were somehow accused of being a part of child molestation rings, for heaven knows what ends.

And there was something called the [Mondale] Act. The government poured money into agencies that went out to look for child abuse. If you pour money in, you're going to find child abuse. They'd created jobs for workers to go out and find child abuse.

The Amiraults [were] an Italian American family run by a woman who had been on welfare. Violet Amirault pulled herself up, clawed herself up into this marvelous position, brought up two children alone. [She ran a] very successful child agency. People relished getting their children in there. Suddenly, one day, there was an anonymous phone call. It was Labor Day, 1984. She was advised that Gerald, her adult son, had been accused of molesting a child.

In 1984—and, indeed, in some places still now—you don't need any more than an accusation. Gerald was taken away two days later to prison. They got him out on bail. No one confirmed the accusation. No one did anything. A pattern was established in all of these cases, and this was typical of the Amiraults. Mrs. Amirault was then sixty. She was then accused. Her adult daughter, Cheryl, was accused. It was alleged to be a family conspiracy to molest children.

They were arrested. They were convicted in two separate trials. They were given enormous sentences. Gerald Amirault, being the male—and you have to understand, it is the rule in all of these cases that gender matters. If you were the male, you were seen as a major perpetrator, although if you were a lone woman, as Margaret Kelly Michaels was, the weight falls on you.

Anyhow, they were sent away to prison. I began writing about them after Mrs. Amirault and her daughter had both served about six years and Gerald had served eight years. A couple of months after the first piece hit the *Wall Street Journal*, the women were released on a plea, and Gerald was kept. There began our fight to free Gerald. The prosecutors fought and fought and fought to get the women back into prison, and they almost won. But by this time, the publicity that had been generated by the writings about this— which were taken up later in the *Boston Globe* and everywhere—was so great, so enormous, a tidal wave of investigation into what really happened.

PRIOR TO THE Amiraults was my very first encounter with this entire matter. I was working as a television commentator at WWOR-TV in New Jersey, doing three times a week some media criticism. I looked up at the screen and I saw [Margaret Kelly Michaels,] this woman in her mid-twenties, rosy, apple cheeks, innocent, accused of something like 280 charges of child sex abuse. "Oh," I thought, "that's very odd." But I didn't think, "What do I know?" I was never interested in work in schools or teachers. It never occurred to me. But something seemed odd about this.

I thought how can one woman, one young, lone woman in an absolutely open place like the child-care center of the church in New Jersey where she worked—how could she have committed these enormous crimes against twenty children, dressed and undressed them. You know what it is to dress and undress even one child every day without getting their socks lost? [To have] twenty children in a perfectly public place, torture them for [seven months], frighten and terrorize them, and yet they never went home and told their parents anything? She covered them with peanut butter, it was alleged, and licked the peanut butter off. Made them eat feces. Made them drink urine. Terrorized them. This did seem strange.

The atmosphere was very like the ayatollah's camp when I raised this to the television news editor. I said, "We should do a story on this. There's something wrong with this case. And there was a wonderful piece by a journalist in the *Village Voice*, Debbie Nathan, who also raised questions." The look on the face of the editor was such that I knew you were not even allowed to raise this. He said, "Don't ever mention this to me again. This is the most hated person in New Jersey." Everywhere in the newsroom I went, I said, "There's something wrong with this story." "How dare you?" [was the response.] I knew there was something sacrosanct about questioning these charges. This should raise questions.

But how did I know? I thought, "Well, maybe the prosecutor knows what he's doing." So I asked to meet the prosecutor. Glenn Goldberg was his name. He was happy to meet with me. Why? Because I was no liberal person. I was a grown-up woman with fairly conservative writing credentials. He told me how much evidence he had against her. It was nonsense. He followed me down the stairs after I raised the questions and he said, "By the way, now I'm going to tell you the real evidence I have against her." "What was that, sir?" He said, "She didn't wear underpants under her jeans." Imagine. I said, "And what did that mean?" He said, "Don't you know?" That was the kind of evidence.

But the other thing was, they sealed the transcript. What are they hiding when they seal a transcript? In a desultory kind of way, the *New York Times* and a couple of other papers went to court to open the record and they said, "No." I found my way to the record. I got somebody to open it for me. And that's when I knew. I read the testimony. I read the entire children's testimony and the interviews. I saw what the jurors did not see. And here's what I saw:

The children were interviewed. They're five [years old]. They're frightened. They wanted to please this adult sitting in front of them, and they don't know what they're there for. But the adult was suddenly showing them a big doll, and the doll has what is called sexually explicit organs. And the interviewer was very persistent and very nice and said to the child, "Do you want to help? Your little friends helped. Do you want to tell us if something bad happened?" "What?" said the children. "Well, you know something bad happened." And the child didn't know.

[It was] just the two of them. [The interviewers] were so certain of their virtue and the rectitude of their cause that they let the tape recorders take this down. They learned better later. They stopped recording these interviews. They would hold up a spoon, saying, "Show us where Kelly molested you—did something bad to you." The child has no idea what's going on, but the child took the spoon and hit the doll here. "Where else?" Child hits the shoulder. "Where else?" Because it's very clear to the child by now that her answers were insufficient. She's not giving the questioner what they wanted. There are "where elses" and "where elses" and "where elses" until the child came to the sex organ, hit the sex organ with the spoon. All the questions stopped. No more "where elses." The questioner got what she wanted and what he wanted.

What's presented to the jury was not this odyssey around the doll's head but only, "Rachel showed us where Kelly molested her with the spoon. She touched the genitals." That was the kind of evidence. When you see in cold print the details of the questioning, then you know. You can't miss it.

[This kind of evidence was admissible] because it was a kind of sacred truth and because this was not hearsay. The prosecutors produce testimony that they dragged from children after hours of questioning and that was simply distorted.

Now, you can ask yourself why did the jury believe these things? How could the jury believe that, as in the Amirault case, old Mrs. Amirault, one of the most upright of citizens, had suddenly turned at the age of sixty into a child molester who raped children? She was accused and convicted of inserting a stick into the body orifice of a little boy, tying him to a tree stark naked in front of everyone, in front of the house in Massachusetts. The children all attested to this, the ones that were part of the case. Who would believe this?

But if you have a prosecutor who tells the jury, "Here are all of these brave children who have come forward to ask that you credit their story because they have endured so much suffering, and if you don't do this, you're betraying the children." It is not easy to find a jury that is stalwart enough to say, "Hey, this really is a pile of nonsense."

WHAT I'M SAYING is an ugly truth most people apprehend. Prosecutors have among them some—many [are] honest, people who know the meaning of integrity—but others, many others, simply want to win their cases and will go down to their last breath, when someone has been acquitted, saying, "He's guilty."

There has to be something in the mental capacities of prosecutors who know, against all of the evidence, they want to hold onto their conviction. And so people are still in prison. Gerald Amirault is still in prison because the State of Massachusetts won't let him go because the integrity of their case—he represents their victory.

MARGARET KELLY MICHAELS—we did get her out, and she won on her first appeal. Today she lives with her four children and has just delivered a fifth child with her husband, a former prosecutor. She's one of the few people that I wrote about who has put her life together in so healthful a way and without being haunted. . . . Remember, there is no one more despised, no one, than the alleged child molester. The Amirault women, when they were thrown into prison, you could not have imagined people more used to comfort and upright status. They were churchgoers—thrown into a prison on a dirty mattress while they waited, being moved to their cell to have people spit at them, call them child abusers. These people were invariably thrown into isolation cells for their own protection.

When you've seen an innocent person, that you know [is innocent] because you've seen the record, in prison, it's a life-altering experience. Margaret Kelly Michaels was sitting there in solitary for two years. I almost fainted, and I don't faint. I went to one of the most secure women's prisons in New Jersey, and it was dismal. This well brought up, highly educated young woman was talking to me about Einstein, and I was about to pass out, looking at where she was. It took a long time, but I did know that if I did not do something about this, life would not really be the same. Anger was everything.

Anger and horror, but anger was everything because the evidence was so doubtless, so overwhelming that these children came in knowing absolutely nothing about what they were talking about. These words were put in their mouths. They were told what happened to them, and they were drilled in what happened to them. And when they took the stand, they believed it. And that's exactly what happened to all of these children.

IT TOOK ME two years to get published. The first piece [was in] *Harper's* magazine. Lewis Lapham, the editor in chief, took a chance, and very quickly, when everybody else turned it down. They had turned it down for the strangest of reasons. I knew almost every editor at the time, and they were filled with commiseration. They said, "Look, but you know, I have a four-year-old child," or, "I just can't do this." Because it was a piece that didn't just raise questions about her guilt—it said this is an innocent person.

It was published in April 1990. I was then at home. I stopped working on television and I was simply doing book writing, freelance stuff, and I was just about to join the *Wall Street Journal*. With Lapham's publication of that, we were able to move. We got money. We got a lawyer [to represent Margaret Kelly Michaels].

I got the wonderful lawyer Morton Stavis to read this, who is now deceased, one of the great liberal civil rights lawyers, and he took some of his students . . . and spent two years putting together [Kelly Michaels's] appeal. They won and she was out.

THE AMIRAULTS' prosecutor didn't see me coming because I was pretty new at it. They didn't know what I'd had to do with the Kelly Michaels's case. They were in another state.

[As a journalist] you have to talk to both sides. You have to talk to the prosecutor. I called him and he was happy to come to the phone because Lawrence Hardoon was the active lead prosecutor and his experiences told him that the press was there for him. The press was there to carry his story out.

In the midst of his telling me how successful this prosecution had been—the Amiraults, don't forget, had been locked away in prison by the time I got there for many years; it was a dead case, they were dead and buried as far as Boston, Massachusetts, was concerned. . . . I said to Mr. Hardoon, "Did it ever occur to you that this case could ever be overturned on appeal?" He said, "Never, it'll never happen."

Well, it wasn't overturned for Gerald, but three months later, Cheryl and Violet walked out of prison. I remember by that time everybody knew who I was and what I had to do with these cases, and the press was very generous.

When Cheryl was released, Gerald Amirault's sister, she had to go back to the prison for a minute the very day of their release. The entire woman's prison population came out to cheer her. These are the same women that had threatened her, spat upon her years earlier when she first came to prison. They ultimately know that something has gone awry and they don't fool around.

Not only am I convinced [that Gerald is innocent, but] everybody is convinced. Let me tell you, the governor's board of pardon in Massachusetts is the toughest parole board in the country. They have reason to be. Tough ex-prosecutors, hard-nosed types, and they had a special parole hearing for Gerald, a commutation petition. Unanimously, they declared that he should receive commutation about two years ago.

The majority of the board then issued a separate opinion that said in essence: This case is based on nonsense, and there is every reason to believe that this person has been falsely sent away. This was completely unknown in the history of governor's parole boards and pardons. That's how much everyone understood about this case, which has been exhaustively looked into.

So Gerald had one foot in the door and was on his way out. It's actually unheard of in Massachusetts history that a governor would not listen to the parole board.

Governor Jane Swift was fighting for her political life. She was acting governor, but she wanted to be governor, and Jane Swift, who already had a terrible reputation as governor, was advised by her political advisers that it would not be good to allow Gerald Amirault out.

She was in a primary. It was just before she had to step down. . . . She made the decision that she knew more [than the parole board did]. She had done her own investigation. The board of pardons and paroles had investigated so thoroughly to make absolutely sure they would make no mistake but there was nothing anybody could do. . . . She put Gerald back in.

GERALD COMPILED a marvelous record going to school in prison. One of the things that has made his life easier is that everybody in the prison system knew he was innocent. They know.

Gerald Amirault [was granted parole in October 2003]. There's only one problem. There's a little law in Massachusetts and elsewhere called the sexually dangerous persons law. The prosecutor can, even after he's paroled, decide she's going to keep him there anyway as a sexually dangerous person. We hope it doesn't happen. We think she'd like to put it behind her finally, but you never know.

I HAVE NO IDEA how many pieces I've written on all these people in the *Journal.* The *Journal* was remarkable in that every quarter of the *Wall Street Journal* supported this. They allowed me so much space on this, but I could not have done it without being impelled by pure rage. Of all of the emotions that you have—pity, it's not that. You're not thinking of the victims. You're not thinking of poor Gerald. That's behind you. What you're thinking about is the prosecutor. What you're thinking about is the totalitarian nature of this enterprise. Black is white. Two and two equal five. A child says, "Nothing happened to me." That was the most continuous theme: nothing happened, nothing happened, nothing happened. And it's never enough.

The Modern Supreme Court

by

EDWARD LAZARUS

In 1988 and 1989, Edward Lazarus served as a clerk to Supreme Court Justice Harry Blackmun. In his book, Closed Chambers: The First Eyewitness Account of the Epic Struggles Inside the Supreme Court, *published by* Times Books in 1998, *Lazarus has offered a rare insider's view of the nation's most powerful court. On June 14, 1998, Mr. Lazarus joined us on* Booknotes *to discuss the Court's internal battles over issues such as the death penalty, abortion, and other landmark decisions. Mr. Lazarus is currently a lawyer in California.*

THE THEME OF my book is the idea that these justices are closed off from one another. . . . The justices themselves are very isolated in their decision-making. They don't talk to one another the way we would expect them to. . . . And, at the same time, the Court is closed off from the American people. We don't know enough about how our most important cases are decided.

I WAS AT THE Court for a year as a law clerk. That's sort of a right-hand assistant to one of the justices. . . . Each justice is entitled to four clerks. The chief justice has only taken three, although he's in fact entitled to an extra clerk. By and large there are thirty-six young law school graduates.

WE ALWAYS STARTED [our days] the same way, which is at about 8:10 in the morning, the four clerks to Justice Blackmun and the justice would go to the main cafeteria at the Supreme Court and we would have breakfast together. That was the ritual by which we really came to know the justice. Amazing things happened at that breakfast, [such as] Justice Blackmun singing the Dartmouth fight song on key.

This is a man who was eighty at the time. I remember the first morning that we had breakfast together. It was a Monday and I ordered pancakes. He took me aside very quietly so that the cook couldn't hear and said, "You know, Eddie, the griddle goes stale over the weekend. You shouldn't have the pancakes on Monday." This was the kind of thing that developed, almost a grandfather to grandson relationship between the justice and me. I remember those breakfasts vividly and always will.

My boss [Justice Blackmun] . . . was there before we had breakfast every morning. I'm guessing he got in at 7:30. I know 'cause I got in just in time for the breakfast, but I know he was always there. And he would leave, I would say, around 6:00 or 6:30, and he would take a huge stack of work home with him. He was at the Court almost every Saturday. He was probably working at home Sunday. I know I worked close to 100 hours a week. I bet the justice worked not far from that.

I FELL IN LOVE with the place when I was there. I, of course, had a high regard for it before I was there. But at the same time, I was quite dismayed by some of the things that I saw. One of the cases I start out with may capture a bit of what I'm talking about: This was a death penalty case where Justice O'Connor was recused . . . so there were only eight justices participating. It's called *Tompkins v. Texas.* This was a case of a black man on trial for his life in Texas for a terrible crime. He had abducted a woman very late at night and gagged her and tied her to a tree while he used her bank card to rob her teller machine.

Those of us who worked on it were pretty sure about two things in this case: One was that the prosecutor had eliminated all the blacks from this black man's jury on purpose. So Tompkins's jury was an all-white jury and the blacks on the jury had been systematically eliminated.

And the second thing we knew—because there had been a confession in the case that had been suppressed at trial but that we saw—was that there was a very strong likelihood that this man had not done this crime on purpose. The woman had choked on the gag, a horrible, horrible death. But Tompkins carried a knife. If he wanted to kill her, he could've done it very easily. In his confession, this man was borderline mentally retarded. His confession rang true, and that was he just meant to tie her up while he used the bank card and then she would be discovered.

You're not supposed to get the death penalty if blacks have been eliminated from your jury or if you didn't kill intentionally. That's the Constitution. Yet on this seemingly easy case, the justices deadlocked, 4 to 4, which meant that the lower-court decision stood and the lower-court decision was allowing this man to proceed to execution.

I shook my head at this case. I did not understand how, in good faith, these eight justices reached a 4-to-4 deadlock on this case. Part of the enterprise of this book was to say, "OK. We got into a terrible spot here where the decisions were so reflexive that this man was basically flushed through the system. How did that happen?" I went back and through five years of research and reporting, and I tried to describe how we got into this terrible predicament of splitting apart ideologically within the Court so deeply that a 4–4 outcome was possible in a case like that.

WEBSTER V. REPRODUCTIVE HEALTH SERVICES was a referendum on *Roe v. Wade* in 1989. It came out as a mishmash. The chief justice joined with three others and said not that *Roe* was overturned, but that a lot more abortion regulation was permissible. The liberals on the other side were saying *Roe* is what *Roe* has always been, very little regulation allowed. O'Connor was in the middle basically dodging all the issues.

Years after I left the Court, I discovered that things had happened that I didn't have any idea about when I was there and that there was documentary evidence to back it up. I pursued that documentary evidence. I found that the conservative group at the Court was caucusing behind the backs of the liberals, trying to reach some agreement before they would circulate anything to the liberals. And in that caucus, the chief circulated a draft that he was hoping everyone would sign on to and Justice O'Connor wouldn't sign on. The other thing that was discovered is that Justice Kennedy actually wanted at that time for *Roe v. Wade* to be overturned. He later changed his mind.

It was my judgment [that Chief Justice Rehnquist was deceitful and surreptitious with *Webster*.] It was also the judgment of Justice Stevens, who said [the chief] was trying to drop *Roe* off the back of a fast-moving train, or something to that effect. What had happened in that case is the chief circulated a draft which, in its terms, claimed that *Roe* still stood. But because of the way it was written, in terms of the technical, legal wording of it, it would have just torn the entire guts of *Roe* out. I felt that that was a very surreptitious and inappropriate way to try and do away with the most important case of the last twenty-five years, whatever one thought of *Roe v. Wade*.

I DID NOT HAVE much personal contact with Chief Justice Rehnquist. . . . But my complaint with the chief justice throughout the book is that he does not believe in deliberation and debate. He doesn't think people's minds get changed. I think that that's fundamentally at odds with the way the Court ought to operate.

DURING THE TERM, the justices meet in their secret conference, usually on Fridays, to discuss the cases to decide, to vote on which cases are going to be heard later on in the year. They walk the inside of the Court. It's like a cloister in a church, almost. There's a red carpet that the justices walk along, from that wing of the building to the suite where they hold their conference, which is at the center in the back, where the chief justice has his offices.

Every week, one of the things that I always remarked on was just watching the justices walk. There are some images that really stick with me, even today. For example, Justice Kennedy was in his mid-fifties then, but he was brand new to the Court and he would just bound down the hallway. You could see the enthusiasm with which he was coming to this job—just feeling on top of the world. Then you had the three octogenarian justices, Blackmun, Brennan, and Marshall, and the image I remember of them is that they would come back out of conference and Brennan and Blackmun would be in the front. They were both short in stature and were quite old, of course, at that time. Marshall, who was a very large man, would be right behind them and would be walking behind them. You never could quite tell whether he was sort of supporting them with a protective umbrella or whether they were a little bit supporting him by holding him up. I think it captured a lot about our term, which was the decline of the liberal way.

The [conferences] were basically an expression of views, not a debate. You'd go around the table, and each justice would say what he or she thought, there would be a vote, and that would be it. Justice Scalia has publicly spoken about this, that there is not an exchange of views and that people's minds do not get changed in conference. That adds, it seems to me, to this atmosphere of division when you're really trying to engage the other side seriously and say there are good points to be made on both sides and they need to be taken account of. The Court wasn't doing that.

I saw Justice O'Connor a bit more than I saw the chief. A very brave woman. She was ill our year with breast cancer, as people know, and I just was admiring of her fortitude. I'm not a huge fan of her jurisprudence, which I think is very idiosyncratic. She holds that center position at the Court and so often her views really just come down to what she thinks about a case. I think that holds the Constitution hostage to her own personal views.

In the *Webster* case she did not join Chief Justice Rehnquist in cutting back sharply on *Roe*. Basically, Justice Scalia let her have it with both guns. Some of what Justice Scalia said was warranted because, in that case, Justice O'Connor's whole opinion was based on the idea of judicial restraint: "We won't ever step outside the narrow confines of a case to speak to an issue more broadly." As Justice Scalia pointed out, when it suits her, Justice O'Connor does that with some frequency. One of the things I complain about in my book is if you're going to be a person of judicial restraint, you have to be that way when it suits your personal views *and* when it doesn't suit your personal views. You can't flip 'em around like cards in a deck.

THERE'S RARELY BEEN a justice who so regularly takes after his colleagues with the tone of disapproval that Justice Scalia has in his opinions. He's someone who cherishes the turn of the phrase, where he can have the ability to write things that just skewer people. He's very effective at it and he seems to enjoy doing it.

He's known as Nino by those who know him. He would send around these memos, zingers really, on cases where he would set forth his view in a page or two of extremely pungent prose. At the Court, if it's after hours, a clerk will walk to each of the nine chambers and slip a manila envelope under the door. That's the way they distribute these things. Those "Ninograms" would come—*shhhwip*—right under the door. There it would be, this very powerful, often hyperbolic analysis of the case. That was a Ninogram. Of course, if you were on the side that Justice Scalia was on, they were very welcome because they usually provided some very cogent thinking. But if you were on the other side, they were darn infuriating.

Personal dislike [among the justices] is something that is very tough for a clerk to gauge; we don't really see that sort of thing. What was going on here, whether it translated into personal dislike or not, was the kind of accusations it's very difficult to recover from. If Justice Brennan accuses Justice Kennedy, as he virtually did, of being a racist, in one particular case, *Patterson v. McLean Credit Union*, and the conservatives accused the liberals of basically being hypocritical idiots, it's really hard if that happens over and over again to just let bygones be bygones and pretend that, "Well, we all really get along." These charges were heartfelt, and so there were deep divisions.

IN ORAL ARGUMENT, each side gets one-half hour to present their case to the Court. So they come up there, they stand in the courtroom—this gem of a room, with the justices up on their dais in their leather chairs rocking back and forth. They start out always with, "May it please the Court," and they make their half-hour presentation. The justices, to a greater or lesser extent, depending on how interested they are in the case, will pepper them with questions.

Then, after the oral argument is over, the justices retire and either later that day or later in the week, meet together in their conference and take a tentative vote. [Then, the senior member of the side that wins assigns the majority opinion. If the chief justice is in the majority, it's the chief justice. If it's not the chief justice, someone else.] And that's how it goes.

[ATTORNEYS PRACTICE before they argue their cases.] I wish some of them would do more, but I think the experienced advocates probably moot their cases two or three times before they get up there. . . . A "moot" is where he'll have a group of colleagues prepare for the case and pretend that they're the justices and hammer him with as tough a question as they can think of.

I think [oral arguments] can matter. Justices can ask the lawyers to answer some nagging question they have about the case, but I think the justices themselves seek to educate one another on the bench. In oral argument, Scalia is trying to get to Kennedy and O'Connor, and say, "This is how I'm thinking about the case and you've gotta be able to answer this if you want to come out the other way."

[Stevens and Scalia were the only two justices who wrote their own first drafts on decisions.] What that means is—and it varies from chambers to chambers, the degree to which the justices are just editing—that law clerks, these young people, greenhorns out of law school, have the job of taking the justice's vote from conference and translating that into an actual opinion that is going to be pored over meticulously by the legal community. When you're doing the first draft of an opinion, you make the choices about what facts to put in, how to characterize those facts, what cases to put in, how to characterize those cases, all kinds of technical legal nuance that is going to be crucially important in future cases and how that opinion is interpreted. Unless a justice is unwrapping all of those choices, as he or she edits the opinion, then too much responsibility is falling to that clerk. I don't think enough of the justices were really unwrapping all of those choices.

[Blackmun did not write drafts but was a meticulous editor.] He sat up there in that justices' library and went over every case, every nuance of that opinion. It was certainly his product when it came out of our chambers. But I still think that the idea of delegating the entire first drafting process to a clerk is too great.

THE "CLERK BACK CHANNEL" is my shorthand reference for the way justices can use their clerks to communicate things. For example, let's say you're drafting an opinion on a close case and you really need Justice Kennedy's vote. One of the things you may decide you're going to do, as a justice, is have your law clerk feel out Justice Kennedy's law clerk and say, "Here's the way I'm thinking about going on this. How does your boss feel about that? Do you have a sense?" It's an informal way for the justices to communicate. One of the things that I felt happened my year was that that informal channel of communication got clogged up by the really bitterly divided ideological factions that the clerks broke into.

[There was an episode between one of O'Connor's clerks and one of Brennan's clerks.] Every Thursday afternoon, it was habit to have a happy hour at the Court. That was not unusual. It was a chance to unwind a little bit. In good weather, they'd take place in a beautiful flagstone courtyard with a fountain. This was at the end of our term, and it was just a symptom of the terrible divisions we were having. They actually broke out into a shoving match [which] was really just an emblem for how we had felt about each other all year. The liberals were frustrated and enraged at what they saw as the conservative ascendancy. I think we were mirroring the justices in this.

As a general matter in the legal world, conservatives think of liberals as weak sentimentalists, suckers for prisoners' rights and highfalutin' concepts that really aren't very well grounded in the Constitution, like the right to privacy. On the other side, liberals have come to think of conservatives as evil. I think that's what the Robert Bork [Supreme Court nomination] fight was all about—that they don't give a damn about civil rights and they want to roll the clock back thirty years. They don't care about due process, etc., etc. This breakdown in the good faith that is necessary for a court to operate was palpable my term.

There was a group of conservative clerks, about ten or so, who were at the Court my year. They called themselves the cabal. This was a group of very conservative clerks who banded together, both socially and politically, to push a conservative agenda at the Court. One of the things that I describe in the book is a civil war that was occurring in our legal culture at that time. I think it continues to this day. In law schools, there's a deep division between those who believe in, for example, Bork's theory of original intent, interpreting the Constitution according to the framers' intent, and those who, more along the lines of Justice Brennan, believe in a more flexible, living Constitution. And this was a group of clerks who were really devoted to the conservative Reaganite agenda and many of whom had clerked for Bork and who were determined to push that agenda on the Court, if they could. . . . Both conservative and liberal clerks, at that young age of twenty-six, twenty-seven, twenty-eight, are really driven by ideology. . . . Sometimes ideology carries away clerks on both sides.

[I REFERRED TO Stevens as a FedEx justice.] Justice Stevens is an extraordinarily bright and personable man, and what I was describing is the breakdown in the collegiality and in the discussion process within the Court. The problem with Justice Stevens, as I saw it, was that he spent a great deal of the winter in Florida [where he has a home.] So he was really communicating to the Court—I used the shorthand—by FedEx. He wasn't like a Brennan or a Marshall or a Blackmun, who were really sort of alienated from the crucial members of the Court: O'Connor and Kennedy. They're the swing votes. There wasn't a lot of influence that was going to be exerted on Kennedy and O'Connor by the left wing; they were just too alienated. Justice Stevens, on the other hand, had the pure brain power and the sway. He had influence. But if he was in Florida, he couldn't exercise it in the same way that he could if he were at the Court. And I felt that something was lacking. I regretted that he wasn't there.

[JUSTICES] ARE [influenced by the media] a little bit. Justice Kennedy invited a reporter to follow him around the morning that he handed down *Planned Parenthood of Southeastern Pennsylvania v. Casey.* You have to wonder why, if the media doesn't matter.

The "Greenhouse Effect" takes its name from Linda Greenhouse, who is the *New York Times* reporter who is generally thought to be liberal in her inclinations. . . . Conservatives felt that Justice Kennedy was excessively concerned with his public image, that he wanted, basically, for Linda Greenhouse to like him, and he was an apostate from conservative positions on a number of important issues. For example, he was thought to be in favor of voluntary school prayer, and yet, in a crucial case, *Lee v. Weisman*, he couldn't bring himself to overturn the Supreme Court precedents which prohibit voluntary school prayer. In the area of abortion, he was thought to be in favor of overturning *Roe v. Wade* and returning the issue of abortion to the states, but in *Planned Parenthood of Pennsylvania v. Casey*, he and Justice O'Connor and Justice Souter banded together to uphold the basic principles of *Roe*, although they did cut back on *Roe* somewhat. The "Greenhouse Effect" was the idea that what lay behind these moderating forces in Kennedy's jurisprudence was not necessarily principle, but a view that he wanted to be liked by the elite liberal press.

THE MARCHES ON the Court—people take note of them. But it's not a huge influence.

[MAIL] HAS A varying effect in different chambers. I know Justice Blackmun read all of his mail because he felt this is the people's Court and he wanted to know how the people felt about the Court's decisions. That's not to say that it affected him like a popularity poll would, but he wanted to have a feeling for what the people were thinking.

WE WILL [see cameras in the Supreme Court]. It's inevitable. But the justices certainly stand firmly against it. I can't for the life of me understand why it's not appropriate to televise those oral arguments.

[The Robert Bork confirmation hearings had an impact on the Court.] The fact that he did not come across well on television may have struck [the justices] as, "Hey, how am I gonna come across on television?" The effect of the Bork hearings was much broader than that, which is that this kind of political campaigning about whether somebody's going to get on the Court or not was, in the view of the Court, unseemly and damaging.

The liberals were willing to go to almost any length to stop him—[by taking all the nuance out of] Judge Bork's position so that he was caricatured. It basically taught the conservatives that the liberals would go to any lengths to protect themselves. As a consequence, conservatives felt, "We're gonna fight fire with fire."

The Court is a political institution. It was designed to be. The way it reflects politics is through the nomination process. We elect our presidents because we think that they have a certain set of beliefs and we think that their appointments to the Supreme Court are going to reflect those beliefs. One of the problems we have is it's also Congress's or the Senate's responsibility to advise and consent to those appointments. When you have a disagreement ideologically, let's say, between a liberal Senate and a conservative president or vice versa, well, they have to reach some kind of compromise candidate. That's appropriate because the country is itself divided. FDR put on like-minded people. Many other presidents have. Sometimes they guessed wrong. For example, Nixon thought that my own former boss was a conservative when he turned out to be much more moderate than Nixon might have thought. But there's nothing wrong with a president saying, "I want somebody who's going to agree with me up there on the Court."

WHAT I WOULD change [about the Court is] the entire deliberative atmosphere, and I think perhaps it is changing a bit for the better. There are four new justices since the time I left. Those justices . . . are people with a very strong sense of the institution itself. I think I would infuse the place with a greater feeling of self-doubt, that, "Hey, maybe I'm wrong in what I think. I want to think about what the other side has to say." I'd foster more debate— so the basic thing I would change would be in the souls of the justices. They'd just have to do a better job.

The Early Years of
the First Female Justice

by

SANDRA DAY O'CONNOR

On September 25, 1981, Sandra Day O'Connor became the first woman to serve on the U.S. Supreme Court, ensuring her more national attention and scrutiny than most justices ever receive. Her memoir Lazy B: Growing Up on a Cattle Ranch in the American Southwest *recounts her life before the Court, especially her childhood years on a family-owned cattle ranch on the Arizona–New Mexico border. Justice O'Connor appeared on* Booknotes *on January 27, 2003, to share stories from her memoir, which was published in 2002 by Random House.*

My BROTHER AND I grew up on the Lazy B Ranch. It ended up being sold in 1993 and it broke my heart. Something that I thought would always be part of me and part of our family and always there for my children and grandchildren and their children was gone, and there wasn't any other way to preserve it except to sit down and see if we could write up some of those memories and make it real.

The ranch is on the Arizona–New Mexico border. The ranch was half in each state, to the south side of the Gila River and to the top of the Peloncillo mountain range. It's a high desert area; it's rather arid and sparse. There are some oak trees and mesquite trees on the higher elevations. It's about 5,000 feet high, even on the flat part. But it has a fairly decent climate: rarely gets below freezing in the winter; it gets fairly hot in the summer, but not unbearably so.

I lived on it from childhood until I went away to school and eventually got married. My brother lived on it always, until it was sold. My father ran it until his death, lived on it. It was started in 1880 by his father, so it had been in the family 113 years by the time it was sold.

The ranch was close to 250 square miles. That's a large area, but of course, you have to realize that grass is very sparse in that area. It's not like having that amount of land that is well-watered and that produces a lot of grass. It had very little.

It was primarily public land. When my grandfather started it in 1880, that area was part of the New Mexico Territory. It was in the area acquired by the United States in the Gadsden Purchase, just before the Civil War, that had belonged to Mexico. The Southern Pacific Railroad wanted to put a line through from New Orleans all the way to Los Angeles, and the best route went through that area, south of the Gila River. Congress eventually approved the Gadsden Purchase. Mr. Gadsden had been sent down to negotiate it. And so in 1880, the land was basically unoccupied, except for the railroad. If somebody wanted to acquire livestock and go out there and develop water, then it was possible to homestead a certain amount of land around the water that was developed, and the rest of the land could just be used.

Arizona became a state in 1912. At that point, coming into the Union, the state was given a certain amount of land and the same with New Mexico. . . . The federal government kept a large amount of land in Arizona and New Mexico, and, of course, a great deal of the land is owned by Indian tribes. So the land that is actually available, in Arizona and New Mexico anyway, for private ownership is less than 10 percent of the land overall.

What happened in time was that leases were negotiated for the state land with the states of Arizona and New Mexico, and the federal lands were administered by the Bureau of Land Management under the Department of Interior. An elaborate system of provisions for parceling out that federal land evolved over time, initially with the passage of the Taylor Grazing Act, and that required sorting out who got what. In the days when my grandfather [settled there], anyone could put cattle on [the land], and many people did, so there might be joint use of a lot of the land. After the passage of the Taylor Grazing Act, the objective was to sort out who should be using what part and not have multiple use, at least grazing rights, going to more than one person for a particular acre of land.

MY EARLIEST recollection is of sound, or the absence of sound. I don't know how many people who live in urban areas today are even aware of how much noise is going on around us all the time, from vehicular traffic, or airplanes, or the sounds of heating and cooling systems working, or of computer systems operating, or telephones ringing. There's just a lot of sound in urban areas. At the Lazy B, there was none of that. We didn't have electricity for years, so there were no motors running, and there was no vehicular traffic to hear. Now, the sounds you did hear were of the cattle, perhaps walking or mooing, making sounds that cattle make, or occasionally birds, and at night, the coyotes or the windmills. We had to get our water from deep underground, and in order to power the withdrawal of the water, we used windmills. When the wind came up, they would turn and creak, and you would hear all the sounds of the machinery of the windmill. The wells at the ranch by the house were 500 feet deep, and suck rods had to go all the way down, and as they moved up and down, you could hear them. But if the wind wasn't blowing and the cattle weren't making any noise, there was no sound. None. It was almost a deafening silence

I was born in 1930. My parents were living at the ranch. My father had taken over management when his father died in order to try to settle the estate, and he never left. He ended up meeting and marrying my mother, who had the courage to say, "All right, yes, let's go live on the ranch." It was very primitive in those days for her. When she had her first child—me—she wanted to go to a hospital. Her parents, by then, were living in El Paso, Texas, so she chose to go to El Paso, some 200-plus miles away, for my birth. We returned to the ranch as quickly as she was able to travel.

Living there was like living on an island, you might say. We were away from everything. We had no neighbors close at hand. There were my parents and the cowboys who helped run the ranch. In those days, cowboys tended to be single men; they seldom had a wife or family. A number of the cowboys at the Lazy B spent their entire lives there; they really were part of our family, part of the working team.

Jim Brister was one of those cowboys, who spent most of his life at the ranch. He came there when he was twenty-four years old. He was from Oklahoma originally. He was a huge redhead with massive shoulders, a strong fellow, and he had married a little woman, who was not five feet tall, named Mae, [who] said that she was eleven years old when they got married. He had worked in the Wild West shows. He learned to ride horses early on and was quite a skillful rider and a fantastic roper. He could just handle a rope like nobody else. He worked in the Wild West shows that were going around the country. He and Mae would follow the Wild West shows, and that's what he did.

It must have been when movies started, silent films or something, that people stopped going to the Wild West shows, and then Jim started working on different ranches around the country. Typically, he would ride the wild string of horses—the tough ones that hadn't been broken. He'd come onto a ranch and break the horses that needed breaking and get them shaped up, and then he might move on to the next ranch. He came to the Lazy B that way. He was still very young. He and Mae showed up, and he went to work and never left.

He was the toughest man I have ever seen in my life and probably the most coordinated man I've ever seen. He could stand pain better than anyone I've seen. . . . You can't ride horses all the time and not end up having some broken bones because the horse will fall or you get thrown or something goes wrong. He had all kinds of injuries, but he never let it stop him. I don't think he ever missed a day of work, no matter whether it was his collarbone broken or what.

One day he came in and he said he had this heck of a toothache; he just couldn't stand it anymore. Well, we didn't have dentists within 150 miles of the Lazy B. He got a piece of baling wire . . . and heated it up on the stove till it was red hot, and jabbed it in his tooth where the root was rotten. He just put it in there. My brother was standing right there. You could smell the burning flesh. It was unbelievable. He never winced and he solved his problem. I don't know how people can be that tough, I really don't.

Rastus was another of the wonderful cowboys who lived his whole life at the Lazy B. . . . He ended up in Lordsburg, New Mexico, and asked around town if anybody could use some help, said he'd like to work on a ranch. . . . He hitched a ride to the Lazy B, and they said, "Yeah, you can do some chores if you want to stay here for awhile," and he did. He never left until he died in his late seventies.

Rastus was amazing in his ability to work with cattle. . . . He knew every cow and every calf on the place, the thousands of them. . . . If a mother cow is nursing a calf . . . the mother won't accept other calves that aren't hers. Her udder will be badly swollen and in need of milking, but she won't accept one. . . . It's something about the inherent nature of cows. [When] a calf had been killed . . . it left the mother without a calf. . . . Rastus went out and took the skin from the dead calf and tied it around one of the dogie calves, so that the mother cow would smell the skin of her own dead calf and accept it. . . . Things like that went on a lot.

[WHEN I WAS SIX] life meant having to go away to school, and that was a very painful time for me. It's hard for ranch families who have children because when it's time for a child to go to school, many ranchers send their wives into town to rent or buy a house to live with the children during the school year, and that means the husband and wife are separated. My father and mother were really deeply in love with each other, and they didn't want to be separated.

My mother's parents were living in El Paso. My Grandmother Wilkey . . . had married at age sixteen herself. She was very young and had plenty of energy. She said she would just be delighted to keep me in El Paso for school, and so that was the arrangement that was made. I went away to school. I would come home at Christmas and over Easter break and in the summers, but other than that, I was staying in El Paso. That was all right, except I was homesick. I really loved the ranch and loved being with my parents, and I didn't want to be away. So I remember those years with considerable pain, actually.

[MY PARENTS] bought books constantly, kept a library. When they ran out of space, they would sometimes give some books to the local library; they were both readers. They loved to subscribe to magazines—*Time* and the *Saturday Evening Post* and the *National Geographic*. We only went to town once a week, and we'd get the mail and groceries. When we'd came back with the mail, there'd be a big battle in the family about who got which magazine first because we were kind of starved for news, and we loved to read everything we could put our hands on. So there was a big race for the mail to see who got what first.

We had an electric generator by the time I was in college, and that ran on some kind of natural gas. My father could start it up at night and run it for a while, and we'd have lights in the evening. But then the REA, the Rural Electrification Act, had been passed during the Franklin Roosevelt administration, and the whole purpose of that was to try to bring electricity to rural areas that didn't have it. In those days, there were many rural areas in America that didn't have electricity.

While electricity did come then to the Duncan Valley and to Verden and to Lordsburg, it did not come out to the ranches. My father made some arrangement with the local REA that he would build the line, put the poles in to their specifications and string the wire to their specs, if he could get hooked up. When I was away at Stanford, we finally got hooked up with the REA. That was very helpful because it was possible to eventually put an electric pump down in the wells and get our water pumped out with that electric energy. My mother could have a refrigerator in the kitchen, run a vacuum cleaner, a washing machine, and all those things that hadn't been easy to do before.

[MY FATHER'S] nature was to want to know how everything worked, and he liked people, regardless of background or wealth or status, high or low. If they were interesting people to talk to, he liked to talk to them. I think I share some of that. He wanted to go to Stanford and never had a chance, and probably that's why that was the only university I wanted to go to. I don't know that that's the case, but we're often influenced by things we don't understand.

I don't think I had a cohesive philosophy of life until I went to Stanford University. I was basically very uneducated, and I went to high school in El Paso. In those days, it wasn't fashionable to get good grades, so I did have good grades, but I tried not to have anybody know about it. I don't think I learned much.

When I went off to Stanford, I was really astounded at the depth of knowledge of my classmates; many of them were really remarkably well-educated compared to me. I just thought I was very deficient, and I'm sure I was.

I finished my major in three years, but I needed some additional credits to count for the undergraduate degree. I applied for early admission at the law school, and to my great surprise, they took me.

I was ignorant and naive about what life for a woman lawyer might be like. It never occurred to me that there weren't women lawyers out there and that it might be hard to get a job as one. I never thought about that. [Growing up on the ranch,] I learned that women could do all right and be accepted if they could do the job. I guess that's why I assumed when I went to law school that I wouldn't have any trouble getting a job.

[MY HUSBAND, JOHN,] grew up in San Francisco. He was a city boy. He knew nothing about ranch life; he had never lived in the country. I was a little concerned about having him get along well with my family, since he knew so little about ranch life. I didn't know whether he'd be accepted by the cowboys, either. I didn't know if he could ride a horse well.

We made a trip out to the ranch one afternoon. They knew we were coming because you could see the car dust for five miles out. We got up to the house, and my mother rushed out to greet us and was so happy to see us and to see John. I said, "Well, where's DA?" [my father] and she said, "He and the men are down in the corral branding some calves. Maybe you'd better go down there and tell him hello."

So, John and I walked down to the corrals, and there was a lot of activity down there. They were branding that day right at the headquarters and had some cattle in the corrals. There was a lot of dust swirling around and bawling of the cattle. They had a branding fire in the middle of one of the corrals. I knew that my father knew we were there—he had seen the car coming— but he never looked over and acknowledged us.

Then, finally, he reached up and touched the brim of his hat. That's the universal sign out in that part of the country that says, "Yeah, I know you're there."

So, finally, he said "Come on over. This must be John." He stuck out his hand, and, of course, it was the hand of a working man. It was tough. When you shook his hand, it was a little like shaking hands with Justice Byron White; You knew you'd had a handshake. It was dirty because he'd been branding and probably a lot of blood all over it and no telling what else. He said, "Glad to meet you, John."

Then my father went over to the fence, and pulled down a piece of baling wire, and straightened it out. He put two or three strands together and made a skewer. There was a bucket down near where they were branding the calves, where the cowboys who were castrating the bull calves just threw the testicles; they just cut them off and threw them in the bucket. My father reached down in the bucket and pulled a couple out. He took his pocketknife out of his pocket and trimmed them up a little bit. They were just a bloody, dirty mess. He stuck some on this skewer, and put it in the branding fire, and cooked the things down in the branding fire for a while.

After he thought they were done, he pulled a skewer out and held it out to John. "Here, John, try these." I think John was pretty astonished. I would have been. But he was great. He plucked them off the end of this baling wire skewer and popped them in his mouth and chewed them up and sort of swallowed hard and said, "Oh, very good, Mr. Day."

[WHEN MY SUPREME COURT nomination was announced, everyone my parents knew] contacted them to tell them how excited they were. So here are these two—who had lived that life for so many years on that isolated ranch—in contact with the world. Reporters came out to the ranch and wanted to talk to them and take their photographs, and the world came to their door. It must have been interesting for them, really, to have all of that communication at that late stage in their lives. I know it was fun for them. It was a great thrill when they came back here and sat in that courtroom. . . . They were in the court on the day I was sworn in September of 1981.

[I HOPE THAT] people who have never experienced life in isolation or in the Southwest may be able to read this book and have some feeling of how it looks, how it smells, how it sounds, how it feels. I thought my upbringing was perfectly normal at the time, but, looking back, I know that it wasn't. It was a special way of life and a way of life that is largely gone these days. You don't find those old cowboys who spend a lifetime on a ranch anymore.

Growing up on a ranch gives you a certain amount of self-confidence in your ability to work things out and not be afraid to tackle something. You learn out there very much how you can't call somebody in to repair anything. You have to do it yourself. So maybe a little of that provided me the sense that I could do this job [of Supreme Court Justice]. I don't think my experience was such that would immediately suggest I could. I'd never been a federal court judge, so maybe I leaned a little bit on that experience as a ranch girl.

America's Black Market
in Sex and Drugs

by

ERIC SCHLOSSER

Over the past thirty years, the American black market has seen unprecedented levels of growth. Americans spend more money on illegal drugs than on cigarettes. In his book Reefer Madness: Sex, Drugs, and Cheap Labor in the American Black Market, *published by Houghton Mifflin in 2003, Eric Schlosser examined the intricacies of the shadow economy by focusing on marijuana, pornography, and illegal migrant workers. Mr. Schlosser, author and* Atlantic Monthly *correspondent, appeared on* Booknotes *on June 15, 2003.*

[THE BLACK MARKET IS] huge. Economists agree that it's really been growing since about 1970. But what its actual size is, nobody knows. I tried to use statistics from a conservative Austrian economist who was doing work for the International Monetary Fund. His estimates were 8 to 10 percent of our gross domestic product. That would be about $1 trillion.

When the IRS in 1998 looked at how much money people were evading in taxes, they came up with an estimate of $200 billion. . . . That would mean about $1.5 trillion in income was not being reported, and that doesn't include illegal activity, so it's huge. It's gigantic.

MARK YOUNG WAS a hippie biker whom I wrote about in the marijuana section of the book. He's no saint, but he's certainly no serial killer.

He's from Indianapolis. He was involved in a marijuana deal. He didn't grow the pot. He didn't sell the pot or distribute it, but he introduced a grower to a distributor and took a cut on some of their sales. When this marijuana-growing operation was shut down, Mark Young refused to cooperate with the government, refused to testify against anybody, refused to admit that he was guilty.

He's a very proud marijuana smoker. And as a result, for his first marijuana crime, he was sentenced to life without parole and sent to a very scary federal penitentiary in Kansas.

I did [go see him], and that was quite an experience. Leavenworth penitentiary is a very scary building, and it was designed to be that way. It was the first federal penitentiary. It's very strange. Its architecture is modeled on that of the U.S. Capitol building, but . . . the Capitol building is our symbol of freedom. . . . That's where they send convicted international terrorists and killers, and here was this hippie biker there for a pot deal.

He's probably about forty-eight now. He was in his mid-thirties when he got sent to prison. After I wrote about him for the *Atlantic Monthly* . . . his life sentence was reduced to twelve years, which is still longer than the typical convicted killer spends in prison in the United States. So in the marijuana section, I'm trying to come to terms with: How do we punish someone more for marijuana in America than for killing somebody with a gun?

It's GENERALLY a certain kind of moralistic conservative who has led the prohibition of marijuana and is in favor of these very tough sentences. . . . And yet, there are other conservatives who come from a much more libertarian tradition and not as much of a moralistic tradition, like William Buckley, Milton Friedman, George Shultz, who have called for the decriminalization of marijuana.

The traditional political labels don't always apply when it comes to the war on drugs. A lot of the tough legislation was eagerly sponsored by liberal Democrats. We've had one president who has admitted to having a joint in his mouth, which was Bill Clinton, and more people were sent to prison, and arrested for marijuana, during the Clinton administration than during any other presidency.

I WROTE ABOUT marijuana and not cocaine for a number of reasons. It's the most widely used illegal drug in the United States. It's the most popular, and it's also the one that we produce here. You can't blame this problem on Colombian cartels. This is an all-American crop. It's being grown not just in Northern California or Hawaii or Kentucky, which are the popular stereotypes of marijuana growing, but I wrote about a very profitable marijuana farm in Indiana. It's being grown widely in Illinois and in Missouri. No one knows for sure, but I believe and I contend in the book, that most of the marijuana being grown in the United States is coming from the Farm Belt, and some people believe it's our largest cash crop in the United States.

Our corn crop is worth about $19 billion. Some people think our marijuana crop may be worth as much as $25 billion. In any event, it's huge, because apples, which is our biggest fruit [crop], that's about $1 billion a year; and so even if it's $5 billion or $10 billion in marijuana, that's a huge, huge American industry. And again, it comes out of the heartland.

[Between 100,000 and 200,000 commercial marijuana growers in the United States] is a rough estimate that comes from an old federal drug-investigative report. Clearly, if 20 million people are smoking it a year, you need a lot of people to grow it. The estimate of 2 million a day smoking it and 20 million a year, these come from government surveys in which people are asked if they smoke marijuana. Most likely, that understates the number considerably, because given the marijuana laws that we have now, I think a fair number of people aren't going to tell the government sincerely and honestly if they're using marijuana or growing it.

It's a very unusual type of crime in the sense that a marijuana crime can be subject to local law, state law, and federal law simultaneously. As a matter of fact, if you're arrested with some marijuana and found innocent under local law or under your state law, the federal government could still prosecute you for the same marijuana and send you to prison.

I wrote about a marijuana grower in Florida who was found innocent or who was given a very minor sentence under state law, and then was prosecuted for the same marijuana under federal law and given a life sentence. It varies—it entirely depends on who arrests you, who decides to prosecute you, and what they decide to prosecute you for. Under federal law, marijuana is illegal in every state of the Union in any amount. So, technically, the federal government could prosecute anybody arrested for marijuana anywhere in the United States. In practical terms, they don't do that. But if there's a prosecutor who doesn't like you and really wants to cause you a hard time, you can be in big trouble even for relatively small amounts of marijuana.

[It's] very, very hard to calculate [how many people are in prison or jail today because of marijuana], and the best estimate I could come up with is about 20,000 in federal prison, 25,000 to 30,000 in state prison. The one area that's looked at is marijuana arrests for possession, just for simple possession of marijuana and who goes to jails in Maryland. They did a study and found that one out of every four people arrested went to jail for at least a night; one out of every six arrested went to jail for at least a week. That's a lot of people when you figure that, nationwide, about 700,000 people are arrested for pot every year, and that's more than for any other drug.

MARIJUANA IS A black market commodity; illegal immigrants are black-market labor. And then, pornography is an example of how a little black market becomes mainstream.

Eleven thousand videos . . . are produced [each year;] different titles. Some of those may be old material respliced together. But that's an extraordinary number of titles.

The number of titles that are rented is [about] 790 million a year, so when you figure an adult population of about 200 million, that's a lot of people renting porn.

Blockbuster [video stores] won't carry porn, so this has been a real boon to independent video stores at a time when they're competing with Blockbuster, fiercely. These are films that they can rent out and earn money from at a time when Blockbuster is driving them out of business left and right. So oddly enough, the mom-and-pop video stores rely a lot more on the revenues from porn than the big companies.

Right now, federal law forbids the production or distribution of obscene material. That's a law that was passed in 1873. But the question is, what's obscene and what's not? I mean, we all have a fairly good notion of what a murder is or what an armed robbery is. That's something few of us would argue about. But an obscenity crime is unique in that it occurs in the mind. So whatever a jury says is obscene is obscene.

The federal government has tried very hard to keep hard-core porn off the market. In the 1980s in particular, under the Reagan and Bush administrations, they really tried to crack down on porn. Unfortunately, juries, even in very conservative communities, kept on saying hard-core porn wasn't obscene. It's kind of a gray area right now. But nevertheless, some very, very big corporations are making a lot of money off of pornography.

These are rough estimates [about the money]: About $460 million, $500 million a year of porn is sold via cable and satellite and upward of $200 million via hotels. So that's a lot of money.

One of the things I look at in the porn section of my book is the public morality and the desire to stamp out vice and these moral crusades and the underlying reality. It's not just about how people are really behaving, but even within the same person, you see this public desire to stamp out vice and then this private desire to indulge in it. One example would be Father Bruce Ritter, who was a member of President Reagan's Meese commission to investigate pornography.

[Ritter] was the head of Covenant House—a place in New York City for runaways, a Catholic charity. One of the runaways came out publicly and said that he had been paid to have sex with Father Ritter. There was a scandal that involved his behavior, and he had to step down.

Ritter was very adamant, by day, that homosexuality should be included in the commission's purview and that homosexuality should be officially condemned. And by night, he was cruising for young male prostitutes. Again and again, you see this kind of obsession with pornography in some people being combined with a real desire to indulge in it.

Now, I'm not saying this of all conservatives, by any means, or of all critics of pornography. There are a lot of people who criticize it, and rightly so, on its content. But when you look at America, we have some of the toughest laws on pornography in the Western world, but we watch more porn, we produce more porn—we have a pornographic culture. The same is true for . . . marijuana. We have some of the toughest marijuana laws in the Western world. You can get a life sentence without parole for a first-time marijuana offense. But we grow more marijuana. We smoke more pot. We write more songs about pot. I think that speaks to very deeply conflicted American psyche and culture on these issues.

If you look at the history of this country, we were founded by Puritans. But at the same time, this country has a very rebellious and iconoclastic history and tradition. I think through all these issues you see this ongoing battle between the Puritan part of our culture and the very rebellious and iconoclastic, dissenting tradition that we have.

American Inventors and Businessmen

Robert Fulton and the Steamboat

by

KIRKPATRICK SALE

After dabbling in painting and designing land mines and submarines, Robert Fulton changed the nature of transportation in America by designing the first successful steamboat. Driven by a desire for wealth and renown, Fulton teamed up with a New York official to establish a monopoly on steamboat travel on the Hudson River. Journalist Kirkpatrick Sale appeared on Booknotes *in November 2001 to talk about* The Fire of His Genius: Robert Fulton and the American Dream, *published that year by* The Free Press.

ROBERT FULTON, when he died at an early age, was compared to the self-consuming tree of Gambia. I don't know if any such tree exists, but that's what was said at his funeral. "Like the self-burning tree of Gambia, he was destroyed by his own genius . . . ." I think that's the key to Fulton's character. That's why I called the subtitle *Robert Fulton and the American Dream*, because it was that American Dream of fame and riches, which he acknowledged right from the beginning he wanted. . . . That's what he was out for, and he would do anything to get there. He got it, but the process ate him up.

The larger theme of *Robert Fulton and the American Dream* is that getting the American Dream is one thing, but in the process, we tend to eat ourselves up and have effects on the rest of the world that we don't even pay any attention to. There are costs to the American Dream.

I live alongside the Hudson River, and so I've wanted to write about the Hudson for some time. . . . I thought about the steamboat that was first used successfully on the Hudson River. That led me back to Fulton. . . . In England, they had steam factories as their industrial revolution, but we had water-powered factories and we didn't need steam factories. The steamboats brought the Industrial Revolution to America.

ROBERT FULTON lived from 1765 to 1815. He created his steamboat in 1807, so he had eight years of fame and fortune, but he loved those eight years. . . . He spent so much time worrying about his fame and going to courts and to legislatures, trying to protect his patent and the monopoly he had on the Hudson River, that [it] ate him up. That was the fire that consumed him far too early. He died much too early in his career and had only eight years to carry out the steamboat legacy.

He came from Lancaster, Pennsylvania. . . . Lancaster was a headquarters for much of the army and prisoners of war during the Revolutionary War. It was a major center of gun manufacturing, so Fulton grew up with all of this matériel and military fervor going on about him. It went into his soul; it struck his soul very deeply, so that when he began his inventive career, he turned almost immediately, after a few dodges here and there, to weapons of war. He invented a submarine, and he invented what he called torpedoes, which were land mines.

The difficulty in writing a biography of someone who is famous only later in life is that all that early history is pretty much forgotten. There's just a shadowy record there. His father, however, was a failure. That seems clear. He tried to establish a farm and that failed, and he was an itinerant salesman in Lancaster without much success. It seems clear that that was one of the motives for Fulton in his drive to be a success. [There is not much known about his mother.] He wrote a few letters to her, but if she wrote to him, those letters didn't survive. She's an anonymous figure.

Fulton had probably six to eight years of schooling before he went to Philadelphia to apprentice to a jeweler. He apparently made hair lockets with pictures in lockets that people wore. Then he became a miniatures painter and set himself up in a studio in Philadelphia. That lasted for only a couple of years before somebody gave him the money to go to England to become a real painter.

When he does get to England and starts painting, we see the same kind of thing: adequate paintings, the ones that survive, but nothing distinguished [or] great about them. He spent five or six years trying to be a painter and failing in England. You could see that somehow he didn't put his fire into that. That wasn't what he thought was going to get him his fame and fortune.

But he created [land mines] and proved that they could work. . . . He went down in the submarine and came back up. He created [the submarine] in

France, and he tried to sell it to the French government, which was at war with England at the time. He was trying to persuade Napoleon, "This is the great thing to blow up the ships of England." Napoleon thought about it, and then he said, "Well, let me see it." Fulton wouldn't let him see it. Fulton said, "I destroyed it," because he didn't want them to copy it without him getting the fame and fortune from it. So Napoleon said, "No, I'm not interested."

Fulton went over to England and said the same thing to the English, "I'll build it for you to destroy the French fleet." The English were interested for a while. Now . . . there was another country involved, which was Fulton's own country, the United States. . . . This was an act of treason to provide a weapon of war that would be used against the United States as well as against France or England. But it didn't bother Fulton. He didn't consider it treasonous because, again, this drive for wealth and fame was eating and propelling him.

[Fulton was in England from 1787 to 1797.] At the end of that, he decided that he would be an inventor or an engineer, as he called himself. He went around trying to invent this and that and the other. He had played with the idea of a steamboat even as early as 1793.

[He lived another seven years in France]. Then he went to England, and he came back to the United States in 1806. In that time he had almost no success, until at the very end when the British government paid him a considerable amount of money, £10,000, for his floating land mines and his submarine, and with that, he became a wealthy man.

FULTON, AT HIS grown age, was about six feet tall, which is four inches taller than the average person back then . . . [and] was a very handsome man. One believes that coming from poverty . . . and with very little schooling, that it was his good looks and the charm that he developed that really got him his early successes.

FULTON MARRIED Harriet Livingston, a cousin of his whom he met during the course of his steamboat ventures . . . [in] 1808, just after his success of the steamboat in 1807. She was not a beautiful woman, but she had apparently a certain charm, and she had spent some years at a school, so she had a modicum of education. But they didn't get along. They had a very sour marriage, and he treated her as baggage that he had to lug around.

They had eventually four kids, but he wrote about the children as if they were Harriet's responsibility. . . . He showed no warmth at all for his children. There is a letter of his in Paris, when he was talking about the first steamboat that he created there, and he referred to the steamboat as his child. It's quite a warm and wonderful description of how his child is getting along and will be able to move about in the world. He never wrote a comparable letter about his real children, ever. His affection was for his steamboat and not for his children.

[THE HUDSON RIVER is] the most beautiful river in America. And it's flat. Now, you don't know about flat rivers. The Hudson is flat from New York to Albany, and that's the extraordinary thing about it. It is like a Scottish loch in that sense, like a lake. Then there are these mountains that go up on either side of it. There are turns and twists. But because of that beauty, it was a river that needed the steamboat.

Now the story here is interesting, because the very first successful steamboat [rode] the Delaware River from Philadelphia to Trenton. That should have been a marvelous success, except that there are no twists and turns to that river, there are no difficult curves, and so sailing boats went up and down without any trouble. The banks of the Delaware are easy for stagecoaches to go on. So the guy who built his steamboat didn't have any customers, because nobody needed to go on a frightening, loud, and ugly steamboat because they could go by sail or by carriage.

On the Hudson, you couldn't do that. It was a long and arduous coach journey to go from New York to Albany because of these mountains in the way. The Hudson twists and the curves are so treacherous, it was difficult for sailboats. That's why the steamboat was necessary for the Hudson River, as it was necessary for the Mississippi and the other rivers of America.

There were other inventions and probably something on the order of fifteen to twenty other steamboats that had been tried before Fulton's. He saw that it might be an instrument for England, and then he went to France and tried to sell it there, but it wasn't a passion with him at all. He toyed with this invention and that invention. He kept on looking at things and borrowing other people's ideas, which is what you have to do, actually, when you're inventing.

FULTON HAD A partner in his steamboat business, who was Robert Livingston, one of the great American statesmen, who had been involved in writing the Declaration and the Constitution. He was a representative of New York State for much of that, and chiefly responsible for getting Napoleon to sign the treaty for the Louisiana Purchase. . . . [Livingston and] Fulton got together in Paris, and Fulton said, "I'll build the boat." Livingston said, "Well, I'll give you the monopoly, and together we'll be partners." Actually, they were financial equals in this because by then, Fulton had enough money to go in [fifty–fifty] with Livingston. He built the boat; and it was a success. Livingston secured the monopoly, and so nobody else was allowed to run steamboats, although other people could easily do so. Building a steamboat that worked was not all that difficult. Livingston was a great patron of the Hudson Valley.

FULTON MET JOEL and Ruth Barlow in 1800. We know something about it, but we don't know enough. Joel Barlow was then a famous American poet who had written a poem about America called "The Vision of Columbus," which was revised and came out in 1807. Joel was living in Paris and had gone there in a land scheme. He stayed in Paris, and he had a considerable amount of money. [Ruth] was his wife, and they were happily married, but they had a habit of bringing other people in [to their relationship and] . . . one of the people they brought in was Robert Fulton. . . . They lived together, the three of them, a *ménage à trois*. The French gave the word to us. It was a threesome, and they lived together for those seven years in Paris.

Barlow might have looked upon Fulton as a son; there was a twenty-year age difference there. . . . But, clearly, it was more than father-son. There was clearly a sexual relationship among them, and we know this from letters that Barlow wrote while Fulton and Ruth were off on holidays in 1802 and 1803. [There] are baby-talk letters full of sexual images, and there is clearly a sexual feeling from Barlow to Fulton. We have no evidence that this was returned. Fulton's letters do not survive from that period. Barlow is encouraging Fulton to have a wonderful summer of sexual pleasure with his wife and says that he must not let his beautiful body be deranged, and if he does anything wrong, Barlow says, he'll come and cut off his penis. He says this in the baby-talk fashion of his letters.

They are bizarre letters, and it was a bizarre arrangement for these three. There was clearly real affection at the bottom of it, because when Barlow and Ruth finally go back to America and settle down in Washington, Fulton goes there often to see them and stay with them. When he got married . . . he thought maybe there could be a *ménage à quatre* with the four of them in Washington. That was his hope, and he wrote so much to Barlow. It didn't happen. His wife, Harriet, would have none of it, and clearly it was a disaster.

THERE'S ANOTHER incident here, too, because while he was in England, Fulton stayed at the castle of the most notorious homosexual in England, Powderham Castle, down in Devon. He stayed there for probably two years, at least a year and a half, painting the portrait of Lord Courtenay, and clearly living within that *ménage* as well.

Now, there's no suggestion anywhere that there was a homosexual relationship between the two of them; however, it is known that Lord Courtenay flaunted his homosexual life there, and he had parties and brought in people. . . . It seems impossible that Fulton could have escaped being a part of that homosexual world, and given his looks and charm, he might have been a willing partner there. He needed that because he had no other means of support, and if Lord Courtenay was going to support him, that was fine.

[This aspect of Fulton's life was known, I think, but not talked about.] They don't teach [this to young kids in school]. They teach them that Fulton invented the steamboat and that it was called the *Clermont.* Neither is true. He didn't invent it; he made the first successful steamboat run. It wasn't called the *Clermont;* it was called the *North River.* They don't teach [kids] about the rest of this.

It's hard to say [how the names of the steamboats were changed]. But in the first biography written by Fulton's friend and his lawyer, Cadwallader Colden, Colden used that name. He said it was called the *Clermont* or the *North River.* I don't know how he got that idea, or he may have just been trying to stay on the good side of the Livingston family, whose family home was called Clermont. But it was never called that on any paper or in any document or in any letter that Fulton wrote.

I TALKED ABOUT Fulton to classes of fifth-graders the other day. There were about 100 kids there, and I told them about Fulton. I told them the truth about Fulton. I [was] gentle on much of it. But they had no trouble getting it. They could see who he was. They saw his brilliance, and they saw the fire, and they saw how it burned him up.

[Historians have created an image of him that is not accurate.] It's the Parson Weems's treatment of George Washington and others that we want our heroes to be heroic. We don't want them to have clay feet. We want them to be perfect. That's very much a part of American history. Probably every nation's history tries to do the same. So the other parts we don't even bother to examine. Now, I have some problem with the question of Fulton's homosexuality. It was clear that he was involved in these relationships. It's not clear that they had any particular effect on his creativity, on his inventiveness, on his work.

[Whether or not Fulton was honest is] an interesting question. I think you could say that he was honest within his own likes. The fact that he was traitorous in offering his weapons of war all around to countries other than his own, I don't think that's dishonesty, exactly. He'd [say] he never saw it as traitorous. People actually said it to him, suggested to him that it was, and he wouldn't believe it. Even Barlow was a bit upset by all of that, but it never touched Fulton.

[THE STEAMBOAT] had more impact than any other invention until Colt perfected his revolver in the 1840s. It was decisive in shaping the course of American history in the first half of the nineteenth century. Not only could it work on the Hudson but it also worked on the Mississippi River system that America acquired in the Louisiana Purchase and that transformed our country. It made America occupy the entire center of the continent, all the way to the Rockies, created a huge economic machine in that area, and brought in massive waves of white settlers. [This] displaced Indians and later the Mexicans, and stamped American culture and economics all over that huge area. [That region] became, in fact, more important than the original thirteen colonies as a political and economic entity. ✕ ✕ ✕ ✕

In addition to allowing the destruction of the native tribes and the native flora and fauna, it enabled cotton to be a successful crop, and slavery to continue to exist. Until then, cotton was a problematic crop. It had some market in England and some use domestically, but it wasn't significant. It is thought by many historians that slavery was about to go out of fashion in the South as it had in the North. There was still slavery both North and South, but it was diminishing. Then along came this instrument that enabled you to carry big loads of cotton . . . up and down the rivers and to do it quickly and economically. So the plantation economy was secured by the steamboat, as was king cotton and slavery, right up until the Civil War.

[ROBERT FULTON's genius when it came to actually building a steamboat came from a] vision of what it should do and what it should look like, which was in some ways flawed, but it was clear enough . . . to build this first boat and have success with it. He was also enough of an artist to draw the inventions that he wanted to create. There are drawings from his patent for the steamboat that he applied for in 1809. He was a skillful artist, and he could design the inventions that he wanted built. He designed the steamboat . . . and he carried out all of its building with great care. He was there in the shop, saw what his workmen were doing, and took care of every detail inside the engine and outside.

THE FAMOUS names of the country in 1807 . . . [were] Lewis and Clark. Lewis and Clark were the new heroes of America, because it was in 1806 that they came back from their momentous journey to the Pacific. There were celebrations of Meriwether Lewis in all the cities, including Washington, where there was a huge banquet in his honor. To that banquet went Barlow and his wife, and Fulton. Barlow and Fulton are recorded as having given toasts, which was then the fashion, to Lewis for his achievement.

But Fulton, by that time, was the new hero because he had created the successful steamboat, and everyone could see that that was going to be an instrument of significance. . . . I don't think anybody was thinking just how important an instrument it was. It took America a few years to understand that. By 1907, the centenary year, Mark Twain, who was on the committee to celebrate this centenary, said that Fulton's achievement had made the rivers useful, before that they were just there.

[THE NEW YORK State Assembly granted the steamboat monopoly to Livingston, but there was no money exchanged to get the monopoly.] This was the idea that commerce would be improved if we could get a steamboat there. In order to get somebody to invent it and put it on the water, you had to give them a monopoly, or else they wouldn't do it.

Livingston persuaded the New York State Legislature to do his bidding. He was a rich and famous patriot and they . . . gave him the monopoly. If he could successfully provide a steamboat, he could have the monopoly on steamboat travel on the Hudson. [Livingston in turn, gave Fulton the monopoly.]

Chief Justice John Marshall broke the steamboat monopoly. The monopoly began in 1807 and was renewed for years, even after Fulton's death. But it was challenged at every point all the time. That took Fulton to court and to legislatures more often than he wished to go. Fulton built twelve or thirteen [steamboats in his life] and there were five of them that plied the Hudson. The others were steam ferries, and there was one boat on Long Island and there were some on the Mississippi. [This was not a national monopoly.] That's why Fulton was so late in going to the Mississippi, because he couldn't get a monopoly on the Mississippi. He managed, with the help of another Livingston, to get a monopoly on New Orleans for New Orleans's waters. That sort of gave him a monopoly on the Mississippi, but it was effectively ignored. There were other people who were putting boats on the Mississippi, and there was very little that Fulton could do about it. . . .

After Fulton's death, a lot of people came, trying to challenge [the monopoly]. Commodore Cornelius Vanderbilt was one of them. . . . Then this went into a state court and finally, to the Supreme Court in 1824. It was then that Marshall declared that the monopoly was odious and that there couldn't be any monopolies in American waters.

[That decision] helped to expand trade enormously. But it had been successfully challenged on the Hudson before that, and successfully challenged on the Mississippi and the Ohio before that. This was a legal assistance, but people were going to build steamboats and use them, no matter what. When that monopoly was finally destroyed, though, it opened the floodgates for the Hudson River. By that time, there were hundreds of steamboats in the Mississippi system and on other rivers in America. [America] had these long rivers that were otherwise, as Mark Twain said, "useless." Not quite, but now they were useful.

[FULTON DIED] of pneumonia. He didn't take care of himself. . . . That fire in his soul was driving him to achieve more fame and more fortune. He had a restless soul that would not even learn to take care of his own health. What is certain is that ten years after his death [his family was destitute]. It's not certain where that money went. Probably his widow had some of it, and she married a rather unscrupulous man who might have taken it all for himself. . . .

[HAVING A STREET created and named after you] . . . is an honor that's rarely been accorded to anybody in New York. But here they made a street [named Fulton Street], and it was a street that went between Fulton's landings on the Hudson, where the steam ferries went to New Jersey, and the other Fulton landing on the East River, where the steam ferries went to Brooklyn and Queens. They just plowed a road between those two points after his death and named it Fulton Street in his honor.

[AFTER I FINISHED the book, I did not like Fulton much.] . . . I had no idea that he was quite the scallywag he was. He certainly got [the fame]. He is known to this day by every child in America, and that is a considerable amount of fame. And Fulton Street is still there, plowing through the middle of Manhattan.

Charles Goodyear
and Rubber Vulcanization

by

CHARLES SLACK

In 1839, Charles Goodyear made a discovery—vulcanization—that turned a novel but nearly useless substance into an indispensable commodity. Goodyear was granted a U.S. patent for his process but had to fight off competitors and spent himself into debt along the way. Author Charles Slack, who told Goodyear's story in Noble Obsession: Charles Goodyear, Thomas Hancock, and the Race to Unlock the Greatest Industrial Secret of the Nineteenth Century, *published by Hyperion, appeared on Booknotes on October 27, 2002.*

THE NOBLE OBSESSION in the title of my book was Charles Goodyear's obsessive quest to find a way to take rubber, which was an industrial curiosity, an industrial sideshow until he got hold of it, and to turn it into a commodity which really changed the world. He went on a quest for about ten years to find the secret and then to perfect it. He did it at tremendous cost to himself and to his family. That was his noble obsession: He was obsessed with rubber.

THE TERM *RUBBER* comes from the eighteenth century. One of the first practical uses, well before vulcanization, was that it was found to be useful for erasing pencil marks—for rubbing them out—and that's where the term comes from.

THOMAS HANCOCK was Charles Goodyear's principal competitor. Charles Goodyear was an American. Thomas Hancock was an Englishman. Thomas

Hancock had been known as the "father of the rubber industry," the early rubber industry, when rubber first began appearing in large quantities in the early 1800s in Europe and America. He was a brilliant inventor and a very good businessman, and he had come through with some very important discoveries and inventions on rubber.

Goodyear, on the other hand, was obscure, poverty stricken, in and out of debtors' prison, ridiculed by virtually everyone, pitied by those who didn't ridicule him. Where their two worlds came into collision was when Goodyear had finally perfected the process and sent over some small samples—foolishly, because he hadn't taken a patent out yet—but sent some samples over to England to try to attract British investors. He always needed money.

They got into the hands of Thomas Hancock, and Hancock decided to see if he could reverse-engineer these samples. He was dumbfounded because he had thought that rubber's great flaw couldn't be solved, and he saw that it could. He spent the next year in his secret laboratory reverse-engineering Goodyear's invention and actually beat Goodyear to the British patent office, which was the most important at the time.

CHARLES GOODYEAR was born in 1800, and he died in 1860. He was born in New Haven, Connecticut. When he was five years old, he moved to Naugatuck, which is about twelve miles up the road due north. The Goodyears were actually founding members of the New Haven colony. His ancestor, Stephen Goodyear, was one of the wealthiest and principal founders of the colony back in the early 1600s.

When Charles was growing up, his father, Amasa Goodyear, was an inventor himself. He produced the buttons worn by American soldiers in the War of 1812. He was a tinkerer and a businessman. He had two principal qualities that he passed on to his son: one was a vision for products that others didn't see and being ahead of his time, and the other was a debilitating lack of business sense, a lack of how to be a businessman. Charles Goodyear inherited both of those.

CHARLES WAS SICK from the time he was a teenager, and perhaps before. He had gone to Philadelphia at the age of seventeen to work as an apprentice for a hardware company and had to leave because he had a physical breakdown. His ailments came under the general umbrella of dyspepsia. . . . He had these various gastric problems, and these plagued him throughout his life.

He also worked with a number of very harsh chemicals, including nitric acid and lead, and there were no safety codes in those days. He was mixing it and molding it with his hands and that, perhaps, contributed. He suffered from gout. He was kind of a physical wreck.

[TO RECOVER FROM his physical breakdown] he'd gone back to Naugatuck. Shortly after he was married, he went back to Philadelphia in 1826 to start what was the first American hardware store that was devoted solely to domestically produced goods. His father produced hay and manure forks which were made of steel and lighter than the other kind and they manufactured other goods and started this hardware store. About 1830, there was a financial panic, and the hardware store basically collapsed. Goodyear had his first stint in debtors' prison.

In Philadelphia, where Goodyear was first imprisoned, creditors had to pay a 20-cent a day fee for a couple of loaves of bread and a blanket to keep you alive. Essentially, they could keep you there indefinitely. Most terms were a period of days, maybe twenty days.

IT WAS ABOUT 1834 when Goodyear came across rubber for the first significant time. He was in the New York offices of the Roxbury India Rubber Company, which had been the first and the biggest American rubber company.

He came across a life preserver, and he decided that he could make a better valve for the life preserver. So he went back home and perfected this valve. He wasn't really thinking about rubber at that time. Then he came back with the valve and tried to sell it to the agent, and the agent said, "Well, this is a great valve, but I've got something to show you." And he took him around to the warehouse, where were just these rank, foul blobs of goo which had been life preservers and caps, and so forth, that had been returned because of the heat.

The way Goodyear told it was this agent said, "If somebody wants to make his mark on the world, he should find a way to prevent this from happening." A light went off or a bell rang for Goodyear and that became his obsession for the rest of his life.

[IN THE EARLY 1800s], rubber had been around for centuries. The South American natives had been using it, and Europeans had been aware of it since the late fifteenth century and sixteenth century. In the early 1800s, it began making a strong appearance in the United States and Europe. There was a great deal of excitement because it was just at the very dawning of the industrial age. There was no other substance like it. It was airtight. It was waterproof. It was elastic. You could stretch it out and it would snap back to its original shape. You could compress it and it would bounce back. It had a seemingly unlimited variety of uses, which later proved to be the case.

In the 1830s, it really took off, and people started investing. I compare it to the Internet boom of the 1990s, where it attracted all sorts of investment from people who weren't sure exactly how it was going to make a profit, but they didn't want to be left out.

Rubber turned out to have a very fatal flaw, which is that when the temperature gets very hot out, rubber becomes sticky, and then if the heat is intensified, it becomes gooey, and then it actually melts and starts to run. And when the weather gets very cold, it starts to crack.

WOBURN IS ABOUT ten miles north of Boston, and Goodyear was living there. He'd been in Roxbury, which is in part of Boston, and had been working with the remnants of the Roxbury India Rubber Company. By that time, the rubber industry had shrunk down to a very few hardy souls who still believed in it.

This was in the early to mid-1830s, and he had a falling out with the Roxbury India Rubber Company and heard about a mill in Woburn, Massachusetts, a few miles away. He moved to Woburn and began working with Nathaniel Hayward, who had been a stable operator but had become enamored of rubber and actually first gave Goodyear the idea to use sulfur in experiments.

Goodyear did experiments wherever he could find heat. Once he knew that heat was an essential element, he began to look for fire wherever he could find it. When he was able to use this mill in Woburn, he would use that. He built an oven there, but he was chronically behind on his payments, so he was not always able to use that.

He would go around to the local blacksmiths and cajole them. He was an excellent beggar. He was convinced of the holiness of his vision and he had no shame about sponging off his fellow residents of Woburn, or anywhere else for use of their fire, or for money. He would go around to the blacksmiths at the end of the day and say, "Can I use your fire before it dies out?" And, of course, some of them agreed.

Goodyear worked in Woburn for several years and came up by accident with the discovery in 1839, and it's not clear how. The specifics are still kind of vague. We have Goodyear's own account of it but his memoirs are written in this sort of third-person elliptical, vague, hard-to-pin-down way.

But it seems that he had been mixing sulfur with rubber and dropped some on a stove and then came back later and was astonished to find that the rubber hadn't melted but it had toughened, and he knew that that was a great discovery. By that time, everybody was fed up with the rubber industry, so he couldn't convince people that he'd come up with this important discovery, and then he also had a very difficult time reproducing it.

VULCANIZATION IS THE term actually devised by a friend of Thomas Hancock's, named for the Roman god of fire, Vulcan. Vulcanization is the process by which rubber is transformed so that it is no longer susceptible to heat or cold. This was Goodyear's great discovery. . . . Rubber has this quality of being pliant and elastic. The chemical properties of rubber really weren't known well into the twentieth century, so everything was trial and error. Even after the process, nobody—Goodyear nor anybody else—really knew exactly what he'd discovered.

One of the most poignant aspects of the Goodyear story is that when he had his eureka moment, it wasn't like his life turned for the better. If anything, he sank deeper into poverty and despair and he became consumed with the fear that he would die before the world recognized this discovery he'd made.

HORACE CUTLER was a minor but very important figure in the Goodyear story, when Goodyear had moved on from Woburn to Springfield, Massachusetts, and was working there on perfecting his process. This was after his discovery of 1839, and he convinced Horace Cutler, who was a shoe manufacturer, to come in with him. Goodyear was very good at convincing people that fame and fortune was right around the corner, and I don't think he was lying. I think he believed that his whole life, and he convinced Horace Cutler to invest, to become a partner with him.

Cutler after a while became fed up, and that was when Horace Day, who is my villain in the story, came in contact with Horace Cutler. He convinced Horace Cutler to come down to New Jersey where Horace Day lived and essentially tell him the secret that he'd learned from his close association with Goodyear. In the course of a couple of days, Cutler basically spilled these secrets which had taken Goodyear years to develop.

Horace Day took that information and tried to reproduce vulcanization, but he had difficulty doing it and it drove him crazy. Vulcanization is a delicate process and even if you have the basic formula, it takes a while to get the exact measurements and the heat and so forth.

He then traveled to Springfield and tried to wheedle his way into Goodyear's mill and wasn't able to get in. Then, once the process became better known and perfected, he made a career out of ripping Goodyear off at every turn. . . . This was after the discovery had been made and Goodyear held the U.S. patent, even though he'd lost out on the English patent. Horace Day had been infringing and infringing, and finally Goodyear's licensees in America, the Goodyear Shoe Association, got together the funds to sue Horace Day for patent infringement in a case that became "the Great India Rubber Case" of 1852. They hired as their attorney Daniel Webster, who was then secretary of state to Millard Fillmore. He was close to seventy years old, suffering from cirrhosis of the liver. He had lost a step or two, to say the least.

Webster really didn't need the publicity to be had from representing Goodyear and his licensees, but he needed the money. That was what he had in common with Charles Goodyear. For all of his august positions, he was a spendthrift and he needed the money. They offered him what was then a phenomenal sum of $10,000, plus another $6,000 if he could win the case.

Patent infringement was rampant, and not just by Horace Day but by others, and they wanted to make an example of Horace Day. Horace Day was a very combative individual. He fought numerous legal battles, not just against Goodyear, but all of his life against any number of people; he was a combative soul. So he didn't back down, and it all culminated in this great trial.

Before the trial, lawyers for both sides took depositions from people, and Horace Day dragged up several individuals who claimed that they, in fact, had invented vulcanization. Horace Day claimed that he had invented vulcanization, Horace Cutler notwithstanding.

Goodyear won resoundingly. It's not clear how much money Goodyear or the associates ever got out of Horace Day, but the judgment came back resoundingly in Goodyear's favor. It was Daniel Webster's final court battle and he won. The decision actually came down shortly before Webster died.

GOODYEAR DIED on the way to visit his daughter, who was herself dying. It's one of the tragic parts of the Goodyear story. He was living in Washington, got news that his daughter was ill in Connecticut, and even though Goodyear himself was in terrible shape, he got on the boat and took this rough voyage. He got as far as New York and his son-in-law met him and gave him the news that his daughter had died. I think this broke whatever remaining spirit he had, and he essentially collapsed and was taken to a New York hotel and died.

HE DIED CLOSE to $200,000 in debt.

[IN THE YEAR] 1860, Goodyear dies; 1861, the Civil War begins. Soldiers went off to battle with rubber tents, rubber ponchos, rubber canteens, and so forth. Rubber was already becoming a major commodity. The benefits of rubber vulcanization were already apparent and so it was widely used. And then, of course, by the twentieth century, rubber—along with oil and food and a few other things—becomes the thing that armies move and live or die on.

CHARLES GOODYEAR, through his almost superhuman perseverance came up with an invention that changed the world. He took a substance which would only have a sideshow type of benefit to people and turned it into, made it capable of becoming, a substance that is a part of everything that we do to this day.

People think mainly, of course, of automobile tires, which vulcanization made possible, but rubber, since it is a poor conductor of electricity, became essential as an insulation for the electrical industry, for telephones, plumbing, aviation. It's an essential component—and that's what Goodyear gave the world.

Andrew Carnegie

by

PETER KRASS

Scottish-born industrialist and philanthropist Andrew Carnegie is one of the best-known figures of America's Gilded Age. Carnegie made his fortune in the steel industry, rebuilding bridges and railroads after the Civil War. Peter Krass, whose great-grandfather worked in one of the magnate's mills, shared Carnegie's story with Booknotes *viewers on November 24, 2002. His biography* Carnegie *was published that year by John Wiley & Sons.*

ANDREW CARNEGIE IS incredibly complex. He typifies the titan of the Gilded Age, and the American public is still fascinated with that time. . . . If you're looking for a character to work with as a biographer, Carnegie's fantastic because he was so complicated. He had an incredible internal conflict, and his behavior was often so contradictory that you just want to dig in and find out what was driving this man.

My great-grandfather worked in a Carnegie mill—now the Duquesne mill—right outside of Pittsburgh. He was a skilled laborer who worked in the furnaces, changing the lining. He lived from 1872 to 1931, so most of his tenure there was post-Carnegie. But even post-Carnegie, life as a steelworker was tough. I actually didn't know about that until I started this project, and an aunt came to me and said, "You're not going to believe this. You've got a great-grandfather who worked in a mill."

CARNEGIE WAS BORN in Scotland in 1835 and died in Lenox, Massachusetts, in 1919. When he died, he had $25 million, based on the dollar back then. And in his will, every penny went to various institutions, and nothing was left for his wife and daughter, who had already been taken care of. At that point, he'd already given away $350 million.

HE MARRIED ONCE. He was fifty-one, so [it was] 1887. She was about twenty years his junior.

There's been some debate whether or not he promised his mother not to marry until she died, because they lived together right up until her death. I'm certain that that promise was made to her because she died in the fall of 1886, and he married in April of 1887. Everything he did was for his mother. He was driven for her to ride in a fancy carriage, to live in a fancy mansion, to have servants.

Growing up in Scotland during a period called the "hungry Forties," [he experienced] an incredible economic downturn. Andrew's father was a hand-loom weaver, and the Industrial Revolution was kicking off in Britain before it reached here. He eventually found himself out of work. The steam-powered looms took over, and it was Andrew's mother who came to the rescue. She started mending shoes at night. She started working during the day in a little grocery shop she set up in the front window of their house. She became his heroine, and his father basically faded completely from the picture. He dedicated his life to reward her for what she had done.

The Carnegies came to the United States in 1848, when Andrew was twelve. The economic situation had gotten so bad in Dunfermline that his parents felt they had no choice. It was his mother who was the driving force for this move. His father would have been very happy to struggle along in Dunfermline, but they were looking for a better life. The town [they moved to] was called Allegheny City. It's now the north side of Pittsburgh. In those days, the nickname was "Slabtown."

Andrew's father, William, tried his hand again at hand-loom weaving, but there was just no market for it. He briefly took a job in a cotton factory but didn't last long at all. His mother again stepped into the void, and she started mending shoes for an English neighbor . . . and saved the day.

IN SCOTLAND, Andrew went to school from about age eight to age twelve, then they emigrated. When he came to the U.S., he had to go to work. However, after he had been working for a few years here, he got a job as a telegraph operator. It was not a grueling job [and] he had free time at night. He went to night school to learn double-entry accounting. He went to the libraries and just read everything he could get his hands on, [especially] history, American politics; there was an incredible amount of self-education.

CARNEGIE MADE his money in a series of phases. Everyone thinks of Andrew Carnegie as a steel magnate, but you really have to go back to the 1850s to start tracking his rise. He didn't get into steel until the mid-1870s. Long before he was in steel, he was an investor, and he bought stocks, bonds, and he got into a bridge-making company, which was what really started to launch him. [That] was his pet of all businesses because during the Civil War, iron bridges were in huge demand, [since] it was so easy for the two sides to burn wooden bridges. He got into iron bridge making, and it started generating huge profits.

He was like an octopus, with each tentacle reached out with each new project. . . . He started taking over the building of the railroads that were going to cross these bridges. In the meantime, he had also invested in an iron-making business. So he used that iron business to buy all the iron he needed for these other endeavors. It was a really neatly interlocked organization he got going.

Then he took it a step further. They wanted to build a bridge at St. Louis, across the Mississippi River, which was an incredible technological feat in those days. It was going to cost a lot of money. Now, railroad companies had been selling bonds to fund their businesses, but never before had bonds been sold to fund a bridge-building project. They decided that's what they needed to do.

Carnegie immediately raised his hand and said, "I'll sell the bonds, too." So, he was building the bridge and the railroads. Now, he's going to sell the bonds to fund this. He went over to England, where he met Junius Morgan, J. P.'s father, and sold these bonds. What he realized was, "I am a great salesman." And so, he went full tilt into bond selling, netted incredibly huge profits, and he used those profits to fund his steelmaking. So what people don't realize is that Carnegie actually made his first fortune as a bond salesman.

AT THE START of the Civil War, the Confederates had basically cut off Washington by sabotaging some railroad lines and bridges. Carnegie's boss at the Pennsylvania Railroad, which was where he was working at the time, was brought into Washington by the secretary of defense to rebuild these lines and open Washington back up so they could get troops in there and protect the city. He brought in Carnegie, who had been his right-hand man, to oversee the field operations.

Carnegie worked night and day. He was the kind of guy who could get a catnap for an hour and go the next twenty-three hours. They were working to rebuild the bridge across the Potomac. They accomplished that and the troops went over. We've got the first battle of Manassas. Carnegie was in charge of getting the troops there by train. Of course, the Union ended up on their heels and retreated. Carnegie was out there getting the troops back on the trains and he took one of the last trains out. He had quite an experience and it actually took its toll on him. He suffered from heat stroke and took a vacation soon thereafter.

He didn't fight. He thought he was sort of immune from ever being recruited or drafted to fight because there was a two-year-old law passed that exempted railroad men and people in crucial positions. But he was drafted, and instead of going to war, he hired a substitute for $850. It was fairly common practice. If you had the money, you did it. In fact, you could buy your way out by spending $300, which went straight to the government. But if you were more patriotic, you would spend the $850 to actually hire a soldier to replace you.

[ANDREW CARNEGIE had just one younger brother,] Tom, who was eight years younger. Andrew was very good about taking care of Tom financially. He brought him into the Pennsylvania Railroad and hired him as his personal secretary. Later they were partners in business together in iron and steel. However, the two had a contentious relationship, as well. To give you an idea of how that relationship ended, Tom died in his mid-forties from complications from being an alcoholic because he was driven so hard by Andrew. The reason he felt such pressure is because Andrew moved to New York and Tom stayed in Pittsburgh, where the business was. So you can imagine, Tom was dealing with all the day-to-day affairs. Not only that, he had Andrew on his back, to make sure it was managed properly.

ANDREW CARNEGIE moved in 1867 to New York City, and he was convinced you had to be in New York because that's where . . . the money was. Anyone who wanted to build a large business had to be there. When he got there, what he found was that you had all these scoundrels like Daniel Drew and Jay Gould. He was expecting the London of the United States, a cultured city, but that's not what he found.

He was feeling a little melancholy about his situation there. . . . Then he sat down in December, the end of the year, and wrote this note where he pledged to himself that he was going to retire in two years, which would put him at the age of thirty-five. He was going to dedicate himself to literary pursuits. He wanted to move to Oxford in England and meet men of letters [and] spend all his surplus income on philanthropy, uplifting the masses.

Carnegie wrote to himself: "Man has an idol. The amassing of wealth is one of the worst species of idolatry. No idol more debasing than the worship of money. Whatever I engage in, I must push inordinately, therefore should I be careful to choose that life which will be the most elevating in its character. To continue much longer overwhelmed by business cares and with most of my thoughts wholly upon the way to make money in the shortest time must degrade me beyond hope of permanent recovery. I will resign business at 35."

That was a reaction to what he saw in New York and he realized that. And yet he also realized that he was so driven internally, he couldn't shut himself down. He had to go 100 percent. So, he was warning himself.

STEEL. THIS IS a great story because it has sort of Machiavellian intrigue to it. The year was 1861, and a boyhood friend of Carnegie's had become a partner in an iron business with two Bavarian brothers. They had a falling out and they invited Carnegie to mediate.

Carnegie ended up getting his brother, Tom, involved because . . . he thought his brother would bring evenhanded management to this company. Carnegie loaned his brother $10,000 to buy into this partnership. However, there had to have been some kind of agreement between Andrew and Tom because when you look at the income records of Andrew within the next couple of years, the money he was making off this iron enterprise is not interest on a loan. It was a tremendous amount of money.

So, before you know it, Carnegie was in the door. [So he started a rival iron business.] There was trouble with the other company. Hs friend finally dropped out, and Andrew said, "We'll start our own company." And now he was competing with his brother Tom.

They ended up merging. . . . When they merged, Andrew eventually had the majority of the business interests. So, now he had this iron business going and it was incredibly profitable, especially during the Civil War and the years after with the railroad boom.

Now we get to the 1870s. Steel has been around for over ten years, so Carnegie was not a pioneer in steel, which is another legend that needs to be dismissed. He had been monitoring it very carefully. By the 1870s, they had worked out a lot of the problems in the manufacturing of steel. A quote from Carnegie is: "Pioneering don't pay."

He was determined to build the most advanced steel mill ever, which he did, just outside of Pittsburgh. He hired this guy, Alexander Holley, who had already built several steel mills, as the most experienced because he always only wanted the best men. . . . He gave Holley carte blanche. What that allowed Holley to do was have form follow function. In other words, this was an incredibly efficient operation.

THE HOMESTEAD tragedy took place in the summer of 1892 when the workers there went on strike for better wages. Ultimately you need to know that thirteen men died. The Pinkertons were brought in to suppress the strike. There are a couple of intriguing things: One is that you had 3,800 men there but only a little over 300 were going to be affected by these wage cuts and yet the entire workforce got behind this strike. . . . The other intrigue is that Carnegie was brutally criticized by the press for being in Scotland at the time of the strike. . . . He had been going to Scotland every summer for years. The day of the strike, July 6, he was in Aberdeen, Scotland, where he had just dedicated a library, receiving a Freedom [award].

Henry Clay Frick was his partner. He was president of the company at this time, and in charge of all the operations. So, Carnegie was over in Scotland; however, there was communication between him and Frick right up until July 4th. Carnegie was right in there planning the campaign to oust the union from the mill. . . . When you look at the letters all together between Frick and Carnegie, there was a lot of waffling on their part. Should we give in to the union? Should we grant them wage raises? Should we recognize the union? [That waffling] led them to mishandle the situation. Events got out of control and men were killed.

CARNEGIE PROTECTED himself throughout the panics of 1873, 1893, and 1907, and he came out stronger. He was a cutting-edge entrepreneurial type who was willing to take risks. On the other hand, he was very conservative with his money and when the 1873 panic hit, he had cash. What he learned from the experience was that he was still in the process of building that mill and now he could build it cheaper because he could get his labor cheaper. He could get all his material cheaper because all these people were suffering [and] struggling, and they would do anything to sell their product or to get a job. So for every downturn, what you find is Carnegie shutting down his mills and making improvements on them; every time there was an economic downturn, he'd come out stronger.

HIS FIRST MAJOR benefaction was in 1873. He gave baths to his hometown of Dunfermline. Then in the 1880s, he gave Dunfermline an impressive library. . . . In 1889, he wrote an essay called "The Gospel of Wealth" where he started to lay out his template for giving. Later in that year, he wrote a second essay on the best uses of wealth, which was now the complete picture of what he thought the wealthy ought to do with their money. From 1890 on, [his philanthropy] started to pick up its pace, but it was when he sold out to Morgan in 1901 for an astounding $480 million that now he had all the money to fund these incredible institutions he set up.

One of the things I respect is that when he retired he was sixty-five years old and he dedicated his life to philanthropy. He cut all ties to the business, and he didn't just give his money away. He had this template, and he was hands-on to make sure it was spent in the best way possible to uplift as much of the American public as he could.

He was hands-on, but when you look at the language of the trusts he set up, he always gave his trustees a free hand and at any time they could vote to change the direction this institution could take. He was also very broad-minded when he did this. When you look at magnates today, I find it discouraging that a lot of them when they retire, they either go to an investment bank or they keep their hand in the cookie jar at their old company. It would be nice to see someone step up in that same manner and just go into it with a template in mind.

From 1901 until his death in 1919, philanthropy was a full-time job. . . . In the beginning, it was he, three secretaries, and his wife, basically, and then some advisers out there to whom he would go. But as the years progressed, the trustees wanted to be more autonomous. He started getting shut out, which was hard for him because he was in the twilight of his career. This was now his entire life.

THERE WAS AN economist who did an article for the *New York Times* back in 1999 . . . and he had a funky formula to estimate what these titans would be worth today. He put John D. Rockefeller at a little over $200 billion and he put Carnegie at a little over $100 billion. And then we'd have Bill Gates at mid-$50s billion, depending on his stock price.

There are a number of major foundations still in existence that Carnegie created. The primary one is the Carnegie Corporation in New York. The Carnegie Institution in Washington, D.C. . . . funds a lot of scientific work. The Carnegie Institute, out in Pittsburgh, is an incredible facility that includes a museum, art museum, museum of natural history, library. Carnegie Mellon University. Over in Scotland, you've got a number of foundations still in existence. So his legacy is still felt by literally millions of people.

The Carnegie Corporation in New York has a fund now at about $2 billion. Several years ago, they gave $15 million to urban libraries. This is exactly what Carnegie himself would want them to do today because libraries were his centerpieces, and he felt that they would best uplift the masses. Giving that kind of money to urban libraries certainly fits right in with what he wanted.

In the world, it would be close to 3,000 libraries [that are in existence today because of his money]. Twenty-seven percent have his name on them. The rest don't. There's this misconception that Carnegie forced his libraries on communities and wanted his name on those buildings, sort of the Ramses II factor, where he built temples all over Egypt and slapped his name on them. That comparison's been made. But that's not true, because it was the communities that would come to him. It was mainly women's clubs, ministers, town councils who would come to Carnegie, request a library. They'd have to fill out an application. It'd have to be okayed by Carnegie's secretaries. Never was his name required to be on the building. In the state of Indiana, which received numerous libraries, not one had his name on the building.

CARNEGIE WAS A self-proclaimed pacifist. During the Spanish-American War in 1898, he joined the anti-imperialist movement because there was a great concern that once we won that war, we were going to take over the Philippines, Cuba, Puerto Rico, and impose ourselves on them. He became a leader, and he wrote letters to anyone who would listen, from Roosevelt to the other presidents in that period of time. These are letters with language you would not believe ... he was calling presidents "bubbleheads," and "cowardly" and "spineless." "You've got to leave the Philippines alone." There is plenty of evidence that he was a pacifist.

He also wanted arbitration treaties with all the other European countries, especially England, Germany, France, so that there would never be war. He wanted everything arbitrated, regardless of what it was. Roosevelt, who was a jingoist, just could not buy into this at all.

While Carnegie was proclaiming himself a pacifist and promoting the anti-imperialist movement, he's urging his managers in Pittsburgh to build a projectiles mill, for the projectiles to go into cannons. . . . Profits were ruling over ideology, at this point.

[THE CARNEGIE Endowment for International Peace] was founded in 1910, and he wanted to use it as an educational institution to educate people on the drawbacks of war. If there was a war in the Balkans, they analyzed it and said, "This is what happened. This is what you could have done to prevent it." When that foundation was created, it was really ridiculed in the press because he gave $10 million to them. They said, "What are you going to do with $10 million in the name of peace." The institute is living off that endowment today; it's active right now.

AT THE BEGINNING of the book I think of Carnegie as a flawed Shakespearean hero. He thought the world was a stage, and while he was on that stage, he wore a number of masks. I just don't think you can reconcile those masks. We go back to his childhood and look at something here.

When he was growing up, his family were political radicals. They were the working classes. They were fighting for the right to vote, the right to own land, better working conditions, and better wages. Then he went to the United States and embraced capitalism. He became a rabid Republican, so this is in complete opposition to his ancestors. Through his whole life [there were] two sides in conflict fighting each other. . . . It seems oversimplified, but you can use that to explain a lot of his contradictory behavior.

Philo T. Farnsworth:
The Inventor of Television

by

DANIEL STASHOWER

While his name might not be recognized by many, Philo T. Farnsworth's legacy lives on in most American homes. Farnsworth was instrumental in the development of electronic television technology. Although he obtained a patent for his design, he spent many years in a legal battle with RCA over control of the patent and never really profited from his invention. On July 21, 2002, author Daniel Stashower appeared on Booknotes. *He discussed Farnsworth and the debate over his designation as the inventor of television, as described in his book,* The Boy Genius and the Mogul: The Untold Story of Television, *published that year by Broadway Books.*

PHILO T. FARNSWORTH, at the age of fourteen, came up with the idea that became electronic television technology. From the moment he got the idea, it became his life's work.

The story goes that [Farnsworth] was fourteen years old and was the son of a Mormon farmer. He was working in a field in Idaho. Sometimes it's a hay field, and he's mowing the hay; sometimes it's potatoes, and he's tilling; sometimes it's beets. But he was working in a field, pushing a horse-drawn cutter back and forth. And his mind was drifting, as it often did, this time on the problem of television, which was an idea he had read about in a magazine.

When he got to the end, he looked back over this field and over the neat lines that he himself had made in the field. And it suddenly occurred to him that it might be possible to invent a device, an extraordinary and unique type of glass tube that would take an image, break it down into easily transmittable lines, just like the rows in the field, send them by means of electricity, and then put them back together at the other end.

This was 1921. Radio was still in its infancy. That's why this idea—the whole concept of television—was very, very new, although a lot of people were thinking about it. A lot of people were working on it. Radio itself was still in a fairly early state. In fact, it had only recently, mostly during World War I, progressed beyond basic communication—ship-to-shore kinds of traffic. Even the idea of the human voice over radio was still fairly new. Philo T. Farnsworth and his family did not, in fact, own a radio at the time. Yet he had this idea, as it was commonly known at the time, to send pictures by means of radio.

JUSTIN TOLMAN was a teacher at Rigby High School in Rigby, Idaho, and among the courses that he taught was senior chemistry. Young Philo T. Farnsworth, who had just moved to the area, was a freshman in high school but desperately wanted to take this senior chemistry course. Every day for a week, Farnsworth camped out and badgered Justin Tolman, "Please let me take the class."

Well, the school year was already halfway done. Tolman thought there was no way this kid, who was only a freshman, could possibly make up the work and keep up with the seniors. Farnsworth said, "Please, please, please." And finally, Tolman said, "I'll let you sit in, but just keep quiet. Just listen to what's going on."

Farnsworth didn't keep quiet. He was in the class and it was soon evident not only that Farnsworth knew more than any of the kids in the class, but Farnsworth was easily on a footing with Tolman himself. Tolman started coming in after school and before class to make sure that Farnsworth was getting the extra education that he needed. And very soon, they moved well beyond the scope of any high school chemistry class.

One day, Tolman was walking down the hall and he heard Farnsworth's voice coming from a study hall. He expected to hear Farnsworth helping his fellow students with their chemistry assignment. Instead, he was expounding on Einstein's theory of relativity, which was fairly new and certainly would not have been on the curriculum of the Rigby High School at that time.

What was miraculous about it, what Tolman so responded to, was that Farnsworth's fellow students were hanging on every word. There was something about this kid, when he started talking about his ideas, people listened. He just caught fire, and he managed to convey the ideas in a thrilling, dynamic, and compelling way.

From the moment that Farnsworth had the idea of electronic television transmission, he was desperate not only to put himself in a position where he would be able to work on the idea—in other words, get together lab equipment and lab facilities—but he was also conscious of the fact that he was just a fourteen-year-old kid. He needed an education.

So in addition to working with this Justin Tolman, the high school chemistry teacher, Farnsworth read everything he could get his hands on. Tolman recalled bringing in a book on cathode rays. Farnsworth just about wore it out before he gave it back to him. Then Farnsworth tried to get himself a college education, and unfortunately his father passed away during these years and Farnsworth was obliged to drop out of college and help to support his family.

He joined the navy and went to school at the Naval Academy in Annapolis, hoping to further his education and, at the same time, lessen some of the financial burden on his family. It didn't work out. It was never a good fit, and among the reasons that Farnsworth just did not feel comfortable in the navy was he came to believe that whatever ideas he had and developed at the time were going to belong to the government. There were other reasons besides, but he very soon got a discharge and was on his way back to Utah. That was 1926.

He married "Pem" Gardner, who at one time was literally the girl next door. Farnsworth had been working whatever odd jobs he could find. At one point, he was sweeping streets in Salt Lake City. [One day] a pair of professional fund-raisers came through. They were raising money for a Community Chest fund-raising campaign in Salt Lake, and they were hiring local kids to help them map out a business survey so they would know how to best coordinate their efforts. One of the people who signed on was Farnsworth and his friend Cliff Gardner. They started to work for these two men. . . . Cliff Gardner was Pem Gardner's brother, and for a time the two families shared a duplex house. They were neighbors.

One night after work at the Community Chest campaign, a man, George Everson, who was one of the two fund-raisers, said to Farnsworth, "You're a very bright young man. Why aren't you in college?" Farnsworth explained that he'd had to drop out but he said he had this great idea. It was a very interesting invention. Almost immediately he regretted that he'd said as much as that because Farnsworth was very, very protective of this idea of television and lived in horror of the day when he was going to pick up a magazine and see that somebody else had the same idea, that somebody else had been able to patent it before him.

Everson got interested in this. A couple nights later, he took Farnsworth out and asked to hear more about the idea, and as was always the case, when Farnsworth started talking about the idea, he suddenly became this brilliant orator and managed to persuade Everson and his partner, Leslie Gorrell, that he had the idea that was going to take the world by storm.

Everson said to him: "Well, I have $6,000 in a special savings account and I've been saving it for something like this. I've been meaning to take a wild flyer on something and this is as wild an idea as I can possibly imagine. I'm going to stake you to the $6,000. If we lose the money, I won't squawk."

Everson lost the money. They spent that much money and much more before any money started coming in, but he never squawked, and that's how Farnsworth got his start. [Farnsworth went to work] almost from the moment that Everson said, "Here let's go, let's start working on this idea of yours."

So they moved first to Hollywood, and then when the money ran out in Hollywood, Everson managed to get them backing by a group of San Francisco bankers and they set up shop in a tiny little lab on Green Street in San Francisco.

Farnsworth was barely in his twenties. When he first signed one of his early agreements with Everson and some of the backers, he wasn't even legally entitled to sign his own contract. Everson had to be appointed Farnsworth's guardian and sign the contract on his behalf. By the time they got to Green Street in San Francisco, where the really important early work on television was done, Farnsworth was barely twenty-one.

[Farnsworth worked on] Green Street in San Francisco from about 1926 to the early 1930s. Then he signed an agreement with Philco, a company that a lot of people assume was named for him but actually was the Philadelphia Storage Battery Company. He was there for a few years in Philadelphia. That didn't work out. Farnsworth went out on his own for a few years and ended up in Fort Wayne.

Capehart was a company in Fort Wayne, very, very big in the manufacture of radios. Much later in the story, Farnsworth and his backers managed to get the money together to buy the facility. They were going to follow the RCA model and manufacture radios—sell radios to generate income that they would use to pour into television research and production. So the Farnsworth company bought Capehart. They moved their base of operations to Fort Wayne, and things appeared to be going very well. It looked as if this was going to work.

DAVID SARNOFF, who began in the mailroom and worked his way up to become the chairman of RCA, the Radio Corporation of America, [was] a man who was also deeply interested in the future of television.

Sarnoff is a fascinating figure, and because Farnsworth and Sarnoff crossed swords over the issue of television and had a long and protracted legal battle, it's very tempting to cast him as the villain of the piece. It's really not that simple. Sarnoff, in many ways, is the archetype of the American immigrant success story. He came to America from Russia at the age of nine in 1900. He did not speak English. He sold Yiddish-language newspapers while teaching himself English. And he got a job in the mailroom of the company that became RCA, literally worked his way up to the top from there.

He was deeply interested in the development of radio, and in 1915, wrote something now legendary called the "Radio Music Box" memo, in which he speculated that it might be a good idea if we used this radio to bring music into American homes. This obviously turned out to be a pretty good idea. RCA did very well with it. But even as RCA began to make millions on radio, Sarnoff already had his eye on television, which was an extension that he considered to be inevitable.

The story that was told for years and burnished many times over was that young David Sarnoff, sitting at this wireless operating station [in John Wannamaker's department store in New York City], became the sole point of contact between the distressed ship *Titanic* and a waiting world, and for seventy-two hours he stayed at his telegraph cage with his earphones on, taking down the lists of survivors, getting information, relaying it to the press, and basically serving as the lone voice on behalf of the sinking ship.

It turned out subsequently that although yes, Sarnoff certainly would have had a hand in relaying the message traffic during the *Titanic* disaster, he was by no means the only voice heard that night or in the days to follow. But what was unique about Sarnoff was that he had the presence of mind and the skill and the wit to turn it to his own advantage and use it to further his own career.

It was 1930, and a reporter from the *New York Times* came and asked him and wanted to trot out the *Titanic* story again, and Sarnoff said, "Let's put that one to bed. The Horatio Alger stuff is out of date. Let's talk about the future."

RCA, the Radio Corporation of America, had been called into being, actually, by the United States government after World War I. They were very concerned about keeping control of some valuable radio patent technology that had been developed in wartime, particularly an alternator that was allowing the human voice to be sent further and more clearly than ever before.

Just after the war, a British firm placed a large order for these alternators, and the government was a little concerned. They had spent a lot of money protecting and developing this technology, and they were concerned about sending it overseas. The Radio Corporation of America was called into being to take charge of the government's electronic patents, and also at one time, those controlled by Westinghouse, AT&T, and General Electric. They all had a patent pool, a cross-licensing agreement, which allowed them to use the technology and protected it from foreign competition for a limited time. So at one time, Philo T. Farnsworth, the kid in the field in Idaho, was literally squaring off against the combined might of AT&T, General Electric, and

Westinghouse. The miracle of the situation is that he succeeded to the extent that he did.

[AT&T, General Electric, RCA, and Westinghouse] were competitors. They were all electronic firms. They were all doing research. At the beginning, RCA didn't do anything but administer these patents. That was Sarnoff's job. That was how Sarnoff became so deeply interested in patent technology or the control and use of these electronic breakthroughs. But they were all competitors, who, by means of this cross-licensing agreement, for a brief time had the right to use each other's scientific advancements without paying royalties on them. This was meant to foster greater development. In fact, it very rapidly became unworkable. And in short order, the government, which had called it into being in the first place, moved to break it up.

[By 1922, radio licenses] had multiplied many times over. Sarnoff's vision, as spelled out in the "Radio Music Box" memo almost a decade earlier, came to pass. Radio had made its way into the American home and was generating huge profits for companies like RCA, General Electric.

[At] the 1939 World's Fair, RCA in general and David Sarnoff in particular intended to raise the curtain on television. Now at that point, they were at the end of a long and protracted legal battle with Philo T. Farnsworth. That same year, 1939, an agreement was hammered out whereby RCA was going to have the right to use Farnsworth's patent technology.

What you have to understand about that is that in Sarnoff's fifty-year career at RCA, the company had never, ever paid to use a patent owned by an outside inventor. Sarnoff liked to say, "We don't pay royalties. We collect royalties." He had his own inventors. He had his own patents. Whatever patents he couldn't buy, he would find a way to get around.

RCA had a great big exhibition hall. Sarnoff himself took the stage. There were RCA microphones and a big banner, and he said: "Now we add radio sight to sound," and television supposedly was on the way.

The following week you could buy a television in a New York store at prices ranging from nearly $400 to $1,000. The price turned out to be way, way too steep for most people. . . . Sarnoff cut the prices. Nobody was buying them.

Then, the year was 1939. America entered World War II and television went into mothballs for the duration of the war. When television finally got off the ground in 1946, 1947, these important early patents of Farnsworth's were coming up for expiration. He never benefited to the extent that he should have. . . . When World War II came along, the Farnsworth television and radio company did a very distinguished job of wartime production, winning several government commendations for their work in aiding with the war effort. But then, when the war effort was finally over, they had a very hard time switching gears, getting back into peacetime production and following their original vision of radio and television production.

In the 1930s, Farnsworth was still in his early thirties, but he liked to say of one of his early companies that his small size enabled him to operate like a speedboat among their juggernauts. But, he added, a speedboat eventually runs out of gas, and unfortunately that is what happened, not only to Farnsworth's company but to Farnsworth himself.

He used himself too hard. He never took a break. He just couldn't shut it off. He prided himself that as a young man he could go to bed thinking about a problem and he would wake up in the middle of the night—"Eureka! I have the answer"—and he would go back to work. But that took a terrible toll very early on.

FARNSWORTH'S ONLY television appearance [was] on the game show "I've Got a Secret." He traveled to New York. He signed in as Dr. X, just in case someone recognized his name. . . . The panelists formed the idea that he was some kind of medical doctor and that he had done some sort of medical breakthrough, and at one point he was asked, "Dr. X, this device of yours, is it painful when used?" Farnsworth didn't skip a beat. He said, "Yes, sometimes it's most painful." The audience gave him a big laugh, but the panelists were unable to guess [what his invention was], which meant that Farnsworth won the top prize, which was $80 and a carton of cigarettes.

[FARNSWORTH WAS] born in 1906, died in 1971. Farnsworth is buried in Fort Wayne. . . . [Sarnoff was] born in 1891, also died in 1971. . . . He had only very recently given up the controls of RCA. He was too ill to carry on. He was largely confined to his home on the Upper West Side of Manhattan and passed away at home, having learned only a short time before that he had, in fact, been asked to give up his board position.

There are many who would disagree, but . . . Sarnoff and RCA were the first [to be in the television business]. . . . It's hard to put an exact figure on it, but there was a payment of about $1 million and an agreement to pay royalties to use Farnsworth technology in RCA television sets. It is difficult to say how much that would have amounted to, but since America entered World War II almost immediately thereafter, it didn't amount to anything, because Farnsworth's early patents had been nailed down in the early 1930s, and a patent of this type only had a useful life of seventeen years.

The patents were expiring very early on, but from the earliest days, the technology that went into the television camera tube, particularly, was a blending of Farnsworth's best work with the best work of Vladimir Zworykin, who was the man who was making it work at RCA.

EVERY COUNTRY in the world has someone that they throw up as the father of television, and all of them have some claim or had a hand in the development of television. In my own house, there has been a debate about who is the father of television. My two-year-old son and I were squarely behind Philo T. Farnsworth. My wife, who was born and raised in Scotland, will swear up and down that it was a man named John Logie Baird, who was a very important figure in the development of television. But what John Logie Baird and many others around the world were working on was a mechanical television technology. In other words, your television was going to have moving parts inside. It was going to have a spinning metal disk called the Nipkow disk. Light would shine through that disk and perform a scanning function.

It was Farnsworth's particular genius to realize at the age of fourteen that wasn't going to work. You had to do it electronically. He would sum it up in a single phrase later on. He said, "For television to work, it must have no moving parts."

For that reason, and also because he managed to nail down the early, crucial patents on what became the electronic television technology that developed into television as we know it today, for my money, the father of television is Philo T. Farnsworth.

The Tuxedo Park
Science Laboratory

by

JENNET CONANT

During World War II, the United States relied heavily upon a crucial new piece of technology: radar. Before the government established the famous MIT Radiation Laboratory, much of the research on this technology took place in the private laboratory of a wealthy New York financier and amateur physicist named Alfred Loomis. In her book Tuxedo Park: A Wall Street Tycoon and the Secret Palace of Science That Changed the Course of World War II, *published by Simon & Schuster in 2002, journalist Jennet Conant told the story of the unlikely sponsor of one of the most significant technological developments of the war. Ms. Conant appeared on* Booknotes *on June 9, 2002.*

ALFRED LEE LOOMIS was a tycoon who lived in Tuxedo Park in the 1920s and the 1930s. He made a fortune on Wall Street and he pursued his hobby, which was physics. He ended up playing a very large role in World War II.

ALFRED LEE LOOMIS's father separated from his mother and then died when Alfred was in college. Alfred felt the burden of having to support his mother and younger sister. Science had always been his first love, but he could not pursue it. In those days, science was certainly not a profession that someone with no money went into, and it was not a lucrative profession. It did not hold promise for any fortune. So he got his degree in law and joined the very proper New York firm of Stimson and Winthrop, which was Henry Stimson's very much white-glove law firm. He did very, very well very quickly. After

World War I, he went on to Wall Street. He could not abide going back into a slow Wall Street law firm.

In many ways, World War I was a pivotal moment in Alfred's life because he had gotten onto a very proper start in this white-glove law firm, and he was following very much in Henry Stimson's footsteps. He had been molded by Henry Stimson, and he was a very nice, proper corporate lawyer.

Then World War I came, and he enlisted. Because he had this incredible bent, this engineering, mechanical, inventing bent and had always played with mechanical devices and was very gifted, Henry Stimson saw to it that he was steered to the Aberdeen Proving Ground. He had an instinct that this young fellow would thrive there. In fact, Loomis did, and he proved himself such an excellent study in tanks and weapons and defense systems that he was very quickly made head of development and research at the Aberdeen Proving Ground.

He proved very gifted at advancing systems that were already there. He made several advances in a recoilless shooting cannon. At that point, Thomas Edison was a very old man and had all kinds of notions about explosives. It was Loomis's job to test many of Edison's wilder notions, some of which he said almost got them killed.

There was no proper means at that time of measuring the velocity of shells fired from guns, which meant, practically speaking, you didn't know how long it would take for them to hit the target. There were various systems for measuring that were very bulky and cumbersome, involving a lot of equipment, [but they were] very slow, and not practical in the field.

Loomis and another scientist came up with a device called the Loomis chronograph—later called the Aberdeen chronograph—which was a very sophisticated, advanced system for measuring the velocity of shells. That was his first proper invention, and he did later get a patent for that. That whetted his interest in science for life.

Loomis was out of Aberdeen in 1919, and his sister, . . . Julia Loomis, had married a very, very promising young banker named Landon Ketchum Thorne, and he was quite the salesman. By the time Loomis came out of World War I, Thorne was already known in the *Wall Street Journal* and the other newspapers as a real up-and-comer, a sharp-eyed deal maker, and he was considered to be one of the most promising young security salesmen on Wall Street.

He had his eye on a firm called Bonbright & Company, which was a very sleepy firm. Most of its big clients had lost their money and the firm had lost its way. Thorne and Loomis partnered up. He talked Loomis into quitting the law firm and joining in with him, even though Loomis was not a banker at that point.

They took over Bonbright in a bloodless coup and went right into public utility financing. Over the next ten years, they would become the absolute leaders in public utility financing on Wall Street. They would write over 15 percent of all the securities issues, billions of dollars in deals, and became phenomenally wealthy and powerful in a very, very short run in the booming 1920s.

At the height of their Wall Street fortunes in the 1930s, Loomis and Landon Thorne were living very large. They went through a period of—well, we're familiar with it from the 1980s, when tycoons start spending their money. They bought an America's Cup yacht, which they raced. Only Vanderbilts and Astors did that in those days.

The following year, 1931, they decided to buy Hilton Head Island, 20,000 acres plus, a huge tract of land. It was then a largely uninhabited island. There was no bridge. It was only reachable by boat. They bought it as a private hunting and fishing reserve, and they had it for nearly twenty years.

Loomis steered Bonbright to this tremendous success. He and Thorne had been underwriting most of the deals and were intimately acquainted with the market fluctuations as they made public offerings on these enormous super-power companies. Their last offering was United Corporation, an enormous superpower. It was done with J. P. Morgan. It was one of the biggest deals of its day, and it went for a huge price—much higher than they had thought it deserved. They felt at that point that the market was out of control. They very quietly began pulling out of the market and putting all their holdings in cash. When Black Thursday hit in 1929, they were sitting on a mountain of cash, and they proceeded to do very well in subsequent years along with other financiers—Bernie Baruch and a few others—who profited in the depression years when others really lost everything.

Loomis is estimated to have made about $50 million between 1929 and 1934. Once he had that fortune, he wanted to return to his old love. He had been doing science all along, first in a backyard laboratory and then a larger one in Tuxedo Park, and he quit Wall Street. He resigned from every board. In 1934, at the age of forty-seven, he became a physicist full-time.

TOWER HOUSE WAS the mansion that Loomis bought in Tuxedo Park. He actually bought it in 1926. It was about a mile from his family home, which was another stately mansion, where he lived with his wife and kids. Tower House was a crumbling old mansion, and he gutted it and turned it into a state-of-the-art deluxe laboratory. He put the most expensive equipment in the world in that laboratory. That was equipment that at the time universities could not afford.

He bought three Shortt clocks. They were very famous astronomical clocks, the most exact clocks in the world. In fact, Big Ben is a Shortt clock. They were fabulously expensive. Over the years, in the late 1920s and throughout the 1930s, while he worked on Wall Street during the day, he would go back to Tuxedo Park on weekends and do experiments in physics with this fabulous equipment in this private scientific playground that he had built for himself.

During this period, he would send first-class tickets and invitations to all of the most famous European scientists, the men he wanted to play with and study with. He met them on trips to Europe he had made with a very famous American physicist named Robert Wood, whom he had met at Aberdeen, and they had teamed up.

He was financing Wood's studies, and Wood was teaching him physics. Wood was a brilliant, eccentric figure; very colorful, very well known in Europe, very highly regarded. They would offer these invitations to Guglielmo Marconi, Albert Einstein. They would say, "Here's a first-class ticket. We'll pick you up in a Rolls. You will come to this fabulous mansion, and you will be hosted at a fabulous scientific conference with black-tie dinners every night and Averell Harriman will drop by for drinks. And then we will do physics during the day in this state-of-the-art laboratory."

The Europeans understood this concept because it was very common in Europe for famous scientists to have laboratories in mansions next to their manor houses. Charles Darwin had had one. A very famous British physicist named Lord Rayleigh had had one. Thomas Merton, another famous physicist, had an enormous laboratory built in a mansion right across the river from his estate. It was also very common in France. And they accepted his invitation, and one by one they came to Tuxedo Park throughout the 1930s—these are the depression years. American universities had no money, and they would be on a lecture tour. So they would accept this first-class steamer ticket. They would come to Tuxedo Park and give a talk. Forty or fifty famous scientists from around America would convene in Tuxedo Park. Then they would go on their lecture circuit, but they had been well financed already by Loomis.

Of course, Loomis gained quite a worldwide reputation in the decade or so that he did this. He knew everybody in the world of physics and biology and chemistry.

DURING THOSE YEARS, he was married to Ellen Farnsworth, his society wife. She was the prettiest debutante of her year in Boston. She was a classic product of her day in Boston, actually very similar to my own grandmother. These ladies were from very learned families. They were well off. Their brothers went to Harvard and they were schooled at home. They were educated in Greek and Latin. They read French and German and Italian. They knew opera. But they couldn't do anything. They couldn't boil water. They were utterly impractical creatures, and quite thwarted because they were very bright. This tended to produce singularly neurotic women, and Ellen Farnsworth was no exception.

She was really far better educated than most women of her day, but utterly unable to run a household. She couldn't function at all. She always had to have five Irish maids around her, to dress her, to bring her tea. She spent many, many afternoons prone, in her bedroom, taking various sorts of draughts to calm her nerves. She was quite a handful and a very old-fashioned woman, considering that she married a very energetic, forward-looking man, who would later become a scientist, so they were ill-suited.

This young couple, the Hobarts, had a house right near theirs, in Tuxedo Park. Loomis had pretty much taken Hobart on as the director of his laboratory. Hobart didn't need to work. He was very wealthy. It was a hobby for him, an occupation, and he was interested in science, as Loomis was. He ran the laboratory, and Ellen Farnsworth Loomis pretty much adopted Hobart's young wife, Manette, as a daughter, almost. So they would have dinner several times a week. They vacationed together. They took cruises together. They were very, very close.

Loomis ended up taking up with his protégé's very young wife—she was some twenty-five years his junior—in a very long, secret affair that began in the late 1930s and ran right through the war years. He built a separate house in Tuxedo Park called the Glass House. It was literally a glass house. It was an experiment in efficient heating and one of the first solar houses, and it had all glass walls, but it was very isolated. It became a meeting place for him and Manette.

Most people believe that Mrs. Loomis must have known. She hated the Glass House, and Alfred would not allow any of the household cleaning staff to enter the house. . . . In those days, of course, it wasn't that uncommon and you didn't say anything.

Loomis [eventually] married Manette. He shocked everybody by marrying Manette the same day of his divorce, in 1945. [He was fifty-seven; she was thirty-six.] It was considered very shocking. I interviewed a number of people that were younger members of Bonbright & Company and Wall Street firms that remembered the scandal surrounding the divorce and wedding. It was just not done. You did not divorce your sickly society wife. You certainly did not try to put her in a mental institution to get her out of the way, which is what Loomis at one point attempted to do with his wife when he was seeing Manette. It was also seen as stealing the wife of his very proper protégé, his best friend, and because they had been in his employ, there was some feeling that he had been marrying an employee. She had worked for Tower House as well, part-time, as the secretary during the war years, and that was just not done.

It was so scandalous at the time that many of his lifelong friends, Henry Stimson's peers, the heads of Winthrop, Stimson, Putnam & Roberts, at that point a very, very powerful law firm, literally snubbed him. People he had known his whole life wouldn't speak to him, turned their backs on him. He was really a social pariah for some years.

ERNEST LAWRENCE [of the Lawrence Livermore Laboratory] . . . was a Berkeley physicist. He happened to visit Tower House in 1936. He was just one of the many physicists who came for a conference there. He was already, in 1936, a formidable figure. In 1930, he had invented the cyclotron, the first atom smasher, and he achieved international acclaim by then.

Loomis and Lawrence took an immediate liking to each other. They literally became best friends over that weekend. By the end of the weekend, Loomis was completely on board in terms of wanting to back Lawrence's research. Lawrence was in constant need of money. He was eager to get on with building these machines, and he spent more than half of his time fundraising, traveling the country, trying to get corporate bigwigs and Rockefellers and people like that to give him money. He was scrounging for parts and supplies, and any kind of funding he could get to pay for the kind of physicists he wanted to have work for him at this giant research laboratory he was putting together at Berkeley.

WINSTON CHURCHILL [charged a group of British scientists] to go to America with all of Britain's top military secrets, and this very precious invention, the cavity magnetron, which held the future for very powerful new radar devices. [They were to] smuggle them across the ocean to America and see if they could convince the Americans, in exchange for all these military secrets and technology, to aid Britain by building [upon] these devices. Britain had done tremendous work, but they were under siege from Germany. They didn't have the men; they didn't have the materials; and they didn't have the money to develop these scientific ideas any further.

America was not in the war. We could not really publicly support them. But we could privately continue the research that they had started, and that is what Churchill was hoping for. It would later develop and flourish under something called the Lend-Lease Act. But this was basically a backdoor way of getting American support.

Loomis personally invited [the British scientists] to Tuxedo Park. They unveiled this cavity magnetron in Tuxedo Park. Loomis privately financed some early research in radar, and then Roosevelt gave them a very large grant. They started this private laboratory at MIT to build most of the radar systems that were put on virtually every airplane and submarine during the war.

During this time, Loomis developed the notion for something called Loran. Whether or not it was based on ideas that he may have gleaned from the British, nobody knows. . . . Anyway, he developed this notion for a long-range radar system, kind of a grid system, where you could track vessels at great distances. It became one of the most important navigational devices during the war and is still used today.

LOOMIS WAS REALLY one of the top scientific generals of World War II. He was appointed head of the radar division by Vannevar Bush in 1940 because he had been conducting secret radar research at his laboratory in 1939, at Bush's request, really. We were not at war yet, and the government couldn't do things overtly. There was no congressional funding for this research because America was not involved in what was then seen as a European conflict. So, much of this research was done by universities, and they were strapped for cash in the 1930s. Loomis was a private financier who was willing to bankroll research. Bush turned to him and said, "If you've got the time, the money, and the resources, would you do me a favor and look into something called microwave radar?" That's very high, powerful short-wave radar. "We think it is going to be quite important in the next war, and we ought to be looking into it."

HENRY STIMSON was Alfred Loomis's first cousin. . . . He became Alfred Loomis's surrogate father and was in charge of his money. He was in charge of making all the decisions on young Loomis's life, and he was a lifelong mentor. During the war years, when Stimson was actually secretary of war to Roosevelt, he was essentially Loomis's mentor, father figure, closest friend. It meant that [Loomis] had ready access to the White House and it was one reason he was so powerful during the war.

Henry Stimson was a lifelong Republican. He'd been secretary of state twice under two administrations, the second one being Herbert Hoover's. And he'd been secretary of war and he served in World War I. Stimson was seventy years old when he entered the White House under Roosevelt as secretary of war, so he was a revered figure. He was a very stern, stiff old Yankee. I don't think he ever could have won a popular election. In fact, he ran for governor of New York and lost resoundingly. But he was really a greatly admired and respected leader, and that is why Roosevelt went to the opposition to draft him as secretary of war. Roosevelt brought in a very famous war cabinet, which was largely Republican, many figures from Washington—McGeorge Bundy, Robert Patterson, many other figures. It was just a brilliant war cabinet, by all accounts, and they were largely Republican.

George Kistiakowsky, who was a famous Harvard chemist . . . came to Loomis with reports that he had heard from other European scientists about war work being done by the Germans, particularly in the area of building a bomb—uranium fission research. He reported this to Loomis, knowing that Loomis was phenomenally well connected not only in the scientific establishment but politically. He wanted that information passed to the top, and Loomis did, in fact, pass that information to Vannevar Bush, who passed it on to Roosevelt. It's part of the reason why uranium research moved as quickly as it did in this country—this nexus of scientists, many of them who had worked for Loomis at Tuxedo Park ten years earlier, in the 1930s, at this laboratory.

Vannevar Bush was a very famous engineer at MIT and just a brilliant scientist in his day. He had invented one of the early computer systems. He was a mathematical genius. He was tapped by Roosevelt to basically head up the civilian-based war effort, a scientific war effort. It was a preparedness effort that he spearheaded before America was actually in the war.

At that point, everybody in government knew it was probably inevitable that we would have to fight, but politically it was not palatable. So Roosevelt could not really yet talk to the American public about entering the war, but we knew we had to start becoming prepared. Our military was way behind—our army, our navy, our radar. We were not in the fight, and we were woefully behind.

Loomis undertook a privately financed study of microwave radar at Tuxedo Park. A year later, in 1940, when the Office of Scientific Research and Development was founded by Franklin D. Roosevelt and Bush was put in charge, Bush immediately tapped a number of men to be his scientific generals. My grandfather, James B. Conant, was his deputy, essentially his number two.

I HAD A GREAT-UNCLE who was a chemist, [William Richards], who worked for Loomis in his laboratory for about fifteen years. He ended up writing a novel about his experience there that was called *Brain Waves and Death*; it was based on the brain-wave experiments that Loomis was doing at the time. *Brain Waves and Death* was published in January of 1940, just as a lot of experiments and war research was being done in this country and abroad.

Richards, who wrote the novel, committed suicide in 1940. His brother also committed suicide, and it was a rather famous event in my family's life that these two very brilliant brothers would commit suicide. Their father had been a Nobel Prize–winning chemist at Harvard and chairman of the department. And my grandfather [James B. Conant] had married the Nobel Prize–winner's daughter and was a chemistry professor and then went on to become president of Harvard University.

Bill Richards's suicide, which corresponded with the publication of his novel, was a terrible event in my grandparents' life because my grandmother was devastated. It was a tragedy. The circumstances surrounding his death were very mysterious. He'd been working for Loomis for fifteen years. And this novel, which was a roman à clef—it was very thinly veiled and somewhat scandalous about Loomis's personal life—detailed all the eccentric professors and experiments that had gone on in this private laboratory. My grandfather, I think, took steps to see that the novel was never published. It was too late, and the novel was published, but it was very hushed up.

This, over the years, gained great lore in my family's life. Every time somebody died and we were at Mount Auburn Cemetery, my father would take us to the grave and say, "That one committed suicide this way, and that one committed suicide that way." As a small child, I was always fascinated by these gruesome events. My grandparents never spoke of them, and you were not allowed to mention them in their presence. I never lost my fascination for that period.

LOOMIS WORKED with a number of brilliant scientists and administrators and lawyers putting together this giant laboratory and running it, all during the war. It was a massive operation—2,000 people at its height. Millions and millions of dollars in congressional funding, and they issued hundreds of thousands of contracts. The number of commercial devices that came out of that laboratory [is amazing.] These were contracts that they were writing by the hour, by the month, and they needed very sophisticated lawyers and businessmen to run it.

One of the lawyers that he hired was a San Francisco attorney named Rowan Gaither who became Ernest Lawrence's closest friend as well. Gaither founded the Rand Corporation and asked Loomis to help be a founding member of it. He and Gaither laid the groundwork for what became the Rand Corporation.

HIS WAS A very close family, and during the war years, Alfred Loomis's son, young Henry Loomis, worked for his father in Tuxedo Park, doing the secret radar work. You have to understand that radar was a brand-new concept; microwave radar wasn't known by anybody. It had to be mobilized very, very quickly. Henry had been on a naval ship in Pearl Harbor, and he was there in Hawaii [when the Japanese attack took place]. They quickly sent him to a radar station in Hawaii, where he began training far more senior officers in microwave radar, which they put up very quickly in Hawaii after Pearl Harbor to bolster their defenses. He rose quite quickly in rank for a very young man.

Henry Loomis was named after Henry Stimson, his godfather. They saw each other quite often. Henry Loomis had been in Kyoto and had studied Japanese art and was a great fan of the ancient civilization. He had been going on and on about this to Henry Stimson. Shortly after, Henry Stimson attended a meeting with General Leslie Groves, Conant, and Robert Oppenheimer, to discuss where the sites for the first bomb would be. One of the original sites had always been Kyoto. Henry Stimson piped up that this would not be a good idea, quoting young Henry Loomis, about the wonderful temples and artwork there, and the site was moved to Hiroshima.

[My grandfather, James Conant, former president of Harvard for twenty-three years was involved in the Manhattan Project and] wanted to drop the bomb. "Wanted to" is a difficult term, but at that moment the prevailing wisdom was that we were war-weary as a nation. The feeling then was that you had to do something to shock the Japanese into backing down.

After the war, my grandfather was among the scientists who became very remorseful and with some of the Los Alamos scientists, he founded the Society for the Prevention of Nuclear Proliferation.

Loomis and Lawrence went the other way. They never suffered any remorse about their role in the development of the bomb, and they proceeded to push for the development of the H-bomb, which my grandfather was adamantly opposed to. So they split very much in the 1950s.

Loomis shuttered Tuxedo Park in 1940, when he went off to start the MIT Radiation Laboratory, and he never really properly returned. And then he sold it in the late 1940s. He died in 1975. He had a stroke and dropped dead, literally on the spot. They found him on the floor.

THIS BOOK HAD endless pleasures [for me], because the character of Tuxedo Park, that community, was great fun, as a backdrop. It was a very cloistered, WASPy, gilded environment, the most unlikely place for somebody to start a secret physics laboratory where he would invite the brilliant scientists of Europe. Then, of course, all of the fleeing Jewish scientists came in, much to the horror of his neighbors, as they came to Tuxedo Park to visit Alfred Loomis.

A Road Trip with
Albert Einstein's Brain

---

by

MICHAEL PATERNITI

Only in America might two men take a 4,000-mile road trip carrying Albert Einstein's brain in a Tupperware container. Einstein, the German-born American scientist and father of the special theory of relativity, died on April 18, 1955. During his autopsy, pathologist Thomas Harvey stole Einstein's brain, storing it in his home for more than forty years. When journalist Michael Paterniti heard the story, he decided to find Harvey and the two ultimately set off on a cross-country journey to return the stolen organ to Einstein's granddaughter. Today, Einstein's brain is housed in the Princeton Medical Center, and Michael Paterniti has written a book about his experience, Driving Mr. Albert: A Road Trip Across America *with Einstein's Brain, published by Dial Press in 2000. A most unusual* Booknotes *interview about this tale occurred on September 24, 2000.*

[ALBERT EINSTEIN WAS] born in 1879 in Germany, grew up, was a decent student, not a floundering student the way some people have said. But he didn't speak, really, until he was three and then when he started speaking, spoke in fully formed sentences. As a baby, he had a big, oversized, sort of lopsided head that terrified his mother and grandmother. His grandmother, when she first saw him as a baby, yelled, "Too big. Much too big."

He grew into kind of a dreamy kid. He was really obsessed with his father and his uncle's factory. They made turbines, and he was really into electricity. So while all the other kids were playing, Einstein would really never go out and play. Only when he was forced to would he go out and act as umpire. He wouldn't really engage in competition. He was much more comfortable devouring these science textbooks that they had around the house.

At the age of ten, he went through this deep religious period where he embraced Judaism, would walk through the streets of the village singing songs to God. But at the age of twelve, he rejected religion as being impossible and full of fake stories because his science training had taught him that the Bible and what existed in the universe didn't corroborate each other.

HE WORKED IN the patent office in Switzerland where he penned, in 1905, five groundbreaking papers, the last being this special theory of relativity, $E = mc^2$.

Between 1905 and 1925, Einstein revolutionized science. He tore apart the temple that Newton had built. But after 1925, he really didn't have any more groundbreaking papers. If he'd left it at 1925, he would have probably left the same scientific legacy that he did. But in the years after 1925, he became a voice of moral authority. He became a known pacifist. . . . And during this time, too, he continued to work. He was in pursuit of a unified theory.

ALBERT EINSTEIN is the hero of this story, at least his brain is. I was the chauffeur on this cross-country trip that took place with Dr. Thomas Stoltz Harvey, the man who did the autopsy on Albert Einstein in April of 1955 and took Einstein's brain.

I'd heard the urban myth, maybe ten years ago now, during the Gulf War. A friend mentioned that Einstein's brain had been stolen from his head during the autopsy. It had been sliced up into about 240 pieces and disseminated around the world, but the mother lode of Einstein's brain was in a garage in Saskatchewan. I just couldn't believe it; I thought it sounded completely insane. But I kept telling the story over and over to people that I knew. I just kept passing the myth on and adding on to it.

Some years later, I was living in New Mexico and I mentioned this story to my landlord at the time, and he said, "Yeah. The guy with Einstein's brain lives next to William in Lawrence, Kansas." "William" turned out to be William Burroughs, the Beat writer, and his neighbor turned out to be Dr. Thomas Harvey, the man with Einstein's brain.

[My landlord] was good friends with William Burroughs. He'd actually lived with William for four years cooking for him. It was just a completely random occurrence.

I said, "You've got to be kidding me. I mean, you're putting me on, right?" And he said, "No. I'll get you his number." So I said, "Yeah, OK, get me his number. Whatever." I really didn't believe it. He did get me his number and I jotted it down on a little shred of paper and I pinned it to the wall in my office next to my phone and I just started dialing the number.

I dialed and dialed and dialed; I literally called that number for three months; no answer. I called at different hours of the day. I don't know why. It was just—the number was there and whenever there was a down moment, I would just dial it. When I finally was about to give up, I dialed it, promising myself that this would be one of the last times, and he picked up the phone.

I said, "Hello. Is this Dr. Thomas Harvey who has Einstein's brain?" And he said, "Yes, it is." I was flabbergasted.

"Would it be all right if I might come visit you sometime?" He said it would be fine; I was very surprised that he was so open. I asked him when might be a good time—I was talking to him in the winter—and he said, "July would be good." July was about seven months away, and I said, "All right. July's good. I'll come see you in July."

I was interested in this man who, for over four decades, had kept Einstein's brain and had virtually disappeared with it. He was fired or left his job—depending on whose story you believe—in 1955 from the Princeton Medical Center. In the intervening years, he took different jobs. He kept moving until he ended up in Lawrence. I just had these huge questions about this man and his booty, his relic, his raison d'être. It was the organizing principle of his life. It was the thing he most believed in.

I called him just prior to our supposed meeting time in July, and the line was disconnected. He had disappeared again. So I didn't see him at his apartment in Lawrence. I was lost again. I spent the next four or five months looking for him, and finally tracked him down. He'd moved back to—just outside of Princeton in Jersey.

When he disappeared in July, [what kept me interested] was the game. It was, "I have to find this man." Obviously, there was a reason why he disappeared again: Why has he vanished and what's it going to take to find him? I was just very caught up at that point in following through and meeting him.

DR. HARVEY HAD been married three times, and he had twelve children and stepchildren from those marriages.

I met him probably around November of 1996. We met in Princeton the first time. He lived just outside of Princeton, and I went to the house and he greeted me wearing a plaid shirt and a sport coat and suspenders and his tie had a little price tag from long ago that said $10 on it. He brought me into the house, his girlfriend's house.

Her name was Cleora. We went down into the basement where he had set up a little makeshift office. We sat by a fire that he'd built and we drank tea, and he just started telling the story of the brain.

I didn't know if the brain was there, and I didn't ask him right away. In one of our subsequent meetings, I asked to see the brain and later found out that it wasn't there, that he kept it in a safe house that was some miles away from that house because all sorts of people, perhaps even like me, had inquired over the years about the brain. I think he felt that it was a dangerous object and he needed to keep it hidden.

I was thirty-two at the time; Dr. Harvey was eighty-four. . . . We would go for meals. We drove by 112 Mercer Street, where Einstein used to live. We talked a lot. We spent a lot of time together. Dr. Harvey mentioned that he had to go back to Lawrence, Kansas, because he had been in a little fender bender before he left and he needed to go back to straighten out some insurance matters. But he also wanted to go out and meet some doctors to whom he'd sent pieces of the brain. He kept talking about wanting to get out into America to see some people. I was listening to him and I just finally said, "You know, I could drive you."

Initially my interest was very personal. At this point, I began to think, "I better take notes. I better keep a record because it may be something worth writing about." At that point, too, I had mentioned it to *Harper's* and they were interested. So I thought, "Well, let's see how it goes."

[WE DROVE A] Buick Skylark with teal-green velour seats. I rented it. He had two bags. He had a plaid bag in which he had clothes and he had a duffel bag, in which I would later find out were parts of the brain put in Tupperware and doused with formaldehyde.

I have never transported famous body parts cross-country . . . but these kinds of stories, these kinds of people, really interest me.

We traveled eleven days, 4,000 total miles . . . from Portland, Maine, until we got to Berkeley, California. I picked Dr. Harvey up in Princeton.

I thought the goal was to give the brain back to Evelyn Einstein, Albert Einstein's granddaughter. I thought Dr. Harvey was facing down some late-in-life guilt about having taken Einstein's brain at the autopsy. Apparently, when it was reported the day after the autopsy, in April of 1955, that Dr. Harvey had Einstein's brain, Hans Albert, Einstein's son, was quite upset. He had no idea that his father's brain was going to be taken. And in the years to follow, the family's anger grew. So I thought that Dr. Harvey felt that, at age eighty-four, it was time to give the brain back to the Einstein family and we were going to see Evelyn, who was one of the lone survivors.

She was adopted by Hans Albert. There were family rumors—and Evelyn herself isn't totally certain whether or not they're true—that she was the product of a relationship that Albert Einstein had with a dancer from New York City. Dr. Charles Boyd got a piece of the brain and tried to match it with Evelyn's skin; he tried to match the DNA. He was unable to do it because the brain was too denatured. So there is this huge question mark in Evelyn's mind about whether or not she is, in fact, the daughter. If you see her physically, she looks like an Einstein. She looks like Albert Einstein, especially in the eyes. It's just an uncanny resemblance.

To me, Dr. Harvey was just a complete enigma. . . . Yet as we rode, he remained the enigma that he was from that first phone call. He, even now, to me, is this hologram. Depending on how the light falls, he looks different. Some people think he's a hero. Some people think he's a thief.

He claims he had permission from the executor of the Einstein estate, Otto Nathan, who before his death in the 1990s, said that he never gave that permission. Though he was present at the autopsy, Nathan said he'd had no idea that Dr. Harvey was actually taking the brain out at the time.

The foreskin of Christ was supposedly kept in a church in Italy, but that was stolen. Walt Whitman's brain was dropped in a laboratory at the turn of the century and was thrown out. JFK's brain has gone missing. Thomas Hardy's heart was taken from his body and sent to his wife and was eaten by their dog. So there's a long, strange history of body parts turned into relics. Napoleon's penis was supposedly kept and was offered for auction in 1972. There was so much controversy that the owner took it back. So it's out there somewhere, we just don't know where.

It is as old as the saints. There's something mythological about, especially, the body parts of mythic human beings. They become relics. In the case of Buddha, if you travel through Southeast Asia, every temple you go to, the fingernail of Buddha is encased in tons of gold, and that somehow gives a holiness to these places.

When it comes to the brain craze that seemed to occupy doctors and medical researchers in the nineteenth and twentieth century, I think people were really searching for the keys to genius, so famous brains were collected and studied. Mussolini's brain was studied in America at Walter Reed by a man named Webb Haymaker, who later tried to get Einstein's brain from Dr. Harvey. There are, in these body parts—and especially in Einstein's brain, there is—this power, whether real or assumed, that has led to all kinds of people trying to get the brain. There is this deep desire to be connected to that kind of genius.

Roger Richmond in Los Angeles, who works with Hebrew University, the trustees of the Einstein estate, basically monitors the world for . . . anybody using the image of Einstein in an ad without permission, anybody using anything having to do with Einstein really without permission. Then he goes after them and chases them down with letters or pursues them in court. . . . Albert Einstein appears in ads all the time with Roger Richmond's blessing and that money goes to Hebrew University. Some portion of it goes to Roger Richmond so that he can run his business.

When I first called him, he thought that the brain was in the Smithsonian and he thought that Dr. Harvey was a crackpot who was just looking for attention by claiming that he had Einstein's brain. But as it turns out, Dr. Harvey was for real. The brain is for real. I think Roger Richmond feels that this is an incredible violation of Einstein the man and Einstein the legend.

I FIGURED THAT once we got in the car with the brain, there would be a lot of one-on-one brain time where Dr. Harvey would reveal the entire story to me and reveal the secrets of Einstein's genius to me, and that didn't happen. Dr. Harvey was not that interested in talking about the brain and not that interested in even acknowledging that it was in the trunk. So with each passing mile, my desire to see the brain, because I couldn't see it, grew greater and greater, until I was just crazy to see it.

There was a point in the road trip after New Mexico where I, out of sheer exhaustion and lack of sleep and contact with other human beings, began to say that we had the brain in the trunk. The reactions to that were some of what kept me going. . . . It was a really wild range of reactions, and it was interesting, because in a way, it reflected America back at me. The whole trip reflected America. There was this very easy assumption that some people made about Einstein—about who he was, about what he discovered without really knowing who he was. It seemed very American to me. We're very quick to know it all, without really knowing it, sometimes.

The first time I saw the brain was when we went to San Jose, and Dr. Harvey gave a little talk to a bunch of schoolkids, and he pulled out the Tupperware with the brain in it. Again, I didn't get close to it. I wasn't able to—after the talk, all the kids rushed the podium. . . . I didn't really get to see it until the very end of the trip when we went to see Evelyn Einstein outside Berkeley, California.

I called her a few times from the road. She was understandably filled with some trepidation about meeting us—Dr. Harvey, the brain, and me.

We get to Evelyn's apartment, which is quite a nice place, looking out over the bay. She had agreed to meet us, finally, because she felt that it was her responsibility to meet us and to accept the brain, if Dr. Harvey was going to give it to her. When we arrived, it was afternoon. She was wearing a Star Trek pin. She had, in her life, worked as a cult deprogrammer. At one point, she worked as a policewoman. She has lived a very full, interesting life.

I'm not sure they were getting along. They were very civil with each other. They talked for a little while about Einstein's life. Then finally, after a time, Dr. Harvey pulled out pieces of the brain and gave a very kind of quick lesson on the brain, delivering the same talk that he'd delivered in San Jose to the schoolkids. And Evelyn—who had all her letters from her grandfather stolen from her; a lot of her photographs she'd lost; who has tried throughout the years to recover something of her grandfather—became quite interested in the brain and really was eager to talk about it.

But after, maybe, ten minutes or so, Dr. Harvey decided that that was it. We had planned to go to dinner with Evelyn, but Dr. Harvey announced that he was instead going to visit an eighty-five-year-old cousin of his in San Mateo and he wanted me to drive him down. So after eleven days and 4,000 miles, I put my foot down and said, "We're here to see Evelyn and she's planned this dinner, and so I think we should stay for dinner and then I can drive you down after dinner. Or they could join us for dinner." But he was insistent. He wanted to go visit his cousin, and so we ended up driving him to public transportation, to a BART subway station, and he got out and we said our good-byes, and Evelyn and I went to dinner. We spent three hours eating, had salmon and sirloin, and had a great dinner and a really nice conversation.

We came back out to the car, assuming that Dr. Harvey had taken the brain. We sat down in the front seat, and then, in a pool of streetlight that was flooding in through the back window, resting on the back velour seat was the Tupperware with the brain in it. We saw it and I said to Evelyn, "How could that be? Is that what we think it is? . . . He guards this thing with his life." I actually got quite nervous. What if this had gotten stolen while we were in there? What if this gets stolen now? It's my responsibility.

So we drove back to her apartment and parked in front, and we opened the Tupperware. A security guard passed, looked in, and then kept moving past, and we stopped a minute and looked up and looked back down. Then I reached in and took a piece that was sealed in paraffin and looked at it and held it up to the light. Evelyn took one and held it up. They weighed what a light beach stone weighs. It was a very strange moment. It didn't seem at all like this was Einstein's brain. It seemed like some disconnected little jewel of paraffin.

DR. HARVEY HAS finally given up the brain.

It might have happened, in part, just after the *Harper's* article. I think he was getting some attention. I think he felt that he had done his job of safeguarding the brain. He knew that perhaps he was at the end of his run with the brain, . . . nearing the end of his own life, and he wanted to make sure it was in the hands of somebody who could take it into the next century. One of the purposes of keeping the brain is that someday there might be technology that will help us understand why Einstein was a genius. It could be that they will clone the brain at some point. So Dr. Harvey, if nothing else, kept the brain and kept it intact. It didn't get dropped on a lab floor and thrown out. It hasn't disappeared. And he turned it over to the man who now sits in his old office at Princeton Medical Center. So the brain has come full circle.

Martin Frankel's Financial Scams

by

ELLEN JOAN POLLOCK

Martin Frankel achieved notoriety as one of the most successful con men of the twentieth century. Born in Toledo, Ohio, Frankel exchanged his failed career as a stockbroker for an elaborate insurance fraud. By the time of his arrest in 1999, Frankel had accumulated over $200 million by laundering money through a fictional investment firm and Catholic charity. On May 16, 2003, Frankel pleaded guilty to twenty-four federal corruption charges. Wall Street Journal *senior reporter Ellen Joan Pollock appeared on* Booknotes *on April 14, 2002, to discuss her biography* The Pretender: How Martin Frankel Fooled the Financial World and Led the Feds on One of the Most Publicized Manhunts in History, *which was published by The Free Press in 2002.*

WHEN MARTIN FRANKEL fled the U.S. in 1999, it attracted a huge amount of attention. Nobody knew who this guy was until he fled, and it quickly became apparent that he had stolen gobs of money. Nobody knew really how much. The real amount is probably about $215 million, but at the time he fled, it looked like it might have been a billion dollars. He had apparently stolen it from a bunch of Southern insurance companies that specialized in selling burial insurance.

The remnants of stuff they found in his mansion, which caught fire shortly after he left, was just fascinating. It looked like he'd involved the Vatican. It looked like he was interested in astrology. It looked like a harem had lived there. It just caught everybody's interest because the scheme had clearly gone on for the better part of a decade, and it was an incredibly wild story. As I worked on it, it became too enticing to give up. It had everything. It had money. It had sex. It had the Vatican. It had some interesting names. And it said a lot about business and human frailty, not to mention greed—human frailty was the big thing that attracted me to the story.

IT STARTED IN the late 1980s, Marty Frankel got a job as a broker for a small brokerage firm run by a guy named John Schulte. And immediately, he ran into problems for two reasons: One was that he could not bring himself to trade, which is really one of the most comical aspects of this; here's this guy who by all accounts really did know a lot about the financial markets, but he couldn't get himself, as he would say, to "pull the trigger." He would identify a stock he wanted to buy, and then he just couldn't do it. He was just paralyzed. And all his short life, he equated this to his test anxiety. And in fact, it is very similar. So he really wasn't doing much at the brokerage firm. And then he had another problem, which is he fell in love with the boss's wife, Sonia Schulte.

John Schulte is a very unusual person. He's sort of maniacal. He is a man who holds a grudge, and when Marty Frankel ran away with his wife, that account [could] never be paid.

That happened in 1986, really quite some time ago. And the man is still angry to this day. He is really, really mad. And in the next few years, there was sort of a battle over who was going to rat out who first. Was Frankel going to get the Securities and Exchange Commission to come after John Schulte, or was John Schulte going to get the SEC to go after Frankel? And Frankel and Sonia, the wife, won.

Sonia was charged with racketeering and securities fraud. She's been accused of helping Frankel all along the way. One of the things she did was create false account statements. Frankel was supposedly trading the assets of these insurance companies he owned through fraudulent means, and he would send [his customers] account statements every month or so, and they were all frauds because he couldn't trade anything. Sonia was accused of creating those statements.

FRANKEL CREATED a trust, which he called the Thunor Trust, after the Scandinavian god Thunor, which is the same, I guess, as Thor. He lied about who put up the money to buy the trust. He said Sonia put up $900,000. At the time, Sonia was making $25,000 a year. He lied and said that a broker who worked for him briefly—who was a kid—had put up a lot of money and that a friend of his brother's had put up a lot of money.

There was money in the trust, and he got that money from investors in his second fund, which was called Creative Partners. He set up sort of a mutual fund. He got people to invest in it, and then he just took the money and he bought this small insurance company in Franklin, Tennessee, setting up this fake trust. Then he took the assets of the insurance companies, paid back the insurers—the investors in Creative Partners—and said he was closing down the fund. So he had a lot of very happy investors in Toledo because they were paid back. But they didn't know that they were paid back with money stolen from a little insurance company in Franklin, Tennessee. It was . . . six or seven [insurance companies that he owned].

[He never made any legitimate money.] He did one trade early on, and he made $18,000. Over time, he made a few other trades, but they were not significant trades. . . . He stole $215 million. That's pretty clear. Stole.

Everybody right now is so wrapped up in [the Enron accounting scandal,] and people are trying to understand accounting, and they are trying to understand these partnerships. [Frankel's scam] was much simpler. He bought these insurance companies—using a fraudulent trust, but he bought them—and he promised the executives of the insurance companies that he was going to invest the assets.

FATHER PETER JACOBS is a priest who's been in and out of trouble with the church for most of his career. Father Jacobs spent most of his career in New York City. He worked in Harlem at a boys' school. He spent a lot of time working with junkies and whores, worked very hard by day. And by night, Father Jacobs partied. He was involved with the glitterati, you know, the literary glittery crowd in New York. At one point he owned a restaurant that was frequented by celebrities. He's friends with Norman Mailer. He's friends with Bianca Jagger.

At one point, Frankel, in an effort to cover over what he was doing, tried to create a charity. Father Jacobs had retired to Rome, dividing his time between New York and Rome. He had many Vatican ties, and he offered to help Frankel make connections with the Vatican and, in fact, did. A lawyer named Tom Bolan, who is a former law partner of Roy Cohn and is a deeply religious man, on Marty Frankel's behest, went and negotiated with the Vatican. He tried to get the Vatican to back this fake charity [called the St. Francis of Assisi Foundation]. Bolan did not realize it was a fake charity, and he met with very senior people at the Vatican. He had a series of meetings with people at the Vatican who were extremely interested in doing business with Martin Frankel.

The one thing they balked at—not immediately, but pretty quickly—was they did not want to be in the insurance business. And so Frankel, frustrated, basically lied. He got another Catholic foundation called the Monitor Ecclesiasticus Foundation, which had a Vatican bank account and did have ties to the Vatican, to agree to be involved with St. Francis. And in fact, the head of that foundation, Monsignor Emilio Colagiovanni, signed several fake affidavits, one of which said that the Holy See was providing funds for St. Francis.

I believe firmly that the monsignor knew that that wasn't true. One of the affidavits said that the Monitor Ecclesiasticus had given a billion dollars to St. Francis, and Monitor Ecclesiasticus is a very small foundation which puts out a journal of canon law. He must have known that wasn't correct.

The monsignor has at various times said different things about these affidavits. Once he said his named was forged. But most of the time, he agreed he had signed it. He was arrested . . . . He's based in Rome but was visiting his elderly sister in Cleveland and was picked up by U.S. law enforcement officials.

FRANKEL SAID HE was going to acquire a bunch more insurance companies, and he hired Robert Strauss's law firm, Akin Gump, to represent him. [Robert Strauss is the former chairman of the Democratic Party and was ambassador to Russia.] He met with Mr. Strauss and Mr. Strauss set it up so that Akin Gump would represent Mr. Frankel's interest.

Mr. Strauss and Mr. Frankel met in May of 1998. It was Memorial Day weekend. They met in Mr. Frankel's apartment at the Watergate, and very soon after, within days, the arrangement was set up. They continued to represent Mr. Frankel through the end of the year, maybe a little bit into 1999.

First, Frankel bought the insurance companies through this trust. Then his idea was that he was going to buy them through the charity, St. Francis and, basically, it failed. He wanted to buy a lot more insurance companies. He wanted to be . . . a billion-dollar company. And he enlisted the help of Akin Gump and got in many doors. People would hear that Bob Strauss and Akin Gump represented these entities [and] the doors swung open.

Akin Gump did not find out that there was anything wrong until Frankel fled. Akin Gump was most active for Frankel's entities in late 1998, but they hadn't resigned the account or anything. When Frankel disappeared in May, Akin Gump was pretty worried about where he'd gone to and was trying to figure out where he'd gone because they were still, to some degree, involved.

ONE OF THE scary things about this story . . . is how many times people tried [unsuccessfully] to blow the whistle on Marty Frankel. Among the first people to do it was his nemesis, John Schulte, who went to the SEC. One of the things John Schulte did was hire a private investigator to go through Frankel's garbage, and he would keep feeding what he was finding to regulators.

Early on, two investors sued Frankel, and their lawyers—a law firm in Toledo called Shumaker, Loop, and Kendrick—took on the case of these investors, even though it wasn't a big moneymaker for them, because they were so outraged. They wrote to the SEC and said, "We know you're investigating him." This is early on, in 1992. "But he's at it again. You have to stop him." Nothing happened.

And then, there was this investigator in Greenwich, years later, where Frankel's neighbors didn't like him. There were cars in and out. There were guards. They were worried about guns. They were worried about drugs, probably unnecessarily. Their kids were in the neighborhood. They were worried that their kids were going to have problems. They hired a private investigator, a former FBI guy. And within twenty-nine hours, he had figured out Frankel's real name, that he'd been banned from the securities industry, that he was probably violating the ban, and that he was breaking the law. He went to the SEC. He went to the U.S. Attorney's Office. And although there's some signs that an investigation was started, nothing really came to fruition.

NEAR THE END, there were two sets of regulators who became suspicious. One unsung hero of this is a guy named Billy Lovelady, who was the Tennessee auditor, who wrote a memo to his bosses saying that he worried that the assets of these insurance companies were being looted. He used the word "looted." He actually figured the whole thing out, and he wrote a memo to his bosses, the insurance commissioner, and other people in the department. It fell into a deep bureaucratic hole. Nothing happened.

[Lovelady figured it out by] looking at the books. Then he realized that the assets were being managed by something called Liberty National Securities, which was Frankel's brokerage firm. He went to public records and thought that Liberty National Securities was a tiny, tiny entity with a capitalization of something like $59,000 and realized: How can this tiny firm be trading these hundreds of millions of dollars in assets? It just didn't seem right to him.

FRANKEL WAS CAUGHT in Germany. It was 1999, four months after he'd fled the U.S. He was in Hamburg. It was Labor Day weekend, or right around that point, and he was kept in a prison there. They didn't quite know what to do with him in Germany. They weren't used to picking up, at that point, internationally known criminals. He was in a prison with a bunch of drug addicts and smugglers, low-level criminals, and he didn't look so good when he came out for hearings.

He fought very hard to stay in Germany. To anyone who would listen, he would talk about how in Germany, he would get a short sentence for the crimes he committed. In the U.S., he was going to be put away for life. That was tantamount to capital punishment. It was an affront to human dignity. He tried to make this huge argument that it was almost immoral for him to be extradited to the United States.

About six or seven people have pleaded guilty, at this point, some [to] serious crimes—lying to the FBI over cars and stuff like that. But Frankel's bodyguard, David Rosse, was just sentenced to ten years in jail for racketeering and money-laundering–related crime.

Frankel has been charged with a bunch of things, including racketeering, racketeering conspiracy, securities fraud, wire fraud. Initially, he was accused of money laundering, which is a lot of what he did. But because he wasn't extradited on those charges, he's not going to be prosecuted on those charges.

I'm assuming that if Frankel is convicted . . . he could spend most of the rest of his life in jail. [As we speak] Frankel is in prison in Rhode Island, awaiting trial.

Sandy Weill and
the Rise of Citicorp

by

MONICA LANGLEY

Sandford Weill worked his way up from being a runner on Wall Street to forging the $83 billion deal that created Citicorp, an uprecedented conglomerate of banks, brokerages, and insurance companies. The year 2002 was the best and worst for Sandy Weill—he was named CEO of the year but was embroiled in the unfolding corporate accountability scandal when Citigroup's telecom analyst, Jack Grubman, admitted to changing his ratings on AT&T. Monica Langley covers Sandy Weill and Citicorp for the Wall Street Journal. *She appeared on* Booknotes *on May 11, 2003, to discuss* Tearing Down the Walls: How Sandy Weill Fought His Way to the Top of the Financial World and Then Nearly Lost It All, *published by The Free Press in 2002.*

Sandy Weill's a larger-than-life figure. He started from nowhere, and today he's the most important financial CEO in the world. President Bush calls him to ask what he sees in the economy. Robert Rubin, the former treasury secretary, works for him. But at the beginning, he was the person least likely to succeed, which is what's so fascinating. You still see that insecurity and worry and fear and [his need for] loving accolades even today, now that he's a billionaire.

He's Jewish and grew up in Bensonhurst. It's really interesting to look back in the 1950s. Wall Street was a very WASPy place, although there were some Jewish firms, like Goldman Sachs and others, but believe it or not, those firms tended to look down upon Eastern European Jews and were more German Jewish. Sandy is the son of Polish immigrants, and so he was the wrong kind of Jew. But his whole life has been a lot of class struggle, not just Jewish, but having no connections, no polish. . . .

Sandy was never able to walk in the front door. Wall Street wouldn't let him in to schmooze with the brokers, and he had no contacts. So he had to go in the back door and work in the back office. He started as a runner at Bear Stearns in the 1950s, even though he had a college degree. And he learned the back office. Then when he got control of a little firm, a two-office firm that he started with three others—[former SEC chairman] Arthur Levitt being one of them—he knew he needed to set up a back office, and he brought in Frank Zarb. They always joked that they were nobodies and they ended up doing very well financially.

GERALD FORD WAS his first trophy director. When Sandy made his first empire, called Shearson, he got Gerald Ford, after he was out of the presidency, to be a director. They have become friends for twenty years, and Gerald Ford has become rich by holding the stock in Sandy's companies. He's very appreciative of Sandy for that.

There's a great story between Jim Robinson and Sandy Weill. Jim Robinson is a patrician, chairman of American Express. He brought in Sandy when he bought Shearson, and they were the exact opposites, and they could not get along. Ultimately, Jim Robinson won out over Sandy Weill over who would control American Express, and it was Sandy's most public defeat in his career. But today they're friendly. [One of Weill's mottoes is] "Don't burn bridges."

He used class struggle to his advantage all the time. If it weren't Jew versus WASP—not that he was doing it overtly—it would be things like the rich versus poor or entrepreneur versus establishment. He felt very entrepreneurial going into American Express, and they were very establishment. . . . A lot of these things he uses to his advantage, and they've been powerful motivators to him.

I CALLED [his wife] Joan the most important merger of his career, and that is pretty significant because he has probably done hundreds of mergers, big and small. She was the one who believed in him when no one would. Her parents didn't want her to marry him when they met in their early twenties. They married early in life, and she has stuck with him. She is the ultimate corporate wife. We've seen a lot of them over years, and she truly is. She has stayed with him through thick and thin and bucks him up when he is really down. She also gives him, I found out, a lot of savvy advice, particularly about people he should trust or not trust. So executives tell me she is very much a power behind the scenes.

Sandy can be a really tough guy that you don't want to cross, and then he has so much emotion. When he sold Shearson and he announced that to his company that he had built from nothing, he broke down and cried. There are a few times in the book where he does break down and cry.

[There's a string of] people that he expected loyalty from that he fired over the years. . . . I think that Sandy uses that to his advantage because he wants them to feel on their toes and feel like they have got to perform for him. He pushes people in the most dramatic fashion. I was calling people in reporting this book, and they were in their offices at five o'clock in the morning. These are people that are multimillionaires running huge empires within Citigroup. And he uses that to advantage to make them want to perform the best they possibly can.

There is a thing about Sandy. Even though he can be a big bully and can be vicious, he also can be charming and have a really sweet side to him, believe it or not. As a writer working on this book, I felt both sides of his personality myself.

SANDY WEILL HAS spent his entire life in the financial industry tearing down walls. He started on Wall Street. It was run like a club more than a business, and he had to break down barriers to even get onto Wall Street. When he made his biggest acquisition of Citicorp and created Citigroup, the world's largest financial empire, he tore down the Glass-Steagall Act and all the banking laws, in effect, to put together this monster.

John Reed was the chairman and CEO of Citicorp [in 1998]. He was a legendary banker. All the ATMs you see on every street corner are because of John Reed. He had the technological vision to do that. He put Citicorp into 100 countries. So Sandy, when he proposed that Travelers, his insurance and securities empire, merge with Citicorp, was getting the benefit of a great institution that had been around a long time. It had had trouble, but before John Reed, [when] it was Walter Wriston [at the helm]. It was a legendary bank.

Back in the days when Sandy was trying to break in on Wall Street he would see the Citibank building, which has legends of finance around it. And they were shutting the doors on Sandy Weill. So Citicorp was very important to Sandy. It was what he called "the mother of all deals." If he could ever do that, then he would have succeeded. John Reed was his way to get Citicorp. He got John Reed to agree. But then in a boardroom showdown, he got rid of him.

This was in the spring of 2000. [It took Sandy] two years. At first, they had a great honeymoon. It was a very quick courtship. They were co-chairmen and co-CEOs. Sandy proposed that. He said, "Let's do this together. We'll share power." When they took the deal to their boards, the Citicorp board and the Travelers board, the boards said, "Oh, my God. Are you kidding? You both have huge egos. You both are used to running your own shows. This will never work." John Reed and Sandy Weill told them, "Yes, it will. We've known each other for thirty years. We'll make it work."

So they did this deal. At the time, it was the biggest merger ever, $83 billion. They did it in six weeks, negotiated only by them and a couple close aides. They didn't want to involve anyone else because they didn't want it to leak out. There would be a lot of potential opposition to this deal because they were breaking down barriers in financial services.

At the beginning, they were very lovey-dovey. "Oh, Sandy, you're so good at operations," Reed would say, "What do you say?" And then Sandy would say to Reed, "Oh, you're so good at strategy. What do you think?" But when it got down to the nitty-gritty of running this company day in and day out, they were so different, they couldn't coexist. It became a struggle.

Sandy just put his nose to the grindstone and got all his people in the most powerful operational positions. John Reed was getting tired of running things, worrying about the bottom line, worrying about the stock price. John Reed thought that they would put this deal together and then leave as soon as the deal was solid, as soon as the merger had happened and it was working well. John Reed understood that they would leave together. Sandy apparently never told him, "Oh, no. That's wrong." But he never told him, "Oh, yes. That's right."

There was one scene on the night before the deal was to be announced in New York, when Sandy's loyal general counsel noticed some language in a filing that said, "And then when the deal is done, they will leave together." He called John Reed's lawyer the night before the deal was to be announced and said, "Wait a minute. This isn't the deal." John Reed's lawyer said, "It is the deal, and that's what John tells me." Sandy's person said, "You may think they're going to ride into the sunset together, but Sandy hasn't told me that." And at that point, it would stop the whole deal, and they said, "Well, it's not really imperative that it be in this SEC filing, so we'll take it out."

That was the beginning, when John Reed should have been aware that Sandy really never intended to leave so quickly. This is Sandy's life. He loves his work.

John Reed . . . lost a bruising battle to Sandy. There was a boardroom showdown in 2000, and he lost. . . .

[HIRING FORMER treasury secretary Robert Rubin,] that was a major coup. Everybody wanted Bob Rubin when he came out of the Clinton administration. And Sandy was Sandy. He can be a salesman, from when he was selling little stocks as a young man on Wall Street, to today. He wooed Rubin, calling him every day, meeting with him every day for thirty days, and finally got Rubin to join on.

Bob Rubin, who came out of the secretary of the treasury job here in Washington, got a $33 million-a-year package to work for Sandy and not have any line responsibility.

Citigroup has a trillion dollars in assets. It's a market capitalization of nearly $200 billion. It is one of the top five largest U.S. companies and the biggest financial conglomerate in the world. It's based in New York City, on Park

Avenue, but it is in 100 countries. Sandy wants to make it what a McDonald's or a Coke is all over the world, so that it stands for financial services.

Citigroup owns a lot, apart from Citibank, which is not everywhere, but you see it on every street corner in New York City. Also, it did own Travelers, and recently divested Travelers, which was a big insurance company. It also owns Citi Cards. Did you know that 20 percent of all credit cards are from Citibank in this country? . . . It owns CitiFinancial, which makes consumer loans. They've obviously named everything "Citi" these days. And then they have something called PFS, which are independent insurance agents that sell to the middle class.

SANDY WEILL loves his planes! He uses his helicopter whenever it's convenient. If he wants to bop down to Washington, he'll take the helicopter. When he was at Travelers, and then he would want to go stop in Greenwich or back to Manhattan, he would use it. He adores, however, his Gulfstream G–4—I guess now it's a G–5—the luxury jet. When he was trying to buy Smith Barney, he didn't like that the seller of Smith Barney had these golden parachutes. But if he was going to give up the golden parachutes, by God, he wanted that Gulfstream that was on order.

Sandy loves his perks, and yet you see that throughout, he can slice you up, cut costs everywhere. When he took over one company, he took out the coffeepots. He made employees water their own plants. And then he goes to these elaborate dinners at night, where there are four different kinds of wine, six courses. He would argue that his perks help him do business and develop the camaraderie with the senior management or with the clients or the people he is doing deals with.

SANDY TURNED seventy on March 16, 2003. He's chairman and CEO of Citigroup, and he has no intention of giving it up anytime soon. When most men or women at the heads of corporations would be going to their golf course, he is committed to stay there until he basically salvages his reputation and Citigroup after the bruising fall this past year they've had with the Wall Street scandals.

[*CHIEF EXECUTIVE* MAGAZINE gave Weill its 2002] CEO of the Year award. The people that preceded him were Michael Dell, Jack Welch—big, heavy hitters. It's not just financial services, it's CEO of the Year. That meant a lot to him. He wanted that for the last few years, and he was afraid he wasn't going to get it. When they called him to tell him that he was going to get CEO of the Year, he started shivering, he was so excited. . . . He flew in his mother-in-law from California, who never wanted Joan to marry Sandy. It was a very big deal.

That very night that he was getting the honor he had coveted for so long, his whole crisis, his whole career was breaking in front of him that exact same day.

[The crisis began with] the testimony on Capitol Hill of Jack Grubman, who was his $20 million-a-year telecom analyst. Jack Grubman was testifying because Enron and WorldCom had gone bankrupt or were scandal ridden. Citigroup's Salomon Smith Barney was the key banker for these institutions, and Grubman was the analyst and the banker on the transactions. So Grubman was hauled into Washington to testify about his involvement.

Sandy was sitting on the floor of the New York Stock Exchange, about to win this award. Everybody was chattering. It was cocktail hour. It's a beautiful black-tie gala. And on the TV screens on the New York Stock Exchange floor, they keep airing the congressional testimony of Grubman. So Sandy was sitting there, about to win the biggest award, and he couldn't help but notice over his shoulder were the TV screens where Jack Grubman was [being asked], "Did you favor big clients over small investors?"

Sandy's rise had come through smaller investors. They said, "Did you favor big clients, the big cats instead of the small investor?" Jack Grubman [responded]: "I don't know if I did that. Maybe." It was a very evasive, dismal performance. Sandy literally broke out in a sweat that night, as this was going on.

Sandy says that he never told Grubman what to write in his reports. However, I guess a lot of people say if your boss tells you, "Take a fresh look" and you know he's on the AT&T board, you know he wants you to say something good. Grubman did change his rating to a positive one on AT&T. Then Salomon Smith Barney got more business underwriting AT&T's stock and other securities offerings. When everything broke down, e-mails were discovered that Grubman was writing to people at the time—"I changed my rating on AT&T to help Sandy win the battle with John Reed and get [Michael] Armstrong's vote because then Sandy would help get my kids into an influential preschool in Manhattan."

It's not final yet, but they negotiated the $1.1 billion settlement for all the securities industry, and Citigroup will pay the largest amount, $300 million, in fines and other restitution.

Suddenly, Sandy was on the fence. He was having to defend his reputation and his company. He went back to the core. He had gotten fat and happy. He lost thirty pounds; I call it the Spitzer diet, named after Eliot Spitzer, the New York attorney general. And he started reading everything again—not reading so much, but talking about everything, wanting to check everything. At the end, when it was finally over and the initial settlement was announced, he said, "Let's go back to work." It was as if, "I've got to do it all over again. Here I am, having to prove my critics wrong again."

THERE WERE A lot of people, when he was under fire and on the front pages of the newspaper, who were privately cheering. There were a lot of people that he has crossed and done deals who don't like him and think it's time for him to get his comeuppance and get what he deserves. There are other people that still think it's very unfair. He's done a lot. He's given a lot of charitable contributions, $100 million to the Cornell Medical Center, now named the New York Weill Cornell Medical Center, a lot to Carnegie Hall. They think he's really tried to help community, the society, as well as making a lot of people rich. If you owned Citigroup stock, you'd be a wealthy person right now.

It's not an easy thing with Sandy. You don't love him or hate him. Even the people that are his best friends strongly dislike certain things about him. Even people who hate him admire certain qualities of his. So a lot of these key executives feel strongly that he is leading them to greatness. The company is a great company.

At the same time, they're all getting very rich. One person said to me, "You hate it the whole time you're getting wealthy." These people all have stock options. Sandy was one of the first believers in stock options back in the 1980s, so people who have stuck with him—even secretaries to a chauffeur can be a millionaire in his empire if they've stuck with him from the beginning.

This year, Sandy took a million-dollar salary, and he refused a bonus because the stock did so poorly. But a couple years ago, he made over $200 million, if you count his salary, his bonus, and the exercise of his stock options.

He was worth more before the Wall Street crisis happened last fall. He was getting close to $2 billion. Now he's in the billion-plus range. That's his worth, based on Citigroup stock. Most of his wealth is tied up in Citigroup stock, which is why he says he's not like some of these people who cashed out of their companies right before they went down. His wealth is integrally involved with how well the company does or doesn't do.

[IN THE END,] I have a mixed opinion. I think Sandy is, in some ways, very likable. Other ways, he's very hard to deal with. I'm not sure I'd want to work for him. I'm glad I wrote a book and he didn't have control of it, which was an ongoing issue with him. I interviewed so many people. I would say, "Do you love him or hate him?" And they'd say, "Both." That's what a lot of people feel about Sandy Weill.

I think that Sandy's life tells the story of Wall Street and the financial industry for the last fifty years. Broader than that, though, it also tells the story of American society because, as you see the moves he's making in business, you also see American society changing. . . . [His story tells you] things about American history and just the pure power of a personality and how that person has changed financial services and New York society.

Our Cultural Heritage

William Minor and
the Oxford English Dictionary

by

SIMON WINCHESTER

What's the connection between the venerable Oxford English Dictionary and American culture? In addition to its being the repository of our national language, Simon Winchester discovered that a major contributor to the OED was an American Civil War physician, Dr. W. C. Minor, who had gone mad and murdered an Englishman. From his British insane asylum, Dr. Minor made thousands of contributions to the dictionary. In his 1998 book, The Professor and the Madman, *published by HarperCollins, Mr. Winchester tells the strange story of the twenty-year relationship between Minor and OED editor James Murray. Simon Winchester's* Booknotes *interview aired on November 8, 1998.*

THE PROFESSOR AND THE MADMAN is about the making of the *Oxford English Dictionary* in the latter half of the nineteenth century and that one of the many, many volunteers who was working to collect illustrative quotations turned out to be, but unbeknown to the editors, a lunatic American murderer who did all the work on the dictionary for [more than] twenty years from a cell in a lunatic asylum outside London.

When it was first conceived, [the *Oxford English Dictionary*] was called the *New English Dictionary.* The basic idea was that in 1857, a man called Richard Chenevix Trench, who was the dean of Westminster and also president of the London Philological Society, gathered the great and the good of the philological establishment of England to a meeting in the London

Library, which still exists in St. James's Square in London, to present a paper called "On Some Deficiencies in Our English Dictionaries."

Dictionaries were a very new phenomenon. When Shakespeare was writing his plays, there were no dictionaries. People didn't look things up. That very phrase, "to look something up," didn't appear in the English language until about 1692. . . . There was no such book, until the early part of the eighteenth century. Then the idea took off, and Samuel Johnson created the first superdictionary, which was published in 1757, a big, two-volume monster of a dictionary, which became the defining state of the art for about 100 years.

Richard Chenevix Trench and his colleagues decided that it wasn't enough, because, majestic a work though Johnson's dictionary was, it simply didn't cover all words. . . . So Dr. Trench made this speech, and he said we needed [to] show what the English language was, because it was clearly becoming a world language. He wanted every single word that existed and ever had existed put between hard covers with a definition, with a pronunciation, with an etymology, and, most important, a set of contextual sentences to show how that word had first appeared in the English language and how it had evolved over the centuries.

So this speech in 1857 was to say, "We're going to do this dictionary in this manner. What I'm appealing for, ladies and gentlemen"—although principally gentlemen in those days—"is volunteers. Anyone in the English-speaking world, in America, in Canada, in England, Scotland, Wales, Ireland, who reads is now being earnestly asked to read very carefully and look for words and quotations that they can lift out of magazines and newspapers and books and manuscripts and whatever that illustrate the use of that word and send them in to us." Millions of quotations started to come in.

[The volunteers did this] totally for nothing, absolutely, and it's still being done today. . . . They began work on it in 1857. They thought it would take ten years and occupy maybe two volumes.

The dictionary . . . took seventy years to make. It was twelve volumes long, a huge thing, 415,000 words defined, 1.8 million quotations assembled to illustrate the words. . . . Yet they had a problem the moment it started to come off the presses, because during the seventy years, thousands of new words had appeared. So in 1933, a new supplement had to be produced, four more in the 1970s and 1980s, and then a totally new dictionary in 1989. This is the crucial thing—English is a living language . . . but the complexity of that is that we have to keep expanding our dictionaries. . . . So the *OED* is now twenty volumes, with three additional volumes produced in the last five years. Now, sensibly, it's going on-line, on CD-ROM. . . .

WILLIAM MINOR [the madman] was born in [1834 in] what is now Sri Lanka, the island of Ceylon. His parents were missionaries, and they came from New Haven, Connecticut . . . and he lived in Sri Lanka until his parents got a bit worried about him because he showed an unnatural interest in the young, naked, prepubescent Singhalese girls playing on the beach. They packed him off back to school in New Haven. . . . He went to Yale, studied medicine, and became a surgeon. It was then that he joined the Union army in 1863, in Connecticut and, for a while, was a soldier in Connecticut.

He was packed off as a surgeon to the front and came down to Virginia. He wasn't a roughy-toughy soldiering man. He did watercolors, played the flute, and was interested in words. Even at an early age, he collected antiquarian books, so he was an aesthete. So it was somewhat surprising that they packed him off to one of the most ferocious of the battles of the Civil War, the Battle of the Wilderness, fought in Orange County, Virginia, in May 1864.

In those days, there were a lot of Irishmen [who] were fighting in both armies, the North and the South, and from the Irish point of view, it was a fairly cynical, mercenary attitude. These Irish people had no interest in the North–South conflict. They wanted to get themselves trained in military ways so they could come back to Ireland and fight against the British. So there were Irishmen at the Battle of the Wilderness, but by this time they were losing their stomach for the fight a bit, and they started deserting in rather large numbers. Well, the American army used to execute deserters, because desertion in the field is probably the most heinous of military crimes. But they were short of men, so they didn't; they would humiliate them in some way [instead].

About the 5th of May, 1864, they caught this young Irishman deserting and they decided to humiliate him by branding him on the cheek with the letter "D." The man they chose to apply the red-hot branding iron was this young, just-down-from-Yale, rather sensitive surgeon, W. C. Minor. This event must have been as horrific for the one as for the other. . . . It clearly pushed W. C. Minor over the edge, and he started then spiraling down into madness. He started behaving in a very peculiar way. . . . He would have been about thirty.

[HE WAS SENT to New York and later a remote part of Florida, but he became more and more ill, so the army] sent him for evaluation and examination to St. Elizabeth's in Washington, D.C., and said, "He clearly is mad. He's homicidal, he's suicidal," and he was suffering from what they then called monomania. They decided that he should leave the army. His parents battled long and hard to make sure that he left the army, but with a pension. [After hearings, the army did agree] that he contracted this illness—if one can be said to contract a mental illness—during his military service, which meant he became a veteran, so he could put "W. C. Minor, U.S. Army, retired lieutenant." He got an army pension for the rest of his life.

His parents were distressed by his madness. He began to imagine all sorts of weird things: People would come into his bedroom at night, force metallic poison-coated biscuits into his mouth. He was pretty loopy. So his parents decided perhaps he'd get on rather better in the somewhat more benign atmosphere of London. . . . They packed him off on a boat to London, and he arrived there in November 1871. . . .

Minor had an appetite for sex and louche behavior—I think he probably had a sort of low-level pedophilic interest. The part of the world that was relatively tolerant of this kind of thing was just over the river in what is now a part of London called Lambeth . . . and from there Minor began to go to the bawdy theaters and the brothels that he liked. . . .

But what worried him all the time was he was pathologically afraid of Irishmen because he remembered vividly what he had done to this Irishman . . . and he was afraid that Irishmen would . . . attack him and avenge the memory of the man in Virginia. On the 17th of February 1872, he was coming home at 2 A.M., presumably from some licentious place, and he heard footsteps behind him. He had his Colt service revolver from America and turned around . . . whoever this person was behind him [he believed] was one of these Irishmen. . . . He fired shots at him and killed him, a killing which was allegedly the first-ever murder by gunfire on the streets of London. He gave himself up to the police and said it was all a terrible mistake. He was charged with murder, and because he was an American, this became something of an international incident. The American minister in London—what we'd now call the ambassador—had to become involved. Brother George came over from New Haven to testify on William's behalf.

The trial was a rather sad affair because W. C. Minor was clearly very, very strange. . . . The upshot of the trial was that in early April 1872, he was found not guilty by virtue of his insanity and was sentenced to be detained—and this rather nice orotund phrase is still used in courts today—"to be detained until Her Majesty's Pleasure be known," which meant, essentially, forever, in this newly built lunatic asylum called Broadmoor.

[The man he killed] was George Merrett . . . from Wiltshire . . . [who] married a woman called Eliza Merrett, and the two of them lived a blameless life with many children. Merrett himself worked as a stoker in a brewery in Lambeth . . . and there's a bizarre little runnel we can go down there, because Eliza Merrett received a letter from Minor about [six] years after he began his sentence.

[The] letter from Minor, who was very contrite, said, "I'm frightfully sorry I shot your husband, and I'm quite wealthy and I'd like to settle money on you and on your children to try and make amends." He settled, I think, £1,000, which was a great deal of money in those days. [Eliza was illiterate and had someone write to him:] "I'm sorry for you being locked up for the rest of your life in this asylum. Perhaps I might visit you." He thought . . . because he had this interest in sex, that it might be rather nice having a woman come and visit his cell. So she . . . was allowed in. The governor was a liberal man and he thought this would be quite therapeutic for his patient. . . . After a few visits one can surmise what kind of thing went on in the cell, but Minor said to Eliza one afternoon, "It's frightfully nice of you to keep coming down to visit me, but would you mind doing a bit of shopping for me in London, specifically pick up packages of books that I'm ordering for the library?" He had two cells at Broadmoor. One he kitted out as a library and the other he did his painting and his watercolors in.

[Eliza Merrett] picked up books from Maggs and Bernard Quaritch shops, which still exist today and which have the records of books being sent across to Broadmoor.

Minor came across the call for OED volunteers around 1882. He wrote to the dictionary and said, "Look, I'm your man. I've got time on my hands. I read. I'm learned and scholarly. This is just the kind of thing I'd like to do." So they said, "Fine. We welcome all volunteers." They never knew who he was. He really simply wrote, "Dr. W. C. Minor, Crowthorne, Berkshire." They thought they were dealing with a doctor with a lot of time on his hands. The way he did it was this: He would take down a volume from his shelf in the prison cell, open it [and] he'd have beside him a folded eight blank pages of paper, a quire of paper. He would come across the first interesting word on maybe the second line of the book. Let's say it's the word "dog." Well, he reasons that the word "dog," which he's going to note down, would be—A, B, C, D—on maybe page two of his eight-page quire. So about halfway down page two, he'd write the word "dog" and note that it appears on page one, line two of this certain book. He'd make sure he left enough room on that page so that if there was a word that began with D-U, it could go underneath it, and something with D-A could go above it.

Positioning the words perfectly and writing in the most minute handwriting, he would build up an index to every single word of interest in that particular book. Then he'd move on to the next book—each one would take him six months—until every single one of his books he had made an index for. The point of this was that he wanted to be able to help the dictionary in real time so that when they came to work at Oxford and were working on the letter D, they could say, "Right, we're looking for quotations of the word 'dog.' W. C. Minor ought to know." So they'd write to him, "Do you have anything on *dog*?" He'd go to his little books and he'd say, "Ah, yes, *dog*. That appears in this book on pages 1, 17, 49, and 163, and it appears again in this book on page 11, 47, and 93." Then, he'd pluck the books down, pull out the quotations, and say, "I think this isn't a particularly good illustration of the word *dog*. I'll send that to Oxford." Oxford got the quotation for the word *dog* at the precise moment that they needed it.

Dr. Minor lived at Broadmoor . . . from 1872 to 1910 . . . about thirty-eight years. . . . So that means he would have worked for twenty-two years on the dictionary from his cell.

He contributed maybe 150,000 entries, of which about 10,000 are in the dictionary. In other words, they culled it down to 10,000 useful words.

[James Murray, the editor of the *OED*,] is another great hero of the story. He's self-educated [and] left school at fourteen. He came from Hawick in Scotland. His father was a linen draper, fairly lower-middle-class occupation. Young James, who was fascinated by every imaginable branch of learning, went and became a schoolteacher and then became a bank clerk in London; and his abiding passion was words, learning languages and studying philology.

James Murray was appointed editor in 1878. He died in 1915 when he was in the middle of the word "take," . . . so, he worked on the dictionary for thirty-seven years.

THE MYTH HAS it that [James Murray] didn't know [that Minor was criminally insane] because Minor would never come up to receive the thanks of the dictionary staff every time they completed a volume. When they finished letter A or B or C, they'd have a party—cheese and rather bad sherry—and they'd invite people like Minor, but he would never come. So Murray decided, "Well, I'll go and visit him," so goes the myth. Murray went and visited Minor and was astonished to find he was a lunatic, a murderer, incarcerated in an asylum.

The truth came out of this box that I found in Connecticut. It turns out that the librarian of Harvard College had been visiting Oxford in about 1890 and . . . went to call on James Murray because he was a great iconic figure of letters. In the conversation with Murray, he said, "I want to say, Professor Murray, among other things, that we in America are very grateful for the kindly way you're treating poor Dr. Minor." And Murray said, "Poor Dr. Minor? What do you mean?" And the Harvard librarian said, "You mean, you don't know?" "Know what?" "Know that he's a convicted murderer-lunatic." "Bless my soul," said Murray. For the next ten years, he didn't let on that he knew. In all the correspondence, he's perfect Victorian rectitude, but then finally he decided he should go and visit, and then they became the best of friends.

I KNEW SOMETHING had gone wrong in Minor's life in 1902 because he was confined to the infirmary in the asylum. [It] was an amazing eureka moment when . . . [I looked at the notes, which] are done in beautiful ink copperplate, but one of the sheets of paper was written in a rather hurried script by one of the asylum guards in pencil. This was unusual, so I knew I was going to read something rather extraordinary. And it said, "Dr. Minor came to the south gate this morning at about 10:55 screaming, 'Quick, quick. I need a doctor.' I"—the attendant or the guard—"said, 'Why, Dr. Minor, what appears to be the problem?' And he said, 'I have just cut off my penis and thrown it in the fire.'"

This is a man who was obsessed with sex but also terribly guilty about his constant cravings. He was a compulsive masturbator, and felt that his penis was the source of all of his problems. Remember, he was a surgeon. He knew how to conduct this operation. So early in the morning, the 3rd of December, 1902, he tied a ligature about the base of his member and, using the same knife that he used to cut out the cards to send to Oxford University Press, which he sharpened on a whetstone the night before, cut it off and threw it in the fire, hoping, thereby, to be rid of all his problems. He lost very little blood, as he was a skilled surgeon.

There's an interesting lexical point in all of this. The day I discovered this . . . I went up to Oxford from Broadmoor. . . . I was telling the story to a number of people. Well, there were two elderly women lexicographers . . . going to the theater in London, so I couldn't contain myself. I had to tell them what I had discovered because they, too, knew that something weird had gone on in Minor's life in 1902. So I told them the story and said, "And then he sliced off his penis and threw it in the fire." Strangers in the compartment were listening and they went, "My God." You know, there was a gasp. But not these two women. They said—and I swear, they said it in unison—"Really?" they said "Autopeotomy." Their only interest was the fact that there was a word, and they said moreover [that] the word *peotomy*—which is the amputation of the penis and which appears in the dictionary—exists, but *autopeotomy,* doing it to yourself, does not. They said, "If you can include this in your book, then we will cite it in the dictionary's third edition and you will be guaranteed fifteen minutes of fame."

[W. C. MINOR was eventually allowed to leave Broadmoor and return to the United States.] He was released as a very elderly and infirm man from St. Elizabeth's in 1919 and went to an old people's home in Hartford, Connecticut, where he died in 1920. He's buried in a very ordinary grave in New Haven, Connecticut.

Dr. Murray is buried in Oxford . . . and his grave is marked in marble and visited by many.

Stephen Crane, Civil War Novelist

by

LINDA H. DAVIS

The Red Badge of Courage, *Stephen Crane's stark portrait of the Civil War, was published in 1895 when Crane was only twenty-four. Despite his talent as a journalist, Crane spent his short life mired in debt, his reputation tarred by rumors about his personal life. He died of tuberculosis at age twenty-eight. In a* Booknotes *interview on September 6, 1998, Linda Davis discussed her biography* Badge of Courage: The Life of Stephen Crane, *published by Houghton Mifflin that same year.*

THE RED BADGE OF COURAGE is considered one of the great novels of the Civil War, if not the greatest novel ever written about the Civil War. . . . I think that the reason it lives and it speaks to us today is that Crane wrote it, as he said, as a psychological portrayal of fear. And even those of us who've never been through combat, never been near a war zone, we all know what it is to be afraid. A. J. Liebling put it best when he called it, "It's about a boy in a dragon's wood, and it's timeless."

[The main character, Henry Fleming,] is a boy who's gone off to join the war, which he thinks is something very romantic because of these very romantic accounts of war he's read as a boy. He leaves his widowed mother on the farm and goes off to fight in the great Civil War. He's very naive and finds the realities of war very different.

Readers get a wonderful sense of place, of what it feels like to live in an army camp at the time, in a makeshift tent, to live on hardtack and coffee, to spend your time endlessly drilling and marching. They'll learn a lot about the tedium of war, not of actual combat, but all the waiting that soldiers go through before they actually get into the fight. They will not learn specifics about particular Civil War battles. The name General Longstreet crops up in one of his Civil War pieces, but that's highly unusual. Crane deliberately omitted all reference to geographical specifics and names and battles, because he wanted to make his battle a type in order to do what he was trying to do, which was, as I said, to portray fear.

CRANE WAS VERY knowledgeable about the Civil War. One of his older brothers, William, was very, very knowledgeable and he learned a lot from him. He read a lot. It's unclear exactly what books and things he might've read growing up. But in the months preceding the actual writing of the war novel, he was reading old issues of *Century* magazine, which for years ran memoirs and pieces on the Civil War—very dry. But they were the sorts of things from which he could pick up a lot of details about army life and camp life. So he was extremely knowledgeable about the facts of the Civil War. Also, when Crane was growing up, there were an awful lot of Civil War veterans around. Crane was born, after all, in 1871.

STEPHEN CRANE was the fourteenth child in his family, but five of them had died before he was born. His mother, Mary Helen Peck Crane, was a minister's daughter. His father, the Reverend Jonathan Townley Crane, was also a Methodist minister. He was fifty-two when Stephen was born and she was forty-five. She died when she was sixty-four years old and Crane was twenty; he died at the age of sixty, when Stephen Crane was eight. . . .

[Crane's mother] was one of the women who went to temperance meetings and traveled around giving lectures on temperance, on the evils of alcohol. She did a lot of public talks about it. She had a brother who had a problem with alcohol, and drinking alcohol was not in keeping with Methodist teaching at that time. And so she did a lot of lecturing.

Agnes was Stephen Crane's beloved older sister. He had a couple of sisters, but she was the one he was very close to. She was very literary and aspired to be a writer herself. She was really a substitute mother for Stephen Crane when he was a little boy. She died of spinal meningitis. Stephen Crane was twelve when his sister died.

STEPHEN CRANE went away to Pennington Seminary when he was thirteen. He was there a couple of years. Then he went to Claverack College and Hudson River Institute—which was a semi-military school—for a couple of years. He was at Lafayette College for one semester and then at Syracuse for one semester—and that's when his experiment with college ended, as he said.

HE WAS NOT always very accurate and precise about time and dates, but he said himself that he began *The Red Badge of Courage* late in his twenty-first year and finished it early in his twenty-second year. Now that would mean the rough draft or a good revised draft. He made alterations after that . . . it's awful to think that somebody could've written a masterpiece essentially in about six months.

He didn't make a lot of money. He was very quick to sign a contract with D. Appleton for *The Red Badge* because he was really poor and really anxious to have the book published. He got a bad deal. Instead of having a lawyer, including his brother William, who was a lawyer, look over the contract, he just signed on the dotted line—the first taker. He got no money up front and he was not going to earn any money until the publisher's costs had been recovered. And there was no provision for foreign rights at all.

One of the Crane scholars did some good digging on that and got the financial records. I didn't do the original research on that. He sometimes would earn as much as 5 cents a word for stories, but he never earned a great deal of money.

THE WORST THING people would say about him was that he was a degenerate, he was a drunk and a drug addict. That came from hack reporters who were jealous of his talent and from the police, whom he had alienated when he went up against one of them on behalf of a prostitute he'd seen falsely arrested in 1896. Ever afterward the cops were out to smear his name. And they did. To this day, a lot of people think that Stephen Crane was an alcoholic and a drug addict because of these rumors that started about him.

I think that a lot of the hack reporters he knew in his days in New York were jealous of his talent. Here was this kid in his early twenties, this brilliant writer who could write circles around most of them with both hands tied behind his back, and that excited a lot of jealousy. He was a very likable person, wasn't anything about his personality. . . . I think it was basically jealousy.

HE GOT TO know Theodore Roosevelt in the summer of 1896 when Roosevelt was police commissioner of New York. They were introduced by a mutual friend. Roosevelt was a big fan of Crane's writing. They had dinner a couple of times. There was a little bit of correspondence. They were really just getting to know each other when Stephen Crane happened to be out on the street one night in New York in a bad neighborhood. He was escorting a chorus girl to the subway or the streetcar and went back to find that one of the two girls who were left on the sidewalk had been falsely arrested by this very corrupt policeman, Charles Becker. He accused her of soliciting. This is 2:00 in the morning. She wasn't soliciting. Crane was keeping his eye on the two girls to make sure they were safe while he was getting the other one safely home. She was hauled off to the police station anyway. Against the advice of the desk sergeant, Crane turned up the next day in court to speak up on this prostitute's behalf. She was a prostitute, as it turned out—Dora Clark—but she was not soliciting when she was with Crane.

It was a big, big mistake for his career. He felt that it was the honorable and the right thing to do, but the cops would not forgive him after that. There was actually an official police hearing afterward a couple of months later. Crane turned up again to testify. The policeman, Becker, was exonerated, but the cops would not forgive Crane after that. He literally could not set foot in New York without the cops trying to arrest him on trumped-up charges. He was finished as a working reporter in New York at the age of twenty-five.

Roosevelt apparently tried to persuade him not to testify at the police hearing, that it would be a big mistake. Crane decided to do it anyway because he felt that it would be dishonorable of him not to. Roosevelt sided with the cops and that was it. They were estranged at that point. A year-and-a-half later, they both turned up in the Spanish-American War—Crane as a reporter, Roosevelt with the Rough Riders at that point.

STEPHEN CRANE did not marry. He had a common-law wife named Cora Taylor who went by the name of Cora Crane. She was actually legally married to a British officer who would not divorce her. And he never had children that we know of.

He had met her in Jacksonville, Florida, before the Spanish-American War. He'd gone down to Jacksonville to report the Spanish-American War for the *New York Journal* and he visited the houses of prostitution in Jacksonville. Hers was the classiest joint in Jacksonville. He was introduced to her there.

Cora was a very attractive woman in person. She had beautiful golden-blond hair, such a beautiful shade of golden-blond that a lot of people thought she dyed her hair, but she didn't. She had beautiful coloring. She was intelligent. She was literate. She absolutely adored him. She was a woman who knew how to take care of herself. She had been well traveled. She was a woman who knew how to function independently, yet was very loyal to him.

Apparently, they fell in love. We don't know an awful lot about how Crane felt about her. None of his letters from her have survived as far as we know; none have ever turned up on the market. She was absolutely crazy about him. He seems to have been in love with her at least for a while, but it's a little questionable about whether or not that just settled into another kind of love later on.

Crane went to the Greco-Turkish War in the spring of 1897 as a correspondent. That lasted only a month. Cora followed him there because she was something of a scarlet woman. They felt when the war was over, they couldn't really settle together in the United States. They couldn't get married because her husband wouldn't divorce her and so they decided to move to England, which was more socially tolerant of such liaisons.

From the time he left England for the Spanish-American War, he was away for nine months altogether. When the Spanish-American War ended during the summer of 1898—we hadn't tied up all the loose ends yet—Stephen Crane disappeared into the bowels of Havana for four months. That's when he was incommunicado—and apparently tried to desert Cora. He went into hiding, first at a hotel, then at a boarding house; communicated with no one except his agent. He took to his room, didn't even see correspondence very much.

STEPHEN AND CORA [ran up] a lot of credit. Even in this day before credit cards, you could run up credit at the local butchers and grocers, with the blacksmith and other people . . . which got them into huge trouble. I've often thought about what life would be like for them now with credit cards and the trouble they would get in now. They were constantly sending flares out to Crane's English agent, the long-suffering James Pinker, asking him to advance them money. He advanced them hundreds of pounds out-of-pocket, which Crane did not earn back before he died.

JOSEPH CONRAD was a great Polish writer who learned to write in English, known for *Heart of Darkness* and *Lord Jim* and *The Secret Sharer*. They met in England, [where] they were both living. They had the same publisher. They were introduced at lunch. Crane expressed a desire to meet Conrad, who was some years older than he was. It turned out that Conrad had read *The Red Badge* and admired Crane's work, and they hit it off and became very great friends.

Crane was in his mid- to late twenties; Conrad was forty, but as his biographer says, "a very old forty." H. G. Wells, the English writer, was living in the same neighborhood that Crane was living in, in East Sussex in England. They were friends, too. They were not as close as Crane and Conrad. Conrad became the great friend of Crane's later years. They would get together when they could for lunch; they would stay at each other's homes, visit each other. They wrote letters.

I SUSPECT CRANE got tuberculosis in the [family] household. You usually get TB by repeated exposure to somebody else with an advanced state of the disease, from repeated exposure for many hours a day, for perhaps a month at a time. There is some evidence that Stephen Crane's older brother, William, had TB. But the details are very vague, so we're not absolutely sure. But it does seem to me that he probably contracted it as a boy, that the TB healed at some point, went into a kind of remission, although he was sickly frequently throughout his adult life. Then he got malaria in the Spanish-American War, which was not great for somebody who had bad lungs to begin with, and the TB started to kick in again.

CORA, HIS COMMON-LAW wife, insisted that he go [to Germany] to try to save his life. There was something called the Nordrach cure or treatment, but Crane's TB was far too advanced to benefit from it. And, in fact, the trip from England, which is where they were living at the time, probably hastened his death by several months because it was so rough, being jostled by carriage, and it took a while to get there.

HE LIVED TO the age of twenty-eight. He died in 1900 in Badenweiler, Germany. . . . He's buried in Elizabeth, New Jersey.

CRANE WAS VERY young and very full of the devil and a lot of fun. He had a wonderful sense of humor. He was very boyish because he was always very young. We both share a fondness for dogs and horses and horseback riding, and a preference for the color red. He loved the company of his friends. He was a wonderful, charming talker. A lot of writers can't talk. Even if they can write beautifully, they can't talk. Crane could talk beautifully. I think he was extremely well-intentioned and kindhearted. He got into a lot of trouble, but he was well-meaning. He was a good friend. And he had that indefinable something we call charisma; he was the sort of person who walked into a room and created a kind of magic. One of his friends said, "He was a very alive person, even when he was sitting and observing in a room and being very quiet." He was so alive that his friend E. R. Woodruff said that the news of his death seemed a mistake.

CORA DID NOT live too many years after Crane—just ten years. She died in 1910 at the age of forty-six.

Sinclair Lewis,
Novelist and Social Critic

by

RICHARD LINGEMAN

Sinclair Lewis achieved great recognition as a novelist for his realistic, often subversive portraits of American society. His first book Main Street, *which exposed the monotony and vacancy of small-town life, was published in 1920. Despite his criticism of American culture, Lewis's books were best-sellers, and in 1930, after turning down the Pulitzer Prize for his novel* Arrowsmith, *he became the first American to win the Nobel Prize for Literature. Richard Lingeman appeared on* Booknotes *on March 10, 2002, to discuss his biography* Sinclair Lewis: Rebel from Main Street, *published by Random House in 2002.*

SINCLAIR LEWIS WAS born in 1885 and died in 1951. He was married twice, once to a New York woman named Grace and the second time to a famous columnist named Dorothy Thompson. He had two boys, one by his first wife. [One son] died in World War II. The second one became an actor, and he died young of a form of cancer.

Lewis wrote twenty-three novels. He was very prolific and was an exceedingly successful writer. In the 1920s, he was a best-seller, and even in his lowest period, in the 1930s, he would sell 50,000 copies, so he made a good living.

He was a man with a fierce sense of injustice and a sense of what was wrong with America and a desire to change it. He could be a rude man. He was very quick-witted [and] had little patience with clichés. In his earlier years, he liked to do monologues at parties. . . . It would often be a character in his next novel. He was witty, truculent, and a bundle of paradoxes.

LEWIS WAS TALL and he was red-haired and he had skin problems. He had acne as a kid, then treated with X-rays. He had a hereditary disposition to skin cancer, and that broke out in the 1920s. He started having these basal cell skin cancer eruptions on his face and he would have to treat them and his face would be all red and covered with scars. H. L. Mencken, his friend, said it looked like a lizard's skin sometimes. . . . He was very self-conscious about it. It was very sad.

HE WAS VOTED [the "most eccentric" out of his Yale class of 1907. People said, who knew him, that he felt that he was the loneliest man in the world.]

Lewis had no fixed address and moved around a lot from boyhood. . . . He lived in the Twin Cities and in Washington to write *Main Street*. After *Main Street* was a big success, he went all over Europe. He lived in Minnesota again, and then he lived in Massachusetts. He never really settled down.

[He grew up in] Sauk Centre, Minnesota,] in the flat part of the state. It was wheat country . . . a typical Minnesota town, with the Swedish farmers and the German farmers and the Yankees, who ran the town.

[Dr. E. J. Lewis, his father,] was a typical country doctor. He was a very meticulous and very punctual man. People said they could set their watches by when he walked to the office at the same time every day. He was a rather stern man, and he could never quite make out what Harry—that was Sinclair Lewis's boyhood name—was. He kept telling Harry, "Why can't you be a normal boy, like every other boy?" Harry was different, and he couldn't [be like the others]. But I think he was a good father.

His birth mother died when he was nearly six. That was a traumatic event in his life. He didn't remember her very well, but that was a loss of tenderness and maternal affection. It was a shock to him, and he became withdrawn afterward. His father married another woman, Isabel Warner, who was a good woman and lavished her maternal instincts on Harry and his two older brothers. She concentrated on him and drew him out of his shell. She did a lot for the town, all these public services, and you see some of her in the female character, the heroine of *Main Street*, Carol Kennicott, who tries similar projects.

LEWIS LIVED [in Sauk Centre] his first seventeen years, then he went away . . . to Oberlin Prep, and then Yale. . . . Oberlin at that time was a very religious place. They were trying to turn out missionaries. He went there for a prep school course, so that he could pass the Yale exams, but he became very religious there . . . and he made a decision for Christ. He was caught up in religion, which is kind of ironic for the man who wrote *Elmer Gantry*, but not really because he later became disillusioned and swung the opposite way. Oberlin—and this sense of faith and of Christianity—inspired and disillusioned him. So when he wrote about the small midwestern colleges, they were based on Oberlin.

When he wrote against religion, he was writing out his own disillusionment, his loss of faith. He said to Upton Sinclair once that, "Oh, religion draws in idealistic young men, and what a waste, when they could be out working to improve the world." He didn't think organized religion was doing anything to help the world . . . so he became quite fanatic for a while, but he quickly cooled. . . . At Yale, he became a Socialist. So that's the story of his Oberlin career.

HE DROPPED OUT of Yale in his junior year, with a friend, a fellow poet and radical named Allan Updegraff. Upton Sinclair, with the money he had made from *The Jungle*, bought this estate along the Hudson, called Hellicon Hall. He was going to set up a cooperative commonwealth there. He got a group of mostly literary people or academic people, and they would live there cooperatively, and each would do certain tasks. Their children would be raised in a common nursery . . . so the women who were writers could be free to work.

Lewis and Updegraff went there, and they thought they would be writers, but they were assigned to be janitors, and they spent most of their time being janitors and trying to cope with this enormous furnace for this mansion.

[LABOR LEADER] Eugene Debs was one of Lewis's idols. When Lewis first moved to Greenwich Village around 1910, he became a member of the Socialist Party and was quite a radical young man. He met Debs there, and he gradually built him up as a kind of a Christ figure in his mind, which Debs was, to the labor movement.

Eugene Debs ran for president five times. In 1912, he got about a million votes. He was quite a powerful speaker and a power figure in American politics for the working people. Lewis admired him a lot, and then Debs went to prison because he opposed World War I and made a speech [to that effect and] there were very strong laws against sedition. . . . Lewis wanted to write a novel about labor, and he thought he would model the character of Debs. . . . Lewis went out to Chicago, where Debs was staying at a sanitarium to recoup his health [after prison], and Debs was willing to cooperate. [Lewis] . . . just couldn't make it go. Then he met some doctors out there, and he decided to do a novel about a doctor, *Arrowsmith*, instead. But he continued to dream of his novel about Debs all through the rest of his writing career.

MAIN STREET WAS a sensation. It compared to *Uncle Tom's Cabin* in the way it provoked a national controversy. It was a little slower in building, but it started in New York and spread west because there wasn't the media that there is today. It had people discussing [whether it] was a true picture of America. Lewis claims in the foreword that this [book] stands for America—this Main Street runs right through all America, and this town of Gopher Prairie sets the standards for all America. People discussed, "Are we provincial? Are we hostile to culture? Are we conformist?" A lot of people who read it were small-town people who had moved to the cities. It soon became a term—a "Main Streeter." If you were a Main Streeter, you were kind of a hick or a provincial. They wanted to read it so they wouldn't be a Main Streeter.

This was a time in America of transition after World War I. America was assuming a new role because it had come through the war and helped win the war. It was suddenly more on the world stage than ever before and it was very strong economically, while Europe was devastated. People abroad, too, were interested in what America was like, so Lewis's books, starting with *Main Street*, were much read abroad, but it caused a great furor and debate in the country. It was a healthy debate; people were seriously discussing, "Should we educate ourselves more and travel more?" The younger generation, who were rebelling against the old ways, took Gopher Prairie as a symbol of what they were rebelling against, the old-time America.

Lewis would always say Gopher Prairie was a composite of small towns, and before he wrote it, he was a great researcher. He traveled all the way west, driving in a car with his wife, Grace, and visiting small towns, but it was Sauk Centre that was . . . imprinted on his consciousness. He had visualized this novel when he had come home from Yale in his sophomore year, and he was sitting around. And as often happens in a small town, you're bored and feel hemmed in, and thwarted, and he invented this idea of the "village virus," something that gets into you, dulls your mind, and makes you stop thinking and go to seed. So he thought he'd write a novel about this. That was back in 1905. He kept it in his mind all those years. Sauk Centre was the irritant that yielded this pearl.

[HE WAS THIRTY-FIVE in 1920 when *Main Street* was published,] and he wrote it right downtown [in Washington, D.C.,] near the Mayflower Hotel . . . [He and Grace] had come east and were gypsies. They said, "Where are we going to live?" New York was too expensive. They thought Washington had a more relaxed, low-key atmosphere . . . which was the Washington of those days. It was a quiet Southern town.

Babbitt was written after *Main Street*, in 1921. It came from two ideas or his two obsessions: One was that he wanted a hero who was a salesman and who was selling just for the sake of selling and making people buy things that they might not want to buy. And, he wanted to write a book set in a medium-sized city, population 200,000 to 500,000 . . . a place like Seattle or

Minneapolis or Hartford or places like that. So his first conception was that Babbitt is all of us at age forty-six, a man who is wondering: Is just buying a new car and buying a better house enough? Isn't there something more in life? Romance? He's a man in a midlife crisis. But I think he also wanted to satirize businessmen.

He started planning it. He went out to the Midwest on a kind of a speaking tour, but would do research for his book. He would talk to people, talk to businessmen and note down the way they talked. He would read the society pages, and he would read trade magazines, and he would go visit real estate offices. Babbitt's a real estate man.

He was developing a system for writing novels, and so after he did the research, he filled this notebook full of stuff. Then he'd add biographies of all the characters, and he would have to get the names for the characters. The name was very important to him. His publisher, Alfred Harcourt, said, "You write to a name." Lewis said, "A character doesn't come alive till I know the name. . . ."

He was great on names like T. Cholmondley Frink, who was the advertising man/poet, Chum Frink. Or Opal Emerson Mudge, who was the New Thought guru. Vergil Gunch who was the very conservative guy who catches Babbitt when he's dallying with this beautiful widow named Tanis Judique and so on. He'd draw up all the names of the characters, and he'd write biographies of them. . . . He drew up seventeen maps of the state . . . in which Zenith, Babbitt's hometown, is located. He drew maps of Zenith, and he drew maps of Babbitt's neighborhood, office, and house, both floors and every room in the house, and they're incredibly detailed.

At first, the people it was satirizing, such as the real estate people and the service club members, they sort of took it in stride, saying, "We all know Babbitts in our profession." But it seemed they gradually became aware it was a subversive book. It was antibusiness and this was during the 1920s, which was a conservative time. . . . So, there was a backlash against *Babbitt*, but a delayed one. It was a sensation when it came out.

[THE WRITER Theodore Dreiser and Lewis had a falling out.] They didn't know each other well, but Lewis always praised Dreiser as a great pioneer [and] a great pathfinder. Dreiser was an older writer to Lewis. Dreiser had written a book about Russia, which he had visited during the tenth anniversary of the revolution. In 1927, Dorothy Thompson, with whom Lewis was just falling in love, had gone to Russia [as well]. She was a foreign correspondent, and later wrote a book.

A New York columnist, F. P. Adams, noticed similarities in their two books, and he made it clear that he thought Dreiser had lifted passages from

Dorothy's book. Lewis was infuriated, and he dragged Dorothy up to his lawyer and said, "We're going to sue Dreiser." Oh, it got very messy, and Dreiser was implying he had been intimate with Dorothy while she was really engaged to Lewis at the time, and that she had given him her notes for him to use. They didn't sue, which was probably fortunate.

At a literary dinner for a Russian writer, Lewis came in. He was a bit four sheets to the wind. He got up, and other people were expressing their respects for Dreiser, and he said, "I will not give my respects to a man who stole 3,000 words from my wife's book." Dreiser said after the dinner, "Say that again, Lewis." Lewis said it again. Dreiser said, "OK, I'm going to slap you." And he slapped him. "Now—are you going to apologize?" And Lewis said, "No, I'm not going to take it back. Hit me again." So Dreiser slapped him again. Then a friend of Dreiser's pinioned Lewis, and Dreiser walked away. So this was a literary fight between two literary giants, and it was headline news all over the country.

I'd say Sinclair Lewis was an alcoholic. It got very bad, where he would go on binges, wherever he would go, drinking for weeks on end. Sometimes he'd go on the wagon. But it broke up the marriage with his first wife. . . . [With] the second wife, it was the same thing, the drinking. He would fight . . . and they would have these awful quarrels. Those were the symptoms of it. . . . Finally, it reached a point where the doctors told him, "You're going to die if you keep drinking like that." That was about 1938. So he did quit for a while.

HE WAS MARRIED to his first wife, Grace, for fourteen years. Their only son was named Wells, after H. G. Wells, [who] was one of the big influences on Lewis's early writing career. Lewis finally did meet Wells in the 1920s, and they became rather friendly.

He was married to Dorothy Thompson in 1929 and they divorced in 1940, eleven years. They had one son, Michael. He did have trouble with drinking. . . . He felt it was his heredity. . . . He actually died of Hodgkin's lymphoma. I don't think he died of the drink, but he died in his early fifties.

[*Arrowsmith*, one of Lewis's twenty-two novels, won the Pulitzer Prize in 1926, and Lewis turned it down.] There was some sense of revenge in it. The judges on the 1921 Pulitzer chose *Main Street*, but then the trustees of the prize at Columbia University had the final say. They overruled it and awarded it to Edith Wharton's *The Age of Innocence*. Lewis felt that it was these old guardists, the conservatives of literature, who thought that he was too critical of America. The terms of the prize said this should represent the highest aspects of the American character, or implied that it should be an uncritical look at America. He thought this would thwart writers [and] that this prize would become so central that it would set standards for American literature.

So, when *Arrowsmith* won the award, he turned it down. He wrote a long letter giving his reasons, but mainly . . . he thought the prize was stultifying and set too conservative standards for American novel writing. American novelists should be free and they shouldn't be herded into a certain kind of writing for right or wrong. I think it was a principled stand he took. A lot of people thought he was a publicity hound.

SINCLAIR LEWIS was a regular contributor to the *Nation* in the 1920s, and he was a friend of the editor, Oswald Garrison Villard. The politics of the *Nation* then dovetailed very comfortably with Lewis's. The *Nation* supported Senator Robert LaFollette, who ran on the Progressive Party ticket in 1924 against Coolidge. Lewis wrote some articles for them, doing mock interviews with the *Main Street* people and asking them who they supported. He'd ask Carol Kennicott, and her husband, Dr. Will Kennicott, and some of the other characters. He asked Babbitt.

[*ELMER GANTRY* WAS published in 1927.] Elmer Gantry went to divinity school and became a minister, but he was bored with that and he gets in trouble, first with drinking and wenching, [and] loses his pulpit. He joins up with this woman evangelist named Sharon Falconer and becomes a traveling evangelist.

In those days, they had the tent show evangelists, and they literally spread the sawdust on the ground, and they'd call for you to decide for Christ, and you'd march up the sawdust trail. Gantry's very successful, but then . . . Falconer dies in a fire. He eventually returns to the organized church, rises in that and becomes a respectable figure, but is more dangerous, in a way, in the end.

MARCELLA POWERS was Lewis's last love. When they met, she was eighteen and he was fifty-four. She was an aspiring actress and an apprentice in a summer stock company. She cued him on his lines. He had gone into acting in the 1930s, and this was in 1939. She became his girlfriend. It lasted through about 1947, and then she married.

He died in 1951 in Rome and is buried in Sauk Centre, next to his mother and father.

William James,
Popular Intellectual

by

LINDA SIMON

William James, American philosopher and psychologist, belonged to a prominent family that included novelist Henry James. In 1872, William James began teaching at Harvard, becoming involved in a new approach to psychology. His treatise, The Principles of Psychology, *received worldwide acclaim and influenced generations of thinkers in Europe and America. Linda Simon, professor of English at Skidmore College, explored this complex figure in* Genuine Reality: A Life of William James, *published in 1998 by Harcourt Brace, and featured on* Booknotes *on June 7, 1998.*

AT THE TURN of the century, William James was probably the most popular intellectual in American life. That doesn't even begin to say what he meant to the people of the time. I think that if I were going to define him in a concise way, I would say he was a liberator of hearts and minds and spirits. He was also a professor of philosophy at Harvard, which seems to contradict that first definition. He was a psychologist who set up experimental psychology in this country, although he did not believe, really, in laboratory work. He was a psychical researcher, and he was the eldest brother of Henry James, the novelist.

THE JAMESES WERE a quirky family. There was Henry James Sr., who was a kind of self-proclaimed philosopher, the mother, Mary, who is still a little bit of a mystery to all of us, and there were four sons and a daughter. The two eldest sons, William and Henry, became enormously well-known intellectuals. The youngest daughter, Alice, is known for her victimization. She wrote a diary that's very interesting. And the two middle sons called themselves failures. They were the expendable members of the James family. But at the time, from the mid-nineteenth century until Henry James died after World War I, the Jameses were enormously influential in American life. They knew everyone. American intellectuals were a rather small circle. They were on the level of Emerson, the Alcotts, Thoreau, all of whom they knew. That's who the Jameses were in terms of our intellectual history. Who they were to each other is a different answer entirely.

William was born in New York City in the Astor House. At the time, it was in lower New York, because that's where New York City was located in 1842. The Astor House was really one of the most elegant hotels. The Jameses had money. The grandfather, whom I'm afraid to tell you was also named William, settled in Albany, and he was reportedly the second richest man in America, second only to John Jacob Astor. Although he had very many children, they ended up with enough money to live independently.

William James didn't get an undergraduate degree. His father thought that colleges were, and this is a quote, "hotbeds of corruption," and none of his children would participate in that. He never studied philosophy formally, which is why to call him a philosopher puts a different meaning on it. He wasn't an academic philosopher. He studied at the Lawrence Scientific School, which was a technical school. He studied chemistry. And he went to the Harvard Medical School; in those days, you could do that without having an undergraduate degree. But he had no formal liberal arts or philosophical education. It's wonderful that that could happen, isn't it?

WILLIAM JAMES was trained as a physician, although he never practiced. He just decided not to practice that. His search for a vocation went on very, very long, far longer than most people's. But he was very open to what we would call alternative medicine, or mind-cure movements, or anything out there that might make one feel better.

William did suffer from depression, but also, he didn't have, really, any sense of a goal in his life for such a long time. He was persuaded by his father that having a goal, no matter what that goal was, would pretty much be pandering to the marketplace. So for James to find an occupation that he could justify really took a very long time. And you can imagine that if you are a twenty-year-old male and your father won't let you go to college the way other young men did and your father didn't want you to train for a profession the way your friends were, that you would feel very despondent. What were you supposed to do?

That was the cause of a lot of James's depression early in his life, which really shouldn't be a surprise to anyone, but it was a surprise to them. Once he got a job and got affirmation and had a community and, especially, a teaching job where he had a feeling of authority, his depressions lightened considerably. Then when he married Alice, that was a big change, also.

LEONORA PIPER was a medium that James investigated throughout his life. There's an interesting story about how he found her. William James had been interested in spiritualism—not spiritualism in terms of séances and table rapping and the sort of low-level popular [kind], but the possibility of real spiritual connections—for a very long time. The Jameses suffered a real tragedy in 1885. They had a son who, at the age of about seventeen months, died of complications from whooping cough. Herman was the third child, and it was a devastating loss, especially for Alice. Alice felt the loss so deeply, as, of course, anyone would. She was kind of a large, sturdy woman, but photographs of her after the child's death show someone that looks just stunned and drained and thin; it was very devastating. She desperately wanted some assurance that Herman still existed in some other realm. Her mother came back from a sitting with Leonora Piper that she had attended with another of her daughters, and she was very, very excited. She felt that Leonora Piper knew things about both the James family and her own family, who were the Gibbenses, that she could not have known unless she was an authentic medium. It was such a vulnerable moment for William and Alice that they rushed to her. Piper was then about twenty-six. She was living in Boston. And she had a very modest kind of personality. Some of the mediums that advertised themselves were really showmen or showwomen, but Leonora Piper was just a woman who was kind and quiet. They attended a séance and, indeed, they were persuaded that she was authentic.

Everybody was sitting around a table, and it was dark or dim. The medium went into a trance state and talked through what is called a "control." She would be talking in the voice of someone from, as they put it, "beyond the veil." Leonora Piper's controls were very arrogant and imperious men, but that didn't seem to bother anybody. The sitters would ask her questions, and then she would respond with messages about or from people that had died. She gave the Jameses information about the burial of their son, Herman, which certainly anybody could have known who knew the family, but which were distinct—the flowers and the way they arranged them and certain things that they did.

James was an empiricist who wanted to believe in what could not be known through experience. He desperately wanted to believe in this spiritual realm, and he conjured up explanations of what this could be. One of them was that there was a "mother-sea" as he put it, in which souls of dead would just merge into this mother-sea. And our minds were constructed almost as kind of sieves. The more receptive of us could have the mother-sea sort of flow into our consciousness. And the more receptive, of course, would be the mediums or maybe ordinary people who were just quasi-receptive to this.

People reading that at the time got very incensed. They said, "No, I want to have my soul separate from other souls. I don't want to merge into a mother-sea. What's the good of that? And if I merged, I might merge with people not of my class." So they were very upset about that and he modified it.

JOHN DEWEY, who was a later famous American philosopher, said that when William James lived, it was James first and no second. He was so enormously influential. Let's do a little chronology just to get all this in place. He published his major works, the works that are kind of iconic, late in his life. *Pragmatism* came out in 1907; *A Pluralistic Universe* and *The Meaning of Truth* and all the other kind of keywords we associate with James came out very, very close to his death.

He was so enormously popular before then that the question is: Why? And not among academics. It would be so wrong to call him an academic philosopher. Even when I say he was an intellectual, I know that some people are hearing, "Uh-oh, that's not for me." He really wanted to speak to and directed his works toward ordinary people, to students, to teachers, elementary school teachers, anybody who was interested in any questions of spirituality or religion and not on a kind of high philosophical vein. "How can I believe in God if science tells me that I should only believe what can be proven?"—a question like that. James felt that what unites us . . . is beyond the empirical. . . . This from the inventor of pluralism. But he believed that there were certain human needs that united us. And one of them was a craving to believe that there was some kind of transcendent spirituality that we could have faith in.

So even though he was grounded in experience and he exhorted people to trust their own experience, they could know the world. They didn't need philosophers to interpret the world for them. They didn't need scientists to prove the world for them. They just needed to look and feel and reflect on what it was to live in the world.

ONE OF THE prevalent maladies, especially among the educated class, was something called neurasthenia. We would call it now "depression" or "being stressed out," or whatever we would say. But the symptoms were very similar. People would feel that they had very little reason to live. They were not very optimistic. They would have related gastrointestinal problems, and low self-esteem, all of those issues. It was a very popular disease. It was almost a badge of intellectualism if you could claim that you were neurasthenic.

There were lots of self-help movements to try to deal with feelings [of depression]. One of them that James felt was very exciting was started by a businessman named Horace Fletcher. He was very overweight, and physically, he felt terrible because he was so very overweight. He was also feeling very pessimistic. He didn't feel that being in business gave him much justification for living. He was discontent. So he walked away from his business, and he traveled. One of the places he traveled to was Japan, and one of the things that he found in Japan was a sense of serenity that he wished he could achieve, but he was neurasthenic and he wasn't at all serene.

About the same time, Fletcher discovered this chew-chew movement that was popularized in England that [Prime Minister William] Gladstone participated in. It meant that you would chew every mouthful of food thirty-two times. That was the rule of it. . . . If you did that, you would reduce the food to liquid, you would lose weight, and also you would eat differently from the way people in the mid-nineteenth century were eating. So instead of eating meat and eggs and fatty foods, you would focus on grains and breads and cereals. I would guarantee this to anyone out there: If you chew your food thirty-two times and cut out fats, you will start losing weight. And Horace Fletcher did, indeed, lose very great amounts of weight. He started feeling better, and so he started exercising. And he found that even though he was then in his fifties and had never done this before, he was stronger and much more at peace with himself.

So he decided that this was not only a dietary help, but this was a spiritual help, that if you could get yourself fit and strong, then your whole mental state would be much better. But not to end it there; if everybody's mental state was much better, society would be utopian. There would be no problems. There would be no need for jails, because people's aggressions would just melt away. Serenity would be the result of this, and, therefore, by chewing your food thirty-two times, you could enact major social reform. James thought that was a wonderful idea. And not only William James, but Henry James did this so assiduously that he claimed, after he did it for years and years, that it really caused a kind of physical breakdown.

WILLIAM DIDN'T want us to [understand life by concepts]. He wanted us to understand life through perception, not by the name that things had. He felt that if we already came to experience with a preconception, a concept of what that experience would be, we wouldn't be open to change. For him, the universe was going to change and we were going to change. And our very interaction with the universe was going to be a reciprocal reaction and, therefore, cause change in us and in the universe.

MANY, MANY [of his] writings had the word "pragmatism" in them, and [there are] many, many definitions of that word in those writings, much to the dismay of his fellow philosophers. Let me tell you the problem he was trying to solve: One was to dissuade philosophers from spending their attention on metaphysical problems that had no apparent consequence. In other words, he was saying to them, "What does it matter? Ask yourself, 'How does it matter?' And if it doesn't matter, then ask a question that does matter." So he was looking to the consequences of a belief or a system of beliefs.

The word "consequences" is a very important word for pragmatism. For James, pragmatism was a way of thinking, of solving problems, of making especially moral decisions that looked to the effect in the community, and in one's own heart, of holding those beliefs or making those decisions. It seems so self-evident to us; we're so used to that. In fact, we've corrupted it and we call it expediency, which is not what he meant at all.

PAULINE GOLDMARK was an infatuation, one among many, but one that James got particular pleasure from. He met her when she was a student at Bryn Mawr. He would go lecturing at many, many colleges and meet many students. She was very bright and spunky. He tended to like women that were forthright and had their own opinions and had a sense of what they were going to do in the world. He became a correspondent with her and friends with her. He was in his early fifties, and it was definitely an infatuation. His letters to her are just so gushy.

[His wife, Alice,] must have [seen these letters] because they exist. The Jameses went through material and destroyed what they didn't want. So [the fact] they exist means that Alice had decided they could stay for posterity.

[WILLIAM JAMES WAS] lean, active, spry; he took great pride in his body. He wanted to be lean and attractive. He loved to buy clothes. When he would go to Europe, he would come home with all kinds of jackets and ties and shirts made to order for himself. He had quite a different time trying to find gifts for his wife or anybody else, but he found loads of clothing for himself.

His wife was frugal. Somebody had to be, but she didn't deny him what he wanted to do. I think it was a wonderful marriage. He could be trying and demanding and egotistical. But he adored her, and he was such an exciting and warm person to be with. So I think it was a very, very good marriage.

JAMES WAS WRITING in a time when people were making these decisions because they were idealists and they were talking about all kinds of high-sounding ideals for why we should, for example, go to war, which James felt we should definitely not be doing. And he wanted to have some influence on those moral decisions.

WILLIAM WAS sixty-eight [when he died]. He had had heart disease for a long, long time. There was heart disease in the family. That is interesting with James, too; he was physically ill for many years. . . . First of all, he was such a good performer, and he had been all his life, in making people feel that he was not ill that even close friends were shocked that he had died. The other thing is that his wife had an autopsy performed just to make sure that this was not psychosomatic.

[IF HE WERE alive today,] I think he'd probably be considered a conservative because he had a hierarchy of what was good, meaningful, important. I don't think he would have patience with the kind of relativism that is out there in terms of what we think when we're making moral decisions. So I do think he would be a little bit conservative. One of the sweetest things that James wrote was that the biggest breach in nature is the breach between human minds. He said there's a kind of outer tolerance—we're all very conversant in outer tolerance—but it's the inner tolerance—that feeling that we actually do empathize, we understand how someone feels—that's what's missing. That, he said, was missing in his own time. Well, if it was missing in his own time, I think it's certainly missing in our own time.

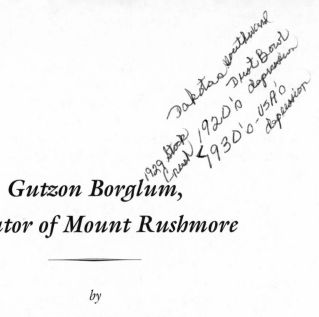

Gutzon Borglum,
Creator of Mount Rushmore

by

JOHN TALIAFERRO

The giant sculpture of Washington, Lincoln, Jefferson, and Roosevelt at Mount Rushmore is one of the most recognizable monuments in the world; less known is the story of its creator, Gutzon Borglum, a first-generation American. One of Borglum's early attempts at larger-than-life carving was Stone Mountain, Georgia, at the behest of the Daughters of the Confederacy. After falling out with the Daughters and the Ku Klux Klan, Borglum made his way to the Black Hills. Booknotes *guest John Taliaferro, a former editor at* Newsweek, *told Borglum's story in an interview on December 15, 2002. His book* Great White Fathers: The Story of the Obsessive Quest to Create Mount Rushmore *was published by PublicAffairs in 2002.*

THIS BOOK IS about Mount Rushmore. I was one of those people who didn't go to Mount Rushmore in the back of a station wagon when I was a child. I went more recently, in the mid-1990s. I was struck in a couple of different ways. One is Mount Rushmore as a work of art, but the other was Mount Rushmore as an artifact. If archaeologists came upon this colossal carving in the Black Hills, in the center of our nation, 10,000 years from now and treated it the way we now treat the pyramids, what does it say about the civilization that created it? Who are these men on the mountain? How did they get here? Who carved it? What are the values behind this?

When I started digging, as an archaeologist I had to know what came before. I wanted to look at the community around Mount Rushmore. Mount Rushmore is a tourist attraction, along with being America's shrine of democracy. It draws 2.5 million people a year. There is an immense community of water slides and paintball courses and reptile gardens that have grown up around Mount Rushmore. I wanted to understand the culture.

Mount Rushmore is in the Black Hills of South Dakota, a long way from a lot of places. In the 1920s, when the idea [to create Mount Rushmore] came to a man named Doane Robinson, South Dakota was in the midst of the Great Depression, a depression that carried over into the depression of the 1930s. He thought, "Well, how can we get Americans to come to our region of the world?" It was conceived as the next leg under the economic table in South Dakota, and it worked.

The idea was conceived in 1924. The sculptor Gutzon Borglum came in 1925. It officially started in 1927. It was finished in 1941, minutes before Pearl Harbor. George Washington, Thomas Jefferson, Theodore Roosevelt, and Abraham Lincoln are [the faces] on the mountain.

Gutzon Borglum is the sculptor of Mount Rushmore. I knew nothing, really, about him until I had been to Mount Rushmore and nothing about him until I started digging into the archives at the Library of Congress. I really had to fight hard not to write a biography of Gutzon Borglum because he is such a terrifically fascinating, complex, colossal figure in his own right, forgotten today in arts circles, one of the great and most important sculptors of the early twentieth century.

[Gutzon Borglum's son,] Lincoln Borglum, was twenty-nine when his father died and he took over what was left of Mount Rushmore. The son was the protégé and went with his father on all of his sculptural jobs, starting with Stone Mountain, Georgia, which was initially a Borglum project. He would tag along with him. He climbed the mountain for the first time with his father as a teenager and eventually became his right-hand man and took over the day-to-day operation. When the father, Gutzon, died in the spring of 1941, the son took over and finished the mountain.

To find Gutzon Borglum's work in this country, start with the Capitol rotunda. There is a wonderful bust of Lincoln. If you look at that, you understand how Borglum got to Mount Rushmore. It was done during the [Theodore] Roosevelt presidency—1908. It's a large head of Lincoln done in marble. If it were a full figure, it would have been on a man twenty-eight feet tall. . . . Borglum did this bust of Lincoln in white marble, and it's a gorgeous treatment of him. Lincoln's son said it was the best piece ever done of him. There's a wonderful sculpture of General Philip Sheridan in [Sheridan] Circle in Washington. Unfortunately, what would have been Borglum's biggest work, even bigger than Mount Rushmore, was never completed and ultimately destroyed, and that is at Stone Mountain, Georgia.

After the Civil War, there was a huge rush to create memorials to the fallen in both the North and the South. The South, after it sort of caught its breath, decided it needed to have its memorials to match those in the North.

Stone Mountain is this huge granite formation sixteen miles outside of Atlanta. The Daughters of the Confederacy thought that it would be nice to have a little shrine there, perhaps a little niche at the bottom where you could ponder the heroes of the lost cause and maybe some busts carved into the side of it. They invited Gutzon Borglum to come down and look at it. He saw this canvas that was acres and acres, hundreds and hundreds of square feet. He conceived a cavalcade of cavalry and artillery marching down the face of the mountain, ending up with Jefferson Davis, Robert E. Lee, and Stonewall Jackson at the fore.

Unfortunately, he fell in with the wrong crowd down there; the Klan was reemerging then, in 1915, same time as the movie *Birth of a Nation* was coming out. Borglum, who liked the political thrust and parry and considered himself a bit of a rebel, joined in with the Klan. When the Klan got to fighting amongst itself, they threw Borglum off the mountain.

Borglum was fired from Stone Mountain because of ego. A man who's going to carve statues into mountains does not have a small ego. He was fired because they thought he wasn't spending enough time there. He was fired because he sided with D. C. Stephenson, who was trying to take over control of the Klan in Atlanta. He was fired because he complained he wasn't getting paid enough. They literally ran him out of town. He destroyed his models so that no one else could follow them. There was an arrest warrant issued, and they chased him out of town, across the Georgia state line. The sheriff and a bunch of Klan thugs chased him [out of] Georgia.

And so, he effectively fled Georgia to South Dakota. Just at the time things were falling apart in Georgia, he was getting letters saying, "We'd like to carve something out here, too."

[At Stone Mountain,] Borglum had gotten partly through the Robert E. Lee head and a little bit into Stonewall Jackson. That was blasted off the mountain. It took to the Nixon administration to complete Stone Mountain. There is a carving of the Confederate generals that Borglum had intended to carve, but they're by an entirely different group of artists.

BORGLUM'S BIRTH parents were Mormon. In fact, his father was a polygamist. His parents were Danish immigrants [who] came over with a wave of Mormon converts in the 1860s, and they all made the long trek out to Utah. His father's wife's sister came over a year later. His father took the sister on as his second wife. Then, the father decided he didn't want to be a Mormon anymore. The prejudice against polygamy was very strong, and the Mormons were greatly persecuted, which is part of the reason why they ended up in Utah. The father decided to abandon one of his wives, and that happened to be Gutzon Borglum's mother. So when Gutzon was six years old, all of a sudden his mother was banished and disappeared from his life.

Borglum married a woman eighteen years older. Pop shrinks would suggest that he was looking for his mother. He stayed married to her a lot longer than he stayed with her. She was an artist. He met her in California. She was a very talented landscape painter, and I think she brought him into the art world out there and encouraged him. They went to Europe together and spent nearly eleven years in Europe, 1890s to the turn of the century, to 1901. Their life together was as husband and wife, but [also] as fellow artists. I think he got to a certain level of talent and maybe didn't need her anymore.

He went to Europe as a painter and came home a sculptor, and the reason was Auguste Rodin. Rodin was, after Michelangelo, probably the most influential sculptor I can think of. Rodin happened to be at his height in Paris, when Borglum showed up. It turned his head and turned his world around, not just because of the sheer talent of Rodin, but Rodin was a celebrity. Rodin didn't respond to anybody else but himself, and he was a very powerful, potent, colorful person. Borglum realized that an artist could be more than an artist and an artist could be a celebrity. . . . When Borglum got back to the United States, Rodin wrote letters to certain people saying, "This guy's good. You ought to pay attention to him." They were real letters of entrée that really gave Borglum a boost when he got back.

He met his second wife on the boat back from Europe. She was coming home from finishing a Ph.D. This was a woman who got a Ph.D. from the University of Berlin, one of the very first women ever to receive a Ph.D. there. She spoke about six different languages. Her parents had been Protestant missionaries in Turkey. He fell in love with her on the boat. They were married more than thirty years. [He had no children by his first wife] and two by his second; his son, Lincoln, and a daughter, Mary Alice.

[MOUNT RUSHMORE cost $989,000 in 1941 money, of which the federal government paid $836,000]. They thought they could raise the money through philanthropy. In the late 1920s, there was a lot of wealth in the United States. But before they got going very far on Mount Rushmore, of course, the stock market crashed, and all of a sudden, the people who had any money had lost it or they were holding onto what they had.

In the summer of 1927, two years before the crash, President Calvin Coolidge was looking for a place to spend his summer vacation. The White House was being renovated. His son had died from a blister he'd gotten playing tennis without socks on the White House lawn, and Grace and Calvin Coolidge were saddened by that and did not want to spend another summer in the White House. They went casting about for a place to stay, and every state in the nation wanted the president, as dull as he was, to come there for summer vacation. Somehow, the Black Hills of South Dakota won that lottery, and Calvin Coolidge and his wife arrived in the summer of 1927.

By a total coincidence, it was when Borglum was just getting to work on Mount Rushmore. . . . It was also the summer of Charles Lindbergh flying the transatlantic flight. Air miracles were on everybody's tongue. Borglum hired a plane, flew over the summer White House, and dropped a note onto the lawn, inviting the president and the first lady to the dedication of Mount Rushmore, and they accepted. Coolidge, like so many others, was taken by Borglum and his talent and his charm and just his forcefulness, and said, "When I get back to Washington, I'm going to tell the secretary of the treasury, Andrew Mellon, to help you out here." So, what should have been a privately funded project ended up being a publicly funded project.

Over seventeen years, Borglum made an average of $10,000 a year on the project. He thought he was only going to work there part-time. After all, they could only work on Mount Rushmore in the warm months. It's a tough winter up there in the Black Hills. He thought he could dash off to other parts of the country, down to Texas where there was a lot of oil money and people wanted big monuments to various causes. He thought he could do that with his left hand, and with his son and others, supervise Mount Rushmore. It didn't work out—he was bound to the mountain, like Prometheus.

[BORGLUM PROMISED women that he'd put a woman somewhere on the mountain.] Just as he was getting to the end of Mount Rushmore, there was a national campaign, a women's movement to get a memorial somewhere of Susan B. Anthony. There was a woman named Rose Arnold Powell who took it on as her life's mission to promote the image of Susan B. Anthony and corresponded with Borglum for years and years. He backhandedly, with sort of a wink and a nod, said, "Yes, we'll find a place somewhere on the mountain for her." She enlisted Eleanor Roosevelt, too, to push for it, and there was actually some legislation drawn up to add Susan B. Anthony to Mount Rushmore. It never got anywhere.

BORGLUM HAD A "noble savage" appreciation of Native Americans, of Indians who were on their reservations. The Pine Ridge Reservation is not far from Mount Rushmore. It is today and has been for a long time, one of the poorest places in America. The Lakota Sioux were one of the fiercest, strongest tribes on the Plains. . . . They had defeated Custer, and the army wanted them to pay for it.

Borglum developed some sympathy for them, went down to the reservation, and did things for them. During the 1930s dust bowl times, he made sure that they got some food and blankets. Mount Rushmore and the Black Hills are the Holy Mount to Native Americans, particularly the Lakota Sioux Indians. Some of their most sacred rituals and ceremonies are held there, their vision quests, their sun dances. There is nothing more sacred to these Indians than the Black Hills.

The tribal registry [today totals] about 30,000–40,000 on the reservation and in the hills. You might remember the Bradley bill. There was a lawsuit filed back in the 1920s saying that . . . the Black Hills had been taken unjustly from the Sioux. It worked all the way through the courts up into the 1980s and it went to the U.S. Court of Claims and an award was given. It was upheld by the Supreme Court, the payment for this breach of treaty.

The Lakota Sioux said, "We don't want this money. We want our Black Hills back. If we take this money it's like wampum. We don't want it." So it sits in a trust fund in Washington, $600 million now. Shannon County, where Pine Ridge Reservation is, is the poorest county in the United States; $600 million dollars would help. But this is the strength and the passion of the Sioux. This is how badly they want the Black Hills back.

Indians who Borglum loved and wanted to help came to him and said, "Look, we have our heroes, too. We want some recognition that we were here first and we had great men also." Borglum, said, "I'll find a place for you where the eagles nest." He was speaking in that white man's version of Indian lingo, but he was a little vague about that and never really did follow through.

Another sculptor showed up in the Black Hills, a man named Korczak Ziolkowski who went on and took that idea and ran with it. . . . His Crazy Horse Memorial, which is many times the size of Mount Rushmore, is a work in progress. It's even more controversial than Mount Rushmore.

It is about twenty miles from Mount Rushmore. It's still being built and will be built for many more generations. This man, Ziolkowski, is dead [but] his children are working on it.

Ziolkowski was a sculptor from Connecticut. He came out and worked for Borglum for about three weeks. Sculptors in general, but sculptors of colossal sculpture [in particular], are pretty headstrong, and they didn't get along. Ziolkowski was fired from the job after three weeks. Borglum said, "Get out of here."

World War II came and nobody did any work on the mountain and Ziolkowski came back in the late 1940s with an even bigger idea. A very controversial [thesis] from a Native American standpoint [is that] Crazy Horse, the great Lakota holy man, chief, and warrior, gave his life to keep white people from the Black Hills. And now they're building this immense memorial, which is to him, but it's an enormous magnet for tourists.

[For] the Indians, carving into their sacred Black Hills is like gouging flesh from the breast of their mother. Even if it's a memorial to one of their greatest leaders, the irony of blowing up the Black Hills to honor Crazy Horse doesn't sit well with Native Americans. A lot of Native Americans support it, [but] I would suggest that a majority don't.

THE FACT THAT the creator of our shrine of democracy also had been a Klansman . . . [shows that] our message of democracy comes from a stew that is not pure. Good people can do bad things. Bad people can do good things. I like that part of the discussion of our American civilization. Nationalism is a complicated subject. . . . This book is much more than just a book about a couple hundred guys chiseling four faces on a big rock. It's really about: Who are these men? Why have we worshipped them? What are the values that they are projecting into the future?

[The Mount Rushmore visitor's center was] completed in 1998 and it is a wonderful structure. Mount Rushmore gets 2.5 million people a year, most of them coming over about a six-month period. Yellowstone Park, which is 2 million acres, gets roughly 3 million visitors a year. . . . So [Rushmore is] packed. It's a city at the end of a long highway. . . . [There is a] wonderful colonnade, and it's like going down the center aisle of a cathedral with these columns. I think they did a wonderful job. There are the flags of all the United States and the territories. When you walk down it and then you come to this viewing terrace at the end, it's like standing at the bow of a ship, all of the parking facilities and the visitor centers are all of a sudden behind you and it's just you and the mountain. You could be in an immense crowd in a summer day of 20,000 or 30,000 people and feel quite alone with this sculpture. I think that's the great achievement of the Park Service.

THE FACE THAT's the hardest to see is Theodore Roosevelt's. [Borglum knew Roosevelt]. He had done a little bit of work, a little bit of carving for Roosevelt for his house at Oyster Bay, Long Island. He did the first Lincoln bust that Eugene Meyer [owner of the *Washington Post*] had commissioned. Roosevelt admired it. It was in the White House briefly, and Roosevelt made sure it got into the rotunda.

Borglum and Roosevelt were in some ways the same person. They [both] were stocky. They [each] had a bristling mustache. They believed in this strenuous life. They were both very athletic, and Borglum worshipped Roosevelt and got to know him personally.

In 1912, Roosevelt decided not to run for reelection. Taft came in. Roosevelt didn't like how Taft had run the White House, [and] decided to run again as a Bull Moose in 1912. Borglum became very involved in his presidential race, and there was an immense amount of personal correspondence. It's hard to imagine Borglum without Roosevelt in the picture as well.

Borglum knew him since he was a police commissioner in New York. Roosevelt got on the mountain because of their personal friendship. Roosevelt died in 1919. Mount Rushmore was conceived in 1925. There was an immense amount of money raised for a Roosevelt memorial. People forget that where the Jefferson Memorial is now in Washington was supposed to be the Roosevelt memorial. They had the money in place to build a Teddy Roosevelt memorial there, but there was the centennial of the death of Jefferson, and some Democrats came forward and [wanted a] Jefferson memorial here.

Borglum . . . wanted to be the guy to do a Roosevelt memorial. It wasn't happening in Washington, and he said, "I'm going to put my guy out here in South Dakota." Remember, Roosevelt, after his wife had died, had gone out and been a rancher in South Dakota briefly. ?, try North Dakota

In the end, Borglum made the selection of Washington, Jefferson, Roosevelt, and Lincoln. His first sketch was of a profile of a Continental soldier, of Washington. Then they thought about adding Lincoln and then one by one Jefferson and Teddy Roosevelt. But I'm sure Roosevelt wouldn't have been there if he and Borglum had not been friends.

KEYSTONE IS THE community closest to Mount Rushmore. It's the little tourist town at the bottom of the mountain. . . . Bill Durst owns or controls most of the businesses in Keystone [and he is the] definition of an entrepreneur. He'd grown up in the Black Hills, and he has, in a sense, taken Borglum's lead and carved out the side of the mountain in Keystone to put in hotels. . . . It's the final shoe dropping on the dream of Gutzon Borglum and the other people in the Black Hills who wanted Mount Rushmore to be carved—that if we build it, they will come. . . . Mount Rushmore, when it was conceived, was remote. You drove across dirt roads. There were scarcely any bridges across the major rivers in the West. You drove for days, and you looked up on the hill and there was this carving. Now, when you drive across South Dakota, it's Reptile Gardens, Bear Country USA. It comes at you for hundreds of miles. Mount Rushmore is the engine that drives that economy.

With all the kitsch and all the tourist culture stuff and even the message of patriotism, all of that aside, Mount Rushmore is a terrific piece of sculpture done by a great American sculptor. To go there and to see it in the early morning light, which is what Borglum intended, to get to see it in the evening when they turn the lights on, to walk around it, to look at the carvings as one would if they were in a museum, is really worthwhile.

WE, AS AMERICANS, put our values and our ideals before the public and say, "This is what we stand for," but we can't guarantee how they will be received. Mount Rushmore is very representative of that. This is . . . our monument of who we are, what we stand for, these four presidents embodying various American values. . . . Not everybody receives that message in the same way, including Native Americans.

Norman Rockwell's Portraits
of America

by

LAURA CLARIDGE

Norman Rockwell's sentimental illustrations of middle-class life were so popular that they became icons of America's values. Born in New York City in 1894, Rockwell began a fifty-year career as a cover illustrator for The Saturday Evening Post *at age twenty. During World War II, he turned to patriotic themes for paintings and posters, creating his* Four Freedoms *series. A well-visited museum in his hometown of Stockbridge, Massachusetts, is dedicated to his work. On December 2, 2001, writer Laura Claridge, a former Naval Academy literature professor, was featured on* Booknotes *to discuss* Normal Rockwell: A Life, *published by Random House.*

[NORMAN ROCKWELL] ... to many people—and by the way, in the world at large, Europe, and the Middle East, and the Far East, as well as America—represents the idea of America in the twentieth century. Now what people mean by that may be very different from what he intended or how he's best "used," but he represents ... the idea of America as a tolerant, generous, capacious country where, on the one hand, the right values obtained—prayer, sobriety—on the other hand, room for people who may not share those values and who, nonetheless, can be invited in. . . .

I GUESS [he was most popular in] the 1950s, although I say that with some hesitation because what surprised me in the research for this book was how popular [he was] from the beginning of his career—I'm talking by 1920, when he was only twenty-six years old, he had made his fortune or was certainly on the way to making it. He was well known. The press on him is voluminous. So this is a man who was famous throughout a good four decades.

HE GREW UP until the last year of junior high in New York City in what now is Harlem, Morningside Heights. But it was a nice, lower-middle-class neighborhood that he then stigmatized later in life as a real dump and the source of all violence, which is interesting.

[His relationship with his mother was] unpleasant. . . . She was a product of a Victorian age and that was replicated in their relationship. . . . She was a coquette who got what she wanted; that she passed on to Rockwell, who, in spite of being Mr. Nice Guy, when he wanted something, definitely got it. I was told that again and again. But she was spoiled, and she also suffered from depression in a period where people weren't very good at analyzing that. I'm sure that influenced the relationship negatively, too.

HE SAID AGAIN and again how he was indebted to Charles Dickens. People, as they often did with Rockwell's self-pronouncements, ignored that. But if you go back, his father read Dickens to him aloud every night for a couple of years when he was seven and eight and learning to draw, and he would actually draw from the Dickens stories. But even more important is that his view of life, and he says this very quietly but seriously a couple of times in his autobiography, "I was taught how to view the world through Dickens, including an insatiable curiosity." I don't doubt that, absolutely. Also, Dickens helped him give form to chaos—anti-city, pro-pastoral ways to act out or to give shape and form and impose narrative form on some of his own psychological bogeys.

[IN HIS MID-TWENTIES,] he was a playboy. He was living a pretty debauched life in an open marriage and experimenting with high society in New Rochelle, New York.

At age twenty, he did his first cover for the *Saturday Evening Post*, the first of what would be 322, which is an extraordinary feat. That was the plum assignment, to get the cover of the *Saturday Evening Post* then.

I don't remember the covers ever being controversial. I remember the civil rights pieces in the 1960s were, and then he actually helped out CORE, which was a radical left racial rights group in New York City. That was a bit controversial. But the *Post* covers—the only thing I remember is . . . there was one with a young girl who you couldn't quite be sure if she was a girl or a boy, and he got a real overspill of letters not so much on that he should have been clear about the gender, but what was he doing making a girl look so sloppy? Or what was he doing making a boy look so connected to girlish things, which I find fascinating.

[HE HAD] THREE children, three marriages, but the three children went with the second marriage. That's interesting. He was a high school dropout at age sixteen and never had any formal education after that, and he married three schoolteachers. That's not very difficult, it seemed to me, to see a kind of fulfilling of something that he valued. And they read to him. One of the requirements, it seems, of marriage for him was that his wife read aloud great novels while he painted. He married [in] 1916 and was divorced in 1930 when the woman left him precipitously for a handsome pilot. What's interesting about that is he almost denied the marriage ever happened, in spite of the fact that it was a fourteen-year-long marriage. His three sons found out about it only in the 1940s when they read an article in the *New Yorker* about his life. He'd never bothered [to tell them], and when they confronted him he said, "Oh, I didn't think it was important." . . . It's a very strong psychological defense of Rockwell's, denial, just a repression.

[He and his first wife, Irene,] had no children. I found out from someone who knew them that she refused to have children, and he very much wanted to.

That's the marriage that . . . embarrassed him very much. [She] ran off with the brother of good friends of theirs in New Rochelle, socialites that had set him up. The socialites took Rockwell to Europe, and while they were gone, the woman of the pair—her brother took Irene away to consummate their affair. When Rockwell got back, Irene notified him she wanted a divorce. It was very public, because he was so well known, and humiliating for him.

He was very discouraged and depressed, and he left New Rochelle for a couple of months and moved back to New York City, the city he supposedly hated so much, he kept returning to, and holed up in a hotel and gave parties and tried to find himself. Then he went out to California after about three months and met and married within weeks his second wife, Mary Barstow.

[They were married for twenty-nine years.] The last eleven years of their marriage, she suffered from really aggravated depression. She not only was hospitalized for it, but she had to have electric shock treatments. And at the end of that marriage, she was not feeling well one day and went up to take a nap—[she] was only fifty-one years old—and he went up to find her when she didn't wake up and she was dead. Apparently, the cause was heart failure. She'd had so much stress on her heart from various reasons—although around town, it was assumed she committed suicide since she had been suicidal for ten years.

There's a picture that shows him just so gray and haggard [after her death]. He was lost. I talked to people around town, a professional photographer there, Clem Kalischer, who said he used to see him looking like death—just walking around town. . . .

HE WAS VOCIFEROUS in announcing to everyone around him that he was not a political man. That was to get out of all the different requests to endorse so-and-so. Also, he didn't want to alienate his audience by saying the wrong choice, the wrong person. But that question interests me is what it means to be political. He was not overtly political. He was, however, a man of very deep convictions. So my own answer would be, at heart, yes. His three sons would quickly say to me, "But don't forget he was avowedly apolitical except for occasional endorsements." He loved Ike the first term, and then afterward, he said he had been a little disappointed in him the second time. He disliked Nixon. So he would make those kinds of statements sotto voce or to friends, but that was about it.

DURING WORLD WAR II, Rockwell was very interested in providing to the war effort, what we would call wartime propaganda pictures, and that's not necessarily a pejorative. It was just used descriptively at the time. He had been a bit young to participate in World War I and also there were illustrators who were just ahead of him, James Montgomery Flagg and [Joe] Leyendecker. So at this time, it was Rockwell's turn, is how he saw it. . . . He did eleven Willie Gillis pictures and instead of showing the glamorous handsome man that Leyendecker used for World War I, he showed this boy-next-door, with the shock of red hair, in this case, neatly combed. . . . There's a quietness about it that's one of Rockwell's attempts to convey the seriousness of war.

THE FOUR FREEDOMS was a series of paintings that Rockwell did to illustrate a combination of the speech [Roosevelt] gave to Congress in January of 1941, and then the meeting he had with Churchill off of Newfoundland, which resulted in the Atlantic Charter. The ideas that were promulgated in those two circumstances became known as the four freedoms, the abstractions: [freedom of speech, freedom of worship, freedom from want, and freedom from fear]. In the long run, they actually became a backing to the U.N.'s charters, too.

He painted those in 1942, and they were published beginning in February of 1943, again, to promote the war effort. The Treasury Department made $133 million off of touring those four paintings in sixteen cities and selling war bonds with the picture of one of them on the cover of one of the war bonds. It was interesting because Rockwell was dying to do those. He wanted to paint those more than anything. He went to a doctor once and apparently during this period he was told to have an operation, and the memo back to himself says "I can't." And then he underlines the line, "This is more important to me than anything I have ever done." It was more than the war effort. He was so idealistic. He was so [supportive of] living that idealistic existence that this was a chance, he thought, to put the big ideas into concrete form.

He never regretted supporting and contributing so heavily to the World War II cause, and he was a major raiser of money for the Office of War Information and the Treasury Department. But by the Vietnam War, not only had he married someone who brought out his most liberal tendencies—a New England schoolteacher—but he himself was so anti-violence, had been all his life. The ambivalence that many people that he trusted felt toward the Vietnam War gave him pause. By the time he had to confront whether he was willing to contribute to the pictorial wartime propaganda for that war, he wasn't convinced it was the right thing. So, finally, because he was, in the end, a very honorable person, he just said, "I'm not the right man for this."

He was invited to what he called a "stag dinner" that apparently President Eisenhower gave to get a little bit of freedom to be himself with men he liked. After, Rockwell painted his portrait and the two hit it off. Then some time later, Rockwell got an invitation in the mail to one of these stag dinners in Washington. And he came. He enjoyed it immensely and spoke of it fondly in years afterward. What was interesting to me was that he was so nervous. By this time he was well established and well loved and certainly a cosmopolitan, a world traveler, but he had to take tranquilizers to get through the dinner. His tuxedo didn't fit, and nothing was right. So I've always taken all of this as a sign that he deeply respected Eisenhower, to care that much for his opinion of how Rockwell conducted himself or looked during that dinner.

[He married] the second Mary, whom we'll call Molly . . . in 1961. The summer of 1959 is when . . . the second wife died.

[That marriage was] very good. It was a calm, even-tempered, even-keeled marriage, the opposite of what he had had for thirty years, I guess. Of course, there were no children, and it was more a question of real deep companionship. She'd had a very rich life herself as a single woman, schoolteacher in a private academy, a very bright woman. She saw this as an adventure, being married to a famous illustrator.

[They rode their bikes together for 4.7 miles a day.] They were that precise. That was Molly's doing. She measured things like that and kept up with it. They did that every day, and it kept them healthy and hardy until the end, when there were a couple of occasions where Rockwell fell off his bike unexplained. He couldn't remember afterward what had happened. One time when they were in the Caribbean, it appears in retrospect, he had . . . little ministrokes. They tried to deny it for a long time, to the point where they also had a routine of going out driving every afternoon, even though Molly was a terrible driver, and the townspeople knew when they'd be driving and watched out for them. And finally, all this had to be given up as Rockwell kept deteriorating.

The triple self-portrait, which he did in 1960—it's fascinating because of its geniality, but at the same time, a real kind of what some people would call a postmodern spin, where he's pretending he's painting himself, but gently mocking himself. If you can see, the actual black and white on the canvas is a younger, more handsome man. He's looking, however, in the mirror as if he's copying what he's seeing, and in the image that's reflected back in that mirror, to add yet another layer of ambiguity, the eyes are whited out.

[Up in the right-hand corner], these are self-portraits, and it's important. A self-portrait of Rembrandt, Dürer, a painting by Picasso that implies self-portraiture in a complicated relationship with the women in his life. So Rockwell was situating himself, Mr. Modest, among these greats as he himself attempted the self-portrait and admitted he didn't know who he was to some extent.

[You can see this painting] in the Norman Rockwell Museum in Stockbridge, Massachusetts, which is a wonderful building. The architect Robert A.M. Stern designed it, and it has an excellent collection, due largely to the insight and foresight of his third wife.

["The Problem We All Live With"] is an extraordinary painting. It was done . . . late in his career in life. Rockwell would have been nearly seventy by then. . . . It's a representation of Ruby Bridges having to go to school when the South was being desegregated. That painting is also at the museum. It was done for *Look* magazine. What I find extraordinary is that it represents this very strong liberal political desire to paint what was happening in the world, that Rockwell was willing to go in that direction fairly late for an artist, to start a very new direction in his work.

[He] died in 1978. He was eighty-four. He lived a long life and was active in his art and [was] a very active man until maybe two years before his death.

[The hardest thing about this book was] deciding what my attitude was toward Rockwell, both as a person and a painter. I vacillated. I started out somewhat dubious. Then I had this kind of epiphany where I so appreciated him. It was a love affair. Then I went to the other extreme again. I had to step back and say, "Wait a minute, what's the proper attitude toward one's subject as a biographer, and how can I best serve him and the project?"

I want to say it was something in his personality [that caused this fluctuation] because he did it with his kids. He did it with anybody who got very close to him. He was a master at creating desire. I would even use the word "manipulating" that relationship so that he invites proximity and intimacy, and you get close, and then you realize that that's as far as it's going to be allowed. And so then there's this kind of coldness. I think that it took me a while to understand that dynamic, even though his oldest son had been expressing that to me in different words for four or five visits. He kept talking about that, when I would say, "Tell me what it's like growing up." He tried to say that. I'd go away disgusted, saying, "Come on, you're sounding like a victim. This was a good father." And [he'd say,] "Yeah." And then I'd go back the next time and say, "So you were a real victim?" And he'd say, "No, no, no. I wouldn't say that." So I think it was a dynamic in Rockwell's personality.

The Forged Poem
of Emily Dickinson

by

SIMON WORRALL

Simon Worrall appeared on Booknotes *on August 18, 2002, to tell the tale of a forged Emily Dickinson poem, which had been unwittingly purchased by the public library in Dickinson's hometown of Amherst, Massachussetts. The culprit was Mark Hofmann, a rare documents dealer who became an expert falsifier, forging at least 1,000 documents—crimes that eventually led to murder. Mr. Worrall's interview tells us more about the great American poet and a forgery that took advantage of the poet's hometown. His book* The Poet and the Murderer: The True Story of Literary Crime and the Art of Forgery *was published in 2002 by Dutton.*

THE POET AND THE MURDERER is about a forged Emily Dickinson poem that was bought by the Jones Library in Amherst. They believed it was a genuine poem.

[The poem] was spotted by the curator of special collections at the Jones Library in April 1997, in a Sotheby's catalog. It was advertised as a genuine Emily Dickinson poem. It was a fourteen-line poem, and the first unpublished Emily Dickinson poem in forty years, which was quite an event. Her manuscripts are very rare and very valuable, and there hadn't been a new poem on the market for some forty years.

THE STORY STARTS in Amherst, which, of course, it should be noted, is Emily Dickinson's birthplace. So the discovery of this brand-new poem, which was up for sale at Sotheby's at the May 1997 auction, was a big event for Amherst, and above all, for the curator of special collections there.

The desire to buy it was motivated not just by wanting to add to the collection that they have of manuscripts, including Dickinson manuscripts. Robert Frost, of course, lived in Amherst. They have a number of those. It was also motivated by a desire to bring this poem home, if you like.

Daniel Lombardo was the curator who organized a fund-raising drive to raise the money. The Jones Library is not a very wealthy library compared with Harvard or Yale, some of the big privately endowed libraries. It was a battle for this little town library—it's not the Amherst College library, it's actually the town's public library. But it has this special collections section where they have a pretty good collection of original manuscripts related to writers connected with Amherst.

EMILY DICKINSON was born in 1830 and died in 1886 . . . of complications with her kidneys.

She's a great poet, and her reputation, I think it's fair to say, has risen progressively since her death in 1886. She was regarded for a long time as just being too difficult and eccentric in terms of the way that she wrote. It's a very modern, expressionist, idiosyncratic way of writing, much more like e. e. cummings than nineteenth-century poets. For a long time, the public just had a lot of trouble with these short, very complex poems that she wrote.

Starting in the 1920s and progressively through the 1950s—a big edition came out in the 1950s—her reputation began to soar. . . . She has overtaken a lot of other candidates for being now regarded as one of the two great American poets.

Her home in Amherst—the Homestead, it's called—has been preserved as a museum and renovated. . . . It was an extraordinary world that she inhabited. She was a very reclusive person. She lived at home at the Homestead—one of the larger houses. It was a very well-to-do family, the Dickinson family, one of the best families in Amherst, an old New England Yankee family.

Emily ended up staying at home really all of her life, except for a couple of short visits. And indeed, for the last twenty-one years of her life, she never left the grounds of the house. She lived there and worked there, wrote her poetry in her bedroom upstairs.

She left a great riddle and a great mystery to the world when she died. She was herself a great riddle and a great mystery in her life because she was so rarely seen. She dressed in white frequently. She was rarely glimpsed. She almost never went into the town. She was a recluse. Howard Hughes is the wrong comparison, but she was as reclusive as Howard Hughes, certainly.

She wasn't known as a poet except to a very small collection of friends and supporters. She had a number of friends who were editors of literary journals or newspapers, and they knew of her work, but she didn't get it published. It was really ten years ahead of the times. Her poems were so modern in their sound and so unlike the kind of poetry that was being written during her life-time that she didn't find an audience at that time. So except for a small number of people, she was entirely unknown to the public.

That changed soon after her death. But her reputation took quite a long time to really become established and for the facts about her life to become clear. And they never have, actually, because she left so little evidence of who she was, apart from these extraordinary poems that were found in a locked box. This was a secret activity for her. The writing of poetry was her private confessional, if you like. It's where she wrote down all of the things that moved her and she cared about most.

She wrote 1,789 poems. I think 700 were found in this locked box, and then another 1,089 were found elsewhere. Some of them had been sent to friends in letters or just as gifts. She wrote poems after somebody had died, she sent a consoling note and often a little poem. None of them had titles. None of them had dates. And only ten of them had been published in her lifetime, and those against her will.

So when she died, her family, initially, and then the world discovered this. It's one of the great literary riddles of the world, actually: "When were these poems written, and to whom were they written?" When William Wordsworth wrote lines written about Tintern Abbey you know how old he was, what was going on in his life, why he wrote the poem. None of this is known about Emily Dickinson.

> *That God cannot*
> *be understood*
> *Everyone agrees*
> *We do not know*
> *His motives nor*
> *Comprehend his deeds*
> *Then why should I*
> *Seek solace in*
> *What I cannot*
> *Know?*
> *Better to play*
> *In winter's sun*
> *Than to fear the*
> *Snow*

THAT IS THE forgery. That is a poem that was forged by Mark Hofmann, an extraordinarily gifted forger, also a double murderer, and hence the title of the book, *The Poet and the Murderer*. That was the poem that appeared in the

Sotheby's catalog in April 1997. And it was seen by the curator of the Jones Library. It's a fourteen-line poem.

The date that the forger, Mark Hofmann, ascribed to it is 1871, which is important because Emily Dickinson was forty-one at that time, and she was writing these kinds of poems. Her great years as an artist, her most prolific years and the years in which she wrote her greatest poetry for which she's remembered were the sort of late 1850s, early 1860s. . . . This is a little bit after that. Her talent started to cool a little bit, her production started to lessen as well, and she did less revision of her poems. And she wrote these kind of little homily pieces, which this is.

As Daniel Lombardo was thinking of buying the poem, he wanted an outside opinion, and he took it to somebody called Ralph Franklin, who was the head of the Beinecke Library at Yale University. Franklin is the world's acknowledged expert on Dickinson's manuscripts, her handwriting, the whole publication history—the history of her "workshop," as it's called.

Franklin looked at the poem, and both he and Lombardo felt it wasn't a great poem. The best comment I heard was if this was Emily, it was Emily on a bad day. But she did write other poems around this time and later that were little homilies, her so-called wisdom pieces. And that led them to think, "Well, OK, in terms of the content, it could be an Emily Dickinson poem."

PERHAPS I SHOULD go back to the beginning of the story, how I got to find out about it. I read a little article in the *New York Times* that said this poem had been found and it was the first unpublished Emily Dickinson for forty years. It was going on sale. And it was a half-page article. . . . I didn't really think twice about it. I happened to read it. Six months later, I read a very small piece in the *New York Times* that said the unpublished Emily Dickinson poem recently purchased by the Jones Library in Amherst for $21,000 has been returned to Sotheby's as a forgery.

I'm a full-time journalist. I'm a magazine writer. And of course, as a magazine writer, you have your antennae up for a great story. I just was intrigued by this and thought, "Who could manage that? Who would?" He'd fooled Sotheby's. He'd fooled the Jones Library. He fooled everybody, whoever this was.

I called up Dan Lombardo, the curator of the Jones Library, who had bought the poem. . . . [Here's] a small-town librarian who thinks he's doing the best thing for his little home library and finds he's enmeshed in this extraordinary story of money, forgery, auction houses, a rare documents dealer in Las Vegas, gun dealers in Salt Lake City. The trail eventually leads back to Mark Hofmann, to a prison cell in Utah.

When I heard the outlines of the story from Daniel Lombardo, in the first forty-five minutes over the phone, I had that classic [feeling]—the hair stands up on the back of your neck. I just couldn't believe that [all this was] behind this Emily Dickinson poem—and there was an irony to me immediately, of course: Here's this most reclusive of people, who didn't publish in her lifetime, who called publication the "auction of the mind of man"—of all people, she became the object of this extraordinary, convoluted literary scam.

MARK HOFMANN was a Mormon, brought up in Salt Lake City, very bright, very gifted young man. As a teenager, he was interested in chemistry and history, science. He went to Utah State University, studied biology, was very interested in science, chess—very rational mind, an inquiring mind. But he was brought up in a very strict Mormon environment, and he became disgruntled with the Mormon Church. He had a lot of questions about what he regarded were problem areas of Mormon doctrine and theology. To put it bluntly, he simply didn't believe many of the founding legends of the Mormon religion.

I think that this inquiring young mind had a lot of questions. The most important thing with teenagers is to keep a dialogue open, and there wasn't one. He was told, "Shut up and believe," to paraphrase it slightly crudely, and I think that generated a great deal of resentment in him and he became a twisted person inside. . . .

He began to forge Mormon documents. He was a brilliant con man and a master of human psychology, one of the great criminal minds, actually, I think, of the twentieth century. He knew what people wanted. It was as though he could look inside your heart and tell what it was that you cared about most, certainly in terms of manuscript collecting. He knew what people wanted, and he created documents that would answer that need.

As far as we know, because the full tally isn't in, [he forged and sold] about 1,000 documents. . . . Initially, they were, above all, Mormon documents. What he did was diabolically cunning. He initially created documents that appeared to authenticate some of the central tenets of the Mormon religion. . . . He sold these to the Mormon Church and thereby won their confidence. He was also himself a well-respected dealer of historical documents in Salt Lake City, genuine historical documents, which he used as a front. He enmeshed the Mormon Church and its hierarchy. It's worth noting here that the president of the Mormon Church, Gordon B. Hinckley, who was involved with many of these transactions, is a figure in the Mormon religion a bit like the pope in Roman Catholicism. Hofmann was eventually dealing on one-on-one terms with Gordon Hinckley, who thought, of course, that he was buying genuine documents.

His real goal and his unique and long history of literary forgery [was that] he intended to use literary forgery, forged documents, to bring down the Mormon Church, to discredit the Mormon Church. . . . It would be as though a disgruntled Catholic were to forge letters by Saint Paul that proved that Saint Paul was a homosexual, let's say. They were that damaging to the church.

HOFMANN WAS A great technician. So it's not the quantity, it's the quality and the technical skill. Most literary forgers, they specialize, as most art forgers. They do Vermeer or they do Monet. Literary forgers tend to specialize as well.

He forged all of the great figures of the Mormon Church—Joseph Smith, Brigham Young, Lucy Smith, the prophet's mother, and the list goes on and on. They found a list in his prison cell in 1989 in Utah where he listed the Mormon forgeries and his non-Mormon forgeries, and on the list of non-Mormon forgeries he did there is every iconic American figure—Abraham Lincoln, George Washington, Martha Washington, Miles Standish, Daniel Boone. Fourth down on that list that was found was the name Emily Dickinson.

Hofmann was a con man as well. He ran what are called Ponzi schemes, using historical documents. He would take money for documents he hadn't produced. He would take money to buy documents that were going to be worth a huge amount of money and then he wouldn't deliver the documents and then, he would run these schemes.

Like all criminals, he started to get too clever and he thought he could never be caught and he started to get greedy. One of the curious things about Hofmann was that his Achilles heel, if you like—and every criminal has some fatal flaw—was that he was a passionate collector of historical children's books, above all British children's books.

When he went to prison, he had America's finest collection of historic children's books, above all he had a first edition of *The Lord of the Rings*, signed by Tolkien. He had the first edition of *The Adventures of Sherlock Holmes*—extraordinary. He had Enid Blyton books. He had Beatrix Potter books signed by the author.

Of all the strange things—and this was his obsession—actually he was collecting them to leave to his children. The roots of his downfall was that he was himself buying at auction and at Sotheby's among others, large numbers of genuine first editions. This was his passion.

His forgeries, he couldn't produce them fast enough to pay for all of the books he was buying, and he started to cut corners. He was about to be exposed and he savagely murdered two people with pipe bombs, and he was then arrested on suspicion of those.

To prove he was a murderer, they had to first prove that he was a forger, that there was a motive for the murders, and the motive was the forgery, and they could not at first find any sign of forgery in the documents.

[THIS DICKINSON poem that Hofmann forged] had passed through the hands of a historical documents dealer [in Las Vegas] called Todd Axelrod, and it was discovered by Daniel Lombardo and later by myself that it had been in Axelrod's possession for a number of years. He exhibited it in his showrooms for sale for $40,000. Then the trail sort of went cold, and years later it popped up at Sotheby's.

One of the reasons the story fascinated me was this extraordinary journey across America that this document had taken and passed through these different hands. [Initially] the main thrust of it was to join the dots together: How did it get from Hofmann to Las Vegas, from Las Vegas to Sotheby's? What did Sotheby's know? What did the dealer in Las Vegas know? Who was telling the truth? Was anyone?

As I SAID earlier, for me it was a story partly of a small-town librarian, who buys this wonderful document and thinks he's doing a great thing for his hometown. Suddenly, Daniel Lombardo is enmeshed in this world of deception and illusion and money and forgery and gun dealers and a double murderer.

He relentlessly went on a mission to find out what was the truth and eventually established enough evidence to confront Sotheby's. They refunded the money.

But his journey is very interesting because the experience for him of buying this forgery and finding that what he thought was going to be the pinnacle of his career and the best thing he ever did for his local community turned out to be this awful event.

He really thought his life was finished in Amherst and his career as a curator would be finished. He was deeply disillusioned by the whole series of events. It shattered all of his illusions about the auction houses, about the manuscript trade, and he gave up the job and left. At one time, he was in pretty bad shape, he felt that his life had melted down.

But as it turned out, this came to be an opportunity and he started a new life as a writer. He's practicing Zen Buddhism. He's living on Cape Cod and is a very, very happy man. So, in a sense, I also wanted the book to be a sort of morality tale, not just another true crime story about an interesting bad man, but a morality tale. The book ends with everybody getting their just rewards. Emily Dickinson wins eternal fame; Daniel Lombardo has a new life; and the forger is where he belongs.

WHEN IT CAME to the book . . . I tried to concentrate on this one forgery, this Emily Dickinson forgery, and the book took on greater depth when I discovered the strange, uncanny parallels between these two people [Dickinson and Hofmann]. They both were one thing on the outside. Emily Dickinson was the well-to-do daughter of a leading family. She was another thing on the inside. They were both geniuses at what they did—her writing poetry, him forging these documents. And what interested me in writing the book was to bring these two characters together, a bit like electricity, and see what sparks would fly.

A Life in Music

by

ISAAC STERN

Russian-born Isaac Stern immigrated to the United States not long after his birth in 1920. Growing up in San Francisco, he began playing the violin with the San Francisco Symphony at age twelve. In his January 23, 2000, visit to Booknotes, *he recounted many of his life experiences, including a Jerusalem concert during the first Gulf War and his campaign to save New York's Carnegie Hall. His memoir is entitled* My First 79 Years *and was published by Knopf in 1999. After a lifetime in music, Mr. Stern passed away in 2001.*

I'M SEVENTY-NINE. I started playing the violin when I was eight. That's seventy-one years playing. And, since I first played on the stage, sixty-seven years. And sixty-four years since I turned professional. The best thing about it is having been married to music all my life. I've talked about this, so it comes somewhat naturally, but it is absolutely true what I'm about to say: There are so many times, and especially in the last ten years, when I've occasionally stopped and said, "Thank you for making me a musician."

There is something that happens to you when you play, and a moment comes—it's not often—when you, the music, all of it disappears into a oneness, a unity. You feel the music going through you and coming out. It is a kind of personal ecstasy that only performers who care desperately about music—not about the instrument, but about music—get to feel. It's what I learned from the time I was fifteen, to listen for in others.

I WAS BORN in a small town in what they called the "pale of Russia." The week that I was born, it happened to be Polish territory. My parents were

Russian, their family was Russian, all my mother's family, all of them, were Russian back two, three generations. They all lived there. My father came from nearby Kiev; there's a little town, Kreminiecz, right near the Polish border. Every week, there were the white Russians, the red Russians, the pink Russians, the blue Russians, the Cossacks, the Poles. Everybody was running back and forth. My bed had had to be moved, depending on where the shooting was, to get away from the window just to make sure that bullets didn't come in over my crib. Probably that is part of my peripatetic tendencies to this day. At least I happen to think so. We left there when I was ten months old and came to San Francisco.

I was very lucky when growing up in San Francisco that my teacher, Naoum Blinder, organized his own quartet in the San Francisco Symphony. Because he was the dominant violinist in town, I met all the musicians, all the first-chair players. From the time I was twelve, thirteen, fourteen, I was playing chamber music with the best musicians in town. I was a new kid on the block and they treated me as a colleague; gave me hell, which was the best thing they could have done.

It taught me to listen to chamber music as a way of joining with others, to listen, to be a part of something that was bigger than I. That experience is what set my whole musical artistic life in motion. When I was fifteen, I heard the Budapest String Quartet just newly arrived in this country.

Then came my first all-Beethoven and Bartok cycles. It swept over me like a stream of golden honey; it opened worlds for me. All the members of the quartet became my friends, particularly the second violinist, Alexander Schneider—Sasha, as we all called him—who became my closest friend when I was fifteen until he died [in 1993].

From that time on, as the kid in San Francisco whom everybody knew and liked—I was lucky—I was invited to the symphony rehearsals. I was invited to come to the opera rehearsals. That's where I first heard my first *Ring* cycle, conducted by Artur Bodanzky, a famous Wagnerian specialist at the time, with local San Francisco singers like Lauritz Melchior and Kirsten Flagstad and Lotte Lehmann. . . .

I'm talking about big, big singers. I heard Rachmaninoff play Beethoven sonatas. I heard Schabel. I heard Kreisler. I heard Yehudi Menuhin when he was a young man. All this music and being involved with the playing of chamber music gave me a clear picture of what I intuited and felt strongly at the time. And as years later went on, I learned the reason why I'm here, why I'm alive.

I went to school for a week when I was a child, and then it was decided that because of practicing, I should have "tutors." I had some people who tried to teach me the rudiments of mathematics and other things. I learned.

Mostly, I found it was very good to argue with older people and because I had a certain talent on the violin, older people gravitated around me. . . . I [made] a lot of friends, older friends. And I read a good deal. I remember reading John Dos Passos at that time, the early books on the American scene. I remember reading *Call of the Wild*, Joseph Conrad, and many, many other books that influenced my early thoughts.

I WAS GIVEN a Guadagnini—it's wonderful, the second line of violin makers in Italy, in the late to the second half of the eighteenth century—when I was sixteen or seventeen. Ms. Lutie Goldstein was a patroness from my early years and was a maiden lady who had great faith in me. And, more or less, she adopted me and took care of my education, and first needs, and travel and so on. She bought me the violin for the princely sum at that time of $6,500. I was given title when she bought the violin. I kept that violin and played my first nine or ten years of concerts on it. That means that I was playing it until I was twenty-four, twenty-five, until I felt that I needed something a little bigger and another man lent me a Strad. Later on, I gathered up my courage and bought the first of my Guarneris. At that time, I think the price was around $65,000.

THE FIRST TIME I went to the Soviet Union, 1956, it was before there was an artistic exchange agreement between the Soviet Union and the United States. My manager, the legendary Sol Hurok—they don't make them like that anymore—he invented a statement that I have to quote. He was the most famous impresario in the business, world-famous. . . . He brought ballet to the United States. He had huge stars like Arthur Rubinstein, Marian Anderson, Roberta Peters, Jan Peerce. He was very careful. He was very successful. He made and lost fortunes, but he was known as a man who had magic at the box office. And somebody once asked him, "Tell me, what is this touch you have in having box office successes?" He said, "There's one thing I know: If people don't want to come, nothing will stop them." Very, very profound remark.

So he tried to find out what would make people want to come. He was a very important person in my formative years. He taught me many lessons. We were very close friends, despite the fact that he was my manager. I used to call him Papa. He liked me personally very, very much. He taught me to always let the local manager make a buck. Don't force the last dollar at the cost of somebody else. There were times when he agreed to concerts with friends of his, Russian friends and others, and they went broke. They couldn't pay. He would pay their bills. He would sometimes pay my fees if they couldn't. And sometimes he and I just simply waited. I learned to have patience.

MY FRIENDS, Eugene Istomin and Leonard Rose—we were the Istomin-Stern-Rose Trio—were invited to play at the [Kennedy] White House. I had been a guest at the first concert that the Kennedys had, which was Pablo Casals. From then on, we were friends and I was at other events at the Kennedy White House. Then they asked us to play on one occasion.

Pierre Salinger, who was Kennedy's press secretary, was a personal friend of mine. His mother had briefly taught me French in San Francisco many years before. . . . Pierre was away from the White House for the couple of days before we came and played, so he didn't have a chance to clue the president in on the niceties of trio chamber music playing.

We played some Schubert, I think, and the president got up at the end of the performance, as he always does, to thank us and said, "And I thank Isaac Stern and his two accompanists." I was ready to drop through the floor. That wasn't the right thing to say, but he realized very quickly he'd made a serious gaffe and turning on full charm, invited us to his private quarters after the reception and charmed both of my friends right out of their clothes. He was wonderful.

[I MET WITH President Johnson in the Oval Office.] There was a discussion that I was having with him about establishing the National Endowment for the Arts. I had begun this discussion with Kennedy, and after his assassination, I kept it up to some degree with Salinger, and then I had a very close friend who was at one time my attorney, Abe Fortas, who became a Supreme Court justice and was the closest adviser to President Johnson.

Abe was an extraordinary man, a Tennessean with this Southern gallantry and a slight, wonderful, little smooth slur to his accent, who was probably one of the greatest legal minds that this country has ever had. I learned a great deal about the history of law from him.

Johnson insisted on putting him on the Court. Through Abe, I continued the discussions with Johnson as to the necessity of having the National Endowment come into being. I remember . . . Johnson saying to me, "I've talked with Abe about this." He says, "I don't know much about music or the arts," he said, "but I promise you one thing, I'm going to keep my cotton-pickin' hands off of it. You take care of it."

. Having that launching was very important at that time. We came in with the enormous budget, I think, of $2.5 million or $3 million, which was a laughable amount to people at the Ford Foundation, who were giving ten times that much. But, slowly, the whole of the NEA grew until it became one of the most important assets to the intellectual and civilized life of this country.

The attacks on it are neither fair, intelligent, or educated. I have no hesitancy in saying all those things about those who have attacked it in the Congress. I pity them because they don't realize to what degree they don't know. They don't recognize the fact that the legacy that the United States will leave as a civilized nation is directly connected with what kind of a civilization its everyday life is.

A civilized life does not exist without the arts. It has nothing to do with economic position. It has nothing to do with social position. It has to do with having young children—and having everybody—realize what a wonderment there is in the creativity of men's minds. What beauty can be in life if you know music, if you can see a painting, see a sculpture, watch a ballet, listen to a song, read a book. All the things that make us non-animal, that make us human. The quality of thought. It is the greatest gift that we were given as a species. It is the greatest responsibility today that we have toward our young people.

I'VE BEEN WITH one company in all its permutations for over fifty years. I signed with Columbia Records in 1945 with Goddard Lieberson, God bless his memory—one of the great giants in producing musical records, a composer and a man knowledgeable about music, and of enormous charm, intelligence, and education. Then Columbia Records became CBS Records, became CBS Classical, became CBS-Sony, and now it's Sony and Sony Classical. And through all those permutations, I've stayed with the company. I don't know how many records. Perhaps 100, 150, maybe more. I don't keep count that way.

THE STRUGGLE TO save Carnegie Hall was a watershed event in my life. The first meeting of the committee that eventually became the first board of Carnegie Hall was in my apartment on Central Park West in New York City on January 10, 1960. I had spent some of the months before—October, November, December—trying to go to people to not allow the hall to be destroyed. That included people from Dean Acheson, who was head of the Rockefeller Brothers Fund at the time, to the Rockefellers, who were involved with Lincoln Center and the development over there. Eventually, all of that proved to be unsuccessful. I decided to form a committee and do it because I could not conceive that this could be allowed to happen.

Carnegie's not a hall. It's a necessary mythology. There are other good halls, there are some good ones, all over the world: Teatro Colón in Argentina, the Great Hall of the Conservatory in Moscow, the Concertgebouw in Amsterdam, some halls in Japan, some symphony halls in Boston. There are fine halls. Only Carnegie—the only one in the world, where every orchestra, every conductor, since 1891, when Tchaikovsky opened the hall, there hasn't been a single major conductor, orchestra, pianist, cellist, singer, violinist who has not appeared at Carnegie Hall. It's the only hall which can say that. It's the center of the musical world.

I WAS IN Jerusalem [during the first Gulf War.] It was just toward the last few days before the ground war began in Iraq. I had been hoping to go because everything in Israel had stopped because of the occasional missiles that were landing there. All public assembly was stopped. I was in the Azores playing concerts and I had called Zubin Mehta and said, "Look, is there any way I can come and help and play?" He said, "Well, we're not allowed to be in the big halls because it's hard to get the people out of there quickly, but we're playing in some small theaters. Let me see. Maybe in a couple of days it'll be possible." I went to play a concert in the early afternoon and I got a message: "Please call Zubin." He said, "It's off. A Scud just landed and all the bans are still on. No public assembly." So I said, "All right. Let me know." So I went back to New York and, of course, within twenty-four hours of getting back to New York, he called. "OK, we can start playing in two days." I said, "I'll come."

So I came and we couldn't play in any of the major halls. We played in little theaters all around the perimeter of Tel Aviv. The last concert was to be in Jerusalem. While in Tel Aviv, there was a Scud warning and I was in a hotel with some friends and we took refuge in the assigned quarters. So I learned a little bit about what happened when a Scud was detected. I knew there was seven minutes at the most from the time they noticed it till it landed somewhere. They couldn't always track it, but they could tell a Scud was approaching Israel. It's a tiny country; it's a spit of land. When I went to Jerusalem for the last concert, it was a Saturday and it was in the Jerusalem Theatre, where their concert hall is. And it was the first time in more than a month that the people in the audience in the hall, including quite a few people from the government, had been together in one room.

I was playing Mozart's G Major Concerto with Zubin conducting with members of the Israel Philharmonic, and I'm playing away, and Zubin suddenly reaches over and stops me. "I think we have to stop." So I looked up and sure enough a man came out of the wings and announced in Hebrew, English, and Arabic that a Scud had been detected on the way and would everybody please put on gas masks. They didn't have to leave, but put gas masks on, because the theater was fairly well built and they considered it fairly safe. Of course, members of the government immediately, quietly— you saw them all scuttle out and disappear and go to their offices. And the orchestra members scattered backstage to call their families, "We're all right. Don't worry. We have our masks. We'll take care of ourselves." I felt this discomfort in the audience and they were reaching down and putting on these masks. And I thought, "What am I here for? I'm here to be useful and I think I'm needed." Those are the two things you get very rarely in your life, to be in a place where you're needed and useful.

So I walked back on stage. I didn't wear the mask. I had it right offstage. But the audience, they were all sitting with masks on. . . . It looked so odd and so out of place. I decided to play some Bach, and I knew approximately that five or six minutes from the time I was going to start to play would be about the time it would take the missile to arrive. So I chose to play some music, a saraband from the "Sonata for Violin Alone in D Minor." Slowly, I could feel the audience starting to relax and listen and sit back, even with the masks on.

I came to the end, and sure enough, the guard came on stage and said, "It's OK. It dropped about fifteen kilometers away. No one was hurt. It's in an uninhabited area." So that got the attention. There was a television crew backstage, a French television crew, that happened to tape some seconds of it and it's received a lot of publicity. For all the years I've played in Israel, I don't think anything got the attention of the people—as a matter of fact, around the world—as much as that moment. It was not something particularly valorous or grand. I was doing what I was there for. It was a little bit like the juggler in *The Juggler of Notre Dame* juggling in front of the statue of Mary. I play the violin for people. I'm there to make them feel better. So that was what I was doing.

Tupac Shakur
and Hip-Hop Culture

by

MICHAEL ERIC DYSON

The hip-hop culture exploded in America in the 1990s, and rap singer Tupac Shakur became an icon for millions of young people. Shakur was born in Harlem in 1971. His string of hit records began in 1982. By 1993, he was in trouble with the law, spending time in jail on various charges. In September 1996, he was killed in a drive-by shooting in Las Vegas, ensuring larger-than-life status among his fans. Cultural critic Michael Eric Dyson was seen on Booknotes *on September 6, 2001, discussing* Holler If You Hear Me: Searching for Tupac Shakur, *published by Basic Civitas Books in 2001.*

[I'M SEARCHING FOR Tupac Shakur] because he's disappeared from the common light of our public life. He's also a murdered figure who still has a shroud of mystery around him. I wanted to find out if I could determine who this real person was, the mythology about him being a thug, about him being a poet, about him being a black revolutionary, his pedigree inherited from his mother. I wanted to figure out what the real Tupac Shakur was about—who was he, what drove him, what passions ignited him, and, ultimately, what was the meaning of his life.

[TUPAC WAS] deeply political. In fact, he began as a very political animal. Tupac began as the kind of rapper who was more associated with the "positive and political rap" of, say, a person like Chuck D. Chuck D is the head rapper of the group Public Enemy, which rose to prominence in the late

1980s and early 1990s in America, and X-Clan, another group from the East that was deeply and profoundly cultural and political, African-centered, conscious of their cultural roots, and deeply determined to bring change to American society. So Tupac initially was just part of that because he was a child of a Black Panther, [something] he talked about. . . . He has a song called *Holler If Ya Hear Me*, from which my book title is taken, where he says, "Just the other day, I got lynched by some crooked cops, and to this day those same cops on the beat getting major pay. But when I get my check, they takin' tax out. So we payin' the pigs to knock the blacks out." Even as he evolved and grew to embrace thug culture, he was always political in the midst of that.

HE WAS A young man who was born in the ghetto of New York, in Harlem, to a mother who was accused along with twenty other Black Panther figures of attempting to blow up fire stations and to bomb railway stations and so on in New York City. She was taken to trial along with her co-defendants. She represented herself and represented the rest of the Panther 21, as they were called, and she showed an enormously intelligent defense of their position and got them off.

A month after that, Tupac was born, named after an Incan conquistador whose body was ripped apart by Spanish conquerors. So here was a very powerful figure, Afeni Shakur, who became the darling of the left liberal wing of American politics for maybe about a year. After that, she was left to her own wits. She became a legal assistant, as it was then known, and tried to support her family but had to go on welfare; had a daughter, Sekyiwa, in 1975, with Mutulu Shakur, who himself was a revolutionary Black Panther.

Tupac was nurtured in an environment where he believed that black people should struggle for self-determination, that they should struggle against white supremacy, that they should oppose it with everything that was in them—their heads, their hearts, their souls, their bodies.

As he grew up, his mother became addicted to crack cocaine. As a result of her addiction, Tupac suffered a series of, shall we say, domestic setbacks. He went from home to home; he was homeless. By the time he was thirteen, he had lived in twenty different places. He went on to become a serious actor, joining the West 127th Street Ensemble Company in New York, where he performed the part of Travis in *A Raisin in the Sun*, the play by Lorraine Hansberry, for Jesse Jackson's 1984 campaign. So early on, he enjoyed the spotlight and enjoyed his camaraderie with these famous black figures.

He went on to leave New York at about the age of fifteen, moved to Baltimore with his mother, and became a member of the Baltimore School for the Arts, which is a very renowned school. He was an enormously gifted actor.

Everybody there says he was tremendous. Even in a school that was known for its extraordinary thespian talent, he stood out because of his spookiness, because of his intensity, because of his mastery of his craft. He also studied ballet and art, began to write poetry, began to rap a bit, met the actress that would eventually become Jada Pinkett Smith, who became one of his close friends. He moved from there at age seventeen to Marin City in California, and there attended what they call Mount Tam High School, one of the elite schools in a very, very nicely sequestered school district. . . . [He] became disillusioned with school because it no longer fit his view of the world, which was, "I'm a young black person trying to struggle for an authentic identity and to articulate my viewpoints about the world, and it's not being supported in school." So he became a rapper after that.

[SHAKUR DIED] September 13th, 1996.

He was murdered in a drive-by. Suge Knight, his record company label head, was driving a 750 black BMW, and Shakur was riding, unfortunately, shotgun, and someone drove up in an automobile and, according to either story, stuck a hand out and fired several rounds into the car door or got out and then actually shot at the car door with Mr. Shakur there, trying to get into the backseat, Mr. Knight pulling him down. Two bullets went through him, and he lingered . . . technically, from the 6th through the 13th—seven days. He died on Friday, September 13th.

He was twenty-five years old.

[People think he's still alive because of], first of all, the kind of numerology that he delved into on his posthumously published album, *Makaveli*. He adopted the Machiavelli character, although he changed the spelling. People thought, well, since Machiavelli in *The Prince* talks about faking one's own death to maintain power, that Tupac Shakur knew that he was going to, quote, "be alleged to have died." Therefore, [they presumed] he faked his own death to escape the rat race he was involved in, to escape the thug life, the viciousness that he had become involved in, and to escape his record contract with a company that had got him out of jail. [They speculated] that now he wanted to leave for greener pastures.

But furthermore, young people believe that Tupac is alive because he's the first black person to integrate this immortal class of figures like JFK and Elvis who are believed to still be alive by their fans. There was something both charismatic and tragic about Tupac at the same time, and many of his fans believe that given his own addiction to drama, that this was the ultimate drama: to escape by pretending that one was dead, so that one could move on in different spheres of one's life. But in the case of Tupac, especially for young black people, I think partly what's going on is the deflection of the reality of death; that is, that people who make some of the decisions and choices he made end up being murdered as a result, as a consequence of the lifestyle that they live. Tupac certainly was a representative of a destructive, as well as edifying, lifestyle for young black people.

SUGE KNIGHT went to prison. The night that Tupac Shakur was murdered, they were attending a Bruce Seldon and Mike Tyson fight in Las Vegas at the MGM. At the MGM, as they were exiting the fight, somebody told Tupac Shakur, "We think we see a guy who snatched one of the Death Row pendants," from one of their fellow artists. Tupac then pursued him. His name was Orlando Anderson. The entourage of Tupac and Suge Knight began to get in kicks and hits and to assail the young man. He pressed no charges. He was allegedly a member of the Crips. Suge Knight was allegedly a member of the Bloods and Tupac was closely allied with him. Anderson was brought up on charges of violating his probation—he had a previous charge involving guns—so he was sent to jail for eight years.

After poring over all of this stuff, I think that what happened that night in the MGM, at the Bruce Seldon–Mike Tyson fight in Vegas, is that when Tupac led the volley of fists against this young man, Orlando Anderson, who was a Crip, part of the rival gang to the Bloods out there in L.A., . . . he sought revenge. Or, at least somebody in the Crips sought revenge that night. As a result of that gang warfare, they rode up on Tupac, so to speak, by drive-by and exacted revenge. But that's just a theory. I have no proof of that at all, but given the kind of gang retribution that goes on very commonly in Los Angeles between the Bloods and the Crips, it would not be a far-fetched theory.

AFENI SHAKUR lives now in Stone Mountain, Georgia, in a house that Tupac bought her with the proceeds from the down payment on his first three albums for Death Row Records. Death Row . . . is now called Tha Row Records, since label head Suge Knight has been released from jail. He was in prison for four years. He went to prison where Tupac was, in Rikers Island, and the Clinton Correctional Facility. Tupac had him sign a three-page, handwritten contract that was the basis of their professional relationship. It was the last company for which Tupac worked. He signed that contract and said, "I need a house for my mother." And so a house was purchased for Tupac's mother, and that's the house in Stone Mountain, Georgia.

Afeni Shakur understands that Tupac was, in the words of Hegel, a world historical figure; he was a very important young man, even though mainstream society may not have been attuned to his importance. She understood that this was a figure who was not only important for African American youth or for pop culture. He is a figure in whom we can see the contesting will of somebody who wants to be smart and intelligent, on the one hand, and on the other hand, got caught up in some self-destructive habits. She sees her son as an exemplar of the best and the brightest of African American culture, and she sees him as a symbol of a generation that continues to fight for legitimacy in a culture that often doesn't recognize it.

Tupac had written his mother a nine-page letter when she indicated that she was in recovery for her crack addiction [which became the song "Dear Mama"]. He said to her, "I appreciate what you've done, but you can't expect me overnight to accept your word that you will stay clean, simply because you said so." This was right when he was becoming famous. He struggled mightily with her decision to go into rehabilitation and whether or not it was a legitimate one. He certainly understood later on that it was.

This was his way of making up with her in public, of forgiving her, of offering an olive branch, so to speak, to bring more tranquillity to their domestic relationship. And so this "Dear Mama" was him speaking from his heart, a gesture of love, a gesture of also criticism, but an acknowledgment that "you are a serious woman, and that there have been serious odds against you."

HE MADE A ton of money and spent a ton of money because he had, some argued, up to forty friends and relatives that he was taking care of at the time of his death. His second album debuted at the top of the charts. His third album, *Me Against the World*, debuted when he was in prison for a conviction of sexual abuse. He had been charged with sodomy and rape, but he was acquitted of those charges and accused of forcibly touching a woman's buttocks.

So this album debuted at the top of the charts, and his next album, *All Eyez on Me*, which was the first double album in the history of hip-hop culture, went on to sell something like 7 million copies. He was extraordinarily popular, made it into a huge sum of money, and spent a huge sum of money because he was a very compassionate young man who believed that he was responsible for taking care of his family.

Death Row Records claimed that Tupac owed them money as a result of his lavish lifestyle, living in the Peninsula Hotel in Los Angeles, California, and the cars that he purchased, and just lavishing gifts on women, and so on. Whereas the estate that was headed by Afeni Shakur, his mother, claimed that he was owed millions of dollars. So they went to court and finally settled by giving the rights of that music to Afeni Shakur and Amaru Records. But he certainly has generated millions of dollars since his death, and his estate continues to collect money.

HIP-HOP IS the term assigned not only to rap music but the larger culture out of which rap music issues. Some say DJ Kool Herc, who is a famous person within rap music, came up with the term. Some say it was somebody else. But the term suggests something about the beat, the rhythm, the passion of urban street life. I was a huge fan of that kind of music because I was a teen father. I knew my son was attracted to that. I wanted to find a way to be able to reach him, to bridge the gulf, generationally speaking, but also because I was a member of a family that was deeply into music. I grew up in Detroit, Michigan, in the inner city. My father and mother listened to everything from blues to jazz and R&B, so I was deeply attracted to the music.

There's a deep division in black America precisely over hip-hop culture and the tremendous tensions that go between the so-called civil rights generation and the hip-hop culture. That's why [in] my book on Martin Luther King Jr., I talked about King and the hip-hop generation. A lot of black people thought, "That's really sacrilegious. How ridiculous is that? And it doesn't have the real intellectual payoff that you might think." My point was not to bring Dr. King down, so-called, to Tupac Shakur's level. They're not moral equivalents. I wasn't that silly. What I was trying to suggest is that some of the same faults and foibles that we forgive King for, we nail these young kids for, and they're in the process of growing up in public.

There's [also] a deep division in black America about the virtue or the value of hip-hop culture. I happen to think that it's a much more complex phenomenon that needs to be supported. It needs to be criticized, to be sure, but also needs to be examined for its complexity. If we have one broad stroke with which we paint the entire culture against the canopy of our disdain, then we're really dismissing what is essentially the most powerful form of popular culture for the last twenty-five years. It's certainly the most invigorating black popular culture of the last, at least, couple of decades.

I HOPE [MY BOOK] educates people about the complexity of this young man. I hope it opens their eyes and their minds to receive some of his messages, while still being critical of him, as I am. I have an entire chapter about his extraordinarily powerful intelligence, the way he read voraciously. He consumed books in a fashion that is associated with professors and not necessarily with ghetto residents. I wanted to reject and repudiate the vicious stereotypes that prevail about not only Tupac but this culture in general.

I'm not suggesting that all of them, or even most of them, read as much as he does, but I think that they are highly intelligent. If you listen to some of the narratives of a person like Mos Def, when he said, "You can laugh and criticize Michael Jackson if you want to. Woody Allen molested and married his stepdaughter. Same press kicking dirt on Michael's name, show Woody and Soon-Yi at the playoff game." So there's high intelligence in there. There's narrative complexity, there's poetic intensity. In Tupac, here was a figure who read widely—feminist theory, he read George Orwell, he read James Baldwin and Nikki Giovanni. He read broadly in self-healing arts, in method acting. I just wanted to suggest that this was a complex, beautiful, self-destructive, confused, edifying young man who brought both the glory and the grief of black culture to live in one body.

I'm critical of the self-destructive choices that he made in regard to talking about women. . . . . I'm critical of him in terms of trying to be a, quote, "real nigger" and reducing an authentic black person to a person who lives in the ghetto. Having come from the ghetto myself, I understand that inclination and appreciate his giving visibility to those who are often denied access to the mainstream culture as legitimately positive people. At the same time, to reduce the complexity of black culture to the ghetto and to suggest that if you're not acting as if you are in the ghetto, or more importantly, that the ghetto is all about being a thug or a pimp or a player, so to speak, [is misdirected]. [The ghetto can also mean] somebody who attends Sunday school or takes lessons with the local musician. To reduce the complexity of the ghetto to even a thug, I think, is misdirected. To see black authenticity linked primarily, or exclusively, to the ghetto is as misled as the bourgeois sensibilities that try to distance black people from the ghetto altogether.

Even Tupac himself, in a song called "I Ain't Mad at You," talked about the extraordinary tensions that result when a person who had formerly been part of a ghetto clique converts to becoming a Muslim and as a result of that doesn't want to associate anymore with that lifestyle. Tupac says, "That's fine, because I'm not mad at you." He says, "I'm not angry at you for wanting to get out the ghetto." There are many up-from-the-ghetto stories in hip-hop culture, similar to Booker T. Washington's *Up from Slavery*, reproduced more than 100 years later, about the upward mobility and the striving of young black people.

America's Mottoes and Pledges

by

BRIAN BURRELL

Among the many expressions that Americans have come to accept out of tradition are "In God We Trust" and "E Pluribus Unum." In his book The Words We Live By: The Creeds, Mottoes, and Pledges That Have Shaped America, *published by The Free Press in 1997, Brian Burrell has examined the origins and significance of some these famous sayings. Mr. Burrell, author and University of Massachusetts lecturer, joined us on* Booknotes *on September 7, 1997.*

I GOT THE IDEA for this book from my father. . . . He's a collector of words, a guy who went around and, when he came to monuments, [would] copy down the inscriptions. When we went to diners, he would copy down the little sayings he found on the placemat menus. This was a collection he put together, which I can vaguely remember from my youth. But as I got older, I would see this collection on his shelf in this three-ring binder and would page through it. I would come upon these outlandish initiation notes and codes of ethics of organizations and inscriptions and mottoes, and I always thought it would make a great book.

[Look at the dollar bill.] There's the Great Seal, which appears to the left and the right of the word "one." And then above the word "one" you have the words "In God We Trust." The things that I was focusing on in the design of the dollar bill are the mottoes, "Annuit Coeptus," "Novus Ordo Seclorum," over in the right "E Pluribus Unum," and then in the middle, what is our official national motto, "In God We Trust." The fact is, that someone had to choose these mottoes and put them on there, and this took a bit of doing.

There's an interesting story behind the mottoes on the Great Seal. We can really attribute this to Charles Thomson, who was the secretary of Congress. He was more or less the factotum, the guy who got things done. In fact, he was the second signer of the Declaration, although we don't give him credit for that because he was merely attesting John Hancock's signature. But he was the second of two signers on July 4th, when the Declaration went out.

Later in the day, on July 4th, 1776, Congress assembled a committee to design a great seal, in other words, to design something that was going to represent the country. Thomas Jefferson, Ben Franklin, and John Adams made it onto that committee, and they had some ideas for what would make a good seal and some good mottoes. But they were all shot down, basically. They could not come to a consensus. Then it went to another committee a few years later, and they couldn't come up with the ideas.

"E Pluribus Unum" is one of the ideas that came out of that process. This was chosen by one of the consultants to the committee, a man named Pierre Eugène du Simitière. It means "one from many." You can find it in Virgil and you can find it in a few other classical writers, but there is a consensus that it seems to have been inspired by Virgil.

Simitière's idea was that this was a country formed out of about six different European nationalities. His idea has evolved over time so that we now think of it in a more multicultural sense: many peoples brought together as one people, as Americans. But originally it had a much more Eurocentric motivation behind it. Of course, others at that time thought it had something to do with thirteen colonies joined as one. That was the other interpretation.

"IN GOD WE TRUST" is our official motto as of 1956. Probably a lot of people, myself included, up until I researched this, thought that "E Pluribus Unum" was the motto because it has appeared on the Great Seal and on our currency practically since the inception. "In God We Trust" first appeared on U.S. currency in 1864, on the two-cent piece. Salmon P. Chase, secretary of the treasury, put it there. A suggestion was made to him that during the time of the Civil War, should the Union not survive, that posterity might look back and think of it as a heathen nation. The suggestion was made then that some acknowledgment of God be made on the currency.

There were several people making this type of suggestion and Chase picked up on it. He went to the man in charge of the mint and said, "Do this," with a couple of coins that were coming up for redesign. The man came back with two coins, one of which was this two-cent piece. He had a couple of suggestions for the mottoes. I believe one suggestion was "God, Our Trust," and Chase rewrote it to say "In God We Trust." Where he got that, it's not perfectly clear. If you go back to the national anthem by Francis

Scott Key in 1814, the very last verse, the one we never sing says, "And this be our motto: In God is our trust."

No one seems to have picked up on that for quite a while, but the expression "In God We Trust" became the motto of some Pennsylvania volunteers in the Civil War. It was a company that distinguished itself in battle and had this as their war cry. Chase perhaps picked it up from that. . . . He got a little bit of flack for it, but on the whole, it was accepted. It began to appear on coinage more and more until 1907, when Theodore Roosevelt thought it shouldn't be there. On the new designs for some $10 gold pieces, he wanted it removed.

You get a very interesting discussion in the *Congressional Record*, if you look back to that period—the pros and cons of having God on our money, commingling God and mammon, as it were. The Congress came down on the side of the motto, that it should be there, it should be restored to all coins on which it had previously appeared. But it had not appeared on paper money yet, and that really takes us to the 1950s, where the suggestion was then made, "If it's on the coins, why isn't it on the dollar bills?"

Again, a big discussion ensued, but it passed a little more easily. In the 1950s, with the Pledge of Allegiance being altered with the addition of the words "under God," and this addition to the currency, as well as our official motto going into effect, it seemed to be the decade in which God made quite an appearance in public life in this country. A lot of people have tried to undo that but have not succeeded to this point.

Teaching U.S. History

by

JAMES W. LOEWEN

After two years of studying some of the most popular high school history textbooks, James Loewen concluded that these books largely omit any ambiguity or conflict from our nation's past, focusing instead on glorifying U.S. history. Mr. Loewen appeared on Booknotes *on March 26, 1995, to discuss his book* Lies My Teacher Told Me: Everything Your American History Textbook Got Wrong, *published by The New Press that same year. Mr. Loewen is a writer in Washington, D.C.*

SOME OF THE lies [my teachers told me], I have to admit, are lies of omissions. I remember learning when I was forty-two years old that the United States had put troops into the Soviet Union in order to support the white side of the "White–Red" civil war that was going on in 1918. I learned that those troops stayed there two years in conjunction with Japanese troops and some British and French naval support. They went all the way to Lake Baikal in the middle of Siberia. We also had troops up in Murmansk and Archangel up near Norway. I thought, how is it that I, a history minor in college, never learned that? So, I went back to my college history book, written by Richard Hofstadter et al., and found everything that Hofstadter had deigned to tell me about that "invasion." It was the following half sentence, speaking about World War I: "American troops were withdrawn from Europe by 1918 with the exception of a contingent from Vladivostok in 1920." So there's a half sentence about how we took our troops out of Vladivostok on April Fool's Day, it turned out, in 1920; nothing at all about how we put them in. That's an example.

I TAUGHT FOR many years at Tougaloo College, a college in Mississippi that is predominantly African American. Then I moved to the University of Vermont, so I went from the blackest to the whitest college in America. When I was at Tougaloo, I was distraught by the fact that my students believed the following myth about Reconstruction: that Reconstruction was that time period when blacks took over the government of the Southern states right after the Civil War, but they were too soon out of slavery, and so they messed up and whites had to take control again. Now, that's a terrible misstatement of what happened in Reconstruction. For one thing, the Southern states were governed by a black–white coalition led by whites; they did not go under black control. For another thing, many of the Southern states, particularly Mississippi, had good government during Reconstruction. In Mississippi, the state government during that time period started the public schools for both races, whites as well as blacks, wrote a terrific new constitution, and did other things.

I thought, what must it do to people to believe erroneously that the one time that they were on the center stage of history in the American past, they messed up? What does that do to your self-concept? So I looked into how had my students learned this. Why did they believe it? Tougaloo is a good college. They had learned what was in their high school state history books, so I put together a coalition of students and faculty, and we wrote a new history of Mississippi called *Mississippi: Conflict and Change*. The state rejected it for public school use—that's another story—but we actually took them to court about that and won a First Amendment victory.

Then I moved to Vermont and realized that in this way, as in so many other ways, Mississippi was not exactly different from the United States as a whole. It was just an exaggeration. In other words, I got interested in American history, not just state history, and realized that it, too, suffers from tremendous distortions and omissions and even lies.

I CALL [historical markers] "lies on the landscape." We've got these markers all over the United States. The first problem with them is what *isn't* commemorated. All kinds of major events go unmarked because they're controversial or because they don't show the United States in the best light.

I was on one of the Finger Lakes teaching a bunch of history teachers. There's a marker there for General Sullivan's raid against the Iroquois during the American Revolution. It's got some very interesting doublespeak in which the marauding Indians messed up the settlers and therefore the army came in and punished the Indians and moved the frontier a couple of hundred miles west. Well, if you think about who were the settlers, the settlers were actually the Iroquois, and part of what Sullivan did was burn their cornfields, destroy their orchards, and tear down their houses. They were the settlers; these were not wandering people; these were not nomads. The marker could best be understood using a phrase from William Buckley: "History is the polemics of the victor."

[To RESEARCH this book,] I'm possibly the only living American who has slogged through twelve high school history textbooks from cover to cover. Besides that, I had to do a lot of research on, . . . for instance, the putting of troops into the Soviet Union, so that I would make sure that I got the facts straight.

I wanted to pick some of the best-seller history texts so that I would cover at least the textbooks that more than half of our students read. There's one book in particular; it used to be called *Rise of the American Nation*, and after we lost the war in Vietnam it got retitled *Triumph of the American Nation*. It has over a fourth of the market by itself. Publishers are leery of divulging sales figures, so it's a little hard to know after that one what's the best-seller, but I tried to include several of the very popular books. I also included two older books. These are called "inquiry textbooks," and they were written during the 1970s, and they were a little different. The other ten books we would call "narrative textbooks." They just tell a straight chronology, and they tell it pretty much in the authorial voice, the kind of omnipresent, omniscient, godlike "here's what happened and then here's what happened next." But the inquiry textbooks include more emphasis on primary sources, and then they ask students questions that, hopefully, get them thinking. These textbooks are no longer in print. The inquiry-text movement didn't find favor with teachers, and it went out of existence.

If you get one-fourth of the market, that is a bonanza and every textbook [author] it seems, and every publisher wants to have that book. Therefore, these books end up as clones of each other. It surprises me. If you think about it, in Washington, D.C., the school board is under black control. The same is true for Detroit, for New York City, for many other cities, and for some districts in Mississippi, for instance, but there is no black-oriented U.S. history. There's no U.S. history that, in fact, is what we might call multicentric. I would say they are all Eurocentric. They are all clones of each other because each one wants to be the next *Triumph of the American Nation*.

IF YOU OR I were going to write a history book, the first thing that Scott Foresman or Macmillan or whoever was engaging us would do is send us five or six competitors, and they would say, "This is what you're up against." I believe they would be saying also, "Make sure your book includes the stuff these books include." The result of that is that the process is supposed to be one in which the textbook is based on the underlying secondary literature in history. There's a terrific secondary literature in history. It's what I read; it's what I based *Lies My Teacher Told Me* on. . . . The textbooks are not based on the huge secondary literature in history. They're based on each other, and thus they repeat some errors that go all the way back to the 1890s. . . . Basically, history textbooks are not reviewed, at least high school textbooks. Even college textbooks are generally not reviewed.

The history profession considers textbooks a little bit dirty; that is, if I were a historian and I were applying for a new job at the University of Washington and I'm already at the University of Vermont, the fact that I might have written a history textbook would not count in my favor if I'm looking for tenure, if I'm looking for advancement. The deans and the history departments are looking for me to write a wonderful monograph on Andrew Jackson or whatever my wonderful monograph is about. They're not looking for a textbook. They consider them kind of dirty, kind of done for profit. At the University of Vermont the former dean made a distinction between scholarship and what he called pedagogy, and textbooks would fit under that latter theme, and get very little credit. The same holds even for the review journals. They're busy; they take their time writing reviews of monographs. They do not bother reviewing textbooks, particularly high school textbooks.

I DEDICATE THIS book to "All American history teachers who teach against their textbooks." That's actually what needs to be done. Now, this is a very interesting point: just think about the titles of textbooks. In chemistry, a high school chemistry textbook is likely to be called *Chemistry* or *Principles of Chemistry* or *Introduction to Chemistry*. The same is true in mathematics. The same is true even in English literature. But in history, very few books are called *American History* or something bland like that. They're called *Rise of the American Nation; Triumph of the American Nation; The Great Experiment; The Great Republic; Land of the Free*. These are real titles.

What is that saying? That we are not just entering another subject; we are not just going to learn about history; we are going to salute it. We are going to salute the flag; it's going to be an exercise in nationalism. I think that's wrong. We develop stronger citizens . . . if we teach history with all of its dirt and its glory, with all of its questions, with its good guys and its bad guys, instead of only good guys.

MY FIRST CHAPTER is about heroes and what textbooks do to heroes, and the two heroes I pick on are Helen Keller and Woodrow Wilson. Both of them did some heroic things and deserve to be treated as heroes. Both of them also are talked about with amazing omissions.

Helen Keller is known to most of us as the famous blind and deaf girl who "overcame." I've asked hundreds of people, mostly my students, also other audiences, to tell me what she did with her life after she overcame. Exactly two people out of over a thousand have known; one of those learned it indirectly from me and the other one is married to a deaf person, and in the deaf community, they do know what she did. But it's very ironic that although we get all these educational films about Helen Keller and although almost every student gets some indoctrination as to this wonderful woman, no one knows what she did once she learned how to read and write and speak.

She became a radical Socialist. She first became a member of the Massachusetts Socialist Party, and when that wasn't far enough left for her, she became a Wobbly, a member of the International Workers of the World, the IWW. The reason she did this is actually related to her blindness, because she wanted to do something to help blind people. She came to realize that blindness is not distributed amongst the social system just randomly. Particularly back then, it was concentrated in the lower class. That's because of industrial accidents that blinded people, it's because of syphilis carried by prostitutes, who were mostly poor, and it's primarily, of course, due to bad medical care. She realized that if she were just to spend the rest of her life working on the Braille alphabet, which she had done some work on improving, or doing other things like that, she was merely treating the symptom, not the cause, so she became a Socialist.

Well, I'm not here to push socialism, but it's very interesting that when she became a Socialist, she was probably the most famous woman on the planet because of all the attention that had been given her when she learned how to speak, when she graduated from Radcliffe College, and so on. Suddenly, from the most famous she became the most notorious, and all these newspapers that had lauded her now proceeded to distance themselves from her and say, "Of course, she's the captive of people around. She really doesn't think independently," and so on.

She took them to task. She wrote letters to them saying, "I blush to think how highly you spoke of me a couple of years ago. How stupid I must have become in the interim." She wrote a letter to the *Brooklyn Eagle*, which was a very major newspaper. It was the newspaper that Walt Whitman [edited] in the nineteenth century, that had been one of these newspapers that now attacked her, and she said, "It is the *Brooklyn Eagle* that is socially blind and deaf." She says, "I may not have been able to see the sweatshops and to see the factories or to hear them, but I have smelled them." In fact, she did go on tours all across America, so she became really quite a humanitarian on behalf of decreasing social stratification.

WILSON ISSUED his Fourteen Points, attempted to argue for democracy at Versailles, also passed various things through the Congress during his Progressive Era as president, but Wilson had at least two, shall we say, feet of clay, two blemishes. One was his incredible racism. He was surely the most racist president since the Civil War ended slavery. He was a white Southerner. When he came to power, which was with the aid of considerable black votes who were trying the Democratic Party and trying its claims for progressivism, he proceeded to segregate Washington, D.C. He segregated the federal cafeterias and federal workplaces. If two people, one white and one black, had been sorting mail together, they now had to be in separate rooms or have a screen between them. He also stopped blacks from various political appointments that had been routinely given them since the days of Lincoln and Grant. It's no coincidence that late in his term, the signals that he was giving off about race relations penetrated the nation, and we had a wave of race riots from about 1917 through at least 1920.

Possibly the first example of bombing civilians by aircraft, certainly the first example in United States history, came about in Tulsa, Oklahoma, when there was a race riot against the black community in 1921. It even included flying an airplane above the black community and dropping dynamite into it, killing more than seventy people. So these were race riots that actually far outdo the riots that we hear so much about in terms of the Rodney King riot in Los Angeles or the Watts riot. . . . Some of the textbooks, let's say maybe five of them, will mention that Woodrow Wilson did some segregation, usually without an active verb. For instance, one textbook actually says that workrooms in the federal government were segregated, and then Woodrow Wilson undid that and called a halt to it. The second statement is just totally false; he never did that.

The other problem with Woodrow Wilson was his invasion of the Soviet Union and of so many countries in Latin America. He put troops into Mexico a total of eleven different times, and also Nicaragua, Haiti, and the Dominican Republic. Some of the things that American soldiers ended up doing and some of the people they ended up supporting have come back to haunt us, from the dictatorship in Haiti, which we helped install, to the Trujillo dictatorship in the Dominican Republic. Now, I'm not trying just to badmouth Woodrow Wilson, but I am suggesting that we need to put him in perspective. We need to be aware of the bad as well as the good, but somehow the textbooks have trouble with any wart, with any blemish on somebody who's supposed to be a hero.

THE RECENT PAST has the potential for being controversial. The Vietnam War is an interesting case in point. If you actually look at public opinion polls on the Vietnam War, you see that for the last ten years at least, 70 percent of the American people believe that the Vietnam War was neither politically correct nor morally correct; that is, it was a mistake for us to do it and it was also morally wrong.

That's a whopping 70–30 majority, so that's not very controversial. Nonetheless, the textbooks leave out everything about the Vietnam War that has any guts to it, that has any controversy to it. For instance, there are maybe half a dozen famous photographs of the Vietnam War. I've asked people who lived through that era to tell me what are these photos, and there's remarkable consensus: the photo of the naked girl having just been napalmed, running along a highway; the photo of the monk burning himself. I have only to cock my hand, and people say, "Oh, yes, that photo." They remember it. The My Lai massacre photo, the famous photo of the evacuation from Saigon.

These are famous photos; they're still used in the news today. Even some of my students have seen them. These are the ones that I concluded are the most important photographs of the war because they moved American public opinion. They also show some of the issues of the war, such as the fact that there were no front lines and that we were firing upon the civilian population.

A typical photo that the textbooks include is a photo of Lyndon Johnson surrounded by happy troops at Cam Ranh Bay, a naval base that we built in Vietnam. It's a very different mood and a much less important image, an image that didn't move American public opinion; it didn't really describe very much about the war in Vietnam. I counted in all twelve books how many of the textbooks included any of these five famous photos. The result: One book included one. Eleven books included none of them. They just included photos like the LBJ photo.

[I asked one of the authors of a high school textbook about this version of Vietnam] and he said, "I call my textbook a McDonald's version of history." I asked him, "What does that mean?" He said, "It means it's bland. If it had any flavor, it wouldn't sell." He believes and his publishers believe, obviously, that if it had any flavor, anything interesting in it, then it would upset some people; that the way to sell the textbook is to make it as bland as possible, as uncontroversial as possible.

THE TEXTBOOKS want to hero-ize everybody, and the number one hero becomes the federal government. . . . This is very unusual because after Watergate and after "Iran-Contragate" and all of our other scandals of the late 1960s and 1970s and even into the 1980s and 1990s, the American people have grown rightly suspicious, or at least thoughtful, about the federal government and don't just think that it always does the right thing.

Our textbooks still present government as the be-all and end-all and the do-gooder of everything. I participated in the civil rights movement. I've mentioned that I was in Mississippi, and there was a poster that the movement offices had up on their walls during the 1964 Mississippi Freedom Summer, which read, "There's a street in Itta Bena called Freedom. There's a town in Mississippi called Liberty. There's a department in Washington called Justice." That's a bitter poster because, of course, there was very little freedom in the little delta town of Itta Bena; there was very little liberty in the nasty Mississippi town of Liberty; and they were arguing, therefore, there's very little justice coming out of Washington.

During the Kennedy administration, the main response of the federal government was made by the FBI. Now, what did the FBI actually do with regard to the civil rights movement? Well, first of all, we have to realize that the FBI didn't have an office in Mississippi and didn't have very many offices in the South at all. When it did, those offices were all staffed by white Southerners. The FBI at this time had not a single black officer. Hoover claimed he did because he counted his two chauffeurs—they were black—but that was it. But beyond that, the FBI claimed that it was not its job to protect or even to investigate threats of violence that came to civil rights workers. J. Edgar Hoover thought that the *Brown v. Board of Education* decision was wrong and outlandish, and he made it his policy to investigate civil rights movement people. He tapped Martin Luther King's phone; he tapped the hotel rooms that civil rights organizers operated out of or met in. FBI agents made a tape of King's phone calls and conversations in his room, often having to do with sex, and sent it to Coretta Scott King, hoping to persuade King to commit suicide. This is a documented fact. I'm not inventing this fact; I'm just citing the professional literature in history. . . . That's the kind of role that the federal government played with regard to the civil rights movement. . . . But what do the textbooks say? They say that the federal government passed the 1964 Civil Rights Bill, the 1965 Voting Rights Bill, and so on.

This has a terrible payoff for the present, I think. . . . There's room for a paranoia that the textbooks feed by telling the black community and, for that matter, the white community that the federal government has always done things for black people. Blacks become paranoid—what are these things? Are they a good idea? And it encourages whites to become racist and say, "If the federal government has always been doing these wonderful things for black folks, haven't we done enough? Why do we need to do more? What's the problem?"

I THINK THERE must be some belief on the part of someone in the publishing houses or in the textbook adoption boards that the way to promote strong citizens is by lying to them, by giving them this feel-good history that just tells them that the United States is the best country that has ever been, and that we never did anything wrong. I don't hold that belief. I think the way to develop strong citizens is to get them involved in the issues of history. They would see that there have been Americans who have argued for positive, wonderful, just principles and are remembered around the world, and there have been Americans that have argued for oppressive principles and are remembered around the world for that. Sometimes even the same Americans have argued on both sides. That, I think, would get students involved with the issues of history, rather than just [reading] rote patriotism.

Presidential Rhetoric

by

WAYNE FIELDS

On April 30, 1789, George Washington gave the first inaugural address. Since then, U.S. presidents have given countless speeches to articulate their visions for the nation. In Union of Words: A History of Presidential Eloquence, *published by The Free Press in 1994, Wayne Fields examined presidential speeches from Washington to Clinton. On April 14, 1996, Mr. Fields appeared on* Booknotes *to discuss his book and the political climate surrounding presidential speeches, as well as the different rhetorical patterns of various presidents. Mr. Fields is an English professor at Washington University in St. Louis.*

FIRST AND FOREMOST, this book is about the story of union, which has always interested me. Union is a commitment, for such a practical and individualistic people as we, to make so prominently and so proudly. Union is one of the most demanding things a nation can seek and conserve. This idea that we are to dedicate ourselves to "a more perfect union" is a fairly remarkable thing, it seems. And then, the test of the presidency is how well that office serves union, that [it is] presidents who make us think of our collective life, the "we" of our national experience.

I STARTED WITH Lincoln, with the whole crisis of a president who is committed to holding the Union together . . . and in an era of secession, having to establish the foundation for a rebirth of that Union. Every president before Lincoln had said, as a means of holding the Union together, "If it ever comes apart, it can't be restored." He had to go against the logic of all those generations of presidents before.

ONE OF THE things that has struck me in retrospect is how many presidents I really didn't have much regard for before I looked at them. My attitude toward their struggle with the office changed that perception. There are speeches by presidents whom I've never thought of as particularly eloquent but, in retrospect, seemed really dramatic moments.

Jerry Ford, for instance, in recent history, is a president whom no one ever really thought of as a terribly articulate man or eloquent speaker. Yet when we listened to the speech that he gave after he had taken the oath of office and just after the dramatic departure of Richard Nixon from Washington, he started out by asking the country to pray for him, and then at the end he said, "Now I want you to pray for Richard Nixon and his family." His voice broke at that moment, and then he continued, his voice breaking a couple of more times, to say, "May the man who helped bring peace to millions find it for himself."

The sincerity of that emotion [struck me], the whole sense that in this moment of his own ascent into the highest office, he was capable of this kind of empathy, this kind of concern. That, in a way, was what we didn't feel during the Nixon years. What we had not felt, especially in the latter stage, was that the president was capable of thinking of much beyond himself in terms of the crisis. It was an important emotional moment for the country to have a president who was empathizing with this pain instead of simply going on with his own celebratory role that day as a newly inaugurated president.

AN INAUGURAL address, particularly one that marks a change in administration, is the most carefully written and elaborately rehearsed speech of any president's career, and it provides a remarkably reliable indication of what matters to a new president and how he wants to be perceived. Presidents have time to work on that speech, that's why I distinguished first inaugurals from second inaugurals—it's the one that they've got the most preparation time for. They know it's coming up; they know the basic terms of the event; and they've got the months between the election and the inauguration to work on it. It's also the time where they are first going to speak with the presidential voice. It's a unique voice. Nobody ever quite has the training for that; they've spoken for narrower interests all the rest of their career, and now to transcend those interests, to rise above that and find the people's voice is one of the great challenges and one that they struggle with most diligently.

George Washington . . . delivered his inaugural address to an audience of congressmen. The beginning is Washington, and almost all of our conception of the office is rooted in that beginning. It's Washington who tells us what the presidency is all about. The audiences [for inaugural addresses] started to expand very early, but the person who was most responsible for enlarging [them] was Andrew Jackson. At that point, we start thinking of the capital in a much more dramatic way, as a center for the people. Jackson had people coming in and out of the White House all the time, just drifting in to see the president. It opened up the sense of government, and his inaugural was extended that way. From the very beginning, there was a sense that this was a public message, even though most of the public would see it in print and not hear it.

The longest inaugural speech was William Henry Harrison's, who spoke about an hour and a half. It was an important speech because it was almost longer than his presidency. He died within the month. There are lots of people who think he died because he was outside too long giving that speech. The shortest speech was probably the last FDR. With his third and fourth inaugurations, Franklin Roosevelt shortened his speeches considerably, and for the fourth, he was in bad health, and so it was a different kind of occasion.

The most colloquial, the most conversational, was probably Truman's, just because his voice was least comfortable with formal kinds of addresses. It had its own kind of eloquence; there was something very moving about Truman's speech, but it was not like John F. Kennedy's. What we get after Franklin Roosevelt in other forms of discourse—inaugurals tend to be different from those—is a lessening of the distance between the speaker and the audience: The president sounds more and more like the audience in his formal address. Ronald Reagan was very good at that, so that his language sounded like our language, his talk sounded like our talk, even though it was much better talk than most of us would give.

THE FIRST president's voice you can hear is Teddy Roosevelt's. . . . We have some recordings of Harding and Coolidge, but there we've got presidents who primarily thought of themselves as speaking on the platform, unless they were actually in a studio—and even there they sound like they were on a platform. They were still overly "oratoricalists." It was not until the "fireside chats" that we get away from that [heavily oratorical style].

The first president to be aware of the broadcast possibility was Hoover, who wasn't very good at using it but understood that it was important, that this was really changing the nature of the office. The person who changed the office in response to radio most effectively was FDR.

The first president to speak on television, at his inaugural, was Truman, but remember that there is a difference between actually having the technology there and having many Americans see it. Television becomes important with Eisenhower, who was our first real television president.

One of the things that happens with broadcast is that what we think of as presidential eloquence takes in all the other aspects of platform performance. People, first with radio, are actually hearing the president's voice in great numbers, and then [with television] they're actually seeing the person deliver it, and there's no way of separating what we see and what we hear from the words that are spoken. So the full persona becomes more a part of the performance than it would have been for, say, Thomas Jefferson, who didn't much like to speak anyway and preferred that people read him. So that the idiosyncrasies of speech, of a president who comes from upstate New York aristocracy, such as FDR, or from Georgia, become a part of our sense of what they say and the relative eloquence of it.

THE PRESIDENT who probably authored more of his material than anybody else, the one that I feel most confident in saying that about is Lincoln, simply because he wrote better than anybody around him. It seems difficult to imagine that those words are somebody else's. But even there, he tried things out on other people, circulated speeches, changed phrases in response to advisers.

Washington's finest rhetorical moments were often scripted by James Madison or Alexander Hamilton. President Monroe's most famous address was largely crafted by his secretary of state, John Quincy Adams. Andrew Jackson's first inaugural included important contributions from his vice president, John C. Calhoun. We actually know more about speechwriters and their effect on speeches now than we knew during the Franklin Roosevelt era, when they tried to remain relatively invisible. Peggy Noonan has written about her own work as a speechwriter [for Ronald Reagan], and there are conferences now in which speechwriters appear and talk about their trade and refer to things that they've written in the past. So we've gotten away from the notion that they have to be anonymous and invisible. You no longer have to keep alive the illusion that they don't exist, that they really are ghosts. The fact is more obvious now, maybe than it was even when we had Madison writing for Washington, that the presidency is a collaborative office. It is a role. It's not just a single person. It is one that draws on lots of people's energy and talent, and has from the very beginning.

A part of the test of the presidency is how well the person who holds that office chooses the words that are going to be spoken. Those words may be crafted by someone else, but the really important thing is that the message be appropriate. That's what I mean about the collaborative work.

It would have been a mistake for Abraham Lincoln to rely on somebody other than himself for most of his writing, because he's the one who knew those words. He was the one with the wisdom for that particular moment. On the other hand, the people who helped Franklin Roosevelt or Ronald Reagan craft their words were important extensions of the personality and goals of those particular presidents.

We tend, for a couple of generations, to measure ourselves against some great historical moment. So that it's the Revolution and George Washington; and then it's the Civil War and Abraham Lincoln; and then it's World War II and FDR. Then we go through a [less tumultuous period], and at the end of that, we're uncertain how to measure ourselves, what the test of our Americanness is, what our model of patriotism is, or of civic virtue is.

For most of the people listening when Reagan was giving his speech at Normandy [for the fortieth anniversary of D-day], World War II was something in a history book. It wasn't real in their experience; what was real war for an American was Vietnam, a very different kind of experience. What Reagan did in that moment at Normandy was to talk about the kind of service that those now-old men in his audience had given there, the kinds of risks they had taken, and the kinds of purposes they were serving. Especially for younger audiences who were far removed from that clear historical moment and had the muddier notions of Vietnam in mind, there was something deeply moving about that. Reagan handled it not by drawing lots of attention to himself, but to the specific acts of heroism of the men in front of him.

ONE OF THE things that I found very interesting was what I call the "Western swing of Teddy Roosevelt." Roosevelt was the first president to really go out to the people to build the presidential case. Andrew Johnson had tried it in his conflicts with Congress; it hadn't worked well. People thought it was very unpresidential. But Roosevelt went on a several-week tour that took him all the way to the West Coast twice, stopping at lots of places like national parks, as well as at universities, and delivering his own Progressive message about America's future.

This was at a time where his standing with his own party was shaky. He'd come to the presidency after the death of William McKinley. He had not been somebody that most of the party leaders would have wanted to be president, and it wasn't clear in his own mind that they were going to nominate him to run again. What he was doing during this time was building support for himself; but he was also getting Americans to think of themselves in this new way which, especially in the West, incorporated lots of the Progressive ideals that became important to his presidency.

NIXON WAS BOTH the most problematic figure for me, and in some ways the most interesting. If the office of the presidency is about holding us together, about union, then a part of what we want in the president is for them to seem together, themselves, in some important way. . . . That's our notion of the presidency. We have this great monolith in the Washington Monument that is the model for the presidency, and not just for George Washington—that singular obelisk that declares just one thing.

On the other hand, what we saw in Richard Nixon was a disintegration of the self of the president, not just of the country he was trying to hold together during that time. Part of what interested me there was the way in which [Americans] remain committed to union when the servant of that union is, as his resignation speeches make clear, coming apart himself.

One of the things that's interesting about the presidency is that inevitably the individuals who hold that office are smaller than the office. They're often driven by relatively petty ambitions or psychological needs of a fairly complicated sort that don't match our notion of what the office represents, or even their own notion of it. One of the things that began to interest me was how they transcended their own limits, in some instances, to fill the office, but other times how they declared themselves.

Nixon was desperate to be taken seriously. He was constantly saying things that invited you to correct him—about not being very bright, about having struggled to get through the bar exam, when we know he was a good student. This sense that everybody else was treating him as though he was insignificant and small and was needing someone to say, "No, he's more than that."

ONE OF THE things that they tried to do in the nineteenth century was to keep the nominee separate from the corrupt and wild process of nomination, so that the nominee was approached by the party after the nomination, even when the nominee has been following it the way Abraham Lincoln had, with hourly telegrams from the convention hall. Then a party was sent to offer the nomination to the candidate, and the candidate accepted, usually with either a formal speech then or some informal remarks in a written letter.

Franklin Roosevelt came to the floor of the 1932 Democratic Convention and said, "You nominated me, and I know it. I accept, and you know that. Let's get on to it." It was the whole idea that they were going to cut through any kind of sham, any kind of empty pretense, and get at the work at hand; that they were in a national crisis, and it would be a waste of time to pretend that we don't know what's gone on, and get on with our business.

Franklin Roosevelt, in his third and fourth campaigns, had a different kind of relationship with the process because nobody else had run [that often]. Everybody had observed the Washington precedent of two terms and then retirement, so that his relationship at those conventions was most distant. One was a recorded message. But after his first presentation before a convention, every candidate realized how much political capital was to be gained by this appearance, how much more effectively the party could be drawn together, and how much of a national audience such a speech could win.

PRESIDENTIAL SPEECH is important in different ways, at different times. We've gone through long periods when we've not had particularly articulate presidents, when there's very little, apart from the drama of the times, that should interest us in the speeches they give. But we do know, from the effectiveness of the Reagan presidency, from the kind of emphasis, for instance, that was placed on Bill Clinton's last State of the Union speech, that we do take what presidents say seriously, even though we sometimes are very cynical and skeptical about all of that.

In this era of sound bites, of presidents making comments that can show up in the short segments on the evening news, the concept of eloquence is changed. The idea of a whole argument in an elaborated speech is more in danger now, I think, than it used to be.

MOST OF WHAT we know about the idea of union nationally, we know from our own efforts to reconcile all of our conflicting natures and interests. We haven't changed as a people, either individually or corporately, but on the one hand, we are very practical. We're very commonsensical. And that's where our suspicions of one another come from. That's where our emphasis upon individual rights and liberties comes from. On the other hand, we are committed to this idea of community that we represent with the word "union." It's not just a union of states; it becomes increasingly a union of people.

These two things are very uncomfortable next to each other, but we are equally committed to both of them, and in each of our historical eras, different kinds of forces have been testing our ability to sustain these two commitments, to be both *pluribus* and *unum*. We've responded in different ways, but the basic struggle has always been the same.

Appendix

Readers can review an online appendix to
Booknotes: On American Character
on the World Wide Web at:

http://www.booknotes.org

Available on the C-SPAN Web page are
- *Complete transcripts of over seven hundred* Booknotes *interviews*
- *Audio and video archives looking back at programs over the past twelve years*

Complete List of C-SPAN Booknotes
(1989-2004)

SEPTEMBER 14, 1988
Pre-BOOKNOTES Interview
with Neil Sheehan
*A Bright Shining Lie: John Paul
Vann and America in Vietnam*
Publisher: Random House

1. APRIL 2, 1989
*[official start of *Booknotes*]
Zbigniew Brzezinski
*Grand Failure: The Birth and
Death of Communism in the
20th Century*
Publisher: Macmillan

2. APRIL 9, 1989
Judy Shelton
*The Coming Soviet Crash: Gor-
bachev's Desperate Pursuit of Credit
in Western Financial Markets*
Publisher: The Free Press

3. APRIL 16, 1989
Bruce Oudes
*From: The President—
Richard Nixon's Secret Files*
Publisher: Harper & Row

4. APRIL 23, 1989
Susan Moeller
*Shooting War: Photography and the
American Experience of Combat*
Publisher: Basic Books

5. APRIL 30, 1989
Henry Brandon
*Special Relationships: A Foreign
Correspondent's Memoirs*
Publisher: Atheneum

6. MAY 7, 1989
David Hackworth
(with Julie Sherman)

*About Face: The Odyssey of an
American Warrior*
Publisher: Simon & Schuster

7. MAY 14, 1989
James Fallows
*More Like Us: Making America
Great Again*
Publisher: Houghton Mifflin
Company

8. MAY 21, 1989
Gregory Fossedal
*The Democratic Imperative:
Exporting the American Revolution*
Publisher: Basic Books

9. MAY 28, 1989
Stanley Karnow
*In Our Image: America's Empire
in the Philippines*
Publisher: Random House

10. JUNE 4, 1989
James MacGregor Burns
The Crosswinds of Freedom
Publisher: Alfred A. Knopf

11. JUNE 11, 1989
Robert Christopher
*Crashing the Gates: The De-
WASPing of America's Power Elite*
Publisher: Simon & Schuster

12. JUNE 18, 1989
Senator Robert Byrd
The Senate: 1789–1989
Publisher: Government Printing
Office

13. JUNE 25, 1989
Elizabeth Colton
*The Jackson Phenomenon: The

Man, The Power, The Message*
Publisher: Doubleday

14. JULY 2, 1989
Nathaniel Branden
*Judgment Day: My Years with
Ayn Rand*
Publisher: Houghton Mifflin
Company

15. JULY 9, 1989
Roger Kennedy
*Orders From France:
The Americans and the
French in a Revolutionary
World (1780–1820)*
Publisher: Alfred A. Knopf

16. JULY 14, 1989
Simon Schama
*Citizens: A Chronicle of the
French Revolution*
Publisher: Alfred A. Knopf

17. JULY 16, 1989
George Wilson
*Mud Soldiers: Life Inside the
New American Army*
Publisher: Scribner

18. JULY 23, 1989
Jeanne Simon
*Codename: Scarlett—Life on the
Campaign Trail by the Wife of a
Presidential Candidate*
Publisher: The Continuum
Publishing Company

19. JULY 30, 1989
Michael Kaufman
*Mad Dreams, Saving Graces—
Poland: A Nation in Conspiracy*
Publisher: Random House

20. AUGUST 6, 1989
Porter McKeever
Adlai Stevenson: His Life and Legacy
Publisher: William Morrow

21. AUGUST 13, 1989
Gary Paul Gates and Bob Schieffer
The Acting President
Publisher: E. P. Dutton

22. AUGUST 20, 1989
Bruce Murray
Journey Into Space—The First Thirty Years of Space Exploration
Publisher: W. W. Norton & Company

23. AUGUST 27, 1989
Jack Germond and Jules Witcover
Whose Broad Stripes and Bright Stars—The Trivial Pursuit of the Presidency 1988
Publisher: Warner Books, Inc.

24. SEPTEMBER 3, 1989
Walter Laquer
The Long Road to Freedom: Russia and Glasnost
Publisher: Scribner

25. SEPTEMBER 10, 1989
Thomas Friedman
From Beirut to Jerusalem
Publisher: Farrar, Straus and Giroux

26. SEPTEMBER 17, 1989
General Ariel Sharon
Warrior: An Autobiography
Publisher: Simon & Schuster

27. SEPTEMBER 24, 1989
George Gilder
Microcosm: The Quantum Revolution in Economics and Technology
Publisher: Simon & Schuster

28. OCTOBER 1, 1989
Mort Rosenblum
Back Home: A Foreign Correspondent Rediscovers America
Publisher: William Morrow

29. OCTOBER 8, 1989
Barbara Ehrenreich
Fear of Falling: The Inner Life of the Middle Class
Publisher: Pantheon Books

30. OCTOBER 15, 1989
Harrison Salisbury
Tiananmen Diary: Thirteen Days in June
Publisher: Little, Brown and Company

31. OCTOBER 22, 1989
Kenneth Adelman
The Great Universal Embrace: Arms Summitry—A Skeptic's Account
Publisher: Simon & Schuster

32. OCTOBER 29, 1989
Reverand Ralph David Abernathy
And the Walls Came Tumbling Down
Publisher: Harper & Row

33. NOVEMBER 5, 1989
Vassily Aksyonov
Say Cheese: Soviets and the Media
Publisher: Random House

34. NOVEMBER 12, 1989
Felix Rodriguez (and John Weisman)
Shadow Warrior: The CIA Hero of a Hundred Unknown Battles
Publisher: Simon & Schuster

35. NOVEMBER 19, 1989
Robin Wright
In the Name of God: The Khomeini Decade
Publisher: Simon & Schuster

36. NOVEMBER 26, 1989
Peter Hennessy
Whitehall
Publisher: The Free Press

37. DECEMBER 3, 1989
Clifford Stoll
The Cuckoo's Egg: Tracking a Spy Through the Maze of Computer Espionage
Publisher: Doubleday

38. DECEMBER 10, 1989
Arthur Grace
Choose Me: Portraits of a Presidential Race
Publisher: University Press of New England

39. DECEMBER 17, 1989
James Reston Jr.
The Lone Star: The Life of John Connally
Publisher: Harper & Row

40. DECEMBER 24, 1989
Richard Rhodes
Farm: A Year in the Life of an American Farmer
Publisher: Simon & Schuster

41. DECEMBER 31, 1989
William Lutz
Doublespeak: From "Revenue Enhancement" to "Terminal Living"—How Government, Business, Advertisers and Others Use Language to Deceive You
Publisher: Harper & Row

42. JANUARY 7, 1990
Sig Mickelson
From Whistle Stop to Sound Bite: Four Decades of Politics and Television
Publisher: Praeger

43. JANUARY 14, 1990
John Barry
The Ambition and the Power—The Fall of Jim Wright: A True Story of Washington
Publisher: Viking

44. JANUARY 21, 1990
Fitzhugh Green
George Bush: An Intimate Portrait
Publisher: Hippocrene Books

45. JANUARY 28, 1990
Charles Fecher, editor
The Diary of H. L. Mencken
Publisher: Alfred A. Knopf

46. FEBRUARY 4, 1990
Jim Mann
Beijing Jeep: The Short, Unhappy Romance of American Business in China
Publisher: Simon & Schuster

47. FEBRUARY 11, 1990
David Burnham
A Law Unto Itself: Power, Politics and the IRS
Publisher: Random House

48. FEBRUARY 18, 1990
Peggy Noonan
What I Saw at the Revolution: A Political Life in the Reagan Era
Publisher: Random House

49. FEBRUARY 25, 1990
Michael Fumento
The Myth of Heterosexual AIDS
Publisher: Basic Books

50. FEBRUARY 27, 1990
Hedley Donovan
Right Places, Right Times: Forty Years in Journalism Not Counting My Paper Route
Publisher: Henry Holt and Company

51. MARCH 4, 1990
Richard Barnet
The Rockets' Red Glare: When America Goes to War—The Presidents and the People
Publisher: Simon & Schuster

52. MARCH 11, 1990
Frederick Kempe
Divorcing the Dictator: America's Bungled Affair with Noriega
Publisher: Putnam

53. MARCH 18, 1990
(Neil Livingstone and)
David Halevy
Inside the PLO
Publisher: William Morrow

54. MARCH 25, 1990
James Abourezk
Advise and Dissent: Memoirs of South Dakota and the U.S. Senate
Publisher: Lawrence Hill Books

55. APRIL 1, 1990
Fred Graham
Happy Talk: Confessions of a TV Newsman
Publisher: W. W. Norton & Company

56. APRIL 9, 1990
Leonard Sussman
Power, the Press and the Technology of Freedom: The Coming Age of ISDN
Publisher: Freedom House

57. APRIL 15, 1990
Helmut Schmidt
Men and Powers: A Political Retrospective
Publisher: Random House

58. APRIL 22, 1990
Michael Barone
Our Country: The Shaping of America from Roosevelt to Reagan
Publisher: The Free Press

59. APRIL 29, 1990
Robert Caro
Means of Ascent: The Years of Lyndon Johnson
Publisher: Alfred A. Knopf

60. MAY 6, 1990
Morley Safer
Flashbacks On Returning to Vietnam
Publisher: Random House

61. MAY 13, 1990
Brian Duffy and Steven Emerson

The Fall of Pan Am 103: Inside the Lockerbie Investigation
Publisher: Putnam

62. MAY 20, 1990
Allister Sparks
The Mind of South Africa
Publisher: Alfred A. Knopf

63. MAY 27, 1990
Bette Bao Lord
Legacies: A Chinese Mosaic
Publisher: Alfred A. Knopf

64. JUNE 3, 1990
Dusko Doder
Gorbachev: Heretic in the Kremlin
Publisher: Viking

65. JUNE 10, 1990
Thomas Sowell
Preferential Policies: An International Perspective
Publisher: William Morrow

66. JUNE 17, 1990
Judith Miller
One, By One, By One: Facing the Holocaust
Publisher: Simon & Schuster

67. JUNE 24, 1990
Kevin Phillips
The Politics of Rich and Poor: Wealth and the Electorate in the Reagan Aftermath
Publisher: Random House

68. JULY 1, 1990
Chris Ogden
Maggie: An Intimate Portrait of a Woman in Power
Publisher: Random House

69. JULY 8, 1990
Denton Watson
Lion in the Lobby: Clarence Mitchell, Jr.'s Struggle for the Passage of Civil Rights Laws
Publisher: William Morrow

70. JULY 15, 1990
Caspar Weinberger
Fighting for Peace: Seven Critical Years in the Pentagon
Publisher: Warner Books, Inc.

71. JULY 22, 1990
Teresa Odendahl
Charity Begins at Home: Generosity and Self-Interest Among the Philanthropic Elite
Publisher: Basic Books

72. JULY 29, 1990
Michael Shapiro

In the Shadow of the Sun: A Korean Year of Love and Sorrow
Publisher: Atlantic Monthly Press

73. AUGUST 5, 1990
Dan Raviv and Yossi Melman
Every Spy a Prince: The Complete History of Israel's Intelligence Community
Publisher: Houghton Mifflin Company

74. AUGUST 12, 1990
Roger Kimball
Tenured Radicals: How Politics Has Corrupted Our Higher Education
Publisher: Harper & Row

75. AUGUST 19, 1990
Tad Szulc
Then and Now: How the World Has Changed Since World War II
Publisher: William Morrow

76. AUGUST 26, 1990
Christopher Wren
The End of the Line: The Failure of Communism in the Soviet Union and China
Publisher: Simon & Schuster

77. SEPTEMBER 2, 1990
Lee Edwards
Missionary for Freedom: The Life and Times of Walter Judd
Publisher: Paragon House

78. SEPTEMBER 9, 1990
Senator Robert Dole
Historical Almanac of the United States Senate
Publisher: Government Printing Office

79. SEPTEMBER 16, 1990
M. L. Farber
Outrage: The Story Behind the Tawana Brawley Hoax
Publisher: Bantam Books

80. SEPTEMBER 23, 1990
Janette Dates
Split Image: African Americans in the Mass Media
Publisher: Howard University Press

81. OCTOBER 14, 1990
Harold Stassen
Eisenhower: Turning the World Toward Peace
Publisher: Merrill Magnus

82. OCTOBER 21, 1990
Tim Weiner

*Blank Check: The Pentagon's
Black Budget*
Publisher: Warner Books, Inc.

83. OCTOBER 28, 1990
Pat Choate
*Agents of Influence: How Japan's
Lobbyists in the United States
Manipulate America's Political
and Economic System*
Publisher: Alfred A. Knopf

84. NOVEMBER 4, 1990
Paul Taylor
*See How They Run: Electing a
President in an Age of Mediaocracy*
Publisher: Alfred A. Knopf

85. NOVEMBER 11, 1990
Blaine Harden
*Africa: Dispatches from a Fragile
Continent*
Publisher: W. W. Norton &
Company

86. NOVEMBER 18, 1990
Jean Edward Smith
*Lucius D. Clay: An American
Life*
Publisher: Henry Holt and
Company

87. NOVEMBER 25, 1990
Martin Mayer
*The Greatest-Ever Bank Robbery:
The Collapse of the Savings and
Loan Industry*
Publisher: Scribner

88. DECEMBER 2, 1990
Carol Barkalow
(with Andrea Raals)
*In the Men's House: An Inside
Account of Life in the Army by
One of West Point's First Female
Graduates*
Publisher: Poseidon Press

89. DECEMBER 9, 1990
Sally Bedell Smith
*In All His Glory: The Life of
William S. Paley, the Legendary
Tycoon and His Brilliant Circle*
Publisher: Simon & Schuster

90. DECEMBER 16, 1990
Shen Tong
*Almost a Revolution: The Story of
a Chinese Student's Journey from
Boyhood to Leadership in
Tiananmen Square*
Publisher: Houghton Mifflin
Company

91. DECEMBER 23, 1990
John and Janet Wallach

*Arafat: In the Eyes of the
Beholder*
Publisher: Lyle Stuart

92. DECEMBER 30, 1990
Garry Wills
*Under God: Religion and
American Politics*
Publisher: Simon & Schuster

93. JANUARY 6, 1991
Ben Wattenberg
*The First Universal Nation:
Leading Indicators and
Ideas About the Surge of
America in the 1990s*
Publisher: The Free Press

94. JANUARY 13, 1991
Daniel Roos
*The Machine That
Changed the World*
Publisher: Macmillan

95. JANUARY 27, 1991
Daniel Yergin
*The Prize: The Epic Quest for
Oil, Money and Power*
Publisher: Simon & Schuster

96. FEBRUARY 3, 1991
Carl Rowan
Breaking Barriers: A Memoir
Publisher: Little, Brown and
Company

97. FEBRUARY 10, 1991
Theodore Hesburgh
(with Jerry Reedy)
*God, Country, Notre Dame:
The Autobiography of
Theodore M. Hesburgh*
Publisher: Doubleday

98. FEBRUARY 17, 1991
Ronald Brownstein
*The Power and the Glitter: The
Hollywood-Washington Connec-
tion*
Publisher: Pantheon Books

99. FEBRUARY 24, 1991
Robert Kuttner
*The End of Laissez-Faire:
National Purpose and the Global
Economy After the Cold War*
Publisher: Alfred A. Knopf

100. MARCH 3, 1991
Haynes Johnson
*Sleepwalking Through History:
America in the Reagan Years*
Publisher: W. W. Norton &
Company

101. MARCH 10, 1991
Georgie Anne Geyer
*Guerrilla Prince: The Untold
Story of Fidel Castro*
Publisher: Little, Brown and
Company

102. MARCH 17, 1991
Leonard Goldenson (with
Marvin Wolf)
*Beating the Odds: The Untold
Story Behind the Rise of ABC:
The Stars, Struggles and Egos That
Transformed Network Television*
Publisher: Scribner

103. MARCH 24, 1991
Richard Brookhiser
*The Way of the WASP: How It
Made America and How It Can
Save It . . . So to Speak*
Publisher: The Free Press

104. MARCH 31, 1991
Dayton Duncan
*Grass Roots: One Year in the Life
of the New Hampshire Presiden-
tial Primary*
Publisher: Penguin

105. APRIL 7, 1991
Tom Wicker
*One of Us: Richard Nixon and
the American Dream*
Publisher: Random House

106. APRIL 14, 1991
William Strauss and Neil Howe
*Generations: The History of
America's Future, 1584–2069*
Publisher: William Morrow

107. APRIL 21, 1991
Robert Shogun
*The Riddle of Power: Presidential
Leadership from Truman to Bush*
Publisher: Dutton

108. APRIL 28, 1991
Caroline Kennedy and
Ellen Alderman
*In Our Defense: The Bill of
Rights in Action*
Publisher: William Morrow

109. MAY 5, 1991
Nick Lemann
*The Promised Land: The Great
Black Migration and How It
Changed America*
Publisher: Alfred A. Knopf

110. MAY 12, 1991 (PART ONE)
Lou Cannon
President Reagan: Role of a

Lifetime
Publisher: Simon & Schuster

III. MAY 19, 1991 (PART TWO)
Lou Cannon
President Reagan: Role of a
Lifetime
Publisher: Simon & Schuster

112. MAY 26, 1991
Robert Reich
The Work of Nations
Publisher: Alfred A. Knopf

113. JUNE 2, 1991
Robert Kaiser
Why Gorbachev Happened: His
Triumphs and His Failure
Publisher: Simon & Schuster

114. JUNE 9, 1991
George Friedman and
Meredith LeBard
The Coming War with Japan
Publisher: St. Martin's Press

115. JUNE 16, 1991
Dixy Lee Ray
Trashing the Planet: How
Science Can Help Us Deal with
Acid Rain, Depletion of the
Ozone, and Nuclear Waste
Among Other Things
Publisher: Regnery Publishing,
Inc.

116. JUNE 23, 1991
Bob Woodward
The Commanders
Publisher: Simon & Schuster

117. JUNE 30, 1991
Roger Gittines
Consequences: John G. Tower—A
Personal and Political Memoir
Publisher: Little, Brown and
Company

118. JULY 7, 1991
Donald Ritchie
Press Gallery: Congress and the
Washington Correspondents
Publisher: Harvard University
Press

119. JULY 14, 1991
Michael Beschloss
The Crisis Years: Kennedy and
Khrushchev, 1960–1963
Publisher: HarperCollins

120. JULY 21, 1991
Alan Ehrenhalt
The United State of Ambition:
Politicians, Power and the

Pursuit of Office
Publisher: Random House

121. JULY 28, 1991
Clark Clifford
Counsel to the President: A Memoir
Publisher: Random House

122. AUGUST 4, 1991
Elaine Sciolino
The Outlaw State: Saddam
Hussein's Quest for Power and
the Gulf Crisis
Publisher: John Wiley &
Sons, Inc.

123. AUGUST 11, 1991
Len Colodny and Robert Gettlin
Silent Coup: The Removal
of a President
Publisher: St. Martin's Press

124. AUGUST 18, 1991
Liz Trotta
Fighting for Air: In the Trenches
with Television News
Publisher: Simon & Schuster

125. AUGUST 25, 1991
E. J. Dionne Jr.
Why Americans Hate Politics
Publisher: Simon & Schuster

126. SEPTEMBER 1, 1991
Andrew and Leslie Cockburn
Dangerous Liaisons: The Inside
Story of the U.S.-Israeli Covert
Relationship
Publisher: HarperCollins

127. SEPTEMBER 8, 1991
Liva Baker
The Justice from Beacon Hill
Publisher: HarperCollins

128. SEPTEMBER 15, 1991
Reuven Frank
Out of Thin Air: The Brief
Wonderful Life of Network News
Publisher: Simon & Schuster

129. SEPTEMBER 22, 1991
Robert Dallek
Lone Star Rising: Lyndon
Johnson and His Times,
1908–1960
Publisher: Oxford University Press

130. SEPTEMBER 29, 1991
Stephen Carter
Reflections of an Affirmative
Action Baby
Publisher: Basic Books

131. OCTOBER 6, 1991
Ken Auletta

Three Blind Mice: How the TV
Networks Lost Their Way
Publisher: Random House

[October 13, 1991: Preempted
by U.S. Senate]

132. OCTOBER 20, 1991
Anthony Lewis
Make No Law: The Sullivan
Case and the First Amendment
Publisher: Random House

133. OCTOBER 27, 1991
Don Oberdorfer
The Turn: From the
Cold War to a New Era—
The United States and the
Soviet Union, 1983–1990
Publisher: Simon & Schuster

134. NOVEMBER 3, 1991
Larry Sabato
Feeding Frenzy: How Attack
Journalism Has Transformed
American Politics
Publisher: The Free Press

135. NOVEMBER 10, 1991
Tina Rosenberg
Children of Cain: Violence and
the Violent in Latin America
Publisher: William Morrow

136. NOVEMBER 17, 1991
Suzanne Garment
Scandal: The Culture of Mistrust
in American Politics
Publisher: Times Books

137. NOVEMBER 24, 1991
James Stewart
Den of Thieves
Publisher: Simon & Schuster

138. DECEMBER 1, 1991
Gary Sick
October Surprise: America's
Hostages in Iran and the Election
of Ronald Reagan
Publisher: Times Books

139. DECEMBER 8, 1991
James Reston
Deadline: A Memoir
Publisher: Random House

140. DECEMBER 15, 1991
Thomas Byrne Edsall and
Mary Edsall
Chain Reaction: The Impact
of Race, Rights and Taxes on
American Politics
Publisher: W. W. Norton &
Company

141. DECEMBER 22, 1991
Martin Gilbert
Churchill: A Life
Publisher: Henry Holt and
Company

142. DECEMBER 29, 1991
Jimmy Breslin
Damon Runyan: A Life
Publisher: Ticknor & Fields

143. JANUARY 5, 1992
Charles Hamilton
*Adam Clayton Powell, Jr.:
The Political Biography of an
American Dilemma*
Publisher: Atheneum

144. JANUARY 12, 1992
August Heckscher
Woodrow Wilson: A Biography
Publisher: Scribner

145. JANUARY 26, 1992
Frederick Downs
*No Longer Enemies, Not Yet
Friends: An American Soldier
Returns to Vietnam*
Publisher: W. W. Norton &
Company

146. FEBRUARY 2, 1992
Robert Cwiklik
*House Rules: A Freshman
Congressman's Initiation to
the Backslapping, Backpedaling,
and Backstabbing Ways of
Washington*
Publisher: Villard Books

147. FEBRUARY 9, 1992
Francis Fukuyama
*The End of History and the
Last Man*
Publisher: The Free Press

148. FEBRUARY 16, 1992
Senator Al Gore
*Earth in the Balance: Ecology
and the Human Spirit*
Publisher: Houghton Mifflin
Company

149. FEBRUARY 23, 1992 (PART ONE)
Richard Nixon
*Seize the Moment: America's
Challenge in a One-Superpower
World*
Publisher: Simon & Schuster

150. MARCH 1, 1992 (PART TWO)
Richard Nixon
*Seize the Moment: America's
Challenge in a One-Superpower
World*
Publisher: Simon & Schuster

151. MARCH 8, 1992
Robert Massie
*Dreadnought: Britain, Germany
and the Coming of the Great War*
Publisher: Random House

152. MARCH 22, 1992
Linda Chavez
*Out of the Barrio: Toward a New
Politics of Hispanic Assimilation*
Publisher: Basic Books

153. MARCH 29, 1992
Nan Robertson
*The Girls in the Balcony: Women,
Men and the New York Times*
Publisher: Random House

154. APRIL 5, 1992
Robert Remini
*Henry Clay: Statesman for
the Union*
Publisher: W. W. Norton &
Company

155. APRIL 12, 1992
Orlando Patterson
*Freedom: Freedom in the
Making of Western Culture*
Publisher: Basic Books

156. APRIL 19, 1992
Paul Hollander
*Anti-Americanism:
Critiques at Home and
Abroad, 1965–1990*
Publisher: Oxford University
Press

157. APRIL 26, 1992
Tinsley Yarbrough
*John Marshall Harlan: Great
Dissenter of the Warren Court*
Publisher: Oxford University
Press

158. MAY 3, 1992
Earl Black and Merle Black
*The Vital South: How Presidents
Are Elected*
Publisher: Harvard University
Press

159. MAY 10, 1992
David Moore
*The Superpollsters: How They
Measure and Manipulate Public
Opinion in America*
Publisher: Four Walls Eight
Windows

160. MAY 17, 1992
Robert Bartley
*The Seven Fat Years and How to
Do it Again*
Publisher: The Free Press

161. MAY 24, 1992
Lewis Puller Jr.
*Fortunate Son: The Autobiogra-
phy of Lewis Puller, Jr.*
Publisher: Grove Weidenfeld

162. MAY 31, 1992
Lester Thurow
*Head to Head: The Coming
Economic Battle Among Japan,
Europe and America*
Publisher: William Morrow

163. JUNE 7, 1992
R. Emmett Tyrrell Jr.
The Conservative Crack-Up
Publisher: Simon & Schuster

164. JUNE 14, 1992
William Lee Miller
*The Business of May Next: James
Madison and the Founding*
Publisher: The University Press
of Virginia

165. JUNE 21, 1992
John Jackley
*Hill Rat: Blowing the Lid Off
Congress*
Publisher: Regnery Publishing,
Inc.

166. JUNE 28, 1992
David Savage
*Turning Right: The Making of
the Rehnquist Supreme Court*
Publisher: John Wiley &
Sons, Inc.

167. JULY 5, 1992
William Rehnquist
*Grand Inquests: The Historic
Impeachments of Justice Samuel
Chase and President Andrew
Johnson*
Publisher: William Morrow

168. JULY 12, 1992
Jeffrey Bell
*Populism and Elitism: Politics in
the Age of Equality*
Publisher: Regnery Publishing,
Inc.

169. JULY 19, 1992
David McCullough
Truman
Publisher: Simon & Schuster

170. JULY 26, 1992
Richard Ben Cramer
*What it Takes: The Way to the
White House*
Publisher: Random House

171. AUGUST 2, 1992
Gilbert Fite

Richard B. Russell, Jr.: Senator from Georgia
Publisher: The University of North Carolina Press

172. AUGUST 9, 1992
Robert Donovan and Ray Scherer
Unsilent Revolution: Television News and American Public Life
Publisher: Cambridge University Press

173. AUGUST 16, 1992
Martin Anderson
Impostors in the Temple: American Intellectuals Are Destroying Our Universities and Cheating Our Students of Their Future
Publisher: Simon & Schuster

174. AUGUST 23, 1992
Mickey Kaus
The End of Equality
Publisher: Basic Books

175. AUGUST 30, 1992
Neil Postman
Technopoly: The Surrender of Culture to Technology
Publisher: Alfred A. Knopf

176. SEPTEMBER 6, 1992
Terry Eastland
Energy in the Executive: The Case for a Strong Presidency
Publisher: The Free Press

177. SEPTEMBER 13, 1992
James Billington
Russia Transformed: Breakthrough to Hope
Publisher: The Free Press

178. SEPTEMBER 20, 1992
Senator Paul Simon
Advise and Consent: Clarence Thomas, Robert Bork and the Intriguing History of the Supreme Court's Nomination Battles
Publisher: National Press Books

179. SEPTEMBER 27, 1992
Walter Isaacson
Kissinger: A Biography
Publisher: Simon & Schuster

[October 4, 1992: Preempted by U.S. House of Representatives]

[October 11, 1992: Preempted by Presidential Debate]

180. OCTOBER 18, 1992
George Will

Restoration: Congress, Term Limits and the Recovery of Deliberative Democracy
Publisher: The Free Press

181. OCTOBER 25, 1992
Susan Faludi
Backlash: The Undeclared War Against American Women
Publisher: Crown

182. NOVEMBER 8, 1992
Barbara Hinkley and Paul Brace
Follow the Leader: Opinion Polls and the Modern Presidents
Publisher: Basic Books

183. NOVEMBER 15, 1992
Derrick Bell
Faces at the Bottom of the Well: The Permanence of Racism
Publisher: Basic Books

184. NOVEMBER 22, 1992
General Norman Schwartzkopf
It Doesn't Take a Hero
Publisher: Bantam Books

185. NOVEMBER 29, 1992
Charles Sykes
A Nation of Victims: The Decay of the American Character
Publisher: St. Martin's Press

186. DECEMBER 6, 1992
Daniel Boorstin
The Creators
Publisher: Random House

187. DECEMBER 13, 1992
Brian Kelly
Adventures in Porkland: How Washington Wastes Your Money and Why They Don't Stop
Publisher: Villard Books

188. DECEMBER 20, 1992
Eric Alterman
Sound and Fury: The Washington Punditocracy and the Collapse of American Politics
Publisher: HarperCollins

189. DECEMBER 27, 1992
Michael Medved
Hollywood vs. America: Popular Culture and the War on Traditional Values
Publisher: HarperCollins

190. JANUARY 3, 1993
Michael Davis and Hunter Clark
Thurgood Marshall: Warrior at the Bar, Rebel on the Bench
Publisher: The Carol Publishing Group

191. JANUARY 10, 1993
Jeffrey Birnbaum
The Lobbyists: How Influence Peddlers Get Their Way in Washington
Publisher: Times Books

192. JANUARY 17, 1993
P. F. Bentley
Clinton: Portrait of Victory
Publisher: Warner Books, Inc.

193. JANUARY 24, 1993
Robert Gilbert
The Mortal Presidency: Illness and Anguish in the White House
Publisher: Basic Books

194. JANUARY 30, 1993
Benjamin Stein
License to Steal: The Untold Story of Michael Milken and the Conspiracy to Bilk the Nation
Publisher: Simon & Schuster

195. FEBRUARY 7, 1993
Jack Nelson
Terror in the Night: The Klan's Campaign Against the Jews
Publisher: Simon & Schuster

196. FEBRUARY 14, 1993
Nathan Miller
Theodore Roosevelt: A Life
Publisher: William Morrow

197. FEBRUARY 21, 1993
Richard Norton Smith
Patriarch: George Washington and the New American Nation
Publisher: Houghton Mifflin Company

198. FEBRUARY 28, 1993
Kay Mills
This Little Light of Mine: The Life of Fannie Lou Hamer
Publisher: Dutton

199. MARCH 6, 1993
Alex Dragnich
Serbs and Croats: The Struggle in Yugoslavia
Publisher: Harcourt Brace Jovanovich

200. MARCH 13, 1993
Paul Kennedy
Preparing for the Twenty-First Century
Publisher: Random House

201. MARCH 21, 1993
Deborah Shapley
Promise and Power: The Life and Times of Robert McNamara

Publisher: Little, Brown and
Company

202. MARCH 28, 1993
Michael Kelly
*Martyrs' Day: Chronicle of a
Small War*
Publisher: Random House

203. APRIL 4, 1993
Nadine Cohodas
*Strom Thurmond and the Politics
of Southern Change*
Publisher: Simon & Schuster

204. APRIL 11, 1993
Blanche Wiesen Cook
*Eleanor Roosevelt: Volume 1,
1884–1933*
Publisher: Viking

205. APRIL 18, 1993
Douglas Brinkley
*The Majic Bus: An American
Odyssey*
Publisher: Harcourt Brace

206. APRIL 25, 1993
Lisa Belkin
*First, Do No Harm: The Dra-
matic Story of Real Doctors and
Patients Making Impossible
Choices at a Big-City Hospital*
Publisher: Simon & Schuster

207. MAY 2, 1993
Marshall DeBruhl
*Sword of San Jacinto: A Life of
Sam Houston*
Publisher: Random House

208. MAY 9, 1993
Charles Adams
*For Good and Evil:
The Impact of Taxes on the
Course of Civilization*
Publisher: Madison Books

209. MAY 16, 1993
Anna Quindlen
*Thinking Out Loud: On the
Personal, the Political, the Public
and the Private*
Publisher: Random House

210. MAY 23, 1993
George Ball
*The Passionate Attachment:
America's Involvement with
Israel, 1947 to the Present*
Publisher: W. W. Norton &
Company

211. MAY 30, 1993
Douglas Davis
*The Five Myths of Television
Power: Or, Why the Medium is*

Not the Message
Publisher: Simon & Schuster

212. JUNE 6, 1993
Bowyer Bell
*The Irish Troubles: A Generation
of Violence, 1967–1992*
Publisher: St. Martin's Press

213. JUNE 13, 1993
David Brock
The Real Anita Hill
Publisher: The Free Press

214. JUNE 20, 1993
Howard Kurtz
*Media Circus: The Trouble with
America's Newspapers*
Publisher: Times Books

215. JUNE 27, 1993
George Shultz
*Turmoil and Triumph: My Years
as Secretary of State*
Publisher: Scribner

216. JULY 4, 1993
Joel Krieger
*The Oxford Companion to
Politics of the World*
Publisher: Oxford University
Press

217. JULY 11, 1993
David Halberstam
The Fifties
Publisher: Villard Books

218. JULY 18, 1993
Molly Moore
*A Woman at War: Storming
Kuwait with the U.S. Marines*
Publisher: Scribner

219. JULY 25, 1993
David Remnick
*Lenin's Tomb: The Last Days of
the Soviet Empire*
Publisher: Random House

220. AUGUST 1, 1993
Alexander Brook
*The Hard Way: The Odyssey of a
Weekly Newspaper Editor*
Publisher: Bridge Works

221. AUGUST 8, 1993
Tom Rosenstiel
*Strange Bedfellows: How Televi-
sion and the Presidential Candidates Changed American Politics,
1992*
Publisher: Hyperion

222. AUGUST 15, 1993
Lewis Lapham
The Wish for Kings: Democracy

at Bay
Publisher: Grove Press

223. AUGUST 22, 1993
Harold Holzer
The Lincoln Douglas Debates
Publisher: HarperCollins

224. AUGUST 29, 1993
Peter Macdonald
Giap: The Victor in Vietnam
Publisher: W. W. Norton &
Company

225. SEPTEMBER 5, 1993
Joseph Ellis
*Passionate Sage: The Character
and Legacy of John Adams*
Publisher: W. W. Norton &
Company

226. SEPTEMBER 12, 1993
Ronald Kessler
*The FBI: Inside the World's Most
Powerful Law Enforcement
Agency*
Publisher: Pocket Books

227. SEPTEMBER 19, 1993
Madeline Cartwright
*For the Children: Lessons from a
Visionary Principal; How We
Can Save Our Public School*
Publisher: Doubleday

228. SEPTEMBER 26, 1993
Malcolm Browne
*Muddy Boots and Red Socks: A
Reporter's Life*
Publisher: Times Books

229. OCTOBER 3, 1993
Peter Skerry
*Mexican-Americans: The
Ambivalent Minority*
Publisher: The Free Press

230. OCTOBER 10, 1993
Alan Brinkley
*The Unfinished Nation: A Concise
History of the American People*
Publisher: Alfred A. Knopf

231. OCTOBER 17, 1993
Christopher Hitchens
For the Sake of Argument
Publisher: Verso

232. OCTOBER 24, 1993
William F. Buckley Jr.
*Happy Days Were Here Again:
Reflections of a Libertarian
Journalist*
Publisher: Random House

233. OCTOBER 31, 1993
Andrew Nagorski
The Birth of Freedom: Shaping

*Lives and Societies in the New
Eastern Europe*
Publisher: Simon & Schuster

234. NOVEMBER 7, 1993
Charles Mee
*Playing God: Seven Fateful
Moments When Great Men Met
to Change the World*
Publisher: Simon & Schuster

235. NOVEMBER 14, 1993
Herbert Block
Herblock: A Cartoonist's Life
Publisher: Macmillan

[November 21, 1993: Pre-
empted by U.S. House of
Representatives]

236. NOVEMBER 28, 1993
Betty Friedan
The Fountain of Age
Publisher: Simon & Schuster

237. DECEMBER 5, 1993
Margaret Thatcher
The Downing Street Years
Publisher: HarperCollins

238. DECEMBER 12, 1993
Richard Reeves
*President Kennedy: Profile of
Power*
Publisher: Simon & Schuster

239. DECEMBER 19, 1993
John Podhoretz
*Hell of a Ride: Backstage at the
White House Follies, 1989–1993*
Publisher: Simon & Schuster

240. DECEMBER 26, 1993
Willard Sterne Randall
Thomas Jefferson: A Life
Publisher: Henry Holt and
Company

241. JANUARY 2, 1994
David Levering Lewis
*DuBois: The Biography of a Race,
1868–1919*
Publisher: Henry Holt and
Company

242. JANUARY 9, 1994
William Bennett
*The Book of Virtues: A Treasury
of Great Moral Stories*
Publisher: Simon & Schuster

243. JANUARY 16, 1994
Carolyn Barta
*Perot and His People: Disrupting
the Balance of Political Power*
Publisher: The Summit Group

244. JANUARY 23, 1994
Gary Hymel (co-author with
Tip O'Neill)
*All Politics is Local and Other
Rules of the Game*
Publisher: Times Books

245. JANUARY 30, 1994
William Chafe
*Never Stop Running: Allard
Lowenstein and the Struggle to
Save American Liberalism*
Publisher: Basic Books

246. FEBRUARY 6, 1994
Stanley Weintraub
Disraeli: A Biography
Publisher: Dutton

247. FEBRUARY 13, 1994
Bill Emmott
*Japanophobia: The Myth of the
Invincible Japanese*
Publisher: Times Books

248. FEBRUARY 20, 1994
Peter Arnett
*Live from the Battlefield:
From Vietnam to Baghdad, 35
Years in the World's War Zones*
Publisher: Simon & Schuster

249. FEBRUARY 27, 1994
Stephen Lesher
*George Wallace:
American Populist*
Publisher: Addison-Wesley

250. MARCH 6, 1994
Nathan McCall
*Makes Me Wanna Holler: A
Young Black Man in America*
Publisher: Random House

251. MARCH 13, 1994
Norman Ornstein
*Debt and Taxes: How America
Got into Its Budget Mess and
What to Do About It*
Publisher: Times Books

252. MARCH 20, 1994
Clare Brandt
*The Man in the Mirror:
A Life of Benedict Arnold*
Publisher: Random House

253. MARCH 27, 1994
John Corry
*My Times: Adventures
in the News Trade*
Publisher: Putnam

254. APRIL 3, 1994
Andrew Young
*A Way Out of No Way: The
Spiritual Memoirs of Andrew
Young*

Publisher: Thomas Nelson
Communications

[April 10, 1994 *Booknotes*
Fifth Anniversary Special]

255. APRIL 17, 1994
James Cannon
*Time and Chance: Gerald Ford's
Appointment with History*
Publisher: HarperCollins

[April 24, 1994: Encore *Booknotes*
Richard Nixon (PART TWO)]

256. MAY 1, 1994
Howell Raines
*Fly Fishing Through the Midlife
Crisis*
Publisher: William Morrow

257. MAY 8, 1994
John Keegan
A History of Warfare
Publisher: Alfred A. Knopf

258. MAY 15, 1994
Forrest McDonald
*The American Presidency:
An Intellectual History*
Publisher: University of Kansas
Press

259. MAY 22, 1994
James McPherson
*What They Fought For,
1861–1865*
Publisher: Louisiana State
University Press

260. MAY 29, 1994
Pete Hamill
A Drinking Life: A Memoir
Publisher: Little, Brown and
Company

261. JUNE 5, 1994
Stephen Ambrose
*D-Day: June 6, 1944: The
Climactic Battle of World War II*
Publisher: Simon & Schuster

262. JUNE 12, 1994
Mark Neely
*The Last Best Hope of Earth:
Abraham Lincoln and the
Promise of America*
Publisher: Harvard University
Press

263. JUNE 19, 1994
Sam Roberts
Who We Are: A Portrait of America
Publisher: Times Books

264. JUNE 26, 1994
Lani Guinier
The Tyranny of the Majority:

Fundamental Fairness in
Representative Democracy
Publisher: Martin Kessler Books

265. JULY 3, 1994
Murray Kempton
Rebellions, Perversities,
and Main Events
Publisher: Times Books

266. JULY 10, 1994
Cal Thomas
The Things That Matter Most
Publisher: HarperCollins

267. JULY 17, 1994
David Hackett Fischer
Paul Revere's Ride
Publisher: Oxford University
Press

268. JULY 24, 1994
Dan Quayle
Standing Firm
Publisher: HarperCollins

269. JULY 31, 1994
Colman McCarthy
All of One Peace: Essays on
Nonviolence
Publisher: Rutgers University
Press

270. AUGUST 7, 1994
Peter Collier
The Roosevelts:
An American Saga
Publisher: Simon & Schuster

271. AUGUST 14, 1994
Merrill Peterson
Lincoln in American Memory
Publisher: Oxford University
Press

272. AUGUST 21, 1994
Hugh Pearson
The Shadow of the Panther:
Huey Newton and the Price
of Black Power in America
Publisher: Addison-Wesley

273. AUGUST 28, 1994
John Leo
Two Steps Ahead of the
Thought Police
Publisher: Simon & Schuster

274. SEPTEMBER 4, 1994
Paul Weaver
News and the Culture of Lying:
How Journalism Really Works
Publisher: The Free Press

275. SEPTEMBER 11, 1994
Shelby Foote
Stars in Their Courses:

The Gettysburg Campaign
Publisher: Modern Library

276. SEPTEMBER 18, 1994
Irving Bartlett
John C. Calhoun: A Biography
Publisher: W. W. Norton &
Company

277. SEPTEMBER 25, 1994
Ben Yagoda
Will Rogers: A Biography
Publisher: Alfred A. Knopf

278. OCTOBER 2, 1994
Harry Jaffe and Tom Sherwood
Dream City: Race,
Power and the Decline
of Washington, D.C.
Publisher: Simon & Schuster

279. OCTOBER 9, 1994
Henry Louis Gates Jr.
Colored People: A Memoir
Publisher: Alfred A. Knopf

280. OCTOBER 16, 1994
Nicholas Kristof and
Sheryl Wudunn
China Wakes: The Struggle for
the Soul of a Rising Power
Publisher: Times Books

281. OCTOBER 23, 1994
Liz Carpenter
Unplanned Parenthood
Publisher: Random House

282. OCTOBER 30, 1994
David Frum
Dead Right
Publisher: Basic Books

283. NOVEMBER 6, 1994
Bill Thomas
Club Fed: Power, Money, Sex
and Violence on Capitol Hill
Publisher: Scribner

284. NOVEMBER 13, 1994
John Kenneth Galbraith
A Journey Through Economic
Time: A Firsthand View
Publisher: Houghton Mifflin
Company

285. NOVEMBER 20, 1994
Milton Friedman
Introduction to F. A. Hayek's
Road to Serfdom
Publisher: University of
Chicago Press

286. NOVEMBER 27, 1994
Melba Pattillo Beals
Warriors Don't Cry: A Searing
Memoir of the Battle to Integrate

Little Rock's Central High
Publisher: Pocket Books

287. DECEMBER 4, 1994
Charles Murray
The Bell Curve: Intelligence and
Class Structure in American Life
Publisher: The Free Press

288. DECEMBER 11, 1994
Elizabeth Drew
On the Edge: The Clinton
Presidency
Publisher: Simon & Schuster

289. DECEMBER 18, 1994
Peter Robinson
Snapshots From Hell:
The Making of an MBA
Publisher: Warner Books, Inc.

290. DECEMBER 25, 1994
Glenn Frankel
Beyond the Promised Land: Jews
and Arabs on a Hard Road to a
New Israel
Publisher: Simon & Schuster

291. JANUARY 1, 1995
Doris Kearns Goodwin
No Ordinary Time: Franklin
and Eleanor Roosevelt: The
Home Front in World War II
Publisher: Simon & Schuster

292. JANUARY 8, 1995
Robert Wright
The Moral Animal: Why We Are
the Way We Are: The New Science
of Evolutionary Psychology
Publisher: Pantheon Books

293. JANUARY 15, 1995
Anthony Cave Brown
Treason in the Blood: H. St. John
Philby, Kim Philby, and the Spy
Case of the Century
Publisher: Houghton Mifflin
Company

294. JANUARY 22, 1995
Marvin Olasky
The Tragedy of American
Compassion
Publisher: Regnery Publishing,
Inc.

295. JANUARY 29, 1995
Steven Waldman
The Bill: How the Adventures
of Clinton's National Service
Bill Reveal What is Corrupt,
Comic, Cynical and Noble
about Washington
Publisher: Viking

296. FEBRUARY 5, 1995
Stanton Evans
*The Theme is Freedom: Religion,
Politics and the American Tradi-
tion*
Publisher: Regnery Publishing,
Inc.

297. FEBRUARY 12, 1995
Philip Howard
*The Death of Common Sense:
How Law is Suffocating America*
Publisher: Random House

298. FEBRUARY 19, 1995
Jimmy Carter
*Always a Reckoning and
Other Poems*
Publisher: Times Books

299. FEBRUARY 26, 1995
Alan Ryan
Author, Introduction
Democracy in America
Publisher: Alfred A. Knopf

300. MARCH 5, 1995
Lynn Sherr
*Failure is Impossible:
Susan B. Anthony in
Her Own Words*
Publisher: Times Books

301. MARCH 12, 1995
Donald Kagan
On the Origins of War
Publisher: Doubleday

302. MARCH 19, 1995
Neil Baldwin
Edison: Inventing the Century
Publisher: Hyperion

303. MARCH 26, 1995
James Loewen
*Lies My Teacher Told Me:
Everything Your American
History Textbook Got Wrong*
Publisher: The New Press

304. APRIL 2, 1995
Gertrude Himmelfarb
*The De-Moralization of Society:
From Victorian Virtues to
Modern Values*
Publisher: Alfred A. Knopf

305. APRIL 9, 1995
Stanley Greenberg
*Middle Class Dreams: The
Politics and Power of the New
American Majority*
Publisher: Times Books

306. APRIL 16, 1995
Alvin and Heidi Toffler
Creating a New Civilization:

The Politics of the Third Wave
Publisher: Turner Publishing, Inc.

307. APRIL 23, 1995
Robert McNamara
*In Retrospect: The Tragedy and
Lessons of Vietnam*
Publisher: Times Books

308. APRIL 30, 1995
Michael Klare
*Rogue States and Nuclear Out-
laws: America's Search for a New
Foreign Policy*
Publisher: Farrar, Straus and
Giroux

309. MAY 7, 1995
David Maraniss
*First in His Class:
A Biography of Bill Clinton*
Publisher: Simon & Schuster

310. MAY 14, 1995
Tim Penny and Major Garrett
Common Cents
Publisher: Little, Brown and
Company

311. MAY 21, 1995
Linn Washington
Black Judges on Justice
Publisher: The New Press

312. MAY 28, 1995
John Niven
Salmon P. Chase: A Biography
Publisher: Oxford University
Press

313. MAY 4, 1995
Hanan Ashrawi
This Side of Peace
Publisher: Simon & Schuster

314. JUNE 11, 1995
Peter Brimelow
*Alien Nation: Common Sense
About America's Immigration
Disaster*
Publisher: Random House

315. JUNE 18, 1995
Yuri Shvets
*Washington Station: My Life as
a KGB Spy in America*
Publisher: Simon & Schuster

316. JUNE 25, 1995
Norman Mailer
*Oswald's Tale:
An American Mystery*
Publisher: Random House

317. JULY 2, 1995
Ari Hoogenboom
Rutherford B. Hayes:

Warrior and President
Publisher: University Press of
Kansas

318. JULY 9, 1995
DeWayne Wickham
*Woodholme: A Black Man's
Story of Growing Up Alone*
Publisher: Farrar, Straus and
Giroux

319. JULY 16, 1995
Armstrong Williams
*Beyond Blame: How We
Can Succeed by Breaking
he Dependency Barrier*
Publisher: The Free Press

320. JULY 23, 1995
Newt Gingrich
To Renew America
Publisher: HarperCollins

321. JULY 30, 1995
John Hockenberry
*Moving Violations: A Memoir:
War Zones, Wheelchairs, and
Declarations of Independence*
Publisher: Hyperion

322. AUGUST 6, 1995
Marc Fisher
*After the Wall: Germany,
the Germans and the Burdens
of History*
Publisher: Simon & Schuster

323. AUGUST 13, 1995
Robert D. Richardson Jr.
Emerson: The Mind on Fire
Publisher: University of
California Press

324. AUGUST 20, 1995
Cartha "Deke" DeLoach
*Hoover's FBI: The Inside
Story by Hoover's Trusted
Lieutenant*
Publisher: Regnery Publishing,
Inc.

325. AUGUST 27, 1995
Robert Timberg
The Nightingale's Song
Publisher: Simon & Schuster

326. SEPTEMBER 3, 1995
Robert Leckie
*Okinawa: The Last Battle of
World War II*
Publisher: Viking

327. SEPTEMBER 10, 1995
Emory Thomas
Robert E. Lee: A Biography
Publisher: W. W. Norton &
Company

328. SEPTEMBER 17, 1995
Elsa Walsh
*Divided Lives: The Public
and Private Struggles of
Three Accomplished Women*
Publisher: Simon & Schuster

329. SEPTEMBER 24, 1995
Irving Kristol
*Neoconservatism: The Autobio-
graphy of an Idea*
Publisher: The Free Press

330. OCTOBER 1, 1995
Andrew Sullivan
*Virtually Normal: An Argument
About Homosexuality*
Publisher: Alfred A. Knopf

331. OCTOBER 8, 1995
Susan Eisenhower
*Breaking Free: A Memoir
of Love*
Publisher: Farrar, Straus and
Giroux

332. OCTOBER 15, 1995
Nicholas Basbanes
*A Gentle Madness: Bibliophiles,
Bibliomanes, and the Eternal
Passion for Books*
Publisher: Henry Holt and
Company

333. OCTOBER 22, 1995
David Fromkin
*In The Time of Americans: The
Generation that Changed
America's Role in the World*
Publisher: Alfred A. Knopf

334. OCTOBER 29, 1995
Ben Bradlee
*A Good Life: Newspapering and
Other Adventures*
Publisher: Simon & Schuster

335. NOVEMBER 5, 1995
Marlin Fitzwater
*Call the Briefing! Reagan and
Bush, Sam and Helen: A Decade
with Presidents and the Press*
Publisher: Times Books

336. NOVEMBER 12, 1995
Pierre Salinger
P. S., A Memoir
Publisher: St. Martin's Press

337. NOVEMBER 19, 1995
bell hooks
Killing Rage: Ending Racism
Publisher: Henry Holt and
Company

338. NOVEMBER 26, 1995
Sanford Ungar
*Fresh Blood: The New
American Immigrants*
Publisher: Simon & Schuster

339. DECEMBER 3, 1995
James Baker
(with Thomas DeFrank)
*The Politics of Diplomacy:
Revolution, War and Peace,
1989–1992*
Publisher: Putnam

340. DECEMBER 10, 1995
David Brinkley
A Memoir
Publisher: Alfred A. Knopf

341. DECEMBER 17, 1995
Evan Thomas
*The Very Best Men—Four Who
Dared: The Early Years of the CIA*
Publisher: Simon & Schuster

342. DECEMBER 24, 1995
David Herbert Donald
Lincoln
Publisher: Simon & Schuster

343. DECEMBER 31, 1995
Charles Kuralt
Charles Kuralt's America
Publisher: Putnam

344. JANUARY 7, 1996
Colin Powell
My American Journey
Publisher: Random House

345. JANUARY 14, 1996
William Prochnau
Once Upon a Distant War
Publisher: Times Books

346. JANUARY 21, 1996
Michael Kinsley
Big Babies
Publisher: William Morrow

347. JANUARY 28, 1996
Carlo D'Este
Patton: A Genius for War
Publisher: HarperCollins

348. FEBRUARY 4, 1996
Dennis Prager
Think a Second Time
Publisher: HarperCollins

349. FEBRUARY 11, 1996
Lance Banning
*The Sacred Fire of Liberty:
James Madison and the Found-
ing of the Federal Republic*

Publisher: Cornell University
Press

350. FEBRUARY 18, 1996
Dan Balz
(with Ronald Brownstein)
*Storming the Gates: Protest
Politics and Republican Revival*
Publisher: Little, Brown and
Company

351. FEBRUARY 25, 1996
H. W. Brands
*The Reckless Decade:
America in the 1890s*
Publisher: St. Martin's Press

352. MARCH 3, 1996
Hillary Rodham Clinton
*It Takes a Village: And Other
Lessons Children Teach Us*
Publisher: Simon & Schuster

353. MARCH 10, 1996
Johanna Neuman
*Lights, Camera, War:
Is Media Technology Driving
International Politics?*
Publisher: St. Martin's Press

354. MARCH 17, 1996
Clarence Page
*Showing My Color: Impolite
Essays on Race & Identity*
Publisher: HarperCollins

355. MARCH 24, 1996
Robert Merry
*Taking on the World: Joseph
and Stewart Alsop—Guardians
of the American Century*
Publisher: Viking

356. MARCH 31, 1996
Fox Butterfield
*All God's Children:
The Bosket Family and the
American Tradition of Violence*
Publisher: Alfred A. Knopf

357. APRIL 7, 1996
Jean Baker
*The Stevensons: A Biography
of an American Family*
Publisher: W. W. Norton &
Company

358. APRIL 14, 1996
Wayne Fields
*Union of Words: A History of
Presidential Eloquence*
Publisher: The Free Press

359. APRIL 21, 1996
Robert Kaplan

The Ends of the Earth: A Journey at the Dawn of the 21ˢᵗ Century
Publisher: Simon & Schuster

360. APRIL 28, 1996
David Reynolds
Walt Whitman's America: A Cultural Biography
Publisher: Alfred A. Knopf

361. MAY 5, 1996
David Broder
(with Haynes Johnson)
The System: The American Way of Politics at the Breaking Point
Publisher: Little, Brown and Company

362. MAY 12, 1996
Stanley Crouch
The All-American Skin Game, or the Decoy of Race: The Long and Short of It, 1990–1994
Publisher: Pantheon Books

363. MAY 19, 1996
Michael Sandel
Democracy's Discontent: America in Search of a Public Philosophy
Publisher: Harvard University Press

364. MAY 26, 1996
Noa Ben Artzi-Pelossof
In the Name of Sorrow and Hope
Publisher: Alfred A. Knopf

365. JUNE 2, 1996
James Thomas Flexner
Maverick's Progress: An Autobiography
Publisher: Fordham University Press

366. JUNE 9, 1996
Christopher Matthews
Kennedy and Nixon: The Rivalry that Shaped Postwar America
Publisher: Simon & Schuster

367. JUNE 16, 1996
Albert Murray
Blue Devils of Nada: A Contemporary American Approach to Aesthetic Statement
Publisher: Pantheon Books

368. JUNE 23, 1996
Seymour Martin Lipset
American Exceptionalism: A Double-Edged Sword
Publisher: W. W. Norton & Company

369. JUNE 30, 1996
Glenn Simpson
(with Larry Sabato)
Dirty Little Secrets: The Persistence of Corruption in American Politics
Publisher: Times Books

370. JULY 7, 1996
Paul Greenberg
No Surprises: Two Decades of Clinton Watching
Publisher: Brassey's

371. JULY 14, 1996
Ted Sorensen
Why I Am a Democrat
Publisher: Henry Holt and Company

372. JULY 21, 1996
Eleanor Randolph
Waking the Tempests: Ordinary Life in New Russia
Publisher: Simon & Schuster

373. JULY 28, 1996
James Lardner
Crusader: The Hell-Raising Police Career of Detective David Durk
Publisher: Random House

374. AUGUST 4, 1996
Denis Brian
Einstein: A Life
Publisher: John Wiley & Sons, Inc.

[August 11 and August 18, 1996: Preempted by Reform Party Convention]

375. AUGUST 25, 1996
Eleanor Clift and Tom Brazaitis
War Without Bloodshed: The Art of Politics
Publisher: Scribner

376. SEPTEMBER 1, 1996
Drew Gilpin Faust
Mothers of Invention: Women of the Slaveholding South in the American Civil War
Publisher: The University of North Carolina Press

377. SEPTEMBER 8, 1996
Donald Warren
Radio Priest: Charles Coughlin, the Father of Hate Radio
Publisher: The Free Press

378. SEPTEMBER 15, 1996
Lloyd Kramer
Lafayette in Two Worlds

Publisher: The University of North Carolina Press

379. SEPTEMBER 22, 1996
Michael Elliott
The Day Before Yesterday: Reconsidering America's Past, Rediscovering the Present
Publisher: Simon & Schuster

380. SEPTEMBER 29, 1996
Monica Crowley
Nixon off the Record: His Candid Commentary on People and Politics
Publisher: Random House

[October 6, 1996: Preempted by Presidential Debate in Hartford, CT]

381. OCTOBER 13, 1996
Louise Barnett
Touched by Fire: The Life, Death and Mythic Afterlife of George Armstrong Custer
Publisher: Henry Holt and Company

382. OCTOBER 20, 1996
David Friedman
Hidden Order: The Economics of Everyday Life
Publisher: HarperBusiness

383. OCTOBER 27, 1996
Paul Hendrickson
The Living and the Dead: Robert McNamara and Five Lives of a Lost War
Publisher: Alfred A. Knopf

384. NOVEMBER 3, 1996
Andrew Ferguson
Fools' Names, Fools' Faces
Publisher: Atlantic Monthly Press

385. NOVEMBER 10, 1996
Leon Dash
Rosa Lee: A Mother and Her Family in Urban America
Publisher: Basic Books

386. NOVEMBER 17, 1996
Conor Cruise O'Brien
The Long Affair: Thomas Jefferson and the French Revolution, 1785–1800
Publisher: University of Chicago Press

387. NOVEMBER 24, 1996
Mikhail Gorbachev

Memoirs
Publisher: Doubleday

388. DECEMBER 1, 1996
Robert Bork
Slouching Towards Gomorrah:
Modern Liberalism and Ameri-
can Decline
Publisher: HarperCollins

389. DECEMBER 8, 1996
Nell Irvin Painter
Sojourner Truth: A Life, A
Symbol
Publisher: W. W. Norton &
Company

390. DECEMBER 15, 1996
President Bill Clinton
Between Hope and History:
Meeting America's Challenges for
the 21st Century
Publisher: Times Books

391. DECEMBER 22, 1996
David Denby
Great Books: My Adventures
with Homer, Rousseau, Woolf
and Other Indestructible Writers
of the Western World
Publisher: Simon & Schuster

392. DECEMBER 29, 1996
Stanley Wolpert
Nehru: A Tryst with Destiny
Publisher: Oxford University Press

393. JANUARY 5, 1997
Edward Jay Epstein
Dossier: The Secret History of
Armand Hammer
Publisher: Random House

394. JANUARY 12, 1997
Robert Ferrell
The Strange Deaths of
President Harding
Publisher: University of
Missouri Press

395. JANUARY 19, 1997
Alfred Zacher
Trial and Triumph: Presidential
Power in the Second Term
Publisher: Midpoint Trade Books

396. JANUARY 26, 1997
David Boaz
Libertarianism: A Primer
Publisher: The Free Press

397. FEBRUARY 2, 1997
Henry Grunwald
One Man's America: A Journalist's
Search for the Heart of His Coun-

try
Publisher: Doubleday

398. FEBRUARY 9, 1997
John Brady
Bad Boy: The Life and
Politics of Lee Atwater
Publisher: Addison-Wesley

399. FEBRUARY 16, 1997
Katharine Graham
Personal History
Publisher: Alfred A. Knopf

400. FEBRUARY 23, 1997
(PART ONE)
Sam Tanenhaus
Whittaker Chambers: A Biogra-
phy
Publisher: Random House

401. MARCH 2, 1997 (PART TWO)
Sam Tanenhaus
Whittaker Chambers: A Biogra-
phy
Publisher: Random House

402. MARCH 9, 1997
Sarah Gordon
Passage to Union: How the
Railroads Transformed American
Life, 1829–1929
Publisher: Ivan R. Dee

403. MARCH 16, 1997
John Fialka
War By Other Means: Economic
Espionage in America
Publisher: W. W. Norton &
Company

404. MARCH 23, 1997
Jon Katz
Virtuous Reality: How America
Surrendered Discussion of Moral
Values to Opportunists, Nitwits
and Blockheads like William
Bennett
Publisher: Random House

405. MARCH 30, 1997
Claude Andrew Clegg III
An Original Man: The Life and
Times of Elijah Muhammad
Publisher: St. Martin's Press

406. APRIL 6, 1997
Keith Richburg
Out of America: A Black Man
Confronts Africa
Publisher: Basic Books

407. APRIL 13, 1997
David Horowitz
Radical Son:

A Generational Odyssey
Publisher: The Free Press

408. APRIL 20, 1997
Leonard Garment
Crazy Rhythm: My Journey From
Brooklyn, Jazz, and Wall Street,
to Nixon's White House, Water-
gate and Beyond
Publisher: Times Books

409. APRIL 27, 1997
Stephen Oates
The Approaching Fury: Voices of
the Storm, 1820–1861
Publisher: HarperCollins

410. MAY 4, 1997
Christopher Buckley
Wry Martinis
Publisher: Random House

411. MAY 11, 1997
Richard Bernstein
(with Ross Munro)
The Coming Conflict with China
Publisher: Alfred A. Knopf

412. MAY 18, 1997
Anne Matthews
Bright College Years: Inside the
American Campus Today
Publisher: Simon & Schuster

413. MAY 25, 1997
Jane Holtz Kay
Asphalt Nation: How the Auto-
mobile Took Over America, and
How We Can Take it Back
Publisher: Crown Publishers

414. JUNE 1, 1997
Jill Krementz
The Writer's Desk
Publisher: Random House

415. JUNE 8, 1997
Pavel Palazchenko
My Years with Gorbachev and
Shevardnadze: The Memoir of a
Soviet Interpreter
Publisher: Penn State Press

416. JUNE 15, 1997
Walter McDougall
Promised Land, Crusader State:
The American Encounter with
the World Since 1776
Publisher: Houghton Mifflin
Company

417. JUNE 22, 1997
James Humes
Confessions of a White House
Ghostwriter: Five Presidents and
other Political Adventures

Publisher: Regnery Publishing,
Inc.

418. JUNE 29, 1997
Walter Cronkite
A Reporter's Life
Publisher: Alfred A. Knopf

419. JULY 6, 1997
Jack Rakove
*Original Meanings:
Politics and Ideas in the
Making of the Constitution*
Publisher: Alfred A. Knopf

420. JULY 13, 1997
Tom Clancy
General Fred Franks (Ret.)
*Into the Storm: A Study
in Command*
Publisher: Putnam

421. JULY 20, 1997
Robert Hughes
*American Visions: The Epic
History of Art in America*
Publisher: Alfred A. Knopf

422. JULY 27, 1997
Sylvia Jukes Morris
*Rage for Fame: The Ascent of
Clare Boothe Luce*
Publisher: Random House

423. AUGUST 3, 1997
LeAlan Jones
(and Lloyd Newman)
*Our America: Life and Death
on the South Side of Chicago*
Publisher: Scribner

424. AUGUST 10, 1997
James Tobin
*Ernie Pyle's War: America's
Eyewitness to World War II*
Publisher: The Free Press

425. AUGUST 17, 1997
Pauline Maier
*American Scripture:
Making the Declaration
of Independence*
Publisher: Alfred A. Knopf

426. AUGUST 24, 1997
Peter Maas
*Underboss: Sammy
The Bull Gravano's Story
of Life in the Mafia*
Publisher: HarperCollins

427. AUGUST 31, 1997
Frank McCourt
Angela's Ashes: A Memoir
Publisher: Scribner

428. SEPTEMBER 7, 1997
Brian Burrell
*The Words We Live By: The
Creeds, Mottoes, and Pledges
That Have Shaped America*
Publisher: The Free Press

429. SEPTEMBER 14, 1997
John Toland
*Captured By History: One Man's
Vision of Our Tumultuous Century*
Publisher: St. Martin's Press

430. SEPTEMBER 21, 1997
Peter Gomes
*The Good Book: Reading the
Bible with Mind and Heart*
Publisher: William Morrow

431. SEPTEMBER 28, 1997
John Berendt
*Midnight in the Garden of Good
and Evil: A Savannah Story*
Publisher: Random House

432. OCTOBER 5, 1997
Howard Gardner
*Extraordinary Minds: Portraits
of Four Exceptional Individuals
and an Examination of Our
Own Extraordinariness*
Publisher: Basic Books

433. OCTOBER 12, 1997
Geoffrey Perret
*Ulysses S. Grant:
Soldier and President*
Publisher: Random House

434. OCTOBER 19, 1997
Nat Hentoff
Speaking Freely: A Memoir
Publisher: Alfred A. Knopf

435. OCTOBER 26, 1997
Alan Schom
Napoleon Bonaparte
Publisher: HarperCollins

436. NOVEMBER 2, 1997
Thomas West
*Vindicating the Founders:
Race, Sex, Class, and Justice
in the Origins of America*
Publisher: Rowman &
Littlefield

[November 9, 1997:
Preempted by coverage of the
U.S. House of Representatives]

437. NOVEMBER 16, 1997
David Gelertner
*Drawing Life: Surviving
the Unabomber*
Publisher: The Free Press

438. NOVEMBER 23, 1997
Anita Hill
Speaking Truth to Power
Publisher: Doubleday

439. NOVEMBER 30, 1997
Jeff Shesol
*Mutual Contempt: Lyndon
Johnson, Robert Kennedy, and
the Feud that Defined a Decade*
Publisher: W. W. Norton &
Company

440. DECEMBER 7, 1997
Tim Russert
*Meet the Press: 50 Years of
History in the Making*
Publisher: McGraw Hill

441. DECEMBER 14, 1997
Susan Butler
*East to the Dawn:
The Life of Amelia Earhart*
Publisher: Addison Wesley
Longman

442. DECEMBER 21, 1997
Jim Hightower
*There's Nothing in the Middle
of the Road But Yellow Stripes
and Dead Armadillos*
Publisher: HarperCollins

443. DECEMBER 28, 1997
Sally Quinn
*The Party: A Guide to
Adventurous Entertaining*
Publisher: Simon & Schuster

444. JANUARY 4, 1998
Paul Nagel
*John Quincy Adams: A Public
Life, A Private Life*
Publisher: Alfred A. Knopf

445. JANUARY 11, 1998
Iris Chang
*The Rape of Nanking:
The Forgotten Holocaust
of World War II*
Publisher: Basic Books

446. JANUARY 18, 1998
Allan Metcalf
(with David Barnhart)
America In So Many Words
Publisher: Houghton Mifflin
Company

447. JANUARY 25, 1998
Daniel Pipes
*Conspiracy: How the
Paranoid Style Flourishes
and Where it Comes From*
Publisher: The Free Press

448. FEBRUARY I, 1998
Roger Simon
Showtime: The American
Political Circus and the
Race for the White House
Publisher: Times Books

449. FEBRUARY 8, 1998
Carol Reardon
Pickett's Charge in History
and Memory
Publisher: The University of
North Carolina Press

450. FEBRUARY 15, 1998
Joseph Hernon
Profiles in Character:
Hubris and Heroism in
the U.S. Senate, 1789–1990
Publisher: M. E. Sharpe Inc.

451. FEBRUARY 22, 1998
William Gildea
Where the Game Matters Most
Publisher: Little, Brown and
Company

452. MARCH I, 1998
John Lukacs
The Hitler of History
Publisher: Alfred A. Knopf

453. MARCH 8, 1998
John Marszalek
The Petticoat Affair:
Manners, Mutiny and
Sex in Andrew Jackson's
White House
Publisher: The Free Press

454. MARCH 15, 1998
Randall Robinson
Defending the Spirit:
A Black Life in America
Publisher: Dutton

455. MARCH 22, 1998
Ernest Lefever
The Irony of Virtue:
Ethics and American Power
Publisher: Westview Press

456. MARCH 29, 1998
Douglas Wilson
Honor's Voice: The Transforma-
tion of Abraham Lincoln
Publisher: Alfred A. Knopf

457. APRIL 5, 1998
Paul Johnson
A History of the American People
Publisher: HarperCollins

458. APRIL 12, 1998
Taylor Branch
Pillar of Fire: America in the

King Years 1963–65
Publisher: Simon & Schuster

459. APRIL 19, 1998
John S. D. Eisenhower
Agent of Destiny: The Life and
Times of General Winfield Scott
Publisher: The Free Press

460. APRIL 26, 1998
Molly Ivins
You Got to Dance with
Them What Brung You:
Politics in the Clinton Years
Publisher: Random House

461. MAY 3, 1998
David Aikman
Great Souls: Six Who
Changed the Century
Publisher: Word Publishing

462. MAY 10, 1998
Arthur J. Schlesinger Jr.
The Disuniting of America
Publisher: W. W. Norton &
Company

463. MAY 17, 1998
Patrick Buchanan
The Great Betrayal: How Ameri-
can Sovereignty and Social Justice
are Being Sacrificed to the Gods
of the Global Economy
Publisher: Little, Brown and
Company

464. MAY 24, 1998
Jill Ker Conway
When Memory Speaks:
Reflections on Autobiography
Publisher: Alfred A. Knopf

465. MAY 31, 1998
Max Boot
Out of Order: Arrogance,
Corruption, and Incompetence
on the Bench
Publisher: Basic Books

466. JUNE 7, 1998
Linda Simon
Genuine Reality:
A Life of William James
Publisher: Harcourt Brace

467. JUNE 14, 1998
Edward Lazarus
Closed Chambers: The First
Eyewitness Account of the Epic
Struggles Inside the Supreme
Court
Publisher: Times Books

468. JUNE 21, 1998
Ron Chernow

Titan: The Life of
John D. Rockefeller, Sr.
Publisher: Random House

469. JUNE 28, 1998
Edward Larson
Summer for the Gods:
The Scopes Trial and
America's Continuing Debate
over Science and Religion
Publisher: Basic Books

470. JULY 5, 1998
Andrew Carroll
Letters of a Nation: A Collection
of Extraordinary American Letters
Publisher: Kodansha

471. JULY 12, 1998
John Lewis
Walking With the Wind:
A Memoir of the Movement
Publisher: Simon & Schuster

472. JULY 19, 1998
Ben Procter
William Randolph Hearst:
The Early Years, 1863–1910
Publisher: Oxford University
Press

473. JULY 26, 1998
Richard Holbrooke
To End a War
Publisher: Random House

474. AUGUST 2, 1998
Carolyn Graglia
Domestic Tranquility:
A Brief Against Feminism
Publisher: Spence

475. AUGUST 9, 1998
Roy Reed
Faubus: The Life and Times
of An American Prodigal
Publisher: University of
Arkansas Press

476. AUGUST 16, 1998
Patricia O'Toole
Money and Morals in America
Publisher: Potter

477. AUGUST 23, 1998
Barbara Crossette
The Great Hill Stations of Asia
Publisher: Westview Press

478. AUGUST 30, 1998
Robert Sobel
Coolidge: An American Enigma
Publisher: Regnery Publishing,
Inc.

479. SEPTEMBER 6, 1998
Linda H. Davis
Badge of Courage:
The Life of Stephen Crane
Publisher: Houghton Mifflin
Company

480. SEPTEMBER 13, 1998
Arnold A. Rogow
A Fatal Friendship: Alexander
Hamilton and Aaron Burr
Publisher: Hill and Wang

481. SEPTEMBER 20, 1998
Larry Tye
The Father of Spin:
Edward L. Bernays and The
Birth of Public Relations
Publisher: Crown Publishers

482. SEPTEMBER 27, 1998
Balint Vazsonyi
America's 30 Years War:
Who Is Winning?
Publisher: Regnery Publishing,
Inc.

483. OCTOBER 4, 1998
George Bush and Brent Scowcroft
A World Transformed
Publisher: Alfred A. Knopf

484. OCTOBER 11, 1998
Juan Williams
Thurgood Marshall:
American Revolutionary
Publisher: Times Books

485. OCTOBER 18, 1998
Christopher Dickey
Summer of Deliverance:
A Memoir of Father and Son
Publisher: Simon & Schuster

486. OCTOBER 25, 1998
Dorothy Herrmann
Helen Keller: A Life
Publisher: Alfred A. Knopf

487. NOVEMBER 1, 1998
Charles Lewis
The Buying of the Congress:
How Special Interests Have
Stolen Your Right to Life,
Liberty, and the Pursuit
of Happiness
Publisher: Avon Books

488. NOVEMBER 8, 1998
Simon Winchester
The Professor and the
Madman: A Tale of Murder,
Insanity, and the Making of the
Oxford English Dictionary
Publisher: HarperCollins

489. NOVEMBER 15, 1998
Eric Foner
The Story of American Freedom
Publisher: W. W. Norton &
Company

490. NOVEMBER 2, 19982
Philip Gourevitch
We wish to inform you
that tomorrow we will
be killed with our families:
Stories from Rwanda
Publisher: Farrar, Straus and
Giroux

491. NOVEMBER 29, 1998
Melissa Muller
Anne Frank: The Biography
Publisher: Metropolitan Books

492. DECEMBER 6, 1998
Shelby Steele
A Dream Deferred:
The Second Betrayal of
Black Freedom in America
Publisher: HarperCollins

493. DECEMBER 13, 1998
William Greider
Fortress America:
The American Military and
the Consequences of Peace
Publisher: PublicAffairs

494. DECEMBER 20, 1998
Scott Berg
Lindbergh
Publisher: The Putnam Publish-
ing Group

495. DECEMBER 27, 1998
Peter Jennings
The Century
Publisher: Doubleday

496. JANUARY 3, 1999
P. J. O'Rourke
Eat the Rich
Publisher: Grove Atlantic

497. JANUARY 10, 1999
John Morris
Get the Picture: A Personal
History of Photojournalism
Publisher: Random House

498. JANUARY 17, 1999
Dava Sobel
Longitude: The True Story
of a Lone Genius Who Solved
the Greatest Scientific Problem
of His Time
Publisher: Walker & Company

499. JANUARY 24, 1999
Michael Ignatieff

Isaiah Berlin: A Life
Publisher: Metropolitan Books

500. JANUARY 31, 1999
Peter Kann and Frances
FitzGerald
Reporting Vietnam
Publisher: Library of America

501. FEBRUARY 7, 1999
Harold Evans
The American Century
Publisher: Alfred A. Knopf

502. FEBRUARY 14, 1999
Virginia Postrel
The Future and Its Enemies
Publisher: The Free Press

503. FEBRUARY 21, 1999
Annette Gordon-Reed
Thomas Jefferson
and Sally Hemings:
An American Controversy
Publisher: The University Press
of Virginia

504. FEBRUARY 28, 1999
Robert Famighetti
World Almanac and
Book of Facts 1999
Publisher: World Almanac
Books

505. MARCH 7, 1999
Tom Brokaw
The Greatest Generation
Publisher: Random House

506. MARCH 14, 1999
Allen Weinstein
The Haunted Wood:
Soviet Espionage in America—
The Stalin Era
Publisher: Random House

507. MARCH 21, 1999
Richard Shenkman
Presidential Ambition: How the
Presidents Gained Power, Kept
Power, and Got Things Done
Publisher: HarperCollins

508. MARCH 28, 1999
Norman Podhoretz
Ex-Friends: Falling Out with
Allen Ginsberg, Lionel and Diana
Trilling, Lillian Hellman, Han-
nah Arendt, and Norman Mailer
Publisher: The Free Press

[April 4, 1999: Tenth
Anniversary Special]

509. APRIL 11, 1999
Amity Shlaes

*The Greedy Hand: How Taxes
Drive Americans Crazy and
What to do About it*
Publisher: Random House

510. APRIL 18, 1999
Max Frankel
*The Times of My Life and My
Life with the Times*
Publisher: Random House

511. APRIL 25, 1999
Randall Kenan
*Walking on Water: Black
American Lives at the Turn
of the Twenty-First Century*
Publisher: Alfred A. Knopf

512. MAY 2, 1999
Mary Soames, editor
*Winston and Clementine: The
Personal Letters of the Churchills*
Publisher: Houghton Mifflin
Company

513. MAY 9, 1999
Betty Boyd Caroli
The Roosevelt Women
Publisher: Basic Books

514. MAY 16, 1999
T. R. Reid
*Confucius Lives Next Door:
What Living in the East Teaches
us About Living in the West*
Publisher: Random House

515. MAY 23, 1999
Jean Strouse
Morgan: American Financier
Publisher: Random House

516. MAY 30, 1999
Bill Gertz
*Betrayal: How the Clinton
Administration Undermined
American Security*
Publisher: Regnery Publishing,
Inc.

517. JUNE 6, 1999
Roger Mudd
Great Minds of History
Publisher: John Wiley &
Sons, Inc.

518. JUNE 13, 1999
Joseph Stevens
The Rebirth of a Nation
Publisher: Bantam Books

519. JUNE 20, 1999
David Kennedy
*Freedom from Fear: The Ameri-
can People in Depression and War*

Publisher: Oxford University
Press

520. JUNE 27, 1999
Jon Margolis
*The Last Innocent Year:
America in 1964*
Publisher: William Morrow &
Company

521. JULY 4, 1999
Floyd Flake
The Way of the Bootstrapper
Publisher: HarperSanFrancisco

522. JULY 11, 1999
Michael Korda
*Another Life: A Memoir
of Other People*
Publisher: Random House

523. JULY 18, 1999
Michael Cottman
*The Wreck of the Henrietta
Marie: An African-American's
Spiritual Journey to Uncover a
Sunken Slave Ship's Past*
Publisher: Harmony/Crown
Books

524. JULY 25, 1999
Dan Rather
*Deadlines and Datelines: Essays
at the Turn of the Century*
Publisher: William Morrow

525. AUGUST 1, 1999
Richard Gephardt
*An Even Better Place:
America in the 21st Century*
Publisher: PublicAffairs

526. AUGUST 8, 1999
H. W. Crocker
Robert E. Lee on Leadership
Publisher: Forum/Prima
Publishing

527. AUGUST 15, 1999
Elizabeth Norman
*We Band of Angels: The Untold
Story of American Nurses
Trapped on Bataan by the
Japanese*
Publisher: Random House

528. AUGUST 22, 1999
David Atkinson
*Leaving the Bench: Supreme
Court Justices at the End*
Publisher: University of Kansas
Press

529. AUGUST 29, 1999
Mark Pendergrast
The History of Coffee and How

it Transformed Our World
Publisher: Basic Books

530. SEPTEMBER 5, 1999
Leslie Chang
*Beyond the Narrow Gate:
The Journey of Four Chinese
Women From the Middle King-
dom to Middle America*
Publisher: Dutton

531. SEPTEMBER 12, 1999
Jay Parini
Robert Frost: A Life
Publisher: Henry Holt and
Company

532. SEPTEMBER 19, 1999
Richard Cohen
Rostenkowski
Publisher: Ivan R. Dee

533. SEPTEMBER 26, 1999
Linda McMurry
*To Keep the Waters Troubled:
The Life of Ida B. Wells*
Publisher: Oxford University
Press

534. OCTOBER 3, 1999
James Glassman
*Dow 36,000: The New Strategy
for Profiting from the Coming
Rise in the Stock Market*
Publisher: Times Books

535. OCTOBER 10, 1999
Stuart Rochester
*Honor Bound: American Prisoners
of War in Southeast Asia,
1961–1973*
Publisher: Naval Institute Press

536. OCTOBER 17, 1999
Witold Rybczynski
*A Clearing in the Distance:
Frederick Law Olmsted and
America in the 19th Century*
Publisher: Scribner

537. OCTOBER 24, 1999
Michael Kammen
*American Culture, American
Tastes: Social Change and the
20th Century*
Publisher: Alfred A. Knopf

538. OCTOBER 31, 1999
Patrick Tyler
*A Great Wall: Six Presidents and
China, An Investigative History*
Publisher: PublicAffairs

539. NOVEMBER 7, 1999
Eugene Robinson
Coal to Cream: A Black

Man's Journey Beyond Color
to an Affirmation of Race
Publisher: The Free Press

540. NOVEMBER 14, 1999
Fred Maroon
The Nixon Years, 1969–1974,
White House to Watergate
Publisher: Abbeville Press

541. NOVEMBER 21, 1999
Alfred Young
The Shoemaker and the
Tea Party: Memory and the
American Revolution
Publisher: Beacon Press

542. NOVEMBER 28, 1999
Winston Churchill
The Great Republic:
A History of America
Publisher: Random House

543. DECEMBER 5, 1999
Edmund Morris
Dutch: A Memoir of
Ronald Reagan
Publisher: Random House

544. DECEMBER 12, 1999
Michael Patrick MacDonald
All Souls: A Family
Story from Southie
Publisher: Beacon Press

545. DECEMBER 19, 1999
Robert Conquest
Reflections on a Ravaged Century
Publisher: W. W. Norton &
Company

546. DECEMBER 26, 1999
Tom Wheeler
Leadership Lessons
from the Civil War
Publisher: Current Books/
Doubleday

547. JANUARY 2, 2000
Thomas Keneally (PART ONE)
The Great Shame and the
Triumph of the Irish in the
English-Speaking World
Publisher: Nan A. Talese/
Doubleday

548. JANUARY 9, 2000
Thomas Keneally (PART TWO)
The Great Shame and the
Triumph of the Irish in the
English-Speaking World
Publisher: Nan A. Talese/
Doubleday

549. JANUARY 16, 2000
William Least Heat-Moon

River-Horse:
A Voyage Across America
Publisher: Houghton Mifflin
Company

550. JANUARY 23, 2000
Isaac Stern
My First 79 Years
Publisher: Alfred A. Knopf

551. JANUARY 30, 2000
Robert Novak
Completing the Revolution:
A Vision for Victory in 2000
Publisher: The Free Press

552. FEBRUARY 6, 2000
Arthur Herman
Joseph McCarthy: Reexamining
the Life and Legacy of America's
Most Hated Senator
Publisher: The Free Press

553. FEBRUARY 13, 2000
Arianna Huffington
How to Overthrow the
Government
Publisher: Regan
Books/HarperCollins

554. FEBRUARY 20, 2000
Cornel West
The Cornel West Reader
Publisher: Basic *Civitas* Books

555. FEBRUARY 27, 2000
Gina Kolata
Flu: The Story of the Great
Influenza Pandemic of 1918
and the Search for the Virus
that Caused It
Publisher: Farrar, Straus and
Giroux

556. MARCH 5, 2000
David Haward Bain
Empire Express: Building the
First Transcontinental
Railroad
Publisher: Viking

557. MARCH 12, 2000
Howard Zinn
A People's History of the United
States, 1492-Present
Publisher: HarperCollins

558. MARCH 19, 2000
Loung Ung
First They Killed My
Father: A Daughter of
Cambodia Remembers
Publisher: HarperCollins

559. MARCH 26, 2000
John Dower

Embracing Defeat: Japan in
the Wake of World War II
Publisher: W. W. Norton &
Company

560. APRIL 2, 2000
Philip Short
Mao: A Life
Publisher: Henry Holt and
Company

561. APRIL 9, 2000
Tavis Smiley
Doing What's Right:
How to Fight for What
You Believe In—And
Make A Difference
Publisher: Doubleday

562. APRIL 16, 2000
Allen Guelzo
Abraham Lincoln:
Redeemer President
Publisher: William Eerdmans
Publishing Co.

563. APRIL 23, 2000
Walter Mosley
Workin' on the Chain Gang:
Shaking Off the Dead Hand of
History
Publisher: Ballantine Books

564. APRIL 30, 2000
Ward Connerly
Creating Equal: My Fight
Against Race Preferences
Publisher: Encounter Books

565. MAY 7, 2000
David Wise
Cassidy's Run: The Secret
Spy War Over Nerve Gas
Publisher: Random House

566. MAY 14, 2000
Stephanie Gutmann
The Kinder, Gentler Military:
Can America's Gender-Neutral
Fighting Force Still Win Wars?
Publisher: Scribner

567. MAY 21, 2000
James Perry
A Bohemian Brigade:
The Civil War Correspondents—
Mostly Rough, Sometimes Ready
Publisher: John Wiley & Sons,
Inc.

568. MAY 28, 2000
David Crosby
Stand and Be Counted:
Making Music, Making History
Publisher: HarperSanFrancisco

569. JUNE 4, 2000
Zachary Karabell
The Last Campaign: How Harry Truman Won the 1948 Election
Publisher: Alfred A. Knopf

570. JUNE 11, 2000
Dan Baum
Citizen Coors: An American Dynasty
Publisher: William Morrow

571. JUNE 18, 2000
Joyce Appleby
Inheriting the Revolution: The First Generation of Americans
Publisher: Belknap/Harvard

572. JUNE 25, 2000
Francis Wheen
Karl Marx: A Life
Publisher: W. W. Norton & Company

[July 2, 2000: Preempted by coverage of the Libertarian Party Convention]

573. JULY 9, 2000
James Bradley
Flags of Our Fathers
Publisher: Bantam Books

574. JULY 16, 2000
Brooks Simpson
Ulysses S. Grant: Triumph Over Adversity
Publisher: Houghton Mifflin Company

575. JULY 23, 2000
Elizabeth Taylor
American Pharaoh: Mayor Richard J. Daley
Publisher: Little, Brown and Company

576. JULY 30, 2000
David Brooks
Bobos in Paradise: The New Upper Class and How They Got There
Publisher: Simon & Schuster

577. AUGUST 6, 2000
Paul Jeffers
An Honest President: The Life and Presidencies of Grover Cleveland
Publisher: William Morrow/Avon Books

578. AUGUST 13, 2000
Jane Alexander
Command Performance: An Actress in the Theater of Politics
Publisher: PublicAffairs

579. AUGUST 20, 2000
Harry Stein
How I Accidentally Joined the Vast Right-Wing Conspiracy (And Found Inner Peace)
Publisher: Delacorte Press

580. AUGUST 27, 2000
Ted Gup
The Book of Honor: Covert Lives and Classified Deaths at the CIA
Publisher: Doubleday

581. SEPTEMBER 3, 2000
Harold Bloom
How to Read and Why
Publisher: Scribner

582. SEPTEMBER 10, 2000
Lerone Bennett
Forced Into Glory: Abraham Lincoln's White Dream
Publisher: Johnson Publishing

583. SEPTEMBER 17, 2000
Alan Murray
The Wealth of Choices: How the New Economy Puts Power in Your Hands and Money in Your Pocket
Publisher: Crown Business

584. SEPTEMBER 24, 2000
Michael Paterniti
Driving Mr. Albert: A Trip Across America with Einstein's Brain
Publisher: The Dial Press

585. OCTOBER 1, 2000
Nina Easton
Gang of Five: Leaders at the Center of the Conservative Crusade
Publisher: Simon & Schuster

586. OCTOBER 8, 2000
Diane Ravitch
Left Back: A Century of Failed School Reforms
Publisher: Simon & Schuster

587. OCTOBER 15, 2000
Rick Bragg
Somebody Told Me: The Newspaper Stories of Rick Bragg
Publisher: University of Alabama Press

588. OCTOBER 22, 2000
Karen Armstrong
Islam: A Short History
Publisher: Modern Library

[October 29, 2000: Preempted by coverage of the U.S. House of Representatives]

589. NOVEMBER 5, 2000
Bonnie Angelo
First Mothers: The Women Who Shaped the Presidents
Publisher: William Morrow

590. NOVEMBER 12, 2000
William Duiker
Ho Chi Minh: A Life
Publisher: Hyperion

591. NOVEMBER 19, 2000
Maya Lin
Boundaries
Publisher: Simon & Schuster

592. NOVEMBER 26, 2000
Murray Sperber
Beer and Circus: How Big-Time College Sports Is Crippling Undergraduate Education
Publisher: Henry Holt and Company

[December 3, 2000: Preempted by coverage of Campaign 2000]

593. DECEMBER 10, 2000
Frank Rich
Ghost Light: A Memoir
Publisher: Random House

594. DECEMBER 17, 2000
Harvey Mansfield, Editor & Translator of a new edition of Alexis de Tocqueville's *Democracy in America*
Publisher: University of Chicago Press

595. DECEMBER 24, 2000
Robert Putnam
Bowling Alone: The Collapse and Revival of American Community
Publisher: Simon & Schuster

596. DECEMBER 31, 2000
Peter Hitchens
The Abolition of Britain: From Winston Churchill to Princess Diana
Publisher: Encounter Books

597. JANUARY 7, 2001
Martin Goldsmith
The Inextinguishable Symphony: A True Story of Music and Love in Nazi Germany
Publisher: John Wiley & Sons, Inc.

598. JANUARY 14, 2001
Dinesh D'Souza
*The Virtue of Prosperity:
Finding Values in an Age
of Techno-Affluence*
Publisher: The Free Press

599. JANUARY 21, 2001
Robert Scigliano, editor
The Federalist
Publisher: Modern Library

600. JANUARY 28, 2001
Arlen Specter
*Passion for Truth: From Finding
JFK's Single Bullet to Question-
ing Anita Hill to Impeaching
Clinton*
Publisher: William Morrow

601. FEBRUARY 4, 2001 (PART ONE)
Kurt Eichenwald
The Informant: A True Story
Publisher: Broadway Books

602. FEBRUARY 11, 2001
(PART TWO)
Kurt Eichenwald
The Informant: A True Story
Publisher: Broadway Books

603. FEBRUARY 18, 2001
Maurizio Viroli
*Niccolo's Smile:
A Biography of Machiavelli*
Publisher: Farrar, Straus and
Giroux

604. FEBRUARY 25, 2001
Bernard Weisberger
*America Afire: Jefferson,
Adams, and the Revolutionary
Election of 1800*
Publisher: William Morrow

605. MARCH 4, 2001
Dick Gregory
Callus on My Soul: A Memoir
Publisher: Longstreet Press

606. MARCH 11, 2001
Jeffrey Meyers
*Orwell: Wintry Conscience
of a Generation*
Publisher: W. W. Norton &
Company

607. MARCH 18, 2001
Jason Epstein
*Book Business: Publishing:
Past, Present, and Future*
Publisher: W.W. Norton &
Company

608. MARCH 25, 2001
Reese Schonfeld

*Me and Ted Against the World:
The Unauthorized Story of the
Founding of CNN*
Publisher: Cliff Street Books
(HarperCollins)

609. APRIL 1, 2001
Don Hewitt
*Tell Me A Story: 50 Years
and 60 Minutes in Television*
Publisher: PublicAffairs

610. APRIL 8, 2001
William Cooper
Jefferson Davis, American
Publisher: Alfred A. Knopf

611. APRIL 15, 2001
Andrew Burstein
*America's Jubilee: How in 1826
A Generation Remembered Fifty
Years of Independence*
Publisher: Alfred A. Knopf

612. APRIL 22, 2001
Emily Bernard
*Remember Me to Harlem:
The Letters of Langston Hughes
and Carl Van Vechten,
1925–1964*
Publisher: Alfred A. Knopf

613. APRIL 29, 2001
Kiron Skinner
*Reagan In His Own Hand:
The Writings of Ronald Reagan
That Reveal His Revolutionary
Vision for America*
Publisher: The Free Press

614. MAY 6, 2001
Susan Dunn
*The Three Roosevelts:
Patrician Leaders Who
Transformed America*
Publisher: Atlantic Monthly Press

615. MAY 13, 2001
Robert Slayton
*Empire Statesman: The Rise
and Redemption of Al Smith*
Publisher: The Free Press

616. MAY 20, 2001
John Farrell
*Tip O'Neill and the
Democratic Century*
Publisher: Little, Brown and
Company

617. MAY 27, 2001
Diane McWhorter
*Carry Me Home: Birmingham,
Alabama—The Climactic Battle
of the Civil Rights Revolution*
Publisher: Simon & Schuster

618. JUNE 3, 2001
Rick Perlstein
*Before the Storm: Barry Goldwater
and the Unmaking of the Ameri-
can Consensus*
Publisher: Hill & Wang

619. JUNE 10, 2001
Morton Kondracke
*Saving Milly: Love, Politics,
and Parkinson's Disease*
Publisher: PublicAffairs

620. JUNE 17, 2001
Edward Said
*Reflections on Exile and
Other Essays*
Publisher: Harvard University
Press

621. JUNE 24, 2001
Alma Guillermoprieto
*Looking for History:
Dispatches from Latin America*
Publisher: Pantheon Books

622. JULY 1, 2001
Daniel Schorr
*Staying Tuned: A Life
in Journalism*
Publisher: Pocket Books

623. JULY 8, 2001
Alan Ebenstein
Friedrich Hayek: A Biography
Publisher: St. Martin's Press

624. JULY 15, 2001
Sally Satel
*PC, M.D.: How Political
Correctness is Corrupting Medi-
cine*
Publisher: Basic Books

625. JULY 22, 2001
Jeff Greenfield
*Oh, Waiter! One Order of Crow:
Inside the Strangest Presidential
Election Finish in American
History*
Publisher: Putman

626. JULY 29, 2001
Jay Winik
*April 1865: The Month
That Saved America*
Publisher: HarperCollins

627. AUGUST 5, 2001
Tom Philpott
*Glory Denied: The Saga of
Jim Thompson, America's
Longest-Held Prisoner of War*
Publisher: W. W. Norton &
Company

628. AUGUST 12, 2001
Roger Wilkins
Jefferson's Pillow: The Founding Fathers and the Dilemma of Black Patriotism
Publisher: Beacon Press

629. AUGUST 19, 2001
Walter Berns
Making Patriots
Publisher: University of Chicago Press

630. AUGUST 26, 2001
Thomas Fleming
The New Dealers' War: F.D.R. and the War Within World War II
Publisher: Basic Books

631. SEPTEMBER 2, 2001
Herbert Bix
Hirohito and the Making of Modern Japan
Publisher: HarperCollins

632. SEPTEMBER 9, 2001
Irvin Molotsky
The Flag, The Poet and The Song: The Story of the Star-Spangled Banner
Publisher: Dutton

633. SEPTEMBER 16, 2001
James Bamford
Body of Secrets: Anatomy of the Ultra-Secret National Security Agency From the Cold War Through the Dawn of a New Century
Publisher: Doubleday
and
Jeffrey Richelson
The Wizards of Langley: Inside the CIA's Directorate of Science and Technology
Publisher: Westview Press

634. SEPTEMBER 23, 2001
John Steele Gordon
The Business of America: Tales from the Marketplace—American Enterprise from the Settling of New England to the Breakup of AT&T
Publisher: Walker & Company

635. SEPTEMBER 30, 2001
Hampton Sides
Ghost Soldiers: The Forgotten Epic Story of World War II's Most Dramatic Mission
Publisher: Doubleday

636. OCTOBER 7, 2001
Midge Decter
An Old Wife's Tale: My Seven Decades in Love and War
Publisher: Regan Books

637. OCTOBER 14, 2001
Fran Grace
Carry A. Nation: Retelling the Life
Publisher: Indiana University Press

638. OCTOBER 21, 2001
Stephen Kinzer
Crescent and Star: Turkey Between Two Worlds
Publisher: Farrar, Straus and Giroux

639. OCTOBER 28, 2001
Ted Yeatman
Frank and Jesse James: The Story Behind the Legend
Publisher: Cumberland House Publishing Inc.

640. NOVEMBER 4, 2001
Michael Eric Dyson
Holler If You Hear Me: Searching for Tupac Shakur
Publisher: Basic *Civitas* Books

641. NOVEMBER 11, 2001
Joseph Persico
Roosevelt's Secret War: FDR and World War II Espionage
Publisher: Random House

642. NOVEMBER 18, 2001
Daniel Pink
Free Agent Nation: How America's New Independent Workers are Transforming the Way We Live
Publisher: Warner Books, Inc.

643. NOVEMBER 25, 2001
Kirkpatrick Sale
The Fire of His Genius: Robert Fulton and the American Dream
Publisher: The Free Press

644. DECEMBER 2, 2001
Laura Claridge
Norman Rockwell: A Life
Publisher: Random House

645. DECEMBER 9, 2001
Phyllis Lee Levin
Edith and Woodrow: The Wilson White House
Publisher: Scribner

646. DECEMBER 16, 2001
Peter Bergen
Holy War, Inc.: Inside the Secret World of Osama bin Laden
Publisher: The Free Press

647. DECEMBER 23, 2001
Vernon Jordan
Vernon Can Read! A Memoir
Publisher: PublicAffairs

648. DECEMBER 30, 2001
Bernard Lewis
What Went Wrong?: Western Impact and Middle Eastern Response
Publisher: Oxford University Press

649. JANUARY 6, 2002
Bill Press
Spin This!: All The Ways We Don't Tell the Truth
Publisher: Pocket Books

650. JANUARY 13, 2002
Jeffrey Hart
Smiling Through the Cultural Catastrophe: Toward the Revival of Higher Education
Publisher: Yale University Press

651. JANUARY 20, 2002
John Laurence
The Cat From Hue: A Vietnam War Story
Publisher: PublicAffairs

652. JANUARY 27, 2002
Sandra Day O'Connor
Lazy B: Growing Up On a Cattle Ranch in the American Southwest
Publisher: Random House

653. FEBRUARY 3, 2002
Ralph Nader
Crashing the Party: How to Tell the Truth and Still Run for President
Publisher: Thomas Dunne Books/St. Martin's Press

654. FEBRUARY 10, 2002
Steve Neal
Harry and Ike: The Partnership That Remade the Postwar World
Publisher: Scribner

655. FEBRUARY 17, 2002
Edward Steers Jr.
Blood on the Moon: The Assassination of Abraham Lincoln
Publisher: University Press of Kentucky

656. FEBRUARY 24, 2002
Kent Newmyer
John Marshall and the Heroic Age of the Supreme Court
Publisher: Louisiana State University Press

657. MARCH 3, 2002
Randall Kennedy
Nigger: The Strange Career
of a Troublesome Word
Publisher: Pantheon Books

658. MARCH 10, 2002
Richard Lingeman
Sinclair Lewis:
Rebel From Main Street
Publisher: Random House

659. MARCH 17, 2002
Michael Novak
On Two Wings: Humble Faith
and Common Sense at the
American Founding
Publisher: Encounter Books

660. MARCH 24, 2002
Jon Ronson
Them: Adventures with Extremists
Publisher: Simon & Schuster

661. MARCH 31, 2002
Frank Wu
Yellow: Race in America
Beyond Black and White
Publisher: Basic Books

662. APRIL 7, 2002
Leonard Downie Jr.
(with Robert Kaiser)
The News About the News:
American Journalism in Peril
Publisher: Alfred A. Knopf

663. APRIL 14, 2002
Ellen Joan Pollock
The Pretender: How Martin
Frankel Fooled the Financial
World and Led the Feds on
One of the Most Publicized
Manhunts in History
Publisher: Wall Street Journal
Books

664. APRIL 21, 2002
Gordon Wood
The American Revolution:
A History
Publisher: Modern Library

665. APRIL 28, 2002
Robert Skidelsky
John Maynard Keynes:
Fighting for Freedom,
Publisher: Viking

666. MAY 5, 2002
Sarah Brady
A Good Fight
Publisher: PublicAffairs

667. MAY 12, 2002
Jennifer Toth

What Happened to Johnnie
Jordan? The Story of A
Child Turning Violent
Publisher: The Free Press

668. MAY 19, 2002
James Srodes
Franklin: The Essential
Founding Father
Publisher: Regnery
Publishing, Inc.

669. MAY 26, 2002
Richard John Neuhaus
As I Lay Dying: Meditations
Upon Returning
Publisher: Basic Books

670. JUNE 2, 2002
Richard Posner
Public Intellectuals:
A Study of Decline
Publisher: Harvard
University Press

671. JUNE 9, 2002
Jennet Conant
Tuxedo Park: A Wall Street
Tycoon and the Secret Palace
of Science that Changed the
Course of World War II
Publisher: Simon & Schuster

672. JUNE 16, 2002
Samantha Power
A Problem From Hell: America
and the Age of Genocide
Publisher: Basic Books

673. JUNE 23, 2002
Diana Preston
Lusitania: An Epic Tragedy
Publisher: Walker
& Company

674. JUNE 30, 2002
John Leonard
Lonesome Rangers:
Homeless Minds, Promised
Lands, Fugitive Cultures
Publisher: The New Press

675. JULY 7, 2002
Sandra Mackey
The Reckoning: Iraq and the
Legacy of Saddam Hussein
Publisher: W. W. Norton &
Company

676. JULY 14, 2002
Nguyen Cao Ky
Buddha's Child: My Fight
to Save Vietnam
Publisher: St. Martin's Press

677. JULY 21, 2002
Daniel Stashower
The Boy Genius and the Mogul:
The Untold Story of Television
Publisher: Broadway Books

678. JULY 28, 2002
Beppe Severgnini
Ciao America! An Italian
Discovers the U.S.
Publisher: Broadway Books

679. AUGUST 4, 2002
Glenn Loury
The Anatomy of Racial Inequal-
ity
Publisher: Harvard University
Press

680. AUGUST 11, 2002
Ann Coulter
Slander: Liberal Lies
About the American Right
Publisher: Crown Publishers

681. AUGUST 17, 2002
Simon Worrall
The Poet and the Murderer
Publisher: Dutton

682. AUGUST 25, 2002
Michael Oren
Six Days of War: June 1967
and the Making of the Modern
Middle East
Publisher: Oxford University
Press

683. SEPTEMBER 1, 2002
Winston Groom
A Storm in Flanders: The Ypres
Salient, 1914–1918—Tragedy
and Triumph on the Western Front
Publisher: Atlantic Monthly Press

684. SEPTEMBER 8, 2002
Dennis Hutchinson
The Forgotten Memoir of
John Knox: A Year in the Life
of a Supreme Court Clerk in
FDR's Washington
Publisher: University of Chicago
Press

685. SEPTEMBER 15, 2002
Arnold Ludwig
King of the Mountain: The
Nature of Political Leadership
Publisher: University Press of
Kentucky

686. SEPTEMBER 22, 2002
Eliot Cohen
Supreme Command:
Soldiers, Statesmen, and

Leadership in Wartime
Publisher: The Free Press

687. SEPTEMBER 29, 2002
Pete Davies
American Road: The Story of An Epic Transcontinental Journey at the Dawn of the Motor Age
Publisher: Henry Holt and Company

688. OCTOBER 6, 2002
Zig Ziglar
Zig: The Autobiography of Zig Ziglar
Publisher: Doubleday

689. OCTOBER 13, 2002
Linda Greenlaw
The Lobster Chronicles: Life On a Very Small Island
Publisher: Hyperion

690. OCTOBER 20, 2002
Michael Mandelbaum
The Ideas That Conquered the World: Peace, Democracy, and Free Markets in the Twenty-first Century
Publisher: PublicAffairs

691. OCTOBER 27, 2002
Charles Slack
Noble Obsession: Charles Goodyear, Thomas Hancock, and the Race to Unlock the Greatest Industrial Secret of the Nineteenth Century
Publisher: Hyperion

692. NOVEMBER 3, 2002
Caryle Murphy
Passion for Islam: Shaping the Modern Middle East: The Egyptian Experience
Publisher: Scribner

693. NOVEMBER 10, 2002
Frank Williams
Judging Lincoln
Publisher: Southern Illinois University Press

694. NOVEMBER 17, 2002
Rick Atkinson
An Army at Dawn: The War in North Africa, 1941–1943
Publisher: Henry Holt and Company

695. NOVEMBER 24, 2002
Peter Krass
Carnegie
Publisher: John Wiley & Sons, Inc.

696. DECEMBER 1, 2002
Bruce Feiler
Abraham: A Journey to

the Heart of Three Faiths
Publisher: William Morrow

697. DECEMBER 8, 2002
Michelle Malkin
Invasion: How America Still Welcomes Terrorists, Criminals and Other Foreign Menaces to Our Shores
Publisher: Regnery Publishing, Inc.

698. DECEMBER 15, 2002
John Taliaferro
Great White Fathers: The Story of the Obsessive Quest to Create Mt. Rushmore
Publisher: PublicAffairs

699. DECEMBER 22, 2002
Diana Walker
Public and Private: Twenty Years Photographing the Presidency
Publisher: National Geographic Insight

700. DECEMBER 29, 2002
Margaret MacMillan
Paris 1919: Six Months That Changed the World
Publisher: Random House

701. JANUARY 5, 2003
Hugh Price
Achievement Matters: Getting Your Child the Best Education Possible
Publisher: Kensington Publishing Corp.

702. JANUARY 12, 2003
Andrew Roberts
Napoleon and Wellington: The Battle of Waterloo and the Great Commanders Who Fought It
Publisher: Simon & Schuster

703. JANUARY 19, 2003
Warren Zimmermann
First Great Triumph: How Five Americans Made Their Country a World Power
Publisher: Farrar, Straus and Giroux

704. JANUARY 26, 2003
Robert Coram
Boyd: The Fighter Pilot Who Changed the Art of War
Publisher: Little, Brown and Company

705. FEBRUARY 2, 2003
Stephen Schwartz
The Two Faces of Islam: The House of Sa'ud from

Tradition to Terror
Publisher: Doubleday

706. FEBRUARY 9, 2003
Amy Chua
World on Fire: How Exporting Free Market Democracy Breeds Ethnic Hatred and Global Instability
Publisher: Doubleday

707. FEBRUARY 16, 2003
Robert Kagan
Of Paradise and Power: America and Europe in the New World Order
Publisher: Alfred A. Knopf

708. FEBRUARY 23, 2003
Joy Hakim
Freedom: A History of US
Publisher: Oxford University Press

709. MARCH 2, 2003
John McWhorter
Authentically Black: Essays for the Black Silent Majority
Publisher: Gotham Books

710. MARCH 9, 2003
Dana Priest
The Mission: Waging War and Keeping Peace with America's Military
Publisher: W. W. Norton & Company

711. MARCH 16, 2003
Michael Howard
The First World War
Publisher: Oxford University Press

712. MARCH 23, 2003
Bernard Bailyn
To Begin the World Anew: The Genius and Ambiguities of the American Founders
Publisher: Alfred A. Knopf

713. MARCH 30, 2003
Mona Charen
Useful Idiots: How Liberals Got It Wrong in the Cold War and Still Blame America First
Publisher: Regnery Publishing, Inc.

714. APRIL 6, 2003
Roy Morris Jr.
Fraud of the Century: Rutherford B. Hayes, Samuel Tilden, and the Stolen Election of 1876
Publisher: Simon & Schuster

715. APRIL 13, 2003
Philip Taubman
*Secret Empire: Eisenhower, The
CIA, and The Hidden Story of
America's Space Espionage*
Publisher: Simon & Schuster

716. APRIL 20, 2003 (PART ONE)
William Taubman
Khrushchev: The Man and His Era
Publisher: W. W. Norton &
Company

717. APRIL 27, 2003 (PART TWO)
William Taubman
Khrushchev: The Man and His Era
Publisher: W. W. Norton &
Company

718. MAY 4, 2003
Dorothy Rabinowitz
*No Crueler Tyrannies:
Accusation, False Witness, and
Other Terrors of Our Times*
Publisher: Wall Street Journal
Books

719. MAY 11, 2003
Monica Langley
*Tearing Down the Walls: How
Sandy Weill Fought His Way to
the Top of the Financial World
. . . And Then Nearly Lost it All*
Publisher: Wall Street Journal
Books

720. MAY 18, 2003
Paul Theroux
*Dark Star Safari: Overland
from Cairo to Cape Town*
Publisher: Houghton Mifflin
Company

721. MAY 25, 2003
Anne Applebaum
Gulag: A History
Publisher: Doubleday

722. JUNE 1, 2003
Raymond Strother
*Falling Up: How a Redneck
Helped Invent Political Consult-
ing*
Publisher: Louisiana State
University Press

723. JUNE 8, 2003
Azar Nafisi
*Reading Lolita in Tehran:
A Memoir in Books*
Publisher: Random House

724. JUNE 15, 2003
Eric Schlosser
*Reefer Madness: Sex,
Drugs, and Cheap Labor in
the American Black Market*

Publisher: Houghton Mifflin
Company

725. JUNE 22, 2003
Paul Berman
Terror and Liberalism
Publisher: W. W. Norton &
Company

726. JUNE 29, 2003
Vartan Gregorian
*The Road to Home:
My Life and Times*
Publisher: Simon & Schuster

727. JULY 6, 2003
Jon Kukla
*Wilderness So Immense:
The Louisiana Purchase
and the Destiny of America*
Publisher: Alfred A. Knopf

728. JULY 13, 2003
Willard Scott
*The Older the Fiddle,
the Better the Tune: The Joys
of Reaching a Certain Age*
Publisher: Hyperion

729. JULY 20, 2003
Connie Bruck
*When Hollywood Had a King:
The Reign of Lew Wasserman,
Who Leveraged Talent into
Power and Influence*
Publisher: Random House

730. JULY 27, 2003
Kenneth Ackerman
*Dark Horse: The Surprise
Election and Political Murder of
President James A. Garfield*
Publisher: Carroll & Graff
Publishers

731. AUGUST 3, 2003
Dorothy Height
*Open Wide the Freedom Gates:
A Memoir*
Publisher: PublicAffairs

732. AUGUST 10, 2003
Gretchen Rubin
*Forty Ways to Look at
Winston Churchill: A Brief
Account of a Long Life*
Publisher: Ballantine Books

733. AUGUST 17, 2003
David Lipsky
*Absolutely American:
Four Years at West Point*
Publisher: Houghton Mifflin
Company

734. AUGUST 24, 2003
Adam Bellow

*In Praise of Nepotism:
A Natural History*
Publisher: Doubleday

735. AUGUST 31, 2003
Robert Darnton
*George Washington's False Teeth:
An Unconventional Guide to the
Eighteenth Century*
Publisher: W. W. Norton &
Company

736. SEPTEMBER 7, 2003
Michael Parenti
*The Assassination of Julius Caesar:
A People's History of Ancient Rome*
Publisher: The New Press

737. SEPTEMBER 14, 2003
Erik Larson
*The Devil in the White City:
Murder, Magic, and Madness at
the Fair that Changed America*
Publisher: Crown Publishers

738. SEPTEMBER 21, 2003
Eric Rauchway
*Murdering McKinley: The Making
of Theodore Roosevelt's America*
Publisher: Hill & Wang

739. SEPTEMBER 28, 2003
Victor Davis Hanson
Mexifornia: A State of Becoming
Publisher: Encounter Books

740. OCTOBER 5, 2003
David Von Drehle
*Triangle: The Fire
That Changed America*
Publisher: Atlantic Monthly Press

741. OCTOBER 12, 2003
Jessica Stern
*Terror in the Name of God:
Why Religious Militants Kill*
Publisher: HarperCollins

742. OCTOBER 19, 2003
Lance William Morrow
Evil: An Investigation
Publisher: Basic Books

743. OCTOBER 26, 2003
Jill Jonnes
*Empires of Light: Edison,
Tesla, Westinghouse, and the
Race to Electrify the World*
Publisher: Random House

744. NOVEMBER 2, 2003
James Bovard
*Terrorism and Tyranny: Trampling
Freedom, Justice, and Peace to Rid
the World of Evil*
Publisher: Palgrave Macmillan

745. NOVEMBER 9, 2003
Rich Lowry
*Legacy: Paying the Price
for the Clinton Years*
Publisher: Regnery Publishing,
Inc.

746. NOVEMBER 16, 2003
Michael Moore
Dude, Where's My Country?
Publisher: Warner Books, Inc.

747. NOVEMBER 23, 2003
Tom Coburn
*Breach of Trust: How Washington
Turns Outsiders into Insiders*
Publisher: WND Books

748. NOVEMBER 30, 2003
Tom Daschle
*Like No Other Time:
The 107th Congress and
the Two Years That Changed
America Forever*
Publisher: Crown

749. DECEMBER 7, 2003
Richard Pipes
Vixi: Memoirs of a Non-Belonger
Publisher: Yale University Press

750. DECEMBER 14, 2003
Gail Collins
*America's Women: 400 Years
of Dolls, Drudges, Helpmates,
and Heroines*
Publisher: William Morrow

751. DECEMBER 21, 2003
Matthew Pinsker
Lincoln's Sanctuary: Abraham

Lincoln and the Soldiers' Home
Publisher: Oxford University
Press

752. DECEMBER 28, 2003
Carl Cannon
*The Pursuit of Happiness
in Times of War*
Publisher: Rowman &
Littlefield

753. JANUARY 4, 2004
Brenda Wineapple
Hawthorne: A Life
Publisher: Alfred A. Knopf

754. JANUARY 11, 2004
Walter Mears
*Deadlines Past: Forty Years
of Presidential Campaigning:
A Reporter's Story*
Publisher: Andrews McMeel

755. JANUARY 18, 2004
John Siegenthaler
James K. Polk
Publisher: Times Books

756. JANUARY 25, 2004
Nathaniel Philbrick
*Sea of Glory: America's
Voyage of Discovery:
The U.S. Exploring Expedition,
1838–1842*
Publisher: Simon & Schuster

756. MARCH 14, 2004
John W. Dean
Warren G. Harding
Publisher: Times Books

757. FEBRUARY 1, 2004
Abigail Thernstrom (and
Stephan Thernstrom)
*No Excuses:
Closing the Racial Gap
in Learning*
Publisher: Simon & Schuster

758. FEBRUARY 8, 2004
Nikki Giovanni
*The Collected Poetry of Nikki
Giovanni: 1968–1998*
Publisher: William Morrow

759. FEBRUARY 15, 2004
Kenneth Silverman
*Lightning Man:
The Accursed Life of
Samuel F. B. Morse*
Publisher: Alfred A. Knopf

760. FEBRUARY 22, 2004
John Meacham
*Franklin and Winston:
An Intimate Portrait of an
Epic Friendship*
Publisher: Random House

761. FEBRUARY 29, 2004
George Soros
*The Bubble of American
Supremacy: Correcting the Misuse
of American Power*
Publisher: PublicAffairs

762. MARCH 7, 2004
Richard Perle (and David Frum)
*An End to Evil: How to Win the
War on Terror*
Publisher: Random House

Index

PublicAffairs is a publishing house founded in 1997. It is a tribute to the standards, values, and flair of three persons who have served as mentors to countless reporters, writers, editors, and book people of all kinds, including me.

I. F. STONE, proprietor of *I. F. Stone's Weekly*, combined a commitment to the First Amendment with entrepreneurial zeal and reporting skill and became one of the great independent journalists in American history. At the age of eighty, Izzy published *The Trial of Socrates*, which was a national bestseller. He wrote the book after he taught himself ancient Greek.

BENJAMIN C. BRADLEE was for nearly thirty years the charismatic editorial leader of *The Washington Post*. It was Ben who gave the *Post* the range and courage to pursue such historic issues as Watergate. He supported his reporters with a tenacity that made them fearless and it is no accident that so many became authors of influential, best-selling books.

ROBERT L. BERNSTEIN, the chief executive of Random House for more than a quarter century, guided one of the nation's premier publishing houses. Bob was personally responsible for many books of political dissent and argument that challenged tyranny around the globe. He is also the founder and longtime chair of Human Rights Watch, one of the most respected human rights organizations in the world.

For fifty years, the banner of Public Affairs Press was carried by its owner, Morris B. Schnapper, who published Gandhi, Nasser, Toynbee, Truman, and about 1,500 other authors. In 1983, Schnapper was described by *The Washington Post* as "a redoubtable gadfly." His legacy will endure in the books to come.

Peter Osnos, *Publisher*